ROTHMANS
RUGBY LEA
YEARBOOK 1988-89

**Raymond Fletcher
and David Howes**

ROTHMANS

Queen Anne Press

A *Queen Anne Press* BOOK

© **Rothmans Publications Ltd**

First published in Great Britain in 1988 by
Queen Anne Press, a division of
Macdonald & Co (Publishers) Ltd
3rd Floor
Greater London House
Hampstead Road
London NW1 7QX

A member of Maxwell Pergamon Publishing Corporation plc

Front Cover: Great Britain second row man Paul Medley is subjected to a two-man Papua New Guinea tackle in the World Cup-rated Whitbread Trophy encounter at Wigan in October 1987.

Back Cover: Greenalls Man of Steel 1988, Widnes and Great Britain winger Martin Offiah, supported by Mike O'Neill and Andy Currier (right).

ACKNOWLEDGEMENTS
The compilers would like to acknowledge the assistance of the Rugby League Record Keepers' Club, club secretaries and individuals in providing material as a further source of reference for accuracy.

PHOTOGRAPHS
Modern day domestic photographs in this *Rothmans Rugby League Yearbook* are from the files of the *Rugby Leaguer,* the only weekly newspaper dedicated solely to the 13-a-side code. The compilers acknowledge the co-operation of Chief Photographer Gerald Webster and his staff.
The colour photographs on the front and back covers, plus a number of black-and-white contributions, are by freelance photographer Andrew Varley.
Photographic contributions have also been made by *Rugby League Week* in Sydney, *Wigan Observer, Oldham Evening Chronicle* and *Eddie Rolmanis.*

British Library Cataloguing in Publication Data
Rothmans Rugby League Yearbook — 1988-89
    1. Rugby football — Great Britain —
    Periodicals
    796.33.3.0941 GV945.9.G7

ISBN 0 356 15882 9

Photoset by New Rush Filmsetters, London

Reproduced, printed and bound in Great Britain by
Hazell Watson & Viney Ltd., Aylesbury, Bucks.
Member of the BPCC Group

Rothmans Rugby League Yearbook 1988-89

CONTENTS

EDITORIAL PREFACE

With the increasing interest in overseas rugby league we have for the first time included extensive records of the game in France and Australia plus New Zealand's brief tour of Papua New Guinea and Australia. We thank the officials of all four countries for their help in supplying and checking records.

This year's issue has been particularly demanding because both David Howes and I have had to compress the work into a shorter time due to our involvement in Great Britain's tour of Australasia. David had the honour of being appointed the tour business manager.

His much earlier departure Down Under allows me full responsibility for this editorial and the opportunity in his absence to pay a long overdue tribute. At each launching of the *Rothmans Rugby League Yearbook* he thanks many people for their help and co-operation, including myself, while I sit quietly by.

Thus no mention is made of his own part in the publication. At the risk of being accused of mutual back-slapping I would like to place on record my appreciation of his expertise in dealing with promotion and other matters that leave me free to compile the records. Despite eight years of compiling the Yearbook under often intense pressure to meet deadlines, would you believe not one real disagreement?

Perhaps we have reserved that for our long-suffering wives, to whom we apologise without promising things will get better.

Thanks are also due to club officials, the staff at RL headquarters, the RL Record Keepers' Club and a few individuals who have helped in any way.

In particular, I would again like to make special mention of George Bennison, whose help in the last few hectic weeks was invaluable. The gentle persuasion of house editor Celia Kent also helped us to meet deadlines.

● Facts and figures in this Yearbook as at 1 June 1988.

RAYMOND FLETCHER, of the *Yorkshire Post*

FOREWORD

Eight years ago Rothmans launched a rugby league yearbook. It is rewarding to know that since then the book has become firmly established as the definitive reference work for the sport.

The fact that every year we pay tribute to the co-authors does not mean we praise them from habit. We praise them because they deserve recognition for the loyalty and enthusiasm they put into their annual task. It is a loyalty which pervades all aspects of the game of rugby league.

The year was not without the occasional incident, which took the game off the sports pages and onto the news pages of the National Press. But action was swift and effective, demonstrating just why the sport has managed to retain such a favourable image. Long may it remain.

Rugby League adopt contract system

Widnes take title in stylish celebration

Schofield signed for record fee

Mass brawl stuns York

Bishop's £100,000 move is cancelled

Victory for Wigan in Shelford battle

Holmes bows out as injuries take toll

MEMORIES

1987-88 HEADLINES
Behind the facts and figures of the 1987-88 season were a selection of stories which made the headlines:

ATTENDANCE BOOM
A massive all-round increase in attendances was recorded. The new, streamlined Stones Bitter championship which was reduced from 16 to 14 clubs showed a 20 per cent rise in average attendances. A bigger Division Two — 20 clubs instead of 18 — produced an even greater average increase of 40 per cent.

RECORD TRANSFERS
Leeds twice broke the record transfer fee by signing Hull Test players Lee Crooks and Garry Schofield. They signed Crooks for £150,000 in June and then captured Schofield for £155,000 in October.

The previous record cash fee was £130,000 for Andy Gregory's move from Warrington to Wigan in 1987.

SHELFORD COURT MOVE
A High Court judge cleared Adrian Shelford to play for Wigan after ruling that the New Zealand Test forward had not signed a binding contract with St. Helens. The Saints had announced his capture earlier in the year and were very bitter when Wigan revealed in August that he had signed for them. It began a legal battle which kept Shelford out of action until December.

BISHOP SHOCKS ST. HELENS
The Saints called a Press conference in September to announce the securing of the Wales rugby union international scrum half David Bishop. But just before he was about to sign a reported £100,000 contract the deal was called off on medical advice. It is believed his fitness check up revealed that a broken neck injury sustained six years earlier had not healed sufficiently.

UNION CAPTURES
Four rugby union internationals turned professional during the season.

Welsh prop Stuart Evans left Neath for St. Helens; Peter Williams, the Orrell and England stand off joined Salford; Kelso and Scotland centre Alan Tait went to Widnes and Mark Brooke-Cowden, the New Zealand forward, signed for Leeds.

Williams made even bigger headlines when he was a controversial inclusion in Great Britain's standby tour squad after only three matches.

But the biggest impact was made by a non-international. Former Rosslyn Park RU winger Martin Offiah broke the Widnes try record and finished at the top of the game's tryscoring list with 44.

CONTRACTS REVOLUTION
A new players' contract system and the introduction of an independent transfer tribunal brought about the biggest change in the signing of players this century. From the close season of 1987 a player could arrange his own contract which need not tie him to one club indefinitely.

If a player wished to move at the end of his contract period a transfer fee would still have to be paid, but if the clubs failed to agree on a sum the decision would be made by a tribunal.

BOROUGH CHANGES
Blackpool Borough became Springfield Borough and then Chorley Borough in a chequered 12 months.

Despite strong objections from Wigan RLFC, Borough received RL Council approval to share Wigan Athletic's soccer ground at Springfield Park. They began the season as Springfield Borough and reached fourth place in Division Two but attendances were below expectation.

At the end of the season they made another move — to Chorley.

COLTS SCRAPPED

The long dispute between Colts and Youth officials was resolved by a Sports Council mediator who recommended the scrapping of the professional clubs' Colts League for Under-19 players.

A development programme for youth rugby is being introduced in 1988-89 with the co-operation of the Rugby League and the British Amateur RL Association.

BRAWLS MAR SEASON

A series of brawls marred the season.

● Bradford Northern and Castleford were involved in a Yorkshire Cup final replay brawl. Referee Kevin Allatt sin binned a player from each side and sent another from each team to the sin bin following separate incidents.

● A York-Dewsbury brawl made even bigger news by the intrusion on the field of home director Albert Bond. Referee Alan Burke sent off two players from each side following the disturbance and later dismissed another Dewsbury player.

● A Warrington-Wigan league game was disrupted by two brawls and other incidents, referee Kevin Allatt dismissing two from each side and sending another Warrington player to the sin bin.

● The Widnes-Warrington Premiership semi-final produced the worst scenes of all with spectators involved as a brawl spilled over the touchline. A little boy was hurt and Warrington winger Des Drummond faces police action after hitting a spectator. Referee John McDonald sent a Warrington player to the sin bin.

Warrington were fined a record £10,000. It included £2,500 for the latest incident, the £2,500 suspended fine imposed following their earlier brawl with Wigan plus another £5,000 suspended for a year. Widnes were fined £500 with another £2,500 suspended.

JUNE

Leeds hand over a world record £150,000 for Hull skipper Lee Crooks .... New Zealand Test stand off Shane Cooper agrees terms with St. Helens .... Second row Test man Alan Rathbone leaves Warrington to join Leeds in a £32,500 deal .... Rochdale Hornets packman Brian Dunn moves to Leigh .... Widnes pull off a double Rugby Union coup, signing winger Martin Offiah from Rosslyn Park and Orrell's back row forward Chris Ashurst .... Warrington pay Bradford Northern £40,000 for stand off John Woods .... Oldham appoint a new four-man steering committee to pave the way for the formation of a limited company .... Winger Mike Taylor listed at £25,000 by Oldham .... Hull chase French Test loose forward Thierry Bernabe .... Leeds recruit Australian Test prop Peter Tunks .... Keighley's future at Lawkholme Lane assured by the sale of the ground to a local motor company .... Wakefield Trinity cut the £110,000 asking fee on full back Gary Spencer by £20,000 .... Castleford sign St. George duo, centre Michael Beattie and Tongan forward John Fifita .... Oldham appoint Rochdale Hornets coach Eric Fitzsimons as new supremo, with Bradford Northern's Mal Graham returning to Watersheddings as assistant player-coach .... Salford offer Mick McTigue at £45,000 and Martin Foy at £10,000 .... Featherstone Rovers ask £150,000 for scrum half Deryck Fox and £60,000 for skipper Peter Smith .... Eric Hughes appointed coach of Rochdale Hornets .... Hull K.R. announce plans to sell Craven Park for supermaket development and move to another East Hull site .... Wigan fail in a bid to land Australian Test centre Gene Miles .... Brian Lockwood resigns as coach of Batley .... Castleford full back Darren Coen joins Dewsbury for £2,500 .... St. Helens prop Tony Burke asks for a move and is listed at £85,000 .... Danny Sheehan given the role of coach of York after a spell as caretaker .... Hull ask £40,000 for New Zealand

11

full back Gary Kemble .... Cleared to play in Sydney for Cronulla only for the summer, Warrington half back Paul Bishop causes an international row by signing a three-year contract .... Chris Forster appointed coach of Bramley .... Blackpool Borough refused permission at the League's AGM to be retitled Wigan Springfield .... The annual meeting also rejects a proposal by Salford and Leigh for the promotion and relegation figure to be reduced from three to two .... The Rugby League introduces a new contract system to replace the traditional retain and transfer system .... Hunslet agree terms for Brisbane utility back Trevor Benson and Canterbury Bankstown packman David Gillespie .... Lance Todd Trophy winner Graham Eadie comes out of retirement to rejoin Halifax .... Manly stand off Martin Meredith signs for Halifax.

JULY

Hull turn down a £6,000 offer from Leeds for full back Gary Kemble .... Auckland announce a first-ever, six-match autumn tour of Britain .... Featherstone Rovers offer Paul Lyman at £150,000 and reject a Hull offer of £15,000 for Peter Smith .... Swinton appoint Peter Smethurst as manager, his third spell with the club .... Leeds secure the services of Canberra centre Peter Jackson .... Great Britain and Wigan stand off Shaun Edwards turns down a summer stay with Balmain .... Paul Daley given the role of coach at Batley .... St. Helens set up a three-year deal with New Zealand Test forward Adrian Shelford who causes concern by lining up a contract with Sydney Premiership outfit Newcastle .... Leeds offer to swap Errol Johnson for Oldham's Mike Taylor .... Test forward Mick Worrall priced at £65,000 by Oldham .... Leeds sign full back Marty Gurr from Manly .... Bradford Northern list hooker Gary Brentley at £35,000 .... Blackpool Borough given League permission to change their name to Springfield Borough ....

Halifax hand over £20,000 to Oldham for winger Mike Taylor .... New Zealand All Black RU forward Mark Brooke-Cowden joins Leeds .... Bradford Northern sign coach Barry Seabourne's 17-year-old son Peter .... Illawara loose forward Dean Hanson joins Halifax .... Carlisle and former Bradford Northern half back Dean Carroll forced to quit through injury at 22 .... Rochdale Hornets sign Runcorn Highfield stand off Brian Garritty for a club record £25,000 .... Hunslet recruit Queensland forward Mark Hohn .... Leeds and Wakefield Trinity mount a six-man exchange deal estimated to be worth £120,000, Leeds obtaining full back Gary Spencer and stand off John Lyons, Trinity receiving threequarters Andy Mason and Phil Fox, half back Mark Conway and forward Keith Rayne plus cash .... Australian Test loose forward Bob Lindner agrees to rejoin Castleford .... Oldham sign Australian Peter Walsh, player-coach of Lakes United .... Great Britain announce a nine-week, 18-match tour Down Under, highlighted by five Test encounters, three of them World Cup-rated .... Hull and former Test loose forward Steve Norton retires after an 18-year career .... Peter Fox and Alex Murphy retained as coaches of Yorkshire and Lancashire for the annual Rodstock War of the Roses meeting .... Oldham show interest in Wigan centre David Stephenson .... New Zealander James Leuluai returns to Hull on a one-year contract .... Moroccan winger Hussein M'Barki moves from Oldham to Hull .... Champions Wigan issue a World Club Challenge to the eventual winners of the Australian Premiership .... Springfield Borough sign Mansfield Marksman winger Courtney Thompson .... Canterbury Bankstown centre Peter Mortimer joins Hull K.R.

AUGUST

Oldham hand over £20,000 to Warrington for former St. Helens duo Steve Peters and Kevin Meadows .... Hull K.R. sign Manly packman Glen Ryan .... Leeds offer Test men David Creasser and Roy Powell in part exchange for Hull centre Garry Schofield .... Leigh list loose forward John Westhead at £80,000 after absence from training .... Warrington forward Bob Eccles joins Springfield Borough for a club record £25,000, team mate Tony Hodson joining him in a £5,000 move .... Rugby League's first-ever Tribunal Panel to resolve contract disputes is named as Prof. John Wood, Jack Grindrod, David Watkins, Phil Worthington and Vic Bowen .... Graham Idle rejoins Rochdale Hornets .... Warrington open talks with Tim Wilby, player-coach at Le Pontet after service with Leeds and Hull .... Random drug testing to be introduced at first team matches .... Oldham win the chase for top amateur duo, Ian Bates from Dewsbury, and Richard Irving from Huddersfield .... The League reintroduce the sin bin for foul play .... Wigan release South Africans Ray Mordt and Rob Louw .... Hull K.R. sign New Zealand Test prop Ross Taylor .... Keighley recruit Leeds pack pair Trevor Skerrett and Gary Moorby .... Leigh loose forward Milton Huddart announces his retirement .... St. Helens ask £120,000 for skipper Chris Arkwright .... Yorkshire Television announce plans to screen a series of 18 Stones Bitter Championship matches, with transmission to Spain and Italy .... Widnes receive £50,000 from Leeds for Test winger John Basnett .... John Player Special agree a new two-year £320,000 contract, a 76 per cent annual increase .... Wigan lift the Okells Charity Shield with a 44-12 victory over Halifax on the Isle of Man, Riversiders' stand off Shaun Edwards taking the Man of the Match award .... A legal battle looms as Wigan announce the signing of New Zealand forward Adrian Shelford .... Oldham sign Canterbury Bankstown winger Brian McCarthy .... Bradford Northern list utility back Steve Evans .... The first Tribunal sitting fixes Ged Byrne's transfer fee at £40,000, Salford seeking £75,000 and Wigan offering £20,000 .... Halifax hand over £15,000 for Leeds utility back Ian Wilkinson .... Great Britain prop Kevin Ward signs a three-year deal with Castleford, as St.

Helens and Leeds show interest .... Hull pay Salford £30,000 for full back Paul Fletcher .... York spend £40,000 on Castleford packman Stuart Horton and Ian Fletcher, plus local scrum half Chris Hammerton.

SEPTEMBER

The Tribunal puts a price of £65,000 on second row man Paul Round, Oldham having offered £20,000 and St. Helens asking £90,000 .... Huddersfield stand off Phil Johnson moves to Bramley .... Sheffield Eagles hand over £1,000 to Whitehaven for the return of loose forward Paul McDermott .... Bradford Northern sign second row man Kelvin Skerrett from Hunslet .... Fylde and Lancashire B RU back David Tanner joins St. Helens .... Halifax recruit Brisbane centre Robert Grogan .... Doncaster rename their ground Bentley Road and then revert to Tattersfield after fans' protests .... St. Helens fork out a reported £60,000 for Wales and Neath prop forward Stuart Evans .... Australian Test full back Garry Jack joins Salford .... Hull pull out of move for Australian Test prop Steve Roach .... Bradford Northern sign New Zealand duo, Test three-quarter Gary Mercer and Junior Kiwi Russell Stewart .... St. Helens threaten court action over Adrian Shelford's signing for Wigan .... Garry Schofield returns home from a summer stay with Balmain to enter a contract dispute with Hull .... Leeds sign Eastern Suburbs winger Steve 'Slippery' Morris .... Castleford grant permission for Kevin Ward to play for Manly in the Sydney Grand Final .... Hull list Garry Schofield at world record £200,000 .... Warrington offer forward Andy Mossop at £20,000 .... Leigh want £60,000 for hooker Gary Hughes .... Half back Paul Bishop listed at £110,000 by Warrington .... The Sports Council set up independent inquiry into under-19 football, including the Colts set-up .... Yorkshire make it a hat-trick of Rodstock War of the Roses victories with a 16-10 success over Lancashire at Wigan .... Bradford Northern show interest in Hull's Garry Schofield .... Castleford transfer list prop Dean Mountain at £25,000 .... York transfer prop Mick

Hughes to Dewsbury .... Salford having twice turned down offers for hooker Paul Groves, St. Helens switch attention to Oldham's Ian Sanderson .... The League and Whitbreads announce plans for a Hall of Fame to be instituted near Leeds in October 1988, part of a new £750,000 sponsorship deal .... Hull's Steve Norton collects a record £41,000 benefit cheque .... Wigan sign New Zealand Test centre, 19-year-old Kevin Iro .... The League's Management Committee shelves the Adrian Shelford dispute until the player can appear personally .... The Committee also rule that Garry Schofield is a registered Hull player .... Welsh RU scrum half David Bishop's four-year, £100,000 deal with St. Helens is abandoned only minutes before the scheduled Press conference following a medical examination .... The Tribunal rules that Kelvin Skerrett was a free agent when leaving Hunslet for Bradford Northern .... Kevin Ward rated the top forward in Manly's 18-8 Grand Final victory over Canberra .... Salford sign Barrow scrum half David Cairns on a three-year contract.

OCTOBER

St. Helens offer Test winger Barry Ledger for sale at £50,000 as a disciplinary measure .... Barrow row forward Mick Worrall stays away from Oldham .... The Board of Appeal agrees that Garry Schofield is a contracted Hull player .... Bramley sign amateur winger Peter Lewis .... Leg injury rules Castleford prop Kevin Ward out of the Manly side to meet Wigan in the inaugural World Club Challenge .... Widnes winger Martin Offiah called up for the Lancashire debut after only eight matches, having scored eight tries .... Wigan win the first-ever Fosters World Club Challenge by beating Manly 8-2 in front of 36,895 fans .... Swinton, still without a win, sack coach Bill Holliday .... Whitehaven dispense with the services of coach Phil Kitchen .... Leigh back John Kerr suspended for three matches after trial by video .... Papua New Guinea tourists arrive in rainy Manchester for a first-ever tour of the professional scene in Britain .... St. Helens are granted a High Court injunction preventing Adrian Shelford from playing for Wigan .... Papua New Guinea open with a 22-16 victory at Featherstone Rovers .... Wigan retain the Grunhalle Lager Lancashire Cup with a 28-16 success over Warrington .... Lancashire coach Alex Murphy turns down a plea by Wigan coach Graham Lowe to rest the six Wigan players in the county squad to meet Papua New Guinea .... Amateur club coach Frank Barrow takes over at Swinton .... Oldham's Mick Worrall makes a £55,000 move to Salford, in preference to Swinton .... St. Helens pay Salford £40,000 for hooker Paul Groves .... Papua New Guinea earn a thrilling 22-22 draw with Lancashire at St. Helens .... Wigan full back Steve Hampson is one of five uncapped players in the 17-man Great Britain squad named for the Test against Papua New Guinea .... Bradford Northern and Castleford battle it out for a 12-12 draw in the John Smiths Yorkshire Cup Final at Leeds .... Swinton, without a win in the Stones Bitter Championship, end Papua New Guinea's unbeaten run with a dour 13-6 victory .... St. Helens hooker Paul Groves called up for his Great Britain debut to replace the injured Kevin Beardmore .... Wigan have a record eight players called up for Test duty, beating their own previous best of seven .... Featherstone Rovers sign ex-Hull K.R. packman Dave Busby .... Cumbria beat Papua New Guinea 22-4 at Whitehaven .... Widnes recruit Australian Test star Dale Shearer .... Tribunal fixes prices of £55,000 on Barrow winger Les Quirk moving to St. Helens and £35,000 on former teammate David Cairns' switch to Salford .... Leigh reduce the asking price on hooker Gary Hughes by £15,000 to £45,000 .... Leeds pay a world record £155,000, for Hull's Test centre Garry Schofield .... Great Britain beat Papua New Guinea 42-0 in a World Cup-rated Whitbread Trophy Bitter Test at Wigan .... Auckland open their historic tour of Britain with a bruising 29-25 success at Leeds .... Adrian Shelford dispute sent to the High Court .... Auckland record a 22-16 victory at Warrington .... Yorkshire beat Papua New Guinea 28-4 at a rainlashed Leeds .... Wigan collect £6,000 winners'prize in the first-ever British Coal Nines tournament on their home ground .... Former Welsh RU skipper Terry Holmes is forced to quit Bradford Northern with a knee injury after only 37 first team appearances .... Papua New Guinea beat a BARLA X111 20-16 at Halifax .... Bradford Northern's 11-2 Yorkshire Cup victory over Castleford marred by a brawl.

NOVEMBER

St. Helens thrash Auckland 52-26 .... Hull sign North Sydney half back Paul McCaffrey .... Leeds discuss exchange of John Holmes and cash for Featherstone Rovers scrum half Deryck Fox .... Featherstone Rovers consider possibility of selling their Post Office Road ground to the local council .... The League clamps down on the numbering of. players' jerseys .... Bramley appoint former former Great Britain hooker Tony Fisher as coach .... John Sheridan quits as team manager of Doncaster after four years .... Hull snatch a 26-24 victory over Auckland with a last ditch try .... Wigan coach Graham Lowe invited to take charge of the Rest of the World side to meet Australia in the 1988 bicentennial celebrations .... Bradford Northern threatened by a cash crisis .... Doncaster make a bid for Hull K.R.'s Andy Kelly .... Auckland beat Wigan 10-6 .... Leeds sign amateur international prop John Fairbank from Elland .... Management Committee deal with Yorkshire Cup final brawl participants, £100 fines being imposed on Castleford's John Joyner, David Plange, Kevin Ward and Gary Hyde, and Bradford Northern's Paul Harkin and Brendan Hill, with Castleford's Michael Beattie and Northern's Karl Fairbank being found not guilty

.... Australian Rod Reddy appointed coach of Barrow .... Graham Heptinstall promoted to team manager at Donacaser .... Featherstone Rovers offer Paul Lyman at £120,000 .... RL Chairman's XIII beat Auckland 12-6 in the last match of the minitour .... Leigh reject £30,000 Oldham bid for scrum half Mike Ford .... Hull fail to land Featherstone Rovers skipper Peter Smith and Auckland forward Dean Lonergan .... Leigh price prop forward Bryan Gelling at £25,000 .... Thirteen players from Hull and Castleford fined £50 each by the Disciplinary Committee for brawling, fines of £30 each being imposed on four players from Whitehaven and Wakefield Trinity .... Leigh sign Orrell RU centre Craig Burrill .... Fines of £100 imposed on five further brawl offenders from the Yorkshire Cup final replay, Bradford Northern's Kelvin Skerrett, David Hobbs and Wayne Heron, and Castleford's Keith England and Kenny Hill .... The League order all First Division clubs to video matches and to send a copy to the referee for educational purposes .... Rochdale Hornets banned from signing players until an outstanding payment to Runcorn Highfield for half back Brian Garritty is settled .... Cash crisis at Bradford Northern worsens as the local council refuse to advance money .... Whitehaven appoint John McFarlane as coach .... Bradford counci¹ appoint a special committee to administer ɒradford Northern's finances .... Stuart Wainman, seeking a return to the amateur game, buys himself back from Wakefield Trinity .... Swinton transfer list the Holliday brothers, skipper Les at £90,000 and Mike at £15,000 .... Leigh ask £120,000 for captain Derek Pyke .... Hull K.R. cut the fee on second row man Andy Kelly by £20,000 to £40,000 .... Great Britain utility star Joe Lydon ruled out of the first nine matches of the 1988 tour Down Under by the completion of a degree course .... Prop Dean Sampson becomes the 14th player from the Castleford-Hull brawl to be fined £50 ....

15

Leigh turn down Swinton suggestion of swapping skippers Derek Pyke and Les Holliday .... Andy Goodway signs a four-year contract with Wigan to end speculation of a move to Australia .... Featherstone Rovers ask a total of £27,500 for hookers Martin Slater and Mark Campbell, winger David Jones and forward Paul Geary.

DECEMBER

Widnes reject a Swinton proposal to swap loose forwards Harry Pinner and Les Holliday .... Hull offer scrum half Kevin Dick at £25,000 and winger Pepi Brand at £10,000 .... Wakefield Trinity ask £40,000 for Great Britain forward Dick Jasiewicz .... St. Helens list hooker Graham Liptrot at £15,000 .... Player of the Year Mark Aston priced at £20,000 by Sheffield Eagles .... Tim Wilby returns to Hull after a four-year stay in France .... Leigh tell Oldham to double their £30,000 bid for scrum half Mike Ford .... National storm as five sent off at York, including four following a brawl, plus home director Albert Bond ordered off the field after protesting to referee Alan Burke .... The four dismissed for brawling — York's Stuart Horton and St. John Ellis, plus Dewsbury's Stuart Morris and Paul Shuttleworth — each banned for four matches, as is Dewsbury's Steve Hinchcliffe who was sent off in a separate late incident .... Oldham up their Mike Ford bid to £45,000 .... Hull list full back Paul Fletcher at £40,000 for disciplinary reasons .... Wigan win a High Court battle to sign New Zealand Test forward Adrian Shelford .... Sheffield Eagles book an Easter date at Sheffield United's Bramall Lane ground, which last staged a Rugby League match 76 years earlier .... Anglo-Aussie summit lined up for Hawaii after potential British tour stars are approached by Australian clubs .... The Management Committee hands out £100 fines to the four players sent off in the York-Dewsbury brawl, plus props Tony Rose (York) and Mick Hughes (Dewsbury); ban

York director Albert Bond for a year and fine each club £2,000, £1,500 suspended for 12 months .... Wigan's Test forward Ian Potter asks for a move and is offered at £75,000 .... Leigh cuts the fee on skipper Derek Pyke to £90,000, while John Westhead and Neil McCulloch settle their differences .... Hard up Bradford Northern offer 22 players for a total of £201,000, headed by hooker Gary Brentley at £35,000 .... Shareholders at Hull K.R. shelve the election of three directors while police investigate claims of ballot rigging .... Springfield Borough sign one-armed Australian forward Kerry Gibson .... Rugby League PRO David Howes appointed business manager for Great Britain's summer tour Down Under .... Warrington ask £85,000 for Great Britain winger Mark Forster and former Under-21 back Brian Carbert .... A disagreement over travelling expenses leads to Swinton's Tex Evans being offered at £45,000 .... York director Albert Bond resigns from the board .... Great Britain winger Phil Ford listed at £120,000 by cash-seeking Bradford Northern .... Hull K.R. hooker Chris Rudd suffers a fractured skull in a road accident .... Wigan's Test centre David Stephenson asks for a move .... Swinton sign Leigh's £25,000-rated packman Bryan Gelling .... Wigan's Joe Lydon banned for four matches after trial by video.

JANUARY

Four players sent off and one sin-binned in the first 20 minutes of the Warrington-Wigan derby on New Year's Day .... Leeds sign Wigan centre David Stephenson for £75,000 .... Hull K.R. recruit St. Helens hooker David Harrison on loan .... The League reintroduce the yellow card to indicate a sin bin dismissal .... York's Tony Rose wins an appeal against his £100 brawl fine .... Leeds sound out Australian Test stars Peter Sterling and Wayne Pearce .... Wakefield Trinity re-sign Hull K.R.'s £40,000-rated second row man Andy Kelly .... Doncaster loose forward

Andy Timson moves to York in exchange for forwards Trevor Hooper, Ian Tansley and £5,000 .... Local council turn down Hull K.R.'s proposed moved to Sutton Park industrial site .... Halifax fail in a bid to re-sign Australian packman Geoff Robinson .... St. Helens back duo Dennis Litherland and Brian Parkes move to Springfield Borough .... Doncaster sack team manager Graham Heptinstall and reinstate John Sheridan .... St. Helens lift the John Player Special Trophy for the first time with 15-14 victory over Leeds at Wigan .... Widnes sign Swinton's New Zealand prop Joe Grima .... Halifax pay club record £65,000 for Swinton loose forward Les Holliday .... Leigh skipper Derek Pyke joins Widnes in exchange for Harry Pinner and £50,000 .... Castleford hand over £7,000 for Halifax utility man Brian Juliff, listing prop Alan Shillito at £25,000 .... Test pack-man Andy Platt asks for a transfer at St. Helens .... Springfield Borough sign Danny Wilson from Swinton and Carlisle's Jimmy Green .... Hull offer Jon Sharp at £50,000 .... Mark Roberts asks to leave Warrington .... Anglo-Aussie meeting in Hawaii agrees that Australian clubs cannot approach a 32-strong squad of British tour candidates .... Also suggests that Los Angeles should stage the September World Cup final and Tokyo should host a May 1989 World Club Championship .... Great Britain coach Malcolm Reilly names three new caps in side to meet France, backs Martin Offiah and Paul Loughlin, plus packman Hugh Waddell .... Swinton agree to swap Mike Holliday for new recruit from Leigh, Bryan Gelling .... Wigan and Warrington each fined a record £3,000, £2,500 of which suspended for a year, for their New Year's Day brawl .... Widnes list centre Trevor Stockley at £25,000 and hooker Ian Gormley at £15,000 .... New Zealand Rugby Union star Charlie McAlister revealed as a trialist with Oldham .... Hull turn down Bradford Northern offer of former utility man Steve Evans in exchange for scrum half Kevin

Dick .... Great Britain beat France 28-14 in Avignon .... Great Britain management de-cide to keep 32 shortlisted tour candidates secret .... Salford City Council grant £15,000 each to Salford and Swinton for schoolboy coaching schemes .... St. Helens offer loose forward Bernard Dwyer at £30,000 .... Mansfield Marksman announce plans to leave Alfreton and return to Mansfield on a new site .... Great Britain coach Malcolm Reilly omits Martin Offiah from the squad for the return French Test, bringing in uncapped winger David Plange.

FEBRUARY

Springfield Borough and landlords Wigan Athletic fall out over payment of ground rent for Springfield Park .... New youth development programme devised jointly by the Rugby Football League and BARLA, under the chairmanship of the Sports Council .... Hull, £400,000 in debt, seek £50,000 loan from the League and are granted £30,000 .... Coach Malcolm Reilly calls up Castleford winger David Plange for his Great Britain debut in the return clash with France .... Mansfield Marksman announce plans to return to a new ground at Mansfield after two years' stay at Alfreton .... Keighley turn down Widnes offer of £7,500 to switch their second round Silk Cut Challenge Cup tie from Lawkholme Lane to Naughton Park .... Granada TV pull out of screening the Scrum-down series .... The League tighten up rules for the import of overseas players for the 1988-89 season, restriction being three per club and one player who qualifies for a British passport .... Leigh sign New Zealand centre Paddy Tuimavave from Swinton .... Wigan stave off the challenge of other top Lancashire clubs to sign 16-year-old scrum half Bobby Goulding from Widnes St. Maries amateur club .... Great Britain defeat France 30-12 at Headingley .... Hull reject £10,000 bid from Bradford Northern for scrum half Kevin Dick .... Hull directors turn down takeover offer from soccer neighbours Hull City .... Swinton complete the signing of Workington Town forward Neil Frazer .... Featherstone Rovers sell their Post Office Road ground to the local council .... Widnes fail in bid to extend Dale Shearer's stay at Naughton Park .... Oldham reject transfer request from newly-capped Great Britain prop Hugh Waddell .... Warrington list Tony Worrall at £15,000 .... Wigan centre Dean Bell a summer contract target for Sydney club Eastern Suburbs .... Wigan axe Ellery Hanley from Silk Cut Challenge Cup tie with Leeds for disciplinary reasons .... Warrington prop Les Boyd announces his retirement after breaking his arm for the second time in the season .... Wigan and Widnes protest at BBC TV screening their third round Silk Cut Challenge Cup tie .... Wigan announce a peace settlement with Ellery Hanley and his selection for the league encounter with Widnes .... Local magistrates turn down Bradford Northern's application for a drinks licence on match days .... New Zealand Maori Rugby Union threequarter Charile McAlister joins Oldham on a three-year contract .... Rochdale Hornets complete the payments for Runcorn Highfield's Brian Garrity and have transfer ban lifted by the League .... Leeds appoint Garry Schofield as captain following Peter Tunks' return to Australia .... Wigan list Ellery Hanley at world record £225,000 on the eve of the league match with Widnes and order him not to report for training .... Bradford Northern take Great Britain winger Phil Ford off the transfer list .... Wakefield Trinity and Whitehaven each fined £700, £500 suspended for a year, for brawling .... Bradford Northern agree new two-year contracts with New Zealand duo Gary Mercer and Russell Stewart .... Salford make double signing from Oldham, Australian Brian McCarthy and utility man Tom Nadiole .... Warrington lose interest in Ellery Hanley after suggestions of part exchange involving Mike Gregory and Paul Cullen .... Hull

skipper James Leuluai issues a public apology from the players for their display in the shock 32-28 defeat by bottom of the table Swinton at the Boulevard .... A host of clubs offer to take Ellery Hanley on a match-by-match rental basis, including Hull, Wakefield Trinity, Featherstone Rovers and Sheffield Eagles .... Halifax coach Chris Anderson decides to leave Thrum Hall to return to Australia at the end of the season.

MARCH
Widnes eye Scotland's record breaking RU full back Gavin Hastings .... Silk Cut Challenge Cup semi-finalists Salford and Hull seek the return of Australian stars Garry Jack and Scott Gale respectively .... The League ignore a plea from Widnes for referee Jim Smith and the two touch judges from the third round Challenge Cup tie with Wigan to be banned from Naughton Park .... Fred Lindop appointed for the Wembley final in his last season before retirement .... Kiwi forward Kevin Tamati ends speculation of a move to Leeds by signing a new two-year contract with Warrington .... Want-away Swinton centre Tex Evans threatens to quit .... Widnes renew chase for Lancashire and Orrell RU centre Gerry Ainscough .... Leeds sign veteran Halifax scrum half Gary Stephens on loan .... Balmain free Scott Gale to play for Hull in the Cup semi-final, but turn down Salford's request for Garry Jack .... Australian Brian McCarthy, freed by Oldham, joins Salford .... Dewsbury scrum half and skipper Paul Shuttleworth listed at club record £50,000 .... Great Britain lose 14-13 in French Under-21 international at Aussillon .... Wigan recruit England B and Lancashire RU winger Mark Preston .... Widnes watch Scotland RU centre Alan Tait .... Ellery Hanley makes peace with Wigan three weeks after being put on the transfer list .... Widnes sign Broughton Park RU winger Brimah Kebbie after assurances about his fitness .... £1.5m improvement scheme announced for

Headingley, Leeds .... Hull second row man Nicky Elgar joins Fulham on loan .... Salford skipper Darren Bloor ruled out of Challenge Cup semi-final by recording of a third sin bin, then wins appeal 24 hours later .... Warrington coach Tony Barrow signs a new two-year contract .... Wigan beat Salford 34-4 to reach Wembley for the third time in five years .... Len Casey resigns as coach of Hull two weeks before their Challenge Cup semi-final with Halifax, alleging lack of support from the Board .... New Zealand order the Iro brothers to return home before being allowed to come back to Britain for the Wembley final .... Warrington offer a short term contract to Manly skipper Paul Vautin .... Swinton turn down a Salford move for Tex Evans .... Leeds sign Littleborough RU winger Stewart Chick .... The French record their first-ever Under-21 international double with an 8-4 success in a mudbath at St. Helens .... Whitehaven sign scrum half Steve Branthwaite from Gosforth RU club .... Bradford Northern decide to stage their clash with Wigan at Bradford City's Valley Parade ground .... St. Helens renew efforts to sign Welsh RU half back Jonathan Davies .... Orrell RU back Peter Williams signs for Salford only an hour after being named in the England RU squad to tour Down Under .... Wakefield Trinity award a new two-year contact to coach David Topliss; appoint a marketing company, SML; and install actor Richard Harris as club president .... Hull appoint Tony Dean and Keith Hepworth as caretaker coaches .... Warrington winger Brian Carbert turns down move to Salford .... Widnes hooker Ian Gormley, on offer at £15,000, signs for Salford .... St. Helens hooker Graham Liptrot rejects a move to Swinton .... Halifax and Hull stage a scoreless draw in the Challenge Cup semi-final at Leeds .... Swinton offer scrum half Martin Lee at £15,000 .... A Tony Anderson try seals a 4-3 Halifax passage to Wembley in the semi-final replay at Elland Road, Leeds ....

Castleford sign New Zealand Test winger Shane Horo .... Huddersfield Barracudas sack coach Jack Addy after a 15-month reign.

APRIL
Australian full back Graham Eadie appointed player-coach of Halifax in succession to fellow countryman Chris Anderson, with Brisbane's Ross Strudwick being installed to the new role of team manager-director .... Great Britain name Salford's RU capture Peter Williams in a 10-man stand-by squad for the tour after only three games, 23 players being selected with three to be added, plus Joe Lydon to join the party halfway through the tour after degree examinations .... Ellery Hanley named as the first-ever black tour captain .... Hull K.R. fan Susan Walford selected as 1988 Traveleads Top Fan, Rugby League's official supporter of the year .... Oldham's Mal Graham resigns as coach, but continues to the end of the season as a player .... Widnes lift the Championship Trophy for the first time for a decade, while Oldham clinch the Second Division title with a one-point victory over title rivals at Wakefield Trinity .... Bradford Northern attract their best crowd of the season by entertaining Wigan at Bradford City's Valley Parade soccer ground .... Irishman Tom O'Donovan appointed as Rugby League's first-ever National Development Officer .... Hull K.R.'s Kiwi Gordon Smith announces his retirement .... St. Helens offer Test forward John Fieldhouse at £95,000 .... Warrington and Wigan plan to stage an American exhibition game in Milwaukee in May 1989 .... Wigan full back Steve Hampson ruled out of a Wembley final for the third time with a broken limb .... Scotland and Kelso RU centre Alan Tait joins Widnes in a 10-year £85,000 deal .... Hull K.R. move for Wales and Pontypool RU pair David Bishop and Mark Ring .... Salford beat Halifax in their last league encounter to condemn Leigh to relegation along with Hunslet and Swinton .... Featherstone

Rovers and Wakefield Trinity join Oldham as promoted clubs .... St. Helens coach Alex Murphy calls for the sin bin to be scrapped .... Castleford sign 16-year-old hooker Graham Southernwood on a club record £40,000 junior contract .... Warrington's Joe Ropati joins Sydney club Manly .... Maurice Bamford steps down as coach of Leeds but stays on as commercial manager .... Leigh cut the fees on loose forward John Westhead by £20,000 to £60,000 and on hooker Gary Hughes from £45,000 to £30,000 .... Great Britain extend the deadline on naming the rest of the tour squad by three days .... Wigan forward Andy Goodway withdraws from the tour because of business commitments .... St. Helens packman Roy Haggerty is promoted from the stand-by squad to replace him .... Castleford sack coach Dave Sampson .... Great Britain decide to fly out Steve Hampson to join the tour when his broken arm is mended .... Hunslet part company with coaches David Ward and Peter Jarvis .... Swinton list winger Derek Bates at £85,000 because of his desire for First Division football .... Great Britain call up Lee Crooks, Des Drummond, Hugh Waddell and Ian Wilkinson for the tour Down Under .... Gary Stephens appointed coach of York .... Wigan lift the Silk Cut Challenge Cup with a record eighth Wembley victory, beating Halifax 32-12.

MAY

Players and fans involved in Widnes-Warrington Premiership semi-final brawl; Warrington winger Des Drummond faces police charges after hitting spectator .... Andy Platt ankle injury delays the St. Helens forward's tour departure .... League say that from next season players who cause trouble off the field will face charges of bringing game into disrepute .... Disciplinary procedure to be streamlined with independent panel meeting weekly .... Halifax sign Jason Ramshaw on a reported £40,000 record three-year contract for a junior player .... Joe Lydon and Des Drummond withdrawn from Great Britain tour squad pending court cases involving incidents with spectators .... Carl Gibson of Leeds brought in as a tour replacement .... Champions Widnes complete big double by beating St. Helens in Stones Bitter Premiership final; Oldham snatch Division Two Premiership Trophy after high-scoring thriller with Featherstone Rovers .... St. Helens sign Australian Test centre Michael O'Connor .... Warrington receive record fine for part in brawl with Widnes, who receive lesser fine .... Australian utility back Andrew Ettingshausen returning to Leeds .... Great Britain beat Papua New Guinea 42-22 .... St. Helens release New Zealand Test centre Mark Elia .... Widnes centre Darren Wright called into tour squad as cover for Shaun Edwards whose knee injury rules him out for several weeks .... Australian Brian Smith appointed coach of Hull .... Bradford Northern release Jeff Grayshon but the 39-year-old prop hopes to continue playing with another club .... Joe Lydon elects to go for trial on spectator charge, ruling him out of joining tour squad .... Britain beat Highlands and Northern Division of Papua 36-18 .... Oldham report loss of £135,000 despite Division Two title and Premiership double .... Malcolm Reilly to take over as Leeds coach after completing contract with Great Britain in August .... Britain beat North Queensland 66-16 .... Springfield Borough become Chorley Borough.

Castleford's David Plange in action against St. Helens on the opening day of the season.

Alan Tomlinson of Hull is tackled by Halifax's Bob Grogan with Keith Neller about to pounce.

CLUBS

The following is a focus on the 34 professional Rugby League clubs, the section providing each club with a profile and an analysis of their 1987-88 campaign on a match by match basis with a summary for each first team player.

KEY
In the individual club profiles the following headings are featured:
First season refers to when the club gained senior league status. In some instances clubs have disbanded and re-formed, sometimes under different titles. For record purposes these changes are ignored except where there has been a break of more than one full season.
Honours. Until they were scrapped in 1970, the Yorkshire and Lancashire Leagues were among the honours in the professional game. Before 1903 they operated under the title of the Yorkshire and Lancashire Senior Competitions. Winners of these senior competitions are listed under Yorkshire and Lancashire League Champions. The pre-1903 Yorkshire Senior Competition should not be confused with the league operating for A-teams in Yorkshire which had the same title.
Coaches. Changes in the appointment of a club's coach during 1987-88 are shown in brackets.
Attendances. Crowds in brackets are at neutral venue.
Appearances. Players' totals are based on official teamsheets submitted to the League after each first team match. + indicates playing substitute appearance.

In the match by match review for each club the following abbreviations are used:

YC	— Yorkshire Cup	A	—	Away
LC	— Lancashire Cup	W	—	Won
SBC	— Stones Bitter Championship	L	—	Lost
SD	— Second Division	D	—	Drawn
JPS	— John Player Special Trophy	dg	—	Drop goal
CC	— Challenge Cup	Fr	—	France
PT	— Premiership Trophy	Aus	—	Australia
SDP	— Second Division Premiership	NZ	—	New Zealand
P	— Preliminary Round	PNG	—	Papua New Guinea
H	— Home	Pr	—	Probationer

BARROW

Ground: Craven Park
Colours: Royal blue jerseys
First Season: 1900-01
Nickname: Shipbuilders
Chairman: Bill Pears
Secretary: Wilf Livingstone
Coach: Dennis Jackson (Feb 1987-Nov 1987)
Rod Reddy (Nov 1987-)

Honours: **Challenge Cup** Winners, 1954-55
Beaten finalists, 1937-38, 1950-51, 1956-57, 1966-67
John Player Trophy Beaten finalists 1980-81
Lancashire Cup Winners, 1954-55, 1983-84
Beaten finalists, 1937-38
Division Two Champions, 1975-76, 1983-84

Records: Attendance: 21,651 v. Salford (League) 15 Apr, 1938
Season
Goals: 135 by J. Ball, 1956-57
Tries: 50 by J. Lewthwaite, 1956-57
Points: 305 by I. Ball, 1979-80
Match
Goals: 12 by F. French v. Maryport, 19 Feb, 1938; W. Horne v. Cardiff, 8 Sep, 1951; S. Tickle v. Kent Invicta, 8 Apr, 1984
Tries: 6 by V. Cumberbatch v. Batley, 21 Nov, 1936; J. Thornburrow v. Maryport, 19 Feb, 1938; F. Castle v. York, 29 Sep, 1951
Points: 28 by K. Jarrett v. Doncaster, 25 Aug, 1970; S. Tickle v. Kent Invicta, 8 Apr 1984
Highest score: 83-3 v. Maryport, 1937-38
Highest against: 71-15 v. St. Helens, 1958-59

1987-88 PLAYERS' SUMMARY

	App	Tries	Goals	Dr	Pts
Blacker, Brian	4	1	—	—	4
Burns, Howard	6	—	—	—	—
Burns, Paul	11 + 3	1	—	—	4
Butcher, Jeffrey	10 + 3	1	—	—	4
Butler, Warren	4 + 1	—	—	—	—
Cairns, David	4	—	—	—	—
Creary, Paul	21	2	—	—	8
Du Toit, Nick	14 + 5	1	—	—	4
Flynn, Malcolm	5	—	—	—	—
Hall, John	1	—	—	—	—
Hewer, Gary	7 + 1	—	—	—	—
Irving, Paul	10	3	2	—	16
James, Mick	20	3	—	—	12
Kay, Anthony	22 + 1	10	—	—	40
Kendall, Dave	10 + 7	—	—	—	—
Kendall, Gary	27	5	—	—	20
Lightfoot, John	6	—	—	—	—
Livesey, Dave	4 + 1	—	—	—	—
Lowden, Syd	12 + 2	2	24	—	56
Maguire, Steve	22 + 2	1	—	2	6
Marwood, Dean	7	—	9	—	18
Morrison, Steve	7	—	—	—	—
Moses, Alan	0 + 1	—	—	—	—
Mossop, Andrew	6	—	—	—	—
Mossop, Steve	26 + 4	—	—	—	—
Pocock, Mark	14	2	—	—	8
Quirk, Les	4	4	—	—	16
Rea, Steve	18 + 2	10	—	2	42
Reddy, Rod	15 + 2	2	—	—	8
Richardson, Dave	0 + 6	—	—	—	—
Shaw, Neil	10 + 2	1	—	—	4
Stott, Phil	12	4	—	—	16
Tickle, Steve	28	5	27	—	74
Trainor, Pat	8 + 2	—	—	—	—
Walker, Russ	11 + 4	2	—	—	8
Williams, Stewart	17 + 2	5	—	—	20
TOTALS:					
36 players		65	62	4	388

Rod Reddy — Barrow's player-coach.

1987-88 MATCH ANALYSIS

Date	Competition	H/A	Opponent	Rlt	Score	Tries	Goals	Attendance	Referee
28.8.87	SD	H	Featherstone R.	W	20-8	Quirk (2), Williams, Kay	Tickle (2)	2172	Hodgson
4.9.87	SD	A	Springfield B.	W	29-6	Quirk, Kay, Rea, Walker, Stott	Tickle (4), Rea (dg)	—	—
13.9.87	LC(1)	H	Wigan	L	2-36	—	Tickle	5950	Bowman
18.9.87	SD	H	Sheffield E.	W	10-8	Stott, Quirk	Tickle	1807	Dockray
27.9.87	SD	A	Keighley	L	10-20	Williams, James	Tickle	—	—
2.10.87	SD	H	Rochdale H.	W	21-6	Rea, Pocock, Du Toit, Irving	Irving (2), Maguire	2047	Tennant
11.10.87	SD	A	Doncaster	D	16-16	Rea, Williams, Reddy	Tickle (2)	—	—
18.10.87	SD	H	Runcorn H.	W	18-7	Rea, Kay, Walker	Tickle (3)	1707	Houghton
25.10.87	SD	A	Oldham	L	8-36	Kay	Tickle (2)	—	—
1.11.87	SD	A	Whitehaven	L	6-16	Rea	Tickle	—	—
8.11.87	SD	H	Doncaster	W	14-10	James, Rea	Tickle (3)	1539	Spencer
12.11.87	JPS(1)	A	Springfield B.	L	2-14	—	Tickle	—	—
22.11.87	SD	A	Rochdale H.	W	11-9	Pocock, Reddy	Tickle, Maguire (dg)	—	—
29.11.87	SD	H	Whitehaven	W	20-16	Tickle, Irving, Creary, Williams	Tickle (2)	2072	Carter
6.12.87	SD	A	Featherstone R.	L	0-36	—	—	—	—
13.12.87	SD	H	Oldham	W	18-14	Irving, Kay, G. Kendall	Tickle (3)	2244	Tennant
20.12.87	SD	A	Bramley	L	4-18	Blacker	—	—	—
3.1.88	SD	H	Workington T.	L	4-6	G. Kendall	—	2027	Whitfield
10.1.88	SD	A	Sheffield E.	L	0-22	—	—	—	—
17.1.88	SD	A	Wakefield T.	L	14-32	G. Kendall, Stott	Lowden (3)	—	—
31.1.88	SCC(1)	A	Rochdale H.	L	4-6	Lowden	—	—	—
7.2.88	SD	H	Keighley	W	14-6	Butcher, Stott, Burns	Lowden	1313	Berry
26.2.88	SD	A	Runcorn H.	L	8-17	G. Kendall	Lowden (2)	—	—
6.3.88	SD	H	Springfield B.	L	0-4	—	—	1188	Hodgson
9.3.88	SD	A	Carlisle	W	10-2	Tickle	Lowden (3)	—	—
13.3.88	SD	H	Huddersfield B.	W	28-10	Rea (2), Tickle, Lowden	Lowden (6)	933	Houghton
20.3.88	SD	A	Bramley	D	12-12	Kay (2)	Lowden (2)	999	Tickle
27.3.88	SD	A	Huddersfield B.	W	22-10	Rea (2), Kay	Lowden (5)	—	—
1.4.88	SD	H	Carlisle	W	16-17	G. Kendall, James, Shaw	Lowden (2)	1410	Bowman
4.4.88	SD	A	Workington T.	L	15-17	Williams, Maquire	Marwood (3), Rea (dg)	—	—
17.4.88	SD	H	Wakefield T.	W	32-16	Tickle (2), Kay (2), Creary	Marwood (6)	1282	Whitfield

25

BATLEY

Ground: Mount Pleasant
Colours: Cerise and fawn jerseys
First Season: 1895-96
Nickname: Gallant Youths
Chairman: Michael Lumb
Secretary: Les Hardy
Coach: Brian Lockwood
(Nov 1985-May 1987)
Paul Daley (July 1987-)
Honours: **Championship** Winners, 1923-24
Challenge Cup Winners, 1896-97,
1897-98, 1900-01
Yorkshire League Winners,
1898-99, 1923-24
Yorkshire Cup Winners, 1912-13
Beaten finalists, 1909-10, 1922-23,
1924-25, 1952-53
Records: Attendance: 23,989 v. Leeds
(RL Cup) 14 Mar, 1925
Season
Goals: 120 by S. Thompson,
1958-59
Tries: 29 by J. Tindall, 1912-13
Points: 281 by J. Perry, 1950-51
Match
Goals: 9 by W. Davies v. Widnes,
27 Mar, 1909; S. Thompson v.
Keighley, 20 Sep, 1958
Tries: 5 by J. Oakland v. Bramley,
19 Dec, 1908; T. Brannan v.
Swinton, 17 Jan, 1920; J. Wale v.
Bramley, 4 Dec, 1926 and v.
Cottingham, 12 Feb, 1927
Points: 26 by J. Perry v. Liverpool
C., 16 Sep, 1951
Highest score: 52-0 v. Widnes,
1908-09
Highest against: 78-9 v. Wakefield
T., 1967-68

1987-88 PLAYERS' SUMMARY

	App	Tries	Goals	Dr	Pts
Agar, Malcolm	16 + 1	2	19	2	48
Arnold, Derek	3 + 1	—	—	—	—
Bartle, Phil	12	1	—	—	4
Bowness, Mark	0 + 1	—	—	—	—
Carroll, John	12	2	—	1	9
Cook, Mark	15	1	—	—	4
Durham, Steve	3 + 3	1	—	—	4
Fenwick, Richard	0 + 1	—	—	—	—
Fortis, Mark	12 + 6	1	—	—	4
Garner, Peter	5 + 2	—	—	—	—
Geary, Paul	15 + 1	5	—	—	20
Harris, Bill	10	—	—	—	—
Hartley, Neil	0 + 1	—	—	—	—
Hemingway, Neil	24 + 1	3	—	—	12
Herring, Phil	4	1	—	—	4
Hinchcliffe, Mark	7	—	—	—	—
Illingworth, Neil	9 + 1	—	—	—	—
Jones, David	10	2	—	—	8
Madden, Shaun	0 + 1	—	—	—	—
McGowan, John	6 + 5	—	—	—	—
McGrath, Damien	16	6	23	1	71
McLeary, Jack	21 + 2	5	—	—	20
Mitchell, Keith	7	1	—	—	4
Parrish, Mick	2	—	6	—	12
Parrish, Steve	11	2	2	1	13
Pickerill, Neil	30	2	—	3	11
Ratcliffe, Paul	1 + 6	—	—	—	—
Reed, Steve	7 + 1	—	—	—	—
Scott, Mark	3	—	—	—	—
Snell, Graham	15 + 1	2	—	—	8
Sowden, Russell	20	3	—	—	12
Speight, Mark	17 + 6	1	—	—	4
Spendler, Mark	16	1	—	—	4
Stainburn, John	9 + 2	1	—	—	4
Storey, Paul	25	3	—	—	12
West, Brian	3	—	—	—	—
Williams, Andy	4	1	—	—	4
Wilson, Simon	32	8	3	1	39
Wragg, Nick	11	1	—	—	4
Yarrow, Julian	1 + 2	—	—	—	—
Trialist	2	—	—	—	—

TOTALS:
41 players		56	53	9	339

1987-88 MATCH ANALYSIS

Date	Competition	H/A	Opponent	Rlt	Score	Tries	Goals	Attendance	Referee
6.9.87	SD	A	Mansfield M.	W	26-10	Carroll, Cook, Wilson, Herring	Agar (5)	—	—
9.9.87	SD	A	Doncaster	W	12-8	Storey	Agar (4)	—	—
13.9.87	YC(1)	A	Featherstone R.	L	6-28	McLeary	Wilson	—	—
20.9.87	SD	H	York	D	16-16	Pickerill, Hemingway, McLeary	Wilson (2)	792	Houghton
4.10.87	SD	H	Keighley	W	17-2	McGrath (2)	McGrath (4), Carroll (dg)	865	Dockray
11.10.87	SD	A	Workington T.	L	4-11	McLeary	—	—	—
18.10.87	SD	H	Doncaster	W	28-16	Hemingway, Mitchell, Sowden, Bartle, McGrath	McGrath (4)	1395	Whitfield
25.10.87	SD	A	Huddersfield B.	L	6-9	Speight	McGrath	—	—
1.11.87	SD	H	Workington T.	L	12-23	Wilson, Carroll, Fortis	—	782	Carter
8.11.87	SD	H	Runcorn H.	L	2-15	—	Agar	754	Bowman
15.11.87	JPS(1)	H	Hunslet	W	18-16	McLeary, Sowden	Agar (5)	1117	Simpson
22.11.87	JPS(2)	H	Oldham	L	0-44	—	—	2808	Cross
29.11.87	SD	A	Keighley	L	6-22	Sowden	Agar	—	—
6.12.87	SD	H	Sheffield E.	L	6-22	Agar	Agar	653	Hodgson
13.12.87	SD	A	Runcorn H.	L	18-23	Wilson, Geary	M. Parrish (4), S. Parrish (dg), Pickerill (dg)	—	—
20.12.87	SD	H	Springfield B.	L	16-20	Storey, Stainburn, S. Parrish	M. Parrish (2)	552	Burke
26.12.87	SD	H	Dewsbury	W	12-6	Pickerill, Wilson	S. Parrish (2)	1309	Tennant
27.12.87	SD	A	Bramley	L	0-4	—	—	—	—
10.1.88	SD	H	Wakefield T.	L	4-18	Wilson	—	1521	McDonald
24.1.88	SD	H	Featherstone R.	L	4-13	Geary	—	1204	Dockray
31.1.88	CC(1)	A	Doncaster	L	10-18	Storey, McLeary	McGrath	—	—
7.2.88	SD	A	Wakefield T.	L	0-14	—	—	—	—
21.2.88	SD	H	Huddersfield B.	L	20-26	Spendler, McGrath, Geary, Jones	McGrath (2)	620	Steele
28.2.88	SD	A	Sheffield E.	W	18-12	Geary (2), Wilson	McGrath (2), Agar (dg), Pickerill (dg)	—	—
6.3.88	SD	H	Bramley	L	13-20	McGrath, Wilson	McGrath, Agar, Wilson (dg)	640	Holgate
13.3.88	SD	A	Springfield B.	L	0-26	—	—	—	—
20.3.88	SD	H	Fulham	L	6-34	Wilson	McGrath	485	Drinkwater
27.3.88	SD	A	York	L	20-33	Snell, Hemmingway, S. Parrish	McGrath (4)	—	—
1.4.88	SD	A	Fulham	L	16-40	McGrath, Jones, Snell	McGrath (1, 1 dg), Agar (dg)	—	—
3.4.88	SD	A	Featherstone R.	L	13-44	Agar, Durham	McGrath, Agar, Pickerill (dg)	—	—
10.4.88	SD	H	Mansfield M.	L	0-8	—	—	459	Holgate
15.4.88	SD	A	Dewsbury	L	10-28	Williams, Wragg	McGrath	—	—

27

BRADFORD NORTHERN

Ground: Odsal Stadium
Colours: White jerseys with red, amber and black hoops
First Season: 1895-96 as "Bradford". Disbanded and became Bradford Northern in 1907-08. Disbanded during 1963-64 and re-formed for start of 1964-65
Nickname: Northern
Chairman: Jack Bates
Secretary: Rita Winter
Coach: Barry Seabourne (May 1985-)
Honours: **Challenge Cup** Winners, 1905-06, 1943-44, 1946-47, 1948-49
Beaten finalists, 1897-98, 1944-45, 1947-48, 1972-73
Championship Beaten finalists, 1947-48, 1951-52
Division One Champions, 1903-04, 1979-80, 1980-81
Division Two Champions, 1973-74
War-time Emergency League Championship winners, 1939-40, 1940-41, 1944-45
Beaten finalists, 1941-42
Yorkshire League Winners, 1899-1900, 1900-01, 1939-40, 1940-41, 1947-48
Yorkshire Cup Winners, 1906-07, 1940-41, 1941-42, 1943-44, 1945-46, 1948-49, 1949-50, 1953-54, 1965-66, 1978-79, 1987-88
Beaten finalists, 1913-14, 1981-82, 1982-83
Premiership Winners, 1977-78
Beaten finalists, 1978-79, 1979-80
John Player Trophy Winners, 1974-75, 1979-80
Records: Attendance: 102,569 Warrington v. Halifax (RL Cup Final replay) 5 May, 1954
Home: 69,429 v. Huddersfield (RL Cup) 14 March, 1953
Season
Goals: 173 by E. Tees, 1971-72
Tries: 63 by J. McLean, 1951-52
Points: 364 by E. Tees, 1971-72

Match
Goals: 14 by J. Phillips v. Batley, 6 Sep, 1952
Tries: 7 by J. Dechan v. Bramley, 13 Oct, 1906
Points: 36 by J. Woods v. Swinton, 13 Oct, 1985
Highest score: 72-9 v. Doncaster, 1973-74; 72-12 v. Hunslet, 1984-85
Highest against: 75-18 v. Leeds, 1931-32

1987-88 PLAYERS' SUMMARY

	App	Tries	Goals	Dr	Pts
Barnett, Steve	0 + 1	—	—	—	—
Clarkson, Allan	3	—	—	—	—
Donlan, Steve	0 + 2	1	—	—	4
Fairbank, Karl	35	15	—	—	60
Fleming, Mark	2	—	—	—	—
Ford, Phil	33 + 1	14	—	2	58
Francis, Richard	21	1	—	—	4
Godfrey, Heath	6 + 3	1	—	—	4
Grayshon, Jeff	9 + 2	—	—	—	—
Grayshon, Paul	1 + 3	—	—	—	—
Hamer, John	0 + 2	—	—	—	—
Harkin, Paul	28	7	—	—	28
Heron, Wayne	17 + 5	3	—	—	12
Hill, Brendan	30 + 5	10	—	—	40
Hobbs, David	28 + 2	6	76	4	180
Holmes, Terry	4	1	—	—	4
McGowan, Steve	34	14	—	—	56
Mercer, Gary	21	13	—	—	52
Moulden, Darren	0 + 2	—	—	—	—
Mumby, Keith	35	6	29	—	82
Noble, Brian	35	4	—	—	16
Parrish, Steve	1	—	—	—	—
Potts, Martin	5	1	—	—	4
Race, Wayne	2	—	—	—	—
Redfearn, David	7 + 9	1	—	—	4
Rhodes, Paul	2 + 7	—	—	—	—
Robinson, Andy	4	—	—	—	—
Roebuck, Neil	13 + 11	1	—	—	4
Sidebottom, Gary	3	—	—	—	—
Simpson, Roger	25 + 3	5	—	—	20
Skerrett, Kelvin	31 + 1	4	—	—	16
Stewart, Russell	19	4	—	—	16
Tuffs, Simon	1	—	—	—	—
TOTALS:					
33 players		112	105	6	664

1987-88 MATCH ANALYSIS

Date	Com-petition	H/A	Opponent	Rlt	Score	Tries	Goals	Atten-dance	Referee
30.8.87	SBC	A	Salford	W	16-12	Fairbank, Ford, Harkin	Mumby (2)	—	—
6.9.87	SBC	H	Widnes	L	8-18	Donlan	Mumby (2)	3091	Allatt
13.9.87	YC(1)	A	Hull K.R.	W	19-12	Simpson (2), Fairbank	Mumby (3), Ford (dg)	—	—
20.9.87	SBC	H	Leeds	W	32-8	Ford (2), Potts, Noble, Fairbank, Holmes	Mumby (4)	6060	Holdsworth
22.9.87	YC(2)	A	Bramley	W	30-6	McGowan (2), Noble (2), Mumby, Fairbank	Mumby (3)	—	—
27.9.87	SBC	A	St. Helens	L	10-38	McGowan (2)	Mumby	—	—
30.9.87	YC(SF)	H	Leeds	W	16-5	Hill, Fairbank, Mumby	Mumby (2)	7730	Tennant
4.10.87	SBC	H	Swinton	W	40-12	Ford (2), Roebuck, Fairbank, Heron, Noble, McGowan	Mumby (6)	2510	Whitfield
11.10.87	SBC	A	Halifax	W	12-10	Hill, Skerrett	Hobbs (1, ldg), Ford (dg)	—	—
17.10.87	YC(F)	Leeds	Castleford	D	12-12	Fairbank	Mumby (2), Hobbs (2)	(10,947)	Allatt
25.10.87	SBC	H	Hull K.R.	W	24-13	Mercer (2), Simpson, Fairbank	Hobbs (4)	3221	Simpson
31.10.87	YC(F) Replay	Elland Rd. Leeds	Castleford	W	11-2	Hill, Heron	Hobbs (1, ldg)	(8175)	Allatt
8.11.87	SBC	H	Leigh	W	24-6	Ford, McGowan, Hill	Hobbs (6)	2963	Tickle
15.11.87	JPS(1)	A	Oldham	L	6-22	Redfearn	Hobbs	—	—
29.11.87	SBC	A	Castleford	L	12-20	Fairbank, Mercer	Hobbs (2)	—	—
6.12.87	SBC	H	Halifax	W	24-8	Ford (2), McGowan, Hill	Hobbs (4)	6735	Cross
13.12.87	SBC	A	Hunslet	W	24-8	Stewart, Ford, Hill, Simpson, Mercer	Hobbs (2)	—	—
20.12.87	SBC	A	Warrington	L	12-18	Heron	Hobbs (4)	—	—
27.12.87	SBC	H	Hull	L	2-5	—	Hobbs	4237	Kendrew
3.1.88	SBC	H	Castleford	W	24-6	Ford, Mumby, Fairbank, McGowan	Hobbs (4)	4108	Lindop
10.1.88	SBC	A	Wigan	W	18-16	Mercer (2), Hill, Stewart	Hobbs	—	—
17.1.88	SBC	H	St. Helens	L	12-13	Stewart, Harkin	Hobbs (2)	6425	Hodgson
24.1.88	SBC	A	Swinton	W	12-8	Mercer, Hobbs	Hobbs (2)	—	—
30.1.88	CC(1)	A	Wigan	L	0-2	—	—	—	—
7.2.88	SBC	A	Widnes	L	4-26	Hill	—	—	—
21.2.88	SBC	H	Warrington	W	28-10	Mercer (2), McGowan (2), Ford	Mumby (4)	3536	Lindop
6.3.88	SBC	A	Hull	W	16-0	Mumby, Ford, Mercer	Hobbs (2)	—	—
20.3.88	SBC	H	Salford	W	34-4	Mercer (3), Hobbs, Harkin, Fairbank	Hobbs (5)	3320	Holdsworth
27.3.88	SBC	A	Leigh	W	20-5	McGowan, Francis, Stewart	Hobbs (4)	—	—
1.4.88	SBC	A	Leeds	W	32-18	Skerrett (2), Mumby, Hobbs, McGowan	Hobbs (5, 2 dg)	—	—
5.4.88	SBC	H	Hunslet	W	32-4	Hobbs, Skerrett, Fairbank, Ford, Mumby	Hobbs (6)	3889	Volante
10.4.88	SBC	H	Wigan (Bradford C. AFC)	L	10-14	Harkin	Hobbs (3)	11,310	Tennant
17.4.88	SBC	A	Hull K.R.	W	46-4	Hobbs (2), Hill (2), Harkin (2), Fairbank (2), Simpson	Hobbs (5)	—	—
24.4.88	PT(1)	H	Leeds	W	32-18	Ford, McGowan, Godfrey, Harkin, Fairbank	Hobbs (6)	7269	McDonald
8.5.88	PT(SF)	A	St. Helens	L	10-24	McGowan	Hobbs (3)	—	—

BRAMLEY

Ground: McLaren Field
Colours: Amber and black jerseys
First Season: 1896-97
Nickname: Villagers
Chairman: Jeff Wine
Secretary: Barry Rennison
Coach: Chris Forster (June 1987-Nov 1987)
      Tony Fisher (Nov 1987-)
Honours: **BBC2 Floodlit Trophy** Winners, 1973-74
Records: Attendance: 12,600 v. Leeds (League) 7 May, 1947
Season
Goals: 130 by J. Wilson, 1961-62
Tries: 34 by P. Lister, 1985-86
Points: 276 by G. Langfield, 1956-57
Match
Goals: 11 by B. Ward v. Doncaster, 1 Sep, 1974
Tries: 7 by J. Sedgewick v. Normanton, 16 Apr, 1906
Points: 28 by B. Ward v. Doncaster, 1 Sep, 1974
Highest score; 52-17 v. Doncaster, 1974-75
Highest against: 92-7 v. Australia, 1921-22

1987-88 PLAYERS' SUMMARY

	App	Tries	Goals	Dr	Pts
Allen, Jamie	2 + 3	—	—	—	—
Aston, Mark	2	—	—	—	—
Barik, Tony	1 + 1	—	—	—	—
Barraclough, Glenn	3 + 7	1	—	—	4
Beale, Graham	1	—	—	—	—
Bibb, Trevor	13	—	15	—	30
Bond, Steve	8 + 2	1	—	—	4
Booth, Simon	2	—	—	—	—
Bowman, Chris	9 + 4	6	—	—	24
Brentley, Gary	8 + 1	1	—	—	4
Carroll, Steve	31	4	12	4	44
Clarkson, Allan	5	—	—	—	—
Crawford, Adrian	18 + 5	1	—	—	4
Denson, Allan	11	3	—	—	12
Duckworth, Ken	4	—	—	—	—
Edmondson, Steve	14 + 11	1	—	—	4
Farrar, Andrew	10	—	—	—	—
Fletcher, Paul	14 + 1	1	—	—	4
Gascoigne, Andy	15 + 1	4	—	—	16
Gibson, Mark	5 + 2	1	—	—	4
Green, Karl	23 + 2	2	—	—	8
Hardisty, Ian	1	—	—	—	—
Hendry, Paul	2 + 2	1	—	—	4
Hobbs, Gary	15	8	—	—	32
Howard, Les	6 + 1	1	—	—	4
Hunter, Damien	4	—	—	—	—
Johnson, Phil	2	—	—	—	—
Kilner, Shaun	5	—	13	—	26
Langley, Paul	3 + 1	—	4	—	8
Lewis, Peter	25	10	—	—	40
Lister, Peter	26	17	27	1	123
Lund, Steve	4	—	—	—	—
Olpherts, Eric	13	1	—	—	4
Owen, Phil	21 + 1	—	—	—	—
Pudsey, Adrian	7	—	—	—	—
Race, Wayne	9	1	—	—	4
Roberts, Lee	2	—	—	—	—
Robinson, Mike	1	—	—	—	—
Savage, Dave	0 + 1	—	—	—	—
Schaumkell, Kevin	3	—	—	—	—
Sharp, Ronnie	6	3	—	—	12
Shipley, Jon	7 + 2	—	—	—	—
Skinner, Matthew	9 + 1	1	—	—	4
Spedding, Paul	23	2	—	—	8
Stutchbury, John	1	—	—	—	—
Tennant, Jeff	20 + 1	—	—	—	—
Watson, Andy	2	2	7	—	22
TOTALS:					
47 players		73	78	5	453

Tony Fisher — Bramley's coach.

1987-88 MATCH ANALYSIS

Date	Com-petition	H/A	Opponent	Rlt	Score	Tries	Goals	Atten-dance	Referee
2.9.87	SD	H	Doncaster	W	20-18	Hobbs, Lister	Kilner (5), Lister	1092	Drinkwater
6.9.87	SD	A	Oldham	L	11-46	Bowman	Bibb (3), Carroll (dg)	—	—
9.9.87	SD	H	Dewsbury	L	14-19	Lister (2)	Bibb (3)	751	Burke
13.9.87	YC(1)	H	Doncaster	W	39-12	Lister (3), Hobbs (2), Bowman, Barraclough	Bibb (5), Carroll (dg)	828	Cross
20.9.87	SD	A	Wakefield T.	L	10-62	Hobbs, Lewis	Bibb	—	—
22.9.87	YC(2)	H	Bradford N.	L	6-30	Lister	Kilner	2181	Kendrew
27.9.87	SD	H	Featherstone R.	L	22-38	Lewis (3), Henry	Kilner (3)	1038	Bowman
7.10.87	SD	A	Sheffield E.	L	10-20	Hobbs	Kilner (3)	—	—
11.10.87	SD	H	Fulham	L	18-26	Gibson, Lister, Bowman	Lister (3)	534	Steele
1.11.87	JPS(P)	A	York	L	2-38	—	Lister	—	—
8.11.87	SD	H	York	L	18-27	Lister (2), Fletcher	Lister (2, ldg), Carroll (dg)	500	Holdsworth
15.11.87	SD	A	Fulham	L	8-16	—	Langley (4)	—	—
22.11.87	SD	A	Carlisle	L	6-20	Lewis	Lister	—	—
29.11.87	SD	A	Rochdale H.	L	20-23	Denson, Crawford, Hobbs	Lister (4)	—	—
6.12.88	SD	H	Mansfield M.	W	12-10	Skinner, Hobbs	Lister (2)	482	Simpson
13.12.87	SD	A	Dewsbury	W	24-22	Lewis (2), Howard, Hobbs, Denson	Lister (2)	—	—
20.12.87	SD	H	Barrow	W	18-4	Carroll, Edmondson	Lister (5)	718	Houghton
26.12.87	SD	A	York	L	16-21	Spedding, Bowman, Lister	Lister (2)	—	—
27.12.87	SD	H	Batley	W	4-0	—	Lister (2)	985	Allatt
3.1.88	SD	H	Sheffield E.	L	6-12	Gasgoine	Lister	864	Drinkwater
10.1.88	SD	A	Doncaster	L	12-22	Denson, Green, Carroll	—	—	—
15.1.88	CC(1)	H	Sheffield E.	L	6-14	Bond	Kilner	1035	Smith
24.1.88	SD	A	Mansfield M.	W	16-8	Bowman, Olpherts, Lewis	Bibb (2)	—	—
7.2.88	SD	H	Whitehaven	L	6-14	Bowman	Bibb	578	Steele
14.2.88	SD	A	Whitehaven	L	0-24	—	—	—	—
2.3.88	SD	H	Carlisle	W	23-13	Carroll, Brentley, Lewis, Lister	Carroll (3, 1 dg)	418	Holdsworth
6.3.88	SD	A	Batley	W	20-13	Lister (2), Sharp	Carroll (4)	—	—
13.3.88	SD	H	Oldham	L	16-36	Lister, Lewis, Gascoigne	Carroll (2)	1639	Whitfield
20.3.88	SD	A	Barrow	D	12-12	Lister, Gascoigne	Carroll (2)	—	—
27.3.88	SD	H	Wakefield T.	W	12-10	Green, Gascoigne	Carroll, Lister	1635	Cross
4.4.88	SD	H	Rochdale H.	W	34-24	Sharp (2), Watson (2), Carroll, Race	Watson (5)	774	Berry
10.4.88	SD	A	Featherstone R.	L	12-40	Spedding, Lister	Trialist (2)	—	—

31

CARLISLE

Ground: Brunton Park
Colours: Blue jerseys with red and white band
First Season: 1981-82. A Carlisle City team entered the League in 1928-29 but withdrew after 10 matches, winning one
Chairman: Alan Tucker
Secretary: Robert Carter
Coach: Roy Lester (June 1986-)
Records: Attendance: 5,903 v. Workington T. (Div. 2) 6 Sep, 1981
Season
Goals: 113 by S. Ferres, 1981-82
Tries: 25 by M. Morgan, 1981-82; G. Peacham, 1984-85
Points: 242 by S. Ferres, 1981-82
Match
Goals: 9 by D. Carroll v. Mansfield M., 16 Mar, 1986
Tries: 4 by G. Peacham v. Workington T., 25 Jan, 1987 and K. Pape v. Rochdale H., 11 Feb, 1987
Points: 21 by D. Carroll v. Mansfield M., 16 Mar, 1986 and v. Fulham, 2 May, 1986
Highest score: 47-18 v Fulham, 1984-85
Highest against: 112-0 v. St. Helens, 1986-87

1987-88 PLAYERS' SUMMARY

	App	Tries	Goals	Dr	Pts
Armstrong, Colin	29 + 1	2	6	1	21
Bond, Gary	0 + 1	—	—	—	—
Bowness, Chris	8	—	—	—	—
Brierley, Steve	13 + 3	—	—	—	—
Coles, Colin	27	4	—	—	16
Courty, Dave	5 + 4	—	—	—	—
Doyle, Mark	27	5	—	—	20
Duffy, Don	9	—	—	—	—
Green, Jimmy	12	—	—	—	—
Green, Kenny	1	—	—	—	—
Kirkby, Steve	21 + 1	2	—	—	8
Langton, Steve	30	11	—	—	44
Lithgow, Paul	9 + 1	1	—	—	4
Little, Alan	6 + 1	—	—	—	—
Maclagan, Alan	1 + 3	—	—	—	—
McAvoy, Brian	3 + 1	1	—	—	4
McMullen, Alan	26 + 1	—	—	—	—
Mills, Steve	32	12	—	—	48
Murdock, Gary	21	2	—	—	8
Murdock, Paul	0 + 6	—	—	—	—
Pape, Kevin	31	22	—	—	88
Peacham, Gary	1	—	—	—	—
Schubert, Gary	33	2	—	—	8
Scott, Tony	15 + 9	1	—	—	4
Stockley, John	1	—	—	—	—
Subritzky, Peter	12	2	—	3	11
Thomason, Malcolm	25	2	—	—	8
Tunstall, Brian	20	—	54	2	110
Vickers, Barry	9	—	24	2	50
Whitchurch, Duncan	2 + 2	—	—	—	—
TOTALS:					
30 players		69	84	8	452

1987-88 MATCH ANALYSIS

Date	Competition	H/A	Opponent	Rlt	Score	Tries	Goals	Attendance	Referee
30.8.87	SD	A	Wakefield T.	L	8-56	Kirkby, Langton	—	—	—
6.9.87	SD	H	Doncaster	D	18-18	Schubert, Langton, Doyle	Tunstall (3)	709	Kendrew
9.9.87	SD	H	Keighley	W	26-12	Langton, Pape, Mills	Tunstall (7)	497	Bowman
13.9.87	LC(1)	A	Whitehaven	L	12-28	Armstrong, Pape	Tunstall (2)	—	—
20.9.87	SD	H	Workington T.	L	12-24	Pape, McAvoy	Tunstall (2)	816	Haigh
27.9.87	SD	A	Rochdale H.	L	5-20	Pape	Subritzky (dg)	—	—
9.10.87	SD	A	Springfield B.	L	9-12	Subritzky	Tunstall (2), Subritzky (dg)	—	—
25.10.87	SD	A	Featherstone R.	W	29-22	Pape (2), Kirkby, Thomason	Tunstall (6), Subritzky (dg)	—	—
8.11.87	SD	A	Huddersfield B.	L	8-16	Pape (2)	—	—	—
15.11.87	JPS(1)	H	Warrington	L	16-22	Pape, Langton	Tunstall (4)	1055	Lindop
22.11.87	SD	H	Bramley	W	20-6	Langton, Pape, Mills	Tunstall (4)	400	Holgate
29.11.87	SD	A	Workington T.	L	2-14	—	Tunstall	—	—
6.12.87	SD	H	Runcorn H.	W	13-11	Pape	Tunstall (4, 1 dg)	507	Tickle
20.12.87	SD	H	Sheffield E.	W	14-12	Mills (2)	Tunstall (3)	559	Simpson
1.1.88	SD	A	Whitehaven	W	6-4	Mills	Tunstall	—	—
10.1.88	SD	H	Springfield B.	W	29-0	Scott, G. Murdoch, Schubert, Thomason	Tunstall (6, 1 dg)	639	Holdsworth
17.1.88	CC(P)	H	Whitehaven	D	8-8	Lithgow	Tunstall (2)	1867	Whitfield
20.1.88	CC(P) Replay	A	Whitehaven	W	22-8	Armstrong, Mills, Pape, Coles	Tunstall (3)	—	—
24.1.88	SD	A	Sheffield E.	L	10-12	Langton, Mills	Tunstall	—	—
31.1.88	CC(1)	A	Hull K.R.	L	6-14	—	Tunstall (3)	—	—
14.2.88	SD	A	Oldham	L	4-26	Pape	—	—	—
21.2.88	SD	A	Doncaster	W	16-6	Pape, Subritzky	Armstrong (4)	—	—
28.2.88	SD	H	Wakefield T.	L	8-22	Mills, Pape	—	920	Spencer
2.3.88	SD	A	Bramley	L	13-23	Pape, Doyle	Armstrong (2, 1 dg)	586	Drinkwater
9.3.88	SD	H	Barrow	L	2-10	—	Vickers	459	Dockray
13.3.88	SD	H	Rochdale H.	L	10-11	Pape (2)	Vickers	—	—
20.3.88	SD	A	Keighley	W	14-10	Pape, Langton	Vickers (3)	—	—
23.3.88	SD	H	Huddersfield B.	W	22-12	Doyle (2), Coles, Pape	Vickers (3)	446	Burke
27.3.88	SD	H	Featherstone R.	W	23-18	Coles (2), Langton, Mills	Vickers (3, 1 dg)	849	Berry
1.4.88	SD	A	Barrow	W	17-16	G. Murdoch, Mills	Vickers (4, 1 dg)	—	—
5.4.88	SD	H	Whitehaven	W	16-7	Langton, Doyle	Vickers (4)	1132	Carter
10.4.88	SD	A	Runcorn H.	W	18-10	Langton, Mills, Pape	Vickers (3)	—	—
17.4.88	SD	H	Oldham	L	16-34	Pape, Langton, Mills	Vickers (2)	2049	Smith

Paul Lithgow of Carlisle is collared against Wakefield Trinity.

CASTLEFORD

Ground:	Wheldon Road
Colours:	Yellow and black jerseys
First Season:	1926-27. There was also a Castleford team from 1896-97 to 1905-06, inclusive
Nickname:	Glassblowers
Chairman:	David Poulter
Secretary:	Denise Cackett
Coach:	David Sampson (May 1987-Apr 1988)
Honours:	**Championship** Beaten finalists, 1938-39, 1968-69 **Challenge Cup** Winners, 1934-35, 1968-69, 1969-70, 1985-86 **Yorkshire League** Winners, 1932-33, 1938-39, 1964-65 **Yorkshire Cup** Winners, 1977-78, 1981-82, 1986-87 Beaten finalists, 1948-49, 1950-51, 1968-69, 1971-72, 1983-84, 1985-86, 1987-88 **Eastern Division** Championship Beaten finalists, 1963-64 **BBC2 Floodlit Trophy** Winners, 1965-66, 1966-67, 1967-68, 1976-77 **John Player Trophy** Winners, 1976-77 **Premiership** Beaten finalists, 1983-84 **Charity Shield** Beaten finalists 1986-87
Records:	Attendance: 25,449 v. Hunslet (RL Cup) 3 Mar, 1935 **Season** Goals: 158 by S. Lloyd, 1976-77 Tries: 36 by K. Howe, 1963-64 Points: 334 by R. Beardmore, 1983-84

Match
Goals: 17 by S. Lloyd v. Millom, 16 Sep, 1973
Tries: 5 by D. Foster v. Hunslet, 10 Nov, 1972; J. Joyner v. Millom, 16 Sep, 1973; S. Fenton v. Dewsbury, 27 Jan, 1978; I. French v. Hunslet, 9 Feb, 1986
Points: 43 by S. Lloyd v. Millom, 16 Sep, 1973
Highest score: 88-5 v. Millom, 1973-74
Highest against: 62-12 v. St. Helens, 1985-86

1987-88 PLAYERS' SUMMARY

	App	Tries	Goals	Dr	Pts
Anderson, Grant	14 + 1	1	—	—	4
Beardmore, Bob	24 + 2	6	63	1	151
Beardmore, Kevin	23	8	—	—	32
Beattie, Michael	20	10	—	—	40
Blackburn, John	2	—	—	—	—
Boothroyd, Giles	12 + 7	6	—	—	24
Crabtree, Paul	0 + 2	—	—	—	—
England, Keith	28 + 2	1	—	—	4
Fifita, John	21 + 3	6	—	—	24
Gill, Steve	0 + 1	—	—	—	—
Hill, Kenny	12 + 4	—	—	—	—
Hyde, Gary	22 + 5	8	—	—	32
Irwin, Shaun	18 + 2	5	—	—	20
Johnson, Barry	11 + 1	1	—	—	4
Jones, Keith	8 + 6	1	—	—	4
Joyner, John	33	3	—	—	12
Juliff, Brian	8 + 3	3	—	—	12
Kear, John	1	—	—	—	—
Ketteridge, Martin	21	1	33	—	70
Lindner, Bob	10	4	—	—	16
Lord, Gary	8	1	—	—	4
Marchant, Tony	32	10	—	—	40
Mountain, Dean	1 + 4	—	—	—	—
Plange, David	28	13	4	—	60
Roockley, David	32 + 2	11	10	—	64
Sampson, Dean	10 + 13	2	—	—	8
Shillito, Alan	11	—	—	—	—
Southernwood, Roy	18 + 7	7	—	—	28
Thornton, Wayne	2 + 3	—	—	—	—
Ward, Kevin	25 + 1	4	—	—	16
TOTALS: 30 players		112	110	1	669

1987-88 MATCH ANALYSIS

Date	Competition	H/A	Opponent	Rlt	Score	Tries	Goals	Attendance	Referee
30.8.87	SBC	H	St. Helens	W	20-10	Marchant, Boothroyd, Sampson, K. Beardmore	Roockley (2)	5443	Lindop
6.9.87	SBC	A	Leigh	L	6-14	Roockley	Roockley	—	—
13.9.87	YC(1)	H	Hunslet	W	32-12	Beattie (2), Joyner, Ward, Marchant, Plange	Plange (4)	4748	Smith
20.9.87	SBC	A	Wigan	L	18-44	Beattie, Roockley, Hyde	Ketteridge (3)	—	—
23.9.87	YC(2)	A	Halifax	W	10-0	K. Beardmore	Ketteridge (3)	—	—
27.9.87	SBC	H	Warrington	L	30-40	Fifita, Marchant, Hyde, Roockley, Plange	Ketteridge (5)	5398	Kershaw
30.9.87	YC(SF)	A	Featherstone R.	W	36-8	Lindner (2), Plange, Marchant, Ward, Southernwood, Beattie	Ketteridge (4)	—	—
4.10.87	SBC	A	Hunslet	W	18-15	Boothroyd, Plange, Sampson	Ketteridge (3)	—	—
17.10.87	YC(F)	Leeds	Bradford N.	D	12-12	Lindner, Plange	Ketteridge (2)	(10,947)	Allatt
25.10.87	SBC	A	Hull	W	37-16	Fifita (3), Beattie (2), Roockley, Joyner	Ketteridge (4), R. Beardmore (dg)	—	—
31.10.87	YC(F) Replay	Elland Road, Leeds	Bradford N.	L	2-11	—	Ketteridge	(8175)	Allatt
8.11.87	SBC	A	Widnes	L	12-31	Roockley, Plange	R. Beardmore (2)	—	—
15.11.87	JPS(1)	A	Featherstone R.	W	34-12	Boothroyd, Roockley, Marchant, Jones, Southernwood, Beattie	Roockley (5)	—	—
21.11.87	JPS(2)	A	Wigan	L	16-26	Lindner, Fifita, Plange	Roockley (2)	—	—
29.11.87	SBC	H	Bradford N.	W	20-12	Fifita, Hyde, Roockley	R. Beardmore (4)	4609	Whitfield
2.12.87	SBC	H	Wigan	W	12-10	K. Beardmore	R. Beardmore (4)	6094	Smith
6.12.87	SBC	A	Leeds	L	0-44	—	—	—	—
13.12.87	SBC	H	Salford	W	14-0	Ward, Beattie	R. Beardmore (3)	3382	Allatt
20.12.87	SBC	H	Leigh	L	18-22	Irwin, Marchant	R. Beardmore (5)	3601	Smith
27.12.87	SBC	A	Hull K.R.	W	28-16	Hyde (2), R. Beardmore, Plange, Boothroyd	R. Beardmore (4)	—	—
3.1.88	SBC	A	Bradford N.	L	6-24	K. Beardmore	R. Beardmore	—	—
10.1.88	SBC	H	Hull	W	32-3	Beattie, K. Beardmore, Plange, R. Beardmore, Marchant	R. Beardmore (6)	3753	Volante
31.1.88	CC(1)	A	Leeds	L	14-22	Beattie, Roockley	R. Beardmore (3)	—	—
7.2.88	SBC	A	Warrington	L	6-32	Roockley	R. Beardmore	—	—
19.2.88	SBC	A	Salford	W	28-12	Southernwood (2), R. Beardmore, Roockley, Hyde	R. Beardmore (2), Ketteridge (2)	—	—
6.3.88	SBC	H	Swinton	W	76-16	K. Beardmore (3), Plange (3), Hyde (2), Roockley, Johnson, Ward, Southernwood, England, R. Beardmore	R. Beardmore (10)	3147	Whitfield
13.3.88	SBC	A	St. Helens	L	6-14	Plange	R. Beardmore	—	—
20.3.88	SBC	H	Halifax	L	6-28	Marchant	R. Beardmore	6797	McDonald
23.3.88	SBC	H	Widnes	L	6-39	Ketteridge	R. Beardmore	3504	Haigh
27.3.88	SBC	H	Hunslet	W	26-14	Southernwood (2), Irwin, Joyner	Ketteridge (5)	2914	Simpson
1.4.88	SBC	A	Halifax	L	12-22	Lord, Marchant	R. Beardmore (2)	—	—
4.4.88	SBC	H	Hull K.R.	W	28-24	R. Beardmore (2), Anderson, Boothroyd	R. Beardmore (6)	3129	Houghton
10.4.88	SBC	A	Swinton	L	14-45	Juliff (2)	R. Beardmore (3)	—	—
17.4.88	SBC	H	Leeds	W	26-12	Irwin (2), Boothroyd, Marchant, Juliff	R. Beardmore (2), Ketteridge	6999	Berry
24.4.88	PT(1)	A	St. Helens	L	8-40	Irwin	R. Beardmore (2)	—	—

35

DEWSBURY

Ground: Crown Flatt
Colours: Red, amber and black jerseys
First Season: 1901-02
Chairman: Rodney Hardcastle
Secretary: Geoff Parrish
Coach: Terry Crook (Apr 1987-)
Honours: **Championship** Winners, 1972-73
Beaten finalists, 1946-47
Division Two Champions, 1904-05
Challenge Cup Winners, 1911-12, 1942-43
Beaten finalists, 1928-29
Yorkshire League Winners, 1946-47
Yorkshire Cup Winners, 1925-26, 1927-28, 1942-43
Beaten finalists, 1918-19, 1921-22, 1940-41, 1972-73
BBC2 Floodlit Trophy Beaten finalists, 1975-76
War League Championship Winners, 1941-42. (1942-43 won final but championship declared null and void because Dewsbury played an ineligible player.)
Beaten finalists, 1943-44
Records: Attendance: 26,584 v. Halifax (Yorkshire Cup) 30 Oct, 1920
Season
Goals: 145 by N. Stephenson, 1972-73
Tries: 40 by D. Thomas, 1906-07
Points: 368 by N. Stephenson, 1972-73
Match
Goals: 10 by J. Ledgard v. Yorkshire Amateurs, 13 Sep, 1947; N. Stephenson v. Blackpool B, 28 Aug, 1972
Tries: 8 by D. Thomas v. Liverpool C, 13 Apr, 1907
Points: 29 by J. Lyman v. Hull, 22 Apr, 1919
Highest score: 72-0 v. Doncaster, 1984-85
Highest against: 82-0 v. Widnes, 1986-87

1987-88 PLAYERS' SUMMARY

	App	Tries	Goals	Dr	Pts
Bailey, Dennis	6	1	—	—	4
Bates, Phil	1 + 8	1	—	—	4
Broxholme, Paul	3	—	—	—	—
Burgess, Mark	9 + 2	—	—	—	—
Clayforth, Shaun	1 + 1	—	—	—	—
Cochrane, Tony	5	4	—	—	16
Cocks, Gary	26	5	—	—	20
Coen, Darren	31	3	1	—	14
Collins, Mick	13 + 1	1	—	—	4
Cooper, Andrew	6	1	—	—	4
Cooper, Paul	15 + 1	2	—	—	8
Corby, David	2	—	—	—	—
Cornell, Paul	2 + 2	—	—	—	—
Dunford, Shaun	5	—	—	—	—
Garforth, David	4 + 10	1	1	—	6
Garner, Peter	3	—	—	—	—
Gregoire, Don	2	2	—	—	8
Hartley, Ian	14 + 6	1	—	—	4
Hinchcliffe, Steve	8 + 6	2	—	—	8
Holden, Barry	32	4	—	—	16
Howley, Pat	22	7	1	—	30
Hoyle, Robert	5 + 1	—	—	—	—
Hughes, Michael	18	1	—	—	4
Jennings, Paul	12 + 1	2	—	—	8
Joyce, Phil	1	—	—	—	—
Keeble, Mick	1 + 1	—	—	—	—
Marsden, Graham	6	—	—	—	—
Moore, John	29	5	—	—	20
Morris, Stuart	13 + 3	5	—	—	20
Overend, Richard	0 + 1	—	—	—	—
Oxley, Richard	1 + 2	—	—	—	—
Richardson, Don	4 + 1	—	—	—	—
Shaw, Alan	11	—	—	—	—
Shuttleworth, Paul	29	4	—	5	21
Spooner, Chris	15	5	—	—	20
Squires, Chris	25	9	—	—	36
Toole, Tim	4 + 2	—	—	—	—
Vasey, Chris	30	11	70	1	185
Womersley, Shaun	2	—	—	—	—

TOTALS:
| 39 players | | 77 | 73 | 6 | 460 |

1987-88 MATCH ANALYSIS

Date	Com-petition	H/A	Opponent	Rlt	Score	Tries	Goals	Atten-dance	Referee
30.8.87	SD	H	Workington T.	L	6-8	Spooner	Vasey	426	Tidball
2.9.87	YC(P)	A	Wakefield T.	L	14-25	Spooner, Moore	Vasey (3)	—	—
6.9.87	SD	H	Wakefield T.	L	0-22	—	—	1283	Smith
9.9.87	SD	A	Bramley	W	19-14	Morris (2), Vasey	Vasey (3), Shuttleworth (dg)	—	—
20.9.87	SD	A	Huddersfield	L	13-22	Spooner, Howley	Vasey (2), Shuttleworth (dg)	—	—
4.10.87	SD	A	Wakefield T.	L	14-32	Cocks, Howley	Vasey (3)	—	—
11.10.87	SD	H	Huddersfield B.	W	14-6	Collins, Squires	Vasey (3)	669	Hodgson
25.10.87	SD	H	Fulham	W	32-10	Spooner (2), Squires, Cocks, Shuttleworth, Bates	Vasey (4)	336	Bowman
1.11.87	SD	A	Mansfield M.	L	5-22	Squires	Vasey (dg)	—	—
8.11.87	SD	A	Featherstone R.	L	24-30	Howley (2), Squires	Vasey (6)	—	—
15.11.87	JPS(1)	H	Doncaster	W	14-12	Howley, Morris, Vasey	Vasey	1081	Kendrew
22.11.87	JPS(2)	A	Salford	L	5-14	—	Vasey (2), Shuttleworth (dg)	—	—
29.11.87	SD	H	Featherstone R.	L	4-15	Moore	—	820	Kershaw
6.12.87	SD	A	York	L	13-24	P. Cooper, Vasey	Vasey (2), Shuttleworth (dg)	—	—
13.12.87	SD	H	Bramley	L	22-24	Squires, Moore, P. Cooper	Vasey (5)	479	Whitfield
20.12.87	SD	A	Fulham	L	0-24	—	—	—	—
26.12.87	SD	A	Batley	L	6-12	Bailey	Howley	—	—
10.1.88	SD	A	Workington T.	L	16-38	Cocks, Coen, Vasey	Vasey (2)	—	—
17.1.88	SD	H	Mansfield M.	L	27-31	Cochrane (2), Squires, Jennings, Holden	Vasey (3), Shuttleworth (dg)	451	Cross
24.1.88	SD	A	Doncaster	L	12-18	Moore, Cochrane	Vasey (2)	—	—
31.1.88	CC(1)	H	Widnes	L	10-38	Jennings, A. Cooper	Coen	1980	Bowman
7.2.88	SD	H	Doncaster	W	16-6	Cochrane, Morris, Coen	Vasey (2)	893	Dockray
21.2.88	50	A	Springfield B.	L	12-32	Morris, Holden	Vasey (2)	—	—
28.2.88	SD	H	York	W	10-6	Squires, Vasey	Vasey	742	Simpson
6.3.88	SD	A	Sheffield E.	L	16-18	Vasey, Coen, Moore	Vasey (2)	—	—
13.3.88	SD	A	Keighley	L	4-24	Hughes	—	—	—
20.3.88	SD	A	Runcorn H.	W	10-6	Vasey	Vasey (3)	—	—
27.3.88	SD	H	Springfield B.	W	20-11	Vasey, Squires, Cocks	Vasey (4)	514	Burke
4.4.88	SD	H	Keighley	L	22-32	Hinchcliffe (2), Cocks, Hartley	Vasey (3)	753	Hodgson
7.4.88	SD	H	Runcorn H.	W	10-6	Howley	Vasey (3)	378	Tidball
15.4.88	SD	H	Batley	W	28-10	Vasey (2), Holden, Squires, Gregoire	Vasey (4)	866	Drinkwater
17.4.88	SD	H	Sheffield E.	W	42-16	Shuttleworth (3), Holden, Garforth, Vasey, Howley, Gregoire	Vasey (4), Garforth	603	Lindop

DONCASTER

Ground:	Tatters Field
Colours:	Blue and yellow jerseys
First Season:	1951-52
Nickname:	Dons
Chairman:	John Desmond
Secretary:	Granville Bowen
Coach:	John Sheridan (June 1984-Nov 1987)
	Graham Heptinstall
	(Nov 1987-Jan 1988)
	John Sheridan (Jan 1988-)
Records:	Attendance: 4,793 v. Wakefield T.

(League) 7 Apr, 1962. There was an attendance of 10,000 for a Challenge Cup tie against Bradford N. at York Road Stadium on 16 Feb, 1952

Season

Goals: 118 by D. Noble, 1985-86
Tries: 20 by N. Turner, 1985-86
Points: 250 by D. Noble, 1986-87

Match

Goals: 9 by D. Towle v. York, 9 Sep, 1967
Tries: 4 by V. Grace v. Rochdale H, 4 Oct, 1952; B. Tasker v. Leeds, 26 Oct, 1963; J. Buckton v. Rochdale H., 30 Aug, 1981; T. Kemp v. Carlisle, 23 Nov, 1986
Points: 20 by K. Jones v. Whitehaven, 13 Mar, 1988
Highest score: 50-6 v, Keighley, 1986-87
Highest against: 75-3 v. Leigh, 1975-76

1987-88 PLAYERS' SUMMARY

	App	Tries	Goals	Dr	Pts
Barrett, Dale	8 + 5	2	—	—	8
Bell, David	5	—	—	—	—
Birkby, Ian	5	—	—	—	—
Carr, Alan	19 + 1	5	—	—	20
Clawson, Martin	2	—	—	—	—
Evans, John	19	1	—	—	4
Gibbon, Mark	30 + 1	5	—	—	20
Grace, Mick	5 + 5	1	—	—	4
Green, John	26 + 1	—	—	—	—
Hooper, Trevor	1	—	—	—	—
Jenkins, Terry	21 + 1	1	—	—	4
Jones, Kevin	32	14	13	2	84
Louis, Steve	11 + 3	4	—	—	16
McCleary, Jack	4	—	—	—	—
Milner, Paul	6 + 2	1	—	—	4
Moore, Garry	1	—	—	—	—
Morris, Geoff	0 + 1	—	—	—	—
Newman, David	1	—	—	—	—
Noble, David	26 + 6	5	75	1	171
O'Reilly, Christopher	0 + 2	—	—	—	—
Parkhouse, Kevin	26 + 4	4	—	—	16
Payne, Phil	31 + 2	2	—	1	9
Pennant, Audley	31	4	—	—	16
Pennant, Milton	2 + 1	—	—	—	—
Pickerill, Clive	3 + 2	—	—	—	—
Pickett, John	4 + 5	1	—	—	4
Roache, Mark	32	8	—	—	32
Robinson, Kevin	8 + 7	—	—	—	—
Sarto, John	5 + 1	—	—	—	—
Smith, Stuart	10 + 1	2	—	—	8
Stutchbury, John	5 + 3	—	—	—	—
Tansley, Ian	5 + 2	—	—	—	—
Timson, Andrew	13 + 1	3	—	—	12
Turner, Neil	32 + 1	11	—	—	44
TOTALS:					
34 players		74	88	4	476

John Green — Doncaster's full back.

1987-88 MATCH ANALYSIS

Date	Competition	H/A	Opponent	Rlt	Score	Tries	Goals	Attendance	Referee
30.8.87	SD	H	York	W	32-12	Timson, Jones, Noble, Barratt, Roache	Noble (6)	2108	Tidball
2.9.87	SD	A	Bramley	L	18-20	Timson, Turner, Carr	Noble (3)	—	—
6.9.87	SD	A	Carlisle	D	18-18	Parkhouse, Timson	Noble (5)	—	—
9.9.87	SD	H	Batley	L	8-12	—	Noble (4)	1497	Lindop
13.9.87	YC(1)	A	Bramley	L	12-39	Parkhouse, A. Pennant	Noble (2)	—	—
20.9.87	SD	A	Whitehaven	L	8-13	Jones	Noble (2)	—	—
27.9.87	SD	H	Oldham	W	20-18	Louis, Jones, Noble	Noble (4)	2060	Holdsworth
4.10.87	SD	A	Fulham	W	17-12	Louis, Gibbon	Noble (4), Jones (dg)	—	—
11.10.87	SD	H	Barrow	D	16-16	Jones (2)	Noble (4)	1637	Allatt
18.10.87	SD	A	Batley	L	16-28	Turner (2), Evans	Noble (2)	—	—
25.10.87	SD	H	Mansfield M.	W	34-10	Turner (2), Roache (2), Milner, Louis	Noble (5)	1482	Hodgson
1.11.87	SD	A	Rochdale H.	L	4-22	Noble	—	—	—
8.11.87	SD	A	Barrow	L	10-14	Louis, Smith	Noble	—	—
15.11.87	JPS(1)	A	Dewsbury	L	12-14	Smith	Noble (4)	—	—
29.11.87	SD	H	Wakefield T.	L	8-26	A. Pennant	Noble (2)	1938	Berry
6.12.87	SD	A	Oldham	L	16-17	Turner (2), Jones	Noble (2)	—	—
13.12.87	SD	H	Featherstone R.	L	12-27	Jones, A. Pennant	Noble (2)	2057	Drinkwater
27.12.87	SD	H	Sheffield E.	L	2-32	—	Noble	1839	Carter
3.1.88	SD	A	York	W	26-12	Parkhouse, A. Pennant, Carr, Jones, Payne	Jones (3)	—	—
10.1.88	SD	H	Bramley	W	22-12	Jones, Pickett, Barratt, Jenkins	Jones (2), Noble	1249	Bowman
17.1.88	SD	A	Featherstone R.	L	8-40	Turner	Jones (2)	—	—
24.1.88	SD	H	Dewsbury	W	18-12	Jones, Grace, Carr	Noble (3)	1108	Holdsworth
31.1.88	CC(1)	H	Batley	W	18-10	Gibbon (2), Jones	Noble (3)	1442	Hodgson
7.2.88	SD	A	Dewsbury	L	6-16	Gibbon	Noble	—	—
14.2.88	CC(2)	H	Mansfield M.	W	16-8	Roache, Payne	Noble (4)	1912	Smith
21.2.88	SD	H	Carlisle	L	6-16	Jones	Noble	1071	Volante
28.2.88	CC(3)	A	Hull	L	12-27	Gibbon	Noble (3), Jones (dg), Payne (dg)	—	—
6.3.88	SD	A	Mansfield M.	L	0-14	—	—	—	—
13.3.88	SD	H	Whitehaven	W	40-12	Turner (2), Roache (2), Jones (2), Carr	Jones (6)	507	Kendrew
20.3.88	SD	A	Wakefield T.	L	0-22	—	—	—	—
27.3.88	SD	H	Rochdale H.	W	21-18	Roache (2), Parkhouse, Turner	Noble (2, 1 dg)	825	Haigh
3.4.88	SD	H	Fulham	L	6-11	Noble	Noble	980	Kershaw
10.4.88	SD	A	Sheffield E. (Sheffield U. AFC)	L	14-30	Noble, Carr	Noble (3)	—	—

FEATHERSTONE ROVERS

Ground: Post Office Road
Colours: Blue and white hooped jerseys
First Season: 1921-22
Nickname: Colliers
Chairman: Richard Evans
Secretary: Terry Jones
Coach: Peter Fox (May 1987-)
Honours: **Challenge Cup** Winners, 1966-67, 1972-73, 1982-83
Beaten finalists, 1951-52, 1973-74
Championship Beaten finalists, 1927-28
Division One Champions, 1976-77
Division Two Champions, 1979-80
Second Division Premiership Beaten finalists, 1987-88
Yorkshire Cup Winners, 1939-40, 1959-60
Beaten finalists, 1928-29, 1963-64, 1966-67, 1969-70, 1970-71, 1976-77, 1977-78
Captain Morgan Trophy Beaten finalists, 1973-74
Records: Attendance: 17,531 v. St. Helens (RL Cup) 21 Mar, 1959
Season
Goals: 163 by S. Quinn, 1979-80
Tries: 31 by C. Woolford, 1958-59
Points: 375 by S. Quinn, 1979-80
Match
Goals: 12 by D. Fox v. Stanningley, 8 Feb, 1964
Tries: 6 by M. Smith v. Doncaster, 13 Apr, 1968
Points: 29 by S. Quinn v. Doncaster, 4 Nov, 1979
Highest score: 66-14 v. Barrow, 1986-87
Highest against: 70-2 v. Halifax, 1940-41

1987-88 PLAYERS' SUMMARY

	App	Tries	Goals	Dr	Pts
Bailey, Howard	5	—	—	—	—
Banks, Alan	11	3	—	—	12
Bannister, Andy	4	3	—	—	12
Barker, Nigel	6 + 3	2	—	—	8
Bastian, John	17 + 7	1	—	—	4
Beach, Danny	3	—	—	—	—
Bell, Keith	28 + 3	5	—	3	23
Bibb, Chris	33 + 1	20	3	—	86
Bradford, Paddy	0 + 2	—	—	—	—
Busby, Dave	1	—	—	—	—
Campbell, Mark	2 + 1	—	—	—	—
Chapman, Tony	1	1	—	—	4
Crossley, John	19 + 16	5	—	—	20
Dakin, Alan	3	—	—	—	—
Denson, Alan	0 + 1	—	—	—	—
Fox, Deryck	38	16	7	9	87
Fox, Martin	0 + 2	—	—	—	—
Geary, Paul	4 + 6	1	—	—	4
Gilbert, John	3	—	—	—	—
Hall, Gary	1 + 1	—	—	—	—
Harrison, Karl	27 + 3	5	—	—	20
Hopkins, Calvin	1 + 2	1	—	—	4
Hughes, Paul	24 + 2	9	—	—	36
Jones, David	12	6	—	—	24
Lidbury, Steve	1	1	—	—	4
Lyman, Paul	30 + 3	17	—	—	68
Marsh, Richard	36	8	—	—	32
Mackintosh, Andy	0 + 3	—	—	—	—
Quinn, Steve	35 + 3	11	127	1	299
Siddall, Gary	30 + 3	4	—	—	16
Slatter, Tim	14 + 1	2	—	—	8
Smales, Ian	9 + 6	3	1	—	14
Smith, Peter	37 + 1	21	—	—	84
Spurr, Bob	3	1	—	—	4
Staniforth, Tony	9	2	—	—	8
Steadman, Graham	30 + 1	17	12	2	94
Sykes, David	18 + 1	3	—	—	12
Wild, Paul	3 + 2	—	—	—	—
Woolford, Neil	9	3	—	—	12

TOTALS:
| 39 players | | 171 | 150 | 15 | 999 |

1987-88 MATCH ANALYSIS

Date	Competition	H/A	Opponent	Rlt	Score	Tries	Goals	Attendance	Referee
28.8.87	SD	A	Barrow	L	8-20	Spurr	Steadman (2)	—	—
2.9.87	SD	A	York	L	20-24	Steadman, Harrison, Hopkins, Jones	Steadman (2)	—	—
6.9.87	SD	H	Whitehaven	W	11-4	Smith	Quinn (3), Fox (dg)	1283	Cross

MATCH ANALYSIS (continued)

Date	Comp	H/A	Opponent	W/L	Score	Tries	Goals	Att	Man
13.9.87	YC(1)	H	Batley	W	28-6	Smith (2), Quinn, Fox, Lyman	Quinn (2), Fox, Steadman	1433	Tidball
20.9.87	SD	H	Rochdale H.	W	56-14	Bibb (3), Steadman (3), Jones (3), Lyman	Quinn (8)	1500	Carter
23.9.87	YC(2)	H	York	W	43-6	Fox (3), Smith, Bibb, Quinn	Quinn (7), Fox (2 dg), Bell (2 dg), Steadman (dg)	1617	Smith
27.9.87	SD	A	Bramley	W	38-22	Lyman (3), Quinn, Slatter, Jones, Smith	Quinn (5)	—	—
30.9.87	YC(SF)	H	Castleford	L	8-36	Jones	Quinn (2)	5329	Lindop
4.10.87	SD	H	Mansfield M.	W	26-10	Staniforth (2), Geary, Slatter, Bibb	Quinn (3)	1340	Tidball
11.10.87	Tour	H	Papua NG	L	16-22	Smith, Marsh, Smales	Fox, Smales	3315	Smith
18.10.87	SD	A	Fulham	L	16-19	Bibb, Lyman, Marsh	Quinn (2)	—	—
25.10.87	SD	H	Carlisle	L	22-29	Smales, Bell, Fox	Quinn (4), Fox	1210	Steele
1.11.87	JPS(P)	H	Thatto Heath	W	34-16	Fox (2), Bell, Marsh, Smith, Barker	Fox (3), Quinn (2)	1045	Cross
8.11.87	SD	H	Dewsbury	W	30-24	Crossley, Smith, Lidbury, Siddall, Bibb, Marsh	Bibb (3)	1353	Lindop
15.11.87	JPS(1)	H	Castleford	L	12-34	Barker, Crossley	Quinn (2)	3376	Spencer
22.11.87	JD	A	Sheffield E.	D	10-10	Hughes, Bibb	Quinn	—	—
29.11.87	SD	A	Dewsbury	W	15-4	Bibb (2), Chapman	Quinn, Fox (dg)	—	—
6.12.87	SD	H	Barrow	W	36-0	Woolford (2), Steadman, Crossley, Lyman, Siddall	Quinn (6)	1268	McDonald
13.12.87	SD	A	Doncaster	W	27-12	Smith, Lyman, Marsh, Bibb	Quinn (5), Fox (dg)	—	—
26.12.87	SD	H	Wakefield T.	W	17-14	Smith (2), Crossley	Quinn (2, 1 dg)	3502	Haigh
1.1.88	SD	A	Wakefield T.	W	21-16	Bibb, Quinn, Bell, Smith	Quinn (2), Fox (dg)	—	—
10.1.88	SD	A	Mansfield M.	W	22-2	Marsh, Hughes, Woolford, Bibb	Quinn (2), Fox (dg), Steadman (dg)	—	—
17.1.88	SD	H	Doncaster	W	40-8	Bibb (2), Fox (2), Steadman, Smith, Lyman	Quinn (6)	2613	Simpson
24.1.88	SD	A	Batley	W	13-4	Smith, Steadman	Quinn (2), Fox (dg)	—	—
31.1.88	CC(1)	H	York	W	32-21	Sykes, Bell, Harrison, Marsh, Smales, Lyman	Quinn (4)	1870	Smith
7.2.88	SD	H	Fulham	W	14-0	Quinn	Quinn (5)	1655	Holgate
14.2.88	CC(2)	A	Hull K.R.	L	26-35	Smith (2), Fox, Bibb	Quinn (3), Steadman (2)	—	—
21.2.88	SD	H	Oldham	D	8-8	Smith	Steadman (2)	3674	Cross
28.2.88	SD	A	Oldham	W	18-15	Lyman, Hughes, Steadman	Quinn (3)	—	—
6.3.88	SD	A	Whitehaven	W	24-14	Lyman, Steadman, Siddall, Hughes	Quinn (3), Fox (dg), Bell (dg)	—	—
13.3.88	SD	H	Sheffield E.	W	40-10	Lyman (3), Fox (2), Crossley, Marsh	Quinn (3), Steadman (3)	1593	Smith
20.3.88	SD	A	Rochdale H.	W	14-12	Steadman (2), Bell	Quinn	—	—
27.3.88	SD	A	Carlisle	L	18-23	Smith (3)	Quinn (3)	—	—
3.4.88	SD	H	Batley	W	44-13	Quinn (2), Fox, Hughes, Bibb, Harrison, Steadman	Quinn (8)	1787	Burke
10.4.88	SD	H	Bramley	W	40-12	Bibb (2), Banks, Hughes, Bastian, Fox, Quinn	Quinn (5), Fox	1683	Drinkwater
17.4.88	SD	H	York	W	64-10	Quinn (2), Steadman (2), Lyman (2), Harrison, Sykes, Bannister, Smith, Hughes	Quinn (10)	2007	Steele
24.4.88	SDP(1)	H	Mansfield M.	W	42-1	Banks (2), Bibb, Siddall, Bannister, Fox, Quinn, Hughes	Quinn (5)	1681	Spencer
8.5.88	SDP(SF)	H	Wakefield T.	W	20-16	Steadman, Harrison, Hughes, Fox	Quinn (2)	4395	Smith
15.5.88	SDP(F)	Man U. FC	Oldham	L	26-28	Steadman (2), Bannister, Sykes	Quinn (5)	—	Whitfield

FULHAM

Ground:	Polytechnic of Central London Stadium, Chiswick
Colours:	Black jerseys with red and white chevron
First Season:	1980-81
Chairman:	Mrs Barbara Close
Secretary:	Tim Lamb
Coach:	Bill Goodwin (Apr 1986-)
Honours:	**Division Two** Champions, 1982-83
Records:	Attendance: 15,013 v. Wakefield T. (RL Cup) 15 Feb, 1981 at Fulham FC

Season

Goals: 136 by S. Diamond, 1982-83
Tries: 27 by J. Crossley, 1982-83
Points: 308 by S. Diamond, 1982-83

Match

Goals: 8 by I. MacCorquodale v. Huddersfield, 12 Oct, 1980
Tries: No player has scored more than 3
Points: 22 by A. Platt, v. Mansfield M., 10 May, 1986
Highest score: 50-5 v. Huyton, 1982-83
Highest against: 72-6 v. Whitehaven, 1986-87

1987-88 PLAYERS' SUMMARY

	App	Tries	Goals	Dr	Pts
Aitken, David	19 + 1	5	—	—	20
Alexander, Adrian	3	—	—	—	—
Bader, Tony	1	—	—	—	—
Bibby, Neil	12 + 4	2	—	—	8
Bridge, Russ	28 + 3	3	—	—	12
Cambriani, Adrian	9	4	—	—	16
Chatterton, Ian	16 + 2	1	—	—	4
Cheetham, Paul	17 + 2	5	—	—	20
Cooper, Dominic	0 + 4	—	—	—	—
Elgar, Nick	6	1	—	—	4
Feighan, Frank	11 + 1	3	—	—	12
Fenn, Colin	21 + 4	—	40	—	80
Fletcher, Jamie	0 + 1	—	—	—	—
Francis, Huw	1	—	—	—	—
Gillan, Dave	29	9	—	—	36
Grimoldby, Nick	29 + 2	3	3	3	21
Guyett, Steve	22 + 2	4	19	—	54
Hanson, Chris	0 + 1	—	—	—	—
Herbert, Justin	0 + 1	—	—	—	—
Hutchison, Mike	29 + 1	2	—	—	8
Johanneson, Lawrence	3 + 6	—	—	—	—
Jones, Charlie	3	—	—	—	—
Keating, Noel	0 + 1	—	—	—	—
Kelly, Shane	13 + 5	3	—	—	12
Lawrie, Geordie	8 + 3	1	—	—	4
Leslie, Roy	1 + 1	—	—	—	—
Manning, Kevin	19 + 5	2	—	—	8
Masa, Santi	9	2	—	1	9
McMullen, Gerry	0 + 1	—	—	—	—
Mighty, Andrew	2	1	—	—	4
Miller, Craig	23 + 1	1	—	—	4
Murphy, Kieron	31	5	—	—	20
O'Riley, Paul	15 + 1	3	—	—	12
Rees, Huw	10 + 1	3	5	—	22
Taylor, Craig	22	2	—	—	8
Wightman, Ian	3 + 3	1	—	—	4
Wing, Jason	1	—	—	—	—

	App	Tries	Goals	Dr	Pts
TOTALS: 37 players		66	67	4	402

Dave Gillan — 29 appearances for Fulham.

1987-88 MATCH ANALYSIS

Date	Competition	H/A	Opponent	Rlt	Score	Tries	Goals	Attendance	Referee
30.8.87	SD	H	Sheffield E.	L	12-20	Rees, Cambriani	Fenn (2)	686	Cross
6.9.87	SD	A	Runcorn H.	L	16-23	Cambriani, Gillan, Feighan	Fenn (2)	—	—
13.9.87	LC(1)	A	Salford	L	4-58	Taylor	—	—	—
20.9.87	SD	H	Keighley	W	34-6	O'Riley (2), Masa, Cambriani, Feighan, Guyett	Fenn (5)	605	Carter
27.9.87	SD	A	Workington T.	L	14-22	Rees, Lawrie	Fenn (3)	—	—
4.10.87	SD	H	Doncaster	L	12-17	Taylor, Grimoldby	Fenn, Rees	822	Houghton
11.10.87	SD	A	Bramley	W	26-18	Murphy (2), Gillan, Bridge	Guyett (5)	—	—
18.10.87	SD	H	Featherstone R.	W	19-16	Gillan, Cambriani, Masa	Guyett (3), Masa (dg)	774	Dockray
25.10.87	SD	A	Dewsbury	L	10-32	Guyett	Rees (3)	—	—
1.11.87	Tour	H	Papua New Guinea	L	4-12	—	Rees, Fenn	1216	Simpson
8.11.87	JPS(P)	A	Oldham	L	8-36	Gillan	Fenn (2)	—	—
15.11.87	SD	H	Bramley	W	16-8	Bridge (2)	Fenn (4)	531	Burke
22.11.87	SD	A	Huddersfield B.	L	14-52	Hutchinson, Kelly	Fenn (3)	—	—
29.11.87	SD	A	Sheffield E.	L	6-16	Manning	Fenn	—	—
6.12.87	SD	H	Workington T.	L	2-12	—	Fenn	565	Spencer
12.12.87	SD	A	Keighley	L	10-33	Feighan, Cheetham	Guyett	—	—
20.12.87	SD	H	Dewsbury	W	24-0	O'Riley, Murphy, Rees, Grimoldby	Guyett (4)	564	Tickle
3.1.88	SD	A	Mansfield M.	L	6-18	Aitken	Guyett	—	—
10.1.88	SD	H	Runcorn H.	W	22-20	Cheetham, Miller, Guyett, Gillan	Guyett (3)	635	Tennant
17.1.88	SD	A	Springfield B.	L	0-17	—	—	—	—
24.1.88	SD	H	York	L	4-36	Aitken	—	603	Haigh
31.1.88	CC(1)	A	Mansfield M.	L	4-16	Guyett	—	712	Holdsworth
7.2.88	SD	A	Featherstone R.	L	0-14	—	—	—	—
14.2.88	SD	H	Wakefield T.	L	12-28	Manning, Bibby	Guyett (2)	551	Hodgson
6.3.88	SD	H	Huddersfield B.	L	10-17	Cheetham, Bibby	Fenn	561	Kendrew
13.3.88	SD	A	Wakefield T.	L	0-32	—	—	—	—
20.3.88	SD	A	Batley	W	34-6	Murphy (2), Cheetham, Elgar, Kenny, Gillan	Fenn (5)	—	—
27.3.88	SD	H	Mansfield M.	L	6-32	Aitken	Fenn	512	Houghton
1.4.88	SD	H	Batley	W	40-16	Gillan (2), Chatterton, Aitken, Wightman, Kelly, Mighty	Fenn (6)	617	Carter
3.4.88	SD	A	Doncaster	W	11-6	Aitken, Cheetham	Grimoldby (1, 1 dg)	—	—
10.4.88	SD	A	York	L	13-34	Gillan, Hutchison	Grimoldby (2, 1 dg)	—	—
17.4.88	SD	H	Springfield B.	W	9-8	Grimoldby	Fenn (2), Grimoldby (dg)	584	Cross

HALIFAX

Ground:	Thrum Hall
Colours:	Blue and white hooped jerseys
First Season:	1895-96
Nickname:	Thrum Hallers
Chairman:	Stan Ackroyd
General Manager:	Tony Beevers
Coach:	Chris Anderson (Nov 1984-May 1988)
	Graham Eadie (May 1988-)
Honours:	**Championship** Winners, 1906-07, 1964-65
	Beaten finalists, 1952-53, 1953-54, 1955-56, 1965-66
	Division One Champions, 1902-03, 1985-86
	War League Beaten finalists, 1942-43, 1944-45
	Challenge Cup Winners, 1902-03, 1903-04, 1930-31, 1938-39, 1986-87
	Beaten finalists, 1920-21, 1940-41, 1941-42, 1948-49, 1953-54, 1955-56, 1987-88
	Yorkshire League Winners, 1908-09, 1920-21, 1952-53, 1953-54, 1955-56, 1957-58
	Eastern Division Championship Winners, 1963-64
	Yorkshire Cup Winners, 1908-09, 1944-45, 1954-55, 1955-56, 1963-64
	Beaten finalists, 1905-06, 1907-08, 1941-42, 1979-80
	John Player Trophy Winners, 1971-72
	Premiership Trophy Beaten finalists, 1985-86
	Charity Shield Winners, 1986-87
	Beaten finalists, 1987-88
Records:	Attendance: 29,153 v. Wigan (RL Cup) 21 Mar, 1959

Season
Goals: 147 by T. Griffiths, 1955-56
Tries: 48 by J. Freeman, 1956-57
Points: 298 by C. Whitfield, 1986-87
Match
Goals: 14 by B. Burton v. Hunslet, 27 Aug, 1972
Tries: 8 by K. Williams v. Dewsbury, 9 Nov, 1957
Points: 31 by B. Burton v. Hunslet, 27 Aug, 1972
Highest score: 76-8 v. Hunslet, 1972-73
Highest against: 64-0 v. Wigan, 1922-23

1987-88 PLAYERS' SUMMARY

	App	Tries	Goals	Dr	Pts
Anderson, Tony	23	17	—	—	68
Beevers, Graham	17 + 5	—	—	—	—
Bell, Peter	5 + 4	1	—	—	4
Dickinson, Roy	4 + 2	—	—	—	—
Dixon, Paul	30 + 2	17	—	—	68
Eadie, Graham	33	9	13	—	62
Fairbank, Dick	9 + 3	6	—	—	24
George, Wilf	24	15	—	—	60
Grogan, Bob	31	5	—	—	20
Hanson, Dean	14 + 2	2	—	—	8
Holliday, Les	11 + 3	4	—	—	16
James, Neil	26 + 2	6	—	—	24
Juliff, Brian	2 + 8	2	—	—	8
Longstaff, Simon	4	1	—	—	4
McCallion, Seamus	35	1	—	—	4
Meredith, Martin	16 + 1	5	—	—	20
Neller, Keith	32 + 1	4	—	—	16
Pendlebury, John	36	4	14	—	44
Ramsden, Andrew	2	—	—	—	—
Riddlesden, Eddie	9 + 1	2	—	—	8
Robinson, Steve	23 + 3	2	—	—	8
St. Hilaire, Darren	0 + 2	—	—	—	—
Scott, Mick	11 + 14	1	—	—	4
Simpson, Andy	1	—	—	—	—
Smith, Steve	4 + 2	—	6	—	12
Stephens, Gary	9	—	—	—	—
Taylor, Mike	18 + 1	7	—	—	28
Whitfield, Colin	27	7	72	3	175
Wilkinson, Ian	29 + 1	14	—	—	56
Wilson, Scott	9 + 1	1	—	—	4
TOTALS:					
30 players		133	105	3	745

1987-88 MATCH ANALYSIS

Date	Competition	H/A	Opponent	Rlt	Score	Tries	Goals	Attendance	Referee
23.8.87	Charity Shield	Isle of Man	Wigan	L	12-44	Dixon, Juliff	Eadie (2)	(4757)	Holdsworth
30.8.87	SBC	A	Widnes	L	6-28	Dixon	Smith	—	—
6.9.87	SBC	H	Warrington	L	10-19	Whitfield (2)	Whitfield	5820	Holdsworth
13.9.87	YC(1)	H	Keighley	W	34-12	Dixon, Wilkinson, Whitfield, Neller, Pendlebury	Whitfield (7)	4086	—

MATCH ANALYSIS (continued)

Date	Comp	H/A	Opponent	Res	Score	Tryscorers	Goalscorers	Att	Referee
20.9.87	SBC	H	Leigh	W	26-18	Taylor, Wilkinson, Longstaff, Pendlebury	Whitfield (5)	5441	Lindop
23.9.87	YC(2)	H	Castleford	L	0-10	—	—	6101	Kershaw
27.9.87	SBC	A	Hull K.R.	L	8-29	Taylor	Eadie (2)	—	—
4.10.87	SBC	H	St. Helens	W	14-12	Wilkinson, Eadie	Whitfield (3)	7021	Carter
11.10.87	SBC	H	Bradford N.	L	10-12	Juliff	Whitfield (3)	8139	Kershaw
18.10.87	SBC	A	Wigan	W	17-14	Fairbank, Whitfield	Whitfield (4, 1 dg)	—	—
1.11.87	SBC	H	Salford	W	29-20	Whitfield, George, Grogan, Wilson, Pendlebury	Whitfield (4, 1 dg)	5231	McDonald
8.11.87	SBC	A	Warrington	L	8-15	Fairbank	Whitfield (2)	—	—
15.11.87	JPS (1)	H	Keighley	W	32-6	Wilkinson (2), James, Fairbank, Meredith, Neller	Eadie (4)	5236	—
22.11.87	JPS(2)	A	Leeds	L	10-20	Anderson, Eadie	Whitfield	—	—
29.11.87	SBC	H	Widnes	L	4-19	Dixon	—	5818	Simpson
6.12.87	SBC	A	Bradford N.	L	8-24	Eadie	Whitfield (2)	—	—
13.12.87	SBC	H	Hull	L	16-20	Wilkinson, Dixon, Taylor	Whitfield (2)	4692	Haigh
26.12.87	SBC	A	Leeds	L	7-12	George	Whitfield (1, 1 dg)	—	—
1.1.88	SBC	H	Swinton	W	36-0	Dixon (2), Wilkinson (2), Eadie, Meredith	Whitfield (6)	5067	Hodgson
5.1.88	SBC	H	Wigan	L	14-16	George, Taylor, Dixon	Whitfield	8210	Holdsworth
10.1.88	SBC	A	Swinton	W	32-12	Taylor (2), James, Dixon, George, Bell, Anderson	Whitfield (2)	—	—
17.1.88	SBC	H	Hull KR.	W	36-13	George (2), Riddlesden, Robinson, Dixon, Hanson, Anderson	Eadie (4)	6034	Tennant
24.1.88	SBC	A	Hunslet	W	42-10	Eadie (2), Wilkinson (2), George, James, Anderson, Hanson	Pendlebury (4), Eadie	—	—
31.1.88	CC(1)	A (at York)	Heworth	W	60-4	George (4), Anderson (3), Dixon (2), James, Neller	Pendlebury (8)	—	—
7.2.88	SBC	A	St. Helens	L	4-16	Whitfield	—	—	—
14.2.88	CC(2)	H	Rochdale H.	W	30-6	Anderson (3), Wilkinson, Dixon, Neller	Whitfield (3)	6538	Tennant
21.2.88	SBC	H	Hunslet	W	46-10	George (4), Anderson, Dixon, Holliday, McCallion, Riddlesden	Whitfield (5)	5338	Allatt
28.2.88	CC(3)	A	Hull K.R.	W	26-4	Dixon (2), Grogan, James, Wilkinson	Whitfield (3)	—	—
6.3.88	SBC	A	Leigh	W	28-14	Eadie (3), Anderson, Whitfield	Whitfield (4)	—	—
13.3.88	SBC	A	Hull	L	12-22	Anderson, Robinson	Whitfield (2)	—	—
20.3.88	SBC	A	Castleford	W	28-6	Wilkinson (2), Grogan, Holliday, Anderson	Whitfield (4)	—	—
26.3.88	CC(SF)	Leeds	Hull	D	0-0	—	—	(20,534)	McDonald
30.3.88	CC(SF) Replay	Elland Rd, Leeds	Hull	W	4-3	Anderson	—	(25,117)	McDonald
1.4.88	SBC	H	Castleford	W	22-12	Fairbank (2), Scott, Grogan	Smith (3)	8364	Spencer
4.4.88	SBC	H	Leeds	L	20-28	Holliday (2), Grogan, Taylor	Smith (2)	9401	Simpson
17.4.88	SBC	A	Salford	L	16-36	Meredith (2), Anderson	Pendlebury (2)	—	—
24.4.88	PT(1)	A	Widnes	L	26-36	Pendlebury, Dixon, Meredith, Fairbank	Whitfield (5)	—	—
30.4.88	CC(F)	Wembley	Wigan	L	12-32	Anderson, James	Whitfield (2)	(94,273)	Lindop

HUDDERSFIELD BARRACUDAS

Ground: Arena 84
Colours: Claret and gold jerseys
First Season: 1895-96; added Barracudas to title
               1984-85
Nickname: Barracudas
Chairman: John Bailey
Secretary: Stuart Greaves
Coaches: Chris Forster (Feb 1985-Dec 1986)
               Jack Addy (Jan 1987-Mar 1988)
               Alan Jones and Neil Whittaker
               (Mar 1988-Apr 1988)
Honours: **Championship** Winners, 1911-12,
               1912-13, 1914-15, 1928-29,
               1929-30, 1948-49, 1961-62
               Beaten finalists, 1913-14, 1919-20,
               1922-23, 1931-32, 1945-46, 1949-50
               Division Two Champions, 1974-75
               Challenge Cup Winners, 1912-13,
               1914-15, 1919-20, 1932-33, 1944-45,
               1952-53
               Beaten finalists, 1934-35, 1961-62
               Yorkshire League Winners,
               1911-12, 1912-13, 1913-14, 1914-15,
               1919-20, 1921-22, 1928-29, 1929-30,
               1948-49, 1949-50, 1951-52
               Eastern Division Beaten finalists,
               1962-63
               Yorkshire Cup Winners, 1909-10,
               1911-12, 1913-14, 1914-15, 1918-19,
               1919-20, 1926-27, 1931-32, 1938-39,
               1950-51, 1952-53, 1957-58
               Beaten finalists, 1910-11, 1923-24,
               1925-26, 1930-31, 1937-38, 1942-43,
               1949-50, 1960-61
Records: Attendance: 35,136 Leeds v.
               Wakefield T. (RL Cup SF)
               19 April 1947. Home: 32,912 v.
               Wigan (League) 4 Mar, 1950
               Season
               Goals: 147 by B. Gronow, 1919-20
               Tries: 80 by A. Rosenfeld, 1913-14
               Points: 330 by B. Gronow, 1919-20

Match
Goals: 18 by M. Holland v.
Swinton Park, 28 Feb, 1914
Tries: 10 by L. Cooper v. Keighley,
17 Nov, 1951
Points: 39 by M. Holland v.
Swinton Park, 28 Feb, 1914
Highest score: 119-2 v. Swinton
Park, 1913-14
Highest against: 64-17 v. Leeds,
1958-59

1987-88 PLAYERS' SUMMARY

	App	Tries	Goals	Dr	Pts
Boothroyd, Alan	18 + 4	1	—	—	4
Bostock, Mick	21	2	3	—	14
Brook, Tim	1 + 1	—	—	—	—
Brooke, Kevin	6	—	—	—	—
Clayton, Peter	1	—	—	—	—
Cockerham, Paul	2	—	—	—	—
Cook, Billy	22 + 5	7	—	—	28
Dickinson, Andy	17 + 5	3	—	—	12
Edwards, Tony	23 + 3	6	—	—	24
Farrell, Tony	27	3	1	—	14
Fitzpatrick, Dennis	5 + 4	—	—	—	—
Gregoire, Don	3	—	—	—	—
Hamilton, Scot	11 + 1	2	—	—	8
Harris, Colin	14	—	—	—	—
Hirst, Bob	5 + 1	1	5	—	14
Huck, Phil	11	2	—	—	8
Johnson, Jimmy	23	5	—	1	21
Kenworthy, Simon	21	5	42	1	105
Knight, Glen	3	1	—	—	4
Lee, Brian	31	7	—	—	28
Meehan, Gary	25 + 1	2	—	1	9
Nelson, David	13 + 6	5	—	—	20
Rodgers, Jeremy	0 + 2	—	—	—	—
St. Hilaire, Lee	23 + 1	2	—	—	8
Scholes, Damien	0 + 3	—	—	—	—
Sedgewick, Peter	8 + 1	4	—	—	16
Sewell, Andrew	0 + 1	—	—	—	—
Simpson, Frank	23 + 4	1	—	—	4
Swale, Graham	3 + 2	—	5	—	10
Thomas, Ian	18 + 1	8	3	—	38
Ventola, Roy	1 + 1	—	—	—	—
Vohland, Wayne	3	—	—	—	—
Wells, Trevor	6	2	—	—	8
Wills, Steve	6 + 7	1	—	—	4
Wood, Neil	9 + 5	3	—	—	12
TOTALS:					
35 players		73	59	3	413

1987-88 MATCH ANALYSIS

Date	Competition	H/A	Opponent	Rlt	Score	Tries	Goals	Attendance	Referee
30.8.87	SD	H	Springfield B.	L	16-22	Lee, Meehan, Nelson	Thomas (2)	486	Bowman
2.9.87	YC(P)	A	Hull	L	8-54	Sedgewick	Hirst (2)	—	—
6.9.87	SD	A	Workington T.	L	10-19	Sedgewick, Nelson	Hirst	—	—
20.9.87	SD	H	Dewsbury	W	22-13	Nelson (2), Lee, Bostock	Bostock (3)	592	Tennant
27.9.87	SD	A	Springfield B.	L	10-32	Sedgewick, Edwards	Hirst	—	—
4.10.87	SD	H	Oldham	L	4-26	Hirst	—	1729	Berry
11.10.87	SD	A	Dewsbury	L	6-14	Lee	Hirst	—	—
18.10.87	SD	H	Mansfield M.	L	12-26	Cook, Kenworthy	Kenworthy (2)	360	Kendrew
25.10.87	SD	H	Batley	W	9-6	Wills	Kenworthy (2), Meehan (dg)	739	Tickle
8.11.87	SD	H	Carlisle	W	16-8	Cook, Lee, Dickenson	Kenworthy, Thomas	377	Burke
15.11.87	JPS(1)	A	Leigh	L	12-28	Edwards, St. Hilaire	Kenworthy (2)	—	—
22.11.87	SD	H	Fulham	W	52-14	Cook (2), Kenworthy (2), Dickinson, Bostock, Meehan, Thomas, Edwards	Kenworthy (8)	453	Lindop
29.11.87	SD	A	Runcorn H.	L	6-20	Cook	Kenworthy	—	—
6.12.87	SD	H	Keighley	L	18-26	Thomas (2), Cook	Kenworthy (3)	715	Steele
13.12.87	SD	A	Mansfield M.	L	8-10	Lee	Kenworthy (2)	—	—
20.12.87	SD	H	Workington T.	L	12-15	Knight, Thomas	Swale (2)	421	Cross
3.1.88	SD	A	Rochdale H.	L	6-8	Johnson	Swale	—	—
10.1.88	SD	H	York	L	20-32	Farrell (2), Johnson, Cook	Swale (2)	542	Allatt
17.1.88	CC(P)	A	Warrington	L	10-48	Edwards, Boothroyd	Farrell	—	—
31.1.88	SD	H	Whitehaven	D	16-16	Johnson, Wood, Dickinson	Kenworthy (2)	336	Burke
14.2.88	SD	A	York	L	0-48	—	—	—	—
21.2.88	SD	A	Batley	W	26-20	Hamilton (2), Edwards, Lee	Kenworthy (5)	—	—
28.2.88	SD	H	Rochdale H.	W	23-22	Huck, Simpson, Edwards, Thomas	Kenworthy (3), Johnson (dg)	920	Berry
6.3.88	SD	A	Fulham	W	17-10	St. Hilaire, Kenworthy, Thomas	Kenworthy (2, 1 dg)	—	—
13.3.88	SD	A	Barrow	L	10-28	Wells (2)	Kenworthy	—	—
20.3.88	SD	A	Oldham	L	0-48	—	—	—	—
23.3.88	SD	A	Carlisle	L	12-22	Wood, Johnson	Kenworthy (2)	—	—
27.3.88	SD	H	Barrow	L	10-22	Thomas, Wood	Kenworthy	417	Imbernon (Fr)
1.4.88	SD	A	Keighley	L	12-26	Thomas, Huck	Kenworthy (2)	—	—
10.4.88	SD	A	Whitehaven	L	16-28	Lee, Kenworthy, Farrell	Kenworthy (2)	—	—
17.4.88	SD	H	Runcorn H.	L	14-16	Sedgewick, Johnson, Nelson	Kenworthy	330	Kershaw

HULL

Ground: The Boulevard
Colours: Irregular black and white hooped jerseys
First Season: 1895-96
Nickname: Airlie Birds
Chairman: John Rawlings
Secretary: Geoff Lythe
Coach: Len Casey (June 1986-Mar 1988) Tony Dean and Keith Hepworth (Mar 1988-Apr 1988)
Honours: **Championship** Winners, 1919-20, 1920-21, 1935-36, 1955-56, 1957-58 Beaten finalists, 1956-57
Division One Champions, 1982-83
Division Two Champions, 1976-77, 1978-79
Challenge Cup Winners, 1913-14, 1981-82
Beaten finalists, 1907-08, 1908-09, 1909-10, 1921-22, 1922-23, 1958-59, 1959-60, 1979-80, 1982-83, 1984-85
Yorkshire League Winners, 1918-19, 1922-23, 1926-27, 1935-36
Yorkshire Cup Winners, 1923-24, 1969-70, 1982-83, 1983-84, 1984-85
Beaten finalists, 1912-13, 1914-15, 1920-21, 1927-28, 1938-39, 1946-47, 1953-54, 1954-55, 1955-56, 1959-60, 1967-68, 1986-87
John Player Trophy Winners 1981-82
Beaten finalists, 1975-76, 1984-85
BBC2 Floodlit Trophy Winners, 1979-80
Premiership Beaten finalists, 1980-81, 1981-82, 1982-83
Records: Attendance: 28,798 v. Leeds (RL Cup) 7 Mar, 1936
Season
Goals: 170 by S. Lloyd, 1978-79
Tries: 52 by J. Harrison, 1914-15
Points: 369 by S. Lloyd, 1978-79

Match
Goals: 14 by J. Kennedy v. Rochdale H., 7 Apr, 1921; S. Lloyd v. Oldham, 10 Sep, 1978
Tries: 7 by C. Sullivan v. Doncaster, 15 Apr, 1968
Points: 36 by J. Kennedy v. Keighley, 29 Jan, 1921
Highest score: 86-0 v. Elland, 1898-99
Highest against: 64-2 v. St. Helens, 1987-88

1987-88 PLAYERS' SUMMARY

	App	Tries	Goals	Dr	Pts
Brand, Michael	9	3	—	—	12
Brooks, David	24 + 1	2	—	—	8
Carroll, John	15 + 2	—	—	—	—
Clarkson, Gary	1	—	—	—	—
Crooks, Steve	16 + 3	—	—	1	1
Dannatt, Andy	9 + 3	1	—	—	4
Dick, Kevin	11 + 5	—	—	—	—
Divorty, Gary	33 + 2	14	—	5	61
Eastwood, Jason	1	—	—	—	—
Eastwood, Paul	33	13	—	—	52
Elgar, Nicky	8 + 21	2	—	—	8
Ellis, Ian	4 + 4	3	—	—	12
Fletcher, Paul	34	8	—	—	32
Gale, Scott	4	1	—	—	4
Hick, Steve	5 + 2	—	8	—	16
Jackson, Lee	9 + 2	—	—	—	—
James, Kevin	2	—	—	—	—
Kerman, Richard	2	—	—	—	—
Leuluai, James	27	3	—	—	12
M'Barki, Hussein	13 + 1	1	—	—	4
McCaffery, Paul	18 + 2	7	—	—	28
O'Hara, Dane	25	7	—	—	28
Patrick, Shaun	20	4	—	—	16
Pearce, Gary	35	6	102	9	237
Price, Richard	7 + 4	1	—	—	4
Proctor, Wayne	4 + 3	1	—	—	4
Puckering, Neil	4 + 5	1	—	—	4
Regan, Terry	25	1	—	1	5
Sharp, Jon	13 + 2	4	—	—	16
Sutton, Mick	2	—	—	—	—
Tomlinson, Alan	21 + 1	3	—	—	12
Vass, Stewart	20	5	—	—	20
Welham, Paul	11 + 4	3	—	—	12
Wilby, Tim	7 + 11	1	—	—	4
Windley, Phil	9 + 3	3	—	—	12

TOTALS:
35 players		98	110	16	628

1987-88 MATCH ANALYSIS

Date	Com-petition	H/A	Opponent	Rlt	Score	Tries	Goals	Atten-dance	Referee
30.8.87	SBC	A	Wigan	L	4-38	Proctor	—	—	—
2.9.87	YC(P)	H	Huddersfield B.	W	54-8	Vass (3), Fletcher (2), Elgar, Eastwood, O'Hara, Pearce	Pearce (9)	2402	Haigh
6.9.87	SBC	H	Salford	W	16-11	Pearce, Fletcher, Dannatt	Pearce (2)	3758	Lindop
13.9.87	YC(1)	A	Leeds	L	24-28	Eastwood (2), Vass, O'Hara	Pearce (3), Divorty (2 dg)	—	—
20.9.87	SBC	H	Widnes	L	18-33	Puckering, Windley, Elgar	Pearce (3)	4576	Kershaw
27.9.87	SBC	A	Swinton	W	15-9	Sharp, Divorty	Pearce (3), Divorty (dg)	—	—
4.10.87	SBC	H	Leigh	W	22-21	Eastwood (2), Gale, Pearce	Pearce (3)	5051	Spencer
11.10.87	SBC	A	Leeds	L	8-28	Divorty	Pearce (2)	—	—
25.10.87	SBC	H	Castleford	L	16-37	Price, Fletcher, Windley	Pearce (2)	4750	Carter
1.11.87	SBC	A	Hunslet	L	17-22	Sharp (2)	Pearce (4, 1 dg)	—	—
4.11.87	Tour	H	Auckland	W	26-24	Ellis (2), Windley, Leuluai, Patrick	Pearce (3)	1921	McDonald
8.11.87	SBC	A	Salford	L	6-20	Divorty	Pearce	—	—
15.11.87	JPS(1)	H	Workington T.	W	42-6	Fletcher (2), Welham (2), Ellis, Tomlinson, Patrick	Hick (7)	2447	Berry
22.11.87	JPS(2)	H	Leigh	W	19-7	Patrick	Pearce (7, 1 dg)	3982	Hodgson
29.11.87	SPS(3)	A	St. Helens	L	16-20	McCaffrey, O'Hara	Pearce (4)	—	—
6.12.87	SBC	A	Widnes	L	22-26	Divorty, O'Hara, McCaffrey	Pearce (5)	—	—
13.12.87	SBC	A	Halifax	W	20-16	Fletcher, Patrick, Eastwood, O'Hara	Pearce (2)	—	—
27.12.87	SBC	A	Bradford N.	W	5-2	—	Pearce (2, 1 dg)	—	—
3.1.88	SBC	H	Hull K.R.	L	2-11	—	Pearce	8186	Kershaw
10.1.88	SBC	A	Castleford	L	3-32	—	Pearce, Regan (dg)	—	—
20.1.88	SBC	H	Warrington	W	22-14	McCaffrey (2), Brooks	Pearce (4), Divorty (dg), Crooks (dg)	3660	Tennant
31.1.88	CC(1)	A	Hunslet	W	27-10	Eastwood (2), Divorty, McCaffrey	Pearce (5, 1 dg)	—	—
7.2.88	SBC	H	Hunslet	W	30-22	Divorty (4), McCaffrey	Pearce (5)	3903	Smith
14.2.88	CC(2)	H	Sheffield E.	W	26-6	Leuluai, Brooks, Vass, Pearce, Brand	Pearce (3)	4544	Carter
17.2.88	SBC	A	St. Helens	L	2-64	—	Hick	—	—
21.2.88	SBC	H	Swinton	L	28-32	Eastwood (2), Fletcher, Divorty, Regan	Pearce (4)	3720	Holdsworth
28.2.88	CC(3)	H	Doncaster	W	27-12	Eastwood, Tomlinson, Pearce, Brand	Pearce (5), Divorty (dg)	6659	Whitfield
2.3.88	SBC	A	Warrington	L	2-36	—	Pearce	—	—
6.3.88	SBC	H	Bradford N.	L	0-16	—	—	4271	Allatt
13.3.88	SBC	H	Halifax	W	22-12	Eastwood, Brand, Tomlinson	Pearce (5)	5096	Volante
20.3.88	SBC	H	Wigan	W	18-12	Leuluai, Divorty, McCaffrey	Pearce (3)	6271	Haigh
26.3.88	CC(SF)	Leeds	Halifax	D	0-0	—	—	(20,534)	McDonald
30.3.88	CC(SF) Replay	Elland Rd, Leeds	Halifax	L	3-4	—	Pearce (1, 1 dg)	(25,117)	McDonald
1.4.88	SBC	A	Hull K.R.	W	21-14	Pearce, Welham, Eastwood	Pearce (3, 3 dg)	—	—
6.4.88	SBC	H	Leeds	W	28-16	Divorty (3), M'Barki, Sharp	Pearce (4)	7024	Haigh
13.4.88	SBC	H	St. Helens	L	8-20	Wilby	Pearce (2)	6175	Whitfield
17.4.88	SBC	A	Leigh	L	9-31	O'Hara (2)	Pearce (dg)	—	—

HULL KINGSTON ROVERS

Ground: Craven Park
Colours: White jerseys with red yoke
First Season: 1899-1900
Nickname: Robins
Chairman: Colin Hutton
Secretary: Ron Turner
Coach: Roger Millward MBE (Mar 1977-)
Honours: **Championship** Winners, 1922-23, 1924-25
Beaten finalists, 1920-21, 1967-68
First Division Champions, 1978-79, 1983-84, 1984-85
Challenge Cup Winners, 1979-80
Beaten finalists, 1904-05, 1924-25, 1963-64, 1980-81, 1985-86
John Player Trophy Winners, 1984-85, Beaten finalists, 1981-82, 1985-86
Premiership Winners, 1980-81, 1983-84, Beaten finalists, 1984-85
Yorkshire League Winners, 1924-25, 1925-26
Yorkshire Cup Winners, 1920-21, 1929-30, 1966-67, 1967-68, 1971-72, 1974-75, 1985-86
Beaten finalists, 1906-07, 1911-12, 1933-34, 1962-63, 1975-76, 1980-81, 1984-85
BBC2 Floodlit Trophy Winners, 1977-78
Beaten finalists, 1979-80
Eastern Division Championship Winners, 1962-63
Charity Shield Beaten finalists, 1985-86
Records: Attendance: 22,282 v. Hull, 7 October, 1922. There was a crowd of 27,670 for a League match v. Hull at Hull City FC's Boothferry Park on 3 April, 1953

Season
Goals: 166 by G. Fairbairn, 1981-82
Tries: 45 by G. Prohm, 1984-85
Points: 366 by S. Hubbard, 1979-80
Match
Goals: 14 by A. Carmichael v. Merthyr Tydfil, 8 Oct, 1910
Tries: 11 by G. West v. Brookland R., 4 Mar, 1905
Points: 53 by G. West v. Brookland R., 4 Mar, 1905
Highest score: 73-5 v. Brookland R., 1904-05
Highest against: 68-0 v. Halifax, 1955-56

1987-88 PLAYERS' SUMMARY

	App	Tries	Goals	Dr	Pts
Beall, Malcolm	16 + 5	1	—	—	4
Burton, Chris	29	3	—	—	12
Clark, Garry	32	12	4	—	56
Ema, Asuquo	30	2	—	—	8
Fairbairn, George	20	3	1	—	14
Fletcher, Mike	28	4	90	—	196
Fletcher, Paul	1	1	—	—	4
Harrison, Dave	8				
Harrison, Des	11 + 8	3	—	—	12
Hogan, Phil	7 + 1	1	—	—	4
Kelly, Andy	0 + 3	—	—	—	—
Lawler, Kenny	3 + 3	—	—	—	—
Laws, David	8 + 2	2	—	—	8
Lydiat, John	8 + 9	2	—	—	8
Matthews, Lee	0 + 2	—	—	—	—
Mortimer, Peter	22	5	—	—	20
Parker, Wayne	31	13	—	14	66
Richardson, Lee	0 + 1	—	—	—	—
Rudd, Chris	16 + 2	4	—	—	16
Ryan, Glen	19	2	—	—	8
Sims, Gary	3 + 1	—	—	—	—
Smith, Gordon	26	2	—	2	10
Smith, Mike	27	5	—	—	20
Smith, Steve	10	5	—	—	20
Speckman, Paul	8 + 3	1	—	1	5
Stead, Ray	20	5	—	—	20
Sullivan, Tony	2	1	—	—	4
Taylor, Ross	17	2	—	—	8
Thompson, Andy	4 + 6	—	—	—	—
Watkinson, David	10 + 5	—	—	—	—
TOTALS:					
30 players		79	95	17	523

1987-88 MATCH ANALYSIS

Date	Competition	H/A	Opponent	Rlt	Score	Tries	Goals	Attendance	Referee
30.8.87	SBC	H	Swinton	W	24-7	Speckman, Stead, Lydiat, Hogan	M. Fletcher (4)	3287	Smith
6.9.87	SBC	A	St. Helens	L	16-31	M. Smith, Stead	M. Fletcher (4)	—	—
13.9.87	YC(1)	H	Bradford N.	L	12-19	G. Smith, Ema	M. Fletcher (2)	3852	Kershaw
20.9.87	SBC	A	Salford	L	32-34	W. Parker (3), Stead, Rudd	M. Fletcher (5), Fairbairn	—	—
27.9.87	SBC	H	Halifax	W	29-8	Clark (2), Ema, Des Harrison	M. Fletcher (5) G. Smith (2 dg), Speckman (dg)	4900	Tennant
4.10.87	SBC	A	Warrington	L	0-36	—	—	—	—
18.10.87	SBC	A	Widnes	L	8-32	W. Parker	M. Fletcher (2)	—	—
25.10.87	SBC	A	Bradford N.	L	13-24	Clark, Lydiat	M. Fletcher (2), W. Parker (dg)	—	—
1.11.87	SBC	H	Warrington	W	17-0	S. Smith	M. Fletcher (6), W. Parker (dg)	3740	Haigh
8.11.87	SBC	H	Hunslet	W	36-12	S. Smith (2), M. Smith, Clark, M. Fletcher, Rudd	M. Fletcher (6)	3513	Shrimpton (NZ)
15.11.87	JPS(1)	H	Rochdale H.	W	30-12	Rudd (2), S. Smith, G. Smith, Clark	M. Fletcher (5)	2308	Houghton
22.11.87	JPS(2)	A	Warrington	L	8-12	Mortimer (2)	—	—	—
29.11.87	SBC	A	Swinton	W	26-18	Sullivan, Beall, Fairbairn	M. Fletcher (7)	—	—
6.12.87	SBC	H	St. Helens	W	25-16	W. Parker, Clark, M. Smith, M. Fletcher	M. Fletcher (4), W. Parker (dg)	4175	Whitfield
13.12.87	SBC	A	Leigh	L	6-13	S. Smith	M. Fletcher	—	—
27.12.87	SBC	H	Castleford	L	16-28	Burton, Fairbairn, Ryan	M. Fletcher (2)	4789	McDonald
3.1.88	SBC	A	Hull	W	11-2	Clark	M. Fletcher (3), W. Parker (dg)	—	—
10.1.88	SBC	H	Salford	W	20-8	Fairbairn, Burton, Clark	M. Fletcher (2), W. Parker (4 dg)	3420	Berry
17.1.88	SBC	A	Halifax	L	13-36	Clark, W. Parker	M. Fletcher (2), W. Parker (dg)	—	—
24.1.88	SBC	H	Leeds	D	8-8	Des Harrison	M. Fletcher (2)	4968	Whitfield
31.1.88	CC(1)	H	Carlisle	W	14-6	W. Parker (2)	M. Fletcher (3)	2908	Lindop
14.2.88	CC(2)	H	Featherstone R.	W	35-26	Mortimer (2), M. Fletcher, Parker, Stead	M. Fletcher (7), Parker (dg)	4743	McDonald
21.2.88	SBC	A	Leeds	L	20-25	Burton, Taylor, Mortimer	M. Fletcher (3), Parker (2 dg)	—	—
28.3.88	CC(3)	H	Halifax	L	4-26	—	M. Fletcher (2)	8837	Lindop
6.3.88	SBC	A	Wigan	L	4-16	Clark	—	—	—
13.3.88	SBC	H	Widnes	W	14-10	Taylor, Des Harrison	M. Fletcher (3)	3568	Simpson
23.3.88	SBC	H	Wigan	W	8-0	M. Fletcher	M. Fletcher (2)	4148	Holdsworth
1.4.88	SBC	H	Hull	L	14-21	M. Smith, W. Parker	M. Fletcher (3)	7076	Lindop
4.4.88	SBC	A	Castleford	L	24-28	Laws, Ryan, W. Parker, M. Smith	Clark (4)	—	—
10.4.88	SBC	H	Leigh	W	23-11	Clark (2), W. Parker, Laws	M. Fletcher (3), W. Parker (dg)	3249	Holdsworth
13.4.88	SBC	A	Hunslet	L	9-10	W. Parker, Stead	W. Parker (dg)	—	—
17.4.88	SBC	H	Bradford N.	L	4-46	M. Fletcher	—	3600	Dockray

HUNSLET

Ground: Elland Road
Colours: Myrtle, flame and white jerseys
First Season: 1895-96. Disbanded at end of 1972-73. Re-formed as New Hunslet in 1973-74. Retitled Hunslet from start of 1979-80
Chairman: Jerry Mason
Secretary: John Moses
Coaches: Peter Jarvis (Nov 1985-Apr 1988) and David Ward (July 1986-Apr 1988)
Honours: **Challenge Cup** Winners, 1907-08, 1933-34
Beaten finalists, 1898-99, 1964-65
Championship Winners, 1907-08, 1937-38
Beaten finalists, 1958-59
Division Two Champions, 1962-63, 1986-87
Second Division Premiership
Beaten finalists, 1986-87
Yorkshire Cup Winners, 1905-06, 1907-08, 1962-63
Beaten finalists, 1908-09, 1929-30, 1931-32, 1944-45, 1956-57, 1965-66
Yorkshire League Winners, 1897-98, 1907-08, 1931-32
Records: Attendance: 54,112 v. Leeds (Championship final) 30 Apr, 1938
Season
Goals: 181 by W. Langton, 1958-59
Tries: 34 by A. Snowden, 1956-57
Points: 380 by W. Langton, 1958-59
Match
Goals: 12 by W. Langton v. Keighley, 18 Aug, 1959
Tries: 7 by G. Dennis v. Bradford N., 20 Jan, 1934
Points: 27 by W. Langton v. Keighley, 18 Aug, 1959
Highest score: 75-5 v. Broughton Rec., 1896-97
Highest against: 76-8 v. Halifax, 1972-73

1987-88 PLAYERS' SUMMARY

	App	Tries	Goals	Dr	Pts
Allen, Michael	5 + 5	—	—	—	—
Anast, Theo	4	—	—	—	—
Bateman, Andrew	9 + 4	3	—	—	12
Bell, Mick	11	1	—	—	4
Benson, Trevor	4	—	—	—	—
Bowden, Chris	17 + 4	1	—	—	4
Coates, Jed	24 + 4	5	—	—	20
Gibson, Phil	5	—	—	—	—
Gillespie, David	19	4	—	—	16
Hohn, Mark	1	—	—	—	—
Irvine, Jimmy	23 + 2	8	—	—	32
Jackson, Mike	0 + 2	—	—	—	—
Kay, Andrew	2 + 3	—	1	—	2
King, Graham	8 + 6	3	—	—	12
Lay, Steven	22 + 1	6	4	—	32
Lowes, James	2	—	—	—	—
Lulham, Ricky	8 + 3	—	—	—	—
Marson, Andrew	9 + 1	—	—	—	—
Mason, Keith	15	1	—	—	4
Milton, Roy	4 + 3	1	—	—	4
Mitchell, Keith	12 + 3	1	—	—	4
Morgan, Paul	5 + 1	—	—	—	—
Nickle, Sonny	11 + 1	3	—	—	12
Penola, Colin	9 + 2	2	—	—	8
Platt, Alan	26	5	59	2	140
Raw, Andrew	3	1	—	—	4
Rowse, Gary	2	—	2	—	4
Rudd, Neil	3	1	—	—	4
Sampson, Roy	19 + 5	3	—	—	12
Senior, Gary	15 + 1	3	—	—	12
Sykes, Andrew	14 + 1	2	—	—	8
Tate, Phil	22 + 2	7	—	—	28
Webb, Terry	24 + 1	3	1	—	14
Wilkinson, Shaun	8	1	—	—	4
Wilson, Warren	15	7	—	—	28
Wood, Mark	10 + 1	—	—	—	—
TOTALS: 36 players		72	67	2	424

David Ward — departed as Hunslet team manager.

1987-88 MATCH ANALYSIS

Date	Competition	H/A	Opponent	Rlt	Score	Tries	Goals	Attendance	Referee
30.8.87	SBC	A	Warrington	L	4-54	Platt	—	—	—
6.9.87	SBC	H	Leeds	L	8-12	Platt	Platt (2)	6156	Tennant
13.9.87	YC(1)	A	Castleford	L	12-32	Coates, Irvine	Platt (2)	—	—
20.9.87	SBC	H	Swinton	D	32-32	Webb (2), Mason, Wilson, Coates	Platt (6)	1187	McDonald
27.9.87	SBC	A	Widnes	L	10-30	Wilson, Tate	Platt	—	—
4.10.87	SBC	H	Castleford	L	15-18	Gillespie, King	Platt (3, 1 dg)	2627	Allatt
11.10.87	SBC	A	Leigh	L	22-28	Bowden, Gillespie, Tate, Sampson	Platt (3)	—	—
18.10.87	SBC	H	Salford	L	12-14	Irvine	Platt (4)	1418	Kershaw
1.11.87	SBC	H	Hull	W	22-17	Platt, Bell, Lay, Irvine	Platt (3)	1382	Holdsworth
8.11.87	SBC	A	Hull K.R.	L	12-36	Wilson, Platt	Platt (2)	—	—
15.11.87	JPS(1)	A	Batley	L	16-18	Wilson, Lay, Sykes	Platt (2)	—	—
22.11.87	SBC	A	Swinton	D	4-4	Rudd	—	—	—
6.12.87	SBC	A	Salford	L	14-21	Irvine (2), Coates	Webb	—	—
13.12.87	SBC	H	Bradford N.	L	8-24	Senior	Rowse (2)	2296	Carter
20.12.87	SBC	H	Wigan	L	10-38	Nickle, Milton	Platt	3582	Haigh
27.12.87	SBC	H	Leigh	W	48-10	Nickle (2), Sampson, Penola, Sykes, Tate, Senior, Gillespie	Platt (8)	2136	Whitfield
1.1.88	SBC	A	Leeds	L	12-28	Platt, Tate	Platt (2)	—	—
10.1.88	SBC	H	Warrington	W	20-16	King, Sampson, Irvine	Platt (4)	2027	Steele
15.1.88	CC(P)		Leigh (at Leigh)	W	23-4	Tate, Senior, Lay, Irvine	Platt (3, 1 dg)	—	—
24.1.88	SBC	H	Halifax	L	10-42	Lay, Coates	Platt	4367	Bowman
31.1.88	CC(1)	H	Hull	L	10-27	Tate	Platt (3)	1892	Drinkwater
7.2.88	SBC	A	Hull	L	22-30	Gillespie, Tate, Lay, Webb	Platt (3)	—	—
21.2.88	SBC	A	Halifax	L	10-46	Mitchell, Penola	Platt	—	—
1.3.88	SBC	A	St. Helens	L	6-70	Bateman	Platt	—	—
6.3.88	SBC	H	St. Helens	L	10-14	Lay, Wilson	Platt	2394	Tennant
27.3.88	SBC	A	Castleford	L	14-26	Irvine, Wilson	Platt (3)	—	—
5.4.88	SBC	A	Bradford N.	L	4-32	Wilson	—	—	—
10.4.88	SBC	H	Widnes	L	14-66	Bateman (2), King	Lay	4552	Kendrew
13.4.88	SBC	H	Hull K.R.	W	10-9	Raw	Lay (3)	688	Spencer
17.4.88	SBC	A	Wigan	L	10-62	Coates, Wilkinson	Kay	—	—

KEIGHLEY

Ground: Lawkholme Lane
Colours: Green, scarlet and white jerseys
First Season: 1901-02
Nickname: Lawkholmers
Chairman: Colin Farrar
Secretary: Martin Lofthouse
Coaches: Colin Dixon and Les Coulter
(July 1986-)
Honours: **Division Two** Champions, 1902-03
Challenge Cup Beaten finalists,
1936-37
Yorkshire Cup Beaten finalists,
1943-44, 1951-52
Records: Attendance: 14,500 v. Halifax
(RL Cup) 3 Mar, 1951
Season
Goals: 155 by B. Jefferson, 1973-74
Tries: 30 by J. Sherburn, 1934-35
Points: 331 by B. Jefferson, 1973-74
Match
Goals: 11 by R. Walker v.
Castleford, 13 Jan, 1906; H. Cook
v. Hull K.R., 31 Oct, 1953
Tries: 5 by I. Jagger v. Castleford,
13 Jan, 1906; S. Stacey v. Liverpool
C., 9 Mar, 1907
Points: 24 by J. Phillips v. Halifax,
5 Oct, 1957
Highest score: 67-0 v. Castleford,
1905-06
Highest against: 92-2 v. Leigh,
1985-86

1987-88 PLAYERS' SUMMARY

	App	Tries	Goals	Dr	Pts
Atkinson, Colin	13 + 1	1	—	—	4
Bardgett, Joe	2 + 2	—	—	—	—
Bragger, Ian	26	12	—	—	48
Butterfield, Jeff	33	10	—	—	40
Cheetham, Paul	1	—	—	—	—
Dixon, Keith	20 + 1	3	27	1	67
Fairbank, Andy	0 + 2	—	—	—	—
Fairbank, John	1	—	—	—	—
Fairbank, Mark	16	4	—	—	16
Fairhurst, Ian	1 + 1	—	—	—	—
Goodier, Frank	14 + 11	2	—	—	8
Hawksworth, Mick	5 + 2	—	—	—	—
Hirst, Carl	32	11	61	2	168
McGregor, Jason	1 + 2	—	—	—	—
McInerney, Mark	10 + 1	—	—	—	—
Manning, Terry	23	9	—	—	36
Moorby, Gary	18 + 3	4	—	—	16
Moses, Paul	16 + 2	2	—	1	9
Newton, Andy	4	—	2	—	4
Proctor, Rob	24	2	—	—	8
Ragan, Mark	32	8	—	1	33
Richardson, Peter	29 + 1	12	—	—	48
Robinson, Kevin	8 + 9	—	—	—	—
Rose, Gary	12 + 1	1	—	—	4
Skerrett, Trevor	26 + 1	1	—	—	4
Tyers, Andy	1 + 2	—	—	—	—
Waller, Vince	11 + 1	1	—	—	4
Walsh, Tim	1 + 1	—	—	—	—
White, Brendan	29 + 1	—	—	—	—
Winterbottom, Ricky	20 + 5	13	—	—	52
Trialist	0 + 1	—	—	—	—

TOTALS:
31 players		96	90	5	569

Trevor Skerrett — Keighley's ex-Test forward.

1987-88 MATCH ANALYSIS

Date	Competition	H/A	Opponent	Rlt	Score	Tries	Goals	Attendance	Referee
30.8.87	SD	H	Mansfield M.	W	30-18	Hirst (2), Richardson, Butterfield, Bragger, Dixon	Dixon (3)	954	Holgate
2.9.87	SD	A	Oldham	L	3-32	—	Dixon (1, 1 dg)	—	—
6.9.87	SD	H	York	W	14-6	Winterbottom (2)	Dixon (3)	972	Tennant
9.9.87	SD	A	Carlisle	L	12-26	Winterbottom, Butterfield	Dixon (2)	—	—
13.9.87	YC(1)	A	Halifax	L	12-34	Ragan, Bragger	Dixon (2)	—	Volante
20.9.87	SD	A	Fulham	L	6-34	Hirst	Hirst	—	—
27.9.87	SD	H	Barrow	W	20-10	Hirst, Dixon	Dixon (6)	1042	Burke
4.10.87	SD	A	Batley	L	2-17	—	Dixon	—	—
18.10.87	SD	H	Workington T.	W	19-11	Butterfield (2), Waller	Newton (2), Dixon, Hirst (dg)	834	Tickle
25.10.87	SD	H	Springfield B.	L	18-20	Proctor, Butterfield, Hirst	Dixon (3)	1037	Tennant
1.11.87	SD	H	Oldham	L	10-12	Ragan	Dixon (2), Hirst (dg), Moses (dg)	1794	Volante
15.11.87	JPS(1)	A	Halifax	L	6-32	Manning	Dixon	—	Holgate
22.11.88	SD	A	Whitehaven	L	10-22	Manning, Bragger	Hirst	—	—
29.11.87	SD	H	Batley	W	22-6	Goodier, Manning, Hirst, Moorby	Hirst (3)	894	Drinkwater
6.12.87	SD	A	Huddersfield B.	W	26-18	Winterbottom (2), Manning (2), Ragan	Hirst (3)	—	—
13.12.87	SD	H	Fulham	W	33-10	Winterbottom (2), Fairbank, Butterfield, Ragan	Hirst (6), Ragan (dg)	766	Dockray
20.12.87	SD	A	York	L	16-19	Hirst (2), Winterbottom	Hirst (2)	—	—
26.12.87	SD	A	Springfield B.	W	20-10	Richardson, Manning, Ragan	Hirst (4)	—	—
1.1.88	SD	A	Runcorn H.	L	16-20	Bragger, Winterbottom, Skerrett	Hirst (2)	—	—
10.1.88	SD	H	Rochdale H.	L	10-15	Richardson (2)	Hirst	1023	Smith
24.1.88	SD	H	Runcorn H.	W	30-6	Atkinson, Winterbottom, Manning, Richardson, Ragan	Hirst (5)	660	Carter
31.1.88	CC(1)	H	Workington T.	W	30-4	Bragger (2), Rose, Winterbottom, Butterfield	Hirst (5)	1248	Tickle
7.2.88	SD	A	Barrow	L	6-14	Bragger	Hirst	—	—
14.2.88	CC(2)	A	Widnes	L	2-16	—	Hirst	3331	Lindop
21.2.88	SD	A	Mansfield M.	L	6-11	Hirst	Hirst	—	—
28.2.88	SD	H	Whitehaven	W	30-18	Dixon, Moorby, Butterfield, Fairbank, Hirst	Hirst (4), Dixon	932	Tennant
6.3.88	SD	A	Rochdale H.	W	14-4	Moses, Bragger, Ragan	Hirst	—	—
13.3.88	SD	H	Dewsbury	W	24-4	Richardson (2), Goodier, Hirst, Manning	Hirst (2)	750	Spencer
20.3.88	SD	H	Carlisle	L	10-14	Bragger (2)	Dixon	859	Steele
27.3.88	SD	A	Workington T.	W	30-17	Bragger, Fairbank, Winterbottom, Butterfield, Manning	Hirst (5)	—	—
1.4.88	SD	H	Huddersfield B.	W	26-12	Richardson (3), Proctor, Bragger	Hirst (3)	892	Tidball
4.4.88	SD	A	Dewsbury	W	32-22	Richardson, Moorby, Ragan, Moses, Butterfield	Hirst (6)	—	—
24.4.88	SDP(1)	A	Oldham	L	24-34	Fairbank, Moorby, Richardson, Winterbottom	Hirst (4)	—	—

LEEDS

Ground:	Headingley
Colours:	Blue and amber jerseys
First Season:	1895-96
Nickname:	Loiners
Chairman:	Bernard Coulby
General Manager:	Joe Warham
Coach:	Maurice Bamford (Dec 1986-Apr 1988)

Honours: **Championship** Winners, 1960-61,
1968-69, 1971-72
Beaten finalists, 1914-15, 1928-29,
1929-30, 1930-31, 1937-38, 1969-70,
1972-73
League Leaders Trophy Winners,
1966-67, 1967-68, 1968-69, 1969-70,
1971-72
Challenge Cup Winners, 1909-10,
1922-23, 1931-32, 1935-36, 1940-41,
1941-42, 1956-57, 1967-68, 1976-77,
1977-78
Beaten finalists, 1942-43, 1946-47,
1970-71, 1971-72
Yorkshire League Winners,
1901-02, 1927-28, 1930-31, 1933-34,
1934-35, 1936-37, 1937-38, 1950-51,
1954-55, 1956-57, 1960-61, 1966-67,
1967-68, 1968-69, 1969-70
Yorkshire Cup Winners, 1921-22,
1928-29, 1930-31, 1932-33, 1934-35,
1935-36, 1937-38, 1958-59, 1968-69,
1970-71, 1972-73, 1973-74, 1975-76,
1976-77, 1979-80, 1980-81
Beaten finalists, 1919-20, 1947-48,
1961-62, 1964-65
BBC2 Floodlit Trophy Winners,
1970-71
John Player Trophy Winners,
1972-73, 1983-84
Beaten finalists, 1982-83, 1987-88
Premiership Winners, 1974-75,
1978-79

Records: Attendance: 40,175 v. Bradford N.
(League) 21 May, 1947

Season
Goals: 166 by B.L. Jones, 1956-57
Tries: 63 by E. Harris, 1935-36
Points: 431 by B.L. Jones, 1956-57
Match
Goals: 13 by B.L. Jones v.
Blackpool B., 19 Aug, 1957
Tries: 8 by F. Webster v. Coventry,
12 Apr, 1913; E. Harris v. Bradford
N., 14 Sep, 1931
Points: 31 by B.L. Jones v.
Bradford N., 22 Aug, 1956
Highest score: 102-0 v. Coventry,
1912-13
Highest against: 71-0 v. Wakefield
T., 1945-46

1987-88 PLAYERS' SUMMARY

	App	Tries	Goals	Dr	Pts
Ashton, Ray	20 + 5	5	—	1	21
Basnett, John	31	7	—	—	28
Brooke-Cowden, Mark	12 + 8	3	—	—	12
Creasser, David	22	14	43	—	142
Crooks, Lee	14 + 1	4	28	2	74
Delaney, Paul	1 + 2	1	—	—	4
Fairbank, John	13 + 6	—	—	—	—
Fawcett, Vince	0 + 3	2	—	—	8
Gibson, Carl	31 + 4	21	—	—	84
Gill, Paul	2	—	4	—	8
Gunn, Richard	8 + 3	1	—	—	4
Gurr, Marty	28	11	—	—	44
Heron, David	33 + 1	3	—	—	12
Holmes, John	4 + 1	1	—	—	4
Jackson, Peter	19 + 2	5	—	—	20
Johnson, Errol	10 + 3	3	—	—	12
Lord, Mark	1 + 1	—	—	—	—
Lyons, John	15 + 7	3	—	—	12
Maskill, Colin	30 + 2	3	17	1	47
Medley, Paul	23 + 4	12	—	—	48
Morris, Steve	19	10	—	—	40
Powell, Roy	35 + 3	2	—	—	8
Pratt, Richard	17	4	—	—	16
Price, Gary	9 + 1	1	—	—	4
Rathbone, Alan	1	—	—	—	—
Rayne, Kevin	23 + 8	—	—	—	—
Schofield, Garry	27	22	4	—	96
Spencer, Gary	8	4	—	—	16
Smithson, Mark	1	—	—	—	—
Stephens, Gary	1	—	—	—	—
Stephenson, David	13	1	29	—	62
Stevens, Darren	2	1	—	—	4
Tunks, Peter	24	4	—	—	16
Wilson, Mark	10 + 2	—	—	—	—
TOTALS:					
34 players		148	125	4	846

1987-88 MATCH ANALYSIS

Date	Competition	H/A	Opponent	Rlt	Score	Tries	Goals	Attendance	Referee
30.8.87	SBC	H	Leigh	W	38-12	Creasser, Crooks, Ashton, Medley, Basnett, Johnson, Gibson	Creasser (3), Crooks (2)	7576	Kershaw
6.9.87	SBC	A	Hunslet	W	12-8	Medley, Gibson	Creasser, Crooks	—	—
13.9.87	YC(1)	H	Hull	W	28-24	Gibson (2), Tunks, Crooks	Crooks (6)	7704	Lindop
20.9.87	SBC	A	Bradford N.	L	8-32	Creasser, Brooke-Cowden	—	—	—
23.9.87	YC(2)	H	Wakefield T.	W	36-8	Spencer (2), Creasser, Gibson, Pratt, Heron	Crooks (6)	6693	Berry
27.9.87	SBC	H	Salford	W	60-6	Medley (2), Creasser (2), Gibson (2), Ashton, Brooke-Cowden, Pratt, Basnett	Creasser (10)	6583	Smith
30.9.87	YC(SF)	A	Bradford N.	L	5-16	Medley	Crooks (dg)	—	—
4.10.87	SBC	A	Wigan	L	6-26	Gurr	Creasser	—	—
11.10.87	SBC	H	Hull	W	28-8	Medley (2), Morris, Tunks, Gurr	Creasser (4)	8373	Simpson
18.10.87	SBC	A	Warrington	D	20-20	Creasser, Morris, Lyons	Creasser (4)	—	—
25.10.87	Tour	H	Auckland	L	25-29	Schofield (2), Spencer (2)	Creasser (4), Crooks (dg)	6639	Lindop
1.11.87	SBC	H	Wigan	D	18-18	Crooks, Schofield, Creasser	Crooks (2), Creasser	14,246	Smith
8.11.87	SBC	H	St. Helens	W	24-21	Crooks, Gibson, Gurr, Schofield	Crooks (4)	10,414	Hodgson
15.11.87	JPS(1)	A	Whitehaven	W	18-14	Jackson (2), Morris	Crooks (3)	—	—
22.11.87	JPS(2)	H	Halifax	W	20-10	Creasser, Schofield, Jackson	Crooks (4)	13,498	Holdsworth
29.11.87	JPS(3)	A	Springfield B.	W	22-12	Creasser (2), Gibson, Morris	Creasser (3)	—	—
6.12.87	SBC	H	Castleford	W	44-0	Morris (3), Schofield (2), Tunks, Gibson, Ashton	Maskill (6)	10,716	Kershaw
12.12.87	JPS(SF)	Bolton Wigan W. F.C.		W	19-6	Medley, Schofield, Maskill	Maskill (3), Ashton (dg)	(13,538)	Tennant
26.12.87	SBC	H	Halifax	W	12-7	Powell, Morris	Creasser (2)	15,295	Lindop
1.1.88	SBC	H	Hunslet	W	28-12	Creasser (2), Basnett, Jackson, Morris	Creasser (4)	10,047	Simpson
9.1.88	JPS(F)	Wigan St. Helens		L	14-15	Creasser, Jackson	Creasser (3)	(16,669)	Lindop
13.1.88	CC(P)	A	Kells (at Whitehaven)	W	28-0	Gibson (2), Schofield, Gurr, Stephenson, Lyons	Creasser (2)	—	—
17.1.88	SBC	H	Widnes	W	26-21	Schofield (2), Maskill, Stephenson	Stephenson (5)	12,439	Holdsworth
24.1.88	SBC	A	Hull K.R.	D	8-8	Gibson	Stephenson (2)	—	—
31.1.88	CC(1)	H	Castleford	W	22-14	Medley (3), Schofield	Stephenson (3)	14,757	Spencer
7.2.88	SBC	A	Leigh	L	6-18	Schofield	Stephenson	—	—
14.2.88	CC(2)	A	Wigan	L	14-30	Schofield, Medley, Tunks	Stephenson	—	—
21.2.88	SBC	H	Hull K.R.	W	25-20	Maskill, Heron, Brooke-Cowden, Morris	Stephenson (4), Maskill (dg)	8353	Kendrew
6.3.88	SBC	A	Salford	L	10-14	Gurr (2)	Stephenson	—	—
13.3.88	SBC	H	Warrington	W	30-10	Basnett (2), Gurr, Pratt, Gibson, Ashton	Stephenson (2), Maskill	7357	McDonald
20.3.88	SBC	A	Widnes	L	6-32	Lyons	Schofield	—	—
27.3.88	SBC	H	Swinton	W	32-6	Gurr (2), Gibson, Delaney, Powell, Fawcett	Maskill (4)	6541	Smith
1.4.88	SBC	H	Bradford N.	L	18-32	Gibson, Johnson, Schofield	Stephenson (2), Schofield	10,893	Whitfield
4.4.88	SBC	A	Halifax	W	28-20	Schofield (2), Gibson, Gunn, Creasser	Stephenson (3), Creasser	—	—
6.4.88	SBC	A	Hull	L	16-28	Basnett, Fawcett, Johnson	Schofield (2)	—	—
10.4.88	SBC	A	St. Helens	W	28-23	Price, Holmes, Basnett, Pratt, Gurr	Gill (4)	—	—
13.4.88	SBC	A	Swinton	W	34-22	Schofield (4), Gibson (3)	Stephenson (3)	—	—
17.4.88	SBC	A	Castleford	L	12-26	Gurr, Ashton	Maskill (2)	—	—
24.4.88	PT(1)	A	Bradford N.	L	18-32	Gibson, Schofield, Heron	Stephenson (2), Maskill	—	—

LEIGH

Ground: Hilton Park
Colours: Red and white jerseys
First Season: 1895-96
Chairman: Brian Sharples
Secretary: Bernadette Knowles
Coach: Billy Benyon (Dec 1986-)
Honours: **Championship** Winners, 1905-06
Division One Champions, 1981-82
Division Two Champions, 1977-78, 1985-86
Challenge Cup Winners, 1920-21, 1970-71
Lancashire Cup Winners, 1952-53, 1955-56, 1970-71, 1981-82
Beaten finalists, 1905-06, 1909-10, 1920-21, 1922-23, 1949-50, 1951-52, 1963-64, 1969-70
BBC2 Trophy Winners, 1969-70, 1972-73
Beaten finalists, 1967-68, 1976-77
Records: Attendance: 31,324 v. St. Helens (RL Cup) 14 Mar, 1953
Season
Goals: 173 by C. Johnson, 1985-86
Tries: 49 by S. Halliwell, 1985-86
Points: 400 by C. Johnson, 1985-86
Match
Goals: 15 by M. Stacey v. Doncaster, 28 Mar, 1976
Tries: 6 by J. Wood v. York, 4 Oct, 1947
Points: 38 by J. Woods v. Blackpool B., 11 Sep, 1977
Highest score: 92-2 v. Keighley, 1985-86
Highest against: 60-8 v. Salford, 1940

1987-88 PLAYERS' SUMMARY

	App	Tries	Goals	Dr	Pts
Atherton, Wayne	3 + 2	—	—	—	—
Burke, Paul	0 + 2	—	—	—	—
Burrill, Craig	12 + 1	2	9	—	26
Clarke, Jeff	18 + 2	1	—	—	4
Collier, Andy	11 + 9	3	—	—	12
Cooper, Mark	0 + 1	—	—	—	—
Cottrell, Tony	20 + 2	2	—	—	8
Dean, Mick	27	5	—	—	20
Dowling, Tony	1	—	—	—	—
Dunn, Brian	27 + 1	5	—	—	20
Earner, Adrian	3 + 1	—	—	—	—
Evans, David	21 + 2	1	—	—	4
Ford, Michael	17	4	—	1	17
Frame, Mark	3 + 1	—	—	—	—
Gelling, Bryan	9	—	—	—	—
Henderson, John	12 + 1	5	—	—	20
Holliday, Michael	1 + 1	—	—	—	—
Horo, Shane	15	9	—	—	36
Jeffrey, Ian	28	8	—	—	32
Johnson, Chris	23 + 2	3	35	6	88
Johnson, Phil	22 + 5	3	32	1	77
Kerr, John	21 + 3	12	—	—	48
Lang, Shaun	0 + 1	—	—	—	—
McCulloch, Neil	31	10	—	—	40
Manfredi, Tony	2	—	—	—	—
Melling, Alex	1	—	—	—	—
O'Toole, David	1	—	—	—	—
Owen, Ivor	3 + 4	—	—	—	—
Peters, Steve	3	1	—	—	4
Pinner, Harry	11	—	—	—	—
Pyke, Derek	17	1	—	—	4
Riding, Colin	1	—	—	—	—
Round, Mick	8	3	—	—	12
Ruane, David	7 + 2	4	—	—	16
Standish, Wayne	6	2	—	—	8
Thomas, Mark	2	—	—	—	—
Tuimavave, Paddy	4 + 2	1	—	—	4
Webb, Carl	2	—	—	—	—
Westhead, John	10 + 2	1	—	—	4

TOTALS:
39 players 86 76 8 504

Harry Pinner — signed from Widnes.

1987-88 MATCH ANALYSIS

Date	Competition	H/A	Opponent	Rlt	Score	Tries	Goals	Attendance	Referee
30.8.87	SBC	A	Leeds	L	12-38	Standish, Kerr	C. Johnson (2)	—	—
6.9.87	SBC	H	Castleford	W	14-6	C. Johnson, Jeffrey	C. Johnson (3)	3605	McDonald
13.9.87	LC(1)	H	St. Helens	W	27-21	McCulloch, Jeffrey, Henderson, Standish, Collier	P. Johnson (3), C. Johnson (dg)	7747	Spencer
20.9.87	SBC	A	Halifax	L	18-26	Kerr (2), McCulloch	C. Johnson (3)	—	—
23.9.87	LC(2)	A	Swinton	L	14-22	Kerr (2), McCulloch	C. Johnson	—	—
27.9.87	SBC	H	Wigan	L	8-36	Pyke	C. Johnson (2)	11,378	Whitfield
4.10.87	SBC	A	Hull	L	21-22	Cottrell, Jeffrey, Henderson, Ford	C. Johnson (2, 1 dg)	—	—
11.10.87	SBC	H	Hunslet	W	28-22	Henderson (3), McCulloch, Ford	C. Johnson (3), P. Johnson	3233	Cross
18.10.87	SBC	A	St. Helens	L	14-23	P. Johnson, Round	C. Johnson (3)	—	—
1.11.87	SBC	H	Widnes	L	12-19	Jeffrey, McCulloch	P. Johnson (2)	3971	Tennant
8.11.87	SBC	A	Bradford N.	L	6-24	—	P. Johnson (3)	—	—
15.11.87	JPS(1)	H	Huddersfield B.	W	28-12	McCulloch, Westhead, Cottrell, Horo, Dean	P. Johnson (4)	2082	Haigh
22.11.87	JPS(2)	A	Hull	L	7-19	Collier	P. Johnson (1, 1 dg)	—	—
6.12.87	SBC	A	Wigan	L	24-34	Horo (2), Kerr, Ford	P. Johnson (4)	—	—
13.12.87	SBC	H	Hull K.R.	W	13-6	Ford, Horo	P. Johnson (2), Ford (dg)	2727	Holdsworth
20.12.87	SBC	A	Castleford	W	22-18	Burrill, Dean, Kerr, McCulloch, Horo	P. Johnson	—	—
27.12.87	SBC	A	Hunslet	L	10-48	Dunn, Horo	P. Johnson	—	—
1.1.88	SBC	H	Salford	W	18-0	Dean, McCulloch, Horo, Kerr	C. Johnson	3818	Spencer
10.1.88	SBC	A	Widnes	L	8-14	P. Johnson	P. Johnson (2)	—	—
17.1.88	SBC	H	Swinton	W	22-16	Horo, Kerr, C. Johnson	P. Johnson (5)	3320	Tickle
31.1.88	CC(1)	H	St. Helens	L	12-22	Kerr (2)	P. Johnson (2)	8813	Allatt
7.2.88	SBC	H	Leeds	W	18-6	Burrill, Horo, Evans	Burrill (3)	4515	McDonald
14.2.88	SBC	A	Swinton	L	20-28	Jeffrey, Clarke, Dunn	Burrill (4)	—	—
21.2.88	SBC	H	St. Helens	L	12-50	Dean, Jeffrey	Burrill (2)	6439	Simpson
6.3.88	SBC	H	Halifax	L	14-28	Jeffrey, P. Johnson, McCulloch	P. Johnson	4760	Tickle
20.3.88	SBC	A	Warrington	L	6-10	Jeffrey	C. Johnson	—	—
23.3.88	SBC	A	Salford	L	21-28	Tuimavave, Ruane, Collier	C. Johnson (4, 1 dg)	—	—
27.3.88	SBC	H	Bradford N.	L	5-20	Dunn	C. Johnson (dg)	3394	Kershaw
4.4.88	SBC	H	Warrington	W	28-5	Dunn, Peters, C. Johnson, Kerr, Ruane	C. Johnson (4)	4069	Haigh
10.4.88	SBC	A	Hull K.R.	L	11-23	Dunn, McCulloch	C. Johnson (1, 1 dg)	—	—
17.4.88	SBC	H	Hull	W	31-9	Ruane (2), Round (2), Dean	C. Johnson (5, 1 dg)	3482	Tennant

MANSFIELD MARKSMAN

Ground: Alfreton Sports Stadium
Colours: Green and yellow hooped jerseys
First Season: 1984-85
Chairman: Paul Tomlinson
General
  Manager: David Parker
Coach: Jim Crellin (Dec 1986-)
Records: Attendance: 2,291 v. Wakefield T.
(Div. 2) 9 Sep, 1984
Season
Goals: 63 by C. Sanderson, 1984-85
Tries: 13 by S. Nicholson,
    K. Whiteman, 1984-85
Points: 136 by C. Sanderson,
1984-85
Match
Goals: 7 by B. Holden v. Keighley,
10 Mar, 1985
Tries: 4 by K. Whiteman v.
Doncaster, 4 Nov, 1984
Points: 18 by B. Holden v.
Keighley, 10 Mar, 1985;
M. Howarth v. Dewsbury, 17 Jan,
1988
Highest score: 54-10 v. Doncaster,
1984-85
Highest against: 76-6 v. Leigh,
1985-86

1987-88 PLAYERS' SUMMARY

	App	Tries	Goals	Dr	Pts
Chadwick, Darren	2	1	—	—	4
Chadwick, Les	19	—	—	—	—
Clark, Rob	24 + 2	2	6	1	21
Cochrane, Tony	7 + 7	3	—	—	12
Cook, Mark	1	—	—	—	—
Davies, Paul	1	—	—	—	—
Deakin, Chris	7 + 3	1	—	—	4
Duffy, Andy	13 + 5	—	—	—	—
Edge, Phil	19 + 1	4	—	—	16
Grix, Wayne	1	1	—	—	4
Hawkyard, Kevin	0 + 1	—	—	—	—
Hough, Mick	20 + 4	3	—	—	12
Howarth, Mick	16 + 2	5	27	—	74
Ince, Ian	17	1	—	—	4
Johnson, Willie	9	1	—	—	4
Lamb, Derek	26	3	24	—	60
Marshall, Nigel	5 + 2	3	—	—	12
Mattison, Neil	33	5	—	—	20
Mehand, Mike	0 + 1	—	—	—	—
Moore, Ian	1 + 2	—	—	—	—
Morgan, Kevin	14	3	3	—	18
Platt, Billy	20 + 5	3	—	5	17
Rudd, Neil	6 + 1	3	—	—	12
Sanderson, Mark	26	2	10	2	30
Sealey, Camrel	30	9	—	—	36
Sheldon, Mick	1 + 1	—	—	—	—
Simpson, Colin	10 + 2	2	6	—	20
Stones, Chris	3	—	—	—	—
Swift, Mick	0 + 1	—	—	—	—
Tupaea, Ashley	26	7	—	—	28
Tupaea, Shane	33	8	—	—	32
Warburton, Joe	30 + 2	10	—	—	40
Whitehead, Craig	22 + 5	2	—	—	8
Willis, Chris	0 + 1	—	—	—	—
TOTALS:					
34 players		82	76	8	488

Mansfield Marksman prop Mick Hough scores against Doncaster.

1987-88 MATCH ANALYSIS

Date	Competition	H/A	Opponent	Rlt	Score	Tries	Goals	Attendance	Referee
30.8.87	SD	A	Keighley	L	18-30	Grix, Chadwick, Sealey	Morgan (3)	—	—
2.9.87	SD	H	Sheffield E.	L	8-32	Warburton	Simpson (2)	227	Tennant
6.9.87	SD	H	Batley	L	10-26	Warburton, Simpson	Simpson	252	Spencer
13.9.87	YC(1)	H	York	L	18-23	Warburton, Cochrane, Morgan	Sanderson (3)	256	Kendrew
20.9.87	SD	A	Runcorn H.	L	16-28	Warburton, S. Tupaea, Deakin	Lamb (2)	—	—
27.9.87	SD	H	Wakefield T.	D	20-20	Sealey (2), A. Tupaea	Lamb (4)	567	Cross
4.10.87	SD	A	Featherstone R.	L	10-26	S. Tupaea, Cochrane	Lamb	—	—
11.10.87	SD	H	York	W	10-8	Edge	Lamb (3)	310	Burke
18.10.87	SD	A	Huddersfield B.	W	26-12	Sealey (2), Edge, Platt, Hough	Lamb (2), Clarke	—	—
25.10.87	SD	A	Doncaster	L	10-34	Simpson, S. Tupaea	Clark	—	—
1.11.87	SD	H	Dewsbury	W	22-5	A. Tupaea, Edge, Warburton, Whitehead	Sanderson (3)	367	Spencer
8.11.87	SD	A	Sheffield E.	W	30-10	Morgan, S. Tupaea, A. Tupaea, Sealey, Edge	Sanderson (4), Lamb	—	—
15.11.87	JPS(1)	A	Runcorn H.	W	6-4	Mattison	Lamb	—	—
22.11.87	JPS(2)	A	St. Helens	L	0-40	—	—	—	—
6.12.87	SD	A	Bramley	L	10-12	Cochrane, Morgan	Lamb	—	—
13.12.87	SD	H	Huddersfield B.	W	10-8	Clarke, Lamb	Lamb	341	Smith
20.12.87	SD	A	Wakefield T.	L	12-16	Sanderson, S. Tupaea	Lamb (2)	—	—
27.12.87	SD	H	Runcorn H.	W	18-4	Warburton, Howarth, Sealey	Lamb (2), Clarke	309	Dockray
3.1.88	SD	H	Fulham	W	18-6	A. Tupaea (2), Howarth	Howarth (3)	391	Holdsworth
10.1.88	SD	H	Featherstone R.	L	2-22	—	Howarth	724	Carter
17.1.88	SD	A	Dewsbury	W	31-27	Howarth (2), Marshall (2), Sealey	Howarth (5), Platt (dg)	—	—
24.1.88	SD	H	Bramley	L	8-16	Marshall, Sealey	—	289	Holgate
31.1.88	CC(1)	A	Fulham	W	16-4	A. Tupaea, Platt, Mattison	Simpson (2)	—	—
7.2.88	SD	A	Springfield B.	L	7-14	S. Tupaea	Simpson, Sanderson (dg)	—	—
14.2.88	CC(2)	A	Doncaster	L	8-16	S. Tupaea	Clark (2)	—	—
21.2.88	SD	H	Keighley	W	11-6	Clark, Howarth	Clark, Sanderson (dg)	253	Hodgson
28.2.88	SD	A	Workington T.	W	32-12	Warburton (3), S. Tupaea, Mattinson	Howarth (6)	—	—
6.3.88	SD	H	Doncaster	W	14-0	Sanderson, Hough	Howarth (3)	493	Drinkwater
13.3.88	SD	A	York	L	8-16	Lamb	Howarth (2)	—	—
20.3.88	SD	H	Workington T.	W	20-10	Rudd (2), Mattinson, A. Tupaea	Howarth (2)	229	Tidball
27.3.88	SD	A	Fulham	W	32-6	Whitehead, Platt, Lamb, Rudd, Ince, Hough	Lamb (4)	—	—
3.4.88	SD	H	Springfield B.	W	18-6	Warburton, Mattinson, Johnson	Howarth (2), Platt (2 dg)	227	Steele
10.4.88	SD	A	Batley	W	8-0	—	Howarth (3), Clark (dg), Platt (dg)	—	—
24.4.88	SDP(1)	A	Featherstone R.	L	1-42	—	Platt (dg)	—	—

61

OLDHAM

Ground:	Watersheddings
Colours:	Red and white hooped jerseys
First Season:	1895-96
Nickname:	Roughyeds
Chairman:	Harvey Ashworth
Secretary:	Anita Lees
Coach:	Eric Fitzsimons (June 1987-)
	Mal Graham (June 1987-Apr 1988)
Honours:	**Championship** Winners, 1909-10, 1910-11,1956-57
	Beaten finalists, 1906-07, 1907-08, 1908-09, 1921-22, 1954-55
	Division One Champions, 1904-05
	Division Two Champions, 1963-64, 1981-82, 1987-88
	Second Division Premiership Winners, 1987-88
	Challenge Cup Winners, 1898-99, 1924-25, 1926-27
	Beaten finalists, 1906-07, 1911-12, 1923-24, 1925-26
	Lancashire League Winners, 1897-98, 1900-01, 1907-08, 1909-10, 1921-22, 1956-57, 1957-58
	Lancashire Cup Winners, 1907-08, 1910-11, 1913-14, 1919-20, 1924-25, 1933-34, 1956-57, 1957-58, 1958-59
	Beaten finalists, 1908-09, 1911-12, 1918-19, 1921-22, 1954-55, 1966-67, 1968-69, 1986-87
Records:	Attendance: 28,000 v. Huddersfield (League) 24 Feb, 1912
	Season
	Goals: 200 by B. Ganley, 1957-58
	Tries: 49 by R. Farrar, 1921-22
	Points: 412 by B. Ganley, 1957-58

Match
Goals: 14 by B. Ganley v. Liverpool C., 4 Apr, 1959
Tries: 7 by Miller v. Barry, 31 Oct, 1908
Points: 30 by A. Johnson v. Widnes, 9 Apr, 1928
Highest score: 67-6 v. Liverpool C., 1958-59
Highest against: 67-11 v. Hull K.R., 1978-79

1987-88 PLAYERS' SUMMARY

	App	Tries	Goals	Dr	Pts
Atkinson, Keith	13 + 1	6	62	—	148
Bardsley, Mick	3 + 6	—	—	—	—
Bates, Ian	1 + 1	1	—	—	4
Burke, Mick	30	7	4	1	37
Casey, Leo	4 + 4	3	—	—	12
Clawson, Neil	26	2	—	—	8
Copeland, Tony	1 + 1	—	—	—	—
Edwards, Jeff	6	—	1	—	2
Flanagan, Terry	18 + 13	6	—	1	25
Ford, Mike	19	9	—	3	39
Foy, Des	26 + 1	21	—	—	84
Graham, Mal	38	16	—	—	64
Hall, Martin	3	2	—	—	8
Hawkyard, Colin	27 + 5	3	—	—	12
Irving, Richard	12 + 3	2	—	—	8
Kirwan, Paddy	9	2	—	—	8
Lord, Paul	7 + 2	5	—	—	20
Marsden, Bob	0 + 1	—	—	—	—
McAlister, Charlie	18	9	15	—	66
McCarthy, Brian	15 + 2	10	—	—	40
Meadows, Kevin	38	16	—	—	64
Morrison, Tony	1 + 3	—	—	—	—
Myler, Chris	0 + 2	—	—	—	—
Nadiole, Tom	1 + 2	—	—	—	—
Peters, Steve	13	—	—	—	—
Robinson, Steve	8	1	—	—	4
Round, Paul	26 + 6	16	—	—	64
Sanderson, Ian	27	4	—	—	16
Sherman, Paul	0 + 1	—	—	—	—
Sherratt, Ian	12 + 2	2	—	—	8
Waddell, Hugh	35 + 1	7	—	—	28
Walsh, Peter	29 + 2	14	62	—	180
Warnecke, Gary	23 + 2	7	—	—	28
Worrall, Mick	5	2	2	—	12
TOTALS:					
34 players		173	146	5	989

1987-88 MATCH ANALYSIS

Date	Competition	H/A	Opponent	Rlt	Score	Tries	Goals	Attendance	Referee
30.8.87	SD	A	Whitehaven	W	20-6	Kirwan, Sherratt, Waddell	Atkinson (3), Worrall	—	—
2.9.87	SD	H	Keighley	W	32-3	Irving, Sanderson, Round, Graham	Atkinson (8)	3724	Carter
6.9.87	SD	H	Bramley	W	46-11	Worrall (2), Graham, Sanderson, Meadows, Atkinson, Flanagan, Round	Atkinson (7)	2851	Houghton
13.9.87	LC(1)	A	Warrington	L	8-42	Meadows	Atkinson (2)	—	—
20.9.87	SD	H	Springfield B.	W	22-20	Hawkyard, Meadows, Flanagan	Atkinson (4), Worrall	3114	Tickle

MATCH ANALYSIS (continued)

Date	Comp	V	Opponent	R	Score	Tries	Goals	Att	Referee
27.9.87	SD	A	Doncaster	L	18-20	Meadows, Bates, Round, Clawson	Edwards	—	—
4.10.87	SD	A	Huddersfield B.	W	26-4	McCarthy (2), Walsh, Round, Graham	Atkinson (3)	—	—
11.10.87	SD	H	Sheffield E.	W	44-20	Burke (2), Round (2), McCarthy, Walsh, Graham, Kirwan	Walsh (6)	3774	Bowman
25.10.87	SD	H	Barrow	W	36-8	Waddell, Burke, Walsh, Foy, Sanderson	Walsh (6)	3929	Shrimpton (NZ)
1.11.87	SD	A	Keighley	W	12-10	Walsh, McCarthy	Walsh (2)	—	—
8.11.87	JPS(P)	H	Fulham	W	36-8	Round (2), Hawkyard, Sanderson, Walsh, McCarthy	Walsh (6)	3197	Carter
14.11.87	JPS(1)	H	Bradford N.	W	22-6	Walsh, McCarthy, Round, Robinson	Walsh (3)	4858	Smith
22.11.87	JPS(2)	A	Batley	W	44-0	Round (3), Foy, Waddell, McCarthy, Warnecke, Burke	Walsh (3), Burke (3)	—	—
28.11.87	JPS(3)	A	Warrington	W	14-10	Flanagan, Round	Walsh (3)	—	—
6.12.87	SD	H	Doncaster	W	17-16	Hall (2), McCarthy	Walsh (2), Burke (dg)	3551	Tidball
12.12.87	SD	A	Barrow	L	14-18	Foy, Warnecke	Walsh (3)	—	—
19.12.87	JPS(SF)	Wigan	St. Helens	L	8-18	McCarthy, Warnecke	—	(8136)	Smith
27.12.87	SD	H	Rochdale H.	W	24-12	Foy, Hawkyard, Waddell, Meadows	Walsh (4)	4866	Steele
3.1.88	SD	A	Springfield B.	W	20-4	McCarthy, Warnecke, McAllister	Walsh (4)	—	—
10.1.88	SD	H	Whitehaven	W	28-20	Foy, Walsh, Meadows, Waddell	Walsh (6)	3803	Dockray
17.1.88	SD	A	Runcorn H.	W	34-8	Meadows (3), Foy (2), Warnecke, Graham	Walsh (2), Burke	—	—
24.1.88	SD	H	Wakefield T.	L	10-28	Ford, McAllister	Walsh	5106	Volante
31.1.88	CC(1)	A	Warrington	L	6-17	Lord	Walsh	—	—
7.2.88	SD	A	Workington T.	W	16-8	Clawson, Round, Foy	Walsh, McAllister	—	—
14.2.88	SD	H	Carlisle	W	26-4	McAllister, Graham, Flanagan, Round, Meadows	Walsh (3)	3356	Holgate
21.2.88	SD	A	Featherstone R.	D	8-8	Warnecke	Walsh (2)	—	—
28.2.88	SD	H	Featherstone R.	L	15-18	Walsh, McAlister	Walsh (3), Ford (dg)	5804	Houghton
6.3.88	SD	H	Workington T.	W	38-10	Foy (2), Atkinson (2), Flanagan, Ford, Meadows, Lord	Atkinson (3)	2866	Carter
13.3.88	SD	A	Bramley	W	36-16	Ford (2), Graham, Burke, Meadows, Waddell	Atkinson (6)	—	—
20.3.88	SD	H	Huddersfield B.	W	48-0	Ford (2), McAlister (2), Burke, Round, Warnecke, Graham, Walsh	Atkinson (6)	2930	Hodgson
27.3.88	SD	A	Sheffield E.	W	28-15	Graham (2), Atkinson, Walsh (2)	Atkinson (4)	—	—
1.4.88	SD	A	Rochdale H.	W	58-6	Foy (3), Ford (2), Walsh (2), Casey, Atkinson, Graham, Irving	Atkinson (6), Walsh	—	—
4.4.88	SD	H	Runcorn H.	W	38-4	Graham (2), Sherratt, Lord, Casey, Foy	Atkinson (7)	3406	Dockray
10.4.88	SD	A	Wakefield T.	W	23-22	Meadows, Ford, Foy, Atkinson	Atkinson (3), Flanagan (dg)	—	—
17.4.88	SD	A	Carlisle	W	34-16	Foy (2), Lord (2), Casey, McAlister	McAlister (5)	—	—
24.4.88	SDP(1)	H	Keighley	W	34-24	Graham (2), McAlister, Meadows (2), Burke, Foy	McAlister (2), Ford (2 dg)	3701	Smith
8.5.88	SDP(SF)	H	Springfield B.	W	18-10	McAlister, Graham, Foy	McAlister (3)	4667	Tennant
15.5.88	SDP(F)	Man U. FC	Featherstone R.	W	28-26	Foy (2), Flanagan, Meadows, Walsh	McAlister (4)	—	Whitfield

ROCHDALE HORNETS

Ground:	Athletic Ground. Moved to Spotland, Rochdale AFC, at start of 1988-89 season.
Colours:	White jerseys with blue and red band
First Season:	1895-96
Nickname:	Hornets
Chairman:	Len Stansfield
Secretary:	Paul Reynolds
Coach:	Eric Fitzsimons (June 1986-June 1987) Eric Hughes (June 1987-)
Honours:	**Challenge Cup** Winners, 1921-22 **Lancashire League** Winners, 1918-19 **Lancashire Cup** Winners, 1911-12, 1914-15, 1918-19 Beaten finalists, 1912-13, 1919-20, 1965-66 **John Player Trophy** Beaten finalists 1973-74 **BBC2 Floodlit Trophy** Beaten finalists 1971-72
Records:	Attendance: 41,831 Wigan v. Oldham (RL Cup Final) 12 Apr 1924 Home: 26,664 v. Oldham (RL Cup) 25 Mar, 1922 **Season** Goals: 115 by K. Harcombe, 1985-86 Tries: 30 by J. Williams, 1934-35 Points: 235 by G. Starkey, 1966-67 **Match** Goals: 10 by H. Lees v. Glasshoughton, 19 Feb, 1938 Tries: 5 by J. Corsi v. Barrow, 31 Dec, 1921 and v. Broughton Moor, 25 Feb, 1922; J. Williams v. St Helens, 4 Apr, 1933; N. Brelsford v. Whitehaven, 3 Sep, 1972 Points: 27 by F. Blincow v. Normanton, 17 Oct, 1903 Highest score: 75-13 v. Broughton M., 1914-15 Highest against: 79-2 v. Hull, 1920-21

1987-88 PLAYERS' SUMMARY

	App	Tries	Goals	Dr	Pts
Aspey, Steve	2	—	—	—	—
Barrow, Scott	22 + 1	5	—	—	20
Brown, David	3 + 2	—	—	—	—
Broxton, Paul	1	1	—	—	4
Byron, Gerry	23	1	—	—	4
Cartwright, Phil	25	4	—	—	16
Causey, Mark	30 + 1	6	—	—	24
Clucas, Geoff	2 + 2	—	—	—	—
Connell, Pomare	1 + 1	—	—	—	—
Cowie, Neil	25 + 3	6	—	—	24
Diamond, Jason	4 + 1	—	—	—	—
Dobson, Mark	6 + 2	—	—	—	—
Dwyer, Mark	4 + 1	1	—	—	4
Fairhurst, Alan	19 + 1	—	2	4	8
Garritty, Brian	22	5	—	—	20
Hitchen, Gary	4 + 1	—	2	—	4
Hoare, Shaun	1 + 4	—	—	—	—
Hughes, Eric	16	—	—	—	—
Idle, Graham	26 + 2	—	—	—	—
Lowe, Kevin	3 + 1	—	—	—	—
Marriott, Carl	0 + 1	—	—	—	—
McGinty, Bob	11	—	—	—	—
Mellor, Terry	15 + 9	—	—	—	—
Nanyn, Mick	5	1	—	—	4
Nash, Steve	0 + 1	—	—	—	—
O'Neill, Sean	0 + 1	—	—	—	—
Ruane, Andy	30	12	15	2	80
Ruane, Dennis	7 + 1	—	3	—	6
Sanderson, Mark	21 + 5	1	—	—	4
Sawyer, Aaron	21 + 2	7	—	—	28
Stapleton, John	4 + 1	—	—	—	—
Stokes, Bob	4	—	—	—	—
Vaafusu, Olsen	19	2	—	—	8
Williams, Dean	19 + 1	6	—	—	24
Wood, David	21 + 1	1	39	2	84
TOTALS: 35 players		59	61	8	366

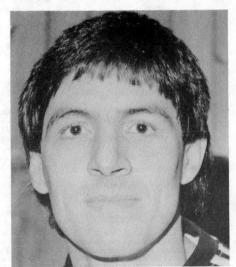

Eric Hughes — Rochdale Hornets' coach.

1987-88 MATCH ANALYSIS

Date	Competition	H/A	Opponent	Rlt	Score	Tries	Goals	Attendance	Referee
30.8.87	SD	H	Runcorn H.	L	0-8	—	—	1138	Burke
2.9.87	SD	H	Springfield B.	W	8-6	Dwyer	Wood (2)	894	Allatt
6.9.87	SD	A	Sheffield E.	L	8-22	Causey, Garritty	—	—	—
13.9.87	LC(1)	A	Swinton	L	20-38	A. Ruane (2), Garritty	Wood (4)	—	—
20.9.87	SD	A	Featherstone R.	L	14-56	Sawyer, Garritty	Wood (3)	—	—
27.9.87	SD	H	Carlisle	W	20-5	Cartwright, Barrow, A. Ruane	Wood (4)	748	Hodgson
2.10.87	SD	A	Barrow	L	6-21	Wood	Wood	—	—
11.10.87	SD	H	Whitehaven	W	20-12	Barrow (2), Sanderson	Wood (4)	828	McDonald
25.10.87	SD	H	Sheffield E.	W	7-2	Cowie	Wood, A. Ruane (dg)	923	Holdsworth
1.11.87	SD	H	Doncaster	W	22-4	Vaafusu, Broxton, Garritty	Wood (4, 1 dg), Fairhurst (dg)	1293	Dockray
8.11.87	SD	A	Springfield B.	L	11-20	Causey, A. Ruane	Wood, Fairhurst (dg)	—	—
15.11.87	JPS(1)	A	Hull K.R.	L	12-30	Cowie, A. Ruane	Wood (2)	—	—
22.11.87	SD	H	Barrow	L	9-11	A. Ruane	Wood (2, 1 dg)	924	Bowman
29.11.87	SD	H	Bramley	W	23-20	A. Ruane (2), Cowie, Garritty	Wood (3), Fairhurst (dg)	907	Volante
6.12.87	SD	A	Wakefield T.	L	2-30	—	Wood	—	—
20.12.87	SD	A	Whitehaven	L	2-26	—	Wood	—	—
27.12.87	SD	A	Oldham	L	12-24	Sawyer, Cartwright	A. Ruane (2)	—	—
3.1.88	SD	H	Huddersfield B.	W	8-6	Williams	Fairhurst (2)	700	Bowman
10.1.88	SD	A	Keighley	L	15-10	Causey (2), Cowie	A. Ruane, Fairhurst (dg)	—	—
17.1.88	SD	H	Workington T.	W	18-8	Sawyer, Vaafusu, Barrow	A. Ruane (3)	811	Allatt
31.1.88	CC(1)	H	Barrow	W	6-4	Ruane	A. Ruane	964	Cross
14.2.88	CC(2)	A	Halifax	L	6-30	Williams	Wood	—	—
28.2.88	SD	A	Huddersfield B.	L	22-23	Sawyer (2), Williams, Causey	Wood (3)	—	—
6.3.88	SD	H	Keighley	L	4-14	A. Ruane	—	803	Kershaw
9.3.88	SD	H	Wakefield T.	L	8-18	Williams	D. Ruane (2)	1106	Burke
13.3.88	SD	A	Carlisle	W	11-10	Cowie, Williams	D. Ruane, A. Ruane (dg)	—	—
20.3.88	SD	H	Featherstone R.	L	12-14	Cartwright, Williams, Wood (2)	—	950	Bowman
27.3.88	SD	A	Doncaster	L	18-21	Cowie, Cartwright, A. Ruane	A. Ruane (3)	—	—
1.4.88	SD	H	Oldham	L	6-58	Sawyer	Hitchen	3260	Drinkwater
4.4.88	SD	A	Bramley	L	24-34	Byron, Barrow, Sawyer, A. Ruane	A. Ruane (3), Hitchen	—	—
13.4.88	SD	A	Runcorn H.	L	8-16	Causey	A. Ruane (2)	—	—
17.4.88	SD	A	Workington T.	L	4-13	Nanyn	—	—	—

RUNCORN HIGHFIELD

Ground: Canal Street
Colours: Black jerseys
First Season: 1922-23 as Wigan Highfield.
Became London Highfield in
1933-34. Became Liverpool Stanley
in 1934-35 and changed to
Liverpool City in 1951-52. Became
Huyton in 1968-69 and changed to
Runcorn Highfield in 1984-85.
There was also a Liverpool City in
1906-07
Chairman: Terry Hughes
Secretary: Tony Almond
Coach: Bill Ashurst (Apr 1987-)
Honours: **Lancashire League** Winners,
1935-36
Records: Attendance: 14,000 v. Widnes
(Championship semi-final) 2 May,
1936 at Prescott Road
Season
Goals: 126 by P. Wood, 1984-85
Tries: 28 by J. Maloney, 1930-31
Points: 240 by P. Wood, 1984-85
Match
Goals: 11 by P. Wood v. Batley,
21 Oct, 1984
Tries: 5 by J. Maloney v. Bramley,
25 Apr, 1931
Points: 24 by T. Rose v.
Workington T., 4 Oct, 1987
Highest score: 59-11 v. Bramley,
1933-34
Highest against: 73-0 v.
Warrington, 1950-51

1987-88 PLAYERS' SUMMARY

	App	Tries	Goals	Dr	Pts
Ashall, Paul	5 + 1	1	—	—	4
Ashcroft, Keith	5 + 2	—	—	—	—
Blackwood, Bob	0 + 1	—	—	—	—
Blythin, Kevin	7 + 8	4	—	—	16
Booth, John	10 + 3	—	—	—	—
Campbell, Danny	6 + 2	—	—	—	—
Cogger, Jamie	14	5	—	—	20
Cogger, John	16 + 3	9	—	—	36
Compton, David	5 + 2	1	—	—	4
Daley, Arthur	7 + 1	—	—	—	—
Day, Sean	3	1	7	—	18
Dean, Geoff	26	4	—	—	16
Dooley, Jim	3 + 5	—	—	—	—
Durnin, Paul	18	3	—	—	12
Ewer, Steve	5 + 1	4	—	—	16
Fitzpatrick, Paul	2 + 1	—	—	—	—
Frazer, Paul	21 + 1	3	—	—	12
Gibson, Kerry	1 + 1	—	—	—	—
Glover, Mick	4 + 6	1	—	—	4
Hunt, David	21	—	—	—	—
Hunter, Clive	24	4	—	—	16
Jackson, Tony	5	1	1	—	6
Marsden, Peter	12 + 2	1	—	—	4
Middlehurst, Chris	25 + 3	3	8	9	37
Moore, Mike	4 + 4	1	—	—	4
Moylan, Steve	24 + 1	1	—	—	4
Pojunas, Chris	8	—	—	—	—
Prescott, Eric	14 + 6	—	—	1	1
Rawlinson, Tommy	28	8	—	—	32
Rose, Terry	24	9	45	—	126
Shaw, Glyn	13 + 4	—	—	—	—
Shaw, Mark	12	1	6	—	16
Smith, Ian	29	7	—	—	28
Walls, David	2 + 1	1	—	—	4
Trialist	0 + 1	—	—	—	—

TOTALS:

	App	Tries	Goals	Dr	Pts
35 players		73	67	10	436

Glyn Shaw — 13 full appearances.

1987-88 MATCH ANALYSIS

Date	Com-petition	H/A	Opponent	Rlt	Score	Tries	Goals	Atten-dance	Referee
30.8.87	SD	A	Rochdale H.	W	8-0	Rawlinson	Rose (2)	—	—
6.9.87	SD	H	Fulham	W	23-16	Dean (2), Blythen, Rose	Rose (3), Middlehurst (dg)	350	Tickle
13.9.87	LC(1)	H	Widnes	L	6-40	Rose	Rose	2679	Burke
20.9.87	SD	H	Mansfield M.	W	28-16	Ewer (2), Jamie Cogger, Jackson, Moore	Rose (4)	347	Berry
27.9.87	SD	A	York	W	19-16	Hunter, Rose, Middlehurst	Rose (3), Middlehurst (dg)	—	—
4.10.87	SD	H	Workington T.	W	41-4	Ewer (2), Rose (2), Fraser, Rawlinson	Rose (8), Middlehurst (dg)	510	Drinkwater
18.10.87	SD	A	Barrow	L	7-18	Rose	Rose, Middlehurst (dg)	—	—
1.11.87	SD	H	Springfield B.	W	26-20	Moylan, Smith, Hunter, Rawlinson	Rose (4), Middlehurst (2 dg)	412	Shrimpton (NZ)
8.11.87	SD	A	Batley	W	15-2	Rawlinson, Blythen	Rose (3), Middlehurst (dg)	—	—
15.11.87	JPS(1)	H	Mansfield M.	L	4-6	—	Rose (2)	514	Dockray
29.11.87	SD	H	Huddersfield B.	W	20-6	Smith (2), Fraser, Shaw	Rose (2)	610	Holgate
6.12.87	SD	A	Carlisle	L	11-13	Jamie Cogger, Rawlinson	Rose, Middlehurst (dg)	—	—
13.12.87	SD	H	Batley	W	23-18	Jamie Cogger (2), Rawlinson, Durnin	Shaw (3), Prescott (dg)	330	Kershaw
27.12.87	SD	A	Mansfield M.	L	4-18	Marsden	—	—	—
1.1.88	SD	H	Keighley	W	20-16	Durnin, Hunter, Smith, Rose	Rose (2)	440	Burke
10.1.88	SD	A	Fulham	L	20-22	Jamie Cogger, Rawlinson, Blythen, Smith	Rose (2)	—	—
17.1.88	SD	H	Oldham	L	8-34	Blythen	Shaw (2)	2400	Spencer
24.1.88	SD	A	Keighley	L	6-30	Dean	Jackson	—	—
31.1.88	CC(1)	H	Springfield B.	L	6-8	John Cogger	Shaw	550	Haigh
14.2.88	SD	A	Whitehaven	L	6-26	John Cogger	Rose	—	—
26.2.88	SD	H	Barrow	W	17-8	Fraser, Rose, John Cogger	Day (2), Middlehurst (dg)	270	McDonald
6.3.88	SD	H	York	L	18-20	Day, Rose, John Cogger	Day (3)	312	Kershaw
13.3.88	SD	A	Workington T.	L	12-32	John Cogger (2)	Day (2)	—	—
20.3.88	SD	H	Dewsbury	L	6-10	John Cogger	Rose	168	Carter
27.3.88	SD	H	Whitehaven	W	24-18	Dean, Glover, Rawlinson, Durnin, John Cogger	Rose (2)	209	Allatt
1.4.88	SD	A	Springfield B.	L	6-20	Crompton	Middlehurst	—	—
4.4.88	SD	A	Oldham	L	4-38	Ashall	—	—	—
7.4.88	SD	A	Dewsbury	L	6-10	Walls	Middlehurst	—	—
10.4.88	SD	H	Carlisle	L	10-18	Hunter	Middlehurst (2), Rose	500	Tidball
13.4.88	SD	H	Rochdale H.	W	16-8	Smith (2), John Cogger	Rose (2)	350	Simpson
17.4.88	SD	A	Huddersfield B.	W	16-14	Middlehurst (2)	Middlehurst (4)	—	—

ST. HELENS

Ground: Knowsley Road
Colours: White jerseys with red V
First Season: 1895-96
Nickname: Saints
Chairman: Lawrie Prescott
Secretary: Geoff Sutcliffe
Coach: Alex Murphy (Nov 1985-)
Honours: **Championship** Winners, 1931-32, 1952-53, 1958-59, 1965-66, 1969-70, 1970-71
Beaten finalists, 1964-65, 1966-67, 1971-72
Division One Champions, 1974-75
League Leaders Trophy Winners, 1964-65, 1965-66
Club Championship (Merit Table) Beaten finalists, 1973-74
Challenge Cup Winners, 1955-56, 1960-61, 1965-66, 1971-72, 1975-76
Beaten finalists, 1896-97, 1914-15, 1929-30, 1952-53, 1977-78, 1986-87
Lancashire Cup Winners, 1926-27, 1953-54, 1960-61, 1961-62, 1962-63, 1963-64, 1964-65, 1967-68, 1968-69, 1984-85
Beaten finalists, 1932-33, 1952-53, 1956-57, 1958-59, 1959-60, 1970-71, 1982-83
Lancashire League Winners, 1929-30, 1931-32, 1952-53, 1959-60, 1964-65, 1965-66, 1966-67, 1968-69
John Player Trophy Winners, 1987-88
Premiership Winners, 1975-76, 1976-77, 1984-85
Beaten finalists, 1974-75, 1987-88
Western Division Championship Winners, 1963-64
BBC2 Trophy Winners, 1971-72, 1975-76
Beaten finalists, 1965-66, 1968-69, 1970-71, 1977-78, 1978-79
Records: Attendance: 35,695 v. Wigan (League) 26 Dec, 1949
Season
Goals: 214 by K. Coslett, 1971-72
Tries: 62 by T. Van Vollenhoven, 1958-59
Points: 452 by K. Coslett, 1971-72

Match
Goals: 16 by P. Loughlin v. Carlisle, 14 Sep, 1986
Tries: 6 by A. Ellaby v. Barrow, 5 Mar, 1932; S. Llewellyn v. Castleford, 3 Mar, 1956 and v. Liverpool C., 20 Aug, 1956; T. Vollenhoven v. Wakefield T., 21 Dec, 1957 and v. Blackpool B., 23 Apr, 1962; F. Myler v. Maryport, 1 Sep, 1969; S. Cooper v. Hull, 17 Feb, 1988
Points: 40 by P. Loughlin v. Carlisle, 14 Sep, 1986
Highest score: 112-0 v. Carlisle, 1986-87
Highest against: 78-3 v. Warrington, 1908-09

1987-88 PLAYERS' SUMMARY

	App	Tries	Goals	Dr	Pts
Allen, Shaun	2 + 5	—	—	—	—
Arkwright, Chris	20 + 3	8	—	—	32
Bailey, Mark	11	3	—	—	12
Burke, Tony	38	5	—	—	20
Cooper, Shane	21	11	—	—	44
Devine, Shaun	2	—	—	—	—
Doherty, Paul	1 + 4	1	—	—	4
Dwyer, Bernard	4 + 9	4	—	—	16
Elia, Mark	31 + 1	20	—	—	80
Evans, Stuart	27 + 4	1	—	—	4
Fieldhouse, John	10 + 7	4	—	—	16
Forber, Paul	33 + 3	7	2	—	32
Groves, Paul	30	9	—	—	36
Haggerty, Roy	37 + 2	5	—	13	33
Harrison, David	5	1	—	—	4
Holding, Neil	25 + 2	8	—	4	36
Jones, Paul	0 + 4	—	—	—	—
Large, David	11 + 2	3	—	—	12
Ledger, Barry	20 + 1	11	—	—	44
Liptrot, Graham	3	—	—	—	—
Litherland, Dennis	1 + 2	1	—	—	4
Loughlin, Paul	37 + 1	8	111	—	254
McCormack, Kevin	14 + 2	9	—	—	36
Neill, Jonathan	2 + 5	—	—	—	—
Platt, Andy	29	12	1	—	50
Quirk, Les	25	16	—	—	64
Southward, Phil	1 + 1	—	—	—	—
Souto, Peter	4	1	—	—	4
Tanner, David	28 + 5	5	45	—	110
Veivers, Phil	35	11	—	1	45
TOTALS:					
30 players		164	159	18	992

1987-88 MATCH ANALYSIS

Date	Competition	H/A	Opponent	Rlt	Score	Tries	Goals	Attendance	Referee
30.8.87	SBC	A	Castleford	L	10-20	Arkwright	Loughlin (3)	—	—
6.9.87	SBC	H	Hull K.R.	W	31-16	Elia (2), Haggerty, McCormack, Veivers	Loughlin (5), Haggerty (dg)	5273	Whitfield
13.9.87	LC(1)	A	Leigh	L	21-27	Elia (2), Forber, Loughlin	Loughlin (2), Holding (dg)	—	—
20.9.87	SBC	A	Warrington	L	20-24	Harrison, Haggerty, Bailey	Loughlin (4)	—	—
27.9.87	SBC	H	Bradford N.	W	38-10	Large (2), Arkwright, Litherland, Veivers, Platt, Bailey	Loughlin (4), Haggerty (2 dg)	6762	McDonald
4.10.87	SBC	A	Halifax	L	12-14	Quirk, Elia	Platt, Tanner	—	—
18.10.87	SBC	H	Leigh	W	23-14	Burke (2), Elia	Loughlin (5), Haggerty (dg)	7212	Holdsworth
25.10.87	SBC	A	Salford	W	18-8	Quirk (3)	Forber (2), Loughlin	—	—
1.11.87	Tour	H	Auckland	W	52-26	Quirk (3), Platt (2), Veivers, Evans, Bailey, Ledger	Tanner (8)	5901	Allatt
8.11.87	SBC	A	Leeds	L	21-24	McCormack (2), Arkwright	Loughlin (3), Tanner, Haggerty (dg)	—	—
14.11.87	JPS(1)	H	Widnes	W	12-10	Quirk	Loughlin (3), Haggerty (2 dg)	7322	Kershaw
22.11.87	JPS(2)	H	Mansfield M.	W	40-0	Elia (2), Forber, Fieldhouse, Veivers, Burke, Cooper	Loughlin (4), Tanner (2)	4966	McDonald
29.11.87	JPS(3)	H	Hull	W	20-16	McCormack, Quirk, Groves	Tanner (3), Loughlin	7400	Kendrew
6.12.87	SBC	A	Hull K.R.	L	16-25	McCormack (2), Elia	Loughlin (2)	—	—
13.12.87	SBC	H	Warrington	W	17-14	Tanner, Platt, Quirk	Tanner, Loughlin, Holding (dg)	8303	Lindop
19.12.87	JPS(SF)	Wigan	Oldham	W	18-8	Platt, Haggerty, Cooper	Loughlin (3)	(8136)	Smith
27.12.87	SBC	A	Wigan	W	32-22	Veivers (2), McCormack, Tanner, Quirk	Loughlin (6)	—	—
3.1.88	SBC	H	Widnes	W	25-0	Loughlin (2), Souto, Quirk	Tanner (2), Loughlin (2), Haggerty (dg)	12,938	Tennant
9.1.88	JPS(F)	Wigan	Leeds	W	15-14	Loughlin (2)	Loughlin (3), Holding (dg)	(16,669)	Lindop
17.1.88	SBC	A	Bradford N.	W	13-12	Tanner, Holding	Loughlin (2), Holding (dg)	—	—
31.1.88	CC(1)	A	Leigh	W	22-12	Elia (2), Quirk, Veivers	Loughlin (3)	—	—
7.2.88	SBC	H	Halifax	W	16-4	Elia (2), Veivers	Tanner (2)	10,476	Kershaw
13.2.88	CC(2)	A	Warrington	W	24-20	Fieldhouse (2), Quirk, Forber	Loughlin (3), Tanner	—	—
17.2.88	SBC	H	Hull	W	64-2	Cooper (6), Ledger (3), Dwyer, Arkwright	Loughlin (7), Tanner (3)	6569	Haigh
21.2.88	SBC	A	Leigh	W	50-12	Arkwright (2), Ledger, Groves, Haggerty, Burke, Fieldhouse, Elia	Tanner (7), Loughlin (2)	—	—
28.2.88	CC(3)	A	Salford	L	18-22	Burke, Loughlin, Dwyer	Loughlin (2), Tanner	—	—
1.3.88	SBC	H	Hunslet	W	70-6	Arkwright (2), Elia (2), Tanner (2), Ledger (2), Holding (2), Forber, Veivers, Cooper	Tanner (5), Loughlin (4)	4783	Burke
6.3.88	SBC	A	Hunslet	W	14-10	Dwyer, Groves	Loughlin (2), Haggerty (2 dg)	—	—
13.3.88	SBC	H	Castleford	W	14-6	Large, Cooper	Loughlin (3)	6083	Lindop
16.3.88	SBC	H	Salford	W	24-10	Cooper, Forber, Ledger, Dwyer	Loughlin (3), Tanner	6376	Houghton
20.3.88	SBC	A	Swinton	W	34-18	Holding, Platt, Veivers, Forber, Groves	Loughlin (5), Tanner (2)	—	—
1.4.88	SBC	H	Wigan	L	9-10	Doherty	Loughlin, Tanner, Haggerty (dg)	2182	Kendrew

(continued on page 92)

69

SALFORD

Ground:	The Willows
Colours:	Red jerseys
First Season:	1896-97
Nickname:	Red Devils
Chairman:	John Wilkinson
Secretary:	Graham McCarty
Coach:	Kevin Ashcroft (May 1984-)

Honours: **Championship** Winners, 1913-14, 1932-33, 1936-37, 1938-39
Beaten finalists, 1933-34
Division One Champions, 1973-74, 1975-76
Challenge Cup Winners, 1937-38
Beaten finalists, 1899-1900, 1901-02, 1902-03, 1905-06, 1938-39, 1968-69
Lancashire League Winners, 1932-33, 1933-34, 1934-35, 1936-37, 1938-39
Lancashire Cup Winners, 1931-32, 1934-35, 1935-36, 1936-37, 1972-73
Beaten finalists, 1929-30, 1938-39, 1973-74, 1974-75, 1975-76
Premiership Beaten finalists, 1975-76
John Player Trophy Beaten finalists 1972-73
BBC2 Trophy Winners, 1974-75

Records: Attendance: 26,470 v. Warrington (RL Cup) 13 Feb, 1937
Season
Goals: 221 by D. Watkins, 1972-73
Tries: 46 by K. Fielding, 1973-74
Points: 493 by D. Watkins, 1972-73
Match
Goals: 13 by A. Risman v. Bramley, 5 Apr, 1933 and v. Broughton R., 18 May, 1940; D. Watkins v. Keighley, 7 Jan, 1972; S. Rule v. Doncaster, 4 Sep, 1981
Tries: 6 by F. Miles v. Lees, 5 Mar, 1898; E. Bone v. Goole, 29 Mar, 1902; J. Hilton v. Leigh, 7 Oct, 1939

Points: 39 by J. Lomas v. Liverpool C., 2 Feb, 1907
Highest score: 78-0 v. Liverpool C., 1906-07
Highest against: 63-5 v. Wigan, 1924-25

1987-88 PLAYERS' SUMMARY

	App	Tries	Goals	Dr	Pts
Austin, Greg	16	8	—	—	32
Beckett, Adrian	1	—	—	—	—
Bentley, Keith	13 + 1	2	—	—	8
Blacker, Brian	3 + 1	2	—	—	8
Blease, Ian	24 + 6	5	—	—	20
Bloor, Darren	28 + 3	8	—	1	33
Bullough, David	12 + 1	1	—	—	4
Burgess, Andy	1 + 3	—	—	—	—
Cairns, David	24	2	—	—	8
Disley, Gary	9 + 2	—	—	—	—
Fazackerley, John	5 + 2	—	—	—	—
Fox, Kevin	1	1	—	—	4
Gibson, Steve	31	13	—	—	52
Gill, Mick	1	—	—	—	—
Glynn, Peter	15 + 7	—	—	1	1
Gormley, Ian	5	1	—	—	4
Griffiths, David	0 + 1	—	—	—	—
Groves, Paul	3 + 2	1	—	—	4
Herbert, Steve	34	3	—	—	12
Jack, Garry	16	3	—	—	12
Jones, Ken	32	9	79	—	194
Lamb, Nigel	2	—	—	—	—
McCarthy, Brian	1 + 1	—	—	—	—
McTigue, Mick	28	4	—	—	16
Major, David	19 + 8	1	—	—	4
Marsh, Ian	6 + 1	1	—	—	4
Moran, Mark	21 + 2	1	—	—	4
Nadiole, Tom	1 + 2	—	—	—	—
Needham, David	2	—	—	—	—
O'Loughlin, Jason	1	1	—	—	4
O'Loughlin, Keiron	27	3	—	—	12
O'Shea, Terry	10 + 5	1	3	—	10
Potts, Ian	1	1	—	—	4
Ratcliffe, David	5 + 1	—	—	—	—
Regan, Peter	3	—	—	—	—
Shaw, David	13 + 3	2	—	—	8
Walsh, Joe	4	—	—	—	—
Warhurst, Glen	1	—	—	—	—
Whiteley, Chris	2	—	—	—	—
Williams, Peter	5	5	—	—	20
Wiltshire, Roy	3 + 1	—	—	—	—
Worrall, Mick	24	8	6	—	44
Worrall, Tony	2 + 1	—	—	—	—

TOTALS:
43 players		87	88	2	526

1987-88 MATCH ANALYSIS

Date	Competition	H/A	Opponent	Rlt	Score	Tries	Goals	Attendance	Referee
30.8.87	SBC	H	Bradford N.	L	12-16	Herbert	Jones (4)	2514	Kendrew
6.9.87	SBC	A	Hull	L	11-16	Jones	Jones (3), Glynn (dg)	—	—
13.9.87	LC(1)	H	Fulham	W	58-4	Bloor (3), Major, Jones, McTigue, Groves, Bullough, Blacker, Gibson	Jones (9)	1640	Drinkwater
20.9.87	SBC	H	Hull K.R.	W	34-32	Jones (2), Blease, Gibson, Marsh, Blacker	Jones (5)	2005	Allatt
23.9.87	LC(2)	A	Wigan	L	2-42	—	Jones	—	—
27.9.87	SBC	A	Leeds	L	6-60	McTigue	Jones	—	—
4.10.87	SBC	H	Widnes	L	0-18	—	—	4190	Holdsworth
18.10.87	SBC	A	Hunslet	W	14-12	Austin (2), O'Shea	Jones	—	—
25.10.87	SBC	H	St. Helens	L	8-18	Worrall	Jones (2)	4549	Cross
1.11.87	SBC	A	Halifax	L	20-29	Austin (2), Worrall, K. O'Loughlin	Jones, Worrall	—	—
8.11.87	SBC	H	Hull	W	20-6	Gibson, K. O'Loughlin, Blease	Jones (4)	2395	Whitfield
15.11.87	JPS(1)	A	Swinton	W	18-12	Jack, Austin, McTigue	Jones (2), Worrall	—	—
22.11.87	JPS(2)	H	Dewsbury	W	14-5	Blease, Gibson	Jones (3)	2129	Tickle
29.11.87	JPS(3)	H	Wigan	L	12-16	Austin, Cairns	Worrall (2)	7986	Haigh
6.12.87	SBC	H	Hunslet	W	21-14	Bloor, Moran, McTigue	Jones (4), Bloor (dg)	2000	Bowman
13.12.87	SBC	A	Castleford	L	0-14	—	—	—	—
27.12.87	SBC	H	Swinton	W	36-8	Shaw, Bloor, Jones, Blease, Worrall, Jack	Jones (6)	4498	Kershaw
1.1.88	SBC	A	Leigh	L	0-18	—	—	—	—
10.1.88	SBC	A	Hull K.R.	L	8-20	Jack, Herbert	—	—	—
17.1.88	SBC	H	Wigan	L	6-14	Gibson	Worrall	6459	Lindop
24.1.88	SBC	A	Widnes	L	2-22	—	Worrall	—	—
31.1.88	CC(1)	H	Swinton	W	16-6	Worrall, Austin	Jones (4)	3425	Houghton
14.2.88	CC(2)	A	Springfield B.	W	12-10	K. O'Loughlin, Gibson	Jones (2)	2352	Whitfield
19.2.88	SBC	H	Castleford	L	12-28	Gibson, Austin	Jones (2)	2304	Bowman
28.2.88	CC(3)	H	St. Helens	W	22-18	Worrall (2), Gibson, Jones	Jones (3)	7964	McDonald
6.3.88	SBC	H	Leeds	W	14-10	Gibson, Bloor	O'Shea (3)	3548	Volante
12.3.88	CC(SF)	Bolton	Wigan	L	4-34	Blease	—	(20,783)	Holdsworth
16.3.88	SBC	A	St. Helens	L	10-24	Jones (2)	Jones	—	—
20.3.88	SBC	A	Bradford N.	L	4-34	Shaw	—	—	—
23.3.88	SBC	H	Leigh	W	28-21	Gibson (3), Bentley, Williams	Jones (4)	3421	Spencer
27.3.88	SBC	H	Warrington	L	14-34	Herbert, Gormley	Jones (3)	4118	Kendrew
1.4.88	SBC	A	Swinton	W	10-6	Williams, Bloor	Jones	—	—
10.4.88	SBC	A	Warrington	W	20-19	Williams, Cairns, Worrall	Jones (4)	—	—
13.4.88	SBC	A	Wigan	L	22-52	J. O'Loughlin, Jones, Fox, Potts	Jones (3)	—	—
17.4.88	SBC	H	Halifax	W	36-16	Williams (2), Bloor, Gibson, Bentley, Worrall	Jones (6)	6716	Haigh

SHEFFIELD EAGLES

Ground:	Owlerton Stadium
Colours:	White, claret and gold jerseys, white shorts
First Season:	1984-85
Nickname:	Eagles
Managing Director:	Gary Hetherington
Secretary:	Julie Bush
Coach:	Gary Hetherington (July 1986-)
Records:	Attendance: 2,316 v. Oldham (Div.2), 27 Mar, 1988 There was an attendance of 2,397 in a Div.2 match against Doncaster at Sheffield United FC's ground on 10 April, 1988.

Season
Goals: 79 by R. Rafferty, 1985-86
Tries: 17 by S. Lidbury, 1986-87
Points: 186 by R. Rafferty, 1985-86
Match
Goals: 12 by R. Rafferty at Fulham, 21 Sep, 1986
Tries: No player has scored more than 3
Points: 32 by R. Rafferty at Fulham, 21 Sep, 1986
Highest score: 68-14 at Fulham, 1986-87
Highest against: 62-11 v. Warrington, 1985-86

1987-88 PLAYERS' SUMMARY

	App	Tries	Goals	Dr	Pts
Aston, Mark	16 + 2	—	—	—	—
Bridgeman, Derek	29 + 2	6	—	—	24
Broadbent, Paul	13 + 7	—	—	—	—
Close, David	25 + 1	7	24	2	78
Cook, Michael	28 + 1	4	—	—	16
Dickinson, Andy	6 + 1	—	—	—	—
Farrell, Kevin	3 + 1	1	—	—	4
Fleming, Mark	8 + 1	—	—	1	1
Gamson, Mark	27 + 2	4	—	—	16
Gearin, Paul	21 + 1	5	8	—	36
Glancy, John	30	5	—	—	20
Hamilton, Scott	1	—	—	—	—
Hetherington, Gary	1 + 3	1	—	—	4
Hytch, Peter	9 + 2	—	—	—	—
Kellett, Neil	18 + 8	7	—	—	28
Lidbury, Steve	31	14	—	—	56
Lloyd, Chris	0 + 1	—	—	—	—
McDermott, Chris	4 + 3	1	—	—	4
McDermott, Paul	26 + 5	8	—	—	32
Nelson, David	30	7	—	—	28
Parkes, Stephen	5	—	—	—	—
Powell, Darryl	32	9	—	1	37
Rafferty, Roy	23	10	46	—	132
Smith, Gary	23 + 3	5	—	—	20
Vohland, Wayne	1 + 1	—	—	—	—
Ward, Martin	0 + 1	—	—	—	—
Wilders, Peter	18 + 8	1	—	—	4
Wilkinson, Marcel	3 + 1	1	—	—	4
Wilson, Andrew	4	2	—	—	8
Young, Andrew	7 + 4	2	—	—	8

TOTALS:
30 players		100	78	4	560

Gary Hetherington — Sheffield team manager.

1987-88 MATCH ANALYSIS

Date	Competition	H/A	Opponent	Rlt	Score	Tries	Goals	Attendance	Referee
28.8.87	SD	A	Fulham	W	20-12	Powell (2), Glancy, Rafferty	Rafferty (2)	—	—
2.9.87	SD	A	Mansfield M.	W	32-8	Glancy, Wilson, Close, Farrell, Rafferty	Rafferty (4), Close (2)	—	—
6.9.87	SD	H	Rochdale H.	W	22-8	Bridgeman, Kellett, Rafferty, Powell	Rafferty (3)	752	Haigh
13.9.87	YC(1)	A	Wakefield T.	L	18-32	Hetherington, Powell, Wilson	Rafferty (3)	—	—
18.9.87	SD	A	Barrow	L	8-10	Close	Rafferty (2)	—	—
27.9.87	SD	H	Whitehaven	W	18-13	Nelson (2), Bridgeman	Rafferty (2), Close (dg), Powell (dg)	721	Kendrew
4.10.87	SD	A	York	W	20-17	Rafferty (3), Close	Rafferty (2)	—	—
7.10.87	SD	H	Bramley	W	20-10	Rafferty (2), Powell	Rafferty (4)	426	Lindop
11.10.87	SD	A	Oldham	L	20-44	Wilder, Wilkinson, Nelson, P. McDermott	Rafferty (2)	—	—
18.10.87	SD	H	Wakefield T.	L	12-14	Rafferty, Close	Rafferty (2)	1183	Drinkwater
25.10.87	SD	A	Rochdale H.	L	2-7	—	Rafferty	—	—
8.11.87	SD	H	Mansfield M.	L	10-30	P. McDermott, C. McDermott	Rafferty	495	Steele
15.11.87	JPS(1)	A	Wigan	L	8-34	Close	Rafferty (2)	—	—
22.11.87	SD	H	Featherstone R.	D	10-10	Gamson, Nelson	Close	785	Berry
29.11.87	SD	H	Fulham	W	16-6	Kellett, Lidbury, Glancy	Close (2)	466	Smith
6.12.87	SD	A	Batley	W	22-6	P. McDermott, Smith, Lidbury, Powell	Close (3)	—	—
13.12.87	SD	H	York	W	45-16	Lidbury (2), Powell, P. McDermott, Nelson, Gamson, Close, Cook	Close (6, 1 dg)	480	Volante
20.12.87	SD	A	Carlisle	L	12-14	Smith, Gamson	Close (2)	—	—
27.12.87	SD	A	Doncaster	W	32-2	Lidbury (2), Cook, Bridgeman, P. McDermott, Gearin	Close (4)	—	—
3.1.88	SD	A	Bramley	W	12-6	Bridgeman (2), Kellett	—	—	—
10.1.88	SD	H	Barrow	W	22-0	Bridgeman, Glancy, Gearin, Lidbury	Close (3)	483	Kershaw
15.1.88	CC(P)	A	Bramley	W	14-6	Nelson, P. McDermott, Lidbury	Close	—	—
24.1.88	SD	H	Carlisle	W	12-10	Lidbury, P. McDermott	Rafferty (2)	446	Smith
31.1.88	CC(1)	A	Wakefield T.	W	14-10	Glancy, Cook	Rafferty (3)	—	—
14.2.88	CC(2)	A	Hull	L	6-26	Smith	Rafferty	—	—
21.2.88	SD	A	Wakefield T.	L	6-14	Close	Rafferty	—	—
28.2.88	SD	H	Batley	L	12-18	Kellett, Gamson	Rafferty (2)	583	Cross
6.3.88	SD	H	Dewsbury	W	18-16	Gearin, Powell, Smith	Rafferty (3)	462	Steele
13.3.88	SD	A	Featherstone R.	L	10-40	Rafferty, Gearin	Rafferty	—	—
20.3.88	SD	A	Whitehaven	W	16-14	Lidbury, Nelson, P. McDermott	Gearin (2)	—	—
27.3.88	SD	H	Oldham	L	15-28	Smith, Young, Lidbury	Gearin, Fleming (dg)	2316	Holdsworth
10.4.88	SD	H	Doncaster (Sheffield U. AFC)	W	30-14	Lidbury (2), Cook, Gearin, Powell	Gearin (5)	2397	Tickle
17.4.88	SD	A	Dewsbury	L	16-42	Young, Kellett, Lidbury	Rafferty (2)	—	—
24.4.88	SDP(1)	A	Springfield B.	L	10-11	Kellett (2)	Rafferty	—	—

SPRINGFIELD BOROUGH

Ground: Springfield Park, Wigan. Moved to Victory Park, Chorley, at start of 1988-89 season.

Colours: Tangerine jerseys with black and white broad bands

First Season: 1954-55 as Blackpool Borough. Changed to Springfield Borough in 1987-88 and became Chorley Borough at start of 1988-89.

Chairman: Mike Marsland

Secretary: Deryk Brown

Coach: Stan Gittins (Nov 1985-)

Honours: **John Player Trophy** Beaten finalists, 1976-77

Records: Attendance: 7,614 v. Castleford (RL Cup) 14 Mar, 1964. There was an attendance of 21,000 in an RL Cup-tie against Leigh on Blackpool FC ground on 9 Mar, 1957

Season
Goals: 98 by M. Smith, 1987-88
Tries: 30 by T. Frodsham, 1985-86
Points: 201 by P. Fearis, 1957-58

Match
Goals: 11 by N. Turley v. Carlisle, 26 Apr, 1984;
Tries: 4 by T. Wilkshire v. Bradford N, 14 Jan, 1961;
J. Stockley v. Doncaster, 1 Apr, 1984
T. Frodsham v. Bridgend, 14 Apr, 1985 and v. Mansfield M., 30 Nov, 1986
Points: 27 by N. Turley v. Carlisle, 26 Apr, 1984
Highest score: 54-0 v. Carlisle, 1985-86
Highest against: 77-8 v. Wigan, 1963-64

1986-87 PLAYERS' SUMMARY

	App	Tries	Goals	Dr	Pts
Bacon, David	21 + 1	1	—	—	4
Bamber, Simon	27 + 5	4	—	—	16
Bimson, Geoff	12 + 2	1	—	—	4
Briscoe, Carl	28 + 3	11	—	—	44
Brennan, Steve	6	—	—	—	—
Brown, David	2 + 1	—	—	—	—
Broxton, Paul	2	—	—	—	—
Donlan, Steve	19 + 1	2	—	—	8
Duane, Ian	15 + 3	3	—	—	12
Eccles, Bob	30 + 1	4	—	3	19
Eccles, Cliff	21 + 6	4	—	—	16
Emson, John	13 + 2	1	—	—	4
Frodsham, Tommy	15	11	—	—	44
French, Gary	6	3	—	—	12
Gamble, Paul	5	—	—	—	—
Ganley, Chris	16 + 1	2	—	—	8
Garner, Steve	30	2	—	—	8
Green, Jimmy	8 + 3	—	—	—	—
Griffiths, Steve	6 + 1	2	—	—	8
Grundy, Tracy	2 + 3	—	—	—	—
Hankinson, Paul	3	1	—	—	4
Hodson, Tony	7 + 3	2	—	—	8
Howarth, Roy	8 + 4	—	1	—	2
Jamieson, Geoff	1	—	—	—	—
Karalius, Graham	9 + 7	1	—	—	4
Litherland, Denis	17	6	—	—	24
Maloney, Dave	4 + 1	2	—	—	8
Melling, Steve	6 + 1	2	—	—	8
McFarland, Dave	1	1	—	—	4
McKenzie, Ian	15	3	—	—	12
Nanyn, Mick	6 + 3	—	—	—	—
O'Hara, Mike	1	—	—	—	—
Parkes, Brian	8	—	—	—	—
Price, Billy	2 + 8	1	—	—	4
Roberts, Paul	0 + 2	—	—	—	—
Seabrook, Derrick	1	—	—	—	—
Smith, Joe	3	—	—	—	—
Smith, Mike	34	—	96	2	194
Stewart, Michael	28	8	—	—	32
Swindells, Adrian	1 + 1	—	—	—	—
Thompson, Courtney	11	1	—	—	4
Viller, Mark	5	2	—	—	8
Wilson, Danny	4	—	—	—	—
Winnard, Ian	5	1	—	—	4
Wood, David	4 + 1	2	1	—	10
TOTALS: 45 players		84	98	5	537

1987-88 MATCH ANALYSIS

Date	Competition	H/A	Opponent	Rlt	Score	Tries	Goals	Attendance	Referee
30.8.87	SD	A	Huddersfield B.	W	22-16	Thompson, Hodson, Briscoe, Melling	Smith (3)	—	—
2.9.87	SD	A	Rochdale H.	L	6-8	Bamber	Smith	—	—
4.9.87	SD	H	Barrow	L	6-29	Melling	Howarth	2431	Simpson
13.9.87	LC(1)	A	Workington T.	L	10-12	Briscoe	Smith (3)	—	—
20.9.87	SD	A	Oldham	L	20-22	R. Eccles, Duane, Hodson	Smith (4)	—	—
27.9.87	SD	H	Huddersfield B.	W	32-10	Bamber, C. Eccles, Duane, Frodsham, Price	Smith (6)	721	Steele
4.10.87	SD	A	Whitehaven	W	13-12	French, Frodsham	Smith (2), R. Eccles (dg)	—	—
9.10.87	SD	H	Carlisle	W	12-9	French	Smith (4)	549	Haigh
18.10.87	SD	A	York	W	24-10	Briscoe (2), Frodsham, C. Eccles	Smith (4)	—	—
25.10.87	SD	A	Keighley	W	20-18	Frodsham (2), Duane, French	Smith (2)	—	—
1.11.87	SD	A	Runcorn H.	L	20-26	Stewart (2), R. Eccles, Frodsham	Smith (2)	—	—
8.11.87	SD	H	Rochdale H.	W	20-11	Bacon, Frodsham, Bamber	Smith (4)	631	Kendrew
13.11.87	JPS(1)	H	Barrow	W	14-2	Bimson	Smith (5)	629	Volante
22.11.87	JPS(2)	H	Wakefield T.	W	14-8	Frodsham, R. Eccles	Smith (3)	1265	Carter
29.11.87	JPS(3)	H	Leeds	L	12-22	Frodsham, McKenzie	Smith (2)	3894	Spencer
20.12.87	SD	A	Batley	W	20-16	Ganley, Frodsham, McKenzie	Smith (4)	—	—
26.12.87	SD	H	Keighley	L	10-20	Frodsham	Smith (3)	1031	Holgate
3.1.88	SD	H	Oldham	L	4-20	—	Smith (2)	2562	Houghton
10.1.88	SD	A	Carlisle	L	0-29	—	—	—	—
17.1.88	SD	H	Fulham	W	17-0	Winnard, Donlan, McFarland	Smith (2), R. Eccles (dg)	532	Drinkwater
24.1.88	SD	A	Workington T.	W	12-6	R. Eccles	Smith (4)	—	—
31.1.88	CC(1)	A	Runcorn H.	W	8-6	Stewart	Smith (2)	—	—
7.2.88	SD	H	Mansfield M.	W	14-7	Briscoe, Garner	Smith (3)	546	Volante
14.2.88	CC(2)	A	Salford	L	10-12	C. Eccles	Smith (3)	—	—
21.2.88	SD	H	Dewsbury	W	32-12	Briscoe (2), Litherland (2), Stewart, Bamber	Smith (4)	420	Tidball
6.3.88	SD	A	Barrow	W	4-0	Stewart	—	—	—
13.3.88	SD	H	Batley	W	26-0	Litherland (2), Maloney, Garner, McKenzie	Smith (3)	366	Kershaw
20.3.88	SD	H	York	W	22-12	Donlan, Emson, Griffiths, Maloney	Smith (3)	404	Dockray
27.3.88	SD	A	Dewsbury	L	11-20	Briscoe, Litherland	Smith (1, 1 dg)	—	—
1.4.88	SD	H	Runcorn H.	W	20-6	C. Eccles, Briscoe, Stewart	Smith (4)	513	Tennant
3.4.88	SD	A	Mansfield M.	L	6-18	Stewart	Smith	—	—
8.4.88	SD	H	Workington T.	W	11-6	Griffiths, Briscoe	Wood, R. Eccles (dg)	337	Burke
14.4.88	SD	H	Whitehaven	W	36-4	Wood (2), Viller, Litherland, Karalius, Ganley, Hankinson	Smith (4)	—	Berry
17.4.88	SD	A	Fulham	L	8-9	Stewart	Smith (2)	—	—
24.4.88	SDP(1)	H	Sheffield E.	W	11-10	Viller	Smith (3, 1 dg)	530	Allatt
8.5.88	SDP(SF)	A	Oldham	L	10-18	Briscoe	Smith (3)	—	—

SWINTON

Ground: Station Road
Colours: Blue jerseys with white V
First Season: 1896-97
Nickname: Lions
Chairman: John Way
Secretary: Steve Moyes
Coach: Bill Holliday and Mike Peers
             (June 1986-Oct 1987)
             Frank Barrow (Oct 1987-)
Honours: **Championship** Winners, 1926-27,
             1927-28, 1930-31, 1934-35
             Beaten finalists, 1924-25, 1932-33
             War League Beaten finalists,
             1939-40
             Division One Champions, 1962-63,
             1963-64
             Division Two Champions, 1984-85
             Second Division Premiership
             Winners 1986-87
             Challenge Cup Winners, 1899-1900,
             1925-26, 1927-28
             Beaten finalists, 1926-27, 1931-32
             Lancashire League Winners,
             1924-25, 1927-28, 1928-29, 1930-31,
             1960-61
             Lancashire War League Winners,
             1939-40
             Lancashire Cup Winners, 1925-26,
             1927-28, 1939-40, 1969-70
             Beaten finalists, 1910-11, 1923-24,
             1931-32, 1960-61, 1961-62, 1962-63,
             1964-65, 1972-73
             BBC Trophy Beaten finalists,
             1966-67
             Western Division Championship
             Beaten finalists, 1963-64
Records: Attendance: 44,621 Wigan v.
             Warrington (RL Cup SF) 7 Apr,
             1951
             Season
             Goals: 128 by A. Blan, 1960-61
             Tries: 42 by J. Stopford, 1963-64
             Points: 283 by A. Blan, 1960-61
             Match
             Goals: 12 by K. Gowers v.
             Liverpool C., 3 Oct, 1959

Tries: 5 by T. Bevan v.
Morecambe, 10 Sep, 1898; W.
Wallwork v. Widnes, 15 Dec, 1900;
J. Evans v. Bradford N., 30 Sep,
1922; H. Halsall v. St. Helens, 24
Jan, 1925; R. Cracknell v.
Whitehaven Rec., 11 Feb, 1928; R.
Lewis v. Keighley, 12 Jan, 1946; J.
Stopford v. Bramley, 22 Dec, 1962;
A. Buckley v. Salford, Apr 8, 1964
Points: 29 by B. McMahon v.
Dewsbury, 15 Aug, 1959
Highest score: 76-4 v. Pontefract,
1906-07
Highest against: 76-3 v.
Huddersfield, 1945-46; 76-16 v.
Castleford, 1987-88

1987-88 PLAYERS' SUMMARY

	App	Tries	Goals	Dr	Pts
Abram, Darren	2	—	—	—	—
Ainsworth, Gary	30	8	—	—	32
Allen, John	19	2	—	—	8
Bate, Derek	21	7	—	—	28
Bibby, Bernard	0 + 1	—	—	—	—
Brown, Andrew	1	—	—	—	—
Cassidy, Frank	22 + 1	9	—	2	38
Derbyshire, Alan	3 + 3	—	—	—	—
Evans, Tex	24	13	—	—	52
Forber, Gary	8 + 1	—	—	—	—
Frazer, Neil	10 + 1	—	—	—	—
Frodsham, Tommy	13 + 1	8	—	—	32
Gelling, Bryan	15	2	—	—	8
Grima, Joe	17	1	—	—	4
Hewitt, Tony	25 + 5	4	—	—	16
Holliday, Les	7	3	—	2	14
Holliday, Michael	4 + 1	—	—	—	—
Horrocks, John	4 + 1	2	—	—	8
Howarth, Roy	7	—	—	—	—
Johnson, William	2 + 1	—	—	—	—
Lee, Martin	4	—	—	—	—
Maloney, David	12 + 2	3	—	—	12
McFarland, David	7 + 1	—	—	—	—
Meadows, Mark	9 + 5	2	—	—	8
Melling, Alex	7	—	—	—	—
Mooney, Frank	14 + 1	—	—	—	—
Muller, Roby	12 + 1	1	—	—	4
Percival, John	2	—	—	—	—
Ranson, Scott	17	10	—	—	40
Rippon, Andrew	2 + 1	—	4	—	8
Scott, Terence	5 + 3	2	—	—	8
Sheals, Mark	15 + 4	—	—	—	—
Skeech, Ian	2 + 2	—	—	—	—
Snape, Steven	33	8	1	—	34
Topping, Paul	28 + 1	4	67	—	150
Tuimavave, Paddy	6 + 1	1	—	—	4
Viller, Mark	7 + 4	—	3	—	6
Wilson, Danny	12	1	—	1	5
Wright, Terence	1 + 2	—	—	—	—
TOTALS:					
39 players		91	75	5	519

1987-88 MATCH ANALYSIS

Date	Com-petition	H/A	Opponent	Rlt	Score	Tries	Goals	Atten-dance	Referee
30.8.87	SBC	A	Hull K.R.	L	7-24	Evans	Topping, Cassidy (dg)	—	—
6.9.87	SBC	H	Wigan	L	8-26	Evans	Topping (2)	5640	Kershaw
13.9.87	LC(1)	H	Rochdale H.	W	38-20	Snape (3), Cassidy (2), Hewitt	Topping (7)	1443	Simpson
20.9.87	SBC	A	Hunslet	D	32-32	Cassidy (2), Bate, Snape, Muller	Topping (6)	—	—
23.9.87	LC(2)	H	Leigh	W	22-14	L. Holliday, Allen, Meadows, Evans	Topping (3)	3824	McDonald
27.9.87	SBC	H	Hull	L	9-15	Evans	Topping (2), L. Holliday (dg)	2134	Allatt
30.9.87	LC(SF)	A	Warrington	L	6-44	Ainsworth	Topping	—	—
4.10.87	SBC	A	Bradford N.	L	12-40	Cassidy, Maloney, Evans	—	—	—
18.10.87	Tour	H	Papua New Guinea	W	13-6	Ainsworth, Horrocks, Maloney	Wilson (dg)	2132	Carter
25.10.87	SBC	A	Widnes	W	21-20	Wilson, L. Holliday, Hewitt, Evans	Topping (2), L. Holliday (dg)	—	—
31.10.87	JPS(P)	A	Heworth	W	32-5	Evans, Topping, L. Holliday, Horrocks, Snape, Maloney	Topping (4)	—	—
15.11.87	JPS(1)	H	Salford	L	12-18	Hewitt, Evans	Topping (2)	3459	Tennant
22.11.87	SBC	H	Hunslet	D	4-4	Evans	—	1488	Steele
29.11.87	SBC	H	Hull K.R.	L	18-26	Evans (3)	Viller (3)	1755	Lindop
6.12.87	SBC	A	Warrington	L	12-39	Cassidy, Hewitt	Rippon (2)	—	—
13.12.87	SBC	H	Widnes	L	12-52	Grima, Ainsworth	Rippon (2)	2781	McDonald
27.12.87	SBC	A	Salford	L	8-36	Ranson (2)	—	—	—
1.1.88	SBC	A	Halifax	L	0-36	—	—	—	—
10.1.88	SBC	H	Halifax	L	12-32	Allen, Tuimavave	Topping (2)	3672	Haigh
17.1.88	SBC	A	Leigh	L	16-22	Topping, Bate	Topping (4)	—	—
24.1.88	SBC	A	Bradford N.	L	8-12	Frodsham	Topping (2)	4367	Berry
31.1.88	CC(1)	A	Salford	L	6-16	Gelling	Snape	—	—
14.2.88	SBC	H	Leigh	W	28-20	Gelling, Bate, Ainsworth, Topping, Cassidy, Ranson	Topping (2)	2989	Dockray
21.2.88	SBC	A	Hull	W	32-28	Frodsham (2), Bate, Evans, Ranson	Topping (6)	—	—
28.2.88	SBC	H	Warrington	L	18-22	Frodsham (2), Ainsworth	Topping (3)	2890	Tickle
6.3.88	SBC	A	Castleford	L	16-76	Ranson, Scott, Ainsworth	Topping (2)	—	—
20.3.88	SBC	H	St. Helens	L	18-34	Ranson, Cassidy, Meadows	Topping (3)	3933	Lindop
27.3.88	SBC	A	Leeds	L	6-32	Scott	Topping	—	—
1.4.88	SBC	H	Salford	L	6-10	Bate	Topping	3841	Allatt
4.4.88	SBC	A	Wigan	L	16-42	Frodsham (2), Ranson	Topping (2)	—	—
10.4.88	SBC	H	Castleford	W	45-14	Ainsworth (2), Ranson (2), Snape, Topping, Cassidy, Bate	Topping (6), Cassidy (dg)	1494	Whitfield
13.4.88	SBC	H	Leeds	L	22-34	Snape (2), Frodsham, Bate	Topping (3)	1849	Kendrew
17.4.88	SBC	A	St. Helens	L	4-52	Ranson	—	—	—

WAKEFIELD TRINITY

Ground: Belle Vue
Colours: White jerseys with red and blue band
First Season: 1895-96
Nickname: Dreadnoughts
Chairman: Rodney Walker
Secretary: Alan Pearman
Coach: David Topliss (May 1987-)
Honours: **Championship** Winners, 1966-67, 1967-68
Beaten finalists, 1959-60, 1961-62
Division Two Champions, 1903-04
Challenge Cup Winners, 1908-09, 1945-46, 1959-60, 1961-62, 1962-63
Beaten finalists, 1913-14, 1967-68, 1978-79
Yorkshire League Winners, 1909-10, 1910-11, 1945-46, 1958-59, 1959-60, 1961-62, 1965-66
Yorkshire Cup Winners, 1910-11, 1924-25, 1946-47, 1947-48, 1951-52, 1956-57, 1960-61, 1961-62, 1964-65
Beaten finalists, 1926-27, 1932-33, 1934-35, 1936-37, 1939-40, 1945-46, 1958-59, 1973-74, 1974-75
John Player Trophy Beaten finalists, 1971-72
Records: Attendance: 37,906 Leeds v. Huddersfield (RL Cup SF) 21 March, 1936
Home: 28,254 v. Wigan (RL Cup) 24 Mar, 1962
Season
Goals: 163 by N. Fox, 1961-62
Tries: 38 by F. Smith, 1959-60, D. Smith, 1973-74
Points: 407 by N. Fox, 1961-62

Match
Goals: 12 by N. Fox v. Workington T., 19 Sep, 1970 and v. Batley, 26 Aug, 1967; B. Ward v. Hunslet, 6 Feb, 1971
Tries: 7 by F. Smith v. Keighley, 25 Apr, 1959; K. Slater v. Hunslet, 6 Feb, 1971
Points: 33 by N. Fox v. Batley, 26 Aug, 1967
Highest score: 78-9 v. Batley, 1967-68
Highest against: 72-6 v. Wigan, 1986-87

1987-88 PLAYERS' SUMMARY

	App	Tries	Goals	Dr	Pts
Bell, Nigel	33 + 2	10	—	—	40
Conway, Billy	30	3	—	—	12
Conway, Mark	35	20	18	1	117
Douglas, Ian	33 + 1	5	—	—	20
Eden, Phil	30	12	—	—	48
Fletcher, Andrew	2 + 1	—	—	—	—
Fox, Phil	32	17	—	—	68
Haggerty, Gary	17 + 5	7	—	—	28
Haigh, Paul	1	—	—	—	—
Halliwell, Steve	31 + 4	15	4	—	68
Harcombe, Kevin	31	3	116	—	244
Hendry, Paul	1	—	—	—	—
Hopkinson, Ian	4 + 9	1	—	—	4
Jasiewicz, Dick	12 + 1	5	—	—	20
Jowitt, Ian	1	—	—	—	—
Kelly, Andy	17	1	—	—	4
Kelly, Neil	0 + 2	—	—	—	—
Lennon, Greg	8	5	—	—	20
Mallinder, Paul	24 + 6	5	—	—	20
Mason, Andy	31	14	—	—	56
Price, Gary	10 + 3	1	—	—	4
Rayne, Keith	30 + 3	10	—	—	40
Rotherforth, Lindsay	3 + 1	2	—	—	8
Russell, Julian	1	—	—	—	—
Sheldon, Ian	22 + 7	6	—	—	24
Thompson, John	5 + 2	—	—	—	—
Thornton, Gary	1 + 1	1	—	—	4
Topliss, David	8 + 4	1	—	—	4
Van Bellen, Gary	23 + 8	2	—	—	8
Walker, Andrew	5 + 1	—	—	—	—
TOTALS:					
30 players		146	138	1	861

1987-88 MATCH ANALYSIS

Date	Com- petition	H/A	Opponent	Rlt	Score	Tries	Goals	Atten- dance	Referee
30.8.87	SD	H	Carlisle	W	56-8	Mason (2), Halliwell (2), M. Conway (2), Douglas, Jasiewicz, Hopkinson, Fox	Harcombe (8)	1746	Haigh
2.9.87	YC(P)	H	Dewsbury	W	25-14	Sheldon, Rayne, M. Conway, Bell	Harcombe (4), M. Conway (dg)	1723	Dockray
6.9.87	SD	A	Dewsbury	W	22-0	Bell, Mason, Topliss, Fox	Harcombe (3)	—	—
13.9.87	YC(1)	H	Sheffield E.	W	32-18	Fox, Halliwell, Mason, Jasiewicz, M. Conway, Mallinder	Harcombe (4)	2111	Tennant

MATCH ANALYSIS (continued)

Date	Comp	H/A	Opponent	Res	Score	Scorers	Goals	Att	Ref
20.9.87	SD	H	Bramley	W	62-10	Fox (3), Lennon, W. Conway, M. Conway, Douglas, Bell, Harcombe, Sheldon, Eden	Harcombe (9)	2000	Whitfield
23.9.87	YC(2)	A	Leeds	L	8-36	Halliwell	Harcombe (2)	—	—
27.9.87	SD	A	Mansfield M.	D	20-20	Eden (3), Sheldon	M. Conway (2)	—	—
4.10.87	SD	H	Dewsbury	W	32-14	Lennon (2), Jasiewicz, Rayne, Bell, Van Bellen	Halliwell (4)	1975	Holgate
18.10.87	SD	A	Sheffield E.	W	14-12	Fox, M. Conway	M. Conway (3)	—	—
25.10.87	SD	H	Whitehaven	W	30-16	M. Conway (2), Mason (2), Jasiewicz, Douglas	M. Conway (3)	1350	Burke
8.11.87	SD	A	Whitehaven	L	10-18	M. Conway	Harcombe (3)	—	—
15.11.87	JPS(1)	H	York	D	22-22	M. Conway, Jasiewicz, Bell	Harcombe (5)	1864	Whitfield
18.11.87	JPS(1) Replay	A	York	W	30-6	Eden (2), Harcombe, Lennon, Bell	Harcombe (5)	—	—
22.11.87	JPS(2)	A	Springfield B.	L	8-14	Rayne	Harcombe (2)	—	—
29.11.87	SD	A	Doncaster	W	26-8	W. Conway, Mallinder, Eden, Lennon, Halliwell	Harcombe (3)	—	—
6.12.87	SD	H	Rochdale H.	W	30-2	Fox (2), Halliwell, Eden, Rotherforth, Harcombe	Harcombe (3)	1800	Tennant
20.12.87	SD	H	Mansfield M.	W	16-12	Rayne, Van Bellen, Rotherforth	Harcombe (2)	1747	Spencer
26.12.87	SD	A	Featherstone R.	L	14-17	Mallinder, Douglas	Harcombe (3)	—	—
1.1.88	SD	H	Featherstone R.	L	16-21	Mallinder, Rayne, Haggerty	Harcombe (2)	4350	Tickle
10.1.88	SD	A	Batley	W	18-4	Thornton, Sheldon, Halliwell	M. Conway (3)	—	—
17.1.88	SD	H	Barrow	W	32-14	M. Conway, Mason, Kelly, Bell	Harcombe (8)	1950	Berry
24.1.88	SD	A	Oldham	W	28-10	Fox (2), Rayne, Mason	Harcombe (6)	—	—
31.1.88	CC(1)	H	Sheffield E.	L	10-14	Haggerty	Harcombe (3)	2371	Kesha (NZ)
7.2.88	SD	H	Batley	W	14-0	M. Conway, Fox	Harcombe (3)	1900	Tickle
14.2.88	SD	A	Fulham	W	28-12	Halliwell (2), M. Conway, Fox, Haggerty	Harcombe (2), M. Conway (2)	—	—
21.2.88	SD	H	Sheffield E.	W	14-6	Douglas, Haggerty, Sheldon	M. Conway	2028	Houghton
28.2.88	SD	A	Carlisle	W	22-8	Sheldon, M. Conway, Mallinder, Mason	Harcombe (3)	—	—
9.3.88	SD	A	Rochdale H.	W	18-8	Halliwell (2), W. Conway	Harcombe (3)	—	—
13.3.88	SD	H	Fulham	W	32-0	Mason (3), Fox, Rayne, Eden	Harcombe (4)	1550	Allatt
20.3.88	SD	H	Doncaster	W	22-0	M. Conway (2), Rayne	Harcombe (5)	2650	Volante
27.3.88	SD	A	Bramley	L	10-12	Fox	Harcombe (3)	—	—
1.4.88	SD	H	York	W	34-12	Rayne (2), Mason (2), M. Conway	Harcombe (7)	2260	Holgate
4.4.88	SD	A	York	L	8-17	M. Conway	Harcombe (2)	—	—
10.4.88	SD	H	Oldham	L	22-23	M. Conway (2), Price, Halliwell	Harcombe (3)	6522	Bowman
17.4.88	SD	A	Barrow	L	16-32	Fox, Haggerty, Eden	Harcombe, M. Conway	—	—
24.4.88	SDP(1)	H	York	W	44-23	Bell (2), Eden (2), Halliwell (2), Haggerty, Fox	Harcombe (5), M. Conway	1986	Tennant
8.5.88	SDP(SF)	A	Featherstone R.	L	16-20	Haggerty, Bell, Halliwell	M. Conway (2)	—	—

WARRINGTON

Ground: Wilderspool
Colours: White jerseys with primrose and blue hoop
First Season: 1895-96
Nickname: Wire
Chairman: Peter Higham
General
  Manager: Ron Close
Coach: Tony Barrow (Mar 1986-)
Honours: **Championship** Winners, 1947-48, 1953-54, 1954-55
Beaten finalists, 1925-26, 1934-35, 1936-37, 1948-49, 1950-51, 1960-61
League Leaders Trophy Winners, 1972-73
Club Championship (Merit Table) Winners, 1973-74
Challenge Cup Winners, 1904-05, 1906-07, 1949-50, 1953-54, 1973-74
Beaten finalists, 1900-01, 1903-04, 1912-13, 1927-28, 1932-33, 1935-36, 1974-75
Lancashire League Winners, 1937-38, 1947-48, 1948-49, 1950-51, 1953-54, 1954-55, 1955-56, 1967-68
Lancashire Cup Winners, 1921-22, 1929-30, 1932-33, 1937-38, 1959-60, 1965-66, 1980-81, 1982-83
Beaten finalists, 1906-07, 1948-49, 1950-51, 1967-68, 1985-86, 1987-88
John Player Trophy Winners, 1973-74, 1977-78, 1980-81
Beaten finalists, 1978-79, 1986-87
Premiership Trophy Winners, 1985-86
Beaten finalists 1976-77, 1986-87
Captain Morgan Trophy Winners, 1973-74
BBC2 Trophy Beaten finalists, 1974-75
Records: Attendance: 35,000 Wigan v. Leigh (Lancs. Cup Final) 29 Oct, 1949
Home: 34,304 v. Wigan (League) 22 Jan, 1949

Season
Goals: 170 by S. Hesford, 1978-79
Tries: 66 by B. Bevan, 1952-53
Points: 363 by H. Bath, 1952-53
Match
Goals: 14 by H. Palin v. Liverpool C., 13 Sep, 1950
Tries: 7 by B. Bevan v. Leigh, 29 Mar, 1948 and v. Bramley, 22 Apr, 1953
Points: 33 by G. Thomas v. St. Helens, 12 Apr, 1909
Highest score: 78-3 v. St. Helens, 1908-09
Highest against: 68-14 v. Hunslet, 1927-28

1987-88 PLAYERS' SUMMARY

	App	Tries	Goals	Dr	Pts
Bacon, Michael	2 + 1	—	—	—	—
Boyd, Les	10 + 2	2	—	—	8
Carbert, Brian	6	3	—	—	12
Crompton, Martin	17	2	—	1	9
Cullen, Paul	27 + 1	7	—	—	28
Drummond, Des	31	18	—	—	72
Duane, Ronnie	13 + 1	3	—	—	12
Forster, Mark	22 + 1	8	1	—	34
Gregory, Mike	28 + 3	8	—	—	32
Harmon, Neil	11 + 8	1	—	—	4
Holden, Keith	22	3	—	1	13
Humphries, Tony	21 + 2	3	—	—	12
Jackson, Bob	19 + 2	2	1	—	10
Jackson, Mark	0 + 3	—	—	—	—
Johnson, Brian	34 + 1	10	—	—	40
Knight, Mark	1 + 4	1	—	—	4
Lyon, David	22 + 3	8	—	—	32
McGinty, Billy	24 + 2	6	—	—	24
Percival, Ian	0 + 1	1	—	—	4
Peters, Barry	18 + 8	4	—	—	16
Roberts, Mark	29 + 3	13	—	—	52
Ropati, Joe	25	11	—	—	44
Roskell, Mark	11 + 1	3	—	—	12
Sanderson, Gary	25 + 9	3	—	—	12
Tamati, Kevin	30 + 3	2	—	—	8
Thorniley, Tony	2 + 2	2	—	—	8
Thursfield, John	2 + 2	—	—	—	—
Turner, Robert	2 + 4	—	4	1	9
Webb, Carl	16 + 1	—	—	—	—
Woods, John	37	13	147	5	351
TOTALS:					
30 players		137	153	8	862

1987-88 MATCH ANALYSIS

Date	Competition	H/A	Opponent	Rlt	Score	Tries	Goals	Attendance	Referee
30.8.87	SBC	H	Hunslet	W	54-4	Roberts (3), Humphries (2), Peters, McGinty, R. Jackson, Tamati	Woods (9)	4123	Whitfield
6.9.87	SBC	A	Halifax	W	19-10	Ropati, Roberts, Johnson	Woods (3), Holden (dg)	—	—
13.9.87	LC(1)	H	Oldham	W	42-8	Cullen (3), Ropati (2), Drummond, Johnson	Woods (6), Jackson	5615	Hodgson
20.9.87	SBC	H	St. Helens	W	24-20	Drummond (2), Humphries, Peters	Woods (4)	5969	Kendrew
23.9.87	LC(2)	A	Workington T.	W	50-10	Roberts (3), Thorniley (2), Roskell, Sanderson, Drummond, McGinty	Woods (7)	—	—
27.9.87	SBC	A	Castleford	W	40-30	Woods (3), Drummond (2), Johnson, Carbert	Woods (6)	—	—
30.9.87	LC(SF)	H	Swinton	W	44-6	Roberts (2), Drummond, Gregory, Woods, Carbert	Woods (10)	5296	Whitfield
4.10.87	SBC	H	Hull K.R.	W	36-0	Drummond (3), Carbert, Woods, Holden, Harmon	Woods (4)	4204	McDonald
11.10.87	LC(F)	St. Helens	Wigan	L	16-28	Forster (2), Gregory	Woods (2)	(20,234)	Lindop
18.10.87	SBC	H	Leeds	D	20-20	Drummond, Holden, Gregory	Woods (4)	5023	Bowman
27.10.87	Tour	H	Auckland	L	16-22	Roberts, Drummond	Turner (4)	3897	Whitfield
1.11.87	SBC	A	Hull K.R.	L	0-17	—	—	—	—
8.11.87	SBC	H	Halifax	W	15-8	Duane	Woods (5, 1 dg)	6140	Berry
15.11.87	JPS(1)	A	Carlisle	W	22-16	Peters, Woods, Lyon	Woods (5)	—	—
22.11.87	JPS(2)	H	Hull K.R.	W	12-8	Holden, Johnson	Woods (2)	4550	Allatt
28.11.87	JPS(3)	H	Oldham	L	10-14	Cullen	Woods (3)	5152	Holdsworth
6.12.87	SBC	H	Swinton	W	39-12	Duane (2), Forster (2), Knight, Drummond	Woods (7), Crompton (dg)	3875	Holdsworth
13.12.87	SBC	A	St. Helens	L	14-17	Drummond, Woods	Woods (3)	—	—
20.12.87	SBC	H	Bradford N.	W	18-12	Crompton, Lyon, Roberts	Woods (3)	4521	Lindop
27.12.87	SBC	A	Widnes	L	17-20	Cullen, Drummond	Woods (4, 1 dg)	—	—
1.1.88	SBC	H	Wigan	D	15-15	McGinty, Johnson	Woods (3, 1 dg)	10,056	Allatt
10.1.88	SBC	A	Hunslet	L	16-20	Johnson, Sanderson, Tamati	Woods (2)	—	—
17.1.88	CC(P)	H	Huddersfield B.	W	48-10	Lyon (2), Ropati (2), Boyd, Woods, Johnson, McGinty	Woods (8)	3433	Dockray
20.1.88	SBC	A	Hull	L	14-22	Gregory, Woods	Woods (3)	—	—
31.1.88	CC(1)	H	Oldham	W	17-6	Boyd, R. Jackson, Gregory	Woods (2, 1 dg)	6642	Tennant
7.2.88	SBC	H	Castleford	W	32-6	Ropati (3), Gregory (2), Johnson	Woods (4)	3750	Whitfield
13.2.88	CC(2)	H	St. Helens	L	20-24	Lyon, McGinty, Woods, Drummond	Woods (2)	5969	Holdsworth
21.2.88	SBC	A	Bradford N.	L	10-28	Lyon	Woods (3)	—	—
28.2.88	SBC	A	Swinton	W	22-18	Forster, Sanderson, Johnson, Drummond	Woods (3)	—	—
2.3.88	SBC	H	Hull	W	36-2	Roberts, Gregory, Cullen, Forster, Crompton	Woods (8)	3048	McDonald
13.3.88	SBC	A	Leeds	L	10-30	Ropati, Drummond	Forster	—	—
16.3.88	SBC	A	Wigan	W	6-2	Johnson	Woods	—	—
20.3.88	SBC	H	Leigh	W	10-6	Roberts, Woods	Woods	3630	Smith
27.3.88	SBC	A	Salford	W	34-14	Ropati (2), Forster, Lyon, Roskell, Peters	Woods (5)	—	—
1.4.88	SBC	H	Widnes	L	6-35	McGinty	Woods	6863	Tickle
4.4.88	SBC	A	Leigh	L	5-28	—	Woods (2, 1 dg)	—	—
10.4.88	SBC	H	Salford	L	19-20	Percival, Woods, Cullen	Woods (3), Turner (dg)	3412—	Lindop
24.4.88	PT(1)	A	Wigan	W	24-12	Forster, Roskell, Lyon	Woods (6)	—	—
8.5.88	PT(SF)	A	Widnes	L	10-20	Woods	Woods (3)	—	—

81

WHITEHAVEN

Ground:	Recreation Ground
Colours:	Chocolate, blue and gold jerseys
First Season:	1948-49
Nickname:	Haven
Chairman:	David Wigham
Secretary:	Eppie Gibson
Coach:	Phil Kitchin (June 1985-Oct 1987)
	John McFarlane (Nov 1987-May 1988)
Records:	Attendance: 18,500 v. Wakefield T. (RL Cup) 19 Mar, 1960

Season
Goals: 141 by J. McKeown, 1956-57
Tries: 29 by W. Smith, 1956-57
Points: 291 by J. McKeown, 1956-57

Match
Goals: 11 by W. Holliday v. Hunslet, 31 Mar, 1962
Tries: 6 by V. Gribbin v. Doncaster, 18 Nov, 1984
Points: 25 by W. Holliday v. Hunslet, 31 Mar, 1962
Highest score: 72-6 v. Fulham, 1986-87
Highest against: 74-6 v. Wigan, 1986-87

1987-88 PLAYERS' SUMMARY

	App	Tries	Goals	Dr	Pts
Ackerman, Rob	23	5	—	—	20
Amor, Martin	1 + 3	—	—	—	—
Banks, Alan	0 + 2	—	—	—	—
Beckwith, Mark	29 + 1	14	—	—	56
Bell, Ian	22	—	—	—	—
Bell, Todd	0 + 1	—	—	—	—
Brannan, Robert	6	—	2	—	4
Branthwaite, Steve	1	—	—	—	—
Burney, Phil	1 + 1	—	—	—	—
Burney, Steve	10 + 3	—	—	—	—
Cameron, Graham	16 + 3	2	6	2	22
Ditchburn, Tom	1 + 3	—	—	—	—
D'Leny, Tony	0 + 1	—	—	—	—
Fearon, Neil	15 + 6	2	—	—	8
Fisher, Billy	21 + 3	3	—	—	12
Glenn, Ricky	0 + 2	—	—	—	—
Hall, Colin	8 + 1	—	—	—	—
Hetherington, Gary	22 + 2	2	—	—	8
Howland, Kevin	0 + 2	—	—	—	—
Howse, Steve	30	3	—	—	12
Johnston, Frank	11 + 1	—	—	1	1
Lightfoot, David	32	5	—	4	24
Lofthouse, Norman	32	11	6	—	56
McCartney, Duncan	11 + 4	1	—	—	4
McConnell, Ralph	8 + 4	1	—	—	4
Mounsey, Gary	24	7	—	—	28
Richardson, Willie	25 + 5	12	63	—	174
Rose, Tony	18	—	—	—	—
Shelford, Kelly	7 + 1	4	—	—	16
Solarie, Tony	11 + 4	2	—	—	8
Tarawhiti, Clarke	6	2	—	—	8
Tarry, Will	18 + 2	—	—	—	—
Tomlinson, Brian	2	—	—	—	—
Watson, David	18 + 1	6	—	—	24
TOTALS:					
34 players		82	77	7	489

1987-88 MATCH ANALYSIS

Date	Competition	H/A	Opponent	Rlt	Score	Tries	Goals	Attendance	Referee
30.8.87	SD	H	Oldham	L	6-20	—	Richardson (3)	2910	Simpson
6.9.87	SD	A	Featherstone R.	L	4-11	Fisher	—	—	—
13.9.87	LC(1)	H	Carlisle	W	28-12	Richardson (2), Fearon, Mounsey	Richardson (6)	2075	Steele
20.9.87	SD	H	Doncaster	W	13-8	Lofthouse	Richardson (4), Lightfoot (dg)	1944	Holgate
24.9.87	LC(2)	H	Widnes	L	14-20	Hetherington, Cameron	Richardson (3)	3152	Allatt
27.9.87	SD	A	Sheffield E.	L	13-18	Tarawhiti, Richardson	Richardson (2), Lightfoot (dg)	—	—
4.10.87	SD	H	Springfield B.	L	12-13	Lofthouse, Fisher	Richardson, Lightfoot, Cameron (dg)	1966	Kershaw
11.10.87	SD	A	Rochdale H.	L	12-20	Ackerman, Beckwith	Richardson, Lightfoot (dg), Johnston (dg)	—	—
25.10.87	SD	A	Wakefield T.	L	16-30	Beckwith, Lofthouse, Tarawhiti	Richardson (2)	—	—
1.11.87	SD	H	Barrow	W	16-6	Lightfoot (2), Lofthouse	Richardson (2)	2015	Lindop
8.11.87	SD	H	Wakefield T.	W	18-10	Beckwith, McConnell, Shelford	Richardson (3)	2079	Allatt
15.11.87	JPS(1)	H	Leeds	L	14-18	Richardson, Beckwith	Richardson (3)	3663	Drinkwater
22.11.87	SD	H	Keighley	W	22-10	Lofthouse (2), Ackerman, Shelford	Richardson (3)	1783	Houghton
29.11.87	SD	A	Barrow	L	16-20	Beckwith (2), Mounsey	Richardson (2)	—	—
20.12.87	SD	H	Rochdale H.	W	26-2	Ackerman, Lofthouse, Shelford, Richardson	Richardson (5)	1778	Hodgson
26.12.87	SD	A	Workington T.	L	14-20	Shelford	Richardson (5)	—	—
1.1.88	SD	H	Carlisle	L	4-6	Solarie	—	2220	McDonald
10.1.88	SD	A	Oldham	L	20-28	Beckwith (2), Mounsey	Lofthouse (4)	—	—
17.1.88	CC(P)	A	Carlisle	D	8-8	Lightfoot, Ackerman	—	—	—
20.1.88	CC(P) Replay	H	Carlisle	L	8-22	Ackerman	Lofthouse (2)	2614	Whitfield
31.1.88	SD	A	Huddersfield B.	D	16-16	Watson (2), Howse	Brannon (2)	—	—
7.2.88	SD	A	Bramley	W	14-6	Richardson (2), Lofthouse	Richardson	—	—
14.2.88	SD	H	Bramley	W	24-0	Richardson (2), Fearon, Howse, Beckwith	Richardson (2)	1241	Spencer
21.2.88	SD	H	Runcorn H.	W	26-6	Mounsey (3), Lightfoot	Richardson (5)	1200	Tickle
28.2.88	SD	A	Keighley	L	18-30	Watson (2), Beckwith	Richardson (3)	—	—
6.3.88	SD	H	Featherstone R.	L	14-24	Solarie, Mounsey, Howse	Richardson	1533	Haigh
13.3.88	SD	A	Doncaster	L	12-40	Beckwith, Watson	Richardson (2)	—	—
20.3.88	SD	H	Sheffield E.	L	14-16	Cameron, Watson	Richardson (2), Cameron	1089	Holgate
27.3.88	SD	A	Runcorn H.	L	18-24	Hetherington, Lightfoot, Beckwith	Cameron (3)	—	—
1.4.88	SD	H	Workington T.	W	10-0	Lofthouse, McCartney	Cameron	2042	Smith
5.4.88	SD	A	Carlisle	L	7-16	Beckwith	Cameron (1, 1 dg)	—	—
10.4.88	SD	H	Huddersfield B.	W	28-16	Richardson (3), Lofthouse (2), Fisher	Richardson (2)	1010	Dockray
14.4.88	SD	A	Springfield B.	L	4-36	Beckwith	—	—	—

WIDNES

Ground:	Naughton Park
Colours:	White jerseys with black trim
First Season:	1895-96
Nickname:	Chemics
Chairman:	Ray Owen
General Manager:	John Stringer
Coach:	Doug Laughton (Jan 1986-)

Honours: **Division One** Champions, 1977-78, 1987-88

Championship Beaten finalists, 1935-36

Challenge Cup Winners, 1929-30, 1936-37, 1963-64, 1974-75, 1978-79, 1980-81, 1983-84
Beaten finalists, 1933-34, 1949-50, 1975-76, 1976-77, 1981-82

Lancashire League Winners, 1919-20

Lancashire Cup Winners, 1945-46, 1974-75, 1975-76, 1976-77, 1978-79, 1979-80
Beaten finalists, 1928-29, 1939-40, 1955-56, 1971-72, 1981-82, 1983-84

John Player Trophy Winners, 1975-76, 1978-79
Beaten finalists, 1974-75, 1977-78, 1979-80, 1983-84

Premiership Winners, 1979-80, 1981-82, 1982-83, 1987-88
Beaten finalists, 1977-78

BBC2 Floodlit Trophy Winners, 1978-79
Beaten finalists, 1972-73, 1973-74

Western Division Championship Beaten finalists, 1962-63

Records: Attendance: 24,205 v. St. Helens (RL Cup) 16 Feb, 1961

Season
Goals: 140 by M. Burke, 1978-79
Tries: 42 by M. Offiah, 1987-88
Points: 316 by M. Burke, 1978-79

Match
Goals: 11 by R. Whitfield v. Oldham, 28 Oct, 1965
Tries: 5 by E. Cunningham v. Doncaster, 15 Feb, 1981; J. Basnett v. Hunslet, 17 Oct, 1981 and v. Hull K.R., 2 Nov, 1986; D. Hulme v. Dewsbury, 30 Nov, 1986
Points: 27 by H. Dawson v. Liverpool C., 22 Apr, 1957
Highest score: 82-0 v. Dewsbury, 1986-87
Highest against: 60-5 v. Oldham, 1927-28

1987-88 PLAYERS' SUMMARY

	App	Tries	Goals	Dr	Pts
Currier, Andy	16 + 1	11	5	—	54
Dowd, Barry	30	2	20	1	49
Eyres, Richard	32 + 2	6	—	—	24
Gormley, Ian	1	—	—	—	—
Grima, Joe	2 + 12	1	—	—	4
Hulme, David	33	16	—	—	64
Hulme, Paul	34 + 1	7	—	—	28
Linton, Ralph	1 + 2	—	—	—	—
Lloyd, Chris	0 + 1	—	—	—	—
Marsh, David	2 + 1	—	—	—	—
McKenzie, Phil	35	12	—	—	48
Myler, John	17 + 4	2	59	4	130
Myler, Tony	13 + 1	7	—	—	28
Newton, Keith	0 + 2	—	—	—	—
Offiah, Martin	35	42	—	—	168
O'Neill, Mike	33 + 3	4	—	—	16
O'Neill, Steve	27 + 6	—	—	—	—
Pinner, Harry	11 + 1	—	—	1	1
Platt, Duncan	16	4	31	2	80
Pyke, Derek	11	—	—	—	—
Ruane, David	8 + 3	4	—	—	16
Shearer, Dale	14	6	11	—	46
Sorensen, Kurt	32	6	—	—	24
Stockley, Trevor	1 + 5	—	—	—	—
Sullivan, Andy	2 + 3	—	—	—	—
Tait, Alan	0 + 3	1	—	—	4
Thackray, Rick	29	11	—	—	44
Wright, Darren	33	11	—	—	44
TOTALS:					
28 players		153	126	8	872

1987-88 MATCH ANALYSIS

Date	Competition	H/A	Opponent	Rlt	Score	Tries	Goals	Attendance	Referee
30.8.87	SBC	H	Halifax	W	28-6	D. Hulme (2), Sorensen, M. O'Neill, Platt	J. Myler (4)	5818	McDonald
6.9.87	SBC	A	Bradford N.	W	18-8	Platt, Dowd, McKenzie	J. Myler (3)	—	—

MATCH ANALYSIS (continued)

13.9.87	LC(1)	A	Runcorn H.	W	40-6	D. Hulme (2), Offiah (2), A. Myler, J. Myler, D. Wright	J. Myler (6)	—	—
20.9.87	SBC	A	Hull	W	33-18	A. Myler (2), D. Wright, Dowd, Offiah, D. Hulme	J. Myler (4, 1 dg)	—	—
24.9.87	LC(2)	A	Whitehaven	W	20-14	Offiah (2), Platt	J. Myler (4)	—	—
27.9.87	SBC	H	Hunslet	W	30-10	D. Hulme, A. Myler, D. Wright, Offiah, Ruane	J. Myler (5)	3612	Lindop
30.9.87	LC(SF)	H	Wigan	L	12-20	Offiah	J. Myler (4)	7306	Allatt
4.10.87	SBC	A	Salford	W	18-0	Offiah, Thackray, D. Wright	J. Myler (3)	—	—
18.10.87	SBC	H	Hull K.R.	W	32-8	Ruane (2), M. O'Neill (2), D. Wright, Offiah	J. Myler (4)	3612	Lindop
25.10.87	SBC	H	Swinton	L	20-21	Offiah (2), McKenzie	J. Myler (4)	3877	Spencer
1.11.87	SBC	A	Leigh	W	19-12	Offiah, Ruane, Sorensen	J. Myler (3, 1 dg)	—	—
8.11.87	SBC	H	Castleford	W	31-12	Offiah (2), Shearer, D. Wright, Thackray	Dowd (5, 1 dg)	4172	Cross
14.11.87	JPS(1)	A	St. Helens	L	10-12	Offiah, Sorensen	Dowd	—	—
29.11.87	SBC	A	Halifax	W	19-4	A. Myler, P. Hulme, Offiah (2)	Dowd, Pinner (dg)	—	—
6.12.87	SBC	H	Hull	W	26-22	Offiah (2), M. O'Neill, Thackray	Dowd (5)	4042	Allatt
13.12.87	SBC	A	Swinton	W	52-12	Sorensen (2), McKenzie (2), Thackray, D. Hulme, Shearer, Offiah, P. Hulme	Shearer (7), Dowd	—	—
27.12.87	SBC	H	Warrington	W	20-17	Offiah (2), D. Hulme, Shearer	Currier, Shearer	10,775	Smith
3.1.88	SBC	A	St. Helens	L	0-25	—	—	—	—
10.1.88	SBC	H	Leigh	W	14-8	Offiah, Platt, McKenzie	J. Myler	5100	Burke
17.1.88	SBC	A	Leeds	L	21-26	Eyres (2), Shearer	J. Myler (4, 1 dg)	—	—
24.1.88	SBC	H	Salford	W	22-2	Eyres (2), Currier (2)	Shearer (3)	4698	McDonald
31.1.88	CC(1)	A	Dewsbury	W	38-10	Offiah (2), D. Wright, A. Myler, Shearer, D. Hulme, McKenzie	J. Myler (5)	—	—
7.2.88	SBC	H	Bradford N.	W	26-4	Offiah (3), P. Hulme, J. Myler	J. Myler (3)	5096	Haigh
14.2.88	CC(2)	A	Keighley	W	16-2	Thackray (2), Shearer, D. Hulme	—	—	—
21.2.88	SBC	H	Wigan	L	12-16	McKenzie, Grima	J. Myler (2)	12,147	Spencer
27.2.88	CC(3)	A	Wigan	L	1-10	—	J. Myler (dg)	—	—
13.3.88	SBC	A	Hull K.R.	L	10-14	Offiah (2)	Dowd	—	—
20.3.88	SBC	H	Leeds	W	32-6	Offiah (3), D. Wright, Thackray, Currier	Platt (4)	5552	Tennant
23.3.88	SBC	A	Castleford	W	39-6	Currier (4), Eyres, McKenzie, Offiah	Platt (5, 1 dg)	—	—
27.3.88	SBC	A	Wigan	L	2-28	—	Platt	—	—
1.4.88	SBC	A	Warrington	W	35-6	Offiah (2), P. Hulme (2), Currier, Thackray	Platt (5, 1 dg)	—	—
4.4.88	SBC	H	St. Helens	W	16-6	Offiah (3)	Platt, Dowd	12,904	Holdsworth
10.4.88	SBC	A	Hunslet	W	66-14	Thackray (2), P. Hulme (2), Offiah (2), McKenzie (2), D. Hulme, A. Myler	Dowd (5), Platt (4)	—	—
24.4.88	PT(1)	H	Halifax	W	36-26	D. Hulme (2), Eyres, Wright, McKenzie, Offiah	Platt (6)	7679	Holdsworth
8.5.88	PT(SF)	H	Warrington	W	20-10	Thackray, Currier, D. Hulme	Platt (4)	10,343	McDonald
15.5.88	PT(F)	Man U. FC	St. Helens	W	38-14	Wright (2), D. Hulme (2), Tait, McKenzie, Sorensen	Currier (4), Platt	(35,252)	Holdsworth

WIGAN

Ground:	Central Park
Colours:	Cherry and white hooped jerseys
First Season:	1895-96
Nickname:	Riversiders
Chairman:	Maurice Lindsay
Secretary:	Mary Charnock
Coach:	Graham Lowe (Aug 1986-)
Honours:	**Championship** Winners, 1908-09, 1921-22, 1925-26, 1933-34, 1945-46, 1946-47, 1949-50, 1951-52, 1959-60 Beaten finalists, 1909-10, 1910-11, 1911-12, 1912-13, 1923-24, 1970-71

League Leaders Trophy Winners, 1970-71

Division One Champions 1986-87

Challenge Cup Winners, 1923-24, 1928-29, 1947-48, 1950-51, 1957-58, 1958-59, 1964-65, 1984-85, 1987-88 Beaten finalists, 1910-11, 1919-20, 1943-44, 1945-46, 1960-61, 1962-63, 1965-66, 1969-70, 1983-84

Lancashire League Winners, 1901-02, 1908-09, 1910-11, 1911-12, 1912-13, 1913-14, 1914-15, 1920-21, 1922-23, 1923-24, 1925-26, 1945-46, 1946-47, 1949-50, 1951-52, 1958-59, 1961-62, 1969-70

Lancashire War League Winners, 1940-41

Lancashire Cup Winners, 1905-06, 1908-09, 1909-10, 1912-13, 1922-23, 1928-29, 1938-39, 1946-47, 1947-48, 1948-49, 1949-50, 1950-51, 1951-52, 1966-67, 1971-72, 1973-74, 1985-86, 1986-87, 1987-88 Beaten finalists, 1913-14, 1914-15, 1925-26, 1927-28, 1930-31, 1934-35, 1935-36, 1936-37, 1945-46, 1953-54, 1957-58, 1977-78, 1980-81, 1984-85

John Player Trophy Winners, 1982-83, 1985-86, 1986-87

Premiership Winners 1986-87

BBC2 Floodlit Trophy Winners, 1968-69 Beaten finalists, 1969-70

Charity Shield Winners, 1985-86, 1987-88

War League Championship Winners, 1943-44

Records:	Beaten finalists, 1940-41 Attendance: 47,747 v. St. Helens (League) 27 Mar, 1959

Season
Goals: 176 by F. Griffiths, 1958-59
Tries: 62 by J. Ring, 1925-26
Points: 394 by F. Griffiths, 1958-59
Match
Goals: 22 by J. Sullivan v. Flimby & Fothergill, 14 Feb, 1925
Tries: 7 by J. Ring v. Flimby & Fothergill, 14 Feb, 1925; v. Salford, 13 Apr, 1925 and v. Pemberton R., 12 Feb, 1927; G. Ratcliffe v. Liverpool S., 23 Aug, 1947; W. Boston v. Dewsbury, 20 Aug, 1955 and v. Salford, 30 Apr. 1962; G. Vigo v. St. Helens, 21 Aug, 1976
Points: 44 by J. Sullivan v. Flimby & Fothergill, 14 Feb, 1925
Highest score: 116-0 v. Flimby & Fothergill, 1924-25
Highest against: 58-3 v. Leeds, 1972-73

1987-88 PLAYERS' SUMMARY

	App	Tries	Goals	Dr	Pts
Bell, Dean	18 + 2	10	—	—	40
Betts, Dennis	1 + 1	—	—	—	—
Byrne, Ged	29 + 5	7	—	—	28
Case, Brian	31	1	—	—	4
Dermott, Martin	11 + 1	—	—	—	—
Edwards, Shaun	32 + 2	17	—	—	68
Gildart, Ian	14 + 9	1	—	—	4
Gill, Henderson	26 + 2	18	12	—	96
Goodway, Andy	40	23	—	—	92
Gregory, Andy	35	3	12	1	37
Hampson, Steve	40	12	4	—	56
Hanley, Ellery	34	31	—	—	124
Ingram, Dave	0 + 1	—	—	—	—
Iro, Kevin	22	8	7	—	46
Iro, Tony	11	8	—	—	32
Kiss, Nicky	31 + 1	4	—	—	16
Lucas, Ian	15 + 14	—	—	—	—
Lydon, Joe	21 + 1	8	30	—	92
Marshall, Dave	8 + 5	4	—	—	16
Potter, Ian	34 + 1	—	—	—	—
Preston, Mark	6	8	—	—	32
Rodgers, Craig	3 + 1	1	1	—	6
Russell, Richard	18 + 9	3	24	—	60
Shelford, Adrian	20 + 1	—	—	—	—
Stazicker, Gerard	0 + 1	—	—	—	—
Stephenson, David	15	5	59	—	138
Wane, Shaun	16 + 7	1	—	—	4
West, Graeme	28 + 6	4	—	—	16

TOTALS:
28 players		177	149	1	1,007

1987-88 MATCH ANALYSIS

Date	Competition	H/A	Opponent	Rlt	Score	Tries	Goals	Attendance	Referee
23.8.87	Charity Shield	Isle of Man	Halifax	W	44-12	Edwards (2), Bell (2), Hampson (2), Gill	Stephenson (8)	(4757)	Holdsworth
30.8.87	SBC	H	Hull	W	38-4	Edwards (2), Gill, West, Bell, Kiss, Goodway	Stephenson (5)	13,554	Holdsworth
6.9.87	SBC	A	Swinton	W	26-8	Gill (2), Hanley, Byrne	Gill (3), Hampson (2)	—	—
13.9.87	LC(1)	A	Barrow	W	36-2	Hampson, Hanley, Gill, Gregory, Goodway, Russell	Stephenson (6)	—	—
20.9.87	SBC	H	Castleford	W	44-18	Goodway (2), Hanley (2), Byrne, Edwards, Stephenson	Stephenson (8)	12,893	Spencer
23.9.87	LC(2)	H	Salford	W	42-2	Hanley (2), Bell, Edwards, Gill, Goodway, Hampson, Kiss	Stephenson (5)	11,633	Houghton
27.9.87	SBC	A	Leigh	W	36-8	Gill (2), Hampson, West, Hanley, Edwards	Gill (2), Lydon (2), Russell (2)	—	—
30.9.87	LC(SF)	A	Widnes	W	20-12	Edwards, Goodway, Stephenson	Stephenson (4)	—	—
4.10.87	SBC	H	Leeds	W	26-6	Hanley, Stephenson, Edwards, Gill, Hampson	Stephenson (3)	13,530	Lindop
7.10.87	World Club Challenge	H	Manly	W	8-2	—	Stephenson (4)	36,895	Holdsworth
11.10.87	LC(F)	St. Helens	Warrington	W	28-16	Hanley (2), Gill, West	Lydon (5), Stephenson	(20,234)	Lindop
18.10.87	SBC	H	Halifax	L	14-17	Byrne, Stephenson, Marshall	Stephenson	13,353	Allatt
1.11.87	SBC	A	Leeds	D	18-18	Hampson, Gill, Goodway	Russell (2), Gill	—	—
8.11.87	Tour	H	Auckland	L	6-10	—	Stephenson (2), Lydon	10,743	Kershaw
15.11.87	JPS(1)	H	Sheffield E.	W	34-8	Goodway (2), Gill (2), Hanley, Stephenson	Stephenson (5)	7484	Bowman
21.11.87	JPS(2)	H	Castleford	W	26-16	K. Iro, Goodway, Wane, Edwards	Stephenson (5)	9613	Smith
29.11.87	JPS(3)	A	Salford	W	16-12	Edwards (2), Lydon	Stephenson, Lydon	—	—
2.12.87	SBC	A	Castleford	L	10-12	Goodway, West	Lydon	—	—
6.12.87	SBC	H	Leigh	W	34-24	Hanley (2), Lydon, Gildart, Russell, Byrne	Lydon (5)	11,087	Lindop
12.12.87	JPS(SF)	Bolton W. FC	Leeds	L	6-19	Hampson	Stephenson	(13,538)	Tennant
20.12.87	SBC	A	Hunslet	W	38-10	Hanley (4), Marshall (2), Goodway	Russell (5)	—	—
27.12.87	SBC	H	St. Helens	L	22-32	Lydon (2), K. Iro, Goodway	Lydon (3)	23,809	Holdsworth
1.1.88	SBC	A	Warrington	D	15-15	Hanley (2), Hampson	K. Iro, Gregory (dg)	—	—
5.1.88	SBC	A	Halifax	W	16-14	Hanley, T. Iro, K. Iro	Russell (2)	—	—
10.1.88	SBC	H	Bradford N.	L	16-18	Hanley, Byrne	Russell (4)	10,984	Whitfield
17.1.88	SBC	A	Salford	W	14-6	Hanley, K. Iro	Russell (3)	—	—
30.1.88	CC(1)	H	Bradford N.	W	2-0	—	Lydon	9825	Simpson
14.2.88	CC(2)	H	Leeds	W	30-14	K. Iro (2), Goodway, Case, Russell, Hampson	Russell (2), Hampson	25,110	Allatt
21.2.88	SBC	A	Widnes	W	16-12	Kiss, K. Iro, Goodway	Russell (2)	—	—
27.2.88	CC(3)	H	Widnes	W	10-1	T. Iro, Hampson	K. Iro	18,079	Smith
6.3.88	SBC	H	Hull K.R.	W	16-4	Edwards, T. Iro, Goodway	Russell (2)	11,252	Holdsworth
12.3.88	CC(SF)	Bolton	Salford	W	34-4	Edwards (2), K. Iro, T. Iro, Hanley, Kiss	K. Iro (5)	(20,783)	Holdsworth
16.3.88	SBC	H	Warrington	L	2-6	—	Hampson	12,338	Kershaw
20.3.88	SBC	A	Hull	L	12-18	Byrne, Hanley, Gill	—	—	—
23.3.88	SBC	A	Hull K.R.	L	0-8	—	—	—	—
27.3.88	SBC	H	Widnes	W	28-2	Lydon (2), Gregory, Goodway, T. Iro	Lydon (4)	14,236	Volante
1.4.88	SBC	A	St. Helens	W	10-9	Hanley (2)	Lydon	—	—

(continued on page 92)

87

WORKINGTON TOWN

Ground:	Derwent Park
Colours:	White jerseys with blue band
First Season:	1945-46
Nickname:	Town
Chairman:	John Bell
Secretary:	John Bell
Coach:	Norman Turley (Mar 1987-Apr 1988)

Honours: **Championship** Winners, 1950-51
Beaten finalists, 1957-58
Challenge Cup Winners, 1951-52
Beaten finalists, 1954-55, 1957-58
Lancashire Cup Winners, 1977-78
Beaten finalists, 1976-77, 1978-79, 1979-80
Western Division Championship Winners, 1962-63

Records: Attendance: 17,741 v. Wigan (RL Cup) 3 Mar, 1965. There was a crowd of 20,403 at Borough Park for a RL Cup-tie v. St. Helens on 8 Mar, 1952

Season
Goals: 186 by L. Hopkins, 1981-82
Tries: 49 by J. Lawrenson, 1951-52
Points: 438 by L. Hopkins, 1981-82

Match
Goals: 11 by I. MacCorquodale v. Blackpool B., 6 Jan, 1973
Tries: 7 by I. Southward v. Blackpool B., 17 Sep, 1955
Points: 33 by I. Southward v. Blackpool B., 17 Sep, 1955
Highest score: 62-15 v. Hunslet, 1963-64
Highest against: 68-0 at Wigan, 1986-87

1987-88 PLAYERS' SUMMARY

	App	Tries	Goals	Dr	Pts
Atherton, Wayne	5 + 1	1	—	—	4
Beck, David	26 + 1	2	—	—	8
Bower, Ian	1 + 5	1	—	—	4
Burgess, Glen	5 + 5	—	—	1	1
Burns, Howard	6 + 3	4	—	—	16
Clewes, Andrew	6	1	—	—	4
Falcon, Colin	23	7	—	—	28
Frazer, Neil	6 + 1	—	—	—	—
Higgins, Michael	25 + 4	4	—	—	16
Key, Andy	24	2	—	—	8
Law, Andrew	1 + 2	1	—	—	4
Law, Michael	1 + 1	—	—	—	—
Lewis, Ray	0 + 1	—	—	—	—
Lomax, Bill	6 + 1	—	—	—	—
Lowden, David	28 + 1	2	54	2	118
Lynch, Keith	3 + 3	—	—	—	—
Mawson, Mark	14 + 1	5	—	—	20
Newall, John	0 + 1	—	—	—	—
Nixon, Gary	21 + 1	5	—	—	20
Penrice, Paul	25 + 1	7	—	—	28
Phillips, Graeme	1 + 4	—	—	—	—
Priestley, Steve	4	—	—	—	—
Rea, Geoff	28 + 1	4	—	—	16
Riley, Peter	10 + 5	—	—	—	—
Rooney, Neil	15 + 2	2	—	—	8
Shearman, Robert	0 + 1	—	—	—	—
Smith, Gary	30 + 1	4	14	3	47
Stoddart, Peter	20 + 6	—	—	1	1
Sullivan, Joe	8 + 4	2	—	—	8
Tabern, Ray	26	5	—	—	20
Tubman, Keith	32	6	—	—	24
Turley, Norman	16	—	1	7	9

TOTALS:
	App	Tries	Goals	Dr	Pts
32 players		65	69	14	412

1987-88 MATCH ANALYSIS

Date	Competition	H/A	Opponent	Rlt	Score	Tries	Goals	Attendance	Referee
30.8.87	SD	A	Dewsbury	W	8-6	Nixon	Lowden, Turley (dg), Stoddart (dg)	—	—
6.9.87	SD	H	Huddersfield B.	W	19-10	Penrice, Tabern, Nixon	Lowden (3), Turley (dg)	419	Dockray
13.9.87	LC(1)	H	Springfield B.	W	12-10	Smith, Beck	Lowden (2)	549	Holgate
20.9.87	SD	A	Carlisle	W	24-12	Penrice (2), Burns	Lowden (5, 1 dg), Turley (dg)	—	—
23.9.87	LC(2)	H	Warrington	L	10-50	Burns (2)	Lowden	1759	Carter
27.9.87	SD	H	Fulham	W	22-14	Higgins, Rea, Burns	Lowden (4), Turley (2 dg)	566	Haigh
4.10.87	SD	A	Runcorn H.	L	4-41	Rooney	—	—	—
11.10.87	SD	H	Batley	W	11-4	Falcon	Lowden (3), Turley (dg)	614	Tennant
18.10.87	SD	A	Keighley	L	11-19	Lowden	Lowden (3), Smith (dg)	—	—
25.10.87	SD	H	York	L	10-11	Penrice	Lowden (3)	511	Allatt
1.11.87	SD	A	Batley	W	23-12	Rea, Mawson, Smith	Lowden (5), Turley (dg)	—	—
15.11.87	JPS(1)	A	Hull	L	6-42	Tabern	Lowden	—	—
29.11.87	SD	H	Carlisle	W	14-2	Mawson, Falcon	Lowden (3)	764	Houghton
6.12.87	SD	A	Fulham	W	12-2	Mawson, Key	Lowden (2)	—	—
20.12.87	SD	A	Huddersfield B.	W	15-12	Tabern, Key, Tubman	Lowden (1, 1 dg)	—	—
26.12.87	SD	H	Whitehaven	W	20-14	Falcon, Tabern, Higgins	Lowden (3), Turley	2455	Volante
3.1.88	SD	A	Barrow	W	6-4	Rea	Lowden	—	—
10.1.88	SD	H	Dewsbury	W	38-16	Smith, Beck, Rooney, Clewes, Bower, Tubman, Nixon	Lowden (5)	653	Holgate
17.1.88	SD	A	Rochdale H.	L	8-18	Mawson, Nixon	—	—	—
24.1.88	SD	H	Springfield B.	L	6-12	—	Smith (3)	554	Steele
31.1.88	CC(1)	A	Keighley	L	4-30	Falcon	—	—	—
7.2.88	SD	H	Oldham	L	8-16	Penrice, Falcon	—	857	Millet (Fr)
21.2.88	SD	A	York	L	6-44	Tabern	Lowden	—	—
28.2.88	SD	H	Mansfield M.	L	12-32	Falcon (2), Sullivan	—	562	Burke
6.3.88	SD	A	Oldham	L	10-38	Penrice	Lowden (2), Smith	—	—
13.3.88	SD	H	Runcorn H.	W	30-12	Higgins (2), Nixon, Rea, Smith	Smith (5)	488	Cross
20.3.88	SD	A	Mansfield M.	L	10-20	Tubman, Mawson	Smith	—	—
27.3.88	SD	H	Keighley	L	17-30	Atherton, Sullivan	Smith (4), Burgess (dg)	576	Lindop
1.4.88	SD	A	Whitehaven	L	0-10	—	—	—	—
4.4.88	SD	H	Barrow	W	17-15	Tubman (2), A. Law	Lowden (2), Smith (dg)	685	Kershaw
8.4.88	SD	A	Springfield B.	L	6-11	Penrice	Lowden	—	—
17.4.88	SD	H	Rochdale H.	W	13-14	Lowden, Tubman	Lowden (2), Smith (dg)	656	Holdsworth

CLUBS

YORK

Ground:	Wiggington Road
Colours:	Amber and black jerseys
First Season:	1901-02
Nickname:	Wasps
Chairman:	Ted Tebbutt
Secretary:	Ian Clough
Coach:	Danny Sheehan (Mar 1987-Apr 1988)
	Gary Stephens (Apr 1988-)

Honours: **Division Two** Champions, 1980-81
Challenge Cup Beaten finalists, 1930-31
Yorkshire Cup Winners, 1922-23, 1933-34, 1936-37
Beaten finalists, 1935-36, 1957-58, 1978-79

Records: Attendance: 14,689 v. Swinton (RL Cup) 10 Feb, 1934
Season
Goals: 146 by V. Yorke, 1957-58
Tries: 35 by J. Crossley, 1980-81
Points: 318 by G. Steadman, 1984-85
Match
Goals: 11 by V. Yorke v. Whitehaven, 6 Sep, 1958; C. Gibson v. Dewsbury, 28 Sep, 1980
Tries: 6 by R. Hardgrave v. Bramley, 5 Jan, 1935
Points: 26 by G. Steadman v. Batley, 25 Nov, 1984
Highest score: 60-0 v. Barrow, 1971-72; 60-10 v. Workington T., 1986-87
Highest against: 75-3 v. Warrington 1950-51

1987-88 PLAYERS' SUMMARY

	App		Tries	Goals	Dr	Pts
Arnett, Colin	5		—	—	—	—
Atkins, Gary	19	+ 2	10	—	—	40
Carlyle, Brendan	9	+ 4	2	—	—	8
Colley, Mick	7	+ 2	1	—	—	4
Dobson, Steve	9	+ 3	3	—	3	15
Ellis, St. John	29		12	63	—	174
Fletcher, Ian	32		5	—	—	20
Hague, Neil	35		5	—	6	26
Hammerton, Chris	30	+ 4	10	20	5	85
Harrison, Chris	9	+ 2	1	—	—	4
Hooper, Trevor	5		1	—	—	4
Horton, Stuart	12	+ 1	4	—	1	17
Lilley, Mark	0	+ 1	—	—	—	—
Maxwell, Paul	4		—	—	—	—
Miles, Paul	3	+ 1	—	—	—	—
Moulden, Darren	3		—	—	—	—
Mulherin, Paul	26		7	—	—	28
Olsen, Steve	20	+ 2	3	—	—	12
Parrish, Steve	2		—	6	—	12
Paver, Ian	26		3	—	—	12
Phillippo, Peter	6		—	—	—	—
Pitts, Graham	2		—	—	—	—
Pryce, Geoff	26		8	—	—	32
Rhodes, Chris	6	+ 3	—	—	—	—
Robinson, Mike	6	+ 2	—	—	—	—
Rose, Tony	5		—	—	—	—
Shillito, Alan	10	+ 1	2	—	—	8
Stephenson, Nigel	4	+ 27	5	1	1	23
Sullivan, Graham	17	+ 3	1	18	—	40
Tansley, Ian	4	+ 2	1	—	—	4
Timson, Andy	8	+ 1	1	—	—	4
Turner, Paul	1		—	—	—	—
Wheatley, Steve	12	+ 1	1	—	—	4
White, Paul	29	+ 1	11	—	—	44
Wigglesworth, Ian	34		19	—	1	77
TOTALS:						
35 players			116	108	17	697

Neil Hague — 35 appearances.

1987-88 MATCH ANALYSIS

Date	Competition	H/A	Opponent	Rlt	Score	Tries	Goals	Attendance	Referee
30.8.87	SD	A	Doncaster	L	12-32	Hammerton, Hague	Hammerton, Ellis	—	—
2.9.87	SD	H	Featherstone R.	W	24-20	Carlyle, Hammerton, Colley	Hammerton (5, 2 dg)	1682	Smith
6.9.87	SD	A	Keighley	L	6-14	Hammerton	Ellis	—	—
13.9.87	YC(1)	A	Mansfield M.	W	23-18	Ellis, Hague, Tansley, Olsen	Hammerton (2, 1 dg), Ellis	—	—
20.9.87	SD	A	Batley	D	16-16	Harrison, Horton	Hammerton (3), Hague (dg), Stephenson (dg)	—	—
23.9.87	YC(2)	A	Featherstone R.	L	6-43	Ellis	Hammerton	—	—
27.9.87	SD	H	Runcorn H.	L	16-19	Wigglesworth (2), Hooper	Parrish (2)	1363	Simpson
4.10.87	SD	H	Sheffield E.	L	17-20	Ellis, Mulherin	Parrish (4), Hammerton (dg)	1510	Tickle
11.10.87	SD	A	Mansfield M.	L	8-10	Stephenson	Hammerton, Ellis	—	—
18.10.87	SD	H	Springfield B.	L	10-24	Fletcher, Wigglesworth	Stephenson	1056	Holgate
25.10.87	SD	A	Workington T.	W	11-10	Mulherin, Fletcher	Ellis, Wigglesworth (dg)	—	—
1.11.87	JPS(P)	H	Bramley	W	38-2	Ellis (2), Olsen, Wigglesworth, White, Pryce	Ellis (7)	1174	Tickle
8.11.87	SD	A	Bramley	W	27-18	Ellis (2), Atkins, Hague, White	Ellis (3), Horton (dg)	—	—
15.11.87	JPS(1)	A	Wakefield T.	D	22-22	Ellis, Stephenson, Horton	Ellis (5)	—	—
18.11.87	JPS(1) Replay	H	Wakefield T.	L	6-30	Hammerton	Ellis	1467	Whitfield
6.12.87	SD	H	Dewsbury	W	24-13	Ellis, Atkins, Pryce, Paver	Ellis (4)	954	Burke
13.12.87	SD	A	Sheffield E.	L	16-45	Wigglesworth, Pryce	Hammerton (3), Hague (2 dg)	—	—
20.12.87	SD	H	Keighley	W	19-16	Wigglesworth (2)	Hammerton (3), Sullivan (2), Hague (dg)	1202	Bowman
26.12.87	SD	H	Bramley	W	21-16	Hague, Hammerton, White, Wigglesworth	Sullivan (2), Hague (dg)	1253	Berry
3.1.88	SD	H	Doncaster	L	12-26	Wigglesworth, White	Sullivan (2)	1384	Cross
10.1.88	SD	A	Huddersfield B.	W	32-20	White (2), Atkin, Price, Fletcher, Timson, Mulherin	Hammerton, Ellis	—	—
24.1.88	SD	A	Fulham	W	36-4	Horton (2), White (2), Atkins (2), Hammerton	Ellis (4)	—	—
31.1.88	CC(1)	A	Featherstone R.	L	21-32	Ellis (2), Wigglesworth, Atkins	Ellis (2), Hammerton (dg)	—	—
14.2.88	SD	H	Huddersfield B.	W	48-0	Atkins (3), Wigglesworth (2), Hammerton (2), Dobson, Wheatley	Ellis (6)	1223	Houghton
21.2.88	SD	H	Workington T.	W	44-6	White, Pryce, Atkins, Ellis, Fletcher, Mulherin, Stephenson	Ellis (8)	1381	Drinkwater
28.2.88	SD	A	Dewsbury	L	6-10	Fletcher	Ellis	—	—
6.3.88	SD	A	Runcorn H.	W	20-18	Wigglesworth, Mulherin, Hammerton	Ellis (3), Sullivan	—	—
13.3.88	SD	H	Mansfield M.	W	16-8	White, Hammerton, Paver	Sullivan (2)	1182	Berry
20.3.88	SD	A	Springfield B.	L	12-22	Wigglesworth, Olsen	Sullivan (2)	—	—
27.3.88	SD	H	Batley	W	33-20	Wigglesworth (2), White, Pryce, Stephenson	Sullivan (3), Ellis (3), Hague (dg)	1317	Spencer
1.4.88	SD	A	Wakefield T.	L	11-34	Paver	Sullivan (2), Ellis, Dobson (dg)	—	—
4.4.88	SD	H	Wakefield T.	W	17-8	Pryce, Mulherin, Hague	Ellis (2), Dobson (dg)	2253	McDonald
10.4.88	SD	H	Fulham	W	34-13	Wigglesworth (2), Mulherin, Dobson, Sullivan, Stephenson	Ellis (4), Sullivan	1923	Smith
17.4.88	SD	A	Featherstone R.	L	10-64	Carlyle, Pryce	Ellis	—	—
24.4.88	SDP(1)	A	Wakefield T.	L	23-44	Shillito (2), Wigglesworth, Dobson	Ellis (2), Sullivan, Dobson (1 dg)	—	—

91

ST. HELENS MATCH ANALYSIS (continued)

4.4.88	SBC	A	Widnes	L	6-16	Platt	Loughlin	—	—
10.4.88	SBC	H	Leeds	L	23-28	Holding (3), Quirk, Loughlin	Loughlin, Veivers (dg)	6857	McDonald
13.4.88	SBC	A	Hull	W	20-8	Platt (2), Veivers, Elia	Loughlin (2)	—	—
17.4.88	SBC	H	Swinton	W	52-4	McCormack (2), Elia (2), Platt (2), Holding, Ledger, Groves, Loughlin	Loughlin (6)	5969	Spencer
24.4.88	PT(1)	H	Castleford	W	40-8	Groves (3), Quirk, Forber, Ledger, Elia	Tanner (4), Loughlin (2)	7209	Lindop
8.5.88	PT(SF)	H	Bradford N.	W	24-10	Platt, Groves	Loughlin (7), Haggerty (2 dg)	10,541	Whitfield
15.5.88	PT(F)	Man U. FC	Widnes	L	14-38	Ledger, Haggerty	Loughlin (3)	(35,252)	Holdsworth

WIGAN MATCH ANALYSIS (continued)

4.4.88	SBC	H	Swinton	W	42-16	Hanley (3), Gill, Preston, Bell, Rodgers, Hampson	Lydon (3), Gill (2)	11,136	Cross
10.4.88	SBC	A	Bradford N. Bradford C. FC	W	14-10	Marshall, Lydon, Bell	Lydon	—	—
13.4.88	SBC	H	Salford	W	52-22	Goodway (4), Preston (2), Bell (2), Edwards, Gregory	Gregory (4), Gill (2)	10,125	Smith
17.4.88	SBC	H	Hunslet	W	62-10	Preston (5), Goodway (2), Gill (2), Byrne, Bell, Edwards	Gregory (5), Gill, Rodgers	10,972	Tickle
24.4.88	PT(1)	H	Warrington	L	12-24	Hanley	Gregory (2), Gill, Lydon	15,732	Whitfield
30.4.88	CC(F)	Wembley	Halifax	W	32-12	K. Iro (2), T. Iro, Lydon, Gill, Bell, Hanley	Lydon, Gregory	(94,273)	Lindop

Martin Offiah of Widnes — a record-breaker in his first season of rugby league.

RECORDS

LEADING SCORERS FOR 1987-88

TOP TEN TRIES
1. Martin Offiah (Widnes) 44
2. Ellery Hanley (Wigan) 36
3. Garry Schofield (Leeds) 25
4. Carl Gibson (Leeds) 24
5. Andy Goodway (Wigan) 23
   Kevin Pape (Carlisle) 23
7. Shaun Edwards (Wigan) 21
   Des Foy (Oldham) 21
   Peter Smith (Featherstone R.) 21
10. Chris Bibb (Featherstone R.) 20
   Mark Conway (Wakefield T.) 20
   Mark Elia (St. Helens) 20
   Les Quirk (St. Helens) 20

TOP TEN GOALS
(Including drop goals)
1. John Woods (Warrington) 152
2. Steve Quinn (Featherstone R.) 128
3. Kevin Harcombe (Wakefield T.) 116
4. Paul Loughlin (St. Helens) 114
5. Gary Pearce (Hull) 111
6. Mike Smith (Springfield B.) 98
7. David Stephenson (Leeds) 95
8. Mike Fletcher (Hull K.R.) 94
9. David Hobbs (Bradford N.) 83
10. Ken Jones (Salford) 79

TOP FIVE DROP GOALS
1. Wayne Parker (Hull K.R.) 15
2. Roy Haggerty (St. Helens) 13
3. Chris Middlehurst (Runcorn H.) 9
4. Deryck Fox (Featherstone R.) 9
5. Gary Pearce (Hull) 9

TOP FIVE POINTS

	T	G	DG	Pts
1. John Woods (Warrington) .	13	147	5	351
2. Steve Quinn (Featherstone R.)	11	127	1	299
3. Paul Loughlin (St. Helens).	8	114	0	260
4. Kevin Harcombe (Wakefield T.).............	3	116	0	244
5. Gary Pearce (Hull)	6	102	9	237

Key:
SBC .... Stones Bitter Championship
SD .... Second Division
SDP .... Second Division Premiership
LC .... Lancashire Cup
YC .... Yorkshire Cup
JPS .... John Player Special Trophy
CC .... Challenge Cup
PT .... Premiership Trophy
NA .... Non-appearance

OUTSTANDING SCORING FEATS IN 1987-88

INDIVIDUAL
Most tries in a match:
6 by Shane Cooper (St. Helens) v. Hull .... SBC
5 by Mark Preston (Wigan) v. Hunslet .... SBC

Most goals in a match:
10 by Bob Beardmore (Castleford) v. Swinton ..... SBC
    David Creasser (Leeds) v. Salford .... SBC
    Steve Quinn (Featherstone R.) v. York .... SD
    John Woods (Warrington) v. Swinton LC

Most points in a match:
28 by David Creasser (Leeds) v. Salford .... SBC
    Steve Quinn (Featherstone R.) v. York .... SD

TEAM
Highest score:
Castleford 76 v. Swinton 16 .... SBC
● There was a total of 22 matches in which a team scored 50 points or more compared with 36 in the previous season. The other 60-plus scores were:

Home:
St. Helens 70 v. Hunslet 6 .... SBC
St. Helens 64 v. Hull 2 .... SBC
Featherstone R. 64 v. York 10 .... SD
Wakefield T. 62 v. Bramley 10 .... SD
Wigan 62 v. Hunslet 10 .... SBC
Leeds 60 v. Salford 6 .... SBC

Away:
Hunslet 14 v. Widnes 66 .... SBC
Heworth 4 v. Halifax 60 .... CC(1)

Highest score by losing team:
Salford 34 v. Hull K.R. 32 .... SBC
● There was a total of 54 matches in which a team scored 20 points or more and lost compared with 59 in the previous season.

High-scoring draws:
Hunslet 32 v. Swinton 32 .... SBC
Wakefield T. 22 v. York 22 .... JPS(1)
Mansfield M. 20 v. Wakefield T. 20 .... SD
Warrington 20 v. Leeds 20 .... SBC

Scoreless draw:
Halifax 0 v. Hull 0 .... CC(SF)

• From the start of the 1983-84 season, the value of a try was raised from three points to four points. It was decided officially that records for most points in a match, season or career would subsequently include the four-point try and that no attempt would be made to adjust existing records featuring the three-point try.
• Substitute appearances do not count towards players' full appearance records.

RECORD-BREAKING FEATS 1987-88

MARTIN OFFIAH scored a Widnes record 42 tries in a season including a Division One record-equalling 11 successive tryscoring matches.

MIKE SMITH kicked a Springfield Borough record 98 goals in a season.

NORMAN TURLEY finished with a career record 85 one-point drop goals.

PETER LISTER finished the season with a Bramley career record of 103 tries.

SHANE COOPER broke the Division One match record with six tries which equalled the St. Helens club record.

TERRY ROSE broke the Runcorn Highfield match points record with 24.

MICK HOWARTH equalled the Mansfield Marksman record of 18 points in a match.

KEVIN JONES scored a club record 20 points in a match for Doncaster.

HUNSLET and SWINTON were involved in a Division One record high scoring draw when they drew 32-32.

HULL went down to a club record 64-2 defeat when they lost at St. Helens.

CASTLEFORD broke the Division One highest score record of 76-16 which equalled Swinton's worst defeat. It was also Castleford's highest score against a professional side.

WIGAN had a record winning run of 29 matches.

WIDNES equalled the highest Premiership final score with a 38-14 defeat of St. Helens.

WIGAN had a Division One record crowd of 23,809 for the visit of St. Helens.

NEW RECORDS IN DETAIL . . .

MARTIN OFFIAH scored a Widnes record 42 tries in a remarkable first season of rugby league in which he also equalled the Division One record of 11 successive tryscoring matches.
    The former Rosslyn Park rugby union winger equalled stand off Frank Myler's Widnes record of 34 tries in 1958-59 with one try in the 39-6 league win at Castleford on 23 March and beat it with the first of two touchdowns in a 35-6 league win at Warrington on 1 April.

Offiah made his debut at home to Halifax on 30 August when Widnes won 28-6. He did not score in his first two matches but then touched down in 15 successive matches for Widnes, a sequence bettered only by Eric Harris's 17 successive tryscoring matches for Leeds in 1935-36.
    Offiah's run included 11 Division One tryscoring matches to equal the record set by Hull Kingston Rovers centre Gary Prohm in 1985.
    At the end of the season Offiah's total in all matches was 44 including a try each for Great Britain and an RL Chairman's X111. It was the most by a winger since 1973-74 when former England RU international Keith Fielding of Salford scored 49 in his first season.
    Offiah's match-by-match record was as follows:

Widnes		Tries
Halifax	(H)	0
Bradford N	(A)	0
Runcorn H. (LC)	(A)	2
Hull	(A)	1
Whitehaven (LC)	(A)	2
Hunslet	(H)	1
Wigan (LC)	(H)	1
Salford	(A)	1
Hull K.R.	(H)	1
Swinton	(H)	2
Leigh	(A)	1
Castleford	(H)	2
St. Helens (JPS)	(A)	1
Halifax	(A)	2
Hull	(H)	2
Swinton	(A)	1
Warrington	(H)	2
St. Helens	(A)	0
Leigh	(H)	1
Leeds	(A)	0
Salford	(H)	NA
Dewsbury (CC)	(A)	2
Bradford N	(H)	3
Keighley (CC)	(A)	0
Wigan	(H)	0
Wigan (CC)	(A)	0
Hull K.R.	(A)	2
Leeds	(H)	3
Castleford	(A)	1
Wigan	(A)	0
Warrington	(A)	2
St. Helens	(H)	3
Hunslet	(A)	2
Halifax (PT)	(H)	1
Warrington (PT)	(H)	0
St. Helens (PT)	(Man. U. FC)	0
Total		**42**
Lancashire v. Papua New Guinea (H)		**0**
Great Britain v. France	(A)	**1**
RL Chairman's X111 v. Auckland (H)		**1**
GRAND TOTAL		**44**

MIKE SMITH scored a Springfield Borough record 98 goals in his first season as a professional after signing from Wigan St. Patricks.

The old record had stood since 1958-59 when John Maughan kicked 89. Smith equalled it with the last of four goals in Borough's 36-4 Division Two home defeat of Whitehaven on 14 April and beat it with the first of two in the 9-8 league defeat at Fulham on 17 April.

The full-back's total included two drop goals.

Smith's record was achieved in the club's first season as Springfield Borough after changing their title from Blackpool Borough and moving to Wigan. He made his debut with three goals in the 22-16 league win at Huddersfield Barracudas on 30 August.

Smith's match-by-match record was as follows:

		Goals
Huddersfield B.	(A)	3
Runcorn H.	(A)	1
Barrow	(H)	NA
Workington T. (LC)	(A)	3
Oldham	(A)	4
Huddersfield B.	(H)	6
Whitehaven	(A)	2
Carlisle	(H)	4
York	(A)	4
Keighley	(A)	2
Runcorn H.	(A)	2
Rochdale H.	(H)	4
Barrow (JPS)	(H)	5
Wakefield T. (JPS)	(H)	3
Leeds (JPS)	(H)	2
Batley	(A)	4
Keighley	(H)	3
Oldham	(H)	2
Carlisle	(A)	0
Fulham	(H)	2
Workington T.	(A)	4
Runcorn H. (CC)	(A)	2
Mansfield M.	(H)	3
Salford (CC)	(A)	3
Dewsbury	(H)	4
Barrow	(A)	0
Batley	(H)	3
York	(H)	3
Dewsbury	(A)	2(1)
Runcorn H.	(H)	4
Mansfield M.	(A)	1
Workington T.	(H)	NA
Whitehaven	(H)	4
Fulham	(A)	2
Sheffield E. (SDPT)	(H)	4(1)
Oldham (SDPT)	(A)	3
Total		**98 (2)**

( ) Denotes drop goals included in total

NORMAN TURLEY took over as the leader of most one-point drop goals in a career, finishing the season with 85.

Workington Town's player-coach loose forward surpassed the old record of 79 shared by Harry Pinner and Nigel Stephenson.

Turley equalled the record with a drop goal in Town's 8-6 Division Two win at Dewsbury on 30 August and beat it with another in the 19-10 home league win over Huddersfield Barracudas on 6 September.

Pinner achieved the old record during his time at St. Helens and Widnes. He has not added to his total since moving to Leigh. Stephenson finished with 80 after announcing his retirement following a 20-year career with Dewsbury, Bradford Northern, Carlisle, Wakefield Trinity and York.

Turley began his first team career with Warrington in 1974-75, the season drop goals were halved to one point, but it was not until he moved to Blackpool Borough in January 1978 that he scored his first one-pointer.

The following season he scored a then record 18 in one season. He has kicked three drop goals in a match on several occasions.

Turley also had brief spells at Runcorn Highfield and Swinton without adding to his total which is made up as follows:

Blackpool B.
1977-78		4
1978-79		18

Rochdale H.
1979-80		4
1980-81		14
1981-82		3
1982-83		3

Blackpool B.
1983-84		15
1984-85		13

Barrow
1985-86		1
1986-87		2

Workington T.
1986-87		1
1987-88		7

Totals
Blackpool B.		50
Rochdale H.		24
Barrow		3
Workington T.		8

GRAND TOTAL 85

PETER LISTER broke the Bramley try career record when he took his total to 93 with their only touchdown in a 30-6 home defeat against Bradford Northern in the John Smiths Yorkshire Cup second round tie on 22 September.

The previous record holder was utility player Jack

Austin who totalled 92 in two periods at Bramley from 1969-1977 and 1982-83.

Lister was signed from Leeds where he made only one appearance before making his Bramley debut in the centre on 20 September, 1981 when they lost 28-9 away to Hunslet, who were then playing at Batley.

His best season was 1985-86 when he scored a club record 34 tries playing mostly at stand off. He finished third in the try chart, the only time he has been in the top ten.

Lister finished the season with a career total of 103 which included three hat-tricks. His season-by-season totals are as follows:

1981-82	7
1982-83	6
1983-84	13
1984-85	15
1985-86	34
1986-87	11
1987-88	17
Total	**103**

SHANE COOPER broke the Division One match record and equalled St. Helens' best with six tries in Hull's biggest ever defeat of 64-2 on 17 February.

The New Zealand stand off's six touchdowns wiped out ten entries in the record books, the number of times the previous Division One record of five tries had been achieved since the reintroduction of two divisions in 1973.

St. Helens players were also involved on three of those occasions. Winger Roy Mathias twice scored five, against Rochdale Hornets on 17 February 1974 and v. Workington Town on 23 December 1979, while Peter Glynn scored five on the wing against Hull on 16 October 1977.

Others to score five tries in a Division One match were: wingers Steve Fenton (Castleford) v. Dewsbury 27 January 1978; Kevin Meadows (Oldham) at Salford 20 April 1984; John Basnett (Widnes) v. Hull K.R. 2 November 1986; stand off John Woods (Bradford Northern) v. Swinton 13 October 1985; centre Steve Hartley (Hull K.R.) v. Huddersfield 13 April 1979; scrum half Parry Gordon (Warrington) v. Dewsbury 3 March 1974 and loose forward Ellery Hanley (Wigan) v. Bradford Northern 1 March 1987.

Cooper's six tries also equalled the St. Helens record for any competitive match. Others to have scored six are: wingers Alf Ellaby v. Barrow on 5 March 1932; Stewart Llewellyn v. Castleford 3 March 1956 and v. Liverpool City 20 August 1956; Tom Van Vollenhoven v. Wakefield Trinity 21 December 1957 and v. Blackpool Borough 23 April 1962; and centre Frank Myler v. Maryport Amateurs in a Lancashire Cup-tie on 1 September 1969.

TERRY ROSE broke a 56-year-old Runcorn Highfield match record with 24 points in the 41-4 Division Two home victory over Workington Town on 4 October. The centre's total was made up of eight goals and two tries.

The previous record of 20 points was shared by three players, each playing under a different team title.

Winger P. Barnes set the old record with seven goals and two tries for Wigan Highfield in a 41-3 Rugby League Challenge Cup home victory over Featherstone Rovers Juniors on 7 February 1931.

They had changed to London Highfield when prop S. Oakley kicked 10 goals in a 59-11 home league defeat of Bramley on 4 May 1934.

And it was Liverpool City for whom stand off P. Twiss scored seven goals and two tries in a 26-23 league defeat at Warrington on 20 August 1958.

MICK HOWARTH equalled the Mansfield Marksman match record with 18 points from five goals and two tries playing at centre in the 31-27 Division Two win at Dewsbury on 17 January.

Signed from Jubilee Amateurs, Featherstone, it was only the utility back's seventh match for Mansfield, having appeared as a trialist a year earlier.

Barry Holden set the record with 18 points when the second row forward scored seven goals and a try in the 34-22 Division Two home win over Keighley on 3 March 1985.

KEVIN JONES broke the Doncaster match record with 20 points in the 40-12 Division Two home defeat of Whitehaven on 13 March.

The scrum half's total from six goals and two tries beat the 18 points record shared by three players. Full-back David Towle set the old figure with 18 points from a club record nine goals in a 33-14 league win at York on 9 September 1967.

Winger Ian Fortis then scored six goals and two tries in a 30-0 home league defeat of Blackpool Borough on 5 September 1970 and prop David Noble got seven goals and a try in Doncaster's club record 50-6 victory in a Division Two home game against Keighley on 23 March 1987.

HUNSLET and SWINTON produced a Division One record high scoring draw when they drew 32-32 at Elland Road on 20 September.

Each team scored five tries as did Widnes and St. Helens when they were involved in the previous record draw of 28-28 at Naughton Park on 23 April 1984.

The record score draw for a Division Two match is also 32-32 between Huddersfield Barracudas and Keighley on 17 April 1986.

HULL suffered a club record defeat when they lost 64-2 in a Stones Bitter championship match at St. Helens on 17 February. St. Helens also inflicted the previous highest score against Hull with a 57-14 home win in the third round of the John Player Special Trophy on 11

December 1985.

Last season's defeat included 11 tries compared with 10 in 1985.

CASTLEFORD broke the Division One highest score record with their 76-16 home defeat of Swinton on 16 March. It was also Castleford's biggest score against a professional side and equalled Swinton's worst defeat.

Castleford scored 14 tries to beat the 72-12 (12 tries) home win by Bradford Northern over Hunslet on 7 October 1984 and Wigan's 14-try 72-6 win at Wakefield Trinity on 29 March 1987. Wigan's win is the widest Division One margin.

Under the old one league system the highest score was Leeds' 102-0 home defeat of Coventry on 12 April 1913.

Castleford's previous highest score against a professional side was 70-10 at home to Barrow on 22 March 1987 in a Division One match. Their overall record remains the 88-5 home defeat of Millow Amateurs in the first round of the Player's No.6 Trophy on 16 September 1973.

Swinton have conceded 76 points once before, when losing 76-3 at Huddersfield, who scored 18 tries in the league match on 20 April 1946.

WIGAN had a record winning run of 29 matches spanning two seasons. It began with a 16-6 league win at home to Castleford on 15 February 1987 and ended with a 17-14 home league defeat against Halifax on 18 October 1987.

The winning run was made up of 20 Stones Bitter Championship matches, three Premiership matches, four Grunhalle Lager Lancashire Cup-ties, the Okells Charity Shield and the Fosters World Club Challenge. It brought them a total of 974 points against 214.

WIDNES equalled the Premiership final record score with their 38-14 defeat of St. Helens at Old Trafford, Manchester. They scored seven tries, as did Warrington when they beat Halifax 38-10 in the final at Elland Road, Leeds, in 1986.

WIGAN'S Central Park housed a Division One record attendance of 23,809 for the match against St. Helens on 27 December which the Saints won 32-22. The previous record was 21,813 for the Central Park fixture between the same clubs on 26 December 1985.

The record refers to the present era of two divisions which began in 1973. Under the old one-league system the record league crowd was 47,747 for Wigan v. St. Helens on 27 March 1959.

Dean Bell scores for Wigan against Halifax in the Okells Charity Shield match — one of 29 successive wins by the Cherry and Whites.

MILESTONES . . .

JOHN WOODS passed the 3,000 points career mark with his first goal in a 14-point haul when Warrington won 22-14 at Carlisle in the first round of the John Player Special Trophy on 15 November.

His total at the end of the season stood at 3,209 points made up of 351 for Warrington, 421 for Bradford Northern, 2,172 for Leigh and 265 in representative matches.

He has scored 191 tries and 1,292 goals including 20 drop goals.

Woods turned professional with Leigh in December 1975 and made a tryscoring debut on the wing at home to Barrow in an 18-8 Division One victory on 5 September 1976.

He set several scoring records at Leigh before moving to Bradford Northern for £65,000, kicking one goal on his debut at stand off in a 32-7 Division One defeat at Warrington on 1 September 1985.

The Test back broke more records in a two-season stay at Bradford and then moved to Warrington for £40,000 in June 1987, kicking nine goals on his debut at stand off in a 54-4 Division One home defeat of Hunslet on 30 August 1987.

Although generally recognised as a stand off, Woods has also played many matches at centre and full-back.

His list of records is:

John Woods — 3,000 points.

Division One career total of points: 1,978
Division One points in a season: 295 for Leigh in 1983-84.
Division Two points in a match: 38 (13g,4t) for Leigh v. Blackpool B. 11 September 1977.
Leigh points in a match: 38 (13g,4t) v. Blackpool.
Bradford Northern points in a match: 36 (8g,5t) v. Swinton 13 October 1985.

In addition, Woods is the only player to have scored both 100 tries and 500 goals in Division One matches.

Woods has scored three tries in a match on nine occasions, including one five-try feat and four touchdowns twice.

His best goals feat was 13 for Leigh against Blackpool Borough on 11 September 1977. He has kicked 10 on two other occasions.

The match against Blackpool in 1977 also produced his best match points tally of 38. He has also scored 36, 29 and 28 points in a match.

Woods finished as the season's top pointscorer with 355 in 1983-84 and 351 in 1987-88.

Woods' totals are made up as follows:

Leigh	T	G	DG	Pts	
1976-77	5	88	2	193	
1977-78	16	140	0	328	+ 2t,7g GB Under-24s; 2t,2g Lancs.
1978-79	10	85	1	201	+ 4g GB Under-24s; 5g,1t England
1979-80	22	80	2	228	+ 3g, 1t Lancs.
1980-81	14	85	1	213	+ 1t England; 2t Lancs.
1981-82	18	146	1	347	+ 8g,1t GB; 3g England
1982-83	12	48	1	133	
1983-84	27	123	1	355	
1984-85	11	64	2	174	
Bradford N.					
1985-86	13	97	1	247	
1986-87	8	70	2	174	
Warrington					
1987-88	13	147	5	351	
Totals					
Leigh	135	859	11	2,172	
Bradford N.	21	167	3	421	
Warrington	13	147	5	351	
1979 tour	12	62*	1	161*	
Britain	1	13	0	29	
England	2	8	0	22	
GB Under-24s	2	11	0	28	
Lancashire	5	5	0	25	

GRAND TOTALS
191 1,272 20 3,209

* Not including 5 goals in a Test match which are included in the Britain total

LEE CROOKS of Leeds scored the 1,000th point of his career, ironically passing the target with 16 against Hull — the club for whom he scored 947 points.

Crooks' 16 points helped to beat Hull 28-24 in the first round of the John Smiths Yorkshire Cup on 13 September.

He turned professional with Hull on his 17th birthday, 18 September 1980, and made his debut two months later, playing in the second row when Hull had a 15-10 home league win over Salford on 30 November.

Crooks made just five appearances that season, including two as substitute, but established himself the following term when he played in 42 matches and scored 254 points.

When Hull's financial problems forced them to sell Crooks he moved to Leeds in June 1987 for a then world record £150,000 for an individual player.

The Test forward made his debut for Leeds with two goals and a try in a 38-12 home defeat of Leigh on 30 August 1987.

Ironically, his best match tally had been against Leeds when he scored 23 points, including his only try hat-trick, and seven goals in Hull's 35-5 home league victory on 13 October 1982.

Crooks' points total at the end of last season was 1,062 made up of 947 for Hull, 74 for Leeds and 41 in representative matches. He did not score in his first season but since then his annual totals are as follows:

Hull	T	G	DG	Pts	
1981-82........	7	115	3	254	
1982-83........	11	113	2	261	+ 4 g , 1 d g G B
1983-84........	6	36	0	96	+ 2 g G B
1984-85........	4	27	0	70	
1985-86........	9	52	1	141	+ 8 g G B
1986-87........	7	46	5	125	+ 1 g G B
Leeds					
1987-88........	4	28	2	74	
Totals					
Hull............	44	389	11	947	
Leeds..........	4	28	2	74	
Britain.........	0	15	1	31	
1984 Tour....	1	3	0	10	

GRAND TOTALS
49   435   14   1,062

ELLERY HANLEY scored his 1,000th career point, and his 100th career try for Wigan during the season.

The Wigan Test star passed the four-figure mark with a try for Yorkshire against Lancashire at his home ground on 16 September taking his total to 1,003.

Hanley finished the season with 1,135 points from 243 tries and 96 goals including three drop goals. He scored 498 points for Bradford Northern, 518 Wigan and 119 in representative matches.

His 100th try for Wigan came with the second of two touchdowns in the 42-2 home defeat of Salford in the second round of the Grunhalle Lager Lancashire Cup on

23 September. His century was notched up in only 84 matches including one substitute appearance.

Hanley turned professional as a 17-year-old with Bradford on 2 June 1978 from Corpus Christi, Leeds. He made his debut as a substitute, scoring a try in the 30-18 home league defeat of Rochdale Hornets on 26 November 1978.

He was then absent for a period and did not make his full debut until 16 August 1981 when he scored a try in the centre in a 33-5 Yorkshire Cup first round win at Halifax.

Wigan signed him in a then world record £150,000 deal on 16 September 1985. They paid a then record £85,000 plus the transfer of Phil Ford and Steve Donlan.

Hanley made his Wigan debut in the centre in a 32-10 home league victory over Widnes on 22 September 1985.

Hanley's total of 125 tries for Wigan includes a Division One record of 44 in 1986-87. He had held the previous record with 40 for Bradford in 1984-85.

Hanley's best match feat is five tries for Wigan against Bradford in a 60-6 home win on 1 March 1987. It was one of 13 occasions he has scored three tries or more, including five four-try feats and seven hat-tricks.

The tries have continued to flow whether playing at stand off, centre or loose forward and a few appearances on the wing for Great Britain.

His season-by-season scoring figures are as follows:

Bradford N.	T	G	Pts	
1978-79........	1	0	3	
1978-79........	Did not play			
1979-80........	Did not play			
1981-82........	15	41	127	
1982-83........	10	3(1)	35	
1983-84........	12	3(1)	53	+ 1t GB Under-24s
1984-85........	52	36	280	+ 1t England; 2t GB
Wigan				
1985-86........	35	8	156	+ 2t GB; 1t,1dg Yorks.
1986-87........	59	1	238	+ 3t GB; 1t Yorks.
1987-88........	31	0	124	+ 4t GB; 1t Yorks.
Totals				
Bradford N. .	90	83(2)	498	
Wigan	125	9	518	
1984 GB tour	8	3	38*	
Britain.........	15	0	60	
England.......	1	0	4	
GB Under-24s	1	0	4	
Yorkshire.....	3	1(1)	13	

GRAND TOTALS
243   96(3)   1,135
( ) denotes drop goals included in total

* Not including 4 Test tries which are included in Britain total

BOB BEARDMORE passed the 1,000 points mark in Division One with six goals and a try in Castleford's 32-3 home defeat of Hull on 10 January taking his total to 1,007.

At the end of the season the scrum half's total was 1,081 from 76 tries and 409 goals including six drop goals — all for Castleford.

Beardmore's total includes a Division One match record of 38 points from 11 goals and four tries in the 70-10 home defeat of Barrow on 22 March 1987. He had held the previous record with 34 points (11 goals, three tries) against Leeds on 2 October 1983 before losing it to John Woods who scored 36 for Bradford Northern against Swinton.

Beardmore was the top Division One goals and pointscorer in 1982-83 with 105 league goals and 249 points.

Beardmore, who shared a benefit campaign with his twin brother, Kevin, in 1987-88, made his debut for Castleford on 18 November 1979 when they lost 10-8 in the League game at Workington Town.

He did not score in his first season but since then his season-by-season totals have been as follows:

	T	G	DG	Pts
1980-81	12	9	1	55
1981-82	10	11	1	53
1982-83	13	105	0	249
1983-84	12	93	1	235
1984-85	6	28	0	80
1985-86	6	42	0	108
1986-87	11	57	2	160
1987-88	6	58	1	141
Totals	**76**	**403**	**6**	**1,081**

Beardmore also passed 500 goals in all matches for Castleford. He reached the milestone in style with the last of his 10 goals in the 76-16 Division One home defeat of Swinton on 6 March.

His most prolific season was 1983-84 when he kicked 142 to share the leadership with Warrington's Steve Hesford. The only other season he finished in the top ten was a year earlier when he was fourth with 117.

Beardmore's best match tally is 12 in a Division One away fixture against Carlisle at Wakefield Trinity's ground on 8 April 1983. He has twice kicked 11 in a match and 10 on two occasions.

His season-by-season goals totals for Castleford are as follows:

1980-81	10	(1)
1981-82	12	(1)
1982-83	117	
1983-84	142	(2)
1984-85	43	
1985-86	65	(1)
1986-87	65	(3)
1987-88	64	(1)
Total	**518**	**(9)**

( ) denotes drop goals included in totals

GARRY SCHOFIELD scored the 1,000th point of his brief career with a try and goal in Leeds' 32-18 home defeat against Bradford Northern on 1 April. He finished his fifth season with a total of 1,032 from 150 tries and 218 goals including four drop goals. He has scored 824 points for Hull, 96 for Leeds and 112 in representative matches.

A former Hunslet Parkside junior, Schofield signed for Hull soon after captaining the Great Britain amateur youth squad to New Zealand in 1983. He made his professional debut in a 22-22 Division One home draw against Warrington on 21 August 1983.

It was the start of a remarkable first season in which he became the youngest ever to finish at the top of the try chart with 38. He was only 18 years 10 months when the season finished and he became the youngest ever Great Britain tourist to Australasia that year.

Schofield has scored 20 points or more in a match on four occasions, with his best haul being 26 from five goals and four tries for the British Lions in a 44-12 defeat of Central Queensland at Rockhampton on the 1984 tour.

He holds the match record for most Great Britain points against New Zealand with 16 in the second Test at Wigan on 2 November 1985, his four tries equalling the British record for any Test match.

Hull transferred Schofield to Leeds for a world record £155,000 and he scored two debut tries for his home town club in a 29-25 defeat by Auckland at Headingley on 25 October 1987.

Schofield's scoring record does not include points scored during his spells with Balmain in Australia. His 1,032 points as a British registered player is made up as follows:

Hull	T	G	DG	Pts	
1983-84	37	57	0	262	+ 1t GB Under-24s
1984-85	23	104	1	301	
1985-86	15	35	1	131	+ 5t, 2g GB; 1dg Yorks.
1986-87	32	1	0	130	+ 5t, 1dg GB
Leeds					
1987-88	22	4	0	96	+ 3t, 5g GB
Totals					
Hull	107	197	2	824	
Leeds	22	4	0	96	
Britain	15	7	1	75	
1984 tour	5	6	0	32*	
Yorkshire	0	0	1	1	
GB Under-24s	1	0	0	4	

GRAND TOTALS

	150	214	4	1,032

*Not including 2 Test tries which are included in Britain total

KEN JONES took his career points total to 1,006 with two tries and a goal in Salford's 24-10 Division One defeat at St. Helens on 16 March. The winger finished the season with 1,052 points from 65 tries and 402 goals.

He has scored 194 points for Salford, 832 for Swinton and 26 during a loan spell with Wakefield Trinity.

A former Leigh rugby union player and England Colts RU captain, Jones signed for Swinton in November 1981 and made his debut in the centre on 7 February 1982 when he kicked five goals in a 21-12 Division Two home victory over Keighley.

Since then Jones has been mostly on the wing although he played three times at stand off during a five-match loan spell at Wakefield in 1985-86.

Salford signed him from Swinton and he made his debut for them with four goals in a 16-12 Division One home defeat against Bradford Northern on 30 August 1987.

His best match points haul is 23 from seven goals and three tries for Swinton in a 50-8 Division Two home defeat of Batley on 17 April 1983. He has scored one other try hat-trick and twice kicked eight goals in a match. Jones' most prolific season was 1984-85 when he scored 262 points for Swinton, finishing ninth in the goals chart with 87. He was seventh with 110 goals in 1982-83 and 10th with 79 in 1987-88.

His season-by-season totals are as follows:

Swinton	T	G	Pts
1981-82	1	20	43
1982-83	11	110	253
1983-84	14	80	216
1984-85	22	87	262
1985-86	6	10	44
Wakefield T.			
1985-86	0	13	26
Swinton			
1986-87	2	3	14
Salford			
1987-88	9	79	194
Totals			
Swinton	56	310	832
Wakefield T	0	13	26
Salford	9	79	194

GRAND TOTALS

65	402	1,052

GARY HYDE of Castleford scored the 100th Division One try of his career with a touchdown in the 28-12 win at Salford on 19 February.

All of his tries have been for Castleford for whom he made his debut in a league match on 19 November 1978 when he scored a try in a 22-10 win at Huddersfield.

He played centre then, but has also scored many tries on the wing.

Hyde's total of 102 Division One tries includes one four-try feat and two other hat-tricks. When he scored four

tries, the centre also kicked eight goals against Warrington on 3 January 1982 for a then Division One record 28 points.

His best season was 1982-83 when he scored 19 league tries.

Hyde's season-by-season Division One try totals are as follows:

1978-79	10
1979-80	7
1980-81	15
1981-82	10
1982-83	19
1983-84	13
1984-85	7
1985-86	5
1986-87	8
1987-88	8

TOTAL.............102

HENDERSON GILL scored the 100th Division One try of his career with a touchdown in Wigan's 46-12 home defeat of Swinton on 4 April. The Test winger's total at the end of the season was 102 made up of 97 for Wigan and five for Bradford Northern.

The winger made his professional first team debut for Bradford in a 35-10 home league win over Barrow on 3 September 1978 while only 17.

He moved to Rochdale Hornets in August 1980 and stayed in Division Two with them until Wigan signed him in October 1981 for a then record fee for a winger of £30,000. Gill scored a try on his Wigan debut in a 20-15 league win at Barrow on 11 October 1981.

The 1986-87 season was Gill's best Division One campaign when he scored 24 league tries. His total of 102 Division One touchdowns includes six hat-tricks and is made up as follows:

Bradford N.	
1978-79	3
1979-80	2
Rochdale H.	
1980-81	In Div. 2
Wigan	
1981-82	11
1982-83	15
1983-84	7
1984-85	23
1985-86	6
1986-87	24
1987-88	11
Totals	
Bradford N.	5
Wigan	97
GRAND TOTAL	102

PHIL FORD scored the 100th Division One try of his career with one touchdown in Bradford Northern's 32-4 home defeat of Hunslet on 5 April. The Test winger's total stood at 100 at the end of the season made up of 42 for Warrington, 10 Wigan and 48 Bradford.

Ford made his rugby league debut by scoring a try as an unnamed trialist from Cardiff rugby union in Warrington's 10-9 home league defeat of Featherstone Rovers on 11 January 1981.

He moved to Wigan for a then record £40,000 for a winger and made another tryscoring debut with two including the late match-winner in a 20-16 home league defeat of Hull Kingston Rovers on 3 March 1985.

Ford stayed just six months at Wigan before they transferred him and Steve Donlan to Bradford in the then world record £150,000 deal to sign Ellery Hanley.

Ford made his debut for Northern in a 17-12 home league defeat against Hull K.R. on 22 September 1985.

Ford's most prolific league season was 1986-87 with 24 tries putting him second to Hanley's Division One record 44.

Ford has scored two Division One hat-tricks, one each for Warrington and Bradford.

His Division One season-by-season totals are as follows:

Warrington

1980-81	4
1981-82	8
1982-83	9
1983-84	18
1984-85	8

Wigan

1984-85	8
1985-86	2

Bradford N.

1985-86	11
1986-87	24
1987-88	13

Totals

Warrington	42
Wigan	10
Bradford N.	48

GRAND TOTAL **100**

GARRY CLARK scored the 100th try of his career with one in Hull Kingston Rovers' 20-8 Division One home defeat of Salford on 10 January. At the end of the season the Test winger's total of 105 was made up of 90 for Rovers and 15 in representative matches.

A Hull K.R. Colt, Clark signed for Rovers after touring Australia and Papua New Guinea with the 1982 Great Britain Colts squad.

Clark was only 17 years 8 months when he made his debut for Rovers with a try in the 33-10 Division One home defeat of Workington Town on 22 August 1982.

In the next match Clark scored the first of only two hat-tricks for Rovers although he has also achieved the feat for Great Britain Under-24s and England.

On the 1984 Great Britain tour of Australia and New Zealand, Clark scored seven tries in 10 appearances.

In his first two seasons Clark finished 10th in the try charts with 24 tries in 1983-84 being his most prolific season.

Clark's season-by-season tryscoring figures are as follows:

Hull K.R.

1982-83	17	+ 3 GB Under-24s
1983-84	24	
1984-85	16	+ 3 England, 2 GB Under-21s
1985-86	11	
1986-87	10	
1987-88	12	

Totals

Hull K.R.	90
England	3
GB Under-21/24s	5
1984 Tour	7

GRAND TOTAL **105**

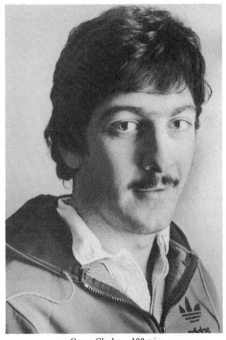

Garry Clark — 100 tries.

PAUL McDERMOTT scored the 100th try of his career in Sheffield Eagles' 30-10 home defeat against Mansfield Marksman on 8 November. His total at the end of the season was 106 made up of 25 for Wakefield Trinity, 47 York, 29 Sheffield, 4 Whitehaven and 1 Keighley.

McDermott began his professional career with Wakefield, joining them from their Colts side and making his senior debut as a back substitute when they lost 12-4 at Rochdale Hornets in a Division One match on 13 March 1977.

McDermott played several matches at full-back before moving to scrum half and loose forward.

He has been involved in several transfers, moving back and forth between Wakefield, York and Sheffield in addition to a spell at Whitehaven and a two-match loan to Keighley.

His try total includes only two hat-tricks, one of them in Sheffield's first ever match when they beat Rochdale 29-10 on 2 September 1984.

His best season was 1980-81 when he finished fourth in the try chart with 23 for York. The only other occasion he finished in the top ten was when he was seventh with 22 for York in 1982-83.

McDermott's season-by-season totals are as follows:

Wakefield T.
1978-79	4
1979-80	15

York
1980-81	23
1981-82	2

Wakefield T.
1981-82	5

York
1982-83	22

Wakefield T.
1983-84	1

Sheffield E.
1984-85	16
1985-86	5

Keighley
1985-86	1

Whitehaven
1985-86	4
1986-87	0

Sheffield E.
1987-88	8

Totals
Wakefield T.	25
York	47
Sheffield E	29
Whitehaven	4
Keighley	1
GRAND TOTAL	**106**

Peter Smith — 100 tries for Featherstone Rovers.

PETER SMITH scored the 100th try of his Featherstone Rovers career with a touchdown in the 40-8 Division Two home defeat of Doncaster on 17 January.

His total at the end of the season was 108.

The back row forward has played all of his professional career with Featherstone, signing from their junior side in May 1972.

He made his debut as a forward substitute on 13 January 1974 in a 17-17 Division One draw at home to Rochdale Hornets. Six days later came his full debut in the second row at Bramley when Rovers had a 16-15 league win.

Smith regained a share in the record for most tries by a Featherstone forward in a season with 21 in 1987-88. He had held the record with 20 in 1976-77 until David Hobbs scored 21 in 1981-82.

Smith's 21 in 1987-88 put him seventh in the try chart, the only time he has finished in the top ten.

His career total, which includes three hat-tricks, would have been much higher but for a series of serious injuries.

Smith made only a few appearances in his first season and did not score. Since then his totals are as follows:

1974-75	3
1975-76	9
1976-77	20
1977-78	8
1978-79	6
1979-80	10
1980-81	7
1981-82	9
1982-83	4
1983-84	0
1984-85	0
1985-86	1
1986-87	10
1987-88	21
Total	**108**

PETER LISTER became the only Bramley player ever to score a century of tries for the club when he touched down twice in the 20-13 Division Two win at Batley on 6 March. He finished the season with a total of 103. Details of Lister's career are in the record section.

LEADING SCORERS 1895-1970

	TRIES	GOALS	POINTS
1895-96	Hurst (Oldham) 28	Lorimer (Manningham) 35	Cooper (Bradford)..........106
			Lorimer (Manningham)...106
1896-97	Hannah (Hunslet)............19	Goldthorpe (Hunslet) 26	Rigg (Halifax)...............112
		Sharpe (Liversedge).........26	
1897-98	Hoskins (Salford) 30	Goldthorpe (Hunslet) 66	Goldthorpe (Hunslet)......135
1898-99	Williams (Oldham) 39	Goldthorpe (Hunslet) 67	Jaques (Hull)................169
1899-00	Williams (Oldham) 36	Cooper (Bradford)...........39	Williams (Oldham).........108
1900-01	Williams (Oldham) 47	Goldthorpe (Hunslet) 44	Williams (Oldham).........141
1901-02	Wilson (Broughton R.).....38	James (Broughton R.) 75	Lomas (Salford).............172
1902-03	Evans (Leeds).................27	Goldthorpe (Hunslet) 48	Davies (Batley)..............136
1903-04	Hogg (Broughton R.).......34	Lomas (Salford) 66	Lomas (Salford).............222
1904-05	Dechan (Bradford)...........31	Ferguson (Oldham)..........50	Lomas (Salford).............146
1905-06	Leytham (Wigan) 40	Ferguson (Oldham)..........49	Leytham (Wigan)...........160
1906-07	Eccles (Halifax)..............41	Lomas (Salford) 86	Lomas (Salford).............280
1907-08	Leytham (Wigan) 44	Goldthorpe (Hunslet)......101	Goldthorpe (Hunslet)......217
1908-09	Miller (Wigan)................49	Lomas (Salford) 88	Lomas (Salford).............272
	Williams (Halifax) 49		
1909-10	Leytham (Wigan) 48	Carmichael (Hull K.R.)....78	Leytham (Wigan)...........232
1910-11	Kitchen (Huddersfield).....40	Carmichael (Hull K.R.)...129	Carmichael (Hull K.R.)...261
	Rosenfeld (Huddersfield) ..40		
	Miller (Wigan)................40		
1911-12	Rosenfeld (Huddersfield) ..78	Carmichael (Hull K.R.)...127	Carmichael (Hull K.R.)...254
1912-13	Rosenfeld (Huddersfield) ..56	Carmichael (Hull K.R.)....93	Thomas (Wigan)............198
1913-14	Rosenfeld (Huddersfield) ..80	Holland (Huddersfield) ...131	Holland (Huddersfield) ...268
1914-15	Rosenfeld (Huddersfield) ..56	Gronow (Huddersfield) ...136	Gronow (Huddersfield) ...284
• Competitive matches suspended during war years			
1918-19	Francis (Hull).................25	Kennedy (Hull) 54	Kennedy (Hull) 135
1919-20	Moorhouse (Huddersfield).39	Gronow (Huddersfield) ...148	Gronow (Huddersfield) ...332
1920-21	Stone (Hull)...................41	Kennedy (Hull) 108	Kennedy (Hull) 264
1921-22	Farrar (Oldham) 49	Sullivan (Wigan)............100	Farrar (Oldham) 213
1922-23	Ring (Wigan) 41	Sullivan (Wigan)............161	Sullivan (Wigan)............349
1923-24	Ring (Wigan) 49	Sullivan (Wigan)............158	Sullivan (Wigan)............319
1924-25	Ring (Wigan) 54	Sullivan (Wigan)............138	Sullivan (Wigan)............282
1925-26	Ring (Wigan) 63	Sullivan (Wigan)............131	Sullivan (Wigan)............274
1926-27	Ellaby (St. Helens) 55	Sullivan (Wigan)............149	Sullivan (Wigan)............322
1927-28	Ellaby (St. Helens) 37	Thompson (Leeds).........106	Thompson (Leeds).........233
1928-29	Brown (Wigan) 44	Sullivan (Wigan)............107	Sullivan (Wigan)............226
	Mills (Huddersfield).........44		
1929-30	Ellaby (St. Helens) 39	Thompson (Leeds).........111	Thompson (Leeds).........243
1930-31	Harris, E. (Leeds)...........58	Sullivan (Wigan)............133	Sullivan (Wigan)............278
1931-32	Mills (Huddersfield).........50	Sullivan (Wigan)............117	Sullivan (Wigan)............249
1932-33	Harris, E. (Leeds)...........57	Sullivan (Wigan)............146	Sullivan (Wigan)............307
1933-34	Brown (Salford) 45	Sullivan (Wigan)............193	Sullivan (Wigan)............404

	TRIES	GOALS	POINTS
1934-35	Morley (Wigan) 49	Sullivan (Wigan)............165	Sullivan (Wigan)............348
1935-36	Harris, E. (Leeds)...........63	Sullivan (Wigan)............117	Sullivan (Wigan)............246
1936-37	Harris, E. (Leeds)...........40	Sullivan (Wigan)............120	Sullivan (Wigan)............258
1937-38	Harris, E. (Leeds)...........45	Sullivan (Wigan)............135	Sullivan (Wigan)............285
1938-39	Markham (Huddersfield)...39	Sullivan (Wigan)............124	Risman (Salford)............267

● For the next six seasons emergency war-time competitions resulted in a reduction of matches and players were allowed to 'guest' for other clubs

	TRIES	GOALS	POINTS
1939-40	Batten (Hunslet) 38	Hodgson (Swinton)..........98	Hodgson (Swinton) 208
1940-41	Walters (Bradford N.)......32	Lockwood (Halifax) 70	Belshaw (Warrington) 174
1941-42	Francis (Barrow) 29	Lockwood (Halifax) 91	Lockwood (Halifax)........185
1942-43	Batten (Hunslet) 24	Lockwood (Halifax) 65	Lockwood (Halifax)........136
1943-44	Lawrenson (Wigan) 21	Horne (Barrow) 57	Horne (Barrow) 144
1944-45	Batten (Bradford N.)........41	Stott (Wakefield T.).........51	Stott (Wakefield T.) 129

● Normal peace-time rugby resumed

	TRIES	GOALS	POINTS
1945-46	Batten (Bradford N.)........35	Ledgard (Dewsbury)........88	Bawden (Huddersfield) ...239
1946-47	Bevan (Warrington) 48	Miller (Hull)................103	Bawden (Huddersfield) ...243
1947-48	Bevan (Warrington) 57	Ward (Wigan) 141	Ward (Wigan) 312
1948-49	Cooper (Huddersfield)......60	Ward (Wigan) 155	Ward (Wigan) 361
1949-50	Nordgren (Wigan) 57	Gee (Wigan) 133	Palin (Warrington) 290
		Palin (Warrington) 133	
1950-51	Bevan (Warrington) 68	Cook (Leeds) 155	Cook (Leeds) 332
1951-52	Cooper (Huddersfield)......71	Ledgard (Leigh) 142	Horne (Barrow) 313
1952-53	Bevan (Warrington) 72	Bath (Warrington)..........170	Bath (Warrington)..........379
1953-54	Bevan (Warrington) 67	Metcalfe (St. Helens)......153	Metcalfe (St. Helens)......369
		Bath (Warrington)..........153	
1954-55	Cooper (Huddersfield)......66	Ledgard (Leigh) 178	Ledgard (Leigh) 374
1955-56	McLean (Bradford N.) 61	Ledgard (Leigh) 155	Bath (Warrington)..........344
1956-57	Boston (Wigan)...............60	Jones (Leeds)................194	Jones (Leeds)................496
1957-58	Sullivan (Wigan) 50	Ganley (Oldham) 219	Ganley (Oldham) 453
1958-59	Vollenhoven (St. Helens) ..62	Ganley (Oldham) 190	Griffiths (Wigan) 394
1959-60	Vollenhoven (St. Helens) ..54	Rhodes (St. Helens) 171	Fox (Wakefield T.) 453
		Fox (Wakefield T.) 171	
1960-61	Vollenhoven (St. Helens) ..59	Rhodes (St. Helens) 145	Rhodes (St. Helens) 338
1961-62	Boston (Wigan)...............51	Fox (Wakefield T.) 183	Fox (Wakefield T.) 456
1962-63	Glastonbury (Work'ton T.)41	Coslett (St. Helens)........156	Coslett (St. Helens)........321
1963-64	Stopford (Swinton) 45	Coslett (St. Helens)........138	Fox (Wakefield T.) 313
1964-65	Lake (Wigan) 40	Kellett (Hull K.R.) 150	Killeen (St. Helens)........360
1965-66	Killeen (St. Helens).........32	Killeen (St. Helens)........120	Killeen (St. Helens)........336
	Lake (Wigan) 32		
1966-67	Young (Hull K.R.).........34	Risman (Leeds) 163	Killeen (St. Helens)........353
	Howe (Castleford) 34		
1967-68	Millward (Hull K.R.).......38	Risman (Leeds) 154	Risman (Leeds) 332
1968-69	Francis (Wigan)..............40	Risman (Leeds) 165	Risman (Leeds) 345
1969-70	Atkinson (Leeds).............38	Tyrer (Wigan)...............167	Tyrer (Wigan)...............385
1970-71	Haigh (Leeds) 40	Coslett (St. Helens)........183	Coslett (St. Helens)........375

LEADING SCORERS 1971-87

TRIES

1971-72

Atkinson (Leeds)	36
Lamb (Bradford N.)	36
Richards (Salford)	35
D. Redfearn (Bradford N.)	35
Sullivan (Hull)	33
Watkins (Salford)	29
Hardisty (Leeds)	27
Brown (Widnes)	27
O'Neill (Widnes)	25
Topliss (Wakefield T.)	24

1972-73

Atkinson (Leeds)	39
Richards (Salford)	38
Charlton (Salford)	33
Topliss (Wakefield T.)	30
Lowe (Hull K.R.)	29
Hardisty (Leeds)	28
A. Smith (Leeds)	28
Dunn (Hull K.R.)	27
D. Redfearn (Bradford N.)	27
N. Stephenson (Dewsbury)	26
Mathias (St. Helens)	26

1973-74

Fielding (Salford)	49
Mathias (St. Helens)	40
D. Smith (Wakefield T.)	38
Eckersley (St. Helens)	26
Fleay (Swinton)	26
Jones (St. Helens)	25
Wilson (St. Helens)	25
Watkins (Salford)	24
Atkinson (Leeds)	23
Lamb (Bradford N.)	22
A. Smith (Leeds)	22
Bevan (Warrington)	22
Ayres (Wigan)	22

1974-75

Dunn (Hull K.R.)	42
Fielding (Salford)	35
Bevan (Warrington)	31
A. Smith (Leeds)	30
Millward (Hull K.R.)	30
Atkinson (Leeds)	29
Richards (Salford)	28
Sullivan (Hull K.R.)	28
Mathias (St. Helens)	27
Dyl (Leeds)	26

1975-76

Richards (Salford)	37
Fielding (Salford)	33
Jones (St. Helens)	31
Briggs (Leigh)	27
D. Smith (Wakefield T.)	26
Burton (Castleford)	25
Clark (Hull)	23
Wright (Workington T.)	22
Barends (York)	21
Boxall (Hull)	21
Holmes (Leeds)	21
Mathias (St. Helens)	21
Butler (Salford)	21

1976-77

Wright (Widnes)	31
Burton (Castleford)	29
D. Smith (Leeds)	28
Fielding (Salford)	27
Dunn (Hull K.R.)	26
Cunningham (St. Helens)	26
Topliss (Wakefield T.)	24
Richards (Salford)	23
Mathias (St. Helens)	23
Barends (York)	22

1977-78

Wright (Widnes)	33
Fielding (Salford)	31
Cunningham (St. Helens)	30
Bevan (Warrington)	30
Fenton (Castleford)	30
Vigo (Wigan)	29
Glynn (St. Helens)	28
D. Smith (Leeds)	28
T. Morgan (York)	27
Burton (Castleford)	27

1978-79

Hartley (Hull K.R.)	35
Wright (Widnes)	28
Barends (Bradford N.)	25
Lowe (Hull K.R.)	25
Prendiville (Hull)	25
Fielding (Salford)	24
D. Redfearn (Bradford N.)	23
Mathias (St. Helens)	22
Bray (Hull)	21
O'Loughlin (Wigan)	21
Sullivan (Hull K.R.)	21

1979-80	
Fielding (Salford)	30
Hubbard (Hull K.R.)	30
Munro (Oldham)	29
Ball (Barrow)	27
Bentley (Widnes)	27
Glynn (St. Helens)	27
Mathias (St. Helens)	27
Bevan (Warrington)	26
D. Redfearn (Bradford N.)	26
D. Smith (Leeds)	24

1980-81	
Crossley (York)	35
Richardson (Castleford)	28
Hubbard (Hull K.R.)	25
Hartley (Hull K.R.)	23
McDermott (York)	23
Slater (Huddersfield)	23
Drummond (Leigh)	20
Ball (Barrow)	19
Bevan (Warrington)	19
Cramp (Huddersfield)	19
Hyde (Castleford)	19
Ramsdale (Wigan)	19

1981-82	
Jones (Workington T.)	31
Drummond (Leigh)	26
Basnett (Widnes)	26
Ashton (Oldham)	26
Morgan (Carlisle)	25
Hartley (Hull K.R.)	23
Hopkins (Workington T.)	23
Day (Hull)	23
Evans (Hull)	22
D. Hobbs (Featherstone R.)	21
Moll (Keighley)	21

1982-83	
Eccles (Warrington)	37
Evans (Hull)	28
Crossley (Fulham)	27
David (Cardiff C.)	26
Topliss (Hull)	24
M'Barki (Fulham)	23
Hyde (Castleford)	22
McDermott (York)	22
Leuluai (Hull)	21
Phil Ford (Warrington)	20
Clark (Hull K.R.)	20

1983-84	
Schofield (Hull)	38
Lydon (Widnes)	28
King (Hunslet)	28
Woods (Leigh)	27
Basnett (Widnes)	26
Gibson (Batley)	26
Herbert (Barrow)	25
Steadman (York)	25
Prohm (Hull K.R.)	25
Clark (Hull K.R.)	24

1984-85	
Hanley (Bradford N.)	55
Prohm (Hull K.R.)	45
Gill (Wigan)	34
Ledger (St. Helens)	30
Meninga (St. Helens)	28
Gibbin (Whitehaven)	27
Gibson (Batley)	26
G. Peacham (Carlisle)	25
Byrne (Salford)	25
Evans (Hull)	24
Ferguson (Wigan)	24

1985-86	
Halliwell (Leigh)	49
Hanley (Wigan)	38
Lister (Bramley)	34
Henderson (Leigh)	31
Frodsham (Blackpool B.)	30
Fox (Leigh)	29
Williams (Barrow)	27
Garrity (Runcorn H.)	24
Gibson (Leeds)	23
Beck (Workington T.)	23

1986-87	
Hanley (Wigan)	63
Schofield (Hull)	37
Gill (Wigan)	32
Bate (Swinton)	31
Ford (Bradford N.)	30
Henderson (Leigh)	27
Edwards (Wigan)	26
Johnson (Warrington)	25
Lydon (Wigan)	24
Dunn (Rochdale H.)	23
Ledger (St. Helens)	23
McCormack (St. Helens)	23

GOALS
(including drop goals)

1971-72

Coslett (St. Helens)	214
Watkins (Salford)	193
Tees (Bradford N.)	173
Dutton (Widnes)	120
Clawson (Hull K.R., Leeds)	120
Gowers (Swinton)	119
Tyrer (Wigan)	117
Larder (Oldham)	114
Whitehead (Warrington)	108
Maloney (York, Hull)	108

1972-73

Watkins (Salford)	221
Coslett (St. Helens)	162
Tees (Bradford N.)	160
Stephenson (Dewsbury)	149
C. Kellett (Featherstone R.)	139
Fox (Wakefield T.)	138
Whitehead (Warrington)	136
Larder (Oldham)	127
Jefferson (Keighley)	120
Quinn (York)	107

1973-74

Watkins (Salford)	183
Whitehead (Warrington)	168
Jefferson (Keighley)	165
Coslett (St. Helens)	134
Mumby (Bradford N.)	131
Dutton (Widnes)	129
Lloyd (Castleford)	121
Quinn (York)	112
Fiddler (Leigh)	111
Holliday (Rochdale H.)	107

1974-75

Fox (Hull K.R.)	146
Coslett (St. Helens)	129
Dutton (Widnes)	122
Lloyd (Castleford)	112
Quinn (York)	112
Hartley (Huddersfield)	110
MacCorquodale (Workington T.)	107
Marshall (Leeds)	107
Mumby (Bradford N.)	96
Fiddler (Salford, Leigh)	85

1975-76

Watkins (Salford)	175
Pimblett (St. Helens)	149
Lloyd (Castleford)	149

Dutton (Widnes)	148
Fairbairn (Wigan)	146
Stacey (Leigh)	137
MacCorquodale (Workington T.)	130
Fox (Hull K.R., York)	102
Marshall (Leeds)	101
Gaitley (New Hunslet)	100

1976-77

Lloyd (Castleford)	163
Quinn (Featherstone R.)	152
Pimblett (St. Helens)	152
Hesford (Warrington)	132
MacCorquodale (Workington T.)	128
Watkins (Salford)	125
Stephenson (Dewsbury)	106
Fairbairn (Wigan)	105
Dutton (Widnes)	97
Woods (Leigh)	90

1977-78

Pimblett (St. Helens)	178
Hesford (Warrington)	158
Woods (Leigh)	149
MacCorquodale (Workington T.)	138
Woods (Widnes)	122
Watkins (Salford)	110
Mumby (Bradford N.)	107
Lloyd (Castleford)	104
Fox (Bradford N.)	95
Oulton (Leeds)	80

1978-79

Lloyd (Hull)	172
Hesford (Warrington)	170
Burke (Widnes)	140
MacCorquodale (Workington T.)	114
Pimblett (St. Helens)	105
Beale (Keighley)	96
Woods (Leigh)	96
Birts (Halifax)	86
Fairbairn (Wigan)	86
Norton (Castleford)	82

1979-80

Quinn (Featherstone R.)	163
Hubbard (Hull K.R.)	138
Rule (Salford)	134
Hesford (Warrington)	128
Burke (Widnes)	127
Ball (Barrow)	119
Diamond (Wakefield T.)	116
Fitzsimons (Oldham)	108
Parrish (Hunslet)	98
Birts (Halifax)	97

1980-81
Hesford (Warrington)......................................147
Quinn (Featherstone R.)..................................123
Diamond (Wakefield T.)..................................112
Burke (Widnes) 110
Hubbard (Hull K.R.)......................................109
Ball (Barrow)..104
Birts (Halifax) 100
Beale (Keighley).. 97
Parrish (Oldham) 95
Fairbairn (Wigan)... 94

1981-82
Hopkins (Workington T.) 190
Fairbairn (Hull K.R.) 168
Parrish (Oldham) 164
Woods (Leigh) 158
Rule (Salford) 130
Dick (Leeds) 125
Quinn (Featherstone R.) 120
Agar (Halifax) 119
Crooks (Hull) 118
Hesford (Warrington)....................................116

1982-83
Diamond (Fulham)..136
Fitzsimons (Hunslet).....................................121
Crooks (Hull)...120
R. Beardmore (Castleford)..............................117
Hesford (Warrington)....................................113
Fenwick (Cardiff C.)......................................111
Jones (Swinton)..110
Whitfield (Wigan)...104
Kilner (Bramley)...104
Quinn (Featherstone R.) 98

1983-84
Hesford (Warrington)....................................142
R. Beardmore (Castleford)..............................142
Hallett (Cardiff C.) 140
Fitzsimons (Hunslet).....................................131
Woods (Leigh) 124
Whitfield (Wigan) 122
Ball (Barrow)...104
Parrish (Oldham) 101
Agar (Halifax) 94
Tickle (Barrow) 91

1984-85
Day (St. Helens)...157
Fairbairn (Hull K.R.) 141
Wood (Runcorn H.) 126
Steadman (York)...122
Griffiths (Salford) 118
Parrish (Oldham) 117
Schofield (Hull) 105
Creasser (Leeds) 102
Agar (Halifax) 87
Jones (Swinton) 87

1985-86
C. Johnson (Leigh)..173
Stephenson (Wigan).......................................128
Noble (Doncaster)...118
Harcombe (Rochdale H.) 115
Kilner (Bramley)ᴵ..110
Dorahy (Hull K.R.).......................................101
Woods (Bradford N.)..................................... 98
Creasser (Leeds).∶... 84
Carroll (Carlisle) 83
Smith (Workington T.)................................... 83

1986-87
Loughlin (St. Helens) 190
Bishop (Warrington)......................................117
Noble (Doncaster)...114
Whitfield (Halifax)..109
Platt (Hunslet)...102
Topping (Swinton) 100
C. Johnson (Leigh) 86
Ketteridge (Castleford) 80
Wood (Rochdale H.)...................................... 80
Quinn (Featherstone R.) 77

DROP GOALS

1974-75 Seabourne (Bradford N.) 10
1975-76 Hancock (Hull)......................................10
1976-77 N. Stephenson (Dewsbury) 16
1977-78 Fiddler (Bramley, Leigh) 10
1978-79 Turley (Blackpool B.) 18
1979-80 Dean (Hunslet) 18
1980-81 Walker (Whitehaven) 22
1981-82 Agar (Halifax) 17
          Donlan (Leigh) 17
1982-83 Pinner (St. Helens).................................13
1983-84 Hallett (Cardiff C.) 29
1984-85 Wood (Runcorn H.) 28
1985-86 Bishop (Warrington) 13
1986-87 Platt (Mansfield M.) 18

POINTS

1971-72 Watkins (Salford)..................................473
1972-73 Watkins (Salford)..................................493
1973-74 Watkins (Salford)..................................438
1974-75 Fox (Hull K.R.).....................................333
1975-76 Watkins (Salford)..................................385
1976-77 Lloyd (Castleford)..................................341
1977-78 Pimblett (St. Helens)..............................381
1978-79 Lloyd (Hull)...373
1979-80 Quinn (Featherstone R.)..........................375
1980-81 Hesford (Warrington)..............................310
1981-82 Hopkins (Workington T.)..........................446
1982-83 Diamond (Fulham) 308
1983-84 Woods (Leigh) 355
1984-85 Day (St. Helens)....................................362
1985-86 C. Johnson (Leigh) 400
1986-87 Loughlin (St. Helens)..............................424

ALL TIME RECORDS

Most goals in a match:
22 by Jim Sullivan (Wigan) v. Flimby & Fothergill (Challenge Cup), 14th February 1925

Most goals in a season:
DAVID WATKINS holds the record for most goals in a season with 221 — all for Salford — in 1972-73. Watkins played and scored a goal in every match that season as follows:

1972

Aug.	19	Leeds ....(H)	5	
	23	Featherstone R. ....(A)	3	
	26	Whitehaven.............................(A)	4	
	28	Swinton ....(H)	1	
Sept.	1	Oldham ....(LC) (H)	10	
	9	Leeds....................................(A)	2	
	15	Rochdale H. ....(LC) (H)	11	
	17	Leigh....................................(A)	6	
	24	Barrow............................(JP) (A)	4	
	29	Huyton ....(H)	10	
Oct.	3	Oldham........................(FT) (A)	4	
	6	Wigan..........................(LC) (A)	4	
	8	Blackpool B. ....(A)	5	
	13	Blackpool B. .... (H)	8	
	21	Swinton..........................(LCF)	5	
Nov.	5	Huyton ....(A)	8	
	10	Rochdale H. .... (H)	6	
	17	Warrington ....(A)	4	
	19	New Zealand..........................(H)	10	
	24	Dewsbury ....(JP) (H)	4	
	26	Workington T. ....(H)	6	
Dec.	1	Barrow..................................(H)	9	
	10	Bradford N. ....(JP) (H)	9	
	13	Oldham..................................(A)	4	
	15	Leigh ....(H)	3	
	24	Bradford N. ....(A)	5	
	26	Workington T. ....(A)	3	
	30	Hull K.R. ....(JP) (A)	5	

1973

Jan.	3	Bradford N...........................(H)	6	
	7	Rochdale H. ....(A)	2	
	12	Featherstone R. ....(H)	4	
	28	Featherstone R..........(RL Cup) (A)	4	
Feb.	2	Whitehaven............................(H)	4	
	11	Barrow..................................(A)	5	
	23	St. Helens ....(H)	3	
Mar.	7	Widnes.................................(A)	3	
	9	Dewsbury..............................(H)	3	
	16	St. Helens ....(A)	2	
	24	Leeds...............................(JP Final)	2	
	30	Warrington ....(H)	1	
Apr.	6	Widnes.................................(H)	4	
	13	Oldham................................(H)	3	
	15	Dewsbury ....(A)	2	

	17	Wigan...................................(A)	3	
	20	Swinton................................(A)	7	
	23	Wigan...................................(H)	3	
	29	Rochdale H. ....(top 16) (H)	2	

	App	Gls
League	34	147
Lancs Cup................................	4	30
John Player..............................	5	24
Tour match	1	10
RL Cup	1	4
Floodlit Cup	1	4
Top 16	1	2
Totals	**47**	**221**

Fastest goals century:
Three players share the record of scoring the fastest 100 goals from the start of a season in terms of number of matches played. They are Bernard Ganley, David Watkins and Steve Quinn, who achieved the century in 18 matches.

Ganley reached 100 goals on 16 November 1957, after playing 17 matches for Oldham and one for Great Britain.

Watkins scored his 100th goal on 17 November 1972, all for Salford.

Quinn scored his 100th goal on 16 December 1979, all for Featherstone Rovers.

Most goals in a career:
JIM SULLIVAN holds the record for most goals in a career with 2,867 between 1921-22 and 1945-46. He scored a century of goals in every season after leaving Welsh Rugby Union for Wigan until the War interrupted the 1939-40 campaign.

The Test full back played all of his club rugby for Wigan apart from War-time appearances with Bradford Northern, Dewsbury and Keighley.

Sullivan's total includes 441 in representative matches, including three tours of Australasia. These figures are accepted by the Record Keepers' Club following research by James Carter and Malcolm Bentley.

Most one-point drop goals in a match:
5 by Danny Wilson (Swinton) v. Hunslet (John Player Special), 6 November 1983.
    Peter Wood (Runcorn H.) v.Batley, 21 October 1984.
    Paul Bishop (Warrington) at Wigan (Premiership semi-final), 11 May 1986.

Most one-point drop goals in a season:
29 by Lyn Hallett (Cardiff C.).....................1983-84

Most one-point drop goals in a career:
85 by Norman Turley (Warrington, Runcorn H., Swinton, Blackpool B., Rochdale H., Barrow, Workington T.) 1974-88

111

Most tries in a match:
11 by George West (Hull K.R.) v Brookland Rovers
Challenge Cup ....4 March 1905

Most tries in a career:
BRIAN BEVAN holds the record for most tries in a career
with 796 between 1946 and 1964. His season-by-season
record is:

1946-47	48
1947-48	57
1948-49	56
1949-50	33
1950-51	68
1951-52	51
1952-53	72
1953-54	67
1954-55	63
1955-56	57
1956-57	17
1957-58	46
1958-59	54
1959-60	40
1960-61	35
1961-62	15
1962-63	10
1963-64	7

Totals

Warrington	740
Blackpool Borough	17
Other Nationalities	26
Other representative matches	13
Grand Total	**796**

The Australian winger played his first game for
Warrington on 17 November 1945 and his last on 23 April
1962 before having two seasons at Blackpool Borough.
His last match for Borough was on 22 February, 1964.

Most tries in a season:
ALBERT ROSENFELD holds the record for most tries
in a season with 80 — all for Huddersfield — in 1913-14.

Rosenfeld's match-by-match record:

1913

Sept.	6	York......................................(A)	4
	8	Warrington ....(H)	2
	13	Leeds ....(H)	5
	20	Halifax.................................(A)	1
	27	Batley..................................(A)	0
Oct.	4	Oldham.................................(H)	2
	11	Rochdale H..........................(A)	0
	18	Bramley.......................(YC) (H)	2
	25	Dewsbury.............................(A)	4
Nov.	1	Halifax.......................(YC) (A)	2
	8	Wigan..................................(A)	1
	15	Dewsbury ....(YC) (H)	3

	19	Bradford N............................(H)	3
	22	Leeds....................................(A)	3
	29	Bradford N.............(Halifax, YCF)	1
Dec.	3	Halifax.................................(H)	3
	6	Hunslet................................(A)	2
	13	Rochdale H. ....(H)	3
	20	Hull K.R..............................(A)	2
	25	Hull ....(A)	1
	26	Wakefield T...........................(H)	3
	27	Hunslet.................................(H)	0
1914			
Jan.	1	St. Helens............................(A)	0
	3	Warrington ....(A)	0
	10	York ....(H)	3
	17	Keighley..............................(A)	2
	24	Dewsbury..............................(H)	1
	31	Batley..................................(H)	0
Feb.	7	Oldham.................................(A)	0
	14	Bramley................................(H)	5
	21	Wigan..................................(H)	3
	28	Swinton Park R..........(RL Cup) (H)	7
Mar.	7	Wakefield T...........................(A)	2
	14	Hull K.R. ....(RL Cup) (A)	2
	18	Bramley................................(A)	3
	21	Widnes ....(RL Cup) (H)	0
	25	Keighley ....(H)	3
	28	Hull K.R. ....(H)	1
	30	Bradford N. ....(A)	1
Apr.	4	Hull................(Leeds, RL Cup SF)	0
	11	Hull.....................(H) did not play	
	13	St. Helens ....(H)	0
	20	Hull ....(Play-off) (H) did not play	
	25	Salford ..(Leeds, Championship final)	0

	App	Tries
League	33	63
Yorks Cup................................	4	8
RL Cup...................................	4	9
Play Off	1	0
Totals	**42**	**80**

Most points in a season:
LEWIS JONES holds the record for most points in a
season with 496 from 194 goals and 36 tries for Leeds and
representative teams in 1956-57.

Jones' match-by-match record:

For Leeds

1956

			Gls	Tries	Pts
Aug.	17	Halifax ....(H)	3	0	6
	22	Bradford N.................(A)	11	3	31
	25	Wigan ....(A)	4	0	8
	27	Featherstone R............(H)	4	1	11
Sept.	1	Wakefield ....(YC) (A)	3	1	9
	8	Dewsbury ....(A)	6	0	12
	15	Warrington ....(H)	7	0	14
	22	Huddersfield...............(A)	3	0	6
	29	York.........................(H)	6	0	12

Oct.	6	Batley.........................(A)	4	2	14
	13	Australia.....................(H)	Did not play		
	20	Hull K.R. ....(A)	Did not play		
	27	Wigan ....(H)	2	0	4
Nov.	3	Hunslet ....(A)	1	0	2
	10	Barrow ....(H)	3	2	12
	17	Halifax ....(A)	4	0	8
	24	Keighley.....................(H)	3	3	15
Dec.	1	Barrow ....(A)	4	0	8
	8	Bramley......................(A)	5	0	10
	15	Doncaster ....(H)	1	2	8
	22	Bradford N (abandoned) (H)	1	1	5
	25	Batley........................(H)	8	1	19
	29	Keighley ....(A)	3	0	6
1957					
Jan.	5	Hull ....(H)	5	2	16
	12	Warrington..................(A)	0	3	9
	19	St. Helens...................(H)	5	1	13
	26	Doncaster...................(A)	Did not play		
Feb.	2	Huddersfield................(H)	6	0	12
	9	Wigan ....(RL Cup) (H)	2	1	7
	16	York ....(A)	7	1	17
	23	Warrington....(RL Cup) (H)	5	1	13
	27	Castleford...................(H)	4	1	11
Mar.	9	Halifax ....(RL Cup) (A)	5	0	10
	16	Wakefield T................(H)	5	1	13
	20	Bradford N ....(H)	5	1	13
	23	Hull...........................(A)	2	0	4
	30	Whitehaven ....(Odsal, RL Cup SF)	1	0	2
Apr.	3	Wakefield T. ....(A)	3	0	6
	6	St. Helens...................(A)	0	0	0
	12	Hull K.R....................(H)	Did not play		
	13	Dewsbury ....(H)	6	2	18
	19	Hunslet ....(H)	5	2	16
	20	Featherstone R.............(A)	2	0	4
	22	Castleford...................(A)	2	0	4
	23	Bramley......................(H)	7	1	17
May	4	Oldham ....(Play-off) (A)	3	0	6
	11	Barrow ...(Wembley, RL Cup final)	0	0	0

Representative matches
For Great Britain:

Jan.	26	France...............(at Leeds)	9	1	21
Mar.	3	France..........(at Toulouse)	5	1	13
Apr.	10	France........(at St. Helens)	7	1	17

For The Rest:

| Oct. | 3 | Britain XIII .....(at Bradford) | 4 | 0 | 8 |

For RL XIII:

| Oct. | 29 | Australia................(Leigh) | 3 | 0 | 6 |

	App	Gls	Tries	Pts
League	36	147	30	384
RL Cup.............................	5	13	2	32
Yorks Cup............................	1	3	1	9
Play-off.............................	1	3	0	6
Representative......................	5	28	3	65
Totals...............................	**48**	**194**	**36**	**496**

Most points in a match:
53 (11t, 10g) by George West (Hull K.R.) v. Brookland Rovers (RL Cup)..............................4 March, 1905

Most points in a career:
NEIL FOX holds the record for most points in a career with 6,220 between 1956 and 1979. This total does not include points scored during a spell of club rugby in New Zealand.

Fox was a month short of his 17th birthday when he made his debut for Wakefield Trinity on 10 April, 1956. Apart from a brief time at Bradford Northern Fox had 19 seasons at Wakefield before moving to a succession of clubs in later years.

After a long career as an international centre Fox moved into the forwards and played his last professional match for Bradford in their opening fixture of the 1979-80 season, on 19 August. That match enabled him to join the elite few who have played first team rugby at 40 years of age.

Fox's season-by-season tally is as follows:

	Gls	Tries	Pts
1955-56.............................	6	0	12
1956-57.............................	54	10	138
1957-58.............................	124	32	344
1958-59.............................	148	28	380
1959-60.............................	171	37	453
1960-61.............................	94	20	248
1961-62.............................	183	30	456
1962 Tour			
Australasia..........................	85	19	227
South Africa	19	4	50
1962-63.............................	125	14	292
1963-64.............................	125	21	313
1964-65.............................	121	13	281
1965-66.............................	98	11	229
1966-67.............................	144	16	336
1967-68.............................	98	18	250
1968-69.............................	95	9	217
1969-70.............................	17	5	49
1970-71.............................	110	12	256
1971-72.............................	84	6	186
1972-73.............................	138	8	300
1973-74.............................	62	8	148
1974-75.............................	146(1)	14	333
1975-76.............................	102(1)	4	215
1976-77.............................	79(1)	6	175
1977-78.............................	95(1)	9	216
1978-79.............................	50	4	112
1979-80.............................	2	0	4

A breakdown of Fox's club and representative totals is as follows:

	App	Gls	Tries	Pts
Wakefield T.	574	1,836	272	4,488
Bradford N.	70	85(1)	12	205
Hull K.R.	59	212(2)	16	470
York	13	42	2	90
Bramley....................	23	73	6	164
Huddersfield..............	21	73(1)	5	160
Club Totals	**760**	**2,321(4)**	**313**	**5,577**

113

RECORDS

			(cont)
Yorkshire..................	17	60	9	147
Britain v. Australia	8	26	3	61
New Zealand.	4	11	1	25
France.........	17	56	10	142
Other representative games including tour	22	101	22	268
Representative Totals.	**68**	**254**	**45**	**643**
Grand Totals	**828**	**2,575(4)**	**358**	**6,220**

( ) Figures in brackets are one point drop goals included in total.

Score-a-match:
The following players have appeared and scored in all of their club's matches in one season:

Jim Hoey (Widnes) 1932-33
Billy Langton (Hunslet) 1958-59
Stuart Ferguson (Leigh) 1970-71
David Watkins (Salford)..............................1972-73
David Watkins (Salford)..............................1973-74
John Woods (Leigh)...................................1977-78
Steve Quinn (Featherstone R.) 1979-80
Mick Parrish (Hunslet) 1979-80
John Gorton (Swinton)..............................1980-81
Mick Parrish (Oldham) 1981-82
Peter Wood (Runcorn H.) 1984-85
David Noble (Doncaster)............................1986-87

Longest scoring run:
DAVID WATKINS holds the record for the longest scoring run, playing and scoring in 92 consecutive matches for Salford from 19 August 1972 to 25 April 1974. He totalled 403 goals, 41 tries and 929 points.

Longest run of appearances:
KEITH ELWELL holds the record for the longest run of appearances with one club with a total of 239 for Widnes. The consecutive run started at Wembley in the 1977 Challenge Cup final against Leeds on 7 May, and ended after he played in a Lancashire Cup-tie at home to St. Helens on 5 September 1982. He was dropped for the match at Featherstone Rovers a week later. Although he went on as a substitute the record refers to full appearances only.
Elwell played as a substitute in the next match and then made a full appearance before his run of all appearances ended at 242.

Highest score:
Huddersfield 119 v. Swinton Park 2 (RL Cup)
.......28 February 1914

Most points in all matches in a season:
1,436 by Leigh from 43 matches in 1985-86 as follows:
34 Division Two matches 1,156
2 Lancashire Cup... 54
4 John Player Special Trophy 161
3 RL Challenge Cup..................................... 65

1,000 points in a League season:
1,156 by Leigh from 34 Division Two matches in 1985-86.
1,126 by Barrow from 34 Division Two matches in 1983-84
1,005 by St. Helens from 38 matches in one-league system in 1958-59.

Longest winning run:
29 by Wigan from February to October, 1987, as follows:
20 Division One, 3 Premiership, 4 Lancashire Cup, Charity Shield and World Club Challenge.

Longest unbeaten run:
38 Cup and League matches by Huddersfield in 1914-15, including three draws. After the interruption by the First World War Huddersfield won their next five competitive matches — 4 Yorkshire Cup ties in 1918-19 and the opening league match of 1919-20.

Longest winning run in the League:
31 matches by Wigan. Last 8 matches of 1969-70 and first 23 of 1970-71.
● In 1978-79 Hull won all of their 26 Division Two matches, the only time a club has won all its league matches in one season.

Longest League losing run:
40 Division Two matches by Doncaster between November 1975 and April 1977. This period included a run of 37 Cup and League defeats.
● In 1906-07 Liverpool City lost all 30 of their league matches, the only time a team playing more than 12 league matches has lost them all. Liverpool also lost their two cup ties and dropped out after only one season. Liverpool did manage a home league draw against Bramley but when they were unable to fulfil a return fixture the match was expunged from league records.

Shaun Edwards, Wembley's youngest ever captain, holds up the Cup watched by Wigan colleague Joe Lydon.

CUPS

RUGBY LEAGUE CHALLENGE CUP

1988 Final

Wigan coach Graham Lowe completed his collection of winners medals in a two-season stay at Central Park by spoiling Halifax supremo Chris Anderson's farewell party.

The Riversiders staged a celebration of their own ... with a display of champagne football to establish a record eighth victory at Wembley. Only Halifax's never-say-die spirit and lack of a reliable goalkicker denied Wigan the record score in a Challenge Cup final.

Six minutes after the interval, Wigan were leading 26-0 and looking certain to surpass the 38 points piled up by Wakefield Trinity in 1960. But the Thrum Hall side rallied in the final 34 minutes, scoring two tries one to keep the margin to 32-12, the 30-point barrier having been broken in a Challenge Cup final for only the fifth time, Wigan having also performed the feat in 1959 against Hull.

Wigan ran in seven tries, several of the touchdowns being of vintage quality. Only two goals were added by a trio of marksmen. Full back Joe Lydon hit the target once from three attempts, Andy Gregory once from two shots, while winger Henderson Gill missed both his attempts.

Gregory was an overwhelming winner of the Lance Todd Trophy as Man of the Match with a dominating scrum-half performance.

After three successive Wembley nail-biting thrillers, the 1988 Silk Cut Challenge Cup final lacked drama but more than compensated with a display of attacking prowess by Britain's glamour club.

The game was also a credit to the discipline of both sides who conceded just four penalties each to give Fred Lindop a happy farewell in his last game as a senior referee.

The opening quarter was scoreless with both sides in a fidgety, fitful mood. Underdogs Halifax were dealt a severe blow in the 20th minute when £65,000 club record signing and pack inspiration Les Holliday had to leave the field with knee ligament trouble, being replaced by veteran Mick Scott. His departure coincided with a change of plan by Wigan as they went on all out attack.

Shaun Edwards, the youngest Wembley captain at just over 21 years 6 months, sprinted into the open to be hauled down within feet of the Halifax line, New Zealand Test centre Kevin Iro powering his way over from acting half back to open the scoring after 27 minutes. After a dull start, the final was all but over in the next 11 minutes.

With scrum half Gregory calling all the shots, Wigan moved into overdrive and cruised to a 16-0 half-time lead. Great Britain wingman Gill scored the second try in the 32nd minute despite the gallant efforts of covering scrum half Steve Robinson. Two minutes later Kevin Iro added his second touchdown after a break by older brother Tony.

Two minutes before the break Lydon, taking the full back role in the absence of the injured Steve Hampson who was missing his third Wembley with a broken limb, touched down after a breathtaking exchange of passes engineered from a Gregory break and an Edwards pivot move.

Pocket battleship Gregory continued to dominate proceedings after the interval, floating a pass to right winger Tony Iro in the 45th minute to allow the New Zealander to stroll in at the corner.

Then came the try of the match ... if not the season. From the kick off, Lydon set off on one of his now famous long runs, cleaving through the Halifax defence on a 60-yard sprint before passing inside to loose forward Ellery Hanley who galloped ahead of blue-and-white defenders to touch down between the posts. There was an extra cheer from the Wigan fans as Gregory added their first goal of the afternoon to push the score to 26-0 after 46 minutes.

With the Challenge Cup record book under threat, Halifax, now destined to become the sixth club in the last 15 years to lose at Wembley 12 months after lifting the Cup, staged a rally. Australian Tony Anderson raced in at the corner for his eighth try of the tournament after strong work by co-centre Ian Wilkinson, celebrating his call up for the Great Britain tour Down Under two days earlier.

New Zealand Test centre Dean Bell touched down in the 65th minute following non-chalant and somewhat fortunate approach work by Hanley, Lydon adding the goal. The last score belonged to Halifax with a Neil James try and Whitfield goal, bringing some respectability to Chris Anderson's last match in charge after a three and a half year reign which had brought Thrum Hall the Championship Trophy and the Challenge Cup, plus runners-up spots at Wembley and in the Premiership.

As per the modern tradition, the 1988 final featured an Antipodean influence. Halifax fielded a record five Australians in captain Graham Eadie, fellow backs Martin Meredith, Tony Anderson, Bob Grogan and pack-man Keith Neller, while Wigan were served by four New Zealanders in Tony and Kevin Iro, Bell and prop forward Adrian Shelford, who escaped an automatic one-match suspension by the League's Disciplinary Committee only two days earlier by not having a sin-bin dismissal recorded. The nine-man contingent fell one short of equalling the 10 overseas players used in the 1985 final between Wigan and Hull.

A capacity crowd of 94,273 paid a world record £1,102,247 to witness Wigan's supreme show to round off coach Lowe's medal collection since his arrival at Central Park in August 1986, his tally being extended to the Challenge Cup, the Championship, the Premiership, the John Player Special Trophy, the Lancashire Cup twice and the Okells Charity Shield.

Ironically, one of the happiest coaches in the stadium was Great Britain's Malcolm Reilly who, after a series of setbacks with his touring party, watched world class displays by Edwards and Lydon, but particularly from Gregory, who maintained an unbeaten record on his fourth appearance at Wembley.

Wigan's four New Zealanders Kevin Iro, Adrian Shelford, Tony Iro and Dean Bell parade round Wembley.

SILK CUT CHALLENGE CUP FINAL

30th April   **Wembley**

HALIFAX 12		WIGAN 32
Graham Eadie, Capt.	1.	Joe Lydon
Martin Meredith	2.	Tony Iro
Tony Anderson	3.	Kevin Iro
Ian Wilkinson	4.	Dean Bell
Colin Whitfield	5.	Henderson Gill
Bob Grogan	6.	Shaun Edwards, Capt.
Steve Robinson	7.	Andy Gregory
Neil James	8.	Brian Case
Seamus McCallion	9.	Nicky Kiss
Keith Neller	10.	Adrian Shelford
Les Holliday	11.	Andy Goodway
Paul Dixon	12.	Ian Potter
John Pendlebury	13.	Ellery Hanley
Dick Fairbank	14.	Ged Byrne
Mick Scott	15.	Shaun Wane

T: Anderson, James
G: Whitfield (2)
Substitutions:
Scott for Holliday (20 min.)
Fairbank for Robinson (46 min.)
Half-time: 0-16
Referee: Fred Lindop (Wakefield)

T: K. Iro (2), T. Iro, Lydon,
    Hanley, Bell, Gill
G: Gregory, Lydon
Substitutions:
Byrne for Edwards (74 min.)
Wane for Potter (76 min.)
Attendance: 94,273
Receipts: £1,102,247

Scorechart

		Scoreline	
Minute	Score	Halifax	Wigan
27:	K. Iro (T)	0	4
32:	Gill (T)	0	8
34:	K. Iro (T)	0	12
38:	Lydon (T)	0	16
45	T. Iro (T)	0	20
46:	Hanley (T)		
	Gregory (G)	0	26
53:	Anderson (T)		
	Whitfield (G)	6	26
65:	Bell (T)		
	Lydon (G)	6	32
67:	James (T)		
	Whitfield (G)	12	32
	Scrums	7	5
	Penalties	4	4

Lance Todd Trophy winner Andy Gregory hugs the cup.

Wigan's Joe Lydon breaks away to set up a great try for Ellery Hanley. Martin Meredith is in vain pursuit.

Shaun Edwards confronted by Halifax's Graham Eadie.

1988 Round by Round

In the six-tie preliminary round, the amateur game was represented by Cumbria Cup winners Kells, Lancashire Cup victors Leigh Miners Welfare, Yorkshire Cup holders West Hull and Slalom Lager National League title holders Heworth. Kells entertained Leeds in front of nearly 6,000 spectators at Whitehaven's Recreation Ground, the visitors running in six tries in a 28-0 success, scrum half John Lyons earning the Silk Cut Award as Man of the Match. Leigh Miners played hosts to Hunslet at Leigh's Hilton Park, the Man of the Match honour going to Tony Dowling who dominated the scrums for the amateurs and gave a non-stop performance in the loose. Victory, however, went to the First Division visitors by 23-4, although it took 22 minutes to break the deadlock before running in four tries, Welfare's reply being a late try from player-coach John Cooke. In an all amateur clash West Hull travelled to York's Wiggington Road ground to meet Heworth, who recorded an 11-4 victory with second row man Andy Smith taking the Silk Cut Award. Sheffield Eagles followed up a recent league win at Bramley with a 14-6 success at McLaren Field, leading 4-0 at the break and tries from Paul McDermott and Steve Lidbury sealing a passage into the first round. Warrington disposed of Second Division Huddersfield Barracudas 48-10 at a mudbound Wilderspool, stand off John Woods contributing 20 points, including his 100th goal of the season. At Carlisle, Cumbrian rivals Whitehaven led with five minutes to go, their two tries coming from David Lightfoot and Rob Ackerman. A Paul Lithgow touchdown forced an 8-8 draw, the replay at Whitehaven three days later producing a 22-8 triumph for Carlisle, with two tries in less than five minutes from centre Steve Mills and winger Colin Coles confirming the visitors' supremacy.

In the first round, favourites Wigan beat fellow Championship title contenders Bradford Northern 2-0 in a dour televised tie at Central Park. Joe Lydon broke the deadlock with a controversial 39th minute penalty goal, awarded after the intervention of a touch judge, full back Steve Hampson taking the Silk Cut Award for an outstanding performance. Holders St. Helens travelled to Leigh to record a 22-12 success after the Hilton Park outfit led 10-6 at half-time with two John Kerr tries. Opposing packmen Andy Platt and Tony Cottrell were sent off before Saints secured victory with tries from Les Quirk, Phil Veivers and Mark Elia. Amateur hopes Heworth were hammered out of the competition 60-4 by 1987 Cup winners Halifax on York's Wiggington Road ground. The Thrum Hall side ran in 11 tries and had four disallowed, winger Wilf George grabbing four touchdowns. In a Manchester derby, Salford beat Swinton 16-6 at the Willows, the scores being pegged at six-apiece until Mick Worrall powered his way over midway through the second half, former Swinton winger Ken Jones adding four goals. League leaders Widnes visited bottom of the Second Division side Dewsbury and recorded a 38-10 victory, two tries inside eight minutes from Great Britain winger Martin Offiah inspiring the Chemics to a 28-0 interval lead. Ever-improving Sheffield Eagles provided the upset of the round by winning 14-10 at Wakefield Trinity. With only 13 minutes left, Trinity full back Kevin Harcombe landed his third penalty goal to put them ahead 10-8. Six minutes from the end, visiting hooker Mick Cook scored a try under the posts, Ron Rafferty adding the goal. Warrington gained revenge for their John Player Special Trophy quarter-final exit by Oldham with a 17-6 victory at Wilderspool. The Wire put the visitors under siege from the kick off, although Oldham contributed the try of the match from winger Paul Ford, playing only his second senior game. Leeds and Castleford provided a five star show for a Headingley crowd of 14,716, Great Britain second row man Paul Medley powering his way over for a hat-trick of tries. The biggest crowd of the day was spellbound as Castleford fought back from 16-4 at half-time to get within two points of the Loiners after 12 minutes of the restart.

Batley full back Paul Storey celebrated his 200th appearance for the club by scoring a try after nine minutes at Doncaster, home hooker Mark Gibbons paving the way for a 18-10 home victory with two opportunist first half tries. Featherstone Rovers stretched their winning run to nine matches with a 32-21 success over York at Post Office Road, highlighted by outstanding performances from packmen Karl Harrison and Peter Smith, although York trailed by only five points after 51 minutes. Veteran forward Billy Platt gained the Silk Cut Award in Mansfield Marksman's 16-4 victory at Fulham, while Second Division Carlisle made Hull K.R. work hard for a 14-6 triumph at Craven Park. Half back Wayne Parker's two tries sealed the Robins' success after Brian Tunstall's third goal on the hour left the Cumbrians trailing only 8-6. Welshman Gary Pearce provided the platform for Hull's 27-10 victory at Hunslet, contributing three goals and a drop goal and creating a try to give the Airlie Birds an 11-2 lead after 17 minutes. Keighley put on their best display of the season to dispose of Workington Town 30-4 at Lawkholme Lane. Centre Ian Bragger opened the scoring after only 51 seconds, Keighley building up a 24-0 half-time lead with prop Brendan White earning the Silk Cut Award. Rochdale Hornets entertained Barrow and held a 6-0 lead until the dying seconds when the Cumbrian's Steve Lowden scored a try but could not add the equalling goal. Runcorn Highfield squandered a host of chances to suffer a fourth successive defeat, Springfield Borough recording an 8-6 away success.

In the second round, more than 25,000 fans saw Wigan dispose of Leeds 30-14 at Central Park. The Loiners led 10-0 inside 12 minutes before the home side rallied to lead 12-10 after 27 minutes. Then Wigan sealed victory with a burst of four tries in a 10-minute spell spanning the break. Tony Iro (twice), Richard Russell and Hampson were the scorers, leaving the Riversiders leading 30-10, Leeds skipper Peter Tunks adding a consolation try in the 72nd minute. In the televised tie, St. Helens gained a last gasp 24-20 victory at Warrington, Great Britain forward John Fieldhouse celebrating his return from a second long lay off with two tries, the second being the match clincher two minutes from time. Warrington assistant coach Les Boyd announced his retirement immediately after the game, suffering a broken arm for the second time in the season. Springfield Borough full back Mile Smith missed a comfortable last minute penalty goal attempt at Salford to deny the Wigan-based side a replay. Salford went through 12-10 after trailing 10-2 with only 14 minutes left. Keiron O'Loughlin and Man of the Match Steve Gibson scored tries and Ken Jones kicked a goal to edge the home side ahead before Smith's miss from 30 yards out. Holders Halifax gained a 30-6 triumph over Second Division Rochdale Hornets at Thrum Hall, taking a 12-0 lead before complacency allowed Hornets to reply with a Dean Williams try and David Wood goal. After the interval Halifax were inspired by Silk Cut Award winner Tony Anderson who made a try for fellow Australian Keith Neller before completing his own hat trick.

Second Division Featherstone Rovers staged a remarkable comeback at Hull K.R. after the Robins had romped to a 25-2 lead inside 24 minutes only to go down 35-26. Second half tries from Deryck Fox, Peter Smith and Chris Bibb brought the Colliers to within three points of the home side who responded in injury time with a try from winger Ray Stead, Man of the Match Mike Fletcher adding the touchline goal kick for a personal tally of 18 points. Across the city, Hull held off the challenge of battling Second Division opponents Sheffield Eagles to record a 26-6 success. Welshman Pearce opened the scoring with a 12th minute penalty goal, before creating a try for James Leuluai, Man of the Match David Brooks adding a touchdown for a 12-0 interval lead. Pearce created a try for Stuart Vass, adding the goal, before the Eagles opened their account with a Gary Smith try and Rafferty goal, Hull rounding off the scoring with tries from Pearce and winger Pepi Brand. Keighley took the lead against top of the table Widnes at Lawkholme Lane with an eighth minute penalty goal from Carl Hirst, tries from Rick Thackray and Dale Shearer giving the Chemics an 8-0 interval lead. In the second half, Keighley enjoyed 90 per cent of the possession but it was Widnes who provided the scores with tries from David Hulme and a second for Thackray for a 16-2 victory. Doncaster clinched a third round place for the first time in 18 years with a 16-8 success over Mansfield Marksman at. Tattersfield. Marksman led 8-0 before a 60-yard solo try from winger Mark Roache in the 28th minute inspired a Doncaster revival aided by the 46th minute dismissal of visiting hooker Joe Warburton and the late sin-binning of veteran loose forward Billy Platt.

Salford provided the shock result of the third round with a 22-18 defeat of high-riding St. Helens at the Willows. The Red Devils produced honest endeavour, aided by untidy St. Helens handling. Silk Cut Award winner Gibson was outstanding as one of the three try scorers, Mick Worrall sealing the surprise victory and Ken Jones adding three goals for a tally of 10 points. Holders Halifax travelled to Hull K.R. to record a 26-4 victory. The Thrum Hall side trailed 4-0 at the break, conceding two Mike Fletcher penalties while facing the strong wind. In the second half, the visitors drew level in nine minutes, went ahead seven minutes later and finally ran in a total of five touchdowns, led by two-try Man of the Match Paul Dixon. A fifth minute penalty goal from Pearce was Hull's only contribution to an opening half hour which saw

Second Division Doncaster leading 12-2 in their bid to reach the semi-finals for the first time. Inspired by front row men Kevin Parkhouse and Mark Gibbon, plus the kicking of former Hull player David Noble, Doncaster let in Paul Eastwood before the interval and Hull continued to rally to take a 20-12 lead 16 minutes into the second half, the final score being 27-12. In the televised tie, Wigan beat Widnes 10-1 at Central Park, the Riversiders being best served by full back Hampson who scored the clinching try, made the other touchdown for Tony Iro and moved a step nearer a Wembley place twice denied him because of injury. Widnes who led through a John Myler drop goal, dominated the first hour but were left to rue two decisions which denied their claims for touchdowns before Wigan's late rally.

In the first semi-final, Wigan were only one point short of equalling Huddersfield's 75-year record for a peace time semi-final score, beating Salford 34-4 at Bolton Wanderers' Burnden Park soccer ground. Relentless rain and Bolton having played at home the previous evening made the pitch a mudbath, but Wigan made light of the atrocious conditions, running in six tries to one. Salford ruled out flu victim Mick Worrall minutes before the kick off and never looked likely to repeat their giant-killing act in the quarter-final defeat of St. Helens, Wigan's five-star show being inspired by two-try, Silk Cut Award winner Shaun Edwards, their newly installed skipper.

Two weeks before the other semi-final, Hull were shocked by the resignation of Len Casey as coach, alleging lack of co-operation from the board. But caretaker coaches Keith Hepworth and Tony Dean restored morale to take them within a finger tip of Wembley. First they held Halifax to a scoreless draw at Leeds where Silk Cut Award winner Terry Regan was outstanding. Both sides failed to produce an effective kicking game, especially when seeking a vital drop goal, Hull missing four attempts and Halifax three. Then in the replay at Elland Road, Leeds, Hull led 3-0 after 65 minutes of a pulsating tie with a Pearce penalty goal and drop goal. Having repelled the more promising Halifax attack with a series of last ditch tackles, Hull went out to a soft touchdown. Halifax prop Keith Neller put in a short kick to the line after the fifth tackle which appeared to be covered, but centre Tony Anderson shot up from nowhere to dive in and get a finger tip try just as Hull kicked for clearance.

1988 RESULTS

Preliminary Round

Bramley	6	Sheffield E.	14
Carlisle	8	Whitehaven	8
Heworth	11	West Hull	4
(at York)			
Kells	0	Leeds	28
(at Whitehaven)			
Leigh Miners	4	Hunslet	23
(at Leigh)			
Warrington	48	Huddersfield	10

Replay

Whitehaven	8	Carlisle	22

First Round

Dewsbury	10	Widnes	38
Doncaster	18	Batley	10
Featherstone R.	32	York	21
Fulham	4	Mansfield M.	16
Heworth	4	Halifax	60
(at York)			
Hull K.R.	14	Carlisle	6
Hunslet	10	Hull	27
Keighley	30	Workington T.	4
Leeds	22	Castleford	14
Leigh	12	St. Helens	22
Rochdale H.	6	Barrow	4
Runcorn H.	6	Springfield B.	8
Salford	16	Swinton	6
Wakefield T.	10	Sheffield E.	14
Warrington	17	Oldham	6
Wigan	2	Bradford N.	0

Second Round

Doncaster	16	Mansfield M.	8
Halifax	30	Rochdale H.	6
Hull	26	Sheffield E.	6
Hull K.R.	35	Featherstone R.	26
Keighley	2	Widnes	16
Salford	12	Springfield B.	10
Warrington	20	St. Helens	24
Wigan	30	Leeds	14

Third Round

Hull	27	Doncaster	12
Hull K.R.	4	Halifax	26
Salford	22	St. Helens	18
Wigan	10	Widnes	1

Semi-Finals

Salford	4	Wigan	34
(at Bolton)			
Halifax	0	Hull	0
(at Leeds)			

Replay

Halifax	4	Hull	3
(at Elland Rd, Leeds)			

Final

Halifax	12	Wigan	32
(at Wembley)			

1988 PRIZES

Round	Per Round		Total
Preliminary	12 ×	£1,200	£14,400
First	16 ×	£1,200	£19,200
Second	8 ×	£1,800	£14,400
Third	4 ×	£3,000	£12,000
Semi-Finals	2 ×	£5,000	£10,000
Runners-up	1 ×	£10,000	£10,000
Winners	1 ×	£18,000	£18,000

Total Prize Money		£98,000
Capital Development Fund		£62,000
Grand Total		£160,000

CHALLENGE CUP ROLL OF HONOUR

Year	Winners		Runners-up		Venue	Attendance	Receipts
1897	Batley	10	St Helens	3	Leeds	13,492	£624.17.7
1898	Batley	7	Bradford	0	Leeds	27,941	£1,586.3.0
1899	Oldham	19	Hunslet	9	Manchester	15,763	£946.16.0
1900	Swinton	16	Salford	8	Manchester	17,864	£1,100.0.0
1901	Batley	6	Warrington	0	Leeds	29,563	£1,644.16.0
1902	Broughton R.	25	Salford	0	Rochdale	15,006	£846.11.0
1903	Halifax	7	Salford	0	Leeds	32,507	£1,834.8.6
1904	Halifax	8	Warrington	3	Salford	17,041	£936.5.6
1905	Warrington	6	Hull K.R.	0	Leeds	19,638	£1,271.18.0
1906	Bradford	5	Salford	0	Leeds	15,834	£920.0.0
1907	Warrington	17	Oldham	3	Broughton	18,500	£1,010.0.0
1908	Hunslet	14	Hull	0	Huddersfield	18,000	£903.0.0
1909	Wakefield T.	17	Hull	0	Leeds	23,587	£1,490.0.0
1910	Leeds	7	Hull	7	Huddersfield	19,413	£1,102.0.0
Replay	Leeds	26	Hull	12	Huddersfield	11,608	£657.0.0
1911	Broughton R.	4	Wigan	0	Salford	8,000	£376.0.0
1912	Dewsbury	8	Oldham	5	Leeds	15,271	£853.0.0
1913	Huddersfield	9	Warrington	5	Leeds	22,754	£1,446.9.6
1914	Hull	6	Wakefield T.	0	Halifax	19,000	£1,035.5.0
1915	Huddersfield	37	St. Helens	3	Oldham	8,000	£472.0.0
1920	Huddersfield	21	Wigan	10	Leeds	14,000	£1,936.0.0
1921	Leigh	13	Halifax	0	Broughton	25,000	£2,700.0.0
1922	Rochdale H.	10	Hull	9	Leeds	32,596	£2,964.0.0
1923	Leeds	28	Hull	3	Wakefield	29,335	£2,390.0.0
1924	Wigan	21	Oldham	4	Rochdale	41,831	£3,712.0.0
1925	Oldham	16	Hull K.R.	3	Leeds	28,335	£2,879.0.0
1926	Swinton	9	Oldham	3	Rochdale	27,000	£2,551.0.0
1927	Oldham	26	Swinton	7	Wigan	33,448	£3,170.0.0
1928	Swinton	5	Warrington	3	Wigan	33,909	£3,158.1.11
1929	Wigan	13	Dewsbury	2	Wembley	41,500	£5,614.0.0
1930	Widnes	10	St. Helens	3	Wembley	36,544	£3,102.0.0
1931	Halifax	22	York	8	Wembley	40,368	£3,908.0.0
1932	Leeds	11	Swinton	8	Wigan	29,000	£2,479.0.0
1933	Huddersfield	21	Warrington	17	Wembley	41,874	£6,465.0.0
1934	Hunslet	11	Widnes	5	Wembley	41,280	£6,686.0.0
1935	Castleford	11	Huddersfield	8	Wembley	39,000	£5,533.0.0
1936	Leeds	18	Warrington	2	Wembley	51,250	£7,070.0.0
1937	Widnes	18	Keighley	5	Wembley	47,699	£6,704.0.0
1938	Salford	7	Barrow	4	Wembley	51,243	£7,174.0.0
1939	Halifax	20	Salford	3	Wembley	55,453	£7,681.0.0
1940	No competition						
1941	Leeds	19	Halifax	2	Bradford	28,500	£1,703.0.0
1942	Leeds	15	Halifax	10	Bradford	15,250	£1,276.0.0
1943	Dewsbury	16	Leeds	9	Dewsbury	10,470	£823.0.0
	Dewsbury	0	Leeds	6	Leeds	16,000	£1,521.0.0
	Dewsbury won on aggregate 16-15						
1944	Bradford	0	Wigan	3	Wigan	22,000	£1,640.0.0
	Bradford	8	Wigan	0	Bradford	30,000	£2,200.0.0
	Bradford won on aggregate 8-3						
1945	Huddersfield	7	Bradford N.	4	Huddersfield	9,041	£1,184.3.7
	Huddersfield	6	Bradford N.	5	Bradford	17,500	£2,050.0.0
	Huddersfield won on aggregate 13-9						

Year	Winners		Runners-up		Venue	Attendance	Receipts
1946	Wakefield T.	13	Wigan	12	Wembley	54,730	£12,013.13.6
1947	Bradford N.	8	Leeds	4	Wembley	77,605	£17,434.5.0
1948	Wigan	8	Bradford N.	3	Wembley	91,465	£21,121.9.9
1949	Bradford N.	12	Halifax	0	Wembley	95,050	£21,930.5.0
1950	Warrington	19	Widnes	0	Wembley	94,249	£24,782.13.0
1951	Wigan	10	Barrow	0	Wembley	94,262	£24,797.19.0
1952	Workington T.	18	Featherstone R.	10	Wembley	72,093	£22,374.2.0
1953	Huddersfield	15	St. Helens	10	Wembley	89,588	£30,865.12.3
1954	Warrington	4	Halifax	4	Wembley	81,841	£29,706.7.3
Replay	Warrington	8	Halifax	4	Bradford	102,569	£18,623.7.0
1955	Barrow	21	Workington T.	12	Wembley	66,513	£27,453.16.0
1956	St. Helens	13	Halifax	2	Wembley	79,341	£29,424.7.6
1957	Leeds	9	Barrow	7	Wembley	76,318	£32,671.14.3
1958	Wigan	13	Workington T.	9	Wembley	66,109	£33,175.17.6
1959	Wigan	30	Hull	13	Wembley	79,811	£35,718.19.9
1960	Wakefield T.	38	Hull	5	Wembley	79,773	£35,754.16.0
1961	St. Helens	12	Wigan	6	Wembley	94,672	£38,479.11.9
1962	Wakefield T.	12	Huddersfield	6	Wembley	81,263	£33,390.18.4
1963	Wakefield T.	25	Wigan	10	Wembley	84,492	£44,521.17.0
1964	Widnes	13	Hull K.R.	5	Wembley	84,488	£44,840.19.0
1965	Wigan	20	Hunslet	16	Wembley	89,016	£48,080.4.0
1966	St. Helens	21	Wigan	2	Wembley	*98,536	£50,409.0.0
1967	Featherstone R.	17	Barrow	12	Wembley	76,290	£53,465.14.0
1968	Leeds	11	Wakefield T.	10	Wembley	87,100	£56,171.16.6
1969	Castleford	11	Salford	6	Wembley	*97,939	£58,848.1.0
1970	Castleford	7	Wigan	2	Wembley	95,255	£89,262.2.0
1971	Leigh	24	Leeds	7	Wembley	85,514	£84,452.15
1972	St. Helens	16	Leeds	13	Wembley	89,495	£86,414.30
1973	Featherstone R.	33	Bradford N.	14	Wembley	72,395	£125,826.40
1974	Warrington	24	Featherstone R.	9	Wembley	77,400	£132,021.05
1975	Widnes	14	Warrington	7	Wembley	85,098	£140,684.45
1976	St. Helens	20	Widnes	5	Wembley	89,982	£190,129.40
1977	Leeds	16	Widnes	7	Wembley	80,871	£241,488.00
1978	Leeds	14	St. Helens	12	Wembley	*96,000	£330,575.00
1979	Widnes	12	Wakefield T.	3	Wembley	94,218	£383,157.00
1980	Hull K.R.	10	Hull	5	Wembley	*95,000	£448,202.90
1981	Widnes	18	Hull K.R.	9	Wembley	92,496	£591,117.00
1982	Hull	14	Widnes	14	Wembley	92,147	£684,500.00
Replay	Hull	18	Widnes	9	Elland Rd., L'ds	41,171	£180,525.00
1983	Featherstone R.	14	Hull	12	Wembley	84,969	£655,510.00
1984	Widnes	19	Wigan	6	Wembley	80,116	£686,171.00
1985	Wigan	28	Hull	24	Wembley	*97,801	£760,322.00
1986	Castleford	15	Hull K.R.	14	Wembley	82,134	£806,676.00
1987	Halifax	19	St. Helens	18	Wembley	91,267	£1,009,206.00
1988	Wigan	32	Halifax	12	Wembley	*94,273	£1,102,247.00

*Indicates a capacity attendance, the limit being fixed annually taking into account variable factors.

RUGBY LEAGUE CHALLENGE CUP .... A REVIEW

1965-66

St. Helens 21 F. Barrow; Vollenhoven, Murphy (1g), Benyon, Killeen (5g, 1t); Harvey, Bishop (1t); Halsall, Sayer, Watson, French, Warlow, Mantle (1t)
Wigan 2 Ashby; Boston, D. Stephens, Ashton, Lake; C. Hill, Parr; Gardiner, Woosey, McTigue, A. Stephens, Gilfedder (1g), Major
Referee: H.G. Hunt (Prestbury)

1966-67

Featherstone R. 17 Wrigglesworth; Thomas (1t), Cotton, Jordan, Greatorex; M. Smith, Dooler (1g); Tonks, Harris, Dixon, A. Morgan (1t), Thompson (1t), Smales (1t, 3g)
Barrow 12 Tees (1g); Burgess, Challinor, Hughes, Murray; Brophy (1t), G. Smith; Kelland, Redhead, Hopwood, Sanderson, Delooze (2g), Watson (1t)
Referee: E. Clay (Leeds)

1967-68

Leeds 11 Risman (4g); Alan Smith, Hynes, Watson, Atkinson (1t); Shoebottom, Seabourne; Clark, Crosby, K. Eyre, Ramsey, A. Eyre, Batten
Wakefield T 10 Cooper, Hirst (2t), Brooke, Coetzer, Batty; Poynton, Owen; Jeanes, Shepherd, D. Fox (2g), Haigh, McLeod, Hawley
Referee: J.P. Hebblethwaite (York)

1968-69

Castleford 11 Edwards; Briggs, Howe (1t), Thomas, Lowndes; Hardisty (1t), Hepworth (1t); Hartley, C. Dickinson, J. Ward, Redfearn (1g), Lockwood, Reilly
Salford 6 K. Gwilliam; Burgess, Whitehead, Hesketh, Jackson; Watkins, Brennan; Ogden, Dickens, Bott, Coulman, Dixon, Hill (3g)
Referee: D.S. Brown (Preston)

1969-70

Castleford 7 Edwards; Briggs, Thomas, Stenton, Lowndes (1t); Hardisty (Hargrave), Hepworth; Hartley, C. Dickinson, Redfearn (2g), Kirkbride, Lockwood, Reilly
Wigan 2 Tyrer (1g) (C. Hill); Jones, Francis, Rowe, Kevin O'Loughlin; D. Hill, Parr; Ashcroft, Burdell, Hogan, Ashurst, D. Robinson, Laughton
Referee: G.F. Lindop (Wakefield)

1970-71

Leigh 24 Eckersley (1t, 1g); Ferguson (5g), Dorrinton (1t), Collins, Walsh; A. Barrow, Murphy (2g) (L. Chisnall); Watts, Ashcroft, Fiddler (1g), Grimes, Clarkson, Smethurst
Leeds 7 Holmes (2g); Langley, Hynes, Cowan (Dyl), Atkinson; Wainwright (1t), Seabourne; J. Burke, Fisher, Barnard, Hick, Haigh, Ramsey
Referee: W.H. Thompson (Huddersfield)

1971-72

St. Helens 16 G. Pimblett; L. Jones (1t), Benyon, Walsh, Wilson; K. Kelly, Heaton; Rees (1t), Greenall, J. Stephens, Mantle, E. Chisnall, Coslett (5g)
Leeds 13 Holmes; Alan Smith, Hynes (Langley), Dyl, Atkinson; Hardisty, Hepworth; Clawson (5g), Fisher, Ramsey, Cookson (1t), Haigh, Batten
Referee: E. Lawrinson (Warrington)

1972-73

Featherstone R. 33 C. Kellett (8g); Coventry, M. Smith (1t) (Hartley) (1t), Newlove (2t), K. Kellett; Mason, Nash (1g); Tonks, Bridges, Farrar (1t), Rhodes (Hollis), Thompson, Stone
Bradford N. 14 Tees (4g); Lamb, Stockwell, Watson, D. Redfearn (1t); Blacker (Treasure), Seabourne; Hogan, Dunn, Earl (Long), Joyce, W. Pattinson, Fearnley (1t)
Referee: M.J. Naughton (Widnes)

1973-74

Warrington 24 Whitehead (7g); M. Philbin, Noonan, Whittle, Bevan; Murphy (2g) (Pickup), Gordon; D. Chisnall, Ashcroft (1t), Brady (Wanbon), Wright, Nicholas (1t), B. Philbin
Featherstone R. 9 Box (3g); Dyas, M. Smith, Hartley, Bray; Newlove (1t), Nash; Tonks, Bridges, Harris, Rhodes (Busfield), Thompson (Stone), Bell
Referee: S. Shepherd (Oldham)

1974-75

Widnes 14 Dutton (5g, 1dg); A. Prescott, George, Aspey, Anderson; Hughes, Bowden; Mills (1t), Elwell, Sheridan, Foran, Adams, Laughton
Warrington 7 Whitehead (2g); M. Philbin, Noonan, Reynolds (W. Briggs), Bevan (1t); Whittle, Gordon; D. Chisnall, Ashcroft, Wanbon, Conroy, Martyn (Nicholas), B. Philbin
Referee: P. Geraghty (York)

1975-76

St. Helens 20 G. Pimblett (3g, 2dg); L. Jones, Cunningham (1t), Noonan, Mathias; Benyon (Glynn 2t), Heaton (1t); Mantle (James), A. Karalius, Coslett, Nicholls, E. Chisnall, Hull
Widnes 5 Dutton (2g); A. Prescott (D. O'Neill); Hughes, George, Jenkins; Eckersley, Bowden; Nelson, Elwell (1dg), Wood, Foran (Sheridan), Adams, Laughton
Referee: R. Moore (Wakefield)

1976-77

Leeds 16 Murrell; Alan Smith (D. Smith), Hague, Dyl (1t), Atkinson (1t); Holmes, Dick (1t, 3g, 1dg); Harrison, Ward, Pitchford, Eccles, Cookson, Fearnley (Dickinson)
Widnes 7 Dutton (2g); S. Wright (George), Aspey (1t), Eckersley, D. O'Neill; Hughes, Bowden; Ramsey, Elwell, Mills, Dearden (Foran), Adams, Laughton
Referee: V. Moss (Manchester)

1977-78
Leeds 14 Oulton (1g); D. Smith (1t), Hague, Dyl,
Atkinson (1t); Holmes (1dg), J. Sanderson (Dick);
Harrison (Dickinson), Ward (2dg), Pitchford,
Cookson (1t), Eccles, Crane
St. Helens 12 G. Pimblett (3g), L. Jones,
Noonan, Glynn, Mathias; Francis (1t),
K. Gwilliam; D. Chisnall, Liptrot (1t), James,
Nicholls, Cunningham, Pinner
Referee: W.H. Thompson (Huddersfield)
1978-79
Widnes 12 Eckersley (1dg); S. Wright (1t),
Aspey, George (Hull), Burke (2g); Hughes (1t),
Bowden; Mills, Elwell (1dg), Shaw, Adams,
Dearden (M. O'Neill), Laughton
Wakefield T. 3 Sheard; Fletcher (1t), K. Smith,
Diamond, Juliff; Topliss, Lampkowski; Burke,
McCurrie, Skerrett, Ashurst, Keith Rayne, Idle
Referee: J.E. Jackson (Pudsey)
1979-80
Hull K.R. 10 Hall; Hubbard (3g, 1t) (Hogan),
M. Smith, Hartley, Sullivan; Millward (1dg),
Agar; Holdstock, Watkinson, Lockwood, Lowe,
Rose (Millington), Casey
Hull 5 Woods; Bray, Walters, Wilby (1t),
Prendiville; Newlove (Hancock), Pickerill;
Tindall, Wileman, Stone (Farrar), Birdsall,
Lloyd (1g), Norton
Referee: G.F. Lindop (Wakefield)
1980-81
Widnes 18 Burke (4g, 1t); S. Wright, George (1t),
Cunningham (J. Myler), Bentley; Hughes,
Gregory (1t); M. O'Neill (Shaw), Elwell,
Lockwood, L. Gorley, E. Prescott, Adams (1dg)
Hull K.R. 9 Hall; Hubbard (3g), M. Smith,
Hogan, Muscroft; Hartley, Harkin; Holdstock
(Millington), Watkinson, Crooks (Proctor), Lowe,
Burton (1t), Casey
Referee: D.G. Kershaw (Easingwold)
1981-82
Hull 14 Kemble; O'Hara (1t), Day, S. Evans,
Prendivile; Topliss, Harkin; Skerrett, Wileman,
Stone, Crane (Crooks), Lloyd (4g), Norton (1t)
Widnes 14 Burke (1g), (A. Myler); S. Wright (1t),
Keiron O'Loughlin, Cunningham (2t), Basnett;
Hughes, Gregory (1g); M. O'Neill, Elwell (1dg),
Lockwood (S. O'Neill), L. Gorley, E. Prescott,
Adams
Referee: G.F. Lindop (Wakefield)
Replay
Hull 18 Kemble (1t); Sullivan, Leuluai, S. Evans,
Prendiville; Topliss (2t), Dean; Tindall, Duke,
Stone, Skerrett, Crooks (1t, 3g), Norton (Crane)
Widnes 9 Burke (3g); S. Wright (1t), Keiron
O'Loughlin, Cunningham, Basnett; Hughes,
Gregory; M. O'Neill, Elwell, Lockwood,
L. Gorley, E. Prescott, Adams
Referee: G.F. Lindop (Wakefield)

1982-83
Featherstone R. 14 N. Barker; Marsden,
Quinn (4g), Gilbert (Lyman), K. Kellett;
A. Banks, Hudson; Gibbins, Handscombe,
Hankins, D. Hobbs (2t), Slatter (Siddall), Smith
Hull 12 Kemble; O'Hara, S. Evans, Leuluai (1t),
Prendiville; Topliss, Harkin (Day), (Crane);
Skerrett, Bridges, Stone, Rose, Crooks (1t, 3g),
Norton
Referee: M.R. Whitfield (Widnes)
1983-84
Widnes 19 Burke (3g); D. Wright, Hughes
(D. Hulme), Lydon (2t), Basnett;
Keiron O'Loughlin (1t), Gregory; S. O'Neill
(1dg), Elwell, K. Tamati, L. Gorley, M. O'Neill
(Whitfield), Adams
Wigan 6 Edwards; Ramsdale, Stephenson,
Whitfield (1g), (Elvin), Gill; Cannon, Stephens;
Hemsley (1t), H. Tamati, Case (Juliff), West,
Scott, Pendlebury
Referee: W.H. Thompson (Huddersfield)
1984-85
Wigan 28 Edwards (1t); Ferguson (2t),
Stephenson (1g), Donlan, Gill (1t, 3g);
Kenny (1t), M. Ford; Courtney, Kiss, Case
(Campbell), West, Dunn, Potter
Hull 24 Kemble; James (1t), S. Evans (1t),
Leuluai (2t), O'Hara (Schofield); Ah Kuoi,
Sterling; Crooks (2g), Patrick, Puckering
(Divorty 1t), Muggleton, Rose, Norton
Referee: R. Campbell (Widnes)
1985-86
Castleford 15 Lord (Roockley); Plange,
Marchant (1t), Hyde, Sandy (1t); Joyner,
R. Beardmore (1t, 1dg); Ward, K. Beardmore
(Horton), Johnson, England, Ketteridge (1g),
French
Hull K.R. 14 Fairbairn; Clark, M. Smith,
Prohm (2t), Laws; Dorahy (1g), Harkin; P.
Johnston, Watkinson, Ema, Kelly (G. Smith),
D. Harrison (Lydiat 1t), Miller
Referee: R. Whitfield (Widnes)
1986-87
Halifax 19 Eadie (1t); Wilson, Whitfield (3g),
Rix, George (1t); C. Anderson (Juliff), Stephens;
Beevers (James), McCallion (1t), Neller, Dixon,
Scott, Pendlebury (1dg)
St. Helens 18 Veivers; Ledger, Loughlin (1t, 3g),
Elia (1t), McCormack; Clark, Holding; Burke,
Liptrot, Fieldhouse, Platt, Haggerty (Round 1t),
Arkwright
Referee: J. Holdsworth (Kippax)

127

THE LANCE TODD TROPHY

The Lance Todd Trophy is presented to the Man of the Match in the Rugby League Challenge Cup Final, the decision being reached by a ballot of members of the Rugby League Writers' Association present at the game.

Lance Todd made his name in Britain as a player with Wigan and as manager of Salford. His untimely death in a road accident on the return journey from a game at Oldham was commemorated by the introduction of the Lance Todd Trophy.

The award was instituted by Australian-born Harry Sunderland, Warrington director Bob Anderton and Yorkshire journalist John Bapty.

Around 1950, the Red Devils' Association at Salford, comprising players and officials who had worked with Todd, raised sufficient funds to provide a trophy and replica for each winner.

Gerry Helme, of Warrington, is the only player to win the trophy twice; Len Killeen, of St. Helens, is the only winger to earn the title; Hull's Tommy Harris the only hooker; and Ray Ashby and Brian Gabbitas the only players to share the honour.

Following the 1954 replay, it was decided by the Red Devils that in future the trophy would be awarded for the Wembley game. In 1954, Gerry Helme had received the trophy for his performance in the Odsal replay. In the 1982 replay at Elland Road, Leeds, the Man of the Match award went to Hull skipper David Topliss, the Lance Todd Trophy having been awarded to Eddie Cunningham, of Widnes, in the drawn Wembley tie.

The 1988 winner, by an overwhelming majority, was Wigan scrum half Andy Gregory.

Andy Gregory of Wigan shows the style that won him the Lance Todd Trophy in the 1988 final.

The Lance Todd Trophy Roll of Honour

Year	Winner	Team	Position
1946	Billy Stott	Wakefield Trinity (v Wigan)	Centre
1947	Willie Davies	Bradford Northern (v Leeds)	Stand off
1948	Frank Whitcombe	Bradford Northern (v Wigan)	Prop
1949	Ernest Ward	Bradford Northern (v Halifax)	Centre
1950	Gerry Helme	Warrington (v Widnes)	Scrum half
1951	Cec Mountford	Wigan (v Barrow)	Stand off
1952	Billy Ivison	Workington T. (v Featherstone R.)	Loose forward
1953	Peter Ramsden	Huddersfield (v St. Helens)	Stand off
1954	Gerry Helme	Warrington (v Halifax)	Scrum half
1955	Jack Grundy	Barrow (v Workington Town)	Second row
1956	Alan Prescott	St. Helens (v Halifax)	Prop
1957	Jeff Stevenson	Leeds (v Barrow)	Scrum half
1958	Rees Thomas	Wigan (v Workington Town)	Scrum half
1959	Brian McTigue	Wigan (v Hull)	Second row
1960	Tommy Harris	Hull (v Wakefield Trinity)	Hooker
1961	Dick Huddart	St. Helens (v Wigan)	Second row
1962	Neil Fox	Wakefield Trinity (v Huddersfield)	Centre
1963	Harold Poynton	Wakefield Trinity (v Wigan)	Stand off
1964	Frank Collier	Widnes (v Hull K.R.)	Prop
1965	Ray Ashby	Wigan	Full back
	Brian Gabbitas	Hunslet	Stand off
1966	Len Killeen	St. Helens (v Wigan)	Winger
1967	Carl Dooler	Featherstone Rovers (v Barrow)	Scrum half
1968	Don Fox	Wakefield Trinity (v Leeds)	Prop
1969	Malcolm Reilly	Castleford (v Salford)	Loose forward
1970	Bill Kirkbride	Castleford (v Wigan)	Second row
1971	Alex Murphy	Leigh (v Leeds)	Scrum half
1972	Kel Coslett	St. Helens (v Leeds)	Loose forward
1973	Steve Nash	Featherstone R. (v Bradford N.)	Scrum half
1974	Derek Whitehead	Warrington (v Featherstone Rovers)	Full back
1975	Ray Dutton	Widnes (v Warrington)	Full back
1976	Geoff Pimblett	St. Helens (v Widnes)	Full back
1977	Steve Pitchford	Leeds (v Widnes)	Prop
1978	George Nicholls	St. Helens (v Leeds)	Second row
1979	David Topliss	Wakefield Trinity (v Widnes)	Stand off
1980	Brian Lockwood	Hull K.R. (v Hull)	Prop
1981	Mick Burke	Widnes (v Hull K.R.)	Full back
1982	Eddie Cunningham	Widnes (v Hull)	Centre
1983	David Hobbs	Featherstone Rovers (v Hull)	Second row
1984	Joe Lydon	Widnes (v Wigan)	Centre
1985	Brett Kenny	Wigan (v Hull)	Stand off
1986	Bob Beardmore	Castleford (v Hull K.R.)	Scrum half
1987	Graham Eadie	Halifax (v St. Helens)	Full back
1988	Andy Gregory	Wigan (v Halifax)	Scrum half

CHALLENGE CUP RECORDS

ALL ROUNDS

TEAM

Highest score:
Huddersfield 119 v. *Swinton Park 2. 1914

INDIVIDUAL

Most goals in a match:
22 by Jim Sullivan (Wigan) v. *Flimby and Fothergill
. . . . 1925

Most tries in a match:
11 by George West (Hull K.R.) v. *Brookland Rovers
. . . . 1905

Most points in a match:
53 (11t,10g) by George West (Hull K.R.) as above.

*Amateur teams

FINAL RECORDS

TEAM

Most wins: 10 by Leeds

Most finals: 18 by Wigan

Highest score:
Wakefield T. 38 v. Hull 5. 1960

Widest margin:
Huddersfield 37 v. St. Helens 3. 1915

Biggest attendance:
102,569 Warrington v. Halifax (Replay) at Bradford
. . . . 1954

INDIVIDUAL

Most goals:
8 by Cyril Kellett (Featherstone R.) v. Bradford N.
. . . . 1973

Most tries:
3 by Bob Wilson (Broughton R.) v. Salford. . . . 1902
Stan Moorhouse (Huddersfield) v. Warrington. 1913
Tom Holliday (Oldham) v. Swinton. 1927

Most points:
20 (7g,2t) by Neil Fox (Wakefield T.) v. Hull. . . 1960

WEMBLEY FACTS

WIGAN made a record 14th appearance at Wembley in the 1988 final against Halifax, recording a record eighth victory at the stadium.

A RECORD 10 overseas players trod the Wembley turf in 1985. Hull fielded six — a record for one club. The Airlie Birds sextet were Australians Peter Sterling and John Muggleton, plus New Zealanders Gary Kemble, James Leuluai, Dane O'Hara and Fred Ah Kuoi. Wigan added Australians John Ferguson and Brett Kenny together with New Zealanders Graeme West and Danny Campbell, who went on as substitute. South African Nick Du Toit was substitute back but did not play.

THE 1985 aggregates of 10 tries and 52 points were both record totals for a Challenge Cup final with Hull's 24 points the most by a losing side. There were also 10 tries in the 1915 final when Huddersfield beat St. Helens 37-3, which is the widest margin. Wakefield Trinity ran up the highest Cup final score when they beat Hull 38-5 in 1960.

WORLD RECORD receipts of £1,102,247 were taken at the 1988 Final between Halifax and Wigan, from a crowd of 94,273.

FIVE players share the record of playing in four Cup-winning sides at Wembley — Alex Murphy, Brian Lockwood, Eric Hughes, Keith Elwell and Mick Adams.
  Murphy was in St. Helens' victorious side of 1961 and as captain led St. Helens (1966), Leigh (1971) and Warrington (1974) to victory. He played in three different positions — stand off, centre and scrum half. Murphy was a scorer in each final with a total of five drop goals and a try.
  Brian Lockwood was in the winning final teams of Castleford (1969 and 1970), Hull K.R. (1980) and Widnes (1981). He also appeared with Widnes in the drawn final of 1982.
  Hughes, Elwell and Adams each played in the Widnes teams that won the Cup in 1975, 1979, 1981 and 1984. They also appeared in the drawn final of 1982.

THE Widnes trio of Eric Hughes, Keith Elwell and Mick Adams each hold the record for most appearances at Wembley...seven. In addition to the five finals mentioned above they were on the losing side in 1976 and 1977.

ERIC ASHTON captained a record six teams at Wembley — Wigan in 1958, 1959, 1961, 1963, 1965 and 1966. His record of three wins (in 1958, 1959, 1965) is shared with Derek Turner (Wakefield Trinity 1960, 1962, 1963) and Alex Murphy (St. Helens 1966, Leigh 1971 and Warrington 1974).

THE YOUNGEST player to appear in a Wembley Cup final was Shaun Edwards who was 17 years, 6 months and 19 days when he played full back for Wigan against Widnes in 1984. He was also the youngest captain at Wembley, leading Wigan to success in the 1988 final against Halifax at the age of 21 years, 6 months and 14 days.

THE OLDEST player at Wembley was Gus Risman, who at 41 years 29 days led Workington Town to victory over Featherstone Rovers in 1952. He played full back.

THE TALLEST player at Wembley was New Zealand Test star Graeme West who captained Wigan in the 1984 and 1985 finals. He measured 6ft. 5in.

SCHOOLBOYS who have appeared in an Under-11 curtain-raiser at Wembley and gone on to play in the major final at the stadium are Joe Lydon, David Hulme, Mike Ford, Neil Puckering and David Plange. Lydon became the first to achieve the feat with Widnes in the 1984 final against Wigan, followed by Hulme who went on as a 72nd minute substitute. Both had played in the first schoolboys' curtain-raiser in 1975 — Lydon for Wigan, and Hulme for Widnes. Ford played scrum half for Wigan in the 1985 final having represented Oldham in the 1977 curtain-raiser. Puckering played for Hull in the 1977 curtain-raiser and for his home town club in the Challenge Cup final of 1985. Plange was in the Hull Schools team of 1976 and played for Castleford in the 1986 final.

CYRIL KELLETT holds the record for most goals in a Challenge Cup final with his eight for Featherstone Rovers in 1973.

In the most remarkable exhibition of kicking seen at Wembley, the veteran full back was successful with every one of his attempts as Bradford Northern crashed 33-14.

Nine years earlier he scored only one for Hull Kingston Rovers in the 13-5 defeat by Widnes.

NEIL FOX — the record aggregate points scorer of all time — piled up the most points in a Challenge Cup final in 1960. His 20 points helped Wakefield Trinity to a 38-5 defeat of Hull. Fox's points came from two tries and seven goals.

His three drop goals for Trinity in the 12-6 victory over Huddersfield two years later was another extraordinary feat in the days when the drop goal was a rarity.

NO player has scored a hat-trick of tries at Wembley, the feat being achieved only three times in the preceding era.

The last to do it was Oldham winger Tom Holliday in the 26-7 defeat of Swinton in 1927.

Bob Wilson, the Broughton Rangers centre and captain, was the first to score three tries, in the 25-0 victory over Salford in 1902.

In between, Stan Moorhouse's three-try feat accounted for all of Huddersfield's points when they beat Warrington 9-5 in 1913. Moorhouse was winger to Harold Wagstaff, recognised as the greatest centre of all time.

MANY great players have gone through an entire career without achieving their ambition of playing at Wembley. Hull's Mike Smith achieved it in his first senior game.

Smith made one of the most remarkable debuts in sporting history when he played in the second row of an injury-hit Boulevard side against Wakefield Trinity in 1960.

In contrast, Freddie Miller signed for Hull in 1932 and

did not play at Wembley until 1952...two years after joining Featherstone Rovers.

A NOTABLE Wembley captain was Gus Risman who led two clubs to victory...14 years apart.

He was captain of Salford when they beat Barrow in 1938. At 41, he led Workington Town to their triumph over Featherstone Rovers in 1952.

PROBABLY the unluckiest Challenge Cup finalist was Dai Davies who appeared in four finals and was on the losing side each time.

Three of those occasions were at Wembley with different clubs. He was a loser with Warrington (1933), Huddersfield (1935) and Keighley (1937).

Before the Wembley era he was also in Warrington's beaten team of 1928.

Steve Norton has played at Wembley four times and has yet to be on the winning side. He was in the beaten Hull teams of 1980, 1983 and 1985 in addition to playing in the 1982 drawn final. In 1970 he was a non-playing substitute for Castleford who won the Cup.

Bill Ramsey was on the losing side in four Wembley finals but gained a winner's medal with Leeds in 1968. He picked up losers' medals with Hunslet (1965), Leeds (1971 and 1972) and Widnes (1977).

A TOTAL of 13 current clubs have yet to play at Wembley ...Batley, Springfield Borough, Bramley, Carlisle, Doncaster, Fulham, Mansfield Marksman, Oldham, Rochdale Hornets, Runcorn Highfield, Sheffield Eagles, Swinton and Whitehaven.

Fate seems to be against Swinton and Oldham. In the five years preceding the move to Wembley, one or the other appeared in the final, twice meeting each other.

Oldham played in four successive finals in that period. Swinton's run of three finals ended when the first Wembley took place in 1929.

They did get through to the final again three years later ...only for it to be played at Wigan!

Steve Norton — four Wembley appearances without winning.

CHALLENGE CUP

Wembley Era Semi-Finals

It is generally felt that it is better to have played at Wembley and lost than never to have played there at all. This makes the semi-final stage of the RL Challenge Cup almost as important as the final with no consolation for the losers.

Of the 13 current clubs who have never appeared at Wembley four have been beaten semi-finalists. They are Oldham (four times), Swinton, Rochdale Hornets (twice) and Whitehaven.

Probably the unluckiest are Oldham. They have reached the penultimate stage four times without being able to realise their ambition. Oldham almost made it in 1964. After drawing 5-5 with Hull K.R. they were winning 17-14 in extra time of the replay when bad light stopped play and they were beaten in the third game.

Swinton did win a semi-final in 1932 but the final that year was switched from Wembley to Wigan!

There have been three occasions when Yorkshire has provided all four semi-finalists in one year — in 1962, 1973 and 1983. Only

once have all four semi-finalists come from west of the Pennines — in 1930.

Until 1962 the two semi-finals were always played on the same Saturday, but with four Yorkshire clubs competing for the first time it was decided to play one mid-week. Both matches were played at Odsal Stadium, Bradford. The first was on a Wednesday evening — without floodlights — when 43,625 saw Wakefield Trinity beat Featherstone Rovers and on the following Saturday there were 31,423 to see Huddersfield beat Hull K.R.

The following year both semi-finals were again played on the same Saturday, but since then they have been staged on different Saturdays.

Some semi-final facts during the Wembley era are:

Biggest attendance: 69,898 Warrington v. Leeds at Bradford in 1950

Biggest aggregate: 104,453 in 1939 (Only other six-figure aggregate was 102,080 in 1951)

Record receipts: £113,679 Halifax v. Hull replay at Elland Road, Leeds in 1988

Lowest attendance: 7,971 Featherstone R. v. Leigh at Leeds in 1974

Highest score and widest margin:
Wigan 34 v. Salford 4 in 1988

CHALLENGE CUP SEMI-FINALS

Year	Winners		Runners-up		Venue	Attendance	Receipts
1929	Dewsbury	9	Castleford	3	Huddersfield	25,000	£1,562
	Wigan	7	St. Helens Recs.	7	Swinton	31,000	£2,209
Replay	Wigan	13	St. Helens Recs.	12	Leigh	21,940	£1,437
1930	Widnes	10	Barrow	3	Warrington	25,500	£1,630
	St. Helens	5	Wigan	5	Swinton	37,169	£2,666
Replay	St. Helens	22	Wigan	10	Leigh	24,000	£1,657
1931	Halifax	11	St. Helens	2	Rochdale	21,674	£1,498
	York	15	Warrington	5	Leeds	32,419	£2,329
1932	Leeds	2	Halifax	2	Huddersfield	31,818	£2,456
Replay	Leeds	9	Halifax	2	Wakefield	21,000	£1,417
	Swinton	7	Wakefield T.	4	Rochdale	21,273	£1,369
●	*Final was played at Wigan, not Wembley*						
1933	Huddersfield	30	Leeds	8	Wakefield	36,359	£2,299
	Warrington	11	St. Helens	5	Swinton	30,373	£2,055
1934	Hunslet	12	Huddersfield	7	Wakefield	27,450	£1,797
	Widnes	7	Oldham	4	Swinton	17,577	£1,050

Year	Winners		Runners-up		Venue	Attendance	Receipts
1935	Castleford	11	Barrow	5	Swinton	24,469	£1,534
	Huddersfield	21	Hull	5	Leeds	37,111	£2,753
1936	Leeds	10	Huddersfield	5	Wakefield	37,906	£2,456
	Warrington	7	Salford	2	Wigan	41,538	£2,796
1937	Keighley	0	Wakefield T.	0	Leeds	39,998	£2,793
Replay	Keighley	5	Wakefield T.	3	Huddersfield	14,400	£1,052
	Widnes	13	Wigan	9	Warrington	29,260	£1,972
1938	Barrow	4	Halifax	2	Huddersfield	31,384	£2,431
	Salford	6	Swinton	0	Belle Vue, Manchester	31,664	£2,396
1939	Halifax	10	Leeds	4	Bradford	64,453	£3,645
	Salford	11	Wigan	2	Rochdale	40,000	£2,154

● *During the war the semi-finals were two-legged and the finals were not played at Wembley*

Year	Winners		Runners-up		Venue	Attendance	Receipts
1946	Wakefield T.	7	Hunslet	3	Leeds	33,000	£4,991
	Wigan	12	Widnes	5	Swinton	36,976	£4,746
1947	Bradford N.	11	Warrington	7	Swinton	33,474	£4,946
	Leeds	21	Wakefield T.	0	Huddersfield	35,136	£6,339
1948	Bradford N.	14	Hunslet	7	Leeds	38,125	£7,437
	Wigan	11	Rochdale H.	0	Swinton	26,004	£4,206
1949	Bradford N.	10	Barrow	0	Swinton	26,572	£4,646
	Halifax	11	Huddersfield	10	Bradford	61,875	£8,638
1950	Warrington	16	Leeds	4	Bradford	69,898	£9,861
	Widnes	8	Bradford N.	0	Wigan	25,390	£3,936
1951	Barrow	14	Leeds	14	Bradford	57,459	£8,248
Replay	Barrow	28	Leeds	13	Huddersfield	31,078	£5,098
	Wigan	3	Warrington	2	Swinton	44,621	£7,358
1952	Featherstone R.	6	Leigh	2	Leeds	35,621	£6,494
	Workington T.	5	Barrow	2	Wigan	31,206	£4,782
1953	Huddersfield	7	Wigan	0	Bradford	58,722	£10,519
	St. Helens	9	Warrington	3	Swinton	38,059	£7,768
1954	Halifax	18	Hunslet	3	Bradford	46,961	£8,243
	Warrington	8	Leeds	4	Swinton	36,993	£7,596
1955	Barrow	9	Hunslet	6	Wigan	25,493	£4,671
	Workington T.	13	Featherstone R.	2	Leeds	33,499	£7,305
1956	Halifax	11	Wigan	10	Bradford	51,889	£9,054
	St. Helens	5	Barrow	5	Swinton	38,897	£7,793
Replay	St. Helens	10	Barrow	5	Wigan	44,731	£7,750
1957	Barrow	2	Leigh	2	Wigan	34,628	£6,340
Replay	Barrow	15	Leigh	10	Swinton	28,081	£5,695
	Leeds	10	Whitehaven	9	Bradford	49,094	£8,987
1958	Wigan	5	Rochdale H.	3	Swinton	28,597	£6,354
	Workington T.	8	Featherstone R.	2	Bradford	31,517	£6,325
1959	Wigan	5	Leigh	0	Swinton	27,906	£6,068
	Hull	15	Featherstone R.	5	Bradford	52,131	£9,776
1960	Wakefield T.	11	Featherstone R.	2	Bradford	55,935	£10,390
	Hull	12	Oldham	9	Swinton	27,545	£6,093
1961	St. Helens	26	Hull	9	Bradford	42,935	£9,231
	Wigan	19	Halifax	10	Swinton	35,118	£7,557
1962	Wakefield T.	9	Featherstone R.	0	Bradford	43,625	£8,496
	Huddersfield	6	Hull K.R.	0	Bradford	31,423	£6,685

Year	Winners		Runners-up		Venue	Attendance	Receipts
1963	Wakefield T.	5	Warrington	2	Swinton	15,565	£3,530
	Wigan	18	Hull K.R.	4	Leeds	21,420	£6,029
1964	Widnes	7	Castleford	7	Swinton	25,603	£5,541
Replay	Widnes	7	Castleford	5	Wakefield	28,739	£5,313
	Hull K.R.	5	Oldham	5	Leeds	28,823	£7,411
Replay	Hull K.R.	14	Oldham	17	Swinton	27,209	£5,929

● *Score after 80 minutes was 14-14, then bad light caused match to be abandoned after 12 minutes of extra time with Oldham winning 17-14*

Year	Winners		Runners-up		Venue	Attendance	Receipts
Second Replay	Hull K.R.	12	Oldham	2	Huddersfield	28,732	£6,183
1965	Wigan	25	Swinton	10	St. Helens	26,658	£6,384
	Hunslet	8	Wakefield T.	0	Leeds	21,262	£6,090
1966	St. Helens	12	Dewsbury	5	Swinton	13,046	£3,102
	Wigan	7	Leeds	2	Huddersfield	22,758	£5,971
1967	Featherstone R.	16	Leeds	8	Huddersfield	20,052	£6,276
	Barrow	14	Dewsbury	9	Swinton	13,744	£4,560
1968	Leeds	25	Wigan	4	Swinton	30,058	£9,845
	Wakefield T.	0	Huddersfield	0	Bradford	21,569	£6,196
Replay	Wakefield T.	15	Huddersfield	10	Leeds	20,983	£6,425
1969	Castleford	16	Wakefield T.	10	Leeds	21,497	£8,477
	Salford	15	Warrington	8	Wigan	20,600	£7,738
1970	Castleford	6	St. Helens	3	Swinton	18,913	£7,171
	Wigan	19	Hull K.R.	8	Leeds	18,495	£7,862
1971	Leeds	19	Castleford	8	Bradford	24,464	£9,120
	Leigh	10	Huddersfield	4	Wigan	14,875	£5,670
1972	St. Helens	10	Warrington	10	Wigan	19,300	£8,250
Replay	St. Helens	10	Warrington	6	Wigan	32,380	£12,604
	Leeds	16	Halifax	3	Bradford	16,680	£6,851
1973	Featherstone R.	17	Castleford	3	Leeds	15,369	£9,454
	Bradford N.	23	Dewsbury	7	Leeds	14,028	£9,221
1974	Warrington	17	Dewsbury	7	Wigan	11,789	£6,821
	Featherstone R.	21	Leigh	14	Leeds	7,971	£4,461
1975	Widnes	13	Wakefield T.	7	Bradford	9,155	£5,856
	Warrington	11	Leeds	4	Wigan	13,168	£9,581
1976	Widnes	15	Featherstone R.	9	Swinton	13,019	£9,078
	St. Helens	5	Keighley	4	Huddersfield	9,829	£6,113
1977	Leeds	7	St. Helens	2	Wigan	12,974	£11,379
	Widnes	14	Hull K.R.	5	Leeds	17,053	£16,068
1978	Leeds	14	Featherstone R.	9	Bradford	12,824	£11,322
	St. Helens	12	Warrington	8	Wigan	16,167	£13,960
1979	Widnes	14	Bradford N.	11	Swinton	14,324	£16,363
	Wakefield T.	9	St. Helens	7	Leeds	12,393	£14,195
1980	Hull K.R.	20	Halifax	7	Leeds	17,910	£31,650
	Hull	10	Widnes	5	Swinton	18,347	£29,415
1981	Widnes	17	Warrington	9	Wigan	12,624	£20,673
	Hull K.R.	22	St. Helens	5	Leeds	17,073	£30,616
1982	Hull	15	Castleford	11	Leeds	21,207	£41,867
	Widnes	11	Leeds	8	Swinton	13,075	£25,796
1983	Featherstone R.	11	Bradford N.	6	Leeds	10,784	£22,579
	Hull	14	Castleford	7	Elland Rd., L'ds	26,031	£65,498

Year	Winners		Runners-up		Venue	Attendance	Receipts
1984	Wigan	14	York	8	Elland Rd., L'ds	17,156	£52,888
	Widnes	15	Leeds	4	Swinton	14,046	£37,183
1985	Wigan	18	Hull K.R.	11	Elland Rd., L'ds	19,275	£70,192
	Hull	10	Castleford	10	Leeds	20,982	£64,163
Replay	Hull	22	Castleford	16	Leeds	20,968	£65,005
1986	Castleford	18	Oldham	7	Wigan	12,430	£38,296
	Hull K.R.	24	Leeds	24	Elland Rd., L'ds	23,866	£83,757
Replay	Hull K.R.	17	Leeds	0	Elland Rd., L'ds	32,485	£113,345
1987	St. Helens	14	Leigh	8	Wigan	13,105	£48,627
	Halifax	12	Widnes	8	Leeds	16,064	£61,260
1988	Wigan	34	Salford	4	Bolton W. FC	20,783	£95,876
	Halifax	0	Hull	0	Leeds	20,534	£82,026
Replay	Halifax	4	Hull	3	Elland Rd., L'ds	25,117	£113,679

NON-LEAGUE CLUBS IN THE CHALLENGE CUP

AMATEUR clubs were invited to compete in the 1986 Rugby League Challenge Cup after a five-year break. The League asked for two of the three county cup competition winners to enter the preliminary round. Cumbria Cup winners Kells were given a bye into the draw for the preliminary round, while Yorkshire victors Dudley Hill met Lancashire winners Simms Cross at Bramley in an eliminator, the White Rose side going through.

The League later decided that from 1987 the Silk Cut Challenge Cup campaign would feature 38 teams, four amateur clubs joining the professionals for a preliminary round of six ties.

In the early years of the Northern Union Challenge Cup — as it was then called — the line between professional and amateur was less clearly defined.

A variety of Leagues also make it difficult to set non-League clubs apart. Fifty-six clubs appeared in the inaugurating first round of 1897 and four others received byes. The complications continued until 1904 when the League format settled down and non-League clubs had to qualify for the first round.

Between 1904 and 1907 there was a preliminary round of up to 14 ties involving mostly non-league clubs. In 1906-07 SAVILLE GREEN beat Bramley 10-0, and NEWINGTON ROVERS drew 3-3 and 13-13 with York before losing 14-5.

Not since 1909 when BEVERLEY beat Ebbw Vale 7-2 has a senior team been knocked out by a non-League club although amateur teams twice had victories in the two-leg era of 1946-54.

RECORDS OF NON-LEAGUE CLUBS IN THE RUGBY LEAGUE CHALLENGE CUP SINCE 1904
(Excluding preliminary rounds before 1908)
Non-League Clubs in Capitals

Victories over Senior Clubs
1905-06
*FEATHERSTONE ROVERS 23 v. Widnes 2
(second round)

1907-08
WHITEHAVEN RECREATION 13 v. St. Helens 8
(Lost 33-5 at Merthyr Tydfil in second round)

1908-09
BEVERLEY 7 v. Ebbw Vale 2
(Lost 53-2 at Halifax in second round)

1945-46
SHARLSTON 12 v. Workington Town 7
(1st leg) (Workington Town won 2nd leg 16-2)

1947-48
RISEHOW and GILLHEAD 10 v. Keighley 2 (2nd leg)
(Keighley won 1st leg 11-0)

*FEATHERSTONE ROVERS are the only non-League club to appear in the third round when they lost 3-0 at Keighley. In the first round they beat BROOKLAND ROVERS 16-5.

There have been several other instances of non-League clubs meeting in the first round. The last occasion was in 1960 when WALNEY CENTRAL beat LOCK LANE 10-5 before losing at Oldham 55-4 in the second round.

In 1964 THAMES BOARD MILLS received a bye when Bradford Northern disbanded, but lost 48-8 at Blackpool Borough in the second round.

Draws against Senior Clubs
1905-06   VICTORIA RANGERS 0 v. Widnes 0
            Widnes won replay 8-3

1906-07   WORKINGTON 3 v. Wakefield Trinity 3
            Wakefield Trinity won replay 16-5

1907-08　WIGAN HIGHFIELD 3 v. Bramley 3
　　　　　Bramley won replay 8-6

1911-12　NORMANTON ST. JOHN'S 6 v. Warring-
　　　　　ton 6. Warrington won replay 75-0

1921-22　Widnes 5 v. WIGAN HIGHFIELD 5
　　　　　Widnes won replay 9-4

1951-52　RYLAND RECS 9 v. Whitehaven 9 (2nd leg)
　　　　　Whitehaven won first leg 16-0

1986-87　KELLS 4 v. Fulham 4
　　　　　Fulham won replay 22-14

RECORD SCORES

Team

Huddersfield 119 v. SWINTON PARK 2 (1913-14)

● This is the highest score in any competitive match in England.

Non-League teams have provided other sides with club records as follows:

Hull K.R.　73 v. BROOKLAND ROVERS 5 (1905)
Rochdale H. 75 v. BROUGHTON MOOR 13 (1915)
Wigan　　　116 v. FLIMBY & FOTHERGILL 0
　　　　　　　　　　　　　　　　　　　　(1925)
Barrow　　83 v. MARYPORT 3 (1938)
Blackpool B. 48 v. THAMES BOARD MILLS 8 (1964)
St. Helens　73 v. WARDLEY 0 (1924 at Swinton)

All told, non-League clubs have conceded 50 points or more on 42 occasions but only once after 1973-74 (B.A.R.L.A.'s first season).
The lowest score by a senior club was in the 0-0 draw between VICTORIA RANGERS and Widnes in 1906.

Individual

Most tries and points:
11 tries (10g) 53 points by George West (Hull K.R.) v. BROOKLAND ROVERS (1905)

Most goals:
22 by Jim Sullivan (Wigan) v. FLIMBY & FOTHERGILL (1925)

● All three feats are records for any competitive matches in England.

HIGHEST NON-LEAGUE SCORES

FEATHERSTONE ROVERS 23 v. Widnes 2 (second round 1906)

Only other 20 score:

LATCHFORD ALBION 20 v. Wigan 40 (1st leg 1954)
Wigan won second leg 41-2

PILKINGTON RECS. 22 v. Castleford 23 (1978)

NON-LEAGUE CLUBS YEAR-BY-YEAR CUP RECORD FROM 1904

● Non-League clubs in block capitals and all first round ties other than where stated.

1903-04　Broughton R. 26 v. PARTON 0
　　　　　Salford 57 v. BROOKLAND ROVERS 0

1904-05　Hull 52 v. LEIGH SHAMROCKS 0
　　　　　Hull KR 73 v. BROOKLAND ROVERS 5
　　　　　Hunslet 22 v. PARTON 3
　　　　　Leeds 20 v. OSSETT 0
　　　　　St. Helens 9 v. ROCHDALE R. 2

1905-06　EGERTON 9 v. LEIGH SHAMROCKS 0
　　　　　FEATHERSTONE ROVERS 16 v.
　　　　　　　　　BROOKLAND ROVERS 5
　　　　　Keighley 13 v. EGREMONT 0
　　　　　VICTORIA RANGERS 0 v. Widnes 0
　　　　　　　　　Replay
　　　　　Widnes 8 v. VICTORIA RANGERS 3
　　　　　　　　　Second round
　　　　　FEATHERSTONE ROVERS 23 v. Widnes 2
　　　　　Salford 38 v. EGERTON 5
　　　　　　　　　Third round
　　　　　Keighley 3 v. FEATHERSTONE ROVERS 0

1906-07　Halifax 45 v. MILLOM 0
　　　　　Huddersfield 38 v.
　　　　　　　　　BRIGHOUSE ST. JAMES 0
　　　　　Keighley 18 v. BROOKLAND ROVERS 0
　　　　　RADCLIFFE RANGERS 0 v. York 13
　　　　　WHITEHAVEN REC 10 v.
　　　　　　　　　SAVILLE GREEN 0
　　　　　WORKINGTON 3 v. Wakefield T. 3
　　　　　　　　　Replay
　　　　　Wakefield T. 16 v. WORKINGTON 5
　　　　　　　　　Second round
　　　　　WHITEHAVEN REC 0 v. Keighley 14

1907-08　Barrow 28 v. MILLOM 5
　　　　　Batley 32 v. BARROW ST. GEORGE 5
　　　　　BEVERLEY 3 v. Merthyr Tydfil 15
　　　　　HALF-ACRE TRINITY 2 v. York 7
　　　　　WHITEHAVEN REC 13 v. St. Helens 8
　　　　　WIGAN HIGHFIELD 3 v. Bramley 3
　　　　　　　　　Replay
　　　　　Bramley 8 v. WIGAN HIGHFIELD 6
　　　　　　　　　Second round
　　　　　Merthyr Tydfil 33 v.
　　　　　　　　　WHITEHAVEN REC 5

1908-09　Barrow 36 v. BARROW ST. GEORGE 0
　　　　　BEVERLEY 7 v. Ebbw Vale 2
　　　　　NORMANTON 10 v. Hull 20
　　　　　Runcorn 23 v. EGREMONT 5
　　　　　PEMBERTON 6 v. Keighley 41
　　　　　　　　　Second round
　　　　　Halifax 53 v. BEVERLEY 2

1909-10	MILLOM 9 v. BROOKLAND ROVERS 4
	PURSTON WHITE HORSE 10 v.
	Halifax 23
	Salford 64 v. YORK IRISH
	NATIONAL LEAGUE 0
	Warrington 31 v. WIGAN HIGHFIELD 3
	Second round
	Warrington 37 v. MILLOM 0
1910-11	BROUGHTON MOOR 6 v. Runcorn 23
	Dewsbury 47 v. YORK GROVE UNITED 0
	NORMANTON ST. JOHN'S 6 v.
	Broughton R. 10
	PEMBERTON 4 v. Bradford N 12
	Widnes 23 v. LANE END UNITED 0
1911-12	BEVERLEY 5 v. Hull KR 34
	Dewsbury 36 v. LANE END UNITED 9
	MILLOM 0 v. Keighley 11
	NORMANTON ST. JOHN'S 6 v.
	Warrington 6
	Replay
	Warrington 75 v.
	NORMANTON ST. JOHN'S 0
	Wigan 35 v. WIGAN HIGHFIELD 10
1912-13	Bradford N 33 v. PEMBERTON 4
	Broughton R 59 v. BARTON 0
	ELLAND 2 v. Wakefield T 15
	Hull 24 v. SEATON 2
	NORMANTON ST. JOHN'S 4 v.
	Oldham 17
	Rochdale H. 15 v.
	FEATHERSTONE ROVERS 3
1913-14	CASTLEFORD 8 v. Wigan 27
	ELLAND 2 v.
	FEATHERSTONE ROVERS 7
	Huddersfield 119 v. SWINTON PARK 2
	Hull KR 62 v. MILLOM 0
	St. Helens 27 v. WIGAN HIGHFIELD 4
	York 45 v. GLASSON RANGERS 0
	Second round
	FEATHERSTONE ROVERS 3 v. Hull 27
1914-15	BRIGHOUSE RANGERS 0 v.
	Salford 26
	BROUGHTON MOOR 6 v. WARDLEY 3
	FEATHERSTONE ROVERS 0 v.
	St. Helens 6
	Keighley 8 v. ASKHAM 5
	WIGAN HIGHFIELD 0 v. Swinton 2
	Second round
	Rochdale H 75 v. BROUGHTON MOOR 13
1919-20	Bramley 13 v. WIGAN HIGHFIELD 0
	FEATHERSTONE ROVERS 2 v.
	Broughton R 17
	Halifax 55 v. BROOKLAND ROVERS 0
	Hull 75 v. BRITISH OIL & CAKE MILLS 2
	Leeds 44 v. MILLOM 5
	Warrington 9 v. ASKHAM-in-FURNESS 0
	Wigan 64 v. HEALEY STREET ADULTS 3

1920-21	ASKHAM 2 v. Bradford N 7
	FEATHERSTONE ROVERS 41 v.
	PENDLEBURY 0
	Oldham 41 v. ELLAND WANDERERS 5
	Swinton 25 v. BRITISH OIL &
	CAKE MILLS 5
	Widnes 41 v. DEARHAM WANDERERS 5
	WIGAN HIGHFIELD 10 v. Broughton R 15
	Second round
	FEATHERSTONE ROVERS 0 v.
	Dewsbury 22
1921-22	ASKHAM 15 v. CADISHEAD 5
	ELLAND WANDERERS 0 v. Oldham 29
	Rochdale H 54 v. BROUGHTON MOOR 2
	Swinton 24 v. BRITISH OIL &
	CAKE MILLS 5
	Widnes 5 v. WIGAN HIGHFIELD 5
	Replay
	WIGAN HIGHFIELD 4 v. Widnes 9
	Second round
	Keighley 15 v. ASKHAM 0
1922-23	NORWOOD 3 v. St. Helens 29
	Salford 16 v. CASTLEFORD 0
	Wakefield T 67 v HENSINGHAM 13
	Wigan Highfield 16 v.
	CADISHEAD & IRLAM 0
	York 40 v. MILLOM 0
1923-24	Barrow 67 v. DEARHAM WANDERERS 3
	Broughton R 34 v. HULL ST. PATRICK'S 0
	WARDLEY 0 v. St. Helens 73
	Warrington 46 v. DALTON 3
	Hull KR 24 v. CASTLEFORD 0
1924-25	BARNSLEY UNITED (Hull) 3 v.
	DALTON 3
	Hunslet 25 v. CASTLEFORD 0
	Leeds 27 v. TWELVE APOSTLES 0
	Wigan 116 v. FLIMBY & FOTHERGILL 0
	Replay
	DALTON 3 v.
	BARNSLEY UNITED (Hull) 2
	Second round
	St. Helens Rec 74 v. DALTON 5
1925-26	Barrow 44 v.
	BARROW CAMBRIDGE ST. 0
	CASTLEFORD 12 v. St. Helens Rec 18
	HENSINGHAM 0 v. Huddersfield 33
	Hull 7 v. PEMBERTON ROVERS 3
	Hull KR 28 v.
	BARNSLEY UNITED (Hull) 0
1926-27	Batley 32 v. COTTINGHAM 5
	Dewsbury 20 v.
	DEARHAM WANDERERS 5
	Wigan 51 v. PEMBERTON ROVERS 11
1927-28	Batley 31 v. COTTINGHAM 2
	Bradford N 17 v. TWELVE APOSTLES 0
	Warrington 43 v. KINSLEY 2
	WHITEHAVEN REC 0 v. Swinton 44

1928-29	Castleford 31 v. WHITEHAVEN REC 7
	Dewsbury 37 v. COTTINGHAM 0
	St. Helens 32 v. LINDLEY 2
	Wigan Highfield 45 v. UNO's DABS 0
1929-30	Halifax 74 v.
	FEATHERSTONE JUNIORS 9
	Hull 44 v. BICKERSHAW HORNETS 10
	Keighley 6 v. GREAT CLIFTON 5
	Leigh 48 v. COTTINGHAM 0
1930-31	Bramley 7 v. GOLDEN LIONS 3
	Huddersfield 60 v.
	BROOKLAND ROVERS 2
	LINDLEY 2 v. Rochdale H 13
	Wigan Highfield 41 v.
	FEATHERSTONE JUNIORS 3
1931-32	Barrow 65 v. LINDLEY 5
	Dewsbury 27 v. UNO's DABS 10
	GREAT CLIFTON 2 v. Broughton R 20
1932-33	ASKERN WELFARE 0 v. Wigan 46
	Halifax 42 v. UNO's DABS 5
	Hull 37 v. HIGGINSHAW 9
	York 35 v. BARROW MARSH HORNETS 6
1933-34	Bramley 20 v. DEARHAM WANDERERS 11
	Hull KR 18 v. WIGAN RANGERS 2
	London Highfield 32 v. HULL ST MARY'S 2
	St. Helens Rec 32 v.
	PENDLEBURY JUNIORS 3
1934-35	Barrow 28 v. SHARLSTON 3
	Castleford 33 v. ASTLEY &
	TYLDESLEY COLLIERIES 4
	MANCHESTER SHIP CANAL 9 v.
	Dewsbury 28
	Rochdale H. 28 v.
	BARROW MARSH HORNETS 18
1935-36	Leigh 49 v. SEATON 4
	Oldham 38 v. HIGGINSHAW 2
1936-37	GOOLE 2 v. Broughton Rangers 14
	Widnes 39 v. HIGGINSHAW 2
1937-38	Rochdale H 50 v. GLASSHOUGHTON 2
	St. Helens 39 v. PENDLEBURY 0
	Barrow 83 v. MARYPORT 3
1938-39	Bradford N 37 v. SEATON 7
	SHARLSTON 5 v. Bramley 23
	Hunslet 48 v.
	UNITED GLASS BLOWERS 5
	Swinton 46 v. HIGGINSHAW 3

1945-46	HULL JUNIORS 0 v. Bramley 29
	Bramley 51 v. HULL JUNIORS 3
	Hull KR 18 v.
	LANGWORTHY JUNIORS 0
	LANGWORTHY JUNIORS 7 v.
	Hull KR 14
	KELLS 0 v. Warrington 3
	Warrington 27 v. KELLS 0
	HIGHER INCE 3 v. Widnes 30
	Widnes 42 v. HIGHER INCE 3
	SHARLSTON 12 v. Workington Town 7
	Workington Town 16 v. SHARLSTON 2
1946-47	WHELDALE COLLIERY 0 v. Halifax 25
	Halifax 20 v. WHELDALE COLLIERY 10
	PEMBERTON ROVERS 6 v. Liverpool S 27
	Liverpool S 20 v. PEMBERTON ROVERS 5
	Warrington 46 v. BROOKLAND ROVERS 3
	BROOKLAND ROVERS 3 v. Warrington 32
	Workington T 48 v. WIDNES DRAGONS 0
	WIDNES DRAGONS 5 v. Workington T 21
1947-48	VINE TAVERN 6 v. Bramley 17
	Bramley 10 v. VINE TAVERN 2
	Keighley 11 v. RISEHOW & GILLHEAD 0
	RISEHOW & GILLHEAD 10 v. Keighley 2
	Rochdale H 13 v. PEMBERTON ROVERS 0
	PEMBERTON ROVERS 0 v. Rochdale H 11
	St. Helens 48 v.
	BUSLINGTHORPE VALE 0
	BUSLINGTHORPE VALE 2 v.
	St. Helens 13
1948-49	NORMANTON 4 v. Belle Vue Rangers 9
	Belle Vue Rangers 12 v. NORMANTON 0
	Oldham 30 v. BROUGHTON MOOR 0
	BROUGHTON MOOR 2 v. Oldham 35
	VINE TAVERN 4 v. York 11
	York 17 v. VINE TAVERN 3
1949-50	WORSLEY BOYS' CLUB 7 v. Hunslet 45
	Hunslet 18 v. WORSLEY BOYS' CLUB 9
	CARDIFF 10 v. Salford 15
	Salford 20 v. CARDIFF 5
	BROUGHTON MOOR 5 v. Wakefield T 28
	Wakefield T 73 v. BROUGHTON MOOR 3
1950-51	LLANELLY 9 v. Barrow 23
	Barrow 39 v. LLANELLY 5
	Batley 41 v. BROUGHTON MOOR 3
	BROUGHTON MOOR 0 v. Batley 36
	Leigh 43 v. LATCHFORD ALBION 0
	LATCHFORD ALBION 0 v. Leigh 19
1951-52	Whitehaven 16 v. RYLANDS RECS 0
	RYLANDS RECS 9 v. Whitehaven 9

1952-53	ORFORD TANNERY 2 v. Warrington 46 Warrington 46 v. ORFORD TANNERY 8 Widnes 28 v. HULL DOCKERS (NDLB) 0 HULL DOCKERS (NDLB) 3 v. Widnes 22

1953-54	LATCHFORD ALBION 20 v. Wigan 40
	Wigan 41 v. LATCHFORD ALBION 2
	Workington T 50 v.
	    WHELDALE COLLIERY 2
	WHELDALE COLLIERY 6 v.
	    Workington T 32

1954-55	Workington T 43 v. DEWSBURY CELTIC 0
1955-56	Keighley 33 v. TRIANGLE VALVE 8 Rochdale H 55 v. STANNINGLEY 0
1956-57	Barrow 53 v. WAKEFIELD LOCOMOTIVE 12 Halifax 48 v. WIDNES ST. MARIE'S 0
1957-58	York 50 v. LOCK LANE 5 Widnes 51 v. ORFORD TANNERY 2
1958-59	York 54 v. ASTLEY & TYLDESLEY COLLIERY 2 Hunslet 55 v. KELLS REC CENTRE 9
1959-60	WALNEY CENTRAL 10 v. LOCK LANE 5 *Second round* Oldham 55 v. WALNEY CENTRAL 4
1960-61	Hull KR 56 v. PILKINGTON RECS 8 DEWSBURY CELTIC 0 v. Castleford 32
1961-62	Hunslet 53 v. OLDHAM ST ANNE'S 10 BROOKHOUSE 4 v. Doncaster 7
1962-63	Liverpool C 11 v. ROOSE 0 IMPERIAL ATHLETIC 4 v. Bramley 15
1963-64	Featherstone R 60 v. STANNINGLEY 4 THAMES BOARD MILLS — a bye *Second round* Blackpool B 48 v. THAMES BOARD MILLS 8
1964-65	Blackpool B 27 v. CROSSFIELD RECS 4 Swinton 48 v. DEWSBURY CELTIC 5
1965-66	Barrow 11 v. CROSSFIELD RECS 2 Widnes 23 v. BROOKHOUSE 5
1966-67	BLACKBROOK 12 v. York 23 BRITISH OIL & CAKE MILLS 9 v. Liverpool C 20

1967-68	LEIGH MINERS' WELFARE 7 v.
	    Halifax 24
	BRITISH OIL & CAKE OILS 6 v.
	    Castleford 9

1968-69	Wigan 61 v. LEIGH MINERS' WELFARE 0 Wakefield T 50 v. ACKWORTH 7
1969-70	Doncaster 22 v. GLASSON RANGERS 4 Huddersfield 15 v. LOCK LANE 10
1970-71	Dewsbury 25 v. BRITISH OIL & CAKE MILLS 3 Hunslet 49 v. THAMES BOARD MILLS 5
1971-72	Bramley 19 v. PILKINGTON RECS 5 DEWSBURY CELTIC 2 v. Featherstone Rovers 34
1972-73	MILLOM 5 v. Hunslet 18 Leigh 27 v. DEWSBURY CELTIC 4
1973-74	LOCK LANE 9 v. Wigan 37 Leigh 63 v. KIPPAX WHITE SWAN 7
1974-75	DEWSBURY CELTIC 15 v. Hull KR 31 New Hunslet 9 v. MAYFIELD 5
1975-76	Leigh 37 v. POINTER PANTHERS 8 Warrington 16 v. LEIGH MINERS' WELFARE 12
1976-77	BEECROFT & WIGHTMAN 2 v. Swinton 10 PILKINGTON RECS 4 v. Wigan 10
1977-78	DEWSBURY CELTIC 5 v. Wigan 15 PILKINGTON RECS 22 v. Castleford 23
1978-79	LEIGH MINERS' WELFARE 10 v. Leigh 23 Oldham 23 v. ACE AMATEURS 5
1979-80	ACE AMATEURS 5 v. Widnes 22 Hull 33 v. MILLOM 10
1980-81	PILKINGTON RECS 7 v. York 18
1985-86	*Preliminary round* Hull 38 v. DUDLEY HILL 10 Hunslet 20 v. KELLS 8
1986-87	*Preliminary round* Castleford 74 v. BLACKBROOK 6 ELLAND 6 v. HEWORTH 10 KELLS 4 v. Fulham 4 *Replays* Fulham 22 v. KELLS 14 *First round* Mansfield M. 14 v. HEWORTH 7
1987-88	*Preliminary round* HEWORTH 11 v. WEST HULL 4 KELLS 0 v. Leeds 28 LEIGH MINERS' WELFARE 4 v. Hunslet 23 *First round* HEWORTH 4 v. Halifax 60

CHALLENGE CUP PROGRESS CHART

Key: W — Winners. F — Beaten finalists. SF — Semi-final. P — Preliminary round.

	1987-88	1986-87	1985-86	1984-85	1983-84	1982-83	1981-82	1980-81	1979-80	1978-79	1977-78	1976-77	1975-76	1974-75	1973-74	1972-73	1971-72	1970-71	1969-70	1968-69	1967-68
BARROW	1	2	2	P	1	2	2	1	2	3	1	2	1	1	1	1	2	1	2	1	1
BATLEY	1	1	1	1	1	1	2	1	1	1	1	1	1	1	1	1	1	1	1	1	1
BRADFORD N.	1	2	3	3	3	SF	3	1	3	SF	3	3	2	3	3	F	2	1	1	2	2
BRAMLEY	P	1	2	3	1	1	1	1	1	2	1	1	1	1	2	1	3	3	2	2	2
CARLISLE	1	2	1	1	P	1	1														
CASTLEFORD	1	1	W	SF	3	SF	SF	2	2	3	3	3	1	1	1	SF	2	SF	W	W	3
DEWSBURY	1	1	1	1	1	1	1	2	1	2	1	3	1	1	SF	SF	1	2	1	1	1
DONCASTER	3	1	2	P	2	1	1	1	1	1	1	1	2	1	1	1	1	1	3	1	1
FEATHERSTONE R.	2	1	1	P	1	W	P	3	1	1	SF	2	SF	1	F	W	2	2	1	2	3
FULHAM	1	1	1	1	2	2	2	1													
HALIFAX	F	W	1	2	1	2	3	2	SF	1	1	1	1	1	1	1	SF	1	1	1	2
HUDDERSFIELD B.	P	1	1	1	1	1	1	1	2	3	3	1	1	1	1	1	2	SF	2	2	SF
HULL	SF	3	1	F	2	F	W	2	F	3	2	2	1	2	1	2	2	3	1	1	1
HULL K.R.	3	3	F	SF	3	1	2	F	W	2	1	SF	2	3	2	2	1	1	SF	1	1
HUNSLET	1	2	1	3	2	3	1	1	1	2	1	2	3	1	2	1	2	1	1	1	1
KEIGHLEY	2	2	1	1	1	1	1	2	1	2	1	1	SF	1	1	1	2	1	2	1	3
LEEDS	2	3	SF	1	SF	2	SF	1	2	1	W	W	3	SF	3	1	F	F	3	3	W
LEIGH	1	SF	3	2	1	1	3	2	1	2	1	1	3	2	SF	2	2	W	3	1	2
MANSFIELD M.	2	2	P	1																	
OLDHAM	1	2	SF	1	2	1	2	3	2	2	2	1	3	3	1	3	1	1	2	2	3
ROCHDALE H.	2	1	2	2	1	1	2	1	2	2	1	2	1	2	2	2	1	1	2	3	1
RUNCORN H.	1	1	1	2	1	2	1	1	1	1	1	1	1	2	1	1	1	1	2	1	1
ST. HELENS	3	F	2	1	3	3	1	SF	2	SF	F	SF	W	2	3	2	W	2	SF	3	1
SALFORD	SF	1	1	2	1	2	1	3	3	1	2	2	2	2	1	1	3	3	F	2	
SHEFFIELD E.	2	1	1	1																	
SPRINGFIELD B.	2	1	2	1	1	1	1	1	1	1	1	1	1	1	1	1	1	1	1	1	1
SWINTON	1	P	P	1	P	2	1	1	1	2	2	1	1	2	1	2	3	3	2	1	1
WAKEFIELD T.	1	2	1	2	2	2	3	3	3	F	2	2	1	SF	1	3	3	1	1	SF	F
WARRINGTON	2	1	2	2	2	3	1	SF	3	1	SF	1	3	F	W	3	SF	2	2	SF	1
WHITEHAVEN	P	3	1	1	1	1	1	1	1	1	1	1	1	1	1	1	1	1	1	1	1
WIDNES	3	SF	3	3	W	1	F	W	SF	W	3	F	F	W	2	2	1	2	1	3	2
WIGAN	W	1	3	W	F	1	2	1	1	2	2	2	2	3	3	2	2	F	2	SF	
WORKINGTON T.	1	P	1	2	2	3	2	2	1	1	2	3	2	2	2	2	1	1	1	2	2
YORK	1	P	2	1	SF	1	1	2	2	1	1	1	2	2	1	1	3	1	1	1	2

JOHN PLAYER SPECIAL TROPHY

1987-88 Final

Neil Holding brought St. Helens a drop of success ... their first-ever haul of the John Player Special Trophy in the competition's 17-year history.

The scrum half's 38th minute drop goal proved to be the vital difference between two equally-matched sides who provided top class entertainment on a rain-soaked, energy-sapping Central Park, Wigan, pitch.

Both teams produced two tries, three goals and two attempted drop goals. Holding's drop shot was the only one on target to give St. Helens a 15-14 victory and the only major honour to have eluded them.

After an early season of brawls and increased dismissals, this John Player epic in front of a national television audience was the perfect advertisement for the game, none of the 12 penalties, six apiece, awarded by Fred Lindop being for foul play.

Cock-a-hoop after their semi-final humiliation of Wigan, big-spending Leeds opened the scoring after 13 minutes with a try and goal from stand off David Creasser. Second row man Roy Powell, a contender for the Man of the Match award, broke through to send Creasser to the line with a perfectly timed pass.

Four minutes later St. Helens centre Paul Loughlin kicked a penalty goal before putting the Saints in front with a try and goal in the 25th minute. The long striding Great Britain Under-21 threequarter slid over between the posts and the try was awarded despite claims of a double movement.

Two minutes later Creasser equalised with a penalty goal before adding to his considerable contribution to a thrilling encounter. Great Britain packman Paul Medley pulled off one of his now famous 'hits' with a crunching tackle on Welsh prop Peter Souto. As the ball shot loose, Leeds hooker Colin Maskill fed Creasser who set up Australian centre Peter Jackson to restore the Yorkshiremen's lead, Creasser adding the goal.

Two minutes before the interval, Holding popped up to drop the goal which was to make all the difference, Leeds turning round with a 14-9 advantage.

Their half-time lead lasted only two minutes, Loughlin heading for the Man of the Match award by scoring his second try and 14th point for the Saints, only one short of the record for a final. Platt and Forber fed the tall centre who moved inside in classic style to leave behind the challenges of John Basnett and Marty Gurr enroute to the Leeds posts, adding the goal to put Saints 15-14 ahead.

In the remaining 38 minutes, the Leeds forwards continually drove into the Saints' half but, despite pre-match planning, only two drop kicks at goal were attempted. Scrum half Ray Ashton's bid barely got off the ground and Garry Schofield's 73rd minute attempt from further out hit an upright.

St. Helens, renowned for their attacking prowess, earned new found recognition for their defensive qualities as Leeds stormed their line in a tremendous second half in which discipline was of the highest order with only two penalties being conceded, both for offside. Saints' loose forward Andy Platt led the way with a staggering 43 tackles overall, well supported by Paul Forber, Tony Burke and captain Shane Cooper.

A jubilant St. Helens coach, Alex Murphy, collected his first trophy since taking over in November 1985 and earmarked the goal-kicking Loughlin as a tour candidate. The same tag was also hung on Leeds packman Powell who stood out in the Central Park mud with his strong running, powerhouse tackling and well-timed distribution.

141

JOHN PLAYER SPECIAL TROPHY FINAL
9 January   **Wigan**

LEEDS 14		**ST. HELENS 15**
Marty Gurr	1.	Phil Veivers
Steve Morris	2.	David Tanner
Garry Schofield	3.	Paul Loughlin
Peter Jackson	4.	Mark Elia
John Basnett	5.	Les Quirk
David Creasser	6.	Shane Cooper, Capt.
Ray Ashton	7.	Neil Holding
Peter Tunks, Capt.	8.	Tony Burke
Colin Maskill	9.	Paul Groves
Kevin Rayne	10.	Peter Souto
Roy Powell	11.	Paul Forber
Paul Medley	12.	Roy Haggerty
David Heron	13.	Andy Platt
Carl Gibson	14.	David Large
John Fairbank	15.	Stuart Evans

T: Creasser, Jackson
G: Creasser (3)
Substitutions:
Gibson for Basnett (70 min.)
Fairbank for Rayne (70 min.)
Referee: Fred Lindop (Wakefield)

T: Loughlin (2)
G: Loughlin (3), Holding (dg)
Substitution:
Evans for Souto (64 min.)
Half-time: 14-9
Attendance: 16,669

Dressing room celebrations for first-ever John Player Special Trophy winners, St. Helens.

Man of the Match Paul Loughlin en route to his second touchdown, leaving Leeds full back Marty Gurr in his wake.

Neil Holding, scorer of the vital drop goal, by-passes Leeds duo Roy Powell (grounded) and Colin Maskill.

1987-88 Round by Round

The two amateur clubs in the four-tie preliminary round were both soundly beaten, St. Helens-based Thatto Heath going down 34-16 at Featherstone Rovers and York's Heworth crashing 32-5 at home to First Division Swinton. Featherstone led 24-2 at half time in the Post Office Road tie, although Thatto Heath had the better of the second half scoring with stand off Norman Barrow scoring two of their three tries. At York's Wiggington Road ground, Swinton's superiority in the backs was reflected by their scoring all but one of their six tries. Winger St. John Ellis scored 22 points, only four short of the club record, in York's 38-2 home defeat of Bramley, whose points came from a Peter Lister penalty goal. Oldham disposed of fellow Second Division side Fulham 36-8, the Watersheddings tie being highlighted by two Paul Round touchdowns and six goals from Australian Peter Walsh, but marred by scrum half Paddy Kirwan being carried off with a broken leg.

In the first round, former Hunslet coach Paul Daley masterminded Batley's progress into the second round for the first time since 1975 with an 18-16 home success over his old club. The turning point came seven minutes from time when Batley hooker Russell Sowden scored under the posts for Malcolm Agar to kick his fifth goal. Three players were sent off and one sin-binned in a bad-tempered tie between Dewsbury and Doncaster at Crown Flatt, the home side coming back from 10-0 down to win 14-12. Kevin Jones and Mark Gibbon, of Doncaster, and Dewsbury's Gary Cocks were dismissed, with home skipper Paul Shuttleworth being sin binned. League title contenders Warrington travelled to Second Division Carlisle to find themselves trailing 8-4 at half-time and 16-8 well into the second half. The Wire pulled back to 16-16 with only minutes left, clinching victory when Australian full back

Brian Johnson put substitute David Lyon in for a try, goalled by John Woods, who had earlier scored the 3,000th point of his career. An 18-point scoring burst early in the second half paved the way for a comfortable 34-12 Castleford success at Featherstone, after the Division Two hosts had held their Division One neighbours in the first half.

A third minute penalty goal by Dave Lowden gave Second Division Workington Town a short-lived lead at Hull, whose front row of Alan Tomlinson, Shaun Patrick and Paul Welham was outstanding, contributing four of the Airlie Birds' seven tries in a 42-6 win. Across the city, Hull K.R. disposed of Rochdale Hornets 30-12, running in 22 points in the first quarter and leading 28-0 at half-time. The Robins could add only a Mike Fletcher penalty goal in the second period, the Hornets coming back with tries from Andy Ruane and Neil Cowie. As with the Yorkshire Cup tie earlier in the season, Keighley conceded ground advantage to neighbours Halifax because of ground safety limitations. There was the consolation of a 5,000-plus crowd as the Second Division side went down 32-6 at Thrum Hall, Halifax's scoresheet featuring two tries from Ian Wilkinson and four goals from full back Graham Eadie. Huddersfield Barracudas led 12-10 at Leigh after an hour but the home side's superior pace proved decisive in the final quarter, taking their try tally to five including a debut touchdown for Kiwi winger Shane Horo. The Man of the Match award went to Huddersfield's Gary Meehan despite the 28-12 defeat.

Second Division title favourites Oldham pulled off the surprise of the round with a 22-6 defeat of Yorkshire Cup winners Bradford Northern at Watersheddings. Oldham retained their unbeaten home record, scoring four tries to one, former Northern packman Mal Graham taking the individual honours. Mansfield Marksman progressed to the second round for the first time in their four-year history in the tournament with a 6-4 victory at Runcorn Highfield, still undefeated at home in the league. In the televised tie, St. Helens beat Widnes 12-10 at Knowsley Road, the decisive try coming in the 71st minute from newly signed winger Les Quirk, his sixth touchdown in eight games. Widnes skipper Kurt Sorensen's controversial try gave the visitors a 4-3 half-time lead, Martin Offiah's last ditch try coming too late to save the Chemics. In the Manchester derby, Swinton went down 18-12 to Salford at Station Road, three players being sent off and two sin-binned. Swinton hooker Gary Ainsworth was the first to go in the 39th minute, Salford veteran Peter Glynn following in first half injury time. The visitors' Dave Bullough was a second half dismissal after they led 12-0 at half time, Australian Test full back Garry Jack having contributed his first try.

Having trailed 22-10 at Wakefield Trinity, York secured a surprise 22-22 draw with an Ellis 35-yard penalty goal, followed by a try from hooker Stuart Horton. In the replay at Wiggington Road, Trinity romped home 30-6 after Chris Hammerton had given York an early lead with a fourth minute try, the visitors touching down five times, with three further scores disallowed. Whitehaven led 14-10 at home to big spending Leeds when referee Dennis Drinkwater awarded an obstruction try to Australian centre Peter Jackson after a kick over by Lee Crooks, clinching an 18-14 victory for the Loiners. Second Division title contenders Sheffield Eagles travelled to Wigan to lead 8-2 after 23 minutes before the Champions let loose with six tries in a 34-8 victory. Springfield Borough recorded the first cup win under their new title with a creditable 14-2 scoreline against Barrow at Springfield Park, the points coming from a Jeff Bimpson try and five Mike Smith goals.

In the second round, Castleford's brawl-hit image was restored with an impressive comeback in the televised tie at Wigan. Trailing 18-0 at the interval, the Yorkshiremen tore back into the game with a classic Bob Lindner try after an 85-yard move, although his 10-minute absence in the sin bin proved costly with Wigan adding their eight second half points to register a 26-16 victory. Prop forwards Crooks and Peter Tunks formed the base for a 20-10 Leeds success over Halifax at Headingley although their three tries came from the backs. Leeds were also well served by second row pair Roy Powell and Paul Medley, Halifax's challenge being diluted by out-of-form Colin Whitfield who missed five shots before hitting his only successful kick. Brave Dewsbury came close to pulling off a shock win at Salford, leading 3-2 at the break and 5-4 after 57 minutes before Salford substitute Ian Blease grabbed the face-saving try in the 74th minute for a 14-5 win.

Hull had a 19-7 win over Leigh with Welsh centre Gary Pearce scoring 15 points from seven goals out of seven attempts and a drop goal. Warrington looked well on the way to victory over visitors Hull K.R. after a two tries in four minute burst midway through the first half. Rovers dominated the second period with Australian centre Peter Mortimer scoring his first two tries for the club, but marksman Fletcher could not find the target from a series of attempts and they went down 12-8. Wakefield Trinity created sufficient chances in the first half of the tie at Springfield Borough to secure victory, but failed to turn their superiority into points and led by only 8-6 at the interval. Borough skipper Bob Eccles clinched a 14-8 success in a dour contest with a try in the 62nd minute. St. Helens cantered to a 40-0 home victory over Second Division Mansfield Marksman, full back Veivers starring in the seven-try romp.

The third round giant killing act was carried out by Second Division pacesetters Oldham who disposed of Warrington 14-10 at

145

Wilderspool. The Watersheddings pack, well led by Man of the Match Neil Clawson, paved the way, vital tries coming either side of half-time from Terry Flanagan and Round, his 14th of the season. Wigan sealed victory at Salford in injury time with Shaun Edwards' second try gaining a 16-12 passage into the semi-finals. Trailing 12-0 at the break, Salford fought back with tries from Greg Austin and David Cairns, plus two goals from Mick Worrall before Edwards' killer blow. Lacklustre Leeds worked hard for their 22-12 win at Springfield Borough, the clinching try coming in the 66th minute from Australian winger Steve Morris after Borough trailed only 10-6 at half-time. Hull belied their lowly league position by holding St. Helens to 20-16 at Knowsley Road, Hooker Paul Groves paid back a huge chunk of his £40,000 transfer fee with a superb 67th minute try, although a try from Dane O'Hara, goalled by Pearce, set up a nerve wracking last five minutes for the Saints.

In the semi-finals, Wigan and Leeds met at Bolton Wanderers' Burnden Park ground with the Riversiders seeking their third successive final appearance. Leeds lost pack ace Crooks after only three minutes with a dislocated shoulder and went 6-0 down to a try from Steve Hampson — Wigan's best player — goalled by David Stephenson. Leeds overcame this early double blow to lead 7-6 on the hour following a try from Man of the Match Medley goalled by Colin Maskill plus a Ray Ashton drop goal. Then Garry Schofield's brilliant solo try put them on the way to a 19-6 victory. Wigan were left to ponder the wisdom of fielding youngsters like Ian Gildart, Ian Lucas and Martin Dermott in such a pressure situation. A week later at Wigan, St. Helens' sixth bid to reach the final looked like ending up as the previous five attempts ... in defeat. Second Division pacesetters Oldham led 8-6 after controlling the first half and dominating the opening 20 minutes of the second period. But in the last

quarter, the Saints forced their way over for tries to Roy Haggerty and skipper Shane Cooper, Paul Loughlin adding both goals for an 18-8 win.

Leeds stand off David Creasser, scorer of 10 points in the 1988 final.

1987-88 PRIZES

Round	Per Team	Total
Preliminary	8 × £ 1,100	£ 8,800
First	16 × £ 1,100	£ 17,600
Second	8 × £ 1,600	£ 12,800
Third	4 × £ 2,825	£ 11,300
Semi-Finals	2 × £ 4,750	£ 9,500
Runners-up	1 × £ 9,000	£ 9,000
Winners	1 × £16,000	£ 16,000

	Total Prizes	£ 85,000
Capital Development Fund		£ 65,000
	Grand Total	£150,000

RESULTS 1987-88

Preliminary Round

Featherstone R.	34	Thatto Heath	16
Heworth	5	Swinton	32
Oldham	36	Fulham	8
York	38	Bramley	2

First Round

Batley	18	Hunslet	16
Carlisle	16	Warrington	22
Dewsbury	14	Doncaster	12
Featherstone R.	12	Castleford	34
*Halifax	32	Keighley	6
Hull	42	Workington T.	6
Hull K.R.	30	Rochdale H.	12
Leigh	28	Huddersfield B.	12
Oldham	22	Bradford N.	6
Runcorn H.	4	Mansfield M.	6
Springfield B.	14	Barrow	2
St. Helens	12	Widnes	10
Swinton	12	Salford	18
Wakefield T.	22	York	22
Whitehaven	14	Leeds	18
Wigan	34	Sheffield E.	8

Replay

| York | 6 | Wakefield T. | 30 |

Second Round

Batley	0	Oldham	44
Hull	19	Leigh	7
Leeds	20	Halifax	10
St. Helens	40	Mansfield M.	0
Salford	14	Dewsbury	5
Springfield B.	14	Wakefield T.	8
Warrington	12	Hull K.R.	8
Wigan	26	Castleford	16

Third Round

St. Helens	20	Hull	16
Salford	12	Wigan	16
Springfield B.	12	Leeds.	22
Warrington	10	Oldham	14

Semi-Finals

Leeds	19	Wigan	6
(at Bolton W. FC)			
Oldham	8	St. Helens	18
(at Wigan)			

Final

| St. Helens | 15 | Leeds | 14 |
| (at Wigan) | | | |

*Keighley forfeited home advantage

JOHN PLAYER SPECIAL TROPHY ROLL OF HONOUR

Season	Winners		Runners-up		Venue	Attendance	Receipts
1971-72	Halifax	22	Wakefield T.	11	Bradford	7,975	£2,545
1972-73	Leeds	12	Salford	7	Huddersfield	10,102	£4,563
1973-74	Warrington	27	Rochdale H.	16	Wigan	9,347	£4,380
1974-75	Bradford N.	3	Widnes	2	Warrington	5,935	£3,305
1975-76	Widnes	19	Hull	13	Leeds	9,035	£6,275
1976-77	Castleford	25	Blackpool B.	15	Salford	4,512	£2,919
1977-78	Warrington	9	Widnes	4	St. Helens	10,258	£8,429
1978-79	Widnes	16	Warrington	4	St. Helens	10,743	£11,709
1979-80	Bradford N.	6	Widnes	0	Leeds	9,909	£11,560
1980-81	Warrington	12	Barrow	5	Wigan	12,820	£21,020
1981-82	Hull	12	Hull K.R.	4	Leeds	25,245	£42,987
1982-83	Wigan	15	Leeds	4	Elland Rd, Leeds	19,553	£49,027
1983-84	Leeds	18	Widnes	10	Wigan	9,510	£19,824
1984-85	Hull K.R.	12	Hull	0	Hull City FC	25,326	£69,555
1985-86	Wigan	11	Hull K.R.	8	Elland Rd, Leeds	17,573	£66,714
1986-87	Wigan	18	Warrington	4	Bolton W. FC	21,144	£86,041
1987-88	St. Helens	15	Leeds	14	Wigan	16,669	£62,232

147

JOHN PLAYER SPECIAL FINAL .... A REVIEW

1971-72
Halifax 22 Hepworth; Rayner, Davies (1t), Willicombe (1t), Kelly (1t); Burton (5g), Baker (Sanderson); Dewhirst, Hawksley, Callon (1t), (Reeves), Fogerty, J. Martin, Halmshaw
Wakefield T. 11 Wraith (Ward); Slater (1t), Marston, Hegarty, Major; Topliss (1t), Harkin; Jeanes, Morgan, Lyons, Harrison (Spencer), Valentine (1t), N. Fox (1g)
Referee: S. Shepherd (Oldham)
1972-73
Leeds 12 Holmes (1g); Alan Smith, Hynes, Dyl, Atkinson (2t); Hardisty, Hepworth; Clawson (2g) (Ward), Fisher (Pickup), Jeanes, Haigh, Cookson, Eccles
Salford 7 Charlton; Colloby, Watkins (2g), Hesketh, Richards; Gill (P. Ward), Banner; Ramshaw, J. Ward, Mackay, Grice (Davies), Kirkbride, Dixon (1t)
Referee: W.H. Thompson (Huddersfield)
1973-74
Warrington 27 Whitehead (6g, 1t); M. Philbin, Noonan (2t), Reynolds (Pickup), Bevan (1t); Whittle, Gordon; D. Chisnall, (Nicholas 1t), Ashcroft, Brady, Wright, Wanbon, B. Philbin
Rochdale H. 16 Crellin; Brelsford (2t), Brophy (1t), Taylor (1t), Aspinall; Butler (Wood), Gartland; Holliday (2g), Harris, Whitehead, Fogerty, Sheffield, Halmshaw
Referee: D.G. Kershaw (York)
1974-75
Bradford N. 3 Carlton (1t); Francis, Ward, Gant, D. Redfearn; Blacker, Seabourne; Earl, Jarvis, Jackson, Joyce, Trotter, Fearnley
Widnes 2 Dutton (1g); A. Prescott, D.O'Neill, Aspey, Anderson; Hughes, Bowden; Mills, Elwell, Sheridan, Adams, Blackwood, Laughton
Referee: G.F. Lindop (Wakefield)
1975-76
Widnes 19 Dutton (3g); A. Prescott, George, Aspey, Jenkins (2t); Hughes, Bowden (1t, 1dg); Mills, Elwell, Wood, Foran, Sheridan, Adams (1t)
Hull 13 Stephenson; A. Macklin, Clark, Portz, Hunter (1t); Hancock, Foulkes (Davidson); Ramsey, Flanagan, Wardell, Boxall (2g), Walker, Crane (2t)
Referee: J.V. Moss (Manchester)
1976-77
Castleford 25 Wraith (1t); Fenton, Joyner (1t), P. Johnson (1t), Briggs; Burton (1t), Stephens (1t); Khan, Spurr, A. Dickinson, Reilly, Lloyd (5g), S. Norton

Blackpool B 15 Reynolds; Robinson, Heritage, Machen (1t), Pitman (Lamb); Marsh, Newall; Hamilton, Allen (1t), Egan (3g, 1t), Gamble, Groves (Hurst), M. Pattinson
Referee: M. J. Naughton (Widnes)
1977-78
Warrington 9 Finnegan; Hesford (3g), Benyon, Wilson, Bevan (1t); K. Kelly, Gordon; Lester, Dalgreen, Nicholas, Martyn, B. Philbin, Potter
Widnes 4 Eckersley; Wright, Aspey, George, Woods (2g); Hughes, Bowden; Ramsey, Elwell, Shaw (Dearden), Adams, Hull, Laughton
Referee: W.H. Thompson (Huddersfield)
1978-79
Widnes 16 Eckersley; Wright (1t), Aspey, Hughes, Burke (3g); Moran, Bowden; Mills, Elwell (2dg), Shaw, Dearden, Hull (1t), Adams (2dg)
Warrington 4 Finnegan; M. Kelly, Hesford (2g), Benyon, Sutton; K. Kelly, (Hunter), Gordon; Lester, Waller, Nicholas, Case, Martyn, A. Gwilliam
Referee: G.F. Lindop (Wakefield)
1979-80
Bradford N. 6 Mumby (1g); Barends, D. Redfearn, D. Parker (1t), Gant; Stephenson (1dg), A. Redfearn; Thompson, Bridges, Forsyth (I. Van Bellen), Grayshon, G. Van Bellen (Ferres), Casey
Widnes 0 Eckersley; Wright, Aspey, George, Burke; Hughes, Bowden; Hogan (Mills), Elwell, Shaw, L. Gorley, Hull, Adams
Referee: W.H. Thompson (Huddersfield)
1980-81
Warrington 12 Hesford (2g, 2dg); Thackray, I. Duane, Bevan (2t); M. Kelly; K. Kelly, A. Gwilliam; Courtney, Waller, Case, Martyn, Potter, Hunter (Eccles)
Barrow 5 Elliott; McConnell, French, Ball (1g), Wainwright; Mason (1t), Cairns; D. Chisnall, Allen (Szymala), Flynn, K. James, Kirkby, Hadley
Referee: W.H. Thompson (Huddersfield)
1981-82
Hull 12 Banks; O'Hara, Harrison, Leuluai, Prendiville; Day, Dean (1dg) (K. Harkin); Skerrett, Wileman (1t), Stone, Crane, L. Crooks (4g), Norton
Hull K.R. 4 Fairbairn (2g); Hubbard, M. Smith, Hogan, Muscroft; Hartley, P. Harkin (Burton); Holdstock (Millington), Watkinson, S. Crooks, Lowe, Casey, Hall
Referee: G.F. Lindop (Wakefield)
1982-83
Wigan 15 Williams; Ramsdale, Stephenson, Whitfield (4g, 1dg), Gill (1t) (Juliff 1t); M. Foy, Fairhurst; Shaw, Kiss, Campbell, West (Case), Scott, Pendlebury

Leeds 4 Hague; Campbell, Wilkinson, Dyl, Andy Smith; Holmes, Dick (2g); Dickinson, Ward, Burke, Sykes, W. Heron, D. Heron
Referee: R. Campbell (Widnes)
1983-84
Leeds 18 Wilkinson; Prendiville, Creasser (5g), D. Bell, Andy Smith; Holmes (1t), Dick (1t); Keith Rayne, Ward (Squire), Kevin Rayne, Moorby, Laurie, Webb
Widnes 10 Burke (1g); Wright, Keiron O'Loughlin, Lydon (1t), Linton (1t); Hughes, Gregory; S. O'Neill, Elwell, K. Tamati, L. Gorley, Whitfield, Adams
Referee: W.H. Thompson (Huddersfield)
1984-85
Hull K.R. 12 Fairbairn; Clark (1t), Robinson, Prohm (1t), Laws; M. Smith, Harkin; Broadhurst, Watkinson, Ema, Burton, Hogan (1t), Miller
Hull 0 Kemble (Schofield); Evans, Ah Kuoi, Leuluai, O'Hara; Topliss, Sterling; Edmonds (Dannatt), Patrick, Rose, L. Crooks, Proctor, Divorty
Referee: S. Wall (Leigh)
1985-86
Wigan 11 Hampson; Mordt, Stephenson (1g), Hanley, Gill (Edwards); Ella, M. Ford (1t); Dowling (1dg), Kiss, Wane (1t), West, Goodway, Potter (Du Toit)

Hull K.R. 8 Lydiat (1t); Clark, M. Smith, Dorahy, Laws (1t); G. Smith, Harkin; P. Johnston (Robinson), Watkinson, Ema, Burton, Kelly, Miller
Referee: J. Holdsworth (Kippax)
1986-87
Wigan 18 Hampson; Stephenson, Lydon, Bell (1t), Gill (2t, 1g); Hanley, Edwards; West, Dermott, Case, Roberts, Potter, Goodway (1t)
Warrington 4 Johnson; Meadows, Cullen, Ropati, Forster (1t); Kelly, Peters (Duane); Boyd, Tamati (Rathbone), Jackson, Sanderson, Roberts, M. Gregory
Referee: J. Holdsworth (Kippax)

Paul Loughlin, 1988 Man of the Match.

JOHN PLAYER SPECIAL MAN OF THE MATCH

Season	Winner	Team	Position
1971-72	Bruce Burton	Halifax (v. Wakefield T.)	Stand off
1972-73	Keith Hepworth	Leeds (v. Salford)	Scrum half
1973-74	Kevin Ashcroft	Warrington (v. Rochdale H.)	Hooker
1974-75	Barry Seabourne	Bradford N. (v. Widnes)	Scrum half
1975-76	Reg Bowden	Widnes (v. Hull)	Scrum half
1976-77	Gary Stephens	Castleford	Scrum half
	Howard Allen	Blackpool B.	Hooker
1977-78	Steve Hesford	Warrington (v. Widnes)	Winger
1978-79	David Eckersley	Widnes (v. Warrington)	Full back
1979-80	Len Casey	Bradford N. (v. Widnes)	Loose forward
1980-81	Tommy Martyn	Warrington (v. Barrow)	Second row
1981-82	Trevor Skerrett	Hull (v. Hull K.R.)	Prop
1982-83	Martin Foy	Wigan (v. Leeds)	Stand off
1983-84	Mark Laurie	Leeds (v. Widnes)	Second row
1984-85	Paul Harkin	Hull K.R. (v. Hull)	Scrum half
1985-86	Paul Harkin	Hull K.R. (v. Wigan)	Scrum half
1986-87	Andy Goodway	Wigan (v. Warrington)	Loose forward
1987-88	Paul Loughlin	St. Helens (v. Leeds)	Centre

JOHN PLAYER SPECIAL TROPHY RECORDS

ALL ROUNDS

TEAM
*Highest score: Castleford 88 v. Millom 5
Biggest attendance: 25,326 Hull v. Hull K.R.
(at Hull C. FC)....... Final 1984-85

INDIVIDUAL
*Most goals: 17 by Sammy Lloyd (Castleford)
Most tries: 6 by Vince Gribbin (Whitehaven) v. Doncaster 1984-85
*Most points: 43 (17g,3t) by Sammy Lloyd (Castleford)
*The above records were achieved in the Castleford v. Millom first round tie in 1973-74.

JOHN PLAYER SPECIAL TROPHY FINAL RECORDS

Most final appearances: 6 by Widnes
Most wins: 3 by Warrington and Wigan
Most tries: No player has scored 3 or more
Most goals: 6 by Derek Whitehead (Warrington) v.
Rochdale H............................ 1973-74
Most points: 15 (6g,1t) by Derek Whitehead (Warrington)
v. Rochdale H......................... 1973-74
Highest score: Warrington 27 v. Rochdale H. 16 1973-74
Widest margin win: Wigan 18 v. Warrington 4 1986-87
Biggest attendance: 25,326 Hull v. Hull K.R.
(at Hull C. FC).............. 1984-85
Biggest receipts: £86,041 Wigan v. Warrington
(at Bolton W. FC).............. 1986-87

●*BEFORE 1977-78 the competition was known as the Player's No. 6 Trophy, then the John Player Trophy. In 1983-84 it became the John Player Special Trophy. It was not until 1979-80 that semi-finals were played at neutral venues.*

St. Helens captain Shane Cooper confronts Leeds defenders Colin Maskill (left) and Dave Heron in the 1988 Central Park Final.

NON-LEAGUE CLUBS IN THE
JOHN PLAYER SPECIAL TROPHY

Amateur clubs have entered the John Player tournament in every season apart from a period between 1981 and 1984. Two figured in the first round up to 1979-80 and one the following season. They were then left out from 1981-82 because the number of professional clubs had grown beyond the mathematically suitable 32.

But the amateurs returned in 1984-85 with two clubs joining the professionals in a small preliminary round.

The fate of the amateurs has varied from the record 88-5 hammering Millom received at Castleford to victories by Cawoods and Myson over Halifax and Batley respectively.

The full list of amateur clubs' results — all first round matches except where stated (P) Preliminary (2) Second Round — is:

Season							Attendance
1971-72		Wigan	33	v	Ace Amateurs (Hull)	9	2,678
		Thames Board Mill (Warr.)	7	v	Huddersfield	27	1,175
1972-73		Bramley	26	v	Pilkington Recs. (St. Helens)	5	616
		Dewsbury	22	v	Dewsbury Celtic	4	1,897
1973-74		Whitehaven	26	v	Dewsbury Celtic	3	1,276
		Castleford	88	v	Millom (Cumbria)	5	1,031
1974-75		Whitehaven	32	v	Lock Lane (Castleford)	6	537
		Doncaster	15	v	Kippax White Swan	6	453
1975-76		Salford	57	v	Mayfield (Rochdale)	3	3,449
		Barrow	16	v	Pilkington Recs. (St. Helens)	9	612
1976-77		Halifax	24	v	Ovenden (Halifax)	4	3,680
		Salford	39	v	Ace Amateurs (Hull)	15	3,037
1977-78		N.D.L.B. (Hull)	4	v	New Hunslet	18	3,845
		Halifax	8	v	Cawoods (Hull)	9	1,168
	(2)	Wakefield T.	31	v	Cawoods (Hull)	7	3,380
1978-79		Leigh Miners Welfare	9	v	Halifax	21	1,621
		Milford (Leeds)	5	v	Dewsbury	38	3,129
1979-80		Pilkington Recs. (St. Helens)	9	v	Wigan	18	6,707
		Blackpool B.	6	v	West Hull	3	555
1980-81		Castleford	30	v	Pilkington Recs. (St. Helens)	17	2,823
1984-85	(P)	Myson (Hull)	2	v	Dewsbury	8	1,572
	(P)	Keighley	24	v	Dudley Hill (Bradford)	10	1,570
1985-86	(P)	Keighley	24	v	Jubilee (Featherstone)	6	1,007
	(P)	West Hull	10	v	Castleford	24	2,500
1986-87	(P)	Batley	2	v	Myson (Hull)	8	687
	(P)	Millom (Cumbria)	4	v	Wakefield T.	18	2,000
		Myson (Hull)	11	v	Swinton	18	1,648
1987-88	(P)	Featherstone R.	34	v	Thatto Heath (St. Helens)	16	1,045
	(P)	Heworth (York)	5	v	Swinton	32	1,063

JOHN PLAYER SPECIAL TROPHY PROGRESS CHART

Key: W — Winners. F — Beaten finalists. SF — Semi-final. P — Preliminary round.

	1987-88	1986-87	1985-86	1984-85	1983-84	1982-83	1981-82	1980-81	1979-80	1978-79	1977-78	1976-77	1975-76	1974-75	1973-74	1972-73	1971-72
BARROW	1	3	2	1	2	3	3	F	1	1	1	1	2	1	1	1	3
BATLEY	2	P	1	1	P	1	1	1	1	1	1	1	2	1	1	2	1
BRADFORD N.	1	3	2	2	1	3	2	1	W	SF	SF	2	1	W	1	3	1
BRAMLEY	P	1	1	3	*	1	1	1	2	1	1	2	1	2	SF	2	2
CARLISLE	1	2	P	P	2	2	2										
CASTLEFORD	2	2	1	2	1	1	2	SF	3	3	2	W	SF	1	2	1	2
DEWSBURY	2	1	1	3	1	1	1	1	1	2	1	1	1	1	3	2	1
DONCASTER	1	2	2	1	1	1	1	1	1	1	1	1	1	2	1	1	1
FEATHERSTONE R.	1	2	P	2	3	1	2	2	2	2	3	2	1	1	1	2	1
FULHAM	P	1	1	1	1	1	1	2									
HALIFAX	2	2	1	SF	1	1	1	3	1	2	1	2	1	1	2	1	W
HUDDERSFIELD B.	1	P	1	1	1	2	2	2	1	1	3	1	3	1	1	2	2
HULL	3	SF	3	F	2	2	W	SF	1	2	1	3	F	1	1	3	3
HULL K.R.	2	1	F	W	2	3	F	2	1	SF	1	1	3	SF	1	SF	2
HUNSLET	1	1	2	P	1	1	1	2	1	1	2	1	2	1	1	1	1
KEIGHLEY	1	1	2	1	2	1	2	1	2	3	2	1	1	2	3	1	2
LEEDS	F	1	1	SF	W	F	3	1	2	1	1	3	2	3	3	W	SF
LEIGH	2	3	SF	1	SF	2	1	3	3	3	3	SF	2	1	2	2	1
MANSFIELD M.	2	1	1	1													
OLDHAM	SF	1	2	2	1	1	SF	1	1	1	2	2	2	2	1	1	1
ROCHDALE H.	1	1	1	2	1	2	1	1	1	1	1	1	1	1	F	1	2
RUNCORN H.	1	1	1	2	2	P	1	1	1	1	1	1	2	1	1	1	1
ST. HELENS	W	3	SF	3	SF	2	1	1	2	2	2	2	3	1	SF	SF	SF
SALFORD	3	1	2	1	2	3	3	2	SF	2	2	2	SF	3	2	F	1
SHEFFIELD E.	1	2	1	1													
SPRINGFIELD B.	3	2	1	1	1	2	P	2	2	1	1	F	1	1	1	1	3
SWINTON	1	2	1	1	3	1	SF	1	1	1	1	1	1	3	1	3	1
WAKEFIELD T.	2	2	2	P	1	1	1	1	SF	3	SF	1	2	2	3	2	F
WARRINGTON	3	F	3	1	2	SF	2	W	3	F	W	1	1	3	W	1	1
WHITEHAVEN	1	1	1	2	P	1	1	3	1	1	1	1	SF	2	1	2	
WIDNES	1	SF	3	3	F	SF	3	3	F	W	F	SF	W	F	1	3	1
WIGAN	SF	W	W	2	3	W	1	1	2	2	3	2	2	2	2	1	3
WORKINGTON T.	1	1	1	1	1	1	2	1	3	2	2	3	3	1	2	1	1
YORK	1	P	3	1	1	2	1	2	2	1	1	3	1	2	2	2	2

*Bramley withdrew from the Trophy while in liquidation, opponents Hull K.R. receiving a bye.

PREMIERSHIP TROPHY

1988 Final

The Stones Bitter Premiership Trophy double-header at Old Trafford, Manchester, was another great success with an 18-try feast of rugby. It provided excellent value for money for a 35,252 crowd paying record final receipts of £232,298. And the sun shone, too, in contrast to the dull, rain-lashed day for the inaugural double-header a year earlier.

Although the spectacular high-scoring Division Two final was a hard act to follow, Widnes did their best to entertain with a record-equalling 38-14 defeat of St. Helens in the Stones Bitter Premiership final. They scored seven tries, as did Warrington when they beat Halifax 38-10 in the 1986 final.

Widnes also achieved a record fourth Premiership success, while sharing with St. Helens the most final appearances of five. In lifting the trophy Widnes became only the third club to complete a Championship-Premiership double in the same season.

David Hulme took the Harry Sunderland Trophy as Man of the Match with a splendid all-round scrum half performance that included two tries and a major role in Widnes' game plan. But there were other strong contenders for the award among the champions.

Andy Currier and Darren Wright were two impressive centres in the classic style. Wright in particular stood out with his hard, straight running that brought him two superb tries. The first was a perfect example of using his winger as a foil. While St. Helens kept a close watch on the threatening pace of Martin Offiah, they allowed Wright to slip away for a superb 40-yard try.

Later in the game Wright covered a similar distance after receiving from David Hulme at a scrum and Saints were left trailing in his wake. Then Wright intercepted a wayward St. Helens pass and gave Phil McKenzie the chance to reveal his exceptional speed for a

hooker and sprint clear for another 40-yard try.

Richard Eyres was another strong candidate for individual honours, impressing with his aggressive running and smart distribution. The loose forward created the openings and provided the passes for both of David Hulme's tries.

Widnes captain Kurt Sorensen began the seven-try rout in the eighth minute as the burly New Zealand prop bumped Neil Holding out of the way and charged in from 20 yards.

Former Scotland rugby union centre Alan Tait had the unique experience of gaining a winners' medal without having played a full game of first team rugby league. His three appearances had all been as substitute in the Premiership including his ninth minute replacement of winger Rick Thackray in the final.

The Scot took the opportunity to open his RL tryscoring account with a 64th minute touchdown after Sorensen and Currier had opened the way for him.

Currier added to his contribution with four goals and Duncan Platt added another. Paul Loughlin had given St. Helens the lead in the sixth minute with the first of his three goals but it was soon wiped out and they were left chasing for the rest of the match.

They had a brief, bright spell midway through the second half when Roy Haggerty nipped in for a try after a whirling dummy and Barry Ledger got their second. They added to the entertainment without posing any threat to Widnes who finished in champion style.

St. Helens won the scrums 14-12 and penalties were 13-6 in their favour.

By completing the double Widnes ensured that Doug Laughton took the Greenalls Coach of the Year award. He had tied with Alex Murphy of St. Helens and the judges decided whoever coached the winning side in the Premiership final would be acclaimed No.1.

STONES BITTER PREMIERSHIP FINAL

15 May   Old Trafford, Manchester

ST. HELENS 14   **WIDNES 38**

Paul Loughlin	1.	Duncan Platt
Barry Ledger	2.	Rick Thackray
David Tanner	3.	Andy Currier
Mark Elia	4.	Darren Wright
Les Quirk	5.	Martin Offiah
Mark Bailey	6.	Barry Dowd
Neil Holding	7.	David Hulme
Tony Burke	8.	Kurt Sorensen, Capt.
Paul Groves, Capt.	9.	Phil McKenzie
Stuart Evans	10.	Joe Grima
Paul Forber	11.	Mike O'Neill
John Fieldhouse	12.	Paul Hulme
Roy Haggerty	13.	Richard Eyres
Shaun Allen	14.	Alan Tait
Bernard Dwyer	15.	Steve O'Neill

T: Ledger, Haggerty
G: Loughlin (3)
Substitutions:
Dwyer for Evans (47 min.)
Allen for Fieldhouse (55 min.)
Half-time: 2-16
Referee: John Holdsworth (Kippax)

T: Wright (2), D. Hulme (2), Tait,
McKenzie, Sorensen
G: Currier (4), Platt
Substitutions:
Tait for Thackray (9 min.)
S. O'Neill for Grima (58 min.)
Attendance: 35,252
Receipts: £232,298

1988 Round by Round

Champions Widnes defeated Wembley finalists Halifax 36-26 in the first round tie at Naughton Park. Great Britain tourist David Hulme was the key figure, scoring two tries and taking the Man of the Match award. The Chemics led 24-8 at the break and, although Halifax hit back with three tries, the home side never looked in danger. Paul Groves staked a strong claim for the Great Britain hooking role in St. Helens' 40-8 hammering of Castleford, scoring a hat-trick of tries and making another. The Yorkshire side could not cope with Saints' high-speed breaks, Groves scoring twice in the opening 19 minutes from Roy Haggerty passes. Wigan prop forward Adrian Shelford put his Wembley place at risk by collecting a third sin bin in the home tie with Warrington, who earned a 24-12 away victory. A niggling en-

counter featured a total of 37 penalties, with the Wire coming back from 6-2 down aided by John Woods kicking six goals from seven attempts. Bradford Northern went 14 points up inside as many minutes against Leeds at Odsal with Great Britain winger Phil Ford setting up a try for tour colleague Karl Fairbank before scoring himself after a glorious 80-yard run. Leeds pulled back to within six points at the interval but could not cope with the powerful Northern pack who laid the foundations for a 32-18 win.

In the semi-finals, Widnes and Warrington met at Naughton Park in a bitter contest which featured Wire winger Des Drummond hitting a spectator, a brawl, crowd trouble and a young boy being knocked over by fighting players. On the football side, Widnes came back from 10-0 down, Woods scoring all the Wire points, the Widnes tally of 20 without further reply coming from tries by Rick

Thackray, Andy Currier and David Hulme, plus four goals from Duncan Platt. Bradford Northern travelled to St. Helens and went down 24-10, all Saints' points coming from their tourists. Tries came from Andy Platt and Groves, Loughlin adding seven goals and Haggerty two drop goals. Northern led 10-8 at the break but faded in the last 10 minutes as Saints secured a record fifth Premiership final appearance.

David Hulme: 1988 final Man of the Match.

1988 Results

First Round

Bradford N.	32	Leeds	18
St. Helens	40	Castleford	8
Widnes	36	Halifax	26
Wigan	12	Warrington	24

Semi-Finals

| St. Helens | 24 | Bradford N. | 10 |
| Widnes | 20 | Warrington | 10 |

Final

| Widnes | 38 | St. Helens | 14 |

(at Old Trafford, Manchester)

1988 Prizes:

| Winners | £9,000 |
| Runners-up | £3,500 |

History

With the reintroduction of two divisions in 1973-74 there was no longer a need for a play-off to decide the championship.

However, it was decided to continue the tradition of an end-of-season play-off, the winners to receive the newly instituted Premiership Trophy.

In the first season of the Premiership, 1974-75, the top 12 Division One clubs and the top four from Division Two went into a first round draw, the luck of the draw operating through to the final, played on a neutral venue.

The following season the play-off was reduced to the top eight clubs in the First Division, the ties being decided on a merit basis i.e. 1st v. 8th, 2nd v. 7th etc. At the semi-final stage the highest placed clubs had the option of when to play at home in the two-legged tie.

In 1978-79 the two-leg system was suspended because of fixture congestion and the higher placed clubs had home advantage right through to the neutrally staged final. Two legs returned the following season, but were finally abolished from 1980-81.

A Second Division Premiership tournament was introduced for the first time in 1986-87.

PREMIERSHIP ROLL OF HONOUR

Year	Winners	Runners-up	Venue	Attendance	Receipts
1975	Leeds 26	St. Helens 11	Wigan 14,531		£7,795
1976	St. Helens 15	Salford 2	Swinton 18,082		£13,138
1977	St. Helens 32	Warrington 20	Swinton 11,178		£11,626
1978	Bradford N. 17	Widnes 8	Swinton 16,813		£18,677
1979	Leeds 24	Bradford N. 2	Huddersfield 19,486		£21,291
1980	Widnes 19	Bradford N. 5	Swinton 10,215		£13,665
1981	Hull K.R. 11	Hull 7	Leeds 29,448		£47,529
1982	Widnes 23	Hull 8	Leeds 12,100		£23,749
1983	Widnes 22	Hull 10	Leeds 17,813		£34,145
1984	Hull K.R. 18	Castleford 10	Leeds 12,515		£31,769
1985	St. Helens 36	Hull K.R. 16	Elland Rd, Leeds 15,518		£46,950
1986	Warrington 38	Halifax 10	Elland Rd, Leeds 13,683		£50,879
1987	Wigan 8	Warrington 0	Old Trafford, Man 38,756		£165,166
1988	Widnes 38	St. Helens 14	Old Trafford, Man 35,252		£232,298

Widnes get to grips with Roy Haggerty of St. Helens.

PREMIERSHIP FINAL . . . . A REVIEW

1974-75
Leeds 26 Holmes (2g) (Marshall 3g); Alan Smith (1t), Hynes (1t, 1dg) (Eccles), Dyl, Atkinson (2t), Mason (1t), Hepworth; Dickinson, Ward, Pitchford, Cookson, Batten, Haigh
St. Helens 11 G. Pimblett; L. Jones (1t), Wilson, Hull, Mathias (1t); Walsh, Heaton (1t); Warlow (Cunningham), A. Karalius, Mantle (K. Gwilliam), E. Chisnall, Nicholls, Coslett (1g)
Referee: W.H. Thompson (Huddersfield)
1975-76
St. Helens 15 G. Pimblett (3g); L. Jones, Glynn (1t), Noonan, Mathias; Benyon, Heaton (K. Gwilliam); Mantle, A. Karalius (1t), James, Nicholls, E. Chisnall (1t), Coslett
Salford 2 Watkins (2dg); Fielding, Richards, Hesketh, Graham; Butler, Nash; Coulman, Raistrick, Sheffield, Knighton (Turnbull), Dixon, E. Prescott
Referee: M. J. Naughton (Widnes)
1976-77
St. Helens 32 G. Pimblett (7g, 1t); L. Jones, Benyon (1t), Cunningham (1t), Mathias (1t), Glynn (Ashton); K. Gwilliam (1t); D. Chisnall, Liptrot, James (1t), Nicholls (A. Karalius), E. Chisnall, Pinner
Warrington 20 Finnegan; Curling, Bevan (Cunliffe), Hesford (4g), M. Kelly; A. Gwilliam (1t), Gordon (1t); Weavill (1t), Price, Case, Martyn (Peers), Lester, B. Philbin (1t)
Referee: G.F. Lindop (Wakefield)

1977-78
Bradford N. 17 Mumby (2g); Barends (1t), Roe (1t), Austin, D. Redfearn (1t); Wolford (1dg), A. Redfearn; I. Van Bellen (Fox), Raistrick, Thompson, Joyce (Forsyth), Trotter, Haigh (1t)
Widnes 8 Eckersley; Wright, Hughes, Aspey (2t), Woods (1g); Gill, Bowden; Mills, Elwell, Shaw (Ramsey) (George), Adams, Hull, Laughton
Referee: J.E. Jackson (Pudsey)
1978-79
Leeds 24 Hague; Alan Smith (1t), D. Smith (1t), Dyl (Fletcher), Atkinson; Dick (7g, 1dg); J. Sanderson, Harrison, Ward (1t), Pitchford, Joyce, Eccles (Adams), Cookson
Bradford N. 2 Mumby; D. Parker, Okulicz, Gant, Spencer; Ferres (1g), A. Redfearn; Thompson, Bridges, Forsyth (I. Van Bellen), Trotter (Mordue), Grayshon, Casey
Referee: W.H. Thompson (Huddersfield)
1979-80
Widnes 19 Burke (1g); Wright (1t), George, Aspey (1t), Bentley (1t); Eckersley (1dg), Bowden; Shaw, Elwell (1t, 1dg), M. O'Neill, L. Gorley (1t), Hull (Hogan), Adams
Bradford N. 5 Mumby (1g); MacLean (Ferres), D. Redfearn (1t), D. Parker, Gant; Stephenson, A. Redfearn; Thompson, Bridges, Forsyth, Clarkson (G. Van Bellen), Grayshon, Hale
Referee: W.H. Thompson (Huddersfield)

Celebration time for the victorious 1988 Widnes team.

Darren Wright dives in for his second Widnes try ahead of Paul Loughlin in the 1988 final.

1980-81
Hull K.R. 11 Proctor; Hubbard (1g), M. Smith (1t), Hogan (1t), Muscroft; Hartley (1t), Harkin; Holdstock, Watkinson, Millington, Lowe, Casey, Hall (Burton)
Hull 7 Woods (2g); Peacham, Elliott, Wilby, Prendiville; Banks, Dean; Tindall, Wileman, Stone, Skerrett (Madley), Crane (1t), Norton
Referee: J. Holdsworth (Leeds)
1981-82
Widnes 23 Burke (4g, 1t); Wright (1t), Kieron O'Loughlin, Cunningham (A. Myler), Basnett (1t); Hughes (1t), Gregory; M. O'Neill, Elwell, Lockwood (Whitfield), L. Gorley, E. Prescott, Adams (1t)
Hull 8 Kemble; O'Hara (Day), Leuluai, S. Evans, Prendiville; Topliss, Harkin; Tindall, Wileman (Lloyd), Stone, Skerrett, Crooks (1t, 2g, 1dg), Norton
Referee: S. Wall (Leigh)
1982-83
Widnes 22 Burke; Linton, Hughes, Lydon (5g), Basnett (2t); A. Myler (1t), Gregory (1t) (Hulme); M. O'Neill, Elwell, L. Gorley, Whitfield (S. O'Neill), Prescott, Adams
Hull 10 Kemble; O'Hara (1t), Day (Solal), Leuluai, S. Evans; Topliss (1t), Dean; Skerrett, Bridges, Stone, Rose, Crooks (2g), Norton (Crane)
Referee: F. Lindop (Wakefield)
1983-84
Hull K.R. 18 Fairbairn; Clark, M. Smith (1t), Prohm (1t), Laws (1t); Dorahy (1t, 1g), Harkin; Holdstock, Rudd, Millington (Robinson), Burton (Lydiat), Broadhurst, Hall

Castleford 10 Roockley; Coen, Marchant, Hyde, Kear (1t); Robinson, R. Beardmore (3g); Ward, Horton, Connell, Crampton, Atkins, Joyner
Referee: R. Campbell (Widnes)
1984-85
St. Helens 36 Veivers (1t); Ledger (2t), Peters, Meninga (2t) (Allen), Day (4g); Arkwright, Holding; Burke (Forber), Ainsworth (1t), P. Gorley, Platt, Haggerty, Pinner (1t)
Hull K.R. 16 Fairbairn (1t, 2g); Clark, Robinson (1t), Prohm, Laws (1t); M. Smith, G. Smith (Harkin); Broadhurst, Watkinson, Ema (Lydiat), Kelly, Hogan, Hall
Referee: S. Wall (Leigh)
1985-86
Warrington 38 Paul Ford (Johnson 1t); Forster (1t), Cullen, R. Duane, Carbert; Bishop (1t, 5g), A. Gregory; Boyd (2t), Tamati (1t), Jackson (1t), Sanderson (McGinty), Roberts, M. Gregory
Halifax 10 Whitfield (3g) (Smith); Riddlesden, T. Anderson, C. Anderson (1t), Wilson; Crossley, Stephens; Scott, McCallion, Robinson, Juliff, James (Bond), Dixon
Referee: F. Lindop (Wakefield)
1986-87
Wigan 8 Hampson; Gill (1g), Stephenson (1g), Bell, Lydon (1t) (Russell); Edwards, Gregory; Case, Kiss, Wane (West), Goodway, Potter, Hanley
Warrington 0 Johnson; Drummond, Ropati, B. Peters, Forster; Cullen, Bishop; Tamati, Roberts (Eccles), Jackson, Humphries (Gregory), Sanderson, Duane
Referee: K. Allatt (Southport)

THE HARRY SUNDERLAND TROPHY

The trophy, in memory of the famous Queenslander, a former Australian Tour Manager, broadcaster and journalist, is presented to the Man of the Match in the end of season Championship or Premiership final.

The award is donated and judged by the Rugby League Writers' Association and is sponsored by Stones Bitter.

The Harry Sunderland Trophy Roll of Honour

Year	Winner	Team	Position
1965	Terry Fogerty	Halifax (v. St. Helens)	Second row
1966	Albert Halsall	St. Helens (v. Halifax)	Prop
1967	Ray Owen	Wakefield T. (v. St. Helens)	Scrum half
1968	Gary Cooper	Wakefield T. (v. Hull K.R.)	Full back
1969	Bev Risman	Leeds (v. Castleford)	Full back
1970	Frank Myler	St. Helens (v. Leeds)	Stand off
1971	Bill Ashurst	Wigan (v. St. Helens)	Second row
1972	Terry Clawson	Leeds (v. St. Helens)	Prop
1973	Mick Stephenson	Dewsbury (v. Leeds)	Hooker
1974	Barry Philbin	Warrington (v. St. Helens)	Loose forward
1975	Mel Mason	Leeds (v. St. Helens)	Stand off
1976	George Nicholls	St. Helens (v. Salford)	Second row
1977	Geoff Pimblett	St. Helens (v. Warrington)	Full back
1978	Bob Haigh	Bradford N. (v. Widnes)	Loose forward
1979	Kevin Dick	Leeds (v. Bradford N.)	Stand off
1980	Mal Aspey	Widnes (v. Bradford N.)	Centre
1981	Len Casey	Hull K.R. (v. Hull)	Second row
1982	Mick Burke	Widnes (v. Hull)	Full back
1983	Tony Myler	Widnes (v. Hull)	Stand off
1984	John Dorahy	Hull K.R. (v. Castleford)	Stand off
1985	Harry Pinner	St. Helens (v. Hull K.R.)	Loose forward
1986	Les Boyd	Warrington (v. Halifax)	Prop
1987	Joe Lydon	Wigan (v. Warrington)	Winger
1988	David Hulme	Widnes (v. St. Helens)	Scrum half

PREMIERSHIP RECORDS First staged 1975

ALL ROUNDS

TEAM

Highest score: Hull K.R. 54 v. Leeds 0..............1984 (Also widest margin)

Biggest attendance: 38,756 Wigan v. Warrington
..........Final at Old Trafford 1987

INDIVIDUAL

Most goals:
9 by Andy Gregory (Widnes) v. Leeds...Round 1 1982
Most points:
22 (7g, 2t) by John Dorahy (Hull K.R.) v. Leeds
..............Round 1 1984
Most tries:
4 by David Hall (Hull K.R.) v. Castleford
..............Round 1 1983
4 by Phil Ford (Wigan) v. Hull...........Round 1 1985
4 by Ellery Hanley (Wigan) v. Hull K.R.
..............Round 1 1986

PREMIERSHIP FINAL RECORDS

TEAM

Most final appearances: 5 by Widnes, St. Helens
Most wins: 4 by Widnes
Highest score:
Warrington 38 v. Halifax 10 (widest margin).......1986
Widnes 38 v. St. Helens 14 1988
Biggest attendance:
38,756 Wigan v. Warrington
(at Old Trafford, Man'r) 1987

INDIVIDUAL

Most tries:
No player has scored 3 or more
Most goals:
8 by Kevin Dick (Leeds) v. Bradford N............1979
Most points: 17 (7g, 1t) by Geoff Pimblett (St. Helens)
v. Warrington..........1977

SECOND DIVISION

PREMIERSHIP TROPHY

1988 Final

Featherstone Rovers went so near to completing the most remarkable comeback in any final before Oldham snatched back the Second Division Premiership Trophy in a marvellous Old Trafford encounter.

Rovers trailed 22-0 after only 32 minutes but made an amazing recovery to lead 24-22 in the 67th minute and when Steve Quinn added a penalty a minute later it seemed they had achieved the near impossible. Then, with only four minutes left, Oldham revealed their fighting qualities for Des Foy to break through and set up an equalising try for Kevin Meadows after linking with Gary Warnecke.

Charlie McAlister tagged on the simple goal to give Oldham their 28-26 win but there was just as much applause for Featherstone's wonderful efforts including a generous ovation from the victors.

Foy's part in the vital last try also snatched the Man of the Match award from Featherstone's Graham Steadman. There had been little to choose between them. Both had scored two tries but with Steadman having played a major part in the revival the Press had just decided to hand him the individual honour when Foy made his decisive break and a spontaneous reaction resulted in a quick change of votes in favour of the Oldham centre.

Foy's pace and faithful support play earned him two of Oldham's first three tries in an opening blitz that cut Featherstone to pieces. The first try came in the 13th minute after receiving from Terry Flanagan, who went in for one himself five minutes later.

Then Foy finished off a spectacular 60-yard move involving second row pair Colin Hawkyard and Mal Graham plus half-back Peter Walsh. Seven minutes later Walsh dashed in

for the fourth try and McAlister added his third goal to make it 22-0 after 32 minutes. Featherstone looked dead but they would not be buried.

Even so there was little indication of what was to follow despite Steadman's first try goaled by Steve Quinn in the 38th minute. A 22-6 half-time lead still looked comfortable enough for Oldham.

And there was no cause to panic when Steadman struck again with a neat kick and follow up for a 51st minute try goaled by Quinn. But when Andy Bannister stormed in for a great 40-yard try and Quinn banged over a touchline goal the alarm bells started ringing.

Oldham were now only 22-18 ahead and they immediately replaced Mick Burke and Ian Sherratt with Richard Irving and Gary Warnecke. It made little difference as Featherstone continued to attack from all sides and swept in for their fourth try, David Sykes getting the touchdown after Steadman and Paul Lyman combined.

Featherstone fans — and many neutrals — sent up a tremendous roar when Quinn's goal put Rovers ahead with 13 minutes left. A minute later the veteran full back completed an immaculate kicking exhibition by making it five out of five with a hefty 45-yard penalty shot.

But this amazing game had one final twist as Oldham stunned gallant Rovers with their late victory rally. Rovers tried desperately to tip the scales yet again but it was just beyond them.

In addition to Steadman, who began at stand off and moved to centre when John Crossley went on as a 46th minute substitute, Rovers were inspired by the non-stop efforts of Deryck Fox. British Lion Mike Ford won the early scrum half honours before tourist standby Fox began to take control.

Scrums were 9-7 to Featherstone and penalties 12-5 in their favour.

SECOND DIVISION PREMIERSHIP TROPHY

15th May   **Old Trafford, Manchester**

FEATHERSTONE ROVERS 26   ### OLDHAM 28

Featherstone Rovers	No.	Oldham
Steve Quinn	1.	Mick Burke
Andy Bannister	2.	Paul Round
David Sykes	3.	Des Foy
Alan Banks	4.	Charlie McAlister
Richard Marsh	5.	Kevin Meadows
Graham Steadman	6.	Peter Walsh
Deryck Fox, Capt.	7.	Mike Ford
Gary Siddall	8.	Ian Sherratt
Keith Bell	9.	Ian Sanderson
Karl Harrison	10.	Hugh Waddell
Paul Hughes	11.	Colin Hawkyard
Peter Smith	12.	Mal Graham, Capt.
Paul Lyman	13.	Peter Flanagan
John Crossley	14.	Richard Irving
John Bastian	15.	Gary Warnecke

T: Steadman (2), Bannister, Sykes
G: Quinn (5)
Substitutions:
Crossley for Marsh (46 min.)
Bastian for Siddall (46 min.)
Half-time: 6-22
Referee: Robin Whitfield (Widnes)

T: Foy (2), Flanagan, Walsh, Meadows
G: McAlister (4)
Substitutions:
Irving for Burke (59 min.)
Warnecke for Sherratt (59 min.)

Featherstone Rovers' Paul Lyman charges at the Oldham defence.

1988 Round by Round

Second Division Champions Oldham were made to battle by vastly-improved Keighley in the first round tie at Watersheddings. The Roughyeds went through 34-24, the visitors scoring 12 points in the last six minutes. Oldham opened with four tries inside 23 minutes, Keighley pulling back to 17-12 before Burke scored a fortunate try to thwart their revival. Featherstone Rovers ran in eight tries in a 42-1 home success over Mansfield Marksman, who were making their debut in the competition. Scrum half Deryck Fox was the inspiration for the Colliers, setting up four tries and scoring one himself. York, having gained a draw at Wakefield Trinity in the Challenge Cup earlier in the year, were in contention again until the later stages when the Belle Vue side pulled away to win 44-23. For Trinity, Nigel Bell, Phil Eden and Steve Halliwell all grabbed two tries, full back Kevin Harcombe adding five goals. Springfield Borough secured a one-point victory over visitors Sheffield Eagles, who scored two tries through Neil Kellett against one by Mark Viller. Ron Rafferty added only one goal compared with Borough's Mike Smith, who contributed three goals and a drop goal.

In the semi-finals Oldham had to work hard for an 18-10 success over Springfield at Watersheddings, leading only 4-2 at the interval. The Roughyeds were still struggling at 14-10 before a fluke try following a Mike Ford kick through sealed victory. In a thrilling derby at Post Office Road, Featherstone Rovers edged home 20-16 to Wakefield Trinity. Rovers were leading 20-10 going into the last 10 minutes when Halliwell touched down, Mark Conway adding the goal. The visitors launched a frantic last ditch assault on the Colliers' line but the home side held out, half backs Fox and Graham Steadman in brilliant form.

1988 Results

First Round

Featherstone R.	42	Mansfield M.	1
Oldham	34	Keighley	24
Springfield B.	11	Sheffield E.	10
Wakefield T.	44	York	23

Semi-Finals

Featherstone R.	20	Wakefield T.	16
Oldham	18	Springfield B.	10

Final

Oldham	28	Featherstone R.	26

(at Old Trafford, Manchester)

1988 Prizes:

Winners	£4,000
Runners-up	£1,500

SECOND DIVISION PREMIERSHIP. . . . A REVIEW

1986-87

Swinton 27 Viller; Bate (1t), Topping (Ratcliffe), Brown, Rippon (3g); Snape, Lee (1t); Grima (1t), M. Holliday (Allen), L. Holliday (1dg)
Hunslet 10 Kay; Tate, Penola, Irvine, Wilson; Coates, King; Sykes, Gibson (Senior), Bateman (2t), Platt (1g) (Mason), Bowden, Jennings
Referee: J. McDonald (Wigan)

SECOND DIVISION PREMIERSHIP ROLL OF HONOUR

Year	Winners	Runners-up	Venue
1987	Swinton 27	Hunslet 10	Old Trafford, Man'r
1988	Oldham 28	Featherstone R....26	Old Trafford, Man'r

Des Foy, Man of the Match in the Division Two final, on the attack for Oldham.

Oldham's Paul Round breaks away in the Division Two final.

LANCASHIRE CUP

1987 Final

Only four days after their strength-sapping World Club Challenge success over top Australian side Manly, irrepressible Wigan marched on to lift the Grunhalle Lager Lancashire Cup for the third successive year with a 28-16 triumph, to extend their winning run to 29 matches.

More than 20,000 fans watched a memorable contest in which Warrington played a major part despite being without seven regular first team players and losing hooker Carl Webb after only seven minutes. The Wire, suffering their first defeat of the season, led for much of the first half and were on equal terms with only 13 minutes left of a marvellously entertaining encounter.

Wigan were at their most formidable just when they might have been expected to have been at their most vulnerable. The previous Wednesday's Anglo-Aussie challenge had been a physically punishing contest with both defences remaining intact. Yet Wigan drew on untapped resources in the final quarter of a pulsating tie at Knowsley Road, St Helens, to score 12 points and extend their record of Lancashire Cup triumphs to 19.

As the thriller entered its final phase, Warrington had pulled back to level the scores at 16-all, centre Mark Forster registering his second touchdown. Wigan stand off Shaun Edwards, an inspiration throughout, ensured that he would collect the Man of the Match award ahead of Warrington skipper Kevin Tamati by making a brilliant break in the 67th minute for Ellery Hanley to claim his second try. Joe Lydon added the simple goal to put Wigan ahead 22-16.

Six minutes from the end, scrum half Andy Gregory and 24th minute substitute Dean Bell combined to send tall New Zealander Graeme West, on for Shaun Wane, galloping free. Lydon, having taken over the kicking role from the replaced David Stephenson, kicked his fifth goal to round off the scoring.

As the game drifted into injury time, Warrington number seven Keith Holden was banished to the sin bin for tripping Lydon, a rare unsavoury moment in a tight, disciplined contest.

Wigan led 14-12 at the interval having twice trailed to a valiant Wire outfit, 0-6 and 4-12. Great Britain threequarter Forster opened the scoring in the 11th minute after an Andy Gregory kick had been charged down. Wigan's Henderson Gill replied with a touchdown in the 17th minute when the defence of his opposite number, Des Drummond, looked suspect, but Warrington regained the lead three minutes later when half backs John Woods and Holden created an opening for loose forward Mike Gregory.

A further three minutes and outstanding Wigan second row pair Andy Goodway and Ian Potter punched a huge hole in the Wire defence for Goodway to feed the supporting Hanley, who touched down by the posts for Stephenson to add the goal.

Two penalties from Lydon edged Wigan in front until Forster's second try in the 51st minute set up level scores, the excellence of both defences making a replay a distinct possibility.

Wigan found those extra reserves to collect yet another piece of silverware while injury-hit Warrington, without a trace of indignity, succumbed.

GRUNHALLE LAGER LANCASHIRE CUP FINAL

11 October   St. Helens

WARRINGTON 16		WIGAN 28
Brian Johnson	1.	Steve Hampson
Des Drummond	2.	Richard Russell
Mark Forster	3.	David Stephenson
Barry Peters	4.	Joe Lydon
Brian Carbert	5.	Henderson Gill
John Woods	6.	Shaun Edwards
Keith Holden	7.	Andy Gregory
Kevin Tamati, Capt.	8.	Brian Case
Carl Webb	9.	Nicky Kiss
Tony Humphries	10.	Shaun Wane
Gary Sanderson	11.	Andy Goodway
Mark Roberts	12.	Ian Potter
Mike Gregory	13.	Ellery Hanley, Capt.
David Lyon	14.	Dean Bell
Neil Harmon	15.	Graeme West

T: Forster (2), Gregory　　　　　　T: Hanley (2), Gill, West
G: Woods (2)　　　　　　　　　　G: Lydon (5), Stephenson
Substitution:　　　　　　　　　　Substitutions:
Harmon for Webb (7 min.)　　　　Bell for Stephenson (24 min.)
Half-time: 12-14　　　　　　　　West for Wane (52 min.)
Referee: Fred Lindop (Wakefield)　Attendance: 20, 237

1987-88 Round by Round

Favourites to retain the county cup, Wigan travelled to Barrow to record a comfortable 36-2 first round victory. The Riversiders ran in six tries, leading 16-2 at the break, with the Cumbrians' solitary reply being a Steve Tickle penalty. St. Helens paraded new £60,000 Welsh RU capture Stuart Evans but squandered a 21-11 lead by conceding three tries in a 10-minute spell in the last quarter to allow hosts Leigh a 27-21 passage into the second round. Derby rivals Runcorn Highfield and Widnes met at Canal Street in the first round for the second successive season, the Chemics again recording a big win, this time by 40-6. The tie erupted in the last 10 minutes with the dismissal of Runcorn's Paul Durnin and Widnes back Trevor Stockley, then the sin-binning of Terry Rose (Runcorn) and the visitors' Richard Eyres, before the sending off of

home forward Tony Jackson. Salford's new recruit Ken Jones bagged 22 of the Red Devils' 58 points piled up against Second Division visitors Fulham who could manage only four in reply.

Swinton registered their first victory of the season with a 38-20 success over Rochdale Hornets at Station Road, Steve Snape collecting a hat-trick of tries and Paul Topping contributing seven goals. Former Widnes hooker Andy Ruane touched down twice for the Hornets. Tempers were frayed in Warrington's 42-8 hammering of Second Division title favourites Oldham at Wilderspool. Former Wire half back Steve Peters was sent off in the first half, while four players — Warrington's Mark Roberts, Kevin Tamati and Des Drummond, plus Oldham's Paul Round — were sent to the sin bin. In the Cumbrian derby between Whitehaven and Carlisle at the Recreation Ground, the home side's supremacy in the backs paved the way for a 28-12 victory, with threequarter Willie Richardson amassing 20 points from two tries and six goals. Workington Town and Springfield Borough fought out a scoreless last quarter after Town's Dave Lowden had kicked a 50-yard penalty goal in the 48th minute of the Derwent Park clash to put the home side 12-10 ahead.

The second round saw high-riding Wigan crush Salford 42-2 at Central Park. Ellery Hanley, with a brace of touchdowns, led the Riversiders' eight-try rout, Salford's sole contribution being a Jones penalty goal. Leigh travelled to Station Road to continue their unwanted record of never beating Swinton in the Lancashire Cup. The Lions earned a 22-14 victory after Leigh had pulled back to trail only 16-14 early in the second half, Swinton's Tex Evans sealing a semi-final place with a 54th minute try. Second Division Whitehaven held a 6-4 lead over Championship pacesetters Widnes before new wing sensation Martin Offiah scored two tries for the visitors, a late Duncan

Platt touchdown killing off the Cumbrians, 20-14. Cumbria's other representative in the last eight, Workington Town, entertained Warrington and were crushed 50-10, Wire packman Mark Roberts registering a hat-trick of tries, while Town had Neil Frazer sent off and skipper Ray Tabern sin-binned.

In the semi-finals, Wigan battled their way to a fourth successive Lancashire Cup final spot with a hard-earned 20-12 victory at Widnes. In a match dominated by fierce tackling, the Riversiders scored three tries to one, the match-winning touchdown coming from Wigan centre David Stephenson when his attempted drop goal did not get off the ground, the Test threequarter dribbling through for the deciding score. At Wilderspool, Warrington cruised to a third final against Wigan in 10 months by disposing of Swinton 44-6. The tie was highlighted by the brilliance of stand off John Woods who tallied 24 points with 10 goals and a try. The Lancashire star was well supported by two-try Mark Roberts and loose forward Mike Gregory.

Warrington scrum half Keith Holden, supported by John Woods, key figures in the 1987 Lancashire Cup Final.

1987 RESULTS

First Round

Barrow	2	Wigan	36
Leigh	27	St. Helens	21
Runcorn H.	6	Widnes	40
Salford	58	Fulham	4
Swinton	38	Rochdale H.	20
Warrington	42	Oldham	8
Whitehaven	28	Carlisle	12
Workington T.	12	Springfield B.	10

Second Round

Swinton	22	Leigh	14
Whitehaven	14	Widnes	20
Wigan	42	Salford	2
Workington T.	10	Warrington	50

Semi-Finals

Warrington	44	Swinton	6
Widnes	12	Wigan	20

Final

Warrington	16	Wigan	28
(at St. Helens)			

1987 Man of the Match Shaun Edwards.

LANCASHIRE CUP ROLL OF HONOUR

Season	Winners		Runners-up		Venue	Attendance	Receipts
1905-06	Wigan	0	Leigh	0	Broughton	16,000	£400
(replay)	Wigan	8	Leigh	0	Broughton	10,000	£200
1906-07	Broughton R.	15	Warrington	6	Wigan	14,048	£392
1907-08	Oldham	16	Broughton R.	9	Rochdale	14,000	£340
1908-09	Wigan	10	Oldham	9	Broughton	20,000	£600
1909-10	Wigan	22	Leigh	5	Broughton	14,000	£296
1910-11	Oldham	4	Swinton	3	Broughton	14,000	£418
1911-12	Rochdale H.	12	Oldham	5	Broughton	20,000	£630
1912-13	Wigan	21	Rochdale H.	5	Salford	6,000	£200
1913-14	Oldham	5	Wigan	0	Broughton	18,000	£610
1914-15	Rochdale H.	3	Wigan	2	Salford	4,000	£475
1915-16 to 1917-18 *Competition suspended*							
1918-19	Rochdale H.	22	Oldham	0	Salford	18,617	£1,365
1919-20	Oldham	7	Rochdale H.	0	Salford	19,000	£1,615
1920-21	Broughton R.	6	Leigh	3	Salford	25,000	£1,800
1921-22	Warrington	7	Oldham	5	Broughton	18,000	£1,200
1922-23	Wigan	20	Leigh	2	Salford	15,000	£1,200
1923-24	St. Helens Recs.	17	Swinton	0	Wigan	25,656	£1,450
1924-25	Oldham	10	St. Helens Recs.	0	Salford	15,000	£1,116
1925-26	Swinton	15	Wigan	11	Broughton	17,000	£1,115
1926-27	St. Helens	10	St. Helens Recs.	2	Warrington	19,439	£1,192
1927-28	Swinton	5	Wigan	2	Oldham	22,000	£1,275
1928-29	Wigan	5	Widnes	4	Warrington	19,000	£1,150
1929-30	Warrington	15	Salford	2	Wigan	21,012	£1,250
1930-31	St. Helens Recs.	18	Wigan	3	Swinton	16,710	£1,030
1931-32	Salford	10	Swinton	8	Broughton	26,471	£1,654

Season	Winners		Runners-up		Venue	Attendance	Receipts
1932-33	Warrington	10	St. Helens	9	Wigan	28,500	£1,675
1933-34	Oldham	12	St. Helens Recs.	0	Swinton	9,085	£516
1934-35	Salford	21	Wigan	12	Swinton	33,544	£2,191
1935-36	Salford	15	Wigan	7	Warrington	16,500	£950
1936-37	Salford	5	Wigan	2	Warrington	17,500	£1,160
1937-38	Warrington	8	Barrow	4	Wigan	14,000	£800
1938-39	Wigan	10	Salford	7	Swinton	27,940	£1,708
1939-40*	Swinton	5	Widnes	4	Widnes	5,500	£269
	Swinton	16	Widnes	11	Swinton	9,000	£446

Swinton won on aggregate 21-15

1940-41 to 1944-45 *Competition suspended during war-time*

Season	Winners		Runners-up		Venue	Attendance	Receipts
1945-46	Widnes	7	Wigan	3	Warrington	28,184	£2,600
1946-47	Wigan	9	Belle Vue R.	3	Swinton	21,618	£2,658
1947-48	Wigan	10	Belle Vue R.	7	Warrington	23,110	£3,043
1948-49	Wigan	14	Warrington	8	Swinton	39,015	£5,518
1949-50	Wigan	20	Leigh	7	Warrington	35,000	£4,751
1950-51	Wigan	28	Warrington	5	Swinton	42,541	£6,222
1951-52	Wigan	14	Leigh	6	Swinton	33,230	£5,432
1952-53	Leigh	22	St. Helens	5	Swinton	34,785	£5,793
1953-54	St. Helens	16	Wigan	8	Swinton	42,793	£6,918
1954-55	Barrow	12	Oldham	2	Swinton	25,204	£4,603
1955-56	Leigh	26	Widnes	9	Wigan	26,507	£4,090
1956-57	Oldham	10	St. Helens	3	Wigan	39,544	£6,274
1957-58	Oldham	13	Wigan	8	Swinton	42,497	£6,918
1958-59	Oldham	12	St. Helens	2	Swinton	38,780	£6,933
1959-60	Warrington	5	St. Helens	4	Wigan	39,237	£6,424
1960-61	St. Helens	15	Swinton	9	Wigan	31,755	£5,337
1961-62	St. Helens	25	Swinton	9	Wigan	30,000	£4,850
1962-63	St. Helens	7	Swinton	4	Wigan	23,523	£4,122
1963-64	St. Helens	15	Leigh	4	Swinton	21,231	£3,857
1964-65	St. Helens	12	Swinton	4	Wigan	17,383	£3,393
1965-66	Warrington	16	Rochdale H.	5	St. Helens	21,360	£3,800
1966-67	Wigan	16	Oldham	13	Swinton	14,193	£3,558
1967-68	St. Helens	2	Warrington	2	Wigan	16,897	£3,886
(replay)	St. Helens	13	Warrington	10	Swinton	7,577	£2,485
1968-69	St. Helens	30	Oldham	2	Wigan	17,008	£4,644
1969-70	Swinton	11	Leigh	2	Wigan	13,532	£3,651
1970-71	Leigh	7	St. Helens	4	Swinton	10,776	£3,136
1971-72	Wigan	15	Widnes	8	St. Helens	6,970	£2,204
1972-73	Salford	25	Swinton	11	Warrington	6,865	£3,321
1973-74	Wigan	19	Salford	9	Warrington	8,012	£2,750
1974-75	Widnes	6	Salford	2	Wigan	7,403	£2,833
1975-76	Widnes	16	Salford	7	Wigan	7,566	£3,880
1976-77	Widnes	16	Workington T.	11	Wigan	8,498	£6,414
1977-78	Workington T.	16	Wigan	13	Warrington	9,548	£5,038
1978-79	Widnes	15	Workington T.	13	Wigan	10,020	£6,261
1979-80	Widnes	11	Workington T.	0	Salford	6,887	£7,100
1980-81	Warrington	26	Wigan	10	St. Helens	6,442	£8,629
1981-82	Leigh	8	Widnes	3	Wigan	9,011	£14,029
1982-83	Warrington	16	St. Helens	0	Wigan	6,462	£11,732
1983-84	Barrow	12	Widnes	8	Wigan	7,007	£13,160
1984-85	St. Helens	26	Wigan	18	Wigan	26,074	£62,139
1985-86	Wigan	34	Warrington	8	St. Helens	19,202	£56,030
1986-87	Wigan	27	Oldham	6	St. Helens	20,180	£60,329
1987-88	Wigan	28	Warrington	16	St. Helens	20,237	£67,339

*Emergency War-time competition

LANCASHIRE CUP FINAL .... A REVIEW
1965-66
Warrington 16 Bootle (2g); Fisher (1t),
Pickavance, Melling (2t), Glover (1t); Aspinall,
Smith; Payne, Oakes, Winslade, Robinson,
Thomas, Hayes
Rochdale H. 5 Pritchard; Pratt, Starkey (1t, 1g),
Chamberlain, Unsworth; Garforth, Fishwick;
Birchall, Ashcroft, Owen, Parr (Drui), Toga,
Baxter
Referee: E. Clay (Leeds)
1966-67
Wigan 16 Ashby; Boston (1t), Ashton (1t),
Holden, Lake; C. Hill, Parr; Gardiner,
Clarke (1t), J. Stephens, Lyon, Gilfedder
(2g, 1t), Major
Oldham 13 McLeod; Dolly, McCormack,
Donovan (1t), Simms; Warburton (5g),
Canning; Wilson, Taylor, Fletcher, Smethurst,
Irving, Mooney
Referee: P. Geraghty (York)
1967-68
St. Helens 2 F. Barrow; Vollenhoven, Whittle,
Benyon, A. Barrow; Douglas, Bishop; Warlow,
Sayer, Watson, Hogan, Mantle, Coslett (1g)
Warrington 2 Affleck; Coupe, Melling, Harvey
(Pickavance), Glover; Aspinall (1g), Gordon;
Ashcroft, Harrison, Brady, Parr, Briggs, Clarke
Referee: G.F. Lindop (Wakefield)
Replay
St. Helens 13 F. Barrow; Vollenhoven, Smith,
Benyon, Jones (1t); Douglas (Houghton 2g),
Bishop; Warlow (1t), Sayer, Watson,
E. Chisnall (1t), Mantle, Coslett (Egan)
Warrington 10 Conroy; Coupe, Melling (1t),
Allen (2g), Glover; Scahill, Gordon (1t);
Ashcroft, Harrison, Price, Parr, Briggs, Clarke
Referee: G.F. Lindop (Wakefield)
1968-69
St. Helens 30 Rhodes; F. Wilson (2t), Benyon,
Myler, Williams (1t); Whittle, Bishop (1t);
Warlow, Sayer, Watson, Rees (1t), E. Chisnall
(1t) Coslett (6g)
Oldham 2 Murphy; Elliott, Larder,
McCormack, Whitehead; Briggs (1g), Canning;
K. Wilson, Taylor, Fletcher (Maders), Irving,
McCourt, Hughes
Referee: W.H. Thompson (Huddersfield)
1969-70
Swinton 11 Gowers; Gomersall, Fleet, Buckley,
M. Philbin (1t); Davies, Kenny (4g); Bate,
D. Clarke, Mackay, Holliday, Smith, Robinson
Leigh 2 Grainey; Tickle, Warburton, Collins,
Stringer (Brown); Eckersley, Murphy (1g);
D. Chisnall, Ashcroft, Watts, Welding, Lyon,
Fiddler
Referee: E. Clay (Leeds)

1970-71
Leigh 7 Ferguson (2g); Tickle (Canning),
L. Chisnall, Collins, Walsh; Eckersley (1t),
Murphy; D. Chisnall, Ashcroft, Watts, Grimes,
Clarkson, Mooney
St. Helens 4 F. Barrow; L. Jones, Benyon,
Walsh, Wilson; Myler, Whittle; Halsall,
A. Karalius, Rees (Prescott), Mantle,
E. Chisnall, Coslett (2g)
Referee: W.H. Thompson (Huddersfield)
1971-72
Wigan 15 Tyrer (3g); Eastham (1t), Francis (1t),
Fuller, Wright (Gandy); D. Hill, Ayres (1t);
Ashcroft, Clarke, Fletcher, Ashurst, Kevin
O'Loughlin, Laughton
Widnes 8 Dutton; Brown, McLoughlin, Aspey
(1g), Gaydon (1t); D. O'Neill (1t), Bowden;
Warlow, Foran, Doughty, Kirwan, Walsh
(Lowe), Nicholls
Referee: W.H. Thompson (Huddersfield)
1972-73
Salford 25 Charlton (1t); Eastham (1t),
Watkins (1t, 5g), Hesketh, Richards (1t); Gill,
Banner (1t); Mackay, Walker, Ward,
Whitehead, Dixon, Prescott
Swinton 11 Jackson; Fleay (1t), Cooke,
Buckley, Gomersall; Kenny (1g) (M. Philbin),
Gowers (3g); Halsall, Evans, Bate, R. Smith
(Holliday), Hoyle, W. Pattinson
Referee: W.H. Thompson (Huddersfield)
1973-74
Wigan 19 Francis; Vigo, D. Hill, Keiron
O'Loughlin (2t), Wright (1t); Cassidy,
Ayres (1g); Smethurst, Clarke, Gray (4g),
Irving, D. Robinson, Cunningham
Salford 9 Charlton; Fielding, Watkins (1t, 3g),
Hesketh, Holland; Gill, Banner; Mackay,
Walker, Davies (Grice), Dixon, Kear
(Knighton), E. Prescott
Referee: W.H. Thompson (Huddersfield)
1974-75
Widnes 6 Dutton (1g); George (1t),
D. O'Neill, Aspey, A. Prescott; Hughes (1dg);
Bowden; Mills, Elwell, J. Stephens, Adams,
Blackwood, Laughton
Salford 2 Charlton; Fielding (1g), Dixon,
Graham, Richards; Taylor, Banner; Mackay,
Devlin, Grice, Knighton, Coulman, E. Prescott
Referee: G.F. Lindop (Wakefield)
1975-76
Widnes 16 Dutton (3g, 1dg); A. Prescott (1t),
George (1t), Aspey (1t), Jenkins; Hughes,
Bowden; Mills, Elwell, Nelson, Foran,
Fitzpatrick (Sheridan), Adams
Salford 7 Watkins (2g); Fielding, Butler,
Hesketh, Richards (1t); Gill, Nash; Fiddler,
Hawksley, Dixon (Mackay), Turnbull,
Knighton, E. Prescott
Referee: W.H. Thompson (Huddersfield)

1976-77
Widnes 16 Dutton (4g, 1dg); Wright (1t),
Aspey, George (1t), A. Prescott; Eckersley,
Bowden (1dg); Ramsey, Elwell, Nelson,
Dearden, Adams, Laughton
Workington T. 11 Charlton; Collister,
Wilkins (1t), Wright, MacCorquodale (4g);
Lauder, Walker; Mills, Banks, Calvin,
Bowman, L. Gorley, W. Pattinson (P. Gorley)
Referee: W.H. Thompson (Huddersfield)
1977-78
Workington T. 16 Charlton (Atkinson);
Collister, Risman, Wright (1t), MacCorquodale
(4g); Wilkins (1t), Walker (2dg); Watts, Banks,
Bowman, L. Gorley, W. Pattinson, P. Gorley
Wigan 13 Swann; Vigo, Davies (Burke 1g),
Willicombe (1t), Hornby; Taylor, Nulty (1t, 1g);
Hogan, Aspinall, Irving, Ashurst (1t),
Blackwood, Melling (Regan)
Referee: W.H. Thompson (Huddersfield)
1978-79
Widnes 15 Eckersley; Wright (1t), Aspey,
George, Burke (3g); Hughes, Bowden; Mills,
Elwell, Shaw, Adams, Dearden (Hull),
Laughton (2t)
Workington T. 13 Charlton; Collister, Risman,
Wilkins (1t), MacCorquodale (1t, 2g), McMillan,
Walker; Beverley, Banks, Bowman, Blackwood,
P. Gorley, W. Pattinson (L. Gorley 1t)
Referee: W.H. Thompson (Huddersfield)
1979-80
Widnes 11 Eckersley; Wright, Aspey, Hughes
(George), Burke (2g); Moran (1t), Bowden;
Hogan, Elwell (1dg), Shaw, L. Gorley, Dearden,
Adams (1t)
Workington T. 0 Charlton; MacCorquodale,
Maughan, Thompson, Beck; Rudd, Walker
(Roper); Beverley, Banks, Wallbanks (Varty),
W. Pattinson, Lewis, Dobie
Referee: W.H. Thompson (Huddersfield)
1980-81
Warrington 26 Finnegan; Thackray (1t),
I. Duane, Bevan (1t), Hesford (7g, 1t);
K. Kelly, A. Gwilliam; Courtney, Waller, Case,
Martyn (1t), Eccles (Potter); Hunter
Wigan 10 Fairbairn (1t, 2g); Ramsdale (1t),
Willicombe, Davies, Hornby; M. Foy, Bolton
(Coyle); Breheny, Pendlebury (M. Smith),
S. O'Neill, Melling, Clough, Hollingsworth
Referee: D. G. Kershaw (York)
1981-82
Leigh 8 Hogan; Drummond, Bilsbury (1t),
Donlan (1dg), Worgan; Woods (2g), Green;
Wilkinson, Tabern, Cooke, Martyn (Platt),
Clarkson, McTigue

Widnes 3 Burke; George, Hughes,
Cunningham, Bentley (1t); Moran, Gregory;
M. O'Neill, Elwell, Lockwood, L. Gorley,
E. Prescott, Adams
Referee: W.H. Thompson (Huddersfield)
1982-83
Warrington 16 Hesford (2g); Fellows (1t),
R. Duane, Bevan, M. Kelly (1t); Cullen,
K. Kelly (1t); Courtney, Webb, Cooke
(D. Chisnall), Eccles (1t), Fieldhouse, Gregory
St. Helens 0 Parkes (Smith); Ledger,
Arkwright, Haggerty, Litherland; Peters,
Holding; James, Liptrot, Bottell (Mathias),
Moorby, P. Gorley, Pinner
Referee: J. Holdsworth (Leeds)
1983-84
Barrow 12 Tickle (1dg); Moore, Whittle,
Ball (3g, 1dg), Milby; McConnell (1t), Cairns;
Hodkinson, Wall, McJennett, Herbert, Szymala,
Mossop
Widnes 8 Burke; Lydon (1t, 2g), Hughes,
Keiron O'Loughlin, Basnett; A. Myler,
Gregory; S. O'Neill, Elwell, K. Tamati,
Whitfield, E. Prescott, Adams
Referee: K. Allatt (Southport)
1984-85
St. Helens 26 Veivers (Haggerty 1t); Ledger,
Allen, Meninga (2t), Day (1t, 5g); Arkwright,
Holding; Burke, Liptrot, P. Gorley, Platt,
Round, Pinner
Wigan 18 Edwards; Ferguson, Stephenson,
Whitfield (3g), Gill (1t) (Pendlebury); Cannon,
Fairhurst; Courtney, Kiss (1t), Case, West (1t),
Wane, Potter
Referee: R. Campbell (Widnes)
1985-86
Wigan 34 Edwards (1t); Henley-Smith
(Hampson), Stephenson (7g), Hanley (1t),
Whitfield; Ella (2t), M. Ford; Dowling, Kiss
(1t), Wane (Case), Du Toit, Goodway, Potter
Warrington 8 Johnson (1t); Carbert (2g), Cullen,
Blake (Forster), Thackray; Kelly, A. Gregory;
Eccles, Webb, Jackson, Boyd (Tamati),
M. Gregory, Rathbone
Referee: J. Holdsworth (Kippax)
1986-87
Wigan 27 Edwards (2t); Lydon (1t, 1dg),
Stephenson, Bell, Gill (5g); Hanley, M. Ford
(1t); West, Dermott, Case, Roberts (Louw),
Potter, Goodway
Oldham 6 M'Barki; Sherman, Bridge (1t),
Warnecke, Taylor; Topliss, Kirwan; Clark,
Flanagan, Hobbs (1g), Nadiole, Worrall, Raper
(Hawkyard)
Referee: J.E. Smith (Halifax)

MAN OF THE MATCH AWARDS

An award for the adjudged man of the match in the Lancashire Cup final was first presented in 1974-75. For four years the award was sponsored by the *Rugby Leaguer* newspaper. From 1978-85 the trophy was presented by Burtonwood Brewery, then from 1986 by Greenall Whitley, as part of their sponsorship of the Lancashire Cup. Under the auspices of the *Rugby Leaguer*, the choice was made by the Editor, while the breweries invited a panel of the Press to make the decision.

Season	Winner	Team	Position
1974-75	Mike Coulman	Salford (v. Widnes)	Second row
1975-76	Mick George	Widnes (v. Salford)	Centre
1976-77	David Eckersley	Widnes (v. Workington T.)	Stand off
1977-78	Arnold Walker	Workington T. (v. Wigan)	Scrum half
1978-79	Arnold Walker	Workington T. (v. Widnes)	Scrum half
1979-80	Mick Adams	Widnes (v. Workington T.)	Loose forward
1980-81	Tony Waller	Warrington (v. Wigan)	Hooker
1981-82	Ray Tabern	Leigh (v. Widnes)	Hooker
1982-83	Steve Hesford	Warrington (v. St. Helens)	Full back
1983-84	David Cairns	Barrow (v. Widnes)	Scrum half
1984-85	Mal Meninga	St. Helens (v. Wigan)	Centre
1985-86	Steve Ella	Wigan (v. Warrington)	Stand off
1986-87	Mike Ford	Wigan (v. Oldham)	Scrum half
1987-88	Shaun Edwards	Wigan (v. Warrington)	Stand off

LANCASHIRE CUP FINAL RECORDS

TEAM

Most appearances: 33 by Wigan
Most wins: 19 by Wigan
Highest score: Wigan 34 v. Warrington 8 1985
Widest margin: St. Helens 30 v. Oldham 2 1968
Biggest attendance:
42,793 St. Helens v. Wigan (at Swinton) 1953

INDIVIDUAL

Most tries:
4 by Brian Nordgren (Wigan) v. Leigh 1949
Most goals:
7 by Jim Ledgard (Leigh) v. Widnes 1955
    Steve Hesford (Warrington) v. Wigan 1980
    David Stephenson (Wigan) v. Warrington .. 1985
Most points:
17 (7g, 1t) by Steve Hesford (Warrington) v. Wigan
    1980

Wigan skipper Ellery Hanley lifts the 1987 Lancashire Cup, Henderson Gill hoisting the base.

YORKSHIRE CUP

1987 Final

The first drawn Yorkshire Cup final for 32 years — Bradford Northern and Castleford finishing 12-apiece at Leeds — gave rise to a replay double controversy.

Immediately after the Headingley final, Castleford protested at the pre-arranged Yorkshire County decision to stage a replay at Hunslet's Elland Road ground two weeks later, forcing the postponement of Castleford's lucrative home league fixture with crowd pullers Wigan the following day. Castleford chairman David Poulter even threatened to withdraw from the county competition in order to fulfil the Wigan encounter, although county officials pointed out that a traditional midweek replay date was ruled out because of fixture congestion due to Great Britain Test and Papua New Guinea tour commitments, plus the new British Coal Nines tournament.

When the replay did take place on the scheduled date, even greater controversy arose when a mass brawl took place on the stroke of half-time. Television cameras captured the fighting which flared up after a John Joyner tackle on Bradford Northern loose forward Wayne Heron and subsided in less than 10 seconds.

Before the second half began Southport referee Kevin Allatt called Joyner and Northern's Karl Fairbank to the centre of the field and sent them to the sin bin for 10 minutes. There continued to be ill-feeling in the second half and two more players were sent to the sin bin, Bradford's Kelvin Skerrett in the 59th minute and Castleford's Tongan forward John Fifita in the last minute.

Mr Allatt later reported 12 players for taking part in the brawl, the dozen being ordered to appear before the League's Management Committee for bringing the game into disrepute.

On the footballing scene, the Headingley final was highlighted by a Man of the Match performance by Northern skipper Paul Harkin, who added the White Rose Trophy to his two John Player Special Trophy final individual awards. Harkin was an inspirational leader for a Bradford side seeking county cup glory for the first time in nine years.

Castleford were rocked by the loss of Test hooker Kevin Beardmore with a leg injury after 55 minutes. His narrow first half scrum supremacy was turned into a substantial deficit after the interval with scrum half Roy Southernwood put into the middle of the front row, Bob Beardmore coming on for his first senior action of the season.

A broken nose sustained by Australian Test loose forward Bob Lindner dulled his effectiveness after a promising first half performance highlighted by the scoring of Castleford's second try to give them a 10-4 half-time lead.

Two tactical substitutions by Northern helped them bounce back to draw level at 10-apiece. The introduction at half-time of young Neil Roebuck for Terry Holmes and Test prop David Hobbs for the veteran Jeff Grayshon had the desired effect. Hobbs was soon adding the goal to a splendid try by Fairbank and then putting Northern in front with a 57th minute penalty goal.

Second row man Martin Ketteridge levelled the scores again with a penalty goal 15 minutes from the end and Castleford, having scored two tries to one, were left to rue not dropping a goal in the final minutes.

In the Elland Road replay, a slimmed-down Brendan Hill scored the opening try of a defence orientated contest and earned the Man of the Match award. Having lost more than a stone since the opening of the season, the 18st Northern prop battered the Castleford defence throughout, forcing a gaping hole with a 15-yard drive to the line after 27 minutes. His first winners' medal after Northern's 11-2 triumph emulated his father David, who was also at prop when the Odsal club won the Yorkshire Cup in 1965.

Front row partner Hobbs was also in form, dropping a vital 48th minute goal after Castleford's Ketteridge had hit a penalty before the break. Hobbs also added the goal to Northern's second try with only four minutes left, the ever eccentric Phil Ford managing to retrieve his own wayward pass before taking advantage of a bewildered Castleford defence to send Wayne Heron crashing over.

Northern skipper Harkin was again outstanding, while full back Keith Mumby fought a magnificent rearguard action with some deadly tackling. Two celebrated players qualified for winners' medals in their absence, broken leg victim Grayshon and recently retired ex-Wales RU skipper Terry Holmes! The Headingley Final turned out to be Holmes' last appearance of a brief, injury-ridden league career.

One in all in...Northern's Brendan Hill, Man of the Match in the replay, falls to Castleford duo David Roockley (left) and Kevin Ward. On hand are teammate Kelvin Skerrett and Castleford's Keith England (upper left) and Kenny Hill.

JOHN SMITHS YORKSHIRE CUP FINAL

17 October   **Leeds**

BRADFORD NORTHERN 12   **CASTLEFORD 12**

Gary Mercer	1.	David Roockley
Phil Ford	2.	David Plange
Steve McGowan	3.	Tony Marchant
Roger Simpson	4.	Michael Beattie
Richard Francis	5.	Gary Hyde
Keith Mumby	6.	John Joyner, Capt
Paul Harkin, Capt.	7.	Roy Southernwood
Jeff Grayshon	8.	Alan Shillito
Brian Noble	9.	Kevin Beardmore
Brendan Hill	10.	Kevin Ward
Kelvin Skerrett	11.	Martin Ketteridge
Karl Fairbank	12.	John Fifita
Terry Holmes	13.	Bob Lindner
Neil Roebuck	14.	Bob Beardmore
David Hobbs	15.	Dean Sampson

T: Fairbank
G: Mumby (2), Hobbs (2)
Substitutions:
Roebuck for Holmes (Half-time)
Hobbs for Grayshon (Half-time)
Half-time: 4-10
Attendance: 10,947

T: Plange, Lindner
G: Ketteridge (2)
Substitutions:
Sampson for K. Beardmore (38 min.)
R. Beardmore for Shillito (55 min.)
Referee: K. Allatt (Southport)

JOHN SMITHS YORKSHIRE CUP FINAL REPLAY

31 October   **Elland Road, Leeds**

BRADFORD NORTHERN 11   **CASTLEFORD 2**

Keith Mumby	1.	David Roockley
Phil Ford	2.	David Plange
Steve McGowan	3.	Tony Marchant
Gary Mercer	4.	Michael Beattie
Roger Simpson	5.	Gary Hyde
Russell Stewart	6.	Roy Southernwood
Paul Harkin, Capt.	7.	Bob Beardmore
David Hobbs	8.	Kevin Ward
Brian Noble	9.	Kenny Hill
Brendan Hill	10.	John Fifita
Kelvin Skerrett	11.	Martin Ketteridge
Karl Fairbank	12.	Keith England
Wayne Heron	13.	John Joyner
Neil Roebuck	14.	Giles Boothroyd
David Redfearn	15.	Dean Sampson

T: Hill, Heron
G: Hobbs (1, 1dg)
Half-time: 4-2
Referee: Kevin Allatt (Southport)
Attendance: 8,175

G: Ketteridge
Substitutions:
Sampson for Fifita (19 min.)
Boothroyd for England (65 min.)

Bradford Northern packman Kelvin Skerrett bursts through a tackle by Castleford hooker Kenny Hill.

1987 Round by Round

The White Rose tournament got off to an explosive start with the preliminary round tie between Wakefield Trinity and Dewsbury. Three players were dismissed, two stretchered off and two more banished to the sin bin in a tough Cup baptism for newly promoted Leeds referee Kevin Dockray. Trinity went through 25-14. In the other preliminary tie, Hull entertained Huddersfield Barracudas who held out for 23 minutes before the Airlie Birds romped to a 54-8 win. Welshman Gary Pearce landed nine goals from 10 attempts, adding a try for a 22-point haul.

In the first round, holders Castleford disposed of newly-promoted Hunslet 32-12 at Wheldon Road, Australian centre Michael Beattie making his debut with two first half tries. Leeds and Hull staged a thriller at Headingley, the unlucky Boulevarders going down two minutes from time to a try created by former skipper Lee Crooks, who added the goal to give the home side a 28-24 victory. Hull led 20-4 at half-time and the Leeds comeback was aided by referee Fred Lindop awarding a series of 17 consecutive penalties in their favour. Hull K.R. went down 19-12 at home to Bradford Northern, inspired by the return of former Welsh RU skipper Terry Holmes, who collected the Man of the Match award. Owing to ground safety restrictions, Keighley switched their tie with Halifax to Thrum Hall, the increased gate revenue compensating for a 34-12 defeat. The Second Division outfit were trailing by only four points well into the second half before losing prop Brendan White, Halifax finding their rhythm to run in three late tries.

Bramley's Peter Lister recorded a hat-trick of tries to equal the club's career try-scoring record of 92, in the 39-12 home success over Doncaster marred only by the sending off of debutant forward Paul Spedding. Former Featherstone Rovers coach Paul Daley returned to Post Office Road with his new charges, Batley, but was on the receiving end of a 28-6 scoreline. The Colliers were inspired by scrum half Deryck Fox who set up two first half tries and then scored a brilliant 45-yard touchdown himself. Entering the Yorkshire Cup competition for the second time, Mansfield Marksman enjoyed home advantage for the first time, visitors York recording a 23-18 success. York substitute Nigel Stephenson took the Man of the Match award, coming on when Mansfield led 18-8 to create tries for Ian Tansley and Steve Olsen before Neil Hague scored the clinching touchdown in the corner. Wakefield Trinity maintained their unbeaten record as Sheffield Eagles lost theirs in a hard fought encounter at Belle Vue, the Eagles leading by 10 points after 54 minutes before Trinity staged a four-try comeback to win 32-18.

In the second round, Castleford continued their defence of the trophy by travelling to Silk Cut Challenge Cup holders Halifax and registering an impressive 10-0 success. Castleford led 8-0 after 21 minutes, with hooker Kevin Beardmore scoring the only try of the game, and then had to defend throughout a typical cup-tie, with full back David Roockley outstanding. Big spending Leeds disposed of Second Division rivals Wakefield Trinity 36-8 at Headingley, four of the Loiners' six tries coming in the last quarter as the visitors ran out of steam, having lost player-coach David Topliss. Former Leeds half back Mark Conway impressed for Trinity, while ex-Belle Vue full back Gary Spencer collected two tries for his new club. Bradford Northern raced to a 30-6 win at Bramley whose one try went to Lister for a club record of 93 tries. Featherstone Rovers gained revenge for a recent league defeat at the hands of York with a 43-6 rout at Post Office Road, scrum half Fox scoring a hat-trick of tries and centre Steve Quinn tallying 18 points against his former club.

In the last four, Bradford Northern ended a run of two successive county cup semi-final defeats by beating Leeds 16-5 at Odsal. Leeds, beaten 32-8 on the same ground 10 days earlier, grabbed a 5-2 lead at the break but were overcome by a Northern outfit spearheaded by ex-Leeds props Jeff Grayshon and Brendan Hill. Drawn at home again, Featherstone Rovers were knocked out by neighbours Castleford — as at the same stage a year earlier — this time by 36-8. Castleford reached the final for the fifth time in seven years after leading only 8-4 at the interval when Australian Test loose forward Bob Lindner created two tries before claiming a brace for himself. Fresh from his Sydney Grand Final triumph, Castleford prop Kevin Ward grabbed the try of the night.

1987 RESULTS

Preliminary Round

Hull	54	Huddersfield B.	8
Wakefield T.	25	Dewsbury	14

First Round

Bramley	39	Doncaster	12
Castleford	32	Hunslet	12
Featherstone R.	28	Batley	6
*Halifax	34	Keighley	12
Hull K.R.	12	Bradford N.	19
Leeds	28	Hull	24
Mansfield M.	18	York	23
Wakefield T.	32	Sheffield E.	18

*Keighley conceded home advantage

Second Round

Bramley	6	Bradford N.	30
Featherstone R.	43	York	6
Halifax	0	Castleford	10
Leeds	36	Wakefield T.	8

Semi-Finals

Bradford N.	16	Leeds	5
Featherstone R.	8	Castleford	36

Final

Bradford N.	12	Castleford	12
(at Leeds)			

Replay

Bradford N.	11	Castleford	2
(at Elland Rd, Leeds)			

YORKSHIRE CUP ROLL OF HONOUR

Year	Winners		Runners-up		Venue	Attendance	Receipts
1905-06	Hunslet	13	Halifax	3	Bradford P.A.	18,500	£465
1906-07	Bradford	8	Hull K.R.	5	Wakefield	10,500	£286
1907-08	Hunslet	17	Halifax	0	Leeds	15,000	£397
1908-09	Halifax	9	Hunslet	5	Wakefield	13,000	£356
1909-10	Huddersfield	21	Batley	0	Leeds	22,000	£778
1910-11	Wakefield T.	8	Huddersfield	2	Leeds	19,000	£696
1911-12	Huddersfield	22	Hull K.R.	10	Wakefield	20,000	£700
1912-13	Batley	17	Hull	3	Leeds	16,000	£523
1913-14	Huddersfield	19	Bradford N.	3	Halifax	12,000	£430
1914-15	Huddersfield	31	Hull	0	Leeds	12,000	£422
1918-19	Huddersfield	14	Dewsbury	8	Leeds	21,500	£1,309
1919-20	Huddersfield	24	Leeds	5	Halifax	24,935	£2,096
1920-21	Hull K.R.	2	Hull	0	Leeds	20,000	£1,926
1921-22	Leeds	11	Dewsbury	3	Halifax	20,000	£1,650
1922-23	York	5	Batley	0	Leeds	33,719	£2,414
1923-24	Hull	10	Huddersfield	4	Leeds	23,300	£1,728
1924-25	Wakefield T.	9	Batley	8	Leeds	25,546	£1,912
1925-26	Dewsbury	2	Huddersfield	0	Wakefield	12,616	£718
1926-27	Huddersfield	10	Wakefield T.	3	Leeds	11,300	£853
1927-28	Dewsbury	8	Hull	2	Leeds	21,700	£1,466
1928-29	Leeds	5	Featherstone R.	0	Wakefield	13,000	£838
1929-30	Hull K.R.	13	Hunslet	7	Leeds	11,000	£687
1930-31	Leeds	10	Huddersfield	2	Halifax	17,812	£1,405
1931-32	Huddersfield	4	Hunslet	2	Leeds	27,000	£1,764
1932-33	Leeds	8	Wakefield T.	0	Huddersfield	17,685	£1,183
1933-34	York	10	Hull K.R.	4	Leeds	22,000	£1,480
1934-35	Leeds	5	Wakefield T.	5	Dewsbury	22,598	£1,529
Replay	Leeds	2	Wakefield T.	2	Huddersfield	10,300	£745
Replay	Leeds	13	Wakefield T.	0	Hunslet	19,304	£1,327
1935-36	Leeds	3	York	0	Halifax	14,616	£1,113
1936-37	York	9	Wakefield T.	2	Leeds	19,000	£1,294
1937-38	Leeds	14	Huddersfield	8	Wakefield	22,000	£1,508
1938-39	Huddersfield	18	Hull	10	Bradford	28,714	£1,534
1939-40	Featherstone R.	12	Wakefield T.	9	Bradford	7,077	£403
1940-41	Bradford N.	15	Dewsbury	5	Huddersfield	13,316	£939
1941-42	Bradford N.	24	Halifax	0	Huddersfield	5,989	£635

Year	Winners		Runners-up		Venue	Attendance	Receipts
1942-43	Dewsbury	7	Huddersfield	0	Dewsbury	11,000	£680
	Huddersfield	2	Dewsbury	0	Huddersfield	6,252	£618
	Dewsbury won on aggregate 7-2						
1943-44	Bradford N.	5	Keighley	2	Bradford	10,251	£757
	Keighley	5	Bradford N.	5	Keighley	8,993	£694
	Bradford N. won on aggregate 10-7						
1944-45	Hunslet	3	Halifax	12	Hunslet	11,213	£744
	Halifax	2	Hunslet	0	Halifax	9,800	£745
	Halifax won on aggregate 14-3						
1945-46	Bradford N.	5	Wakefield T.	2	Halifax	24,292	£1,934
1946-47	Wakefield T.	10	Hull	0	Leeds	34,300	£3,718
1947-48	Wakefield T.	7	Leeds	7	Huddersfield	24,344	£3,461
Replay	Wakefield T.	8	Leeds	7	Bradford	32,000	£3,251
1948-49	Bradford N.	18	Castleford	9	Leeds	31,393	£5,053
1949-50	Bradford N.	11	Huddersfield	4	Leeds	36,000	£6,365
1950-51	Huddersfield	16	Castleford	3	Leeds	28,906	£5,152
1951-52	Wakefield T.	17	Keighley	3	Huddersfield	25,495	£3,347
1952-53	Huddersfield	18	Batley	8	Leeds	14,705	£2,471
1953-54	Bradford N.	7	Hull	2	Leeds	22,147	£3,833
1954-55	Halifax	22	Hull	14	Leeds	25,949	£4,638
1955-56	Halifax	10	Hull	10	Leeds	23,520	£4,385
Replay	Halifax	7	Hull	0	Bradford	14,000	£2,439
1956-57	Wakefield T.	23	Hunslet	5	Leeds	30,942	£5,609
1957-58	Huddersfield	15	York	8	Leeds	22,531	£4,123
1958-59	Leeds	24	Wakefield T.	20	Bradford	26,927	£3,833
1959-60	Featherstone R.	15	Hull	14	Leeds	23,983	£4,156
1960-61	Wakefield T.	16	Huddersfield	10	Leeds	17,456	£2,937
1961-62	Wakefield T.	19	Leeds	9	Bradford	16,329	£2,864
1962-63	Hunslet	12	Hull K.R.	2	Leeds	22,742	£4,514
1963-64	Halifax	10	Featherstone R.	0	Wakefield	13,238	£2,471
1964-65	Wakefield T.	18	Leeds	2	Huddersfield	13,527	£2,707
1965-66	Bradford N.	17	Hunslet	8	Leeds	17,522	£4,359
1966-67	Hull K.R.	25	Featherstone R.	12	Leeds	13,241	£3,482
1967-68	Hull K.R.	8	Hull	7	Leeds	16,729	£5,515
1968-69	Leeds	22	Castleford	11	Wakefield	12,573	£3,746
1969-70	Hull	12	Featherstone R.	9	Leeds	11,089	£3,419
1970-71	Leeds	23	Featherstone R.	7	Bradford	6,753	£1,879
1971-72	Hull K.R.	11	Castleford	7	Wakefield	5,536	£1,589
1972-73	Leeds	36	Dewsbury	9	Bradford	7,806	£2,659
1973-74	Leeds	7	Wakefield T.	2	Leeds	7,621	£3,728
1974-75	Hull K.R.	16	Wakefield T.	13	Leeds	5,823	£3,090
1975-76	Leeds	15	Hull K.R.	11	Leeds	5,743	£3,617
1976-77	Leeds	16	Featherstone R.	12	Leeds	7,645	£5,198
1977-78	Castleford	17	Featherstone R.	7	Leeds	6,318	£4,528
1978-79	Bradford N.	18	York	8	Leeds	10,429	£9,188
1979-80	Leeds	15	Halifax	6	Leeds	9,137	£9,999
1980-81	Leeds	8	Hull K.R.	7	Huddersfield	9,751	£15,578
1981-82	Castleford	10	Bradford N.	5	Leeds	5,852	£10,359
1982-83	Hull	18	Bradford N.	7	Leeds	11,755	£21,950
1983-84	Hull	13	Castleford	2	Elland Rd, Leeds	14,049	£33,572
1984-85	Hull	29	Hull K.R.	12	Hull C. FC	25,237	£68,639
1985-86	Hull K.R.	22	Castleford	18	Leeds	12,686	£36,327
1986-87	Castleford	31	Hull	24	Leeds	11,132	£31,888
1987-88	Bradford N.	12	Castleford	12	Leeds	10,947	£40,283
Replay	Bradford N.	11	Castleford	2	Elland Rd, Leeds	8,175	£30,732

YORKSHIRE CUP FINAL .... A REVIEW

1965-66
Bradford N. 17 Scattergood; Williamson (2t), Brooke (1t), Rhodes, Walker; Stockwell, Smales; Tonkinson, Morgan, Hill, Ashton, Clawson (4g), Rae
Hunslet 8 Langton (1g); Lee (1t), Shelton, Render, Thompson (1t); Preece, Marchant; Hartley, Prior, Baldwinson, Ramsey, Gunney, Ward
Referee: W.E. Lawrinson (Warrington)

1966-67
Hull K.R. 25 C. Kellett (5g); Young (1t), A. Burwell (1t), Moore (1t), Blackmore (1t); Millward, Bunting; F. Fox, Flanagan (1t), Tyson, Holliday, Foster, Major
Featherstone R. 12 D. Kellett; Thomas, Greatorex, Wrigglesworth (1t), Westwood; M. Smith, Dooler; Dixon, Kosanovic, Forsyth (1t), A. Morgan, Lyons, Smales (3g)
Referee: B. Baker (Wigan)

1967-68
Hull K.R. 8 Kellett (1g); Young, Moore, Elliott, A. Burwell (1t); Millward (1t), Cooper; Holliday, Flanagan, Mennell, Lowe, Hickson (Foster), Major
Hull 7 Keegan; Oliver, Doyle-Davidson, Maloney (1g), Stocks; Devonshire, Davidson (1t, 1g); Harrison, McGlone, Broom, Edson, J. Macklin, Sykes
Referee: D.T.H. Davies (Manchester)

1968-69
Leeds 22 Risman (5g); Alan Smith (1t), Hynes, Watson (1t), Atkinson (1t); Shoebottom, Seabourne; Clark, Crosby, K. Eyre, Ramsey (Hick 1t), A. Eyre, Batten
Castleford 11 Edwards; Howe, Hill (1t, 2g), Thomas, Stephens; Hardisty (2g), Hargrave; Hartley, C. Dickinson, Ward, Small, Lockwood (Redfearn), Reilly
Referee: J. Manley (Warrington)

1969-70
Hull 12 Owbridge; Sullivan (1t), Gemmell, Maloney (2g), A. Macklin; Hancock, Davidson; Harrison, McGlone, J. Macklin (1t), Kirchin, Forster, Brown (1g)
Featherstone R. 9 C. Kellett (3g); Newlove, Jordan, M. Smith, Hartley (T. Hudson); D. Kellett, Nash (1t); Tonks, Farrar, Lyons, A. Morgan, Thompson, Smales
Referee: R.L. Thomas (Oldham)

1970-71
Leeds 23 Holmes; Alan Smith (2t), Hynes (4g), Cowan, Atkinson (1t); Wainwright (Langley), Shoebottom; J. Burke, Dunn (1t), Cookson, Ramsey (1t), Haigh, Batten

Featherstone R. 7 C. Kellett (2g); M. Smith, Cotton, Newlove, Hartley (1t); Harding (Coventry), Hudson; Windmill, D. Morgan, Lyons, Rhodes, Thompson, Farrar
Referee: D.S. Brown (Preston)

1971-72
Hull K.R. 11 Markham; Stephenson, Coupland, Kirkpatrick, Longstaff (1t); Millward (4g), Daley; Wiley, Flanagan, Millington, Wallis, Palmer (Cooper), Brown
Castleford 7 Edwards; Foster (1t), S. Norton, Worsley, Lowndes; Hargrave, Stephens; Hartley, Miller, I. Van Bellen (Ackroyd 2g), A. Dickinson, Lockwood, Blakeway
Referee: A. Givvons (Oldham)

1972-73
Leeds 36 Holmes (3t); Alan Smith, Hynes (1g), Dyl (2t), Atkinson (1t); Hardisty (1t), Hepworth (Langley); Clawson (5g) (Fisher), Ward, Ramsey, Cookson, Eccles (1t), Batten
Dewsbury 9 Rushton; Ashcroft (1t), Childe, Day, Yoward; Agar (3g), A. Bates; Bell (Beverley), M. Stephenson, Lowe, Grayshon, J. Bates (Lee), Hankins
Referee: M.J. Naughton (Widnes)

1973-74
Leeds 7 Holmes; Langley (1t) (Marshall 1g), Hynes (1g), Dyl, Atkinson; Hardisty, Hepworth; Jeanes (Ramsey), Ward, Clarkson, Eccles, Cookson, Batten
Wakefield T. 2 Wraith (Sheard); D. Smith, Crook (1g), Hegarty, B. Parker; Topliss, Bonnar; Valentine, Morgan, Bratt, Knowles (Ballantyne), Endersby, Holmes
Referee: M.J. Naughton (Widnes)

1974-75
Hull K.R. 16 Smithies; Sullivan (Dunn 1t), Watson (2t), Coupland, Kirkpatrick (1t); Millward, Stephenson; Millington, Heslop, Rose, Wallis, N. Fox (2g) (Madley), Brown
Wakefield T. 13 Sheard; D. Smith (1t), Crook (2g), Hegarty (1t), Archer; Topliss, Bonnar; Ballantyne, Handscombe, Bratt (1t), Skerrett, A. Tonks (Goodwin), (Holmes), Morgan
Referee: M.J. Naughton (Widnes)

1975-76
Leeds 15 Marshall; Alan Smith, Hague, Dyl (1t), Atkinson; Holmes (4g, 1dg), Hynes; Harrison, Payne, Pitchford, (Dickinson), Eccles, Batten, Cookson (1t)
Hull K.R. 11 Wallace; Dunn, A. Burwell, Watson, Sullivan (1t); Turner, Millward (1dg); Millington, Dickinson, Lyons, Rose, N. Fox (2g, 1t), Hughes (Holdstock)
Referee: J.V. Moss (Manchester)

1976-77
Leeds 16 Marshall (2g); Hague, Hynes, Dyl
(2t), D. Smith; Holmes, Banner; Dickinson,
Ward, Pitchford, Eccles (1t), Burton, Cookson
(1t)
Featherstone R. 12 Box; Bray (1t), Coventry,
Quinn (3g), K. Kellett; Newlove, Fennell;
Gibbins, Bridges, Farrar, Stone, P. Smith (1t),
Bell (Spells)
Referee: M.J. Naughton (Widnes)
1977-78
Castleford 17 Wraith; Richardson, Joyner,
P. Johnson, Fenton; Burton (2t, 1dg), Pickerill
(Stephens); Fisher (Woodall), Spurr, Weston,
Huddlestone, Reilly, Lloyd (5g)
Featherstone R. 7 Marsden; Evans, Gilbert,
Quinn (1g) (N. Tuffs), K. Kellett; Newlove,
Butler; Townend (1g), Bridges, Farrar,
Gibbins, Stone (P. Smith 1t), Bell
Referee: M.J. Naughton (Widnes)
1978-79
Bradford N. 18 Mumby; Barends, Gant (1t),
D. Parker (1t), D. Redfearn; Slater (Wolford),
A. Redfearn (1t); Thompson, Fisher, Forsyth
(Joyce), Fox (3g), Trotter, Haigh (1t)
York 8 G. Smith (1t); T. Morgan, Day
(Crossley), Foster, Nicholson; Banks (2g),
Harkin; Dunkerley, Wileman, Harris, Rhodes,
Hollis (1dg) (Ramshaw), Cooper
Referee: M.J. Naughton (Widnes)
1979-80
Leeds 15 Hague; Alan Smith (2t), D. Smith
(1t), Dyl, Atkinson; Holmes (J. Sanderson),
Dick (3g); Dickinson, Ward, Pitchford, Eccles,
D. Heron (Adams), Cookson
Halifax 6 Birts (3g); Howard (Snee), Garrod,
Cholmondeley, Waites; Blacker, Langton;
Jarvis (Callon), Raistrick, Wood, Scott, Sharp,
Busfield
Referee: M.J. Naughton (Widnes)
1980-81
Leeds 8 Hague; Alan Smith (1t), D. Smith,
Atkinson, Oulton; Holmes, Dick (2g, 1dg);
Harrison, Ward, Pitchford, Eccles, Cookson
(Carroll), D. Heron
Hull K.R. 7 Robinson; McHugh (1t),
M. Smith, Hogan (2g), Youngman; Hall,
Harkin; Holdstock, Price, Crooks (Rose),
Lowe, Casey, Crane
Referee: R. Campbell (Widnes)
1981-82
Castleford 10 Claughton; Richardson, Fenton,
Hyde (1t), Morris; Joyner (1t), R. Beardmore;
Hardy (P. Norton), Spurr, B. Johnson, Finch
(2g), Ward, Timson

Bradford N. 5 Mumby; Barends, Hale,
A. Parker (1t), Gant; Hanley (1g), A. Redfearn;
Grayshon, Noble, Sanderson (D. Redfearn),
G. Van Bellen (Jasiewicz), Idle, Rathbone
Referee: M.R. Whitfield (Widnes)
1982-83
Hull 18 Kemble; Evans (1t), Day, Leuluai,
Prendiville (1t); Topliss, Harkin; Skerrett,
Bridges, Stone, Rose (2t), L. Crooks (2g, 2dg),
Crane (Norton)
Bradford N. 7 Mumby; Barends, Gant,
A. Parker, Pullen (Smith); Whiteman (1t),
Carroll (1g, 2dg); Grayshon, Noble, G. Van
Bellen (Sanderson), Idle, Jasiewicz, Hale
Referee: S. Wall (Leigh)
1983-84
Hull 13 Kemble; Solal, Schofield, Leuluai,
O'Hara (1t); Topliss, Dean; Edmonds,
Wileman, Skerrett, Proctor (1t), L. Crooks,
Crane (1t, 1dg)
Castleford 2 Coen; Fenton, Marchant, Hyde
(Orum), Kear; Joyner, R. Beardmore (1g);
Connell, Horton, Reilly, Timson, James,
England
Referee: W.H. Thompson (Huddersfield)
1984-85
Hull 29 Kemble (2t); Leuluai, Schofield (4g,
1dg), S. Evans (1t), O'Hara; Ah Kuoi,
Sterling; Edmonds, Patrick, L. Crooks (1t),
Norton (1t), Proctor, Divorty (Rose)
Hull K.R. 12 Fairbairn (1t); Clark, Robinson
(1t), Prohm, Laws; M. Smith, Harkin (Rudd);
Broadhurst, Watkinson, Ema (Hartley),
Burton, Kelly, Hall (1t)
Referee: G.F. Lindop (Wakefield)
1985-86
Hull K.R. 22 Fairbairn (Lydiat); Clark (1t),
Dorahy (5g), Prohm, Laws; G. Smith, Harkin;
D. Harrison, Watkinson, Ema, Burton, Hogan
(Kelly), Miller (2t)
Castleford 18 Lord; Plange, Marchant (2t),
Hyde, Spears; Diamond (1g), R. Beardmore
(1t, 2g); Ward, K. Beardmore, B. Johnson,
England, Ketteridge, Joyner
Referee: R. Campbell (Widnes)
1986-87
Castleford 31 Scott; Plange, Marchant, Johns,
Hyde (Lord); Joyner, R. Beardmore (1dg);
Ward (1t), K. Beardmore (2t), B. Johnson,
Ketteridge (1t, 5g), Atkins (1t) (Shillito),
England
Hull 24 Kemble; Brand (2t), Schofield, O'Hara
(2t), Eastwood; Ah Kuoi, Windley; Brown
(Puckering), S. Patrick, Dannatt, Norton
(Divorty), L. Crooks (4g), Sharp
Referee: J. McDonald (Wigan)

181

THE WHITE ROSE TROPHY

First awarded in 1966, the trophy is presented to the adjudged man of the match in the Yorkshire Cup final.

Donated by the late T.E. Smith, of York, the award is organised by the Yorkshire Federation of Rugby League Supporters' Clubs and judged by a panel of the Press.

The trophy is not awarded in replays, although Bradford Northern's Brendan Hill was named Man of the Match in the second game against Castleford in 1987.

Season	Winner	Team	Position
1966-67	Cyril Kellett	Hull K.R. (v. Featherstone R.)	Full back
1967-68	Chris Davidson	Hull (v. Hull K.R.)	Scrum half
1968-69	Barry Seabourne	Leeds (v. Castleford)	Scrum half
1969-70	Joe Brown	Hull (v. Featherstone R.)	Loose forward
1970-71	Syd Hynes	Leeds (v. Featherstone R.)	Centre
1971-72	Ian Markham	Hull K.R. (v. Castleford)	Full back
1972-73	John Holmes	Leeds (v. Dewsbury)	Full back
1973-74	Keith Hepworth	Leeds (v. Wakefield T.)	Scrum half
1974-75	Roger Millward	Hull K.R. (v. Wakefield T.)	Stand off
1975-76	Neil Fox	Hull K.R. (v. Leeds)	Second row
1976-77	Les Dyl	Leeds (v. Featherstone R.)	Centre
1977-78	Bruce Burton	Castleford (v. Featherstone R.)	Stand off
1978-79	Bob Haigh	Bradford N. (v. York)	Loose forward
1979-80	Alan Smith	Leeds (v. Halifax)	Winger
1980-81	Kevin Dick	Leeds (v. Hull K.R.)	Scrum half
1981-82	Barry Johnson	Castleford (v. Bradford N.)	Prop
1982-83	Keith Mumby	Bradford N. (v. Hull)	Full back
1983-84	Mick Crane	Hull (v. Castleford)	Loose forward
1984-85	Peter Sterling	Hull (v. Hull K.R.)	Scrum half
1985-86	Gavin Miller	Hull K.R. (v. Castleford)	Loose forward
1986-87	Kevin Beardmore	Castleford (v. Hull)	Hooker
1987-88	Paul Harkin	Bradford N. (v. Castleford)	Scrum half

YORKSHIRE CUP FINAL RECORDS

TEAM
Most appearances: 20 Huddersfield, Leeds
Most wins: 16 Leeds
Highest score: Leeds 36 v. Dewsbury 9............ 1972
Widest margin win: Huddersfield 31 v. Hull 0... 1914
Biggest attendance:
36,000 Bradford N. v. Huddersfield (at Leeds).. 1949

INDIVIDUAL
Most tries:
4 by Stan Moorhouse (Huddersfield) v. Leeds.... 1919
Most points:
14 (5g, 1t) by Martin Ketteridge (Castleford)
v. Hull 1986
Most goals:
No player has scored more than 5.

1987 Man of the Match Paul Harkin.

WORLD CLUB CHALLENGE

Nearly 37,000 fans packed Central Park, Wigan, to witness the British Champions' defeat of Sydney Premiership winners Manly in the first-ever World Club Challenge.

Fireworks blazed as the Anglo-Aussie title holders ran out to compete for the £20,000 Foster's prize, Wigan taking the world spotlight with a well-deserved 8-2 victory, four penalty goals from David Stephenson outgunning a solitary success by opposite number Michael O'Connor.

The fireworks were on the field as well, with the turning point of a thrilling encounter being the dismissal of Manly second row powerhouse Ron Gibbs in the 45th minute after a touch judge reported the use of the elbow on home Test centre Joe Lydon.

Two players were also sent to the sin bin for 10-minute spells. Manly stand off Cliff Lyons went in the 10th minute, Wigan prop forward Brian Case being temporarily dismissed on the hour. There were also a couple of melees and a barrage of bone-crushing tackles from the game's top two sides in this pulsating world title decider.

No tries were scored, a testimony to the defensive qualities of both sides, particularly in the second half when, after a dour opening 40 minutes, first Wigan and then the visitors applied relentless pressure.

Manly, fresh from their Sydney Premiership victory over Canberra, took the lead after only two minutes when Wigan were caught offside, O'Connor — Australia's top goals and points scorer on the Kangaroo tour a year earlier — stroking home the close range penalty goal.

Within minutes, Manly scrum half Des Hasler was pulled up for stamping on Wigan Test forward Shaun Wane and Stephenson equalled with a 35-yard penalty shot.

When Lyons was sent to the sin bin in the 10th minute, Stephenson squandered the easiest of penalty goal attempts, O'Connor following suit six minutes later when Hasler was obstructed by Ian Potter chasing his kick through.

Great Britain centre Stephenson put Wigan ahead in the 19th minute with a penalty goal after a brief but unsavoury flare-up between Manly's Dale Shearer and home stand off Shaun Edwards. Just before the break, Manly looked certain to break the

Wigan prop Brian Case subjected to a Des Hasler tackle.

183

tryscoring deadlock when hooker Mal Cochrane prised open the Wigan defence for full back Shearer to take the ball at high speed, only for the Riversiders to succeed in turning the Test man onto his back over the line.

Confusion reigned when the timekeepers sounded the half-time hooter five minutes early, referee John Holdsworth restarting the game with a scrum.

Wigan controlled the early part of the second half, Manly becoming increasingly frustrated with the partisan crowd and the sending off of hard man Gibbs, which gave Stephenson the opportunity to add this fourth penalty goal to the one a minute after the interval.

The white hot pressure of the final quarter spilled over with another outbreak of fighting resulting in Case's dismissal to the sin bin, putting the burden on his Central Park

teammates to hold out, backed by the vociferous support of the pro-British crowd.

Among the packed audience — paying a Wigan record £131,000 — were Great Britain management duo Malcolm Reilly and Les Bettinson who must have taken heart from the victorious Wigan team fielding an all-British line up, 10 from Lancashire and three from Yorkshire.

While not decrying Wigan's victory, Manly coach Bobby Fulton pointed out that his side had been forced to enter the contest after a demanding Sydney season, the history-making encounter being staged in front of a patriotic following with a British referee in charge. Few others would have denied Wigan their moment of world glory, fully endorsing club chairman Maurice Lindsay's tireless efforts to get official backing for the challenge match.

WORLD CLUB CHALLENGE

7 October		Wigan
WIGAN 8		**MANLY-WARRINGAH 2**
Steve Hampson	1.	Dale Shearer
Richard Russell	2.	David Ronson
David Stephenson	3.	Darrell Williams
Joe Lydon	4.	Michael O'Connor
Henderson Gill	5.	Stuart Davis
Shaun Edwards	6.	Cliff Lyons
Andy Gregory	7.	Des Hasler
Brian Case	8.	Phil Daley
Nicky Kiss	9.	Mal Cochrane
Shaun Wane	10.	Ian Gately
Andy Goodway	11.	Ron Gibbs
Ian Potter	12.	Owen Cunningham
Ellery Hanley, Capt.	13.	Paul Vautin, Capt.
Ged Byrne	14.	Mark Brokenshire
Graeme West	15.	Jeremy Ticehurst
Ian Gildart	16.	Mark Pocock
Ian Lucas	17.	Paul Shaw

G: Stephenson (4)
Substitution:
Lucas for Case (76min)
Half-time: 4-2
Referee: John Holdsworth (Kippax)
Attendance: 36, 895

G: O'Connor
Substitutions:
Shaw for Cunningham (21 min.)
Ticehurst for Williams (54 min.)
Brokenshire for Gately (55 min.)
Receipts: £131,000

Manly Test stars Michael O'Connor and Des Hasler (right) cover Wigan full back Steve Hampson.

Manly duo Ron Gibbs (left) and Des Hasler oppose Wigan wingman Henderson Gill.

1987 CHARITY SHIELD

Stones Bitter Champions Wigan fully justified the bookmakers odds of only 5-4 to retain the title by swamping Silk Cut Challenge Cup holders Halifax in the third annual Okells Charity Shield encounter on the Isle of Man.

Rampant Wigan ran in seven top class tries in a 44-12 rout of a Thrum Hall outfit who showed immediate signs of missing newly-retired captain and stand off Chris Anderson.

The Australian coach could only sit and watch as the Riversiders made full use of an 11-5 scrum pull, aided by the 11th hour withdrawal of Halifax hooker Seamus McCallion with a leg injury.

Wigan's touchdowns were all scored by backs — Shaun Edwards, Dean Bell and Steve Hampson each grabbing two plus one from Henderson Gill — while winger David Stephenson hit eight goals from nine attempts.

Edwards produced a near faultless performance in the number six jersey to earn the newly instituted Jack Bentley Memorial Trophy as Man of the Match, having lifted the individual honour two years earlier in the inaugural Charity Shield encounter. The Great Britain stand off ruled the midfield, setting up numerous attacks and launching a series of long-range touch finders, as well as touching down twice.

Wigan provided the entertainment value for a record Charity Shield crowd of 4,804, Halifax trailing 22-0 at the interval and conceding another six points before they got on the scoreboard in the 48th minute. In direct contrast to Wigan's free flowing style, that touchdown came when Great Britain forward Paul Dixon ploughed through a mass of defenders for a close range try, Australian full back Graham Eadie adding the goal.

The Yorkshiremen's second try came in a similar fashion when 62nd minute substitute Brian Juliff added impetus to a lacklustre team performance by powering through for Eadie to again add the goal.

Halifax and former Wigan packman John Pendlebury played a variety of roles, starting off at hooker as emergency deputy for the injured McCallion, being well beaten for scrum possession before prop Graham Beevers took over. Pendlebury returned to his usual loose forward position before taking over at stand off when young Andy Simpson was replaced by Juliff. In the 23rd minute, Pendlebury was sin binned for swinging a punch at Andy Gregory and returned to send out a pass which Edwards intercepted to score his second try with a 75 yard sprint to the line.

Edwards' first touchdown was another long distance effort as the 1987 Young Player of the Year shot through near halfway to kick ahead and win the race to score between the posts after only four minutes.

Then Edwards sent out a defence splitting short pass which put fellow Test man Andy Goodway in the clear. The loose forward ran in great style, stepping out of one tackle and getting out his pass as he fell to another, leaving full back Hampson to finish off the 50-yard move in the corner.

Goodway continued to impress with his running and Hampson completed a first class display by scoring Wigan's last try following clever work around the scrum by Gregory. New Zealand Test centre Bell also grabbed two tries, reversing roles with wing partner Gill, who supplied the pass each time. Test winger Gill got his tryscoring reward when Ian Potter created the opportunity at the corner.

Wigan dominated despite the absence of Great Britain skipper Ellery Hanley with a reported calf strain. Riversiders' captain Graeme West received a prize cheque for £5,000 and the Okells Charity Shield as Wigan celebrated an Isle of Man triumph for the second time in three years and their fifth trophy haul inside 10 months.

Man of the Match Shaun Edwards has plenty of Wigan support in the Okells Charity Shield match.

Wigan captain Graeme West holds aloft the Okells Charity Shield trophy.

OKELLS CHARITY SHIELD

23 August   **Douglas Bowl, Isle of Man**

HALIFAX 12		WIGAN 44
Graham Eadie	1.	Steve Hampson
Mike Taylor	2.	David Stephenson
Scott Wilson	3.	Ged Byrne
Tony Anderson	4.	Dean Bell
Wilf George	5.	Henderson Gill
Andy Simpson	6.	Shaun Edwards
Gary Stephens, Capt.	7.	Andy Gregory
Roy Dickinson	8.	Graeme West, Capt.
John Pendlebury	9.	Nicky Kiss
Graham Beevers	10.	Brian Case
Neil James	11.	Ian Gildart
Mick Scott	12.	Ian Potter
Paul Dixon	13.	Andy Goodway
Brian Juliff	14.	Richard Russell
Peter Bell	15.	Shaun Wane

T: Dixon, Juliff
G: Eadie (2)
Substitutions:
Bell for Scott (60 min.)
Juliff for Simpson (62 min.)
Half Time: 0-22
Referee: John Holdsworth (Kippax)

T: Edwards (2), Bell (2),
Hampson (2), Gill
G: Stephenson (8)
Substitutions:
Russell for Byrne (60 min.)
Wane for Gildart (64 min.)
Attendance: 4,804

CHARITY SHIELD ROLL OF HONOUR

Year	Winners		Runners-up		Attendance
1985-86	Wigan	34	Hull K.R.	6	4,066
1986-87	Halifax	9	Castleford	8	3,276
1987-88	Wigan	44	Halifax	12	4,804

CHARITY SHIELD .... A REVIEW

1985-86
Wigan 34 Hampson; P. Ford, Stephenson (7g), Donlan (2t), Gill (2t); Edwards, M. Ford (1t); Courtney (Mayo), Kiss, Campbell, West (Lucas), Du Toit, Wane
Hull K.R. 6 Fairbairn (Lydiat 1g); Clark (1t), Robinson, Prohm, Laws; M. Smith, G. Smith; D. Harrison, Watkinson, Ema, Kelly (Rudd), Burton, Hogan
Referee: R. Campbell (Widnes)

1986-87
Halifax 9 Smith (Wilson); Riddlesden, Whitfield (1t), Hague (1dg), George (1t); C. Anderson, Stephens; Dickinson, McCallion, Juliff, Scott (James), Bell, Dixon
Castleford 8 Roockley; Plange, Lord (1t), Irwin (R. Southernwood), Spears; Joyner (Fletcher), R. Beardmore; Ward, K. Beardmore, Johnson, Ketteridge (2g), Mountain, England
Referee: G. F. Lindop (Wakefield)

MAN OF THE MATCH AWARDS

Season	Winner	Team	Position
1985-86	Shaun Edwards	Wigan (v. Hull K.R.)	Stand off
1986-87	Chris Anderson	Halifax (v. Castleford)	Stand off
1987-88	Shaun Edwards	Wigan (v. Halifax)	Stand off

● From 1987 it became the Jack Bentley Trophy in memory of the former Daily Express Rugby League journalist.

BBC-2 FLOODLIT TROPHY

The BBC-2 Floodlit Trophy competition was launched in 1965. Eight clubs competed in the first year and the total had grown to 22 by 1980 when the competition was abolished as part of the BBC's financial cut-backs.

For 15 years the matches became a regular television feature on Tuesday evenings throughout the early winter months.

Although the format changed slightly over the years, it was basically a knockout competition on the lines of the Challenge Cup.

In 1966 the Floodlit Competition was used to introduce the limited tackle rule, then four tackles, which proved such a great success it was adopted in all other matches before the end of the year.

BBC-2 FLOODLIT TROPHY FINALS
(Only the 1967, at Leeds, and 1972, at Wigan, finals were played on neutral grounds)

Season	Winners		Runners-up		Venue	Attendance	Receipts
1965-66	Castleford	4	St. Helens	0	St. Helens	11,510	£1,548
1966-67	Castleford	7	Swinton	2	Castleford	8,986	£1,692
1967-68	Castleford	8	Leigh	5	Leeds	9,716	£2,099
1968-69	Wigan	7	St. Helens	4	Wigan	13,479	£3,291
1969-70	Leigh	11	Wigan	6	Wigan	12,312	£2,854
1970-71	Leeds	9	St. Helens	5	Leeds	7,612	£2,189
1971-72	St. Helens	8	Rochdale H.	2	St. Helens	9,300	£2,493
1972-73	Leigh	5	Widnes	0	Wigan	4,691	£1,391
1973-74	Bramley	15	Widnes	7	Widnes	4,422	£1,538
1974-75	Salford	0	Warrington	0	Salford	4,473	£1,913
Replay	Salford	10	Warrington	5	Warrington	5,778	£2,434
1975-76	St. Helens	22	Dewsbury	2	St. Helens	3,858	£1,747
1976-77	Castleford	12	Leigh	4	Leigh	5,402	£2,793
1977-78	Hull K.R.	26	St. Helens	11	Hull K.R.	10,099	£6,586
1978-79	Widnes	13	St. Helens	7	St. Helens	10,250	£7,017
1979-80	Hull	13	Hull K.R.	3	Hull	18,500	£16,605

BBC2 FLOODLIT TROPHY .... A REVIEW
1965-66
Castleford 4 Edwards; C. Battye, M. Battye, Willett (2g), Briggs; Hardisty, Millward; Terry, J. Ward, C. Dickinson, Bryant, Taylor, Small
St. Helens 0 F. Barrow; Vollenhoven, Wood, Benyon, Killeen; Murphy, Prosser; French, Dagnall, Watson, Hicks, Mantle, Laughton
Referee: L. Gant (Wakefield)
1966-67
Castleford 7 Edwards; Howe, Stenton, Willett (1g), Austin (1t); Hardisty, Hepworth (1g); Hartley, C. Dickinson, McCartney, Bryant, Small, Walker
Swinton 2 Gowers; Whitehead (1g), Gomersall, Buckley, Davies; Fleet, G. Williams; Halliwell, D. Clarke, Scott (Cummings), Rees, Simpson, Robinson
Referee: J. Manley (Warrington)
1967-68
Castleford 8 Edwards; Harris, Thomas, Stenton, Willett (4g); Hardisty, Hepworth; Hartley, J. Ward, Walton, Bryant (C. Dickinson), Redfearn, Reilly

Leigh 5 Grainey; Tickle (1t), Lewis, Collins, Walsh; Entwistle, A. Murphy; Whitworth, Ashcroft, Major, Welding, M. Murphy, Gilfedder (1g)
Referee: G.F. Lindop (Wakefield)
1968-69
Wigan 7 Tyrer (2g); Francis, Ashton, Ashurst, Rowe; C. Hill (1t), Jackson; J. Stephens, Clarke, Mills, Fogerty (Lyon), Kevin O'Loughlin, Laughton
St. Helens 4 Williams; Wilson, Benyon, Myler, Wills; Whittle, Bishop; Warlow, Sayer, Watson, Mantle, Hogan, Coslett (2g)
Referee: E. Clay (Leeds)
1969-70
Leigh 11 Ferguson (3g) (Lewis); Tickle (1t), Dorrington, Collins, Walsh; Eckersley, Murphy (1g); D. Chisnall, Ashcroft, Watts, Welding, Grimes, Lyon
Wigan 6 C. Hill; Wright, Francis (2g), Rowe, Kevin O'Loughlin; D. Hill (1g), Jackson; J. Stephens, Clarke, Ashcroft, Ashurst, Mills, Laughton
Referee: W.H. Thompson (Huddersfield)

1970-71
Leeds 9 Holmes (2g); Alan Smith, Hynes (1t, 1g), Cowan, Atkinson; Wainwright, Shoebottom; J. Burke, Fisher, Barnard, Haigh, Ramsey, Batten
St. Helens 5 F. Barrow; L. Jones (1t), Benyon, Walsh, Wilson; Whittle, Heaton; Rees, A. Karalius, E. Chisnall, Mantle, E. Prescott, Coslett (1g)
Referee: E. Lawrinson (Warrington)
1971-72
St. Helens 8 G. Pimblett; L. Jones, Benyon, Walsh, Wilson; Kelly, Heaton; Rees, A. Karalius, E. Chisnall, E. Prescott, Mantle, Coslett (4g)
Rochdale H. 2 Chamberlain (1g); Brelsford, Crellin, Taylor, Glover; Myler, Gartland; Birchall, P. Clarke, Brown, Welding, Sheffield (Hodkinson), Delooze
Referee: E. Clay (Leeds)
1972-73
Leigh 5 Hogan; Lawson (1t) (Lester), Atkin, Collins, Stacey; A. Barrow, Sayer (Ryding); Grimes, D. Clarke, Fletcher, Fiddler (1g), F. Barrow, Martyn
Widnes 0 Dutton; A. Prescott, Aspey, Blackwood, McDonnell; Lowe, Ashton; Mills, Elwell, Warlow, Foran, Sheridan, Nicholls
Referee: G.F. Lindop (Wakefield)
1973-74
Bramley 15 Keegan; Goodchild (1t), Bollon, Hughes, Austin (1t); T. Briggs, Ward (1g) (Ashman); D. Briggs, Firth, Cheshire, D. Sampson (1t), Idle, Wolford (2g)
Widnes 7 Dutton (2g); D. O'Neill, Hughes, Aspey, Macko (1t); Warburton, Bowden; Hogan, Elwell, Nelson, Sheridan, Blackwood (Foran) Laughton
Referee: D. G. Kershaw (York)

1974-75
Salford 0 Charlton; Fielding, Hesketh, Graham, Richards; Brophy (Taylor), Banner; Coulman, Devlin, Grice, Knighton, Dixon, E. Prescott
Warrington 0 Whitehead; Sutton, Cunliffe (Lowe), Whittle, Bevan; Briggs, Gordon; D. Chisnall, Ashcroft, Wright, Gaskell, Conroy, B. Philbin (Jewitt)
Referee: W.H. Thompson (Huddersfield)
Replay
Salford 10 Stead; Fielding (1t), Watkins (2g), Hesketh, Richards (1t); Gill, Banner; Grice, Walker, Mackay, Dixon, Knighton, E. Prescott

Warrington 5 Cunliffe; Whitehead (1g), Pickup, Whittle, Bevan (1t); Noonan (Briggs), Gordon; D. Chisnall, Ashcroft, Wanbon, Conroy, Nicholas (Brady), B. Philbin
Referee: W.H. Thompson (Huddersfield)
1975-76
St. Helens 22 G. Pimblett (2g); L. Jones, Benyon (1t), Hull (1t), Mathias (2t); Wilson (1t), Heaton (1dg); Mantle, A. Karalius, James, Nicholls, E. Chisnall, Coslett (1g)
Dewsbury 2 Langley; Hegarty, Chalkley, Simpson, Mitchell; N. Stephenson (1g) (Lee), A. Bates; Beverley, Price, Hankins, Halloran (Artis), Bell, Grayshon
Referee: W.H. Thompson (Huddersfield)
1976-77
Castleford 12 Wraith; Fenton, Joyner, P. Johnson, Walsh (1t); Burton (1t), Stephens; Khan, Spurr, A. Dickinson, Reilly, Lloyd (3g), S. Norton
Leigh 4 Hogan; A. Prescott, Stacey, Woods, Walsh (1t); Taylor, Sayer; D. Chisnall, Ashcroft (1dg), Fletcher, Macko, Grimes, Boyd
Referee: J.E. Jackson (Pudsey)
1977-78
Hull K.R. 26 Hall (4g); Dunn (2t), M. Smith (1t), Watson, Sullivan (1t); Hartley (1t), Millward; Millington, Watkinson, Cunningham (Hughes), Lowe, Rose (1t), Casey
St. Helens 11 G. Pimblett (Platt); L. Jones (Courtney), Noonan, Cunningham (1t), Glynn (2t, 1g); Francis, K. Gwilliam; D. Chisnall, Liptrot, James, Hope, A. Karalius, Pinner
Referee: M. J. Naughton (Widnes)
1978-79
Widnes 13 Eckersley; Wright (2t), Hughes, Aspey, P. Shaw; Burke (2g, 1t), Bowden; Hogan, Elwell, Mills, Adams, Dearden, Laughton
St. Helens 7 G. Pimblett (2g), L. Jones, Glynn, Cunningham, Mathias; Francis, Holding; D. Chisnall (1t), Liptrot, James, Nicholls, Knighton (E. Chisnall), Pinner
Referee: J. McDonald (Wigan)
1979-80
Hull 13 Woods; Bray, G. Evans (1t), Coupland, Dennison (1t, 2g); Newlove, Hepworth; Tindall, Wileman, Farrar, Stone, Boxall (Birdsall 1t), Norton
Hull K.R. 3 Robinson; Hubbard (1t), M. Smith, Watson, Sullivan; Hall, Agar; Holdstock, Tyreman, Lockwood, Clarkson (Hartley), Lowe, Hogan (Millington)
Referee: W.H. Thompson (Huddersfield)

CAPTAIN MORGAN TROPHY

This sponsored competition, with a winners' prize of £3,000, lasted only one season. Entry was restricted to the 16 clubs who won their Yorkshire and Lancashire Cup first round ties. The Lancashire contingent was made up to eight by including the side which lost their first round county Cup-tie by the narrowest margin. The first round of the Captain Morgan Trophy was zoned with clubs being drawn against those in their own county. The remainder of the competition was integrated. The final was on a neutral ground as follows:

1973-74	Warrington	4	Featherstone R.	0	Salford	5,259	£2,265

1973-74
Warrington 4 Whitehead (2g); M. Philbin, Noonan, Reynolds (Pickup), Bevan; Whittle, Gordon; D. Chisnall, Ashcroft, Brady, Wanbon (Price), Wright, Mather

Featherstone R. 0 Box; Coventry, M. Smith, Hartley, Bray; Mason, Wood; Tonks, Bridges, Harris, Gibbins (Stone), Rhodes, Bell
Referee: G.F. Lindop (Wakefield)

Oldham captain Mal Graham holds aloft the Division Two championship trophy.

LEAGUE

1987-88 CHAMPIONSHIP

Widnes became the first club to top the new-style Stones Bitter Championship...lifting the league title for the first time in 10 years.

Reducing the number of clubs from 16 to 14 increased the competition as quality replaced quantity.

The Chemics earned the £20,000 prize with 20 victories in the 26-match campaign, finishing second top points scorers behind St. Helens and second best defenders after Bradford Northern.

Warrington were the early pacesetters with reigning champions Wigan taking over pole position after only three matches. The Riversiders were replaced by Widnes on October 18 after six games, a first round exit from the John Player Special Trophy enabling the Chemics to take advantage of at least one game in hand to retain the lead throughout the winter.

By February 7 Widnes had opened up an eight point margin from nearest rivals Bradford Northern, both having played 18 games, three more than most other clubs. While making progress in the Silk Cut Challenge Cup, the black-and-whites faltered in their bid for title success, losing successive matches at home to Wigan and at Hull K.R.

On March 20 high-scoring St. Helens took over the leadership on points difference, both clubs having played 21 fixtures. The Easter holiday programme was to be decisive with in-form St. Helens a real threat to Widnes' season-long dominance of the league table.

Widnes entered the Easter break leading fellow title contenders by two points, having played two more matches than the Saints. Watched by a Knowsley Road crowd of 21,812, Alex Murphy's men crashed to a 10-9 home defeat at the hands of arch rivals Wigan, despite a two-day training break at Blackpool. Meanwhile across at Warrington, Widnes cruised to a 35-6 success, running in six tries.

The crunch meeting came on Easter Monday with the visit of St. Helens to Widnes. Wing sensation Martin Offiah scored a thrilling hat-trick of tries in a 16-6 Widnes victory in front of more than 13,000 fans. Doug Laughton's side now needed only a draw in their last league match, at Hunslet five days later, to secure the coveted Championship Trophy, last held in 1977-78.

Unaware that the St. Helens challenge was petering out with a 28-23 home defeat by Leeds, the Chemics celebrated title success in champion fashion with a 66-14 12-try romp at Elland Road.

When the campaign was completed a week later, St. Helens, Wigan and Bradford Northern all trailed by four points, the Saints collecting the £8,000 runners-up cheque, on points difference, for the second successive season.

At the other end of the table, the promotion-relegation format returned to three-up, three-down after the one season of adjustment to form the 14-strong First Division.

Newly promoted Hunslet and Swinton made an immediate return to the Second Division, both securing only four victories and two draws. The battle for survival was prolonged to the final 80 minutes of the campaign with Salford and Leigh fighting to avoid the drop.

Leigh needed to beat visitors Hull to draw level on points with Salford, a superior points difference keeping the Hilton Park outfit in the premier set-up. Salford would then need to at least draw with visitors Halifax to secure a future in the Championship. So as not to give Leigh any advantage, Salford put back their traditional three o'clock kick off to match Leigh's 3.30 start.

As Leigh rattled up a 31-9 success over Challenge Cup semi-finalists Hull, Salford were running in six tries against Wembley finalists Halifax and earning a £1,000 per man bonus!

The Second Division title chase was headed by three of the four clubs relegated the previous season — Featherstone Rovers, Oldham and Wakefield Trinity — all of whom led the pack at some stage.

The climax of the 28-match programme came on the penultimate weekend when Oldham travelled to Wakefield, when defeat for the Lancashire side would set up their joint leadership with one match each left to play. In front of Trinity's best crowd of the season — more than 6,500 — Oldham secured a 23-22 success to clinch the title and £10,000 prize money. But not before surviving last second tension as home full back Kevin Harcombe sent a touchline kick at goal just wide!

Oldham celebrated with a three-point lead on runners-up Featherstone Rovers, who collected £4,000 prize money, the champions being the division's top scorers and second best defenders.

In their first season at Wigan FC's Springfield Park, Springfield Borough — formerly Blackpool — finished a creditable fourth while Sheffield Eagles continued their impressive development by clinching fifth spot in their fourth campaign, having previously finished 17th, 12th and sixth in succession.

Batley finished bottom of the pile for the first time in nine years, while Mansfield Marksman, in the bottom three for the past two seasons, climbed to seventh place to qualify for the Second Division Premiership play-off.

Oldham's Mike Ford on the attack against Keighley.

Widnes winger Martin Offiah takes his turn to lift the Stones Bitter championship trophy.

FINAL TABLES 1987-88

STONES BITTER CHAMPIONSHIP

	P.	W.	D.	L.	Dr.	FOR Gls.	Trs.	Pts.	Dr.	AGAINST Gls.	Trs.	Pts.	Pts.
Widnes	26	20	0	6	7	91	113	641	3	52	51	311	40
St. Helens	26	18	0	8	12	104	113	672	1	54	57	337	36
Wigan	26	17	2	7	1	84	113	621	3	56	53	327	36
Bradford N.	26	18	0	8	4	82	90	528	6	51	49	304	36
Leeds	26	15	3	8	1	84	102	577	8	67	77	450	33
Warrington	26	14	2	10	7	92	85	531	6	71	67	416	30
Castleford	26	13	0	13	1	84	84	505	5	85	96	559	26
Halifax	26	12	0	14	3	70	89	499	9	64	75	437	24
Hull K.R.	26	11	1	14	16	76	63	420	8	70	83	480	23
Hull	26	11	0	15	10	63	57	364	7	94	100	595	22
Salford	26	10	0	16	2	61	61	368	7	83	97	561	20
Leigh	26	9	0	17	6	65	70	416	5	91	93	559	18
Swinton	26	4	2	20	4	57	68	390	2	121	134	780	10
Hunslet	26	4	2	20	1	57	62	363	5	111	138	779	10

SECOND DIVISION

	P.	W.	D.	L.	Dr.	FOR Gls.	Trs.	Pts.	Dr.	AGAINST Gls.	Trs.	Pts.	Pts.
Oldham	28	23	1	4	3	116	134	771	5	59	53	335	47
Featherstone R.	28	21	2	5	10	107	122	712	7	57	58	353	44
Wakefield T.	28	20	1	7	0	103	115	666	5	49	53	315	41
Springfield B.	28	18	0	10	4	74	74	448	12	60	56	356	36
Sheffield E.	28	16	1	11	4	67	88	490	7	67	72	429	33
York	28	15	1	12	14	86	93	558	6	82	89	526	31
Mansfield M.	28	15	1	12	7	68	74	439	4	56	74	412	31
Keighley	28	15	0	13	5	78	84	497	2	75	69	428	30
Barrow	28	14	2	12	4	61	64	382	5	72	62	397	30
Workington T.	28	15	0	13	14	65	59	380	5	70	74	441	30
Carlisle	28	14	1	13	8	70	60	388	6	76	72	446	29
Runcorn H.	28	14	0	14	10	63	71	420	3	79	77	469	28
Whitehaven	28	10	1	17	7	63	71	417	6	67	78	452	21
Bramley	28	10	1	17	4	70	64	400	6	89	104	600	21
Dewsbury	28	10	0	18	5	66	70	417	5	73	92	519	20
Doncaster	28	9	2	17	2	72	65	406	6	85	84	512	20
Fulham	28	10	0	18	4	63	63	382	9	85	95	559	20
Rochdale H.	28	10	0	18	8	53	52	322	8	69	92	514	20
Huddersfield B.	28	7	1	20	3	52	69	383	3	81	108	597	15
Batley	28	6	1	21	9	46	51	305	11	94	81	523	13

TWO DIVISION CHAMPIONSHIP ROLL OF HONOUR

	FIRST DIVISION	SECOND DIVISION
1902-03	Halifax	Keighley
1903-04	Bradford	Wakefield Trinity
1904-05	Oldham	Dewsbury
1962-63	Swinton	Hunslet
1963-64	Swinton	Oldham
1973-74	Salford	Bradford Northern
1974-75	St. Helens	Huddersfield
1975-76	Salford	Barrow
1976-77	Featherstone Rovers	Hull
1977-78	Widnes	Leigh
1978-79	Hull Kingston Rovers	Hull
1979-80	Bradford Northern	Featherstone Rovers
1980-81	Bradford Northern	York
1981-82	Leigh	Oldham
1982-83	Hull	Fulham
1983-84	Hull Kingston Rovers	Barrow
1984-85	Hull Kingston Rovers	Swinton
1985-86	Halifax	Leigh
1986-87	Wigan	Hunslet
1987-88	Widnes	Oldham

THE UPS AND DOWNS OF TWO DIVISION FOOTBALL
Since re-introduction of two divisions in 1973-74.

● Figure in brackets indicates position in division.

	RELEGATED	PROMOTED
1973-74	Oldham (13)	Bradford Northern (1)
	Hull K.R. (14)	York (2)
	Leigh (15)	Keighley (3)
	Whitehaven (16)	Halifax (4)
1974-75	York (13)	Huddersfield (1)
	Bramley (14)	Hull K.R. (2)
	Rochdale Hornets (15)	Oldham (3)
	Halifax (16)	Swinton (4)

1975-76	Dewsbury (13) Keighley (14) Huddersfield (15) Swinton (16)	Barrow (1) Rochdale Hornets (2) Workington T. (3) Leigh (4)
1976-77	Rochdale Hornets (13) Leigh (14) Barrow (15) Oldham (16)	Hull (1) Dewsbury (2) Bramley (3) New Hunslet (4)
1977-78	Hull (13) New Hunslet (14) Bramley (15) Dewsbury (16)	Leigh (1) Barrow (2) Rochdale Hornets (3) Huddersfield (4)
1978-79	Barrow (13) Featherstone Rovers (14) Rochdale Hornets (15) Huddersfield (16)	Hull (1) New Hunslet (2) York (3) Blackpool Borough (4)
1979-80	Wigan (13) Hunslet (14) York (15) Blackpool Borough (16)	Featherstone Rovers (1) Halifax (2) Oldham (3) Barrow (4)
1980-81	Halifax (13) Salford (14) Workington T. (15) Oldham (16)	York (1) Wigan (2) Fulham (3) Whitehaven (4)
1981-82	Fulham (13) Wakefield T. (14) York (15) Whitehaven (16)	Oldham (1) Carlisle (2) Workington T. (3) Halifax (4)
1982-83	Barrow (13) Workington T. (14) Halifax (15) Carlisle (16)	Fulham (1) Wakefield T. (2) Salford (3) Whitehaven (4)
1983-84	Fulham (13) Wakefield T. (14) Salford (15) Whitehaven (16)	Barrow (1) Workington T. (2) Hunslet (3) Halifax (4)
1984-85	Barrow (13) Leigh (14) Hunslet (15) Workington T. (16)	Swinton (1) Salford (2) York (3) Dewsbury (4)
1985-86	York (14) Swinton (15) Dewsbury (16)	Leigh (1) Barrow (2) Wakefield T. (3)
1986-87	Oldham (13) Featherstone R. (14) Barrow (15) Wakefield T. (16)	Hunslet (1) Swinton (2)
1987-88	Leigh (14) Swinton (15) Hunslet (16)	Oldham (1) Featherstone R. (2) Wakefield T. (3)

FIRST DIVISION RECORDS
Since reintroduction in 1973

INDIVIDUAL

Match records

Most tries:
6 Shane Cooper (St. Helens) v. Hull Feb 17, 1988

Most goals: 13 Geoff Pimblett (St. Helens) v. Bramley Mar 5, 1978

Most points: 38 (11g, 4t) Bob Beardmore (Castleford) v. Barrow Mar 22, 1987

Season records

Most tries: 44 Ellery Hanley (Wigan) 1986-87
Most goals: 130 Steve Hesford (Warrington) 1978-79
Most points: 295 (101g, 1dg, 23t) John Woods (Leigh) 1983-84

TEAM

Highest score: Castleford 76 v. Swinton 16 Mar 16, 1988

Biggest away win and widest margin: Wakefield T. 6 v. Wigan 72 Mar 29, 1987

Most points by losing team: Hunslet 40 v. Barrow 41 Sep 9, 1984

Scoreless draw: Wigan 0 v. Castleford 0 Jan 26, 1974

Highest score draw: Hunslet 32 v. Swinton 32 Sep 20, 1987

Best opening sequence: 13 wins then a draw by Widnes 1981-82

Longest winning run: 25 by St. Helens Won last 13 of 1985-86 and first 12 of 1986-87. (Also longest unbeaten run.)

Longest losing run: 20 by Whitehaven 1983-84

Longest run without a win: 23, including 3 draws, by Whitehaven 1981-82 (Also worst opening sequence)

Biggest attendance: 23,809 Wigan v. St. Helens Dec 27, 1987

100 Division One tries
165 Keith Fielding (Salford)
160 Ellery Hanley (Bradford N., Wigan)
144 David Smith (Wakefield T., Leeds, Bradford N.)
139 Stuart Wright (Wigan, Widnes)
136 Roy Mathias (St. Helens)
130 John Bevan (Warrington)
126 Steve Hartley (Hull K.R.)
    David Topliss (Wakefield T., Hull, Oldham)
124 John Joyner (Castleford)
122 Maurice Richards (Salford)
    Steve Evans (Featherstone R., Hull, Wakefield T., Bradford N.)
119 John Woods (Leigh, Bradford N., Warrington)
113 David Redfearn (Bradford N.)
103 Keiron O'Loughlin (Wigan, Workington T., Widnes, Salford)
102 Henderson Gill (Bradford N., Wigan)
    Gary Hyde (Castleford)
    Phil Ford (Warrington, Wigan, Bradford N.)

500 Division One goals
845 Steve Hesford (Warrington)
803 Steve Quinn (Featherstone R.)
790 John Woods (Leigh, Bradford N.)
787 George Fairbairn (Wigan, Hull K.R.)
586 Sammy Lloyd (Castleford, Hull)
546 Colin Whitfield (Salford, Wigan, Halifax)

1,000 Division One points
1,978 John Woods (Leigh, Bradford N.)
1,756 Steve Hesford (Warrington)
1,738 Steve Quinn (Featherstone R.)
1,734 George Fairbairn (Wigan, Hull K.R.)
1,324 Colin Whitfield (Salford, Wigan, Halifax)
1,264 Sammy Lloyd (Castleford, Hull)
1,111 Keith Mumby (Bradford N.)
1,109 Mick Burke (Widnes, Oldham)
1,081 Bob Beardmore (Castleford)

20 Division One tries in a season

Season		Player
1973-74	36	Keith Fielding (Salford)
	29	Roy Mathias (St. Helens)
	21	David Smith (Wakefield T.)
1974-75	21	Maurice Richards (Salford)
	21	Roy Mathias (St. Helens)
1975-76	26	Maurice Richards (Salford)
	20	David Smith (Wakefield T.)
1976-77	22	David Topliss (Wakefield T.)
	21	Keith Fielding (Salford)
	21	Ged Dunn (Hull K.R.)
	20	David Smith (Leeds)
	20	Stuart Wright (Widnes)
1977-78	26	Keith Fielding (Salford)
	25	Steve Fenton (Castleford)
	24	Stuart Wright (Widnes)
	20	David Smith (Leeds)
	20	Bruce Burton (Castleford)
	20	John Bevan (Warrington)
1978-79	28	Steve Hartley (Hull K.R.)
1979-80	24	Keith Fielding (Salford)
	21	Roy Mathias (St. Helens)
	21	Steve Hubbard (Hull K.R.)
	20	David Smith (Leeds)
1980-81	20	Steve Hubbard (Hull K.R.)
1981-82		David Hobbs (Featherstone R.) was top scorer with 19 tries.
1982-83	22	Bob Eccles (Warrington)
	20	Steve Evans (Hull)
1983-84	28	Garry Schofield (Hull)
	23	John Woods (Leigh)
	20	James Leuluai (Hull)
1984-85	40	Ellery Hanley (Bradford N.)
	34	Gary Prohm (Hull K.R.)
	23	Henderson Gill (Wigan)
	22	Barry Ledger (St. Helens)
	22	Mal Meninga (St. Helens)
1985-86	22	Ellery Hanley (Wigan)
1986-87	44	Ellery Hanley (Wigan)
	24	Phil Ford (Bradford N.)
	24	Henderson Gill (Wigan)
	23	Garry Schofield (Hull)
	21	John Henderson (Leigh)
1987-88	33	Martin Offiah (Widnes)
	22	Ellery Hanley (Wigan)

Top Division One goalscorers
1973-74 126 David Watkins (Salford)
1974-75   96 Sammy Lloyd (Castleford)
1975-76 118 Sammy Lloyd (Castleford)
1976-77 113 Steve Quinn (Featherstone R.)
1977-78 116 Steve Hesford (Warrington)
1978-79 130 Steve Hesford (Warrington)
1979-80 104 Steve Hubbard (Hull K.R.)
1980-81   96 Steve Diamond (Wakefield T.)
1981-82 110 Steve Quinn (Featherstone R.)
         John Woods (Leigh)
1982-83 105 Bob Beardmore (Castleford)
1983-84 106 Steve Hesford (Warrington)
1984-85 114 Sean Day (St. Helens)
1985-86   85 David Stephenson (Wigan)
1986-87 120 Paul Loughlin (St. Helens)
1987-88   95 John Woods (Warrington)

Top Division One pointscorer 1987-88
218 (91g, 4dg, 8t) John Woods (Warrington)

SECOND DIVISION RECORDS
Since reintroduction in 1973

INDIVIDUAL

Match records

Most tries: 6 Ged Dunn (Hull K.R.) v. New Hunslet Feb 2, 1975

Most goals: 15 Mick Stacey (Leigh) v. Doncaster Mar 28, 1976

Most points: 38 (13g, 4t) John Woods (Leigh) v. Blackpool B. Sep 11, 1977

Season records

Most tries: 48 Steve Halliwell (Leigh) 1985-86

Most goals: 166 Lynn Hopkins (Workington T.) 1981-82

Most points: 395 (163g, 3dg, 22t) Lynn Hopkins (Workington T.) 1981-82

TEAM

Highest score: Leigh 92 v. Keighley 2 Apr 30, 1986 (Also widest margin)

Highest away: Kent Invicta 8 v. Barrow 80 Apr 8, 1984

Most points by losing team:
Hunslet 38 v. Blackpool B. 32 Sep 22, 1985
Carlisle 32 v. Blackpool B. 33 Oct 27, 1985

Highest score draw: Huddersfield B. 32 v. Keighley 32 Apr 17, 1986

Scoreless draw: Dewsbury 0 v. Rochdale H. 0. Jan 30, 1983

Longest winning run: 30 by Leigh in 1985-86. Hull won all 26 matches in 1978-79

Longest losing run: 40 by Doncaster (16 in 1975-76 and 24 in 1976-77)

Biggest attendance: 12,424 Hull v. New Hunslet May 18, 1979

1987-88 Top Division Two scorers
Most tries: 19 Kevin Pape (Carlisle)

Most goals: 94 Steve Quinn (Featherstone R.)

Most points: 219 (93g, 1dg, 8t) Steve Quinn (Featherstone R.)

NB. Division One and Two records do not include scores in abandoned matches that were replayed.

TWO DIVISION SCORING

The following tables show the scoring totals for each two-division season:

DIVISION ONE

Season	Matches each club played	Goals	1-Point drop goals	Tries	Pts
1973-74	30	1,508	—	1,295	6,901
1974-75	30	1,334	48	1,261	6,499
1975-76	30	1,498	53	1,331	7,042
1976-77	30[1]	1,435	91	1,423	7,230
1977-78	30[2]	1,402	99	1,443	7,232
1978-79	30	1,367	119	1,448	7,197
1979-80	30	1,389	131	1,349	6,956
1980-81	30	1,439	147	1,342	7,051
1981-82	30	1,486	132	1,354	7,166
1982-83	30	1,369	64	1,386	6,960
1983-84	30	1,472	108	1,479	8,968
1984-85	30	1,464	84	1,595	9,392
1985-86	30	1,296	80	1,435	8,412
1986-87	30	1,412	90	1,607	9,342
1987-88	26	1,070	75	1,170	6,895

[1] Salford & Leeds played 29 matches — their final match was abandoned and not replayed. This match was expunged from league records.
[2] Featherstone R. & Bradford N. played 29 matches — their final match was cancelled following Featherstone's strike.

DIVISION TWO

1973-74	26	1,054	—	955	4,973
1974-75	26	992	36	919	4,777
1975-76	26	1,034	49	963	5,006
1976-77	26	942	78	1,046	5,100
1977-78	26	976	86	1,020	5,098
1978-79	26	971	114	972	4,972
1979-80	26	1,046	106	1,069	5,405
1980-81	28	1,133	123	1,220	6,049
1981-82	32	1,636	152	1,589	8,189
1982-83	32	1,510	103	1,648	8,067
1983-84	34	1,782	254	1,897	11,406
1984-85	28[1]	1,542	226	1,666	9,974
1985-86	34	1,722	130	2,021	11,658
1986-87	28[1]	1,323	112	1,496	8,742
1987-88	28[2]	1,443	125	1,543	9,183

[1] The 20 clubs played 28 matches each.
[2] The 18 clubs played 28 matches each.

201

FIFTEEN-SEASON TABLE

St. Helens confirmed their position as the most successful Division One side since the reintroduction of two divisions in 1973 in terms of most points gained. They retained the lead with 18 victories taking their 15-season total to 594 points from 446 matches.

The Saints are the only club to have finished in the top eight in each season although their only championship success was in 1974-75. In addition to St. Helens only Widnes, Castleford, Leeds and Warrington have remained in Division One.

Three clubs have spent the entire 15 seasons in Division Two...Batley, Doncaster and Runcorn Highfield.

Bradford Northern, Hull and Leigh were all Division Two champions who went on to win the Division One title only a few seasons after promotion, while Hull Kingston Rovers, Halifax and Wigan are other former lower grade clubs who have won the trophy.

Halifax achieved the quickest Division One championship win when they took the title in 1985-86 in only their second campaign after being promoted.

The highest place gained by a newly-promoted club is third by Hull in 1979-80 after winning the Division Two championship with a 100 per cent record the previous season.

Division One champions who were relegated a few seasons after winning the major title were Salford, Featherstone Rovers and Leigh.

The records of the five clubs who have appeared in Division One throughout the 15 seasons are as follows:

John Joyner — 15 seasons of Division One with Castleford.

	P.	W.	D.	L.	F.	A.	Pts
1. St. Helens	446	288	18	140	9,135	5,825	594
2. Widnes	446	282	17	147	7,811	5,634	581
3. Leeds	445	254	19	172	8,111	6,548	527
4. Warrington	446	250	17	179	7,566	6,279	517
5. Castleford	446	224	23	199	8,053	7,064	471

● Although Bradford Northern and Hull Kingston Rovers have had only 14 seasons in Division One their records compare more favourably with some of the above. Three times champions Rovers have gained 513 points and twice champions Northern 485.

CHAMPIONSHIP PLAY-OFFS

Following the breakaway from the English Rugby Union, 22 clubs formed the Northern Rugby Football League. Each club played 42 matches and Manningham won the first Championship as league leaders in 1895-96.

This format was then abandoned and replaced by the Yorkshire Senior and Lancashire Senior Combination leagues until 1901-02 when 14 clubs broke away to form the Northern Rugby League with Broughton Rangers winning the first Championship.

The following season two divisions were formed with the Division One title going to Halifax (1902-03), Bradford (1903-04), who won a play-off against Salford 5-0 at Halifax after both teams tied with 52 points, and Oldham (1904-05).

In 1905-06 the two divisions were merged with Leigh taking the Championship as league leaders. They won the title on a percentage basis as the 31 clubs did not play the same number of matches. The following season the top four play-off was introduced as a fairer means of deciding the title.

The top club played the fourth-placed, the second meeting the third, with the higher club having home advantage. The final was staged at a neutral venue.

It was not until 1930-31 that all clubs played the same number of league matches, but not all against each other, the top four play-off being a necessity until the reintroduction of two divisions in 1962-63.

This spell of two division football lasted only two seasons and the restoration of the Championship table brought about the introduction of a top-16 play-off, this format continuing until the reappearance of two divisions in 1973-74.

Since then the Championship Trophy has been awarded to the leaders of the First Division, with the Second Division champions receiving a silver bowl.

Slalom Lager launched a three-year sponsorship deal of the Championship and the Premiership in 1980-81 in a £215,000 package, extending the deal for another three years from 1983-84 for £270,000. From 1986-87, the sponsorship was taken over by brewers Bass, under the Stones Bitter banner, in a new £400,000 three-year deal.

CHAMPIONSHIP PLAY-OFF FINALS

Season	Winners		Runners-up		Venue	Attendance	Receipts
Top Four Play-Offs							
1906-07	Halifax	18	Oldham	3	Huddersfield	13,200	£722
1907-08	Hunslet	7	Oldham	7	Salford	14,000	£690
Replay	Hunslet	12	Oldham	2	Wakefield	14,054	£800
1908-09	Wigan	7	Oldham	3	Salford	12,000	£630
1909-10	Oldham	13	Wigan	7	Broughton	10,850	£520
1910-11	Oldham	20	Wigan	7	Broughton	15,543	£717
1911-12	Huddersfield	13	Wigan	5	Halifax	15,000	£591
1912-13	Huddersfield	29	Wigan	2	Wakefield	17,000	£914
1913-14	Salford	5	Huddersfield	3	Leeds	8,091	£474
1914-15	Huddersfield	35	Leeds	2	Wakefield	14,000	£750
COMPETITION SUSPENDED DURING WAR TIME							
1919-20	Hull	3	Huddersfield	2	Leeds	12,900	£1,615
1920-21	Hull	16	Hull K.R.	14	Leeds	10,000	£1,320
1921-22	Wigan	13	Oldham	2	Broughton	26,000	£1,825
1922-23	Hull K.R.	15	Huddersfield	5	Leeds	14,000	£1,370
1923-24	Batley	13	Wigan	7	Broughton	13,729	£968
1924-25	Hull K.R.	9	Swinton	5	Rochdale	21,580	£1,504
1925-26	Wigan	22	Warrington	10	St. Helens	20,000	£1,100
1926-27	Swinton	13	St. Helens Recs.	8	Warrington	24,432	£1,803
1927-28	Swinton	11	Featherstone R.	0	Oldham	15,451	£1,136
1928-29	Huddersfield	2	Leeds	0	Halifax	25,604	£2,028
1929-30	Huddersfield	2	Leeds	2	Wakefield	32,095	£2,111
Replay	Huddersfield	10	Leeds	0	Halifax	18,563	£1,319
1930-31	Swinton	14	Leeds	7	Wigan	31,000	£2,100
1931-32	St. Helens	9	Huddersfield	5	Wakefield	19,386	£943
1932-33	Salford	15	Swinton	5	Wigan	18,000	£1,053
1933-34	Wigan	15	Salford	3	Warrington	31,564	£2,114
1934-35	Swinton	14	Warrington	3	Wigan	27,700	£1,710
1935-36	Hull	21	Widnes	2	Huddersfield	17,276	£1,208

Season	Winners		Runners-up		Venue	Attendance	Receipts
1936-37	Salford	13	Warrington	11	Wigan	31,500	£2,000
1937-38	Hunslet	8	Leeds	2	Elland Rd., Leeds	54,112	£3,572
1938-39	Salford	8	Castleford	6	Man. City FC	69,504	£4,301

WAR-TIME EMERGENCY PLAY-OFFS
For the first two seasons the Yorkshire League and Lancashire League champions met in a two-leg final as follows:

1939-40	Swinton	13	Bradford N.	21	Swinton	4,800	£237
	Bradford N.	16	Swinton	9	Bradford	11,721	£570
	Bradford N. won 37-22 on aggregate						
1940-41	Wigan	6	Bradford N.	17	Wigan	11,245	£640
	Bradford N.	28	Wigan	9	Bradford	20,205	£1,148
	Bradford N. won 45-15 on aggregate						

For the remainder of the War the top four in the War League played-off as follows:

1941-42	Dewsbury	13	Bradford N.	0	Leeds	18,000	£1,121
1942-43	Dewsbury	11	Halifax	3	Dewsbury	7,000	£400
	Halifax	13	Dewsbury	22	Halifax	9,700	£683

Dewsbury won 33-16 on aggregate but the Championship was declared null and void because they had played an ineligible player

1943-44	Wigan	13	Dewsbury	9	Wigan	14,000	£915
	Dewsbury	5	Wigan	12	Dewsbury	9,000	£700
	Wigan won 25-14 on aggregate						
1944-45	Halifax	9	Bradford N.	2	Halifax	9,426	£955
	Bradford N.	24	Halifax	11	Bradford	16,000	£1,850
	Bradford N. won 26-20 on aggregate						
1945-46	Wigan	13	Huddersfield	4	Man. C. FC	67,136	£8,387
1946-47	Wigan	13	Dewsbury	4	Man. C. FC	40,599	£5,895
1947-48	Warrington	15	Bradford N.	5	Man. C. FC	69,143	£9,792
1948-49	Huddersfield	13	Warrington	12	Man. C. FC	75,194	£11,073
1949-50	Wigan	20	Huddersfield	2	Man. C. FC	65,065	£11,500
1950-51	Workington T.	26	Warrington	11	Man. C. FC	61,618	£10,993
1951-52	Wigan	13	Bradford N.	6	Huddersfield Town FC	48,684	£8,215
1952-53	St. Helens	24	Halifax	14	Man. C. FC	51,083	£11,503
1953-54	Warrington	8	Halifax	7	Man. C. FC	36,519	£9,076
1954-55	Warrington	7	Oldham	3	Man. C. FC	49,434	£11,516
1955-56	Hull	10	Halifax	9	Man. C. FC	36,675	£9,179
1956-57	Oldham	15	Hull	14	Bradford	62,199	£12,054
1957-58	Hull	20	Workington T.	3	Bradford	57,699	£11,149
1958-59	St. Helens	44	Hunslet	22	Bradford	52,560	£10,146
1959-60	Wigan	27	Wakefield T.	3	Bradford	83,190	£14,482
1960-61	Leeds	25	Warrington	10	Bradford	52,177	£10,475
1961-62	Huddersfield	14	Wakefield T.	5	Bradford	37,451	£7,979

TWO DIVISIONS 1962-63 and 1963-64

Top Sixteen Play-Offs

1964-65	Halifax	15	St. Helens	7	Swinton	20,786	£6,141
1965-66	St. Helens	35	Halifax	12	Swinton	30,634	£8,750
1966-67	Wakefield T.	7	St. Helens	7	Leeds	20,161	£6,702
Replay	Wakefield T.	21	St. Helens	9	Swinton	33,537	£9,800
1967-68	Wakefield T.	17	Hull K.R.	10	Leeds	22,586	£7,697
1968-69	Leeds	16	Castleford	14	Bradford	28,442	£10,130
1969-70	St. Helens	24	Leeds	12	Bradford	26,358	£9,791
1970-71	St. Helens	16	Wigan	12	Swinton	21,745	£10,200
1971-72	Leeds	9	St. Helens	5	Swinton	24,055	£9,513
1972-73	Dewsbury	22	Leeds	13	Bradford	18,889	£9,479

CHAMPIONSHIP FINAL . . . . A 10-YEAR REVIEW

1961-62 HUDDERSFIELD 14 Dyson (4g); Breen, Deighton, Booth, Wicks (1t); Davies, Smales (1t); Slevin, Close, Noble, Kilroy, Bowman, Ramsden
WAKEFIELD T. 5 Round; F. Smith, Skene, N. Fox (1t, 1g), Hirst; Poynton, Holliday; Wilkinson, Kosanovic, Firth, Briggs, Vines, Turner
Referee: N. T. Railton (Wigan)
TWO DIVISIONS — NO PLAY-OFFS 1963 and 1964

1964-65 HALIFAX 15 James (3g); Jackson (1t), Burnett (2t), Kellett, Freeman; Robinson, Daley; Roberts, Harrison, Scroby, Fogerty, Dixon, Renilson
ST. HELENS 7 F. Barrow; Harvey, Vollenhoven, Northey, Killeen (1t, 2g); Murphy, Smith; Tembey (Warlow), Dagnall, Watson, French, Mantle, Laughton
Referee: D. S. Brown (Dewsbury)

1965-66 ST. HELENS 35 F. Barrow; A. Barrow (1t), Murphy (1g), Benyon, Killeen (3t, 6g); Harvey; Bishop; Halsall (3t), Sayer, Watson, French, Warlow (Hitchen), Mantle
HALIFAX 12 Cooper (3g); Jones, Burnett, Dixon, Freeman; Robinson, Baker (1t); Roberts, Harrison, Scroby, Ramshaw (Duffy), Fogerty (1t), Renilson
Referee: J. Manley (Warrington)

1966-67 WAKEFIELD T. 7 Cooper; Hirst, Brooke, N. Fox (2g), Coetzer; Poynton, Owen (1t); Bath, Prior, Campbell, Clarkson, Haigh, D. Fox
ST. HELENS 7 F. Barrow; Vollenhoven, A. Barrow, Smith, Killeen (2g); Douglas, Bishop; Warlow, Sayer, Watson (1t), French, Hogan (Robinson), Mantle
Referee: G. Philpott (Leeds)

Replay: WAKEFIELD T. 21 Cooper; Hirst (1t), Brooke (2t), N. Fox (3g), Coetzer; Poynton (1t), Owen (1t); Bath, Prior, Campbell, Clarkson, Haigh, D. Fox
ST. HELENS 9 F. Barrow; Vollenhoven (1t), A. Barrow, Smith, Killeen (2g); Douglas, Bishop (1g); Warlow, Sayer, Watson, French, Hogan, Mantle
Referee: J. Manley (Warrington)

1967-68 WAKEFIELD T. 17 G. Cooper; Coetzer, Brooke, N. Fox (1t, 2g), Batty; Poynton (1g), Owen (1t); Jeanes (1t), Shepherd, D. Fox (1g), Haigh, McLeod, Hawley
HULL K.R. 10 Wainwright; C. Young, Moore (1t), A. Burwell, Longstaff (1t); Millward (2g), C. Cooper; L. Foster, Flanagan, Mennell, Lowe, Major, F. Foster
Referee: D. S. Brown (Preston)

1968-69 LEEDS 16 Risman (4g); Cowan (1t), Hynes, Watson, Atkinson (1t); Shoebottom, Seabourne (Langley); Clark (Hick), Crosby, K. Eyre, Joyce, Ramsey (1g), Batten
CASTLEFORD 14 Edwards; Briggs, Howe, Thomas, Lowndes; Hardisty (1t, 1g), Hepworth; Hartley, C. Dickinson (1t), J. Ward, Redfearn (3g), Lockwood, Reilly (Fox)
Referee: W. H. Thompson (Huddersfield)

1969-70 ST. HELENS 24 F. Barrow; L. Jones, Benyon, Walsh (1t, 2g), E. Prescott (2t), Myler, Heaton; Halsall, Sayer (1t), Watson, Mantle, E. Chisnall, Coslett (4g)
LEEDS 12 Holmes (3g); Alan Smith (1t), Hynes, Cowan (1t), Atkinson; Shoebottom, Seabourne; J. Burke, Crosby, A. Eyre, Ramsey (Hick), Eccles, Batten
Referee: W. H. Thompson (Huddersfield)

1970-71 ST. HELENS 16 Pimblett; L. Jones, Benyon (1t), Walsh, Blackwood (1t); Whittle, Heaton; J. Stephens, A. Karalius, Rees (Wanbon), Mantle, E. Chisnall, Coslett (5g)
WIGAN 12 Tyrer (1g); Kevin O'Loughlin; Francis, Rowe, Wright; D. Hill, Ayres; Hogan, Clarke, Fletcher, Ashurst (1t, 2g), Robinson (1t) (Cunningham), Laughton
Referee: E. Lawrinson (Warrington)

1971-72 LEEDS 9 Holmes (Hick); Alan Smith, Langley, Dyl, Atkinson (1t); Hardisty, Barham; Clawson (3g), Ward, Fisher (Pickup), Cookson, Eccles, Batten
ST. HELENS 5 Pimblett; L. Jones (Whittle), Benyon, Walsh (1g), Wilson; Kelly, Heaton; Rees, Greenall (1t), J. Stephens, Mantle, E. Chisnall, Coslett
Referee: S. Shepherd (Oldham)

1972-73 DEWSBURY 22 Rushton; Ashcroft, Clark, N. Stephenson (5g, 1t), Day; Agar (1t), A. Bates; Beverley (Taylor), M. Stephenson (2t), Lowe, Grayshon, J. Bates, Whittington
LEEDS 13 Holmes; Alan Smith, Hynes (1g), Dyl (1t), Atkinson; Hardisty, Hepworth; Clawson (1g), Fisher (Ward), Clarkson (Langley), Cookson (1t), Eccles (1t), Haigh
Referee: H. G. Hunt (Prestbury)

LEAGUE LEADERS TROPHY
While the top 16 play-off decided the Championship between 1964 and 1973 it was decided to honour the top club in the league table with a League Leaders Trophy. The winners were:
1964-65   St. Helens
1965-66   St. Helens
1966-67   Leeds
1967-68   Leeds
1968-69   Leeds
1969-70   Leeds
1970-71   Wigan
1971-72   Leeds
1972-73   Warrington

CLUB CHAMPIONSHIP (Merit Table)
With the reintroduction of two divisions, a complicated merit table and Division Two preliminary rounds system produced a 16 club play-off with the Club Championship finalists as follows:

Season	Winners		Runners-up		Venue	Attendance	Receipts
1973-74	Warrington	13	St. Helens	12	Wigan	18,040	£10,032

This format lasted just one season and was replaced by the Premiership.

CLUB CHAMPIONSHIP FINAL . . . . A REVIEW
1973-74   WARRINGTON 13   Whitehead (2g); M. Philbin (1t), Noonan (1t), Pickup (Lowe), Bevan; Whittle, A. Murphy; D. Chisnall, Ashcroft, Brady (1t), Wanbon (Gaskell), Mather, B. Philbin
ST. HELENS 12   Pimblett; Brown, Wills, Wilson (2t), Mathias; Eckersley, Heaton; Mantle, Liptrot, M. Murphy, E. Chisnall (Warlow), Nicholls, Coslett (3g)
Referee: P. Geraghty (York)

PREMIERSHIP
With the further reintroduction of two divisions in 1973-74, it was declared that the title of Champions would be awarded to the leaders of the First Division.

However, it was also decided to continue the tradition of an end-of-season play-off, the winners to receive the newly instituted Premiership Trophy.
*For full details of the Premiership Trophy see the CUPS section.

Geoff Pimblett — St. Helens full back in the 1974 Club Championship final.

COUNTY LEAGUE
In the early seasons of the code the Lancashire Senior and Yorkshire Senior Competitions, not to be confused with the later reserve leagues, were major leagues. The winners were:

	Lancashire SC	Yorkshire SC
1895-96	Runcorn	Manningham
1896-97	Broughton Rangers	Brighouse Rangers
1897-98	Oldham	Hunslet
1898-99	Broughton Rangers	Batley
1899-00	Runcorn	Bradford
1900-01	Oldham	Bradford
1901-02	Wigan	Leeds

With the introduction of two divisions in 1902-03, the county league competitions were scrapped until they reappeared as the Lancashire League and Yorkshire League in 1907-08. Clubs from the same county played each other home and away to decide the titles. These games were included in the main championship table along with inter-county fixtures. The county leagues continued until 1970, with the exception of war-time interruptions and two seasons when regional leagues with play-offs operated during the 1960s two division era. They were then abolished when a more integrated fixture formula meant clubs did not play all others from the same county, this system later being replaced by the present two division structure.

LANCASHIRE LEAGUE CHAMPIONS

Season	Winners	
1907-08	Oldham	
1908-09	Wigan	
1909-10	Oldham	
1910-11	Wigan	
1911-12	Wigan	
1912-13	Wigan	
1913-14	Wigan	
1914-15	Wigan	
1915-18	Competition Suspended during war-time	
1918-19	Rochdale H.	
1919-20	Widnes	
1920-21	Wigan	
1921-22	Oldham	
1922-23	Wigan	
1923-24	Wigan	
1924-25	Swinton	
1925-26	Wigan	
1926-27	St. Helens R.	
1927-28	Swinton	
1928-29	Swinton	
1929-30	St. Helens	
1930-31	Swinton	
1931-32	St. Helens	
1932-33	Salford	
1933-34	Salford	
1934-35	Salford	
1935-36	Liverpool S.	
1936-37	Salford	
1937-38	Warrington	
1938-39	Salford	
1939-40	Swinton	War Emergency
1940-41	Wigan	Leagues
1941-45	Competition Suspended during war-time	
1945-46	Wigan	
1946-47	Wigan	
1947-48	Warrington	
1948-49	Warrington	
1949-50	Wigan	
1950-51	Warrington	
1951-52	Wigan	
1952-53	St. Helens	
1953-54	Warrington	
1954-55	Warrington	
1955-56	Warrington	
1956-57	Oldham	
1957-58	Oldham	
1958-59	Wigan	
1959-60	St. Helens	
1960-61	Swinton	
1961-62	Wigan	
1962-64	See Regional	

YORKSHIRE LEAGUE CHAMPIONS

Season	Winners	
1907-08	Hunslet	
1908-09	Halifax	
1909-10	Wakefield T.	
1910-11	Wakefield T.	
1911-12	Huddersfield	
1912-13	Huddersfield	
1913-14	Huddersfield	
1914-15	Huddersfield	
1915-18	Competition Suspended during war-time	
1918-19	Hull	
1919-20	Huddersfield	
1920-21	Halifax	
1921-22	Huddersfield	
1922-23	Hull	
1923-24	Batley	
1924-25	Hull K.R.	
1925-26	Hull K.R.	
1926-27	Hull	
1927-28	Leeds	
1928-29	Huddersfield	
1929-30	Huddersfield	
1930-31	Leeds	
1931-32	Hunslet	
1932-33	Castleford	
1933-34	Leeds	
1934-35	Leeds	
1935-36	Hull	
1936-37	Leeds	
1937-38	Leeds	
1938-39	Castleford	
1939-40	Bradford N.	War Emergency
1940-41	Bradford N.	Leagues
1941-45	Competition Suspended during war-time	
1945-46	Wakefield T.	
1946-47	Dewsbury	
1947-48	Bradford N.	
1948-49	Huddersfield	
1949-50	Huddersfield	
1950-51	Leeds	
1951-52	Huddersfield	
1952-53	Halifax	
1953-54	Halifax	
1954-55	Leeds	
1955-56	Halifax	
1956-57	Leeds	
1957-58	Halifax	
1958-59	Wakefield T.	
1959-60	Wakefield T.	
1960-61	Leeds	
1961-62	Wakefield T.	
1962-64	See Regional	

LANCASHIRE LEAGUE CHAMPIONS

Season	Winners
1964-65	St. Helens
1965-66	St. Helens
1966-67	St. Helens
1967-68	Warrington
1968-69	St. Helens
1969-70	Wigan

YORKSHIRE LEAGUE CHAMPIONS

Season	Winners
1964-65	Castleford
1965-66	Wakefield T.
1966-67	Leeds
1967-68	Leeds
1968-69	Leeds
1969-70	Leeds

REGIONAL LEAGUES

DURING the 1962-63 and 1963-64 two divisions campaigns the county leagues were replaced by the Eastern and Western Divisions. Each club played four other clubs home and away. There was then a top four play-off to decide the regional championship. The finals were played at neutral venues as follows:

Eastern Division

1962-63	Hull K.R.	13	Huddersfield	10	Leeds	6,751	£1,342
1963-64	Halifax	20	Castleford	12	Huddersfield	10,798	£1,791

Western Division

1962-63	Workington T.	9	Widnes	9	Wigan	13,588	£2,287
Replay	Workington T.	10	Widnes	0	Wigan	7,584	£1,094
1963-64	St. Helens	10	Swinton	7	Wigan	17,363	£3,053

EASTERN DIVISION FINAL . . . . A REVIEW

1962-63 HULL K.R. 13 Kellett (2g); Paul (2t), Major, B. Burwell, Harris (1t); A. Burwell, Bunting; Coverdale, Flanagan, J. Drake, Tyson, Murphy, Bonner
HUDDERSFIELD 10 Dyson (2g); Senior, Booth, Haywood (1t), Stocks; Deighton, Smales (1t); Rowe, Close, Noble, Kilroy, Bowman, Redfearn
Referee: T. W. Watkinson (Manchester)

1963-64 HALIFAX 20 James (4g); Jackson (2t), Burnett, Kellett, Freeman; Robinson (1t), Marchant; Roberts, Shaw, Scott, Dixon (1t), Fogerty, Renilson
CASTLEFORD 12 Edwards; Howe (1t), G. Ward, Small, Gamble; Hardisty, Hepworth: Hirst, C. Dickinson (1t), Clark (3g), Bryant, Walker, Walton
Referee: R. L. Thomas (Oldham)

WESTERN DIVISION FINAL . . . . A REVIEW

1962-63 WORKINGTON T. 9 Lowden (3g); Glastonbury, O'Neil, Brennan, Pretorious (1t); Archer, Roper; Herbert, Ackerley, W. Martin, Edgar, McLeod, Foster
WIDNES 9 Randall (3g); R. Chisnall, Lowe, Thompson (1t), Heyes; F. Myler, Owen; Hurtsfield, Kemel, E. Bate, R. Bate, Measures, V. Karalius
Referee: M. Coates (Pudsey)

Replay WORKINGTON T. 10 Lowden (2g); Glastonbury (1t), O'Neil, Brennan, Pretorious (1t); Archer, Roper; Herbert, Ackerley, W. Martin, Edgar, McLeod, Foster
WIDNES 0 Randall; A. Hughes, Lowe, Thompson, Heyes; F. Myler, Owen; Hurstfield, Kemel, E. Bate, R. Bate, Measures, V. Karalius
Referee: M. Coates (Pudsey)

1963-64 ST. HELENS 10 Coslett (2g); Vollenhoven, Williams, Northey (1t), Killeen; Harvey, Murphy; Tembey, Burdell, Owen, French (1t), Warlow, Laughton
SWINTON 7 Gowers; Speed, Fleet, Parkinson, Stopford (1t); Williams, Cartwright; Bate, D. Clarke, Halliwell, Morgan, Rees, Blan (2g)
Referee: E. Clay (Leeds)

LEAGUE LEADERS .... A REVIEW

The following is a list of the League leaders since the formation of the Northern Union, with the exception of the three eras of two-division football — 1902-05, 1962-64 and 1973-85 — which are comprehensively featured earlier in this section. From 1896 to 1901, the League was divided into a Lancashire Senior Competition and a Yorkshire Senior Competition, winners of both leagues being listed for those seasons. From 1905 to 1930 not all the clubs played each other, the League being determined on a percentage basis.

LSC — Lancashire Senior Competition
LL — Lancashire League
YSC — Yorkshire Senior Competition
YL — Yorkshire League
WEL — War Emergency League
★ Two points deducted for breach of professional rules
† Decided on a percentage basis after Belle Vue Rangers withdrew shortly before the start of the season.

		P.	W.	D.	L.	F.	A.	Pts.	
1895-96	Manningham	42	33	0	9	367	158	66	
1896-97	Broughton R.	26	19	5	2	201	52	43	LSC
	Brighouse R.	30	22	4	4	213	68	48	YSC
1897-98	Oldham	26	23	1	2	295	94	47	LSC
	Hunslet	30	22	4	4	327	117	48	YSC
1898-99	Broughton R.	26	21	0	5	277	74	42	LSC
	Batley	30	23	2	5	279	75	48	YSC
1899-00	Runcorn	26	22	2	2	232	33	46	LSC
	Bradford	30	24	2	4	324	98	50	YSC
1900-01	Oldham	26	22	1	3	301	67	45	LSC
	Bradford	30	26	1	3	387	100	51★	YSC
1901-02	Broughton R.	26	21	1	4	285	112	43	
1902-05	Two Divisions								
1905-06	Leigh	30	23	2	5	245	130	48	80.00%
1906-07	Halifax	34	27	2	5	649	229	56	82.35%
1907-08	Oldham	32	28	2	2	396	121	58	90.62%
1908-09	Wigan	32	28	0	4	706	207	56	87.50%
1909-10	Oldham	34	29	2	3	604	184	60	88.23%
1910-11	Wigan	34	28	1	5	650	205	57	83.82%
1911-12	Huddersfield	36	31	1	4	996	238	63	87.50%
1912-13	Huddersfield	32	28	0	4	732	217	56	87.50%
1913-14	Huddersfield	34	28	2	4	830	258	58	85.29%
1914-15	Huddersfield	34	28	4	2	888	235	60	88.24%
1915-18	Competitive matches suspended during First World War								
1918-19	Rochdale H.	12	9	0	3	92	52	18	75.00% LL
	Hull	16	13	0	3	392	131	26	81.25% YL
1919-20	Huddersfield	34	29	0	5	759	215	58	85.29%
1920-21	Hull K.R.	32	24	1	7	432	233	49	76.56%
1921-22	Oldham	36	29	1	6	521	201	59	81.94%
1922-23	Hull	36	30	0	6	587	304	60	83.33%
1923-24	Wigan	38	31	0	7	824	228	62	81.57%
1924-25	Swinton	36	30	0	6	499	224	60	83.33%
1925-26	Wigan	38	29	3	6	641	310	61	80.26%
1926-27	St. Helens R.	38	29	3	6	544	235	61	80.26%
1927-28	Swinton	36	27	3	6	439	189	57	79.16%

		P.	W.	D.	L.	F.	A.	Pts.	
1928-29	Huddersfield	38	26	4	8	476	291	56	73.68%
1929-30	St. Helens	40	27	1	12	549	295	55	68.75%
1930-31	Swinton	38	31	2	5	504	156	64	
1931-32	Huddersfield	38	30	1	7	636	368	61	
1932-33	Salford	38	31	2	5	751	165	64	
1933-34	Salford	38	31	1	6	715	281	63	
1934-35	Swinton	38	30	1	7	468	175	61	
1935-36	Hull	38	30	1	7	607	306	61	
1936-37	Salford	38	29	3	6	529	196	61	
1937-38	Hunslet	36	25	3	8	459	301	53	
1938-39	Salford	40	30	3	7	551	191	63	
1939-40	Swinton	22	17	0	5	378	158	34	WEL LL
	Bradford N.	28	21	0	7	574	302	42	WEL YL
1940-41	Wigan	16	15	1	0	297	71	31	WEL LL
	Bradford N.	25	23	1	1	469	126	47	WEL YL
1941-42	Dewsbury	24	19	1	4	431	172	39	81.25% WEL
1942-43	Wigan	16	13	0	3	301	142	26	81.25% WEL
1943-44	Wakefield T.	22	19	0	3	359	97	38	86.36% WEL
1944-45	Bradford N.	20	17	0	3	337	69	34	85.00% WEL
1945-46	Wigan	36	29	2	5	783	219	60	
1946-47	Wigan	36	29	1	6	567	196	59	
1947-48	Wigan	36	31	1	4	776	258	63	
1948-49	Warrington	36	31	0	5	728	247	62	
1949-50	Wigan	36	31	1	4	853	320	63	
1950-51	Warrington	36	30	0	6	738	250	60	
1951-52	Bradford N.	36	28	1	7	758	326	57	
1952-53	St. Helens	36	32	2	2	769	273	66	
1953-54	Halifax	36	30	2	4	538	219	62	
1954-55	Warrington	36	29	2	5	718	321	60	
1955-56	Warrington	34	27	1	6	712	349	55	80.88% †
1956-57	Oldham	38	33	0	5	893	365	66	
1957-58	Oldham	38	33	1	4	803	415	67	
1958-59	St. Helens	38	31	1	6	1005	450	63	
1959-60	St. Helens	38	34	1	3	947	343	69	
1960-61	Leeds	36	30	0	6	620	258	60	
1961-62	Wigan	36	32	1	3	885	283	65	
1962-64	Two Divisions								
1964-65	St. Helens	34	28	0	6	621	226	56	
1965-66	St. Helens	34	28	1	5	521	275	57	
1966-67	Leeds	34	29	0	5	704	373	58	
1967-68	Leeds	34	28	0	6	720	271	56	
1968-69	Leeds	34	29	2	3	775	358	60	
1969-70	Leeds	34	30	0	4	674	314	60	
1970-71	Wigan	34	30	0	4	662	308	60	
1971-72	Leeds	34	28	2	4	750	325	58	
1972-73	Warrington	34	27	2	5	816	400	56	

Graham Lowe: has won all the trophies in two years as Wigan coach.

COACHES

Between June 1987 and June 1988 a total of 13 clubs made first team coaching changes, some more than once. Nine new coaches had their first senior appointments bringing the total of coaches since the start of the 1974-75 season to 194.

This chapter is a compilation of those appointments, featuring a club-by-club coaches register, an index, plus a detailed dossier of the 1987-88 coaches.

CLUB-BY-CLUB REGISTER

The following is a list of coaches each club has had since the start of the 1974-75 season.

BARROW

Frank Foster	May 73 - Apr. 83
Tommy Dawes	May 83 - Feb. 85
Tommy Bishop	Feb. 85 - Apr. 85
Ivor Kelland	May 85 - Feb. 87
Dennis Jackson	Feb. 87 - Nov. 87
Rod Reddy	Nov. 87 -

BATLEY

Don Fox	Nov. 72 - Oct. 74
Alan Hepworth	Nov. 74 - Apr. 75
Dave Cox	May 75 - June 75
Trevor Walker	June 75 - June 77
Albert Fearnley	June 77 - Oct. 77
Dave Stockwell	Oct. 77 - June 79
*Tommy Smales	June 79 - Oct. 81
Trevor Lowe	Oct. 81 - May 82
Terry Crook	June 82 - Nov. 84
George Pieniazek	Nov. 84 - Nov. 85
Brian Lockwood	Nov. 85 - May 87
Paul Daley	July 87 -

*Ex-forward

BRADFORD NORTHERN

Ian Brooke	Jan. 73 - Sept. 75
Roy Francis	Oct. 75 - Apr. 77
Peter Fox	Apr. 77 - May 85
Barry Seabourne	May 85 -

BRAMLEY

Arthur Keegan	May 73 - Sept. 76
Peter Fox	Sept. 76 - Apr. 77
*Tommy Smales	May 77 - Dec. 77
Les Pearce	Jan. 78 - Oct. 78
Don Robinson	Oct. 78 - May 79
Dave Stockwell	June 79 - June 80
Keith Hepworth	June 80 - May 82
Maurice Bamford	May 82 - Oct. 83
Peter Jarvis	Oct. 83 - Apr. 85
Ken Loxton	Apr. 85 - Dec. 85
Allan Agar	Dec. 85 - Apr. 87
Chris Forster	June 87 - Nov. 87
Tony Fisher	Nov. 87 -

*Ex-forward

CARLISLE

Allan Agar	May 81 - June 82
Mick Morgan	July 82 - Feb. 83
John Atkinson	Feb. 83 - Feb. 86
Alan Kellett	Feb. 86 - May 86
Roy Lester	June 86 -

CASTLEFORD

Dave Cox	Apr. 74 - Nov. 74
*Malcolm Reilly	Dec. 74 - May 87
Dave Sampson	May 87 - Apr. 88

*Shortly after his appointment Reilly returned to Australia to fulfil his contract before resuming at Castleford early the next season.

DEWSBURY

Maurice Bamford	June 74 - Oct. 74
Alan Hardisty	Oct. 74 - June 75
Dave Cox	June 75 - July 77
Ron Hill	July 77 - Dec. 77
Lewis Jones	Dec. 77 - Apr. 78
Jeff Grayshon	May 78 - Oct. 78
Alan Lockwood	Oct. 78 - Oct. 80
Bernard Watson	Oct. 80 - Oct. 82
Ray Abbey	Nov. 82 - Apr. 83
*Tommy Smales	May 83 - Feb. 84
Jack Addy	Feb. 84 - Jan. 87
Dave Busfield	Jan. 87 - Apr. 87
Terry Crook	Apr. 87 -

*Ex-forward

DONCASTER

Ted Strawbridge	Feb. 73 - Apr. 75
Derek Edwards	July 75 - Nov. 76
Don Robson	Nov. 76 - Sept. 77
Trevor Lowe	Sept. 77 - Apr. 79
*Tommy Smales	Feb. 78 - Apr. 79
Billy Yates	Apr. 79 - May 80
Don Vines	Sept. 79 - Jan. 80
Bill Kenny	June 80 - May 81
Alan Rhodes	Aug. 81 - Mar. 83
Clive Sullivan M.B.E.	Mar. 83 - May 84
John Sheridan	June 84 - Nov. 87
Graham Heptinstall	Nov. 87 - Jan. 88
John Sheridan	Jan. 88 -

*Ex-forward

FEATHERSTONE ROVERS

*Tommy Smales	July 74 - Sept. 74
Keith Goulding	Sept. 74 - Jan. 76
†Tommy Smales	Feb. 76 - May 76
Keith Cotton	June 76 - Dec. 77
Keith Goulding	Dec. 77 - May 78
Terry Clawson	July 78 - Nov. 78
†Tommy Smales	Nov. 78 - Apr. 79
Paul Daley	May 79 - Jan. 81
Vince Farrar	Feb. 81 - Nov. 82
Allan Agar	Dec. 82 - Oct. 85
George Pieniazek	Nov. 85 - Nov. 86
Paul Daley	Nov. 86 - Apr. 87
Peter Fox	May 87 -

*Ex-forward   †Ex-scrum half

Len Casey — quit as Hull's coach.

FULHAM

Reg Bowden	July 80 - June 84
Roy Lester	June 84 - Apr. 86
Bill Goodwin	Apr. 86 -

HALIFAX

Derek Hallas	Aug. 74 - Oct. 74
Les Pearce	Oct. 74 - Apr. 76
Alan Kellett	May 76 - Apr. 77
Jim Crellin	June 77 - Oct. 77
Harry Fox	Oct. 77 - Feb. 78
Maurice Bamford	Feb. 78 - May 80
Mick Blacker	June 80 - June 82
Ken Roberts	June 82 - Sept. 82
Colin Dixon	Sept. 82 - Nov. 84
Chris Anderson	Nov. 84 - May 88
Graham Eadie	May 88 -

HUDDERSFIELD BARRACUDAS

Brian Smith	Jan. 73 - Mar. 76
Keith Goulding	Mar. 76 - Dec. 76
Bob Tomlinson	Jan. 77 - May 77
Neil Fox	June 77 - Feb. 78
*Roy Francis	-
Keith Goulding	May 78 - July 79
Ian Brooke	July 79 - Mar. 80
Maurice Bamford	May 80 - May 81
Les Sheard	June 81 - Nov. 82
Dave Mortimer	Nov. 82 - Aug. 83
Mel Bedford	Aug. 83 - Nov. 83
Brian Lockwood	Nov. 83 - Feb. 85
Chris Forster	Feb. 85 - Dec. 86
Jack Addy	Jan. 87 - Mar. 88
Allen Jones ⎫ Neil Whittaker ⎬	Mar. 88 -Apr. 88

Although Roy Francis was appointed he was unable to take over and Dave Heppleston stood in until the next appointment.

HULL

David Doyle-Davidson	May 74 - Dec. 77
Arthur Bunting	Jan. 78 - Dec. 85
Kenny Foulkes	Dec. 85 - May 86
Len Casey	June 86 - Mar. 88
Tony Dean ⎫ Keith Hepworth ⎬	Mar. 88 - Apr. 88

HULL KINGSTON ROVERS

Arthur Bunting	Feb. 72 - Nov. 75
Harry Poole	Dec. 75 - Mar. 77
Roger Millward M.B.E.	Mar. 77 -

HUNSLET

Paul Daley	Apr. 74 - Aug. 78
Bill Ramsey	Aug. 78 - Dec. 79
Drew Broatch	Dec. 79 - Apr. 81
Paul Daley	Apr. 81 - Nov. 85
*Peter Jarvis	Nov. 85 - Apr. 88
*David Ward	July 86 - Apr. 88

Joint coaches from July 1986.

KEIGHLEY

Alan Kellett	Jan. 73 - May 75
Roy Sabine	Aug. 75 - Oct. 77
Barry Seabourne	Nov. 77 - Mar. 79
Albert Fearnley (Mgr)	Apr. 79 - Aug. 79
Alan Kellett	Apr. 79 - Apr. 80
Albert Fearnley	May 80 - Feb. 81
Bakary Diabira	Feb. 81 - Sept. 82
Lee Greenwood	Sept. 82 - Oct. 83
Geoff Peggs	Nov. 83 - Sept. 85
Peter Roe	Sept. 85 - July 86
Colin Dixon ⎫ Les Coulter ⎭	July 86 -

LEEDS

Roy Francis	June 74 - May 75
Syd Hynes	June 75 - Apr. 81
Robin Dewhurst	June 81 - Oct. 83
Maurice Bamford	Nov. 83 - Feb. 85
Malcolm Clift	Feb. 85 - May 85
Peter Fox	May 85 - Dec. 86
Maurice Bamford	Dec. 86 - Apr. 88

LEIGH

Eddie Cheetham	May 74 - Mar. 75
Kevin Ashcroft	June 75 - Jan. 77
Bill Kindon	Jan. 77 - Apr. 77
John Mantle	Apr. 77 - Nov. 78
Tom Grainey	Nov. 78 - Dec. 80
*Alex Murphy	Nov. 80 - June 82
*Colin Clarke	June 82 - Dec. 82
Peter Smethurst	Dec. 82 - Apr. 83
Tommy Bishop	June 83 - June 84
John Woods	June 84 - May 85
Alex Murphy	Feb. 85 - Nov. 85
Tommy Dickens	Nov. 85 - Dec. 86
Billy Benyon	Dec. 86 -

From Dec. 80 to June 82 Clarke was officially appointed coach and Murphy manager

MANSFIELD MARKSMAN

Mick Blacker	May 84 - Oct. 85
Bill Kirkbride	Nov. 85 - Mar. 86
Steve Dennison	Apr. 86 - Dec. 86
Jim Crellin	Dec. 86 -

OLDHAM

Jim Challinor	Aug. 74 - Dec. 76
Terry Ramshaw	Jan. 77 - Feb. 77
Dave Cox	July 77 - Dec. 78
Graham Starkey (Mngr)	Jan. 79 - May 81
Bill Francis	June 79 - Dec. 80
Frank Myler	May 81 - Apr. 83
Peter Smethurst	Apr. 83 - Feb. 84
Frank Barrow	Feb. 84 - Feb. 84
Brian Gartland	Mar. 84 - June 84
Frank Myler	June 84 - Apr. 87
*Eric Fitzsimons	June 87 -
*Mal Graham	June 87 - Apr. 88

Joint coaches June 87 - Apr. 88

Maurice Bamford — resigned as Leeds coach.

ROCHDALE HORNETS
Frank Myler	May 71 - Oct. 74
Graham Starkey	Oct. 74 - Nov. 75
Henry Delooze	Nov. 75 - Nov. 76
Kel Coslett	Nov. 76 - Aug. 79
Paul Longstaff	Sept. 79 - May 81
Terry Fogerty	May 81 - Jan. 82
Dick Bonser	Jan. 82 - May 82
Bill Kirkbride	June 82 - Sept. 84
Charlie Birdsall	Sept. 84 - Apr. 86
Eric Fitzsimons	June 86 - June 87
Eric Hughes	June 87 -

RUNCORN HIGHFIELD
Terry Gorman	Aug. 74 - May 77
Geoff Fletcher	Aug. 77 - June 86
Frank Wilson	July 86 - Nov. 86
Arthur Daley / Paul Woods	Nov. 86 - Apr. 87
Bill Ashurst	Apr. 87 -

ST. HELENS
Eric Ashton M.B.E.	May 74 - May 80
Kel Coslett	June 80 - May 82
Billy Benyon	May 82 - Nov. 85
Alex Murphy	Nov. 85 -

SALFORD
Les Bettinson	Dec. 73 - Mar. 77
Colin Dixon	Mar. 77 - Jan. 78
Stan McCormick	Feb. 78 - Mar. 78
Alex Murphy	May 78 - Nov. 80
Kevin Ashcroft	Nov. 80 - Mar. 82
Alan McInnes	Mar. 82 - May 82
Malcolm Aspey	May 82 - Oct. 83
Mike Coulman	Oct. 83 - May 84
Kevin Ashcroft	May 84 -

SHEFFIELD EAGLES
Alan Rhodes	Apr. 84 - May 86
Gary Hetherington	July 86 -

SPRINGFIELD BOROUGH
Tommy Blakeley	Aug. 74 - Apr. 76
Jim Crellin	May 76 - Mar. 77
Joe Egan Jnr.	Mar. 77 - Oct. 77
Albert Fearnley (Mgr)	Nov. 77 - Apr. 79
Bakary Diabira	Nov. 78 - June 79
Graham Rees	June 79 - Mar. 80
Geoff Lyon	July 80 - Aug. 81
Bob Irving	Aug. 81 - Feb. 82
John Mantle	Feb. 82 - Mar. 82
Tommy Dickens	Mar. 82 - Nov. 85
Stan Gittins	Nov. 85 -

SWINTON
Austin Rhodes	June 74 - Nov. 75
Bob Fleet	Nov. 75 - Nov. 76
John Stopford	Nov. 76 - Apr. 77
Terry Gorman	June 77 - Nov. 78
Ken Halliwell	Nov. 78 - Dec. 79
Frank Myler	Jan. 80 - May 81
Tom Grainey	May 81 - Oct. 83
Jim Crellin	Nov. 83 - May 86
Bill Holliday / Mike Peers	June 86 - Oct. 87
Frank Barrow	Oct. 87 -

WAKEFIELD TRINITY
Peter Fox	June 74 - May 76
Geoff Gunney M.B.E.	June 76 - Nov. 76
Brian Lockwood	Nov. 76 - Jan. 78
Ian Brooke	Jan. 78 - Jan. 79
Bill Kirkbride	Jan. 79 - Apr. 80
Ray Batten	Apr. 80 - May 81
Bill Ashurst	June 81 - Apr. 82
Ray Batten	May 82 - July 83
Derek Turner	July 83 - Feb. 84
Bob Haigh	Feb. 84 - May 84
Geoff Wraith	May 84 - Oct. 84
David Lamming	Oct. 84 - Apr. 85
Len Casey	Apr. 85 - June 86
Tony Dean	June 86 - Dec. 86
Trevor Bailey	Dec. 86 - Apr. 87
David Topliss	May 87 -

WARRINGTON

Alex Murphy	May 71 - May 78
Billy Benyon	June 78 - Mar. 82
Kevin Ashcroft	Mar. 82 - May 84
Reg Bowden	June 84 - Mar. 86
Tony Barrow	Mar. 86 -

WHITEHAVEN

Jeff Bawden	May 72 - May 75
Ike Southward	Aug. 75 - June 76
Bill Smith	Aug. 76 - Oct. 78
Ray Dutton	Oct. 78 - Oct. 79
Phil Kitchin	Oct. 79 - Jan. 82
Arnold Walker	Jan. 82 - May 82
Tommy Dawes	June 82 - May 83
Frank Foster	June 83 - June 85
Phil Kitchin	June 85 - Oct. 87
John McFarlane	Oct. 87 - May 88

WIDNES

Vince Karalius	Jan. 72 - May 75
Frank Myler	May 75 - May 78
Doug Laughton	May 78 - Mar. 83
Harry Dawson Colin Tyrer }	Mar. 83 - May 83
*Vince Karalius Harry Dawson }	May 83 - May 84
Eric Hughes	June 84 - Jan. 86
Doug Laughton	Jan. 86 -

Dawson quit as coach in March 1984 with Karalius continuing as team manager.

WIGAN

Ted Toohey	May 74 - Jan. 75
Joe Coan	Jan. 75 - Sept. 76
Vince Karalius	Sept. 76 - Sept. 79
Kel Coslett	Oct. 79 - Apr. 80
George Fairbairn	Apr. 80 - May 81
Maurice Bamford	May 81 - May 82
Alex Murphy	June 82 - Aug. 84
Colin Clarke Alan McInnes }	Aug. 84 - May 86
Graham Lowe	Aug. 86 -

WORKINGTON TOWN

Ike Southward	Aug. 73 - June 75
Paul Charlton	June 75 - June 76
Ike Southward	June 76 - Feb. 78
Sol Roper	Feb. 78 - Apr. 80
Keith Irving	Aug. 80 - Oct. 80
Tommy Bishop	Nov. 80 - June 82
Paul Charlton	July 82 - Dec. 82
Dave Cox	Mar. 83 - Mar. 83
Harry Archer/Bill Smith	May 83 - June 84
Bill Smith	June 84 - Apr. 85
Jackie Davidson	Apr. 85 - Jan. 86
Keith Davies	Feb. 86 - Mar. 87
Norman Turley	Mar. 87 - Apr. 88

YORK

Keith Goulding	Nov. 73 - Sept. 74
Gary Cooper	Dec. 74 - Sept. 76
Mal Dixon	Sept. 76 - Dec. 78
Paul Daley	Jan. 79 - May 79
David Doyle-Davidson	July 79 - July 80
Bill Kirkbride	Aug. 80 - Apr. 82
Alan Hardisty	May 82 - Jan. 83
Phil Lowe	Mar. 83 - Mar. 87
Danny Sheehan	Mar. 87 - Apr. 88
Gary Stephens	Apr. 88 -

REPRESENTATIVE REGISTER

The following is a list of international and county coaches since 1974-75.

GREAT BRITAIN

Jim Challinor	Dec. 71 - Aug. 74 (Inc. tour)
David Watkins	1977 World Championship
Peter Fox	1978
Eric Ashton	1979 tour
Johnny Whiteley	Aug. 80 - Nov. 82
Frank Myler	Dec. 82 - Aug. 84 (Inc. tour)
Maurice Bamford	Oct. 84 - Dec. 86
Malcolm Reilly	Jan. 87 - (Inc. tour)

ENGLAND

Alex Murphy	Jan. 75 - Nov. 75
	(Inc. World Championship tour)
Peter Fox	1976-77
Frank Myler	1977-78
Eric Ashton	1978-79 & 1979-80
Johnny Whiteley	1980-81 & 1981-82
Reg Parker	1984-85
(Mngr)	

WALES

Les Pearce	Jan. 75 - Nov. 75
	(Inc. World Championship tour)
David Watkins ⎱	1976-77
Bill Francis ⎰	
Kel Coslett ⎱	1977-78
Bill Francis ⎰	
Kel Coslett	1978-79 to 1981-82
David Watkins	1982-83, 1984-85

GREAT BRITAIN UNDER-24s

| Johnny Whiteley | 1976-82 |
| Frank Myler | 1983-84 |

GREAT BRITAIN UNDER-21s

| Maurice Bamford | Oct. 84 - Dec. 86 |
| Malcolm Reilly | Jan. 87 - |

CUMBRIA

Ike Southward	1975-76
Frank Foster	1976-77 & 1977-78
Sol Roper	1978-79
Frank Foster	1979-80
Phil Kitchin	1980-81 to 1981-82
Frank Foster	1982-83
Jackie Davidson	1985-86
Phil Kitchin	1986-87 to 1987-88

LANCASHIRE

Alex Murphy	1973-74 to 1977-78
Eric Ashton M.B.E.	1978-79 to 1979-80
Tom Grainey	1980-81 to 1981-82
Doug Laughton	1982-83
Alex Murphy	1985-86 to 1987-88

YORKSHIRE

Johnny Whiteley	1970-71 to 1979-80
Arthur Keegan	1980-81
Johnny Whiteley	1981-82 to 1982-83
Peter Fox	1985-86 to 1987-88

OTHER NATIONALITIES

| Dave Cox | 1974-75 to 1975-76 |

INDEX OF COACHES

The following is an index of the 194 coaches who have held first team coaching posts since the start of the 1974-75 season with the alphabetical listing of clubs they coached in this period.

Ray Abbey (Dewsbury)
Jack Addy (Dewsbury, Huddersfield B.)
Allan Agar (Bramley, Carlisle, Featherstone R.)
Dave Alred (Bridgend)
Chris Anderson (Halifax)
Harry Archer (Workington T.)
Kevin Ashcroft (Leigh, Salford, Warrington)
Eric Ashton M.B.E. (St. Helens)
Bill Ashurst (Runcorn H., Wakefield T.)
Mal Aspey (Salford)
John Atkinson (Carlisle)

Trevor Bailey (Wakefield T.)
Maurice Bamford (Bramley, Dewsbury, Halifax, Huddersfield, Leeds, Wigan)
Frank Barrow (Oldham, Swinton)
Tony Barrow (Warrington)
Ray Batten (Wakefield T.)
Jeff Bawden (Whitehaven)
Mel Bedford (Huddersfield)
Billy Benyon (Leigh, St. Helens, Warrington)
Les Bettinson (Salford)
Charlie Birdsall (Rochdale H.)
Tommy Bishop (Barrow, Leigh, Workington T.)
Mick Blacker (Halifax, Mansfield M.)
Tommy Blakeley (Blackpool B.)
Dick Bonser (Rochdale H.)
Reg Bowden (Fulham, Warrington)
Drew Broatch (Hunslet)
Ian Brooke (Bradford N., Huddersfield, Wakefield T.)
Arthur Bunting (Hull, Hull K.R.)
Dave Busfield (Dewsbury)

Len Casey (Hull, Wakefield T.)
Jim Challinor (Oldham)
Paul Charlton (Workington T.)
Eddie Cheetham (Leigh)
Colin Clarke (Leigh, Wigan)
Terry Clawson (Featherstone R.)
Malcolm Clift (Leeds)
Joe Coan (Wigan)
Gary Cooper (York)
Kel Coslett (Rochdale H., St. Helens, Wigan)
Keith Cotton (Featherstone R.)
Mike Coulman (Salford)
Les Coulter (Keighley)
Dave Cox (Batley, Castleford, Dewsbury, Huyton, Oldham, Workington T.)
Jim Crellin (Blackpool B., Halifax, Mansfield M., Swinton)
Terry Crook (Batley, Dewsbury)

Arthur Daley (Runcorn H.)
Paul Daley (Batley, Featherstone R., Hunslet, York)
Jackie Davidson (Workington T.)
Keith Davies (Workington T.)
Tommy Dawes (Barrow, Whitehaven)
Harry Dawson (Widnes)
Tony Dean (Wakefield T., Hull)
Henry Delooze (Rochdale H.)
Steve Dennison (Mansfield M.)
Robin Dewhurst (Leeds)
Bakary Diabira (Blackpool B., Keighley)
Tommy Dickens (Blackpool B., Leigh)
Colin Dixon (Halifax, Keighley, Salford)
Mal Dixon (York)
David Doyle-Davidson (Hull, York)
Ray Dutton (Whitehaven)

Graham Eadie (Halifax)
Derek Edwards (Doncaster)
Joe Egan Jnr. (Blackpool B.)

George Fairbairn (Wigan)
Vince Farrar (Featherstone R.)
Albert Fearnley (Batley, Blackpool B., Keighley)
Tony Fisher (Bramley)
Eric Fitzsimons (Rochdale H., Oldham)
Bob Fleet (Swinton)
Geoff Fletcher (Huyton)
Terry Fogerty (Rochdale H.)
Chris Forster (Huddersfield B., Bramley)
Frank Foster (Barrow, Whitehaven)
Kenny Foulkes (Hull)
Don Fox (Batley)
Harry Fox (Halifax)

Neil Fox (Huddersfield)
Peter Fox (Bradford N., Bramley, Featherstone R., Leeds, Wakefield T.)
Bill Francis (Oldham)
Roy Francis (Bradford N., Huddersfield, Leeds)

Brian Gartland (Oldham)
Stan Gittins (Blackpool B.)
Bill Goodwin (Fulham, Kent Invicta)
Terry Gorman (Huyton, Swinton)
Keith Goulding (Featherstone R., Huddersfield, York)
Mal Graham (Oldham)
Tom Grainey (Leigh, Swinton)
Jeff Grayshon (Dewsbury)
Lee Greenwood (Keighley)
Geoff Gunney M.B.E.(Wakefield T.)

Bob Haigh (Wakefield T.)
Derek Hallas (Halifax)
Ken Halliwell (Swinton)
Alan Hardisty (Dewsbury, York)
Graham Heptinstall (Doncaster)
Alan Hepworth (Batley)
Keith Hepworth (Bramley, Hull)
Gary Hetherington (Sheffield E.)
Ron Hill (Dewsbury)
Bill Holliday (Swinton)
Eric Hughes (Widnes, Rochdale H.)
Syd Hynes (Leeds)

Bob Irving (Blackpool B.)
Keith Irving (Workington T.)

Dennis Jackson (Barrow)
Peter Jarvis (Bramley, Hunslet)
Allen Jones (Huddersfield B.)
Lewis Jones (Dewsbury)

Vince Karalius (Widnes, Wigan)
Arthur Keegan (Bramley)
Ivor Kelland (Barrow)
Alan Kellett (Carlisle, Halifax, Keighley)
Bill Kenny (Doncaster)
Bill Kindon (Leigh)
Bill Kirkbride (Mansfield M., Rochdale H., Wakefield T., York)
Phil Kitchin (Whitehaven)

Dave Lamming (Wakefield T.)
Steve Lane (Kent Invicta)
Doug Laughton (Widnes)
Roy Lester (Carlisle, Fulham)
Alan Lockwood (Dewsbury)

Brian Lockwood (Batley, Huddersfield,
Wakefield T.)
Paul Longstaff (Rochdale H.)
Graham Lowe (Wigan)
Phil Lowe (York)
Trevor Lowe (Batley, Doncaster)
Ken Loxton (Bramley)
Geoff Lyon (Blackpool B.)

John Mantle (Blackpool B., Cardiff C., Leigh)
Stan McCormick (Salford)
John McFarlane (Whitehaven)
Alan McInnes (Salford, Wigan)
Roger Millward M.B.E. (Hull K.R.)
Mick Morgan (Carlisle)
David Mortimer (Huddersfield)
Alex Murphy (Leigh, St. Helens, Salford,
Warrington, Wigan)
Frank Myler (Oldham, Rochdale H., Swinton,
Widnes)

Les Pearce (Bramley, Halifax)
Mike Peers (Swinton)
Geoff Peggs (Keighley)
George Pieniazek (Batley, Featherstone R.)
Harry Poole (Hull K.R.)

Bill Ramsey (Hunslet)
Terry Ramshaw (Oldham)
Rod Reddy (Barrow)
Graham Rees (Blackpool B.)
Malcolm Reilly (Castleford)
Alan Rhodes (Doncaster, Sheffield E.)
Austin Rhodes (Swinton)
Ken Roberts (Halifax)
Don Robinson (Bramley)
Don Robson (Doncaster)
Peter Roe (Keighley)
Sol Roper (Workington T.)

Roy Sabine (Keighley)
Dave Sampson (Castleford)
Barry Seabourne (Bradford N., Keighley)
Les Sheard (Huddersfield)
Danny Sheehan (York)
John Sheridan (Doncaster)
Tommy Smales [Scrum-half] (Featherstone R.)
Tommy Smales [Forward] (Batley, Bramley,
Dewsbury, Doncaster, Featherstone R.)
Peter Smethurst (Leigh, Oldham)
Bill Smith (Whitehaven, Workington T.)
Brian Smith (Huddersfield)
Ike Southward (Whitehaven, Workington T.)

Graham Starkey (Oldham, Rochdale H.)
Gary Stephens (York)
Dave Stockwell (Bramley, Batley)
John Stopford (Swinton)
Ted Strawbridge (Doncaster)
Clive Sullivan M.B.E. (Doncaster, Hull)

Bob Tomlinson (Huddersfield)
Ted Toohey (Wigan)
David Topliss (Wakefield T.)
Norman Turley (Workington T.)
Derek Turner (Wakefield T.)
Colin Tyrer (Widnes)

Don Vines (Doncaster)

Arnold Walker (Whitehaven)
Trevor Walker (Batley)
David Ward (Hunslet)
John Warlow (Bridgend)
David Watkins (Cardiff C.)
Bernard Watson (Dewsbury)
Neil Whittaker (Huddersfield B.)
Frank Wilson (Runcorn H.)
Jeff Woods (Bridgend)
John Woods (Leigh)
Paul Woods (Runcorn H.)
Geoff Wraith (Wakefield T.)

Billy Yates (Doncaster)

DOSSIER OF 1987-88 COACHES

The following is a dossier of the coaching and
playing careers of coaches holding first team
posts from June 1987 to the end of May 1988.
BF — beaten finalist.

JACK ADDY
Dewsbury: Feb. 84 - Jan. 87 (Promotion)
Huddersfield B: Jan. 87 - Mar. 88
Played for: Dewsbury

CHRIS ANDERSON
Halifax   Nov. 84 - May 88 (Div. 1
champs, RL Cup winners and
BF, Premier BF,
Charity Shield winners and BF)
Played for: Canterbury-Bankstown (Aus.), Widnes,
Hull K.R., Halifax

219

KEVIN ASHCROFT

Leigh:	June 75 - Jan. 77 (Promotion, Floodlit Trophy BF)
Salford:	Nov. 80 - Mar. 82
Warrington:	Mar. 82 - May 84 (Lancs. Cup winners)
Salford:	May 84 - (Promotion)

Played for: Dewsbury, Rochdale H., Leigh, Warrington, Salford

BILL ASHURST

Wakefield T.:	June 81 - Apr. 82
Runcorn H.:	Apr. 87 -

Played for: Wigan, Penrith (Aus.), Wakefield T.

MAURICE BAMFORD

Dewsbury:	Aug. - Oct. 74
Halifax:	Feb. 78 - May 80 (Yorks. Cup BF., Promotion)
Huddersfield:	May 80 - May 81
Wigan:	May 81 - May 82
Bramley:	May 82 - Oct. 83
Leeds:	Nov. 83 - Feb. 85 (John Player winners)
Leeds:	Dec. 86 - Apr. 88 (John Player BF)
Great Britain & Under-21s:	Oct. 84 - Dec. 86

Played for: Dewsbury, Hull, Batley

FRANK BARROW

Oldham:	Feb. 84 - Feb. 84
Swinton:	Oct. 87 -

Played for: St. Helens, Leigh

TONY BARROW

Warrington:	Mar. 86 - (Premier winners and BF, John Player BF., Lancs. Cup BF)

Played for: St. Helens, Leigh

BILLY BENYON

Warrington:	June 78 - Mar. 82 (Lancs. Cup winners, John Player winners and BF)
St. Helens:	May 82 - Nov. 85 (Lancs. Cup winners and BF, Premier winners)
Leigh:	Dec. 86 -

Played for: St. Helens, Warrington

LEN CASEY

Wakefield T.:	Apr. 85 - (Promotion)
Hull:	June 86 - Mar. 88 (Yorks. Cup BF)

Played for: Hull, Hull K.R., Bradford N., Wakefield T.

LES COULTER

Keighley:	July 86 -

Non-professional player

JIM CRELLIN

Blackpool B.:	May 76 - Mar. 77 (John Player BF)
Halifax:	June 77 - Oct. 77
Swinton:	Nov. 83 - May 86 (Div. 2 champs)
Mansfield M.:	Dec. 86 -

Played for: Workington T., Oldham, Rochdale H.

TERRY CROOK

Batley:	June 82 - Nov. 84
Dewsbury:	Apr. 87 -

Played for: Wakefield T., Bramley, Batley

PAUL DALEY

New Hunslet:	Apr. 74 - Aug. 78 (Promotion)
York:	Jan. 79 - May 79 (Promotion)
Featherstone R.:	May 79 - Jan. 81 (Div. 2 champs)
Hunslet:	Apr. 81 - Nov. 85 (Promotion)
Featherstone R.:	Nov. 86 - Apr. 87
Batley:	July 87 -

Played for: Halifax, Bradford N., Hull K.R., Hunslet

TONY DEAN

Wakefield T.:	June - Dec. 86
Hull:	Mar. 88 - Apr. 88

Played for: Batley, Barrow, Hunslet, Hull, Rochdale H.

COLIN DIXON

Salford:	Mar. 77 - Jan. 78
Halifax:	Sept. 82 - Nov. 84 (Promotion)
Keighley:	July 86 -

Played for: Halifax, Salford, Hull KR

GRAHAM EADIE

Halifax:	May 88 -

Played for: Manly (Aust.), Halifax

TONY FISHER

Bramley:	Nov. 87 -

Played for: Bradford N., Leeds, Castleford

ERIC FITZSIMONS
Rochdale H.:   June 86 - June 87
Oldham: June 87 -
                   (Div. 2 champs, Div. 2 Premier
                   winners)
Played for: Oldham, Hunslet, Rochdale H.

CHRIS FORSTER
Huddersfield B.:   Feb. 85 - Dec. 86
Bramley: June 87 - Nov. 87
Played for: Huddersfield, Hull, Bramley

PETER FOX
Featherstone R.:   Jan. 71 - May 74
                   (RL Cup winners & BF)
Wakefield T.:   June 74 - May 76
                   (Yorks. Cup BF)
Bramley: Sept. 76 - Apr. 77 (Promotion)
Bradford N.:   Apr. 77 - May 85 (Div. 1
                   champs (2), Yorks. Cup winners
                   and BF (2), Premier winners
                   and BF (2), John Player winners)
Leeds: May 85 - Dec. 86
Featherstone R.:   May 87 - (Promotion, Div. 2
                   Premier BF)
England: 1977 (2 matches)
Great Britain: 1978 (3 Tests v. Australia)
Yorkshire: 1985-86 to 1987-88
Played for: Featherstone R., Batley, Hull K.R.,
Wakefield T.

STAN GITTINS
Springfield B.:   Nov. 85 -
Played for: Batley, Swinton

BILL GOODWIN
Kent Invicta: Apr. 83 - Nov. 83
Kent Invicta: Aug. 84 - May 85
Fulham: Apr. 86 -
Played for: Doncaster, Featherstone R., Batley

MAL GRAHAM
Oldham: June 87 - Apr. 88
                   (Div. 2 champs)
Played for: Wests, Newtown (Aust.), Hunslet,
Bradford N., Oldham

KEITH HEPWORTH
Bramley: June 80 - May 82
Hull: Mar. 88 - Apr. 88
Played for: Castleford, Leeds, Bramley

GRAHAM HEPTINSTALL
Doncaster: Nov. 87 - Jan. 88
Played for: Non-professional

GARY HETHERINGTON
Sheffield E.:   July 86 -
Played for: York, Leeds, Kent I., Sheffield E.

BILL HOLLIDAY
Swinton: June 86 - Oct. 87 (Promotion,
                   Div. 2 Premier winners)
Played for: Whitehaven, Hull K.R., Swinton,
Rochdale H.

ERIC HUGHES
Widnes: June 84 - Jan. 86
Rochdale H.:   June 87 -
Played for: Widnes, St. Helens, Rochdale H.

DENNIS JACKSON
Barrow: Feb. 87 - Nov. 87
Played for: Barrow, Blackpool B., Whitehaven,
Workington T.

PETER JARVIS
Bramley: Oct. 83 - Apr. 85
Hunslet: Nov. 85 - Apr. 88 (Div. 2
                   champs, Div. 2 Premier BF)
Played for: Hunslet, Bramley, Halifax, Huddersfield

ALLEN JONES
Huddersfield B.:   Mar 88 - Apr. 88
Played for: Non-professional

PHIL KITCHIN
Whitehaven: Oct. 79 - Jan. 82 (Promotion)
Whitehaven: June 85 - Oct. 87
Cumbria: 1980-81, 1981-82, 1986-87,
                   1987-88
Played for: Whitehaven, Workington T.

DOUG LAUGHTON
Widnes: May 78 - Mar. 83
                   (RL Cup winners (2) and BF,
                   Lancs. Cup winners (2) and
                   BF, John Player winners and
                   BF, Premier winners (2))
Widnes: Jan. 86 - (Div. 1 champs,
                   Premier winners)
Played for: Wigan, St. Helens, Widnes

ROY LESTER
Fulham: June 84 - Apr. 86
Carlisle: June 86 -
Played for: Warrington, Leigh, Fulham

221

GRAHAM LOWE
Wigan: Aug. 86 - (RL Cup winners, Lancs. Cup winners (2), John Player winners, Div. 1 champs, Premier winners, Charity Shield winners)

JOHN McFARLANE
Whitehaven: Oct. 87 - May 88
Played for: Whitehaven, Barrow, Workington T.

ROGER MILLWARD M.B.E.
Hull K.R.: Mar. 77 - (Div. 1 champs (3), RL Cup winners and BF (2), John Player winners and BF (2), Premier winners (2) and BF, Yorks. Cup winners and BF (2), Floodlit Trophy winners and BF, Charity Shield BF)
Played for: Castleford, Hull K.R., Cronulla (Aus.)

ALEX MURPHY
Leigh: Nov. 66 - May 71 (RL Cup winners, Lancs. Cup winners and BF, Floodlit Trophy winners and BF)
Warrington: May 71 - May 78 (League Leaders, Club Merit winners, RL Cup winners and BF, John Player winners (2), Floodlit Trophy BF, Capt. Morgan winners, Premier BF)
Salford: May 78 - Nov. 80
Leigh: Nov. 80 - June 82 (Div. 1 champs, Lancs. Cup winners)
Wigan: June 82 - Aug. 84 (John Player winners, RL Cup BF)
Leigh: Feb. 85 - Nov. 85
St. Helens: Nov. 85 - (RL Cup BF, John Player winners, Premier BF)
Lancashire: 1973-74 to 1977-78; 1985-86 to 1987-88 Champions (2)
England: 1975 (including World Championship (European Champions))
Played for: St. Helens, Leigh, Warrington

MIKE PEERS
Swinton: June 86 - Oct. 87 (Promotion, Div. 2 Premier winners)
Played for: Warrington, Swinton

ROD REDDY
Centrals (Aus.): Feb. 86 - Sep. 87
Barrow: Nov. 87 -
Played for: St. George, Illawarra, Centrals (All Aust.), Barrow

MALCOLM REILLY
Castleford: Dec. 74 - May 87 (Yorks. Cup winners (3) and BF (2), Floodlit Trophy winners, John Player winners, Premier BF, RL Cup winners, Charity Shield BF)
Great Britain & Jan 87 -
Under-21s:
Played for: Castleford, Manly (Aus.)

DAVE SAMPSON
Castleford: Apr. 87 - Apr. 88 (Yorks. Cup BF)
Played for: Wakefield T., Bramley, Castleford

BARRY SEABOURNE
Keighley: Nov. 77 - Mar. 79
Bradford N.: May 85 - (Yorks. Cup winners)
Played for: Leeds, Bradford N., Keighley

DANNY SHEEHAN
York: Mar. 87 - Apr. 88
Played for: York

JOHN SHERIDAN
Doncaster: June 84 - Nov. 87
Doncaster: Jan. 88 -
Played for: Castleford

GARY STEPHENS
York: Apr. 88 -
Played for: Castleford, Wigan, Leigh, Halifax, Leeds, Manly (Aust.)

DAVID TOPLISS
Wakefield T.: May 87 - (Promotion)
Played for: Wakefield T., Hull, Oldham

NORMAN TURLEY
Workington T.: Mar. 87 -
Played for: Warrington, Blackpool B., Rochdale H., Swinton, Runcorn H., Barrow, Workington T.

DAVID WARD
Hunslet: July 86 - Apr. 88 (Div. 2 champs, Div. 2 Premier BF)
Played for: Leeds

NEIL WHITTAKER
Huddersfield B.: Mar. 88 - Apr. 88
Played for: Non-professional

Kumul tourists Arnold Krewanty (left) and Mathias Kitimun.

1987 KUMULS

1987 KUMULS

Papua New Guinea's first-ever tour of the British professional scene brought them two victories and a draw from seven encounters.

The Kumuls — named after the islands' Bird of Paradise — bid to balance a lack of size and power with a willingness to play fast, open football. The tourists opened with a four-try haul in a 22-16 success at Featherstone Rovers before staging a thrilling 22-22 encounter with a powerful Lancashire side at St. Helens.

Despite a lack of depth in the 26-man squad, the Papuans built up a lot of hopes — including their own — for a serious challenge in the Whitbread Trophy Bitter Test meeting with Great Britain at Wigan, a World Cup-rated fixture.

Only 14 months earlier, the Kumuls had shocked the Rugby League world by pulling off a 24-22 home victory over New Zealand in a World Cup game, while during the summer the Kiwis had worked hard to earn a 36-22 success, again at Port Moresby.

The tourists' confidence unfortunately evaporated at Wigan's Central Park as Malcolm Reilly's charges carried out a game plan of methodical attack and watertight defence. The outcome was seven British tries, all goalled, and the Papuans not scoring, their first nil in a 12-Test history dating back to October 1979.

Kumul coach Barry Wilson typified the bitter disappointment being experienced by the fast developing national side at not fulfilling their Test potential on the history-making tour, mounted only after months of fund raising activity throughout the islands.

After four successive defeats — including that 42-0 Test hammering, Swinton, Cumbria and Yorkshire — Papua recovered to beat a BARLA XIII 20-16 in an additional fixture staged at Halifax before rounding off the three-week tour with a 12-4 victory over Second Division Fulham at Chiswick.

Rugby League's youngest nation, having been given International Board status in November 1978, were continually learning on a short, but demanding, tour of Britain, followed by a four-match visit to France, highlighted by the Carcassonne Test with France, albeit a 21-4 defeat.

The Papuan authorities had asked for a match itinerary which allowed scope for the development of their uncapped players. The seven fixtures against professional opposition, headed by the Test encounter, featured Second Division Featherstone Rovers and Fulham, newly promoted Second Division Premiership winners Swinton and the three county sides.

The Kumuls faced several problems as tourists. Language, diet, lack of funds, climate and inexperience all provided headaches for the management. Their Harrogate hotel became a haven for a host of Papuan dialects, an abundance of the favoured chicken and pig dishes, and the mass purchase of gloves, scarves and thermal underwear!

On the field, the tourists conceded twice as many points as they scored. Their tally of 70 points in the seven professional encounters was made up of 14 tries and seven goals.

Discipline on and off the field was excellent. The opposition was equally disciplined and no player was sent off or spent time in the sin bin in any tour match.

Centre Bal Numapo was an inspiring captain, finishing as top goals and points scorer from their modest totals. The Kundiawa threequarter showed touches of class and strong leadership, typified by the taking of the last minute penalty goal kick to level the scores in the Lancashire match, rated as their best performance of an educational visit.

There were promising displays from full back Dairi Kovae, already recruited by Australian club side North Sydney; wingers Kepi Saea and Arnold Krewanty; and second row man Bernard Waketsi.

TOUR RESULTS

Date	Result	Score	Opposition	Venue	Attendance
Oct. 11	W	22-16	Featherstone R.	Featherstone	3,315
14	D	22-22	Lancashire	St. Helens	4,202
18	L	6-13	Swinton	Swinton	2,132
20	L	4-22	Cumbria	Whitehaven	3,750
24	L	0-42	GREAT BRITAIN	Wigan	9,121
27	L	4-28	Yorkshire	Leeds	1,908
Nov. 1	W	12-4	Fulham	Fulham	1,216

● In addition, the tourists also played the following amateur opposition.

Oct. 30	W	20-16	BARLA XIII	Halifax	2,700

TOUR SUMMARY

				FOR				AGAINST			
P.	W.	D.	L.	T.	G.	Dr.	Pts.	T.	G.	Dr.	Pts.
7	2	1	4	14	7	0	70	29	15	1	147

TEST SUMMARY

				FOR				AGAINST			
P.	W.	D.	L.	T.	G.	Dr.	Pts.	T.	G.	Dr.	Pts.
1	0	0	0	0	0	0	0	7	7	0	42

TOUR RECORDS

Biggest attendance: 9,121, Test at Wigan
Highest score: 22-16 v. Featherstone R.; 22-22 v. Lancashire
Widest margin: 12-4 v. Fulham
Highest score against: 0-42 by Great Britain
Most tries in a match: No player scored more than one try
Most goals in a match: 3 by Bal Numapo v. Featherstone R.
Most points in a match: 8 by Bal Numapo v. Lancashire
Most tries on tour: 3 by Kepi Saea
Most goals on tour: 5 by Bal Numapo
Most points on tour: 14 by Bal Numapo
Most full appearances: 6 by Lauta Atoi, Arnold Krewanty,
 Kepi Saea and Bernard Waketsi

TOUR PARTY

Managers: Tau Peruka and Miller Ovasuru
Coach: Barry Wilson
Captain: Bal Numapo
Trainer: Sam Susuve
Doctor: Robin Sios

Skipper Bal Numapo.

TOUR PARTY

PLAYER	CLUB	IN BRITAIN					IN FRANCE					TOTALS				
		App	Sub	T	G	Pts	App	Sub	T	G	Pts	App	Sub	T	G	Pts
AKO, Bobby	Hawks, Mt. Hagen	1	2	1	—	4	3	1	—	—	—	4	3	1	—	4
ATOI, Lauta	Dolphins, Bouganville	6	—	1	—	4	4	—	1	—	4	10	—	2	—	8
GAIUS, David	PIC Easts, Rabaul	4	1	—	1	2	1	—	1	—	4	4	2	1	1	6
GISPE, Joe	Sea Eagles, Rabaul	2	—	—	—	—	1	—	—	—	—	3	—	—	—	—
HAILI, Darius	Brothers, Kimbe	4	1	2	—	8	3	1	—	—	—	7	2	2	—	8
HENI, Roy	Wests, Port Moresby	4	—	—	1	2	3	1	—	2	4	7	1	—	3	6
IPU, Mark	Tarangau, Port Moresby	2	1	—	—	—	3	—	1	—	4	5	1	1	—	4
KAMIAK, Elias	Brothers, Mt. Hagen	2	—	—	—	—	—	2	—	—	—	2	2	—	—	—
KAPIA, James	Muruks, Rabaul	2	—	—	—	—	—	—	—	—	—	2	—	—	—	—
KILA, Tony	Air Niugini, Port Moresby	5	—	—	—	—	4	—	2	—	8	9	—	2	—	8
KITIMUN, Mathias	Defence, Port Moresby	4	1	1	—	4	—	2	—	—	—	4	3	1	—	4
KOMBRA, Mathias	Royals, Mendi	4	—	1	—	4	1	2	1	—	4	5	2	2	—	8
KOUORU, Gideon	Wests, Port Moresby	4	—	—	—	—	1	1	—	—	—	5	1	—	—	—
KOVAE, Dairi	North Sydney, Australia	4	2	—	—	—	4	—	2	9	26	8	2	2	9	26
KREWANTY, Arnold	Defence, Port Moresby	6	—	1	—	4	4	—	2	—	8	10	—	3	—	12
LAPAN, Ngala	West Panther Lae	2	1	—	—	—	1	1	—	—	—	3	2	—	—	—
LOMUTOPA, Ati	Country, Goroka	5	—	—	—	—	2	1	—	—	—	7	1	—	—	—
MATMILLO, Michael	Kone Tigers, Port Moresby	2	—	—	—	—	1	1	—	—	—	3	1	—	—	—
MOREA, Mea	DCA, Port Moresby	3	—	—	—	—	2	1	1	—	4	5	1	1	—	4
MOU, Clement	Wests, Port Moresby	1	2	1	—	4	2	—	2	—	8	3	2	3	—	12
NUMAPO, Bal	Brothers, Kundiawa	4	—	1	5	14	2	—	—	—	—	6	—	1	5	14
ROMBUK, Thomas	Tarangau, Lae	1	2	1	—	4	2	—	—	—	—	3	2	1	—	4
SAEA, Kepi	Air Niugini, Port Moresby	6	—	3	—	12	2	—	—	—	—	8	—	3	—	12
TAUMAKU, Arebo	DCA, Port Moresby	4	—	—	—	—	4	—	1	—	4	8	—	1	—	4
TEP, Joe	Defence, Port Moresby	3	1	—	—	—	—	—	—	—	—	4	—	—	—	—
WAKETSI, Bernard	Paga, Port Moresby	6	—	1	—	4	2	—	—	—	—	8	—	1	—	4

● Not including the fixture against BARLA XIII.

Australian-born coach Barry Wilson.

Top try scorer Kepi Saea.

Test prop Ati Lomutopa.

Papua New Guinea 1987 Left to right: Back row: Kapia, Kamiak, Ipu, Waketsi, Tep, Taumaku, Saea, Rombuk, Mou, Morea, Matmillo, Lapan. Middle row: Sam Susuve (Trainer), Brian King (Vice-President), Robin Sios (Doctor), Haili, Koroae, Kitimun, Kombra, Kouoru Kreevanty, Lomuopa, Joe Keviame (Finance Manager), Barry Wilson (Coach). Front row: Heni, Kila, Gispe, Miller Ovasuru (Team Manager), Numapo (Captain), Tau Peruka (Tour Manager), Gaius, Atoi, Ako.

IN FRANCE

Date	Result	Score	Opposition	Venue	Attendance
Nov. 6	D	12-12	Midi-Pyrenees	Toulouse	2,000
			T: Gaius, Atoi		
			G: Heni (2)		
8	W	48-4	Tarn Selection	Albi	2,317
			T: Kila (2), Mou (2), Kombra, Ipu,		
			Kovae, Taumaku		
			G: Kovae (8)		
11	L	14-18	XIII Catalan	Perpignan	2,638
			T: Krewanty (2), Morea.		
			G: Kovae		
15	L	4-21	FRANCE	Carcassonne	4,982

France: Pougeau; Ratier (1t), Delaunay, Fraisse (2t), Pons (1t); Moliner, Bourrel (2g, 1dg); Rabot, Khedimi, Ailleres, Montgaillard, Divet, Laforgue. Subs: Dumas, Verdes.

Papua New Guinea: Kovae (1t); Krewanty, Atoi, Morea, Saea; Numapo, Kila; Ako, Heni, Lomutopa, Waketsi, Taumaku, Kouoru. Subs: Haili, Kombra.

FRENCH TOUR SUMMARY

				FOR			AGAINST			
P.	W.	D.	L.	T.	G.	Dr.	Pts.	T.	G.	Dr.	Pts.
4	1	1	2	14	11	0	78	11	4	3	55

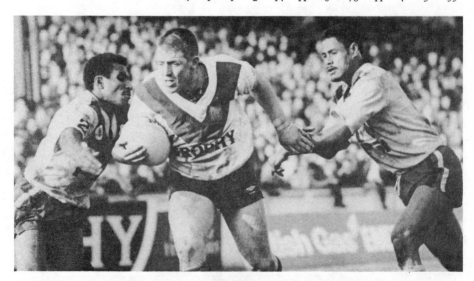

Kumul right wing pair Arnold Krewanty (left) and Lauta Atoi converge on Great Britain scrum half Andy Gregory.

228

Papuan loose forward Arebo Taumaku and prop Ati Lomutopa fail to stop Great Britain try scorer Shaun Edwards.

Double Kumul tackle by David Gaius (left) and Arebo Taumaku on Great Britain prop Brian Case.

MATCH BY MATCH

11 October

FEATHERSTONE R.   16
PAPUA NEW GUINEA   22

1. Kitimun (Kovae)
2. Kapia
3. Atoi
4. Numapo
5. Saea
6. Haili
7. Kila
8. Tep
9. Heni (Rombuk)
10. Lomutopa
11. Kombra
12. Waketsi
13. Taumaku

T: Haili, Kombra, Saea, Rombuk
G: Numapo (3)

Featherstone R.:
Bibb; Jones, Beach, Smales, Marsh; Crossley, Fox; Slatter, Staniforth, Siddal (Geary), Dakin (Bell), Smith, Lyman

T: Smith, Marsh, Smales
G: Fox, Smales

Half-time: 8-12

Referee: Jim Smith (Halifax)
Attendance: 3,315

The Kumuls opened the tour with a confidence-boosting victory at Post Office Road, delighting the crowd with an attacking policy and their ability to keep the ball alive.

Stand off Haili had the distinction of opening the scoring with a seventh minute try, goalled by skipper Numapo, before Fox replied with a penalty goal. Second row man Kombra took advantage of a hesitant home defence to score from 20 yards out, Numapo again adding goal, the Colliers keeping in the picture with a touchdown from captain Smith, the impressive young Smales tagging on a touchline goal to leave the Kumuls 12-8 ahead at the break.

Rovers restarted with a two tries in five minutes, Smales running in from half way and then creating a try for wing partner Marsh to put the tourists 16-12 in arrears.

Showing no signs of jet lag, the Papuans stormed back with classy centre Numapo sending winger Saea over and landing his third goal, substitute Rombuk completing the scoring seven minutes from time with their fourth try.

14 October

St. Helens

LANCASHIRE   22
PAPUA NEW GUINEA   22

1. Kovae
2. Saea (Mou)
3. Morea
4. Atoi
5. Krewanty
6. Numapo
7. Kila
8. Lomutopa
9. Heni
10. Taumaku (Rombuk)
11. Waketsi
12. Kombra
13. Kouoru

T: Waketsi, Krewanty, Saea, Numapo
G: Numapo (2), Heni

Lancashire:
Hampson (Wigan); Drummond (Warrington), Henderson (Leigh), Lydon (Wigan), Offiah (Widnes); Edwards (Wigan), A. Gregory (Wigan), Capt.; Pyke (Leigh), Groves (St. Helens), Round (Oldham), M. Gregory (Warrington), Roberts (Warrington), Arkwright (St. Helens). Substitutions: D. Hulme (Widnes) for A. Gregory, A. Cottrell (Leigh) for Roberts

T: Edwards (2), Roberts, Lydon, Henderson
G: Lydon

Half-time: 10-14

Referee: John Kendrew (Castleford)
Attendance: 4,202

A last minute penalty goal by skipper Numapo earned the Kumuls a well deserved draw with Lancashire in the most entertaining game of the tour. Ironically, kicking had been a weak point of the tourists with three players — Numapo, Heni and Kovae — being used, the first two totalling three from a combined eight attempts.

Papua scored three tries to two in the first half to establish a 14-10 lead at the interval. Early in the second period, a try from Kila pushed the visitors ahead 20-10 before Lydon touched down in the 54th minute.

Wigan teammate Edwards added his second try five minutes later to leave Lancashire trailing by two points. Leigh centre Henderson touched down four minutes from time and it was left to Numapo to step forward to take the last ditch penalty kick to equalise.

18 October

SWINTON	13
PAPUA NEW GUINEA	6

1. Kitimun
2. Kapia (Haili)
3. Morea
4. Kamiak
5. Krewanty
6. Mou
7. Lapan
8. Tep
9. Matmillo
10. Gaius
11. Ako (Ipu)
12. Rombuk
13. Gispe

T: Haili
G: Gaius

Swinton:
Topping; Maloney, Wilson, Snape, Evans; Cassidy, Hewitt; Grima, Melling, Ainsworth, Horrocks, Sheals, Allen (McFarland)

T: Ainsworth, Horrocks, Maloney
G: Wilson (dg)

Half-time: 8-0

Referee: David Carter (Widnes)
Attendance: 2,132

Papua New Guinea lost their unbeaten record in the third outing of the tour with a 13-6 defeat at Swinton, still without a win in the league.

The Station Road fixture was staged with a blackcloth of club politics, a section of the Swinton fans protesting on the terraces about the lack of team strengthening.

The Kumuls fielded virtually a reserve side with the World Cup-rated Test encounter less than a week away and did not discover the flair shown in their two opening matches.

Man of the Match Ainsworth, the Swinton prop, kicked through for the first try after only three minutes, Horrocks also touching down to give the Lions an 8-0 half-time lead. Papua substitute Haili came on for the second period and scored a try within two minutes, goalled by Gaius, before Maloney's 59th minute try and Wilson's late drop goal completed the scoring.

20 October

Whitehaven

CUMBRIA	22
PAPUA NEW GUINEA	4

1. Kitimun
2. Krewanty
3. Atoi
4. Morea (Kovae)
5. Saea
6. Haili
7. Kila (Tep)
8. Ipu
9. Heni
10. Gaius
11. Waketsi
12. Kombra
13. Kouoru

T: Saea

Cumbria:
Lightfoot (Whitehaven); Lofthouse (Whitehaven), Fisher (Whitehaven), Pape (Carlisle), Beck (Workington T.); Rae (Barrow), Cairns (Salford), Capt; Nixon (Workington T.), Falcon (Workington T.), D. Kendall (Barrow), Burney (Whitehaven), Kirkby (Carlisle), Hetherington (Whitehaven). Substitution: Lowden (Workington T.) for Lightfoot, Thomason (Carlisle) did not play.

T: Rae (2), Lofthouse, Beck, Pape
G: Lowden

Half-time: 12-0

Referee: Ray Tennant (Castleford)
Attendance: 3,750

Cumbria beat the tourists at their own game with a display of high speed passing and running, scoring five tries to one.

Papua were also guilty of careless handling and winger Lofthouse set the Cumbrians on the path to victory in the 17th minute with a 70-yard interception try. Three minutes later Barrow stand off Rae grabbed the first of his two tries with a dazzling solo effort and with Nixon, Burney and Kendall providing a solid platform in the pack, the Kumuls struggled to make progress.

There were occasional breaks from threequarters Kovae and Saea before the latter scored a superb long range try in the 50th minute, Cumbria rounding off the scoring with touchdowns from Workington winger Beck and Carlisle centre Pape.

TEST MATCH

The two extremes of the 42-0 scoreline were equally pleasing to Great British coach Malcolm Reilly. His charges had run in seven comfortable tries without needing to be over adventurous, while the sought-for improvement in defence had nilled Papua New Guinea for the first time in their 12-Test history.

Great Britain duly collected two World Cup points and maintained Reilly's unbeaten record. The Kumuls, having promised an entertaining challenge after their high scoring draw against Lancashire, were disappointing.

The tourists were confident of making an impact on the Test scene but could not find the power to trouble a cohesive home unit with a backbone of eight Wigan players, a British Test record.

At least the international newcomers were assured that Great Britain treated them with the greatest respect, maintaining a methodical game plan rather than opting for flambuoyancy which could have turned a hammering into a rout. The obsession of keeping a clean sheet was evident throughout, particularly in the later stages when the British tackling of their lighter counterparts was still as determined and vigorous as the opening quarter.

Skipper Ellery Hanley led by example, finishing as Britain's top tackler with 30. Playing at loose forward in a Test for the first time, the Wigan star also had a hand in the opening try by Phil Ford after only seven minutes, claiming the second himself in the 16th minute. The wearing of the number 13 jersey in his 19th Test appearance took Hanley into the elite band of British Test players to have appeared in four different positions.

Reilly gave Test debuts to three players, Wigan full back Steve Hampson, St. Helens new hooker Paul Groves and Leeds second row man Paul Medley. Hampson justified his selection as a specialist number one without having to cope with any real pressure, while former Under-21 skipper Groves won the scrums 12-10 although his performance in the loose reflected a lack of first class match practice.

Medley displayed his rich potential as a powerpacked runner, scoring a 39th minute touchdown to ease Britain into a 24-0 half-time lead and earning the Whitbread Trophy Bitter Man of the Match award despite having to come off with a knee injury in the 66th minute. His second row partner, Andy Goodway, was so disappointed with his contribution that the Wigan packman left the dressing room issuing threats of premature retirement from the international arena.

Wigan stand off Shaun Edwards was a contender for the individual honours, scoring tries in the 29th and 53rd minutes as well as being one of the busiest players on the pitch.

The most entertaining performance came from winger Ford who, despite a lack of opportunities, opened the scoring and ran delightfully to set up Joe Lydon's try in the 65th minute.

Second row man Bernard Waketsi took the tourists' Man of the Match award with a hard working display, while the handful of Papuans who had been expected to shine at this higher level — including skipper Bal Numapo, full back Dairi Kovae and winger Arnold Krewanty — failed to lift their game.

Wigan centre David Stephenson added the goals to all seven tries although, rarely for a Test match, there were no penalty shots at goal from either side despite a 14-7 penalty count in favour of the visitors.

WHITBREAD TROPHY BITTER TEST

24 October   **Wigan**

GREAT BRITAIN 42

Steve Hampson (Wigan)	1.
Des Drummond (Warrington)	2.
David Stephenson (Wigan)	3.
Joe Lydon (Wigan)	4.
Phil Ford (Bradford N.)	5.
Shaun Edwards (Wigan)	6.
Andy Gregory (Wigan)	7.
Kevin Ward (Castleford)	8.
Paul Groves (St. Helens)	9.
Brian Case (Wigan)	10.
Paul Medley (Leeds)	11.
Andy Goodway (Wigan)	12.
Ellery Hanley (Wigan), Capt.	13.
John Woods (Warrington)	14.
Karl Fairbank (Bradford N.)	15.

T: Edwards (2), Ford, Hanley, Medley, Lydon, Gregory
G: Stephenson (7)
Substitutions:
Woods for Lydon (66 min.)
Fairbank for Medley (66 min.)

PAPUA NEW GUINEA 0

Dairi Kovae
Kepi Saea
Lauta Atoi
Bal Numapo, Capt.
Arnold Krewanty
Darius Haili
Tony Kila
Joe Tep
Roy Heni
Ati Lomutopa
Mathias Kombra
Bernard Waketsi
Arebo Taumaku
Mathias Kitimun
David Gaius

Substitutions:
Gaius for Kombra (Half-time)
Kitimun for Haili (54 min).
Half-time: 24-0
Referee: Francis Desplats (Toulouse)
Attendance: 9,121

Scorechart

		Scoreline	
Minute	*Score*	*GB*	*PNG*
7:	Ford (T)	4	0
	Stephenson (G)	6	0
16:	Hanley (T)	10	0
	Stephenson (G)	12	0
29:	Edwards (T)	16	0
	Stephenson (G)	18	0
39:	Medley (T)	22	0
	Stephenson (G)	24	0
53:	Edwards (T)	28	0
	Stephenson (G)	30	0
65:	Lydon (T)	34	0
	Stephenson (G)	36	0
78:	Gregory (T)	40	0
	Stephenson (G)	42	0
	Scrums	12	10
	Penalties	7	14

Bernard Waketsi, the Kumul's Whitbread Trophy Bitter Man of the Match award winner.

233

27 October

Leeds

YORKSHIRE	28
PAPUA NEW GUINEA	4

1. Kovae
2. Krewanty
3. Atoi
4. Numapo
5. Saea
6. Haili (Lapan)
7. Kila
8. Ipu
9. Taumaku
10. Lomutopa
11. Waketsi
12. Gaius (Ako)
13. Kouoru

T: Atoi

Yorkshire:
Mumby (Bradford N.); Eastwood (Hull), Marchant (Castleford), Gibson (Leeds), Mason (Wakefield T.); Joyner (Castleford), Capt; Fox (Featherstone R.); Hobbs (Bradford N.), McCallion (Halifax), Powell (Leeds), Burton (Hull K.R.), Fairbank (Bradford N.), Dixon (Halifax). Substitutions: Creasser (Leeds) for Marchant, Heron (Leeds) for Fairbank

T: Gibson (3), Fairbank, Marchant, Creasser
G: Hobbs (2)

Half-time: 4-4

Referee: Fred Lindop (Wakefield)
Attendance: 1,908

Leeds threequarter Gibson notched a hat-trick of tries as Yorkshire maintained their 100 per cent record with Peter Fox as coach, his fifth victory.

With the pitch under water in parts and the game played in heavy rain throughout, the Kumuls adapted well to the alien conditions and Atoi's brilliant opening try of the game, covering 90 yards, put them level 4-4 at the break, Yorkshire having replied with a Fairbank try.

Papua, with only four of their Test side being omitted, were overpowered in the second half, the White Rose points coming from Gibson's hat-trick and further tries from Marchant and substitute Creasser, Hobbs adding two goals. The Man of the Match award went to Leeds prop Powell for an industrious performance.

1 November

FULHAM	4
PAPUA NEW GUINEA	12

1. Kitimun
2. Saea
3. Kovae
4. Kamiak (Mou)
5. Krewanty
6. Atoi
7. Lapan
8. Gaius (Ako)
9. Matmillo
10. Lomutopa
11. Waketsi
12. Gispe
13. Kouoru

T: Kitimun, Ako, Mou

Fulham:
Lawrie; Feighan, Rees, Gillan, Cambriani; Guyett, Murphy; Hutchison, Taylor, Miller (Fenn), Grimoldby, Manning (Kelly), O'Riley

G: Rees, Fenn

Half-time: 2-4

Referee: Brian Simpson (Manchester)
Attendance: 1,216

The Kumuls rounded off their history-making tour with a hard-earned victory over Second Division Fulham, mixing enterprising passing with opportunism, two of their three tries coming from the Londoners' defensive errors.

The tourists took the lead when Kitimun was sent over by an excellent pass in the tackle from Kovae, before Rees reduced the half-time deficit with a penalty goal.

Substitute Mou capitalised on a mix up when Fulham backs Lawrie and Guyett both left a high ball to each other, and the tourist dived over for a try. Then Waketsi intercepted and fed second substitute Ako, who scored with his first touch.

The Kumuls' poor goalkicking kept Fulham in the match, but a Fenn penalty goal was all they had to show for a wealth of second half possession.

Auckland captain Ron O'Regan.

AUCKLAND TOUR

AUCKLAND TOUR

Top New Zealand provincial side Auckland mounted their first-ever tour of Britain with a mixed reaction on and off the field.

They gained a 50 per cent record with three wins from six fixtures, highlighted by a surprise 10-6 victory over newly-crowned World Club Challenge winners Wigan.

The pioneering visit lost money with a total of 32,437 fans turning out, only Wigan's 10,743 crowd topping five figures. Particularly disappointing were the attendances of 1,921 for the Hull encounter at the Boulevard and the 3,636 at Leeds for the meeting with the RL Chairman's XIII, coached by Malcolm Reilly in what was termed a tour trial.

Auckland arrived with a good track record, having suffered only one defeat in five seasons and that at the hands of the touring Australians.

An unbeaten nine-match representative campaign in the 1987 New Zealand season had featured the piling up of 412 points, including 73 tries, with the conceding of only 94.

Top scorers in those nine victories had been winger Shane Horo with 14 tries and prop Peter Brown with 118 goals. The duo again topped the charts on the short tour of Britain, each playing in every match.

Horo was the top try scorer with six, twice as many as his nearest rivals, Wigan's new recruit Kevin Iro and former Bramley second row man Dan Lonergan. Brown, a target for Hull, kicked 14 goals, adding a try for a leading points tally of 32, the only other goal scorer being Lonergan with a solitary drop kick.

Auckland's historic visit had been prompted by a desire for international competition after continual domination of the domestic scene. The 22-man squad included six players who had visited Britain two years earlier with the 1985 Kiwis .... Shane Cooper, Marty Crequer, Clayton Friend, James Goulding, Shane Horo and Ron O'Regan, the Auckland skipper.

Of the sextet, Cooper was delaying his arrival for duty with St. Helens, Horo was to join Leigh at the end of the tour, while scrum half Friend was guesting for Auckland after joining North Sydney.

The New Zealanders combined bouts of attractive football with bouts of over-physical play, culminating in brawls in the opening game at Leeds and the finale with the Chairman's XIII, again at Headingley. In the first encounter, forwards Kevin Rayne (Leeds) and tourist Mark Horo were dismissed, while the last match was marred by the sending off of home skipper Lee Crooks and Auckland goalkicker Brown. In addition, a third forward, Steve Kaiser, was dismissed at St. Helens for flooring Paul Forber.

Despite providing a glut of excitement, the mini-tour did not capture the public or the media's imagination. Auckland mounted a thrilling comeback in the opening fixture with Leeds and survived a brave Warrington challenge to maintain their winning record before crashing to a rampant St. Helens side in a 14-try thriller. Weakened Hull sprung a last ditch shock victory in a 50-point encounter, before the New Zealanders beat high flying Wigan, the only disappointing fare being served up in the dull Chairman's XIII meeting.

The half a dozen fixtures produced a total of 254 points, with Auckand contributing and conceding 22 tries. The tourists blamed the lack of promotion at club level for the. lower than required gates and interest. A major factor was Auckland's timing of their inaugural tour, overlapping with the visit by Papua New Guinea and the amateur tour by the Junior Kiwis, and coming so soon after the first-ever World Club Challenge between Wigan and Manly.

TOUR RESULTS

Date		Result	Score	Opposition	Venue	Attendance
Oct.	25	W	29-25	Leeds	Leeds	6,639
	27	W	22-16	Warrington	Warrington	3,897
Nov.	1	L	26-52	St. Helens	St. Helens	5,901
	4	L	24-26	Hull	Hull	1,921
	8	W	10-6	Wigan	Wigan	10,743
	10	L	6-12	RL Chairman's XIII	Leeds	3,636

TOUR SUMMARY

						FOR			AGAINST		
P.	W.	D.	L.	T.	G.	Dr.	Pts.	T.	G.	Dr.	Pts.
6	3	0	3	22	14	1	117	22	24	1	137

TOUR RECORDS

Most appearances: All 6 by Shane Horo, Sam Panapa and Peter Brown

Most tries: 6 by Shane Horo

Most goals: 14 by Peter Brown

Most points: 32 by Peter Brown

Sent off: Mark Horo (v. Leeds) suspended 2 matches; Steve Kaiser (v. St. Helens) suspended 2 matches; Peter Brown (v. RL Chairman's XIII) suspended 2 matches

Opponents sent off: Kevin Rayne (Leeds) suspended 4 matches; Lee Crooks (RL Chairman's XIII) suspended 2 matches

Sin bin: Stever Kaiser (v. Leeds)

Opponents' sin bin: Lee Crooks (Leeds); Des Drummond (Warrington); Shaun Edwards (RL Chairman's XIII)

Auckland's Kiwi back Clayton Friend serves from the scrum against Leeds.

TOUR PARTY

Managers: Bill Nesbitt and Peter McLeod

Coach: Bob Bailey

Captain: Ron O'Regan

Physiotherapist: Graeme Coutts

PLAYER	CLUB	App	Sub	T	G	Pts
BROWN, Peter	Te Atatu	6	—	1	14	32
COOPER, Shane	Mangere East	4	—	2	—	8
CREQUER, Marty	Northcote	4	—	1	—	4
FREEMAN, Gary	Northcote	4	—	1	—	4
FRIEND, Clayton	North Sydney (Aus.)	3	—	1	—	4
GOULDING, James	Richmond	2	—	—	—	—
HOOKER, Lindsay	Mt. Albert	4	—	—	—	—
HORO, Mark	Te Atatu	4	—	1	—	4
HORO, Shane	Northcote	6	—	6	—	24
IRO, Kevin	Mt. Albert	4	—	3	—	12
KAISER, Steve	Te Atatu	3	2	1	—	4
LONERGAN, Dean	Glenora	3	1	3	(1)	13
MANN, George	Mangere East	1	—	—	—	—
MANN, Warren	Mangere East	2	—	—	—	—
NORDMEYER, Rene	Mangere East	2	—	—	—	—
O'REGAN, Ron	Te Atatu	5	—	—	—	—
PATTON, Michael	Glenora	2	2	—	—	—
PANAPA, Sam	Te Atatu	6	—	1	—	4
ROPATI, John	Mangere East	2	—	—	—	—
ROPATI, Peter	Otahuhu	4	1	—	—	—
ROPATI, Tea	Otahuhu	3	—	—	—	—
TUIMAVAVE, Paddy	Mt. Albert	4	1	1	—	4

( ): drop goal

Coach Bob Bailey.

Top goal scorer
Peter Brown.

Marty Crequer.

Te Atatu utility back Sam Panapa, one of three Auckland players to appear in all six tour games.

MATCH BY MATCH

25 October

LEEDS	25
AUCKLAND	29

1. Crequer
2. W. Mann
3. Patton
4. T. Ropati
5. S. Horo (Tuimavave)
6. Panapa
7. Friend
8. Brown
9. Nordmeyer
10. Kaiser
11. P. Ropati (Lonergan)
12. M. Horo
13. O'Regan

T: Crequer, Panapa, Brown, Kaiser, Tuimavave, Lonergan
G: Brown (2), Lonergan (dg)

Leeds:
Spencer; Pratt, Schofield, Jackson, Basnett (Gibson); Creasser, Lyons; Crooks, Stevens (Maskill), Rayne, Smithson, Powell, Heron

T: Spencer (2), Schofield (2)
G: Creasser (4), Crooks (dg)

Half-time: 24-10

Referee: Fred Lindop (Wakefield)
Attendance: 6,639

Great Britain centre Schofield paid the first instalment of his world record transfer fee with two debut tries for Leeds in a thrilling opening to Auckland's first-ever tour of Britain.

The entertaining encounter was marred by a 12th minute brawl which resulted in referee Fred Lindop sending off Leeds prop Rayne and Auckland second row man Mark Horo. Kaiser (Auckland) and Crooks (Leeds) also spent time in the sin bin.

Schofield's brace of tries in his first match since returning from Sydney club duty with Balmain, plus two from full back Spencer, eased Leeds into a 24-10 lead before three tries and a Lonergan drop goal helped push the visitors in front for the first time.

Crooks levelled the scores at 25-apiece, the impressive Crequer feeding Lonergan for the winning try with only minutes to go.

27 October

WARRINGTON	16
AUCKLAND	22

1. Crequer
2. Panapa
3. Iro
4. Tuimavave
5. S. Horo
6. Cooper
7. Freeman
8. Brown
9. Hooker
10. G. Mann (Kaiser)
11. Lonergan
12. M. Horo (Patton)
13. O'Regan

T: Lonergan (2), M. Horo
G: Brown (5)

Warrington:
Johnson; Drummond, Forster (Lyon), Peters, Bacon; Turner, Holden; Tamati, Webb, Humphries, Sanderson (Harmon), Roberts, Gregory

T: Roberts, Drummond
G: Turner (4)

Half-time: 8-14

Referee: Robin Whitfield (Widnes)
Attendance: 3,897

Severely hit by injuries, Warrington showed determination and courage before going down to a strong Auckland side. The Wire recovered from a 12-point deficit to take the lead through a top class Drummond try after 43 minutes.

Drummond's departure to the sin bin after a clash with Mark Horo 15 minutes later proved crucial, the New Zealanders scoring their third try, with two further Brown goals, to clinch their second victory inside three days.

Already devastated by injuries, Warrington put up a brave fight in the first half despite the loss of Great Britain back Forster after only five minutes and the stretchering off of Under-21 international forward Sanderson in the 19th minute.

The powerful Auckland pack laid the foundation for victory, with tries from second pair Lonergan (2) and Horo, plus five goals from prop Brown.

1 November

ST. HELENS	52
AUCKLAND	26

1. J. Ropati
2. Crequer
3. Iro
4. T. Ropati
5. S. Horo
6. Panapa
7. Friend
8. Brown
9. Nordmeyer
10. Goulding (Kaiser)
11. Lonergan
12. P. Ropati
13. O'Regan

T: Iro (2), S. Horo (2), Friend
·G: Brown (3)

St. Helens:
Veivers; Ledger (Litherland), McCormack, Tanner, Quirk; Arkwright, Bailey; Burke (Neil), Liptrot, Evans, Forber, Haggerty, Platt

T: Quirk (3), Platt (2), Veivers, Evans, Bailey, Ledger
G: Tanner (8)

Half-time: 28-16

Referee: Kevin Allatt (Southport)
Attendance: 5,901

St. Helens inflicted defeat on Auckland for the first time on their short tour and for only the second time in five years, the other loss being at the hands of Australia.

Playing polished and relaxed rugby, the Saints ran in nine tries, ex-Barrow winger Quirk registering his second hat-trick in successive matches.

Rugby Union converts Tanner and Evans also took the eye for a rampant St. Helens, the ex-Fylde centre adding eight goals and the latter, formerly with Neath, touching down for the first time in the 13-a-side code.

Auckland played their part in an entertaining encounter and, inspired by Wigan's new capture Iro and scrum half Friend, always maintaind a threat with five high class tries, featuring two each for Iro and winger Shane Horo. Kaiser was sent off 12 minutes from the end for flooring St. Helens packman Forber.

4 November

HULL	26
AUCKLAND	24

1. Patton
2. W. Mann
3. Iro
4. Panapa
5. S. Horo
6. Cooper
7. Freeman
8. Brown
9. Hooker
10. Kaiser
11. Tuimavave
12. P. Ropati
13. O'Regan

T: S. Horo (2), Iro, Cooper, Freeman
G: Brown (2)

Hull:
Pearce; Clarkson, Hick, O'Hara (Windley), M'Barki; Leuluai, Ellis; Tomlinson (Brooks), Patrick, Welham, Elgar, Proctor, Sharp

T: Ellis (2), Windley, Leuluai, Patrick
G: Pearce (3)

Half-time: 6-16

Referee: John McDonald (Wigan)
Attendance: 1,921

Hull gave one of their best displays of a disappointing opening to the season to snatch victory in a see-saw game eight minutes before the end.

Scrum half Ellis, playing his first full senior game, scored two tries and took the Man of the Match award, while the winning touchdown went to hooker Patrick who took a quick tap penalty and drove in from 10 yards.

Auckland ripped through for three long distance tries on their way to a 16-6 interval lead, Hull's reply being a close range try from Windley.

In a hectic finish, Hull's Welsh full back Pearce kicked his third goal to edge the Airlie Birds 22-20 ahead before winger Shane Horo finished off a 75-yard move for his second try, only for Patrick to grab the last ditch winner.

8 November

WIGAN   6
AUCKLAND   10

1. Crequer
2. Panapa
3. Iro
4. Tuimavave
5. S. Horo
6. Freeman
7. Friend
8. Brown
9. Hooker
10. Lonergan (P. Ropati)
11. M. Horo
12. O'Regan
13. Cooper

T: Cooper, S. Horo
G: Brown

Wigan:
Hampson; Marshall, Stephenson, Lydon, Russell; Edwards, Gregory; Lucas, Kiss, Wane, Goodway, Gildart, Hanley

G: Stephenson (2), Lydon

Half-time: 0-10

Referee: Gerry Kershaw (Easingwold)
Attendance: 10,743

Boos echoed round Central Park as Auckland recorded a shock 10-6 victory over a Wigan side giving one of their worst performances for a long time and extending a run of matches without victory to three.

Having lost to St. Helens and Hull in the week, the New Zealanders tackled and spoiled so effectively that Wigan's Test half backs Gregory and Edwards, and only packman Goodway could make any impact.

In contrast, the visiting half backs, Freeman and Friend, enjoyed a field day and were the mainsprings of attacks which brought tries for Cooper and Shane Horo, Brown adding a goal for a 10-0 half-time lead.

Wigan recovered six points after the break with penalty goals from Stephenson (2) and Lydon before winger Marshall had a claim for a last ditch try turned down by referee Gerry Kershaw, a levelling score which would have flattered a Wigan performance riddled with errors.

10 November

Leeds

RL CHAIRMAN'S XIII   12
AUCKLAND   6

1. J. Ropati
2. Panapa
3. T. Ropati
4. Tuimavave (Patton)
5. S. Horo
6. Cooper
7. Freeman
8. Brown
9. Hooker
10. Goulding
11. Kaiser
12. P. Ropati
13. M. Horo

T: S. Horo
G: Brown

RL Chairman's XIII:
J. Myler (Widnes); Ford (Bradford N.), Schofield (Leeds), Whitfield (Halifax), Offiah (Widnes); Edwards (Wigan), Fox (Featherstone R.); Crooks (Leeds, Capt.), McCallion (Halifax), Powell (Leeds), Fairbank (Bradford N.), Roberts (Warrington), Platt (St. Helens). Substitution: Dixon (Halifax) for Roberts. Not used: Forster (Warrington)

T: Offiah, Ford
G: Whitfield (2)

Half-time: 6-2

Referee: John Holdsworth (Kippax)
Attendance: 3,636

An unexciting finale to the six-match tour was marred by the sending off of two players and another being sent to the sin bin. The dull match flared up in the 59th minute with a brief melee which ended with home skipper Crooks and opposite number Brown being dismissed, broken nose victim Roberts, of Warrington, being replaced by Halifax's Dixon. Late in the game, Wigan's Edwards was sin-binned after a clash with Cooper.

Great Britain coach Malcolm Reilly, in charge of the Chairman's XIII as a tour trial, did not learn a lot, the Man of the Match award going to Auckland scrum half Freeman.

One outstanding lesson, however, was the lack of effective use of outstanding wingers Ford and Offiah, who each scored a try with sparse possession. Whitfield contributed two goals, Brown replying with one kick on target before, in the last minute, winger Shane Horo grabbed his sixth try of the tour.

French prop Marc Tisseyre is halted by Great Britain packmen Kevin Ward (upper) and Roy Powell in the 1988 Test at Leeds.

FRANCE

FRANCE

The following is a list of international matches involving France. For matches versus Great Britain see the GREAT BRITAIN section.

France v. Australia Tests

2 Jan. 1938	L	6-35	Paris
16 Jan. 1938	L	11-16	Marseilles
9 Jan. 1949	L	10-29	Marseilles
23 Jan. 1949	L	0-10	Bordeaux
11 Jun. 1951	W	26-15	Sydney
30 Jun. 1951	L	11-23	Brisbane
21 Jul. 1951	W	35-14	Sydney
27 Dec. 1952	L	12-16	Paris
11 Jan. 1953	W	5-0	Bordeaux
25 Jan. 1953	W	13-5	Lyons
11 Jun. 1955	L	8-20	Sydney
2 Jul. 1955	W	29-28	Brisbane
27 Jul. 1955	W	8-5	Sydney
1 Nov. 1956	L	8-15	Paris
23 Dec. 1956	L	6-10	Bordeaux
13 Jan. 1957	L	21-25	Lyons
31 Oct. 1959	L	19-20	Paris
20 Dec. 1959	L	2-17	Bordeaux
20 Jan. 1960	L	8-16	Roanne
11 Jun. 1960	D	8-8	Sydney
2 Jul. 1960	L	6-56	Brisbane
16 Jul. 1960	W	7-5	Sydney
8 Dec. 1963	W	8-5	Bordeaux
22 Dec. 1963	L	9-21	Toulouse
18 Jan. 1964	L	8-16	Paris
13 Jun. 1964	L	6-20	Sydney
4 Jul. 1964	L	2-27	Brisbane
18 Jul. 1964	L	9-35	Sydney
17 Dec. 1967	D	7-7	Marseilles
24 Dec. 1967	W	10-3	Carcassone
7 Jan. 1968	W	16-13	Toulouse
9 Dec. 1973	L	9-21	Perpignan
16 Dec. 1973	L	3-14	Toulouse
26 Nov. 1978	W	13-10	Carcassone
10 Dec. 1978	W	11-10	Toulouse
4 Jul. 1981	L	3-43	Sydney
18 Jul. 1981	L	2-17	Brisbane
5 Dec. 1982	L	4-15	Avignon
18 Dec. 1982	L	9-23	Narbonne
30 Nov. 1986	L	2-44	Perpignan
*13 Dec. 1986	L	0-52	Carcassonne

*Also World Cup

	P	W	D	L	Pts F	Pts A
TOTALS	41	12	2	27	390	784

France v. Australia World Cup

11 Nov. 1954	W	15-5	Nantes
22 Jun. 1957	L	9-26	Sydney
24 Sept. 1960	L	12-13	Wigan
8 Jun. 1968	L	4-37	Brisbane
10 Jun. 1968	L	2-20	Sydney
1 Nov. 1970	W	17-15	Bradford
5 Nov. 1972	L	9-31	Toulouse
22 Jun. 1975	L	6-26	Brisbane
26 Oct. 1975	L	2-41	Perpignan
11 Jun. 1977	L	9-21	Sydney

● Second Test in 1986 also World Cup match.

France v. Australia other matches

1960	L	12-37	Toulouse
11 Nov. 1970	L	4-7	Perpignan

France v. Great Britain Tests
see GREAT BRITAIN section

France v. Great Britain World Cup

7 Nov. 1954	D	13-13	Toulouse
13 Nov. 1954	L	12-16	Paris
15 Jun. 1957	L	5-23	Sydney
1 Oct. 1960	L	7-33	Swinton
2 Jun. 1968	W	7-2	Auckland
28 Oct. 1970	L	0-6	Castleford
1 Nov. 1972	L	4-13	Grenoble
5 Jun. 1977	L	4-23	Auckland

● 1986 (h) and 1987 (a) Tests also World Cup matches.

France v. New Zealand Tests

28 Dec. 1947	L	7-11	Paris
25 Jan. 1948	W	25-7	Bordeaux
4 Aug. 1951	L	15-16	Auckland

23 Dec. 1951	W	8-3	Paris
30 Dec. 1951	W	17-7	Bordeaux
6 Aug. 1955	W	19-9	Auckland
15 Aug. 1955	L	6-11	Auckland
8 Jan. 1956	W	24-7	Toulouse
15 Jan. 1956	L	22-31	Lyons
21 Jan. 1956	W	24-3	Paris
23 Jul. 1960	L	2-9	Auckland
6 Aug. 1960	L	3-9	Auckland
11 Nov. 1961	D	6-6	Bordeaux
18 Nov. 1961	L	2-23	Perpignan
9 Dec. 1961	D	5-5	St. Ouen
25 Jul. 1964	L	16-24	Auckland
1 Aug. 1964	L	8-18	Christchurch
15 Aug. 1964	L	2-10	Auckland
14 Nov. 1965	W	14-3	Marseilles
28 Nov. 1965	W	6-2	Perpignan
12 Dec. 1965	W	28-5	Toulouse
11 Nov. 1971	L	11-27	Perpignan
21 Nov. 1971	L	2-24	Carcassonne
28 Nov. 1971	D	3-3	Toulouse
22 Nov. 1980	W	6-5	Perpignan
7 Dec. 1980	L	3-11	Toulouse
7 Jun. 1981	L	3-26	Auckland
21 Jun. 1981	L	2-25	Auckland
23 Nov. 1985	L	0-22	Marseilles
*7 Dec. 1985	L	0-22	Perpignan

*Also World Cup

	P	W	D	L	Pts F	Pts A
TOTALS	30	10	3	17	289	384

France v. New Zealand World Cup

30 Oct. 1954	W	22-13	Paris
17 Jun. 1957	W	14-10	Brisbane
8 Oct. 1960	L	0-9	Wigan
25 May 1968	W	15-10	Auckland
25 Oct. 1970	L	15-16	Hull
28 Oct. 1972	W	20-9	Marseilles
15 Jun. 1975	L	0-27	Christchurch
17 Oct. 1975	D	12-12	Marseilles
19 Jun. 1977	L	20-28	Auckland

● Second Test in 1985 also World Cup match.

France v. New Zealand other matches

13 Oct. 1960	W	22-11	Paris
15 Nov. 1970	W	16-2	Carcassonne

France v. Papua New Guinea Tests

14 Oct. 1979	W	16-9	Albi
28 Oct. 1979	W	15-2	Carcassonne
25 Jul. 1981	D	13-13	Port Moresby
15 Nov. 1987	W	21-4	Carcassonne

	P	W	D	L	Pts F	Pts A
TOTALS	4	3	1	0	65	28

France v. Papua New Guinea other matches

29 May 1977	L	6-37	Port Moresby

France v. England European Championship

28 Mar. 1935	D	15-15	Paris
16 Feb. 1936	L	7-25	Paris
10 Apr. 1937	L	9-23	Halifax
20 Mar. 1938	L	15-17	Paris
25 Feb. 1939	W	12-9	St. Helens
23 Feb. 1946	L	6-16	Swinton
8 Dec. 1946	L	0-3	Bordeaux
17 May 1947	L	2-5	Leeds
25 Oct. 1947	L	15-20	Huddersfield
11 Apr. 1948	L	10-25	Marseilles
28 Nov. 1948	L	5-12	Bordeaux
12 Mar. 1949	W	12-5	Wembley
4 Dec. 1949	L	5-13	Bordeaux
11 Nov. 1950	L	9-14	Leeds
25 Nov. 1951	W	42-13	Marseilles
11 Apr. 1953	L	13-15	Paris
7 Nov. 1953	L	5-7	Bradford
10 May 1956	W	23-9	Lyons
25 Oct. 1969	D	11-11	Wigan
15 Mar. 1970	W	14-9	Toulouse
19 Jan. 1975	L	9-11	Perpignan
20 Mar. 1977	W	28-15	Carcassonne
5 Mar. 1978	L	11-13	Toulouse
24 Mar. 1979	L	6-12	Warrington

16 Mar. 1980	L	2-4	Narbonne
21 Feb. 1981	W	5-1	Leeds

France v. England World Cup

16 Mar. 1975	L	2-20	Leeds
11 Oct. 1975	L	2-48	Bordeaux

France v. England other matches

*15 Apr. 1934	L	21-32	Paris
17 Nov. 1962	L	6-18	Leeds

* England included Welshmen

France v. Wales European Championship

1 Jan. 1935	W	18-11	Bordeaux
23 Nov. 1935	L	7-41	Llanelli
6 Dec. 1936	L	3-9	Paris
2 Apr. 1938	L	2-18	Llanelli
16 Apr. 1939	W	16-10	Bordeaux
24 Mar. 1946	W	19-7	Bordeaux
18 Jan. 1947	W	14-5	Marseilles
12 Apr. 1947	L	15-17	Swansea
23 Nov. 1947	W	29-21	Bordeaux
20 Mar. 1948	W	20-12	Swansea
23 Oct. 1948	W	12-9	Swansea
10 Apr. 1949	W	11-0	Marseilles
12 Nov. 1949	L	8-16	Swansea
15 Apr. 1951	W	28-13	Marseilles
6 Apr. 1952	W	20-12	Bordeaux

25 Oct. 1952	L	16-22	Leeds
13 Dec. 1953	W	23-22	Marseilles
23 Oct. 1969	W	8-2	Salford
25 Jan. 1970	L	11-15	Perpignan
16 Feb. 1975	L	8-21	Swansea
20 Feb. 1977	W	13-2	Toulouse
15 Jan. 1978	L	7-29	Widnes
4 Feb. 1979	W	15-8	Narbonne
26 Jan. 1980	W	21-7	Widnes
31 Jan. 1981	W	23-5	Narbonne

France v. Wales World Cup

2 Mar. 1975	W	14-7	Toulouse
6 Nov. 1975	L	2-23	Salford

France v. Wales other matches

1 Mar. 1959	W	25-8	Toulouse
17 Feb. 1963	W	23-3	Toulouse
9 Mar. 1969	W	17-13	Paris

France v. Other Nationalities European Championships

15 Jan. 1950	W	8-3	Marseilles
10 Dec. 1950	W	16-3	Bordeaux
3 Nov. 1951	L	14-17	Hull
23 Nov. 1952	L	10-29	Marseilles
18 Oct. 1953	L	10-15	Bordeaux
19 Oct. 1955	L	19-32	Leigh

France v. other international sides

17 Mar. 1934	RL X111	L	16-32	Warrington
6 May 1935	RL X111	L	18-25	Leeds
26 Apr. 1936	Dominion X111	W	8-5	Paris
21 Mar. 1937	Dominion X111	L	3-6	Lyons
1 Nov. 1937	Empire X111	L	0-15	Paris
26 May 1949	Empire X111	W	23-10	Bordeaux
3 Jan. 1954	World X111	W	19-15	Lyons
9 Jan. 1954	U.S.A.	W	31-0	Paris
21 Oct. 1956	RL X111	L	17-18	Marseilles
16 Apr. 1958	RL X111	L	8-19	Leeds
22 Nov. 1958	RL X111	W	26-8	St. Helens
1 Nov. 1962	Eastern Div.	L	16-23	Carcassonne

● France won the European Championship in:
1937-39, 1948-49, 1950-51, 1951-52, 1976-77 and 1980-81.

FRANCE TEAMS . . .
A 20-year review

The following is a compendium of France Test, World Cup and European Championship matches from the start of the 1968-69 season. Only playing substitutes are included on the teamsheet.

Key: (WC): World Cup   t: try   g:goal   dg: one-point drop goal

1968 Great Britain
St. Helens: 30 Nov.

Lost 10-34

Chabert 2g
Ferren
Saboureau
Mantoulan
Marsolan
Calle 1t
Frattini
Marracq
Rebujent
Cabero 1t
De Nadai
Alesina
Armand
Subs: Toujas
  Bonet, G.

1969 England
Wigan: 25 Oct.

Drew 11-11

Cros
Marsolan
Molinier 2t
Gruppi, J. 1t
De Nadai
Capdouze 1g
Garrigue
Ailleres, G.
Begou
Marracq
Biffi
Cremoux
Clar, J.P.
Sub: Sabatie

1970 New Zealand (WC)
Hull: 25 Oct.

Lost 15-16

Cros
Marsolan 2t
Molinier
Ruiz
Bonal, E. 1t
Capdouze 3g
Garrigue
Sabatie
Cabero
Bonet, F.
Mazard
Biffi
Clar, J.P.
Sub: De Nadai

1969 Great Britain
Toulouse: 2 Feb.

Won 13-9

Cros
Marsolan
Andrieu
Mantoulan 1t
Bonnery 1t
Capdouze 2g
Garrigue
Ailleres, G.
Begou
Carias
De Nadai 1t
Mazard
Clar, J.P.
Sub: Marracq

1970 Wales
Perpignan: 25 Jan.

Lost 11-15

Cros
Marsolan
Molinier 1t
Mantoulan 1g
Magagnin
Capdouze 2g
Garrigue 1g
Sabatie
Begou
Ailleres, G.
De Nadai
Mazard
Clar, J.P.
Sub: Biffi

1970 Great Britain (WC)
Castleford: 28 Oct.

Lost 0-6

Cros
Marsolan
Molinier
Ruiz
Bonal, E.
Capdouze
Guiraud, G.
Sabatie
Cabero
De Nadai
Mazard
Cremoux
Clar, J.P.
Subs: Pellerin
  Bonet, F.

1969 Wales
Salford: 23 Oct.

Won 8-2

Cros
Marsolan
Molinier 1t
Mantoulan
Bonnery
Capdouze 1g
Garrigue
Ailleres, G.
Begou 1t
Sabatie
Marracq
Mazard
Clar, J.P.
Sub: Gruppi, J.

1970 England
Toulouse: 15 Mar.

Won 14-9

Cros
Marsolan
Molinier
Gruppi, J. 1t
Magagnin
Capdouze 3g
Garrigue 1g
Ailleres, G.
Cabero
Sabatie
Biffi 1t
De Nadai
Clar, J.P.

1970 Australia (WC)
Bradford: 1 Nov.

Won 17-15

Cros
Marsolan 2t
Molinier
Gruppi, J.
Pellerin
Capdouze 1t, 3g
Garrigue 1g
Sabatie
Cabero
Bonet, F.
De Nadai
Biffi
Clar, J.P.

1971 Great Britain
Toulouse: 7 Feb.
Won 16-8
Cros
Marsolan 1t
Molinier
Gruppi, J.
Bonal, J-M. 1t
Capdouze 5g
Garrigue
Sabatie
Cabero
Sauret
De Nadai
Hermet
Clar, J-P.
Sub: Serrano

1971 Great Britain
St. Helens: 17 Mar.
Lost 2-24
Cros
Marsolan
Molinier
Gruppi, J.
Arne
Pere 1g
Imbert, J-M.
Sabatie
Lavigne
De Nadai
Mazard
Serrano
Clar, J-P.
Sub: Alesina

1971 New Zealand
Perpignan: 11 Nov.
Lost 11-27
Cros
Marsolan 1t
Capdouze
Molinier
Solier
Calle
Camiade 4g
Sabatie
Quintilla
Ribere
Gleyzes
De Nadia
Terrats, R.
Subs: Bonal, E.
Serrano

1971 New Zealand
Carcassonne: 21 Nov.
Lost 2-24
Saboureau
Marsolan
Molinier
Gardon
Guilhem, B.
Capdouze 1g
Guiraund, G.
Theron
Gayral
Sauret
Gleyzes
De Nadai
Cenet
Subs: Alesina
Serrano

1971 New Zealand
Toulouse: 28 Nov.
Drew 3-3
Cros
Marsolan
Molinier 1t
Ruiz
Guilhem, B.
Capdouze
Imbert, J-M.
Zalduendo
Clar, J-P.
Serrano
De Nadai
Gleyzes
Cenet

1972 Great Britain
Toulouse: 6 Feb.
Lost 9-10
Toujas
Alonso
Molinier
Ruiz 1t
Guilhem, B.
Capdouze 2g, 2dg
Imbert, J-M.
Sauret
Clar, J-P.
Sabatie
Gleyzes
Serrano
Cenet

1972 Great Britain
Bradford: 12 Mar.
Lost 10-45
Pierre 1t
Marsolan 1t
Molinier
Ruiz
Laskawiec, C.
Capdouze 2g
Imbert, J-M.
Bonet, F.
Sabatie
Sauret
Gleyzes
Biffi
Serrano
Subs: Fedou, D.
Hermet

1972 New Zealand (WC)
Marseilles: 28 Oct.
Won 20-9
Toujas
Marsolan
Molinier
Ruiz 1t
Bonal, J-M. 2t, 1g
Guilhem, B. 4g
Frattini 1dg
De Nadai
Franc
Garzino
Serrano
Gleyzes
Anglade
Sub: Zalduendo

1972 Great Britain (WC)
Grenoble: 1 Nov.
Lost 4-13
Toujas
Marsolan
Molinier
Ruiz
Bonal, J-M. 1g
Guilhem, B.
Imbert, J-M.
De Nadai
Franc
Sauret
Serrano 1g
Gleyzes
Rodriguez, G.
Sub: Zalduendo

1972 Australia (WC)
Toulouse: 5 Nov.

Lost 9-31

Toujas
Marsolan
Molinier
Ruiz 1t
Bonal, J-M. 3g
Mazare
Frattini
Zalduendo
Franc
Garzino
Serrano
Gleyzes
De Nadai
Subs: Guilhem, B.
    Anglade

1973 Australia
Perpignan: 9 Dec.

Lost 9-21

De Matos
Marsolan
Molinier 1t
Ruiz 1t
Marty, J-C.
Rives, P.
Garrigue 1g, 1dg
Carre
Franc
Thenegal
Cologni
Sauret
Bonet, G.
Subs: Frattini
    Gleyzes

1973 Australia
Toulouse: 16 Dec.

Lost 3-14

Calle
Marsolan
Molinier
Ruiz
Marty, J-C.
Mazare
Garrigue
Carre
Franc 1t
Brunet
Sauret
Gleyzes
Bonet, G.
Subs: Rives, P.
    Serrano

1974 Great Britain
Grenoble: 20 Jan.

Lost 5-24

Pierre, F. 1g
Marsolan
Molinier 1t
Barcelli, A.
Marty, J-C.
Calle
Rives, P.
Moussard
Franc
Garzino
Hermet
Gleyzes
Alesina
Sub: Bonet, G.

1974 Great Britain
Wigan: 17 Feb.

Lost 0-29

Pierre, F.
Alonso
Molinier
Ruiz
Marty, J-C.
Gardon
Imbert, J-M.
Zalduendo
Kaminski, F.
De Nadai
Ledru
Maique
Bonet, G.
Sub: Rouanet

1975 England
Perpignan: 19 Jan.

Lost 9-11

Vigouroux
Bonal, E.
Laskawiec, G.
Solier
Curt 1t
Mazare
Imbert, J-M.
Anglade
Cassin
Kaminski, F.
Serrano 3g
Hermet
Gleyzes
Subs: Terrats
    Zalduendo

1975 Wales
Swansea: 16 Feb.

Lost 8-21

Vigouroux
Bonal, E.
Solier
Terrats
Curt
Molinier 1t
Imbert, J-M. 1dg
Cassin
Gonzales, A.
Serrano 2g
Maique
Hermet
Anglade
Subs: Laskawiec, G.
    Zalduendo

1975 Wales (WC)
Toulouse: 2 March

Won 14-7

Tranier
Bonal, E.
Molinier
Terrats 1t
Curt 1t
Lacoste 1dg
Imbert, J-M. 1dg
De Nadai
Kaminski, F.
Serrano 3dg
Gleyzes
Hermet
Anglade
Sub: Castel, J-L.

1975 England (WC)
Leeds: 16 March

Lost 2-20

Tranier
Bonal, E.
Molinier
Terrats
Curt
Lacoste
Imbert, J-M.
De Nadai
Kaminski, F.
Serrano 1g
Gleyzes
Hermet
Anglade

249

1975 New Zealand (WC)
Christchurch: 15 June
Lost 0-27
Tranier
Dumas, A.
Terrats
Ruiz
Bonal, E.
Calle
Imbert, J-M.
Zalduendo
Gonzales, A.
Cassin
Gleyzes
De Nadai
Mayorgas
Subs: Curt
Hermet

1975 Australia (WC)
Brisbane: 22 June
Lost 6-26
Tranier
Dumas, A.
Ruiz
Terrats
Curt
Calle 3g
Imbert, J-M.
De Nadai
Kaminski, F.
Cassin
Maique
Gleyzes
Anglade
Sub: Zalduendo

1975 England (WC)
Bordeaux: 11 Oct
Lost 2-48
De Matos
Grechi
Ruiz
Terrats
Laffargue
Calle 1g
Imbert, J-M
Garcia
Duthil
Gonzales, M.
Bosc
Tremouille
Bucchi
Subs: Thenegal
Vigouroux

1975 New Zealand (WC)
Marseilles: 17 Oct.
Drew 12-12
Pillon
Grechi
Ruiz
Guilhem, B. 3g
Chauvet 2t
Calle
Imbert, J-M.
Thenegal
Gonzales, A.
Zalduendo
Sauret
Tremouille
Terrats
Sub: Moussard

1975 Australia (WC)
Perpignan: 26 Oct
Lost 2-41
Pillon
Grechi
Ruiz
Guilhem, B. 1g
Chauvet
Calle
Imbert, J-M.
Zalduendo
Gonzales, A.
Thenegal
Sauret
Tremouille
Terrats
Subs: Clergeau
Moussard

1975 Wales (WC)
Salford: 6 Nov.
Lost 2-23
Calle
Grechi
Terrats
Guilhem, B. 1g
Curt
Lacoste
Imbert, J-M.
Alvernhe
Gonzales, A.
Moussard
Tremouille
Sauret
Mayorgas
Sub: Maique

1977 Wales
Toulouse: 20 Feb.
Won 13-2
Guigue
Laskawiec, C. 1t
Guilhem, B. 5g
Bourret
Chauvet
Calle
Alard
Daniel
Bonet, H.
Cassin
Gleyzes
Sauret
Caravaca
Sub: Roosebrouck

1977 England
Carcassonne: 20 Mar.
Won 28-15
Saboureau
Moya
Guigue
Bourret 2t, 5g
Curt
Calle 1t, 1g, 1dg
Alard
Daniel
Bonet, H. 1t
Cassin
Sauret 1t
Cologni
Caravaca

1977 Great Britain (WC)
Auckland: 5 June
Lost 4-23
Guigue
Moya
Laskawiec, C.
Ruiz
Chauvet
Calle 2g
Alard
Cassin
Bonet, H.
Daniel
Sauret
Cologni
Roosebrouck
Sub: Rodriguez, G.

1977 Australia (WC)
Sydney: 11 June
Lost 9-21
Guigue
Moya
Terrats
Bourret
Laskawiec, C. 1t
Calle 3g
Alard
Chantal
Garcia
Cassin
Caravaca
Sauret
Roosebrouck
Subs: Imbert, J-M.
    Rodriguez, G.

1978 England
Toulouse: 5 Mar.
Lost 11-13
Tranier 1t
Sire
Guigue
Guilhem, B. 4g
Baile
Alard
Imbert, J-M.
Cassin
Gonzales, A.
Daniel
Gine
Cologni
Roosebrouck
Sub: Sauret

1979 Wales
Narbonne: 4 Feb
Won 15-8
Tranier 1t
Gonzales, J.M. 1t
Laumond
Bourret 1t, 1dg
Moya 2g
Waligunda 1dg
Alard
Daniel
Malacamp
Castanon
Zalduendo
Hermet
Maique
Sub: Laforgue, G.

1977 New Zealand (WC)
Auckland: 19 June
Lost 20-28
Calle
Moya 4g
Terrats
Ruiz
Guigue 1t
Alard
Imbert, J-M.
Cassin
Garcia
Sauret
Caravaca
Cologni 2t
Roosebrouck 1t
Subs: Imbert, J.
    Moussard

1978 Australia
Carcassonne: 26 Nov.
Won 13-10
Tranier
Moya 5g
Laumond
Naudo 1t
Borreil
Waligunda
Greseque
Daniel
Malacamp
Castanon
Hermet
Zalduendo
Maique

1979 England
Warrington: 24 Mar.
Lost 6-12
Touchagues 3g
Sire
Laumond
Naudo
Moya
Waligunda
Alard
Daniel
Malacamp
Castanon
Zalduendo
Hermet
Maique

1978 Wales
Widnes: 15 Jan.
Lost 7-29
Pillon
Loubet
Bourret 1t, 2g
Guigue
Laffargue
Calle
Imbert, J-M.
Cassin
Gonzales, A.
Lassale
Gine
Rodriguez, G.
Gorse
Sub: Laskawiec, G.

1978 Australia
Toulouse: 10 Dec.
Won 11-10
Tranier
Moya 3g
Laumond
Naudo 1t
Borreil
Waligunda 1dg
Castel, J.L.
Daniel
Malacamp
Castanon
Hermet
Zalduendo
Maique
Subs: Bourret 1dg
    Roosebrouck

1979 Papua New Guinea
Albi: 14 Oct.
Won 16-9
Gaye
Moya
Bourret 1t
Laumond
Nauroy 2t
Waligunda 1t, 2g
Castel, J.L.
Daniel
Malacamp
Chantal
Gine
Hermet
Roosebrouck
Sub: Zalduendo

1979 Papua New Guinea
Carcassonne: 28 Oct.
Won 15-2
Gaye
Gonzales, J.M.
Bourret 3t, 3g
Laumond
Nauroy
Waligunda
Alard
Guigue
Hermet
Gine
Chantal
Daniel
Zalduendo
Subs: Castanon
     Imbert, J.

1980 Wales
Widnes: 26 Jan.
Won 21-7
Pillon
Gonzales, J-M., 1t, 4g
Naudo
Laumond
Rodriguez, S.
Mazare 1dg
Greseque 1t
Chantal
Malacamp
Castanon
Baile
Gine
Roosebrouck 2t

1980 England
Narbonne: 16 Mar.
Lost 2-4
Tranier
Rodriguez, S.
Bourret 1g
Laumond
Gonzales, J.M.
Mazare
Greseque
Chantal
Daniel
Hermet
Gine
Baile
Roosebrouck

1980 New Zealand
Perpignan: 22 Nov.
Won 6-5
Pillon
Sire
Bourret 2t
Laumond
Ratier
Guiraud H.
Greseque
Daniel
Malacamp
Zalduendo
Vila
Hermet
Roosebrouck
Subs: Delaunay
     Garcia

1980 New Zealand
Toulouse: 7 Dec.
Lost 3-11
Pillon
Sire
Bourret 1t
Ratier
Imbert, B.
Guiraud, H.
Greseque
Hermet
Malacamp
Verdieres
Tremouille
Vila
Roosebrouck
Sub: Zalduendo

1981 Wales
Narbonne: 31 Jan.
Won 23-5
Pillon
Rodriguez, S.
Ratier
Naudo
Moya 4g
Guiraud, H.
Greseque 1t
Castanon
Macalli
Chantal
Tremouille 1t
Gine
Roosebrouck 2t
Subs: Fourquet 1t
     Caravaca

1981 England
Leeds: 21 Feb.
Won 5-1
Pillon
Rodriguez. S.
Naudo
Ratier
Moya 1g
Waligunda
Guiraud, H. 1t
Chantal
Macalli
Castanon
Caravaca
Gine
Roosebrouck
Sub: Fourquet

1981 New Zealand
Auckland: 7 June
Lost 3-26
Pillon
Rodriguez, S.
Delaunay
Naudo 1t
Ratier
Guiraud, H.
Alard
Daniel
Macalli
Chantal
Caravaca
Gine
Roosebrouck

1981 New Zealand
Auckland: 21 June
Lost 2-25
Perez, A. 1g
Rodriguez, S.
Fourquet
Delaunay
Ratier
Guiraud, H.
Bezard
Daniel
Macalli
Chantal
Gine
Laforgue
Caravaca
Subs: Imbert, J.
     Gonzales, P.

1981 Australia
Sydney: 4 July
Lost 3-43
Rodriguez, S.
Ratier 1t
Imbert, J.
Fourquet
Imbert, B.
Alard
Greseque
Chantal
Macalli
Castanon
Hermet
Gine
Vila
Sub: Guiraud, H.

1981 Australia
Brisbane: 18 July
Lost 2-17
Pillon
Ratier
Guiraud, H.
Imbert, J.
Rodriguez, S.
Alard
Greseque
Daniel
Macalli
Chantal
Ambert, M.
Caravaca
Roosebrouck
Sub: Perez, A. 1g

1981 Papua New Guinea
Port Moresby: 25 July
Drew 13-13
Pillon
Rodriguez, S. 1t
Caravaca
Guiraud, H.
Ratier
Perez, A. 2g
Greseque
Castanon
Macalli
Chantal
Zalduendo
Ambert, M.
Roosebrouck 2t
Sub: Malacamp

1981 Great Britain
Hull: 6 Dec.
Lost 0-37
Pillon
Rodriguez, S.
Ratier
Costals
Girardet
Waligunda
Scicchitano
Daniel
Macalli
Verdieres
Ambert, M.
Gine
Roosebrouck
Subs: Laville
Bernabe

1981 Great Britain
Marseilles: 20 Dec.
Won 19-2
Perez, A. 3g
Solal 2t
Guigue
Delaunay
Rodriguez, S.
Laville 1dg
Scicchitano 1t
Gine
Macalli
Zalduendo
Laforgue, G.
Ambert, M.
Roosebrouck
Sub: Kaminski, E. 1t

1982 Australia
Avignon: 5 Dec.
Lost 4-15
Perez, A. 2g
Solal
Guigue
Delaunay
Fourcade
Guiraud, H.
Greseque
Daniel
Macalli
Chantal
Ambert, M.
Laforgue, G.
Roosebrouck
Subs: Laumond
Caravaca

1982 Australia
Narbonne: 18 Dec.
Lost 9-23
Guigue
Solal
Delaunay
Laumond
Kaminski, E. 3g
Guiraud, H.
Greseque 1t
Zalduendo
Macalli
Chantal
Cologni
Laforgue, G.
Roosebrouck
Subs: Laville
Caravaca

1983 Great Britain
Carcassonne: 20 Feb.
Lost 5-20
Imbert, J. 1g
Bernard 1t
Guigue
Delaunay
Kaminski, E.
Laville
Greseque
Storer
Macalli
Chantal
Ambert, M.
Laforgue, G.
Roosebrouck
Subs: Cologni
Guiraud, H.

1983 Great Britain
Hull: 6 March
Lost 5-17
Guigue
Solal 1t
Laforgue, F.
Fourquet
Bernard
Guiraud, H.
Scicchitano
Chantal
Macalli
Storer
Laforgue, G.
Baloup 1g
Roosebrouck
Subs: Prunac
Dauphin

FRANCE

1984 Great Britain
Avignon: 29 Jan.
Lost 0-12
Wosniak
Solal
Bernard
Fourquet
Ratier
Perez, A.
Scicchitano
Chantal
Bernabe
Ailleres, P.
Palanque
Laforgue, G.
Baloup
Sub: Caravaca

1984 Great Britain
Leeds: 17 Feb.
Lost 0-10
Wosniak
Solal
Palisses
Fourquet
Bernard
Perez, A.
Scicchitano
Chantal
Trinque
Ailleres, P.
Meurin
Laforgue, G.
Baloup
Sub: Guasch, Bruno

1985 Great Britain
Leeds: 1 Mar.
Lost 4-50
Pallares
Jean
Palisses
Fourquet
Ratier
Perez, A.
Greseque
Chantal
Macalli 1t
Meurin
Ailleres, P.
Laforgue, G.
Baloup
Sub: Titeux

1985 Great Britain
Perpignan: 17 Mar.
Won 24-16
Pallares 4g
Ratier
Fourquet 1t
Palisses
Couston 3t
Laforgue, F.
Greseque
Chantal
Macalli
Titeux
Montgaillard
Verdes
Laforgue, G.
Subs: Mendes
Bernabe

1985 New Zealand
Marseilles: 23 Nov.
Lost 0-22
Pallares
Ratier
Laforgue, F.
Palisses
Couston
Espugna
Greseque
Chantal
Mantese
Titeux
Montgaillard
Palanque
Laforgue, G.
Subs: Perez, A.
Perez, S.

1985 New Zealand (Also WC)
Perpignan: 7 Dec.
Lost 0-22
Pallares
Ratier
Berge
Palisses
Couston
Espugna
Guasch, Bruno
Chantal
Bernabe
Titeux
Montgaillard
Palanque
Laforgue, G.
Subs: Perez, A.
Rabot

1986 Great Britain (Also WC)
Avignon: 16 Feb.
Drew 10-10
Dumas, G. 1t, 3g
Couston
Fourquet
Maury
Laroche
Espugna
Entat
Chantal
Baco
Titeux
Laforgue, G.
Palanque
Bernabe
Subs: Berge
Rabot

1986 Great Britain
Wigan: 1 Mar.
Lost 10-24
Dumas, G. 1g
Couston 2t
Berge
Fourquet
Laroche
Espugna
Entat
Chantal
Baco
Titeux
Laforgue, G.
Palanque
Bernabe
Subs: Pallares
Rabot

1986 Australia
Perpignan: 30 Nov.
Lost 2-44
Dumas, G. 1g
Couston
Palisses
Maury
Ratier
Espugna
Entat
Chantal
Bernabe
Rabot
Laforgue, G.
Titeux
Verdes
Subs: Bret
Laforgue F.

254

1986 Australia (Also WC)
Carcassonne: 13 Dec.
Lost 0-52
Wosniack
Rodriguez, S.
Fourquet
Laforgue, F.
Ratier
Palisses
Scicchitano
Chantal
Bernabe
Titeux
Laforgue, G.
Verdes
Gestas
Subs: Dumas, G.
     Storer

1987 Great Britain (Also WC)
Leeds: 24 Jan.
Lost 4-52
Perez, A. 2g
Couston
Palisses
Ratier
Pons
Espugna
Dumas, G.
Storer
Mantese
Rabot
Verdes
Palanque
Bernabe
Subs: Rocci
     Titeux

1987 Great Britain
Carcassonne: 8 Feb.
Lost 10-20
Perez, A. 3g
Berteloite
Bienes
Moliner
Ratier
Espugna 1t
Scicchitano
Rabot
Trinque
Ailleres, P.
Verdes
Palanque
Bernabe
Sub: Storer

1987 Papua New Guinea
Carcassonne: 15 Nov.
Won 21-4
Pougeau
Ratier 1t
Delaunay
Fraisse 2t
Pons 1t
Moliner
Bourrel 2g,1dg
Rabot
Khedimi
Ailleres, P.
Montgaillard
Divet
Laforgue, G.
Subs: Verdes
     Dumas. G

1988 Great Britain
Avignon: 24 Jan.
Lost 14-28
Pougeau
Ratier 1t
Delaunay
Fraisse
Pons
Espugna
Dumas, G. 3g
Tisseyre
Khedimi
Ailleres, P.
Montgaillard
Verdes 1t
Moliner
Subs: Bienes
     Gestas

1988 Great Britain
Leeds: 6 Feb.
Lost 12-30
Pougeau
Ratier
Delaunay
Fourquet
Pons 1t
Espugna
Bourrel 2g
Tisseyre
Khedimi 1t
Ailleres, P.
Montgaillard
Verdes
Gestas
Sub: Moliner

Britain's Andy Gregory scores against France at Headingley in 1988.

FRANCE REGISTER . . .
1968-88
The following is an index of players who have appeared for France in Test, World Cup or European Championship matches, toured Australasia or been a member of a World Cup squad since the start of the 1968-69 season.

World Cup matches are in bold letters except when they double as Test matches. Substitute appearances are in lower case letters.

In 1975 the World Cup was in two sections and the index refers only to those who were members of the squad Down Under.

Key: A – Australia, B-Britain, E – England, NZ – New Zealand, PNG – Papua New Guinea, W – Wales.

AILLERES, Georges
Appearances: 1969 B,W,E: 1970 W,E.
AILLERES, Pierre
Appearances: 1984 B2; 1985 B; 1987 B,PNG; 1988 B2
ALARD, GUY
Tours: 1981
World Cup: 1977
Appearances: 1977 W,E,**B,A,NZ**; 1978 E; 1979 W,E,PNG; 1981 NZ,A2
ALESINA, Adolphe
Appearances: 1968 B; 1971 b,nz; 1974 B
ALONSO, Richard
Appearances: 1972 B; 1974 B
ALVERNHE, Yves
Appearances: 1975 **W**
AMBERT, Marc
Tours: 1981
Appearances: 1981 A,PNG,B2; 1982 A; 1983 B
ANDRIEU, Guy
Appearances: 1969 B
ANGLADE, Michel
World Cup: 1972, 1975
Appearances: 1972 **NZ,a**; 1975 E,W,**W,E,A**
ARMAND, Jean-Marie
Appearances: 1968 B
ARNE, Rene
Appearances: 1971 B

BACO, Patrick
Appearances: 1986 B2
BAILE, Christian
World Cup: 1977
Appearances: 1978 E; 1980 W,E
BALOUP, Dominique
Appearances: 1983 B; 1984 B2; 1985 B

BARCELLI, Aime
Appearances: 1974 B
BEGOU, Yves
Appearances: 1969 B,W,E; 1970 W
BERGE, Denis
Appearances: 1985 NZ; 1986 b,B
BERNABE, Thiery
Appearances: 1981 b; 1984 B; 1985 b,NZ; 1986 B2,A2; 1987 B2
BERNARD: Didier
Tours: 1981
Appearances: 1983 B2; 1984 B2
BERTELOITE, Gaston
Appearances: 1987 B
BEZARD, Jean-Louis
Tours: 1981
Appearances: 1981 NZ
BIENES, Denis
Appearances: 1987 B; 1988 b
BIFFI, Roger
World Cup: 1970
Appearances: 1969 E; 1970 W,E,**NZ,A**; 1972 B
BONAL, Elie
World Cup: 1970, 1972, 1975
Appearances: 1970 **NZ,B**; 1971 nz; 1975 E,W,**W,E,NZ**
BONAL, Jean-Marie
World Cup: 1972
Appearances: 1971 B; 1972 **NZ,B,A**
BONET, Floreal
World Cup: 1970
Appearances: 1970 **NZ,b,A**; 1972 B
BONET, Georges
Appearances: 1968 b; 1973 A2; 1974 B,b
BONET, Herve
World Cup: 1977
Appearances: 1977 W,E,**B**
BONNERY, Louis
Appearances: 1969 B,W
BORREIL, Gerard
Appearances: 1978 A2
BOSC, Jean-Marie
Appearances: 1975 **E**
BOURREL, Frederic
Appearances: 1987 PNG; 1988 B
BOURRET, Jean-Marc
World Cup: 1977
Appearances: 1977 W,E,**A**; 1978 W,A; 1979 W,PNG2; 1980 E,NZ2
BRET, Serge
Appearances: 1986 a
BRIAL, Jean-Louis
World Cup: 1977
BRUNET, Lambert
Appearances: 1973 A
BUCCHI, Guy
Appearances: 1975 **E**

CABERO, Jacques
World Cup: 1970
Appearances: 1968 B; 1970 E,NZ,B,A; 1971 B
CALLE, Jose
World Cup: 1975, 1977
Appearances: 1968 B; 1971 NZ; 1973 A; 1974 B;
1975 **NZ2,A2,E,W**
CAMIADE, Daniel
Appearances: 1971 NZ
CAPDOUZE, Jean
World Cup: 1970
Appearances: 1969 B,W,E; 1970 W,E,**NZ,B,A**;
1971 B,NZ3; 1972 B2
CARAVACA, Manuel
Tours: 1981
World Cup: 1977
Appearances: 1977 W,E,**A,NZ**; 1981 w,E,NZ2,PNG;
1982 a2; 1984 b
CARIAS, Patrick
Appearances: 1969 B
CARRE, Christian
Appearances: 1973 A2
CASSIN, Michel
World Cup: 1975, 1977
Appearances: 1975 E,W,**NZ,A**; 1977 W,E,B,A,NZ;
1978 W,E
CASTANON, Delphin
Tours: 1981
Appearances: 1978 A2; 1979 W,E,png; 1980 W;
1981 W,E,A,PNG
CASTEL, Jean-Louis
Appearances: 1975 w; 1978 A; 1979 PNG
CENET, Guy
Appearances: 1971 NZ2; 1972 B
CHABERT, Yves
Appearances: 1968 B
CHANTAL, Max
Tours: 1981
World Cup: 1977
Appearances: 1977 A; 1979 PNG2; 1980 W,E;
1981 W,E,NZ2,A2,PNG; 1982 A2; 1983 B2;
1984 B2; 1985 B2,NZ2; 1986 B2,A2
CHAUVET, Patrick
World Cup: 1977
Appearances: 1975 **NZ,A**; 1977 W,**B**
CLAR, Jean-Pierre
World Cup: 1970
Appearances: 1969 B,W,E; 1970 W,E,**NZ,B,A**;
1971 B2,NZ; 1972 B
CLERGEAU, Philippe
Appearances: 1975 a
COLOGNI, Jean-Jacques
World Cup: 1977
Appearances: 1973 A; 1977 E,**B,NZ**; 1978 E; 1982 A;
1983 b

COQUAND, R.
World Cup: 1970
COSTALS, Serge
Appearances: 1981 B
COUSTON, Didier
Appearances: 1985 B,NZ2; 1986 B2,A; 1987 B
CREMOUX, Gerard
World Cup: 1970 •
Appearances: 1969 E; 1970 **B**
CROS, Jean-Pierre
World Cup: 1970
Appearances: 1969 B,W,E; 1970 W,E,**NZ,B,A**;
1971 B2,NZ
CURT, Bernard
World Cup: 1975
Appearances: 1975 E,W,**W2,E,a,A**; 1977 E

DANIEL, Henri
Tours: 1981
World Cup: 1977
Appearances: 1977 W,E,B; 1978 E,A2;
1979 W,E,PNG2; 1980 E,NZ; 1981 NZ2,A,B2;
1982 A
DAUPHIN, Serge
Appearances: 1983 b
DELAUNAY, Guy
Tours: 1981
Appearances: 1980 nz; 1981 NZ2,B; 1982 A2; 1983 B;
1987 PNG; 1988 B2
De MATOS, Maurice
Appearances: 1973 A; 1975 **E**
De NADAI, Francis
World Cup: 1970, 1972, 1975
Appearances: 1968 B; 1969 B,E; 1970 W,E,**nz,B,A**;
1971 B2,NZ3; 1972 **NZ,B,A**; 1974 B;
1975 **W,E,NZ,A**
DIVET, Daniel
Appearances: 1987 PNG
DUMAS, Andre
World Cup: 1975
Appearances: 1975 **NZ,A**
DUMAS, Gilles
Appearances: 1986 B2,A,a; 1987 B,png; 1988 B
DUTHIL, Francis
Appearances: 1975 E

ENTAT, Patrick
Appearances: 1986 B2,A
ESPUGNA, Dominique
Appearances: 1985 NZ2; 1986 B2,A; 1987 B2; 1988 B2

FEDOU, Daniel
Appearances: 1972 b
FERREN, Andre
Appearances: 1968 B
FOURCADE, Philippe
Appearances: 1982 A
FOURQUET, Philippe
Tours: 1981
Appearances: 1981 e,NZ,A; 1983 B; 1984 B2; 1985 B2;
  1986 B2,A; 1988 B
FRAISSE, David
Appearances: 1987 PNG; 1988 B
FRANC, Jacques
World Cup: 1972
Appearances: 1972 **NZ,B,A:** 1973 A2; 1974 B
FRATTINI, Marius
World Cup: 1972
Appearances: 1968 B; 1972 **NZ,A;** 1973 a

GARCIA, Guy
World Cup: 1977
Appearances: 1975 **E;** 1977 **A,NZ;** 1980 nz
GARDON, Roger
Appearances: 1971 NZ; 1974 B
GARRIGUE, Roger
World Cup: 1970
Appearances: 1969 B,W,E; 1970 W,E,**NZ,A;** 1971 B;
  1973 A2
GARZINO, Jacques
World Cup: 1972
Appearances: 1972 **NZ,A;** 1974 B
GAYE, Bernard
Appearances: 1979 PNG2
GAYRAL, Jacques
Appearances: 1971 NZ
GESTAS, Philippe
Appearances: 1986 A; 1988 bB
GINE, Jose
Tours: 1981
Appearances: 1978 W,E; 1979 PNG2; 1980 W,E;
  1981 W,E,NZ2,A,B2
GIRARDET, Laurent
Tours: 1981
Appearances: 1981 B
GLEYZES, Serge
World Cup: 1972, 1975
Appearances: 1971 NZ3; 1972 B2,**NZ,B,A:** 1973 aA;
  1974 B; 1975 E,**W,E,NZ,A:** 1977 W
GONZALES, Antoine
World Cup: 1975
Appearances: 1975, W**NZ2,A,W;** 1978 W,E
GONZALES, Jean-Marc
Appearances: 1979 W,PNG; 1980 W,E
GONZALES, Michel
Appearances: 1975 **E**
GONZALES, Pierre
Tours: 1981
Appearances: 1981 nz

GORSE, Roland
Appearances: 1978 W
GRECHI, Jean Francois
Appearances: 1975 **E,NZ,A,W**
GRESEQUE, Ivan
Tours: 1981
Appearances: 1978 A; 1980 W,E,NZ2;
  1981 W,A2,PNG: 1982 A2; 1983 B; 1985 B2,NZ
GRUPPI, Jacques
World Cup: 1970
Appearances: 1969 w,E; 1970 W,**A;** 1971 B2
GUASCH, Bruno
Appearances: 1984 b; 1985 NZ2
GUIGUE, Jacques
World Cup: 1977
Appearances: 1977, W,E,**B,A,NZ;** 1978 W,E;
  1979 PNG: 1981 B; 1982 A2; 1983 B2
GUILHEM, Bernard
World Cup: 1972
Appearances: 1971 NZ2; 1972 B,**NZ,B,a;**
  1975 **NZ,A,W;** 1977 W; 1978 E
GUIRAUD, Germain
Appearances: 1970 **B;** 1971 NZ
GUIRAUD, Herve
Tours: 1981
Appearances: 1980 NZ2; 1981 W,E,NZ2,Aa,PNG;
  1982 A2; 1983 bB

HERMET, Didier
Tours: 1981
World Cup: 1975
Appearances: 1971 B; 1972 B; 1974 B;
  1975 E,W,**W,E,nz;** 1978 A2; 1979 W,E,PNG2

IMBERT, Bernard
Tours: 1981
Appearances: 1980 NZ; 1981 A
IMBERT, Jacky
Tours: 1981
World Cup: 1977
Appearances: 1977 **nz;** 1979 png; 1981 nz,A2; 1983 B
IMBERT, Jean-Marie
World Cup: 1972, 1975, 1977
Appearances: 1971 B,NZ; 1972 B2,**B;** 1974 B;
  1975 E,W,**W2,E,NZ2,A2,E;** 1977 **a,NZ;**
  1978 W,E

JEAN, Bernard
Appearances: 1985 B

KAMINSKI, Etienne
Appearances; 1981 b; 1982 A; 1983 B
KAMINSKI, Fernand
World Cup: 1975
Appearances: 1974 B; 1975 E,**W,E,A**
KHEDIMI, Mathieu
Appearances; 1987 PNG; 1988 B2

LACOSTE, Jean-Pierre
Appearances: 1975 **W2,E**
LAFFARGUE, Michel
Appearances: 1975 **E;** 1978 W
LAFORGUE, Francis
Appearances: 1983 B; 1985 B,NZ; 1986 aA
LAFORGUE, Guy
Tours: 1981
Appearances: 1979 w; 1981 NZ,B; 1982 A2; 1983 B2;
  1984 B2; 1985 B2,NZ2; 1986 B2,A2; 1987 PNG
LAROCHE, Paul
Appearances: 1986 B2
LASKAWIEC, Christian
World Cup: 1977
Appearances: 1972 B; 1977 **W,B,A**
LASKAWIEC, Gabriel
Appearances: 1975 E,w; 1978 w
LASSALE, Christian
Appearances: 1978 W
LAUMOND, Christian
Appearances: 1978 A2; 1979 W,E,PNG2;
  1980 W,E,NZ; 1982 aA
LAVIGNE, Guy
Appearances: 1971 B
LAVILLE, Michel
Appearances: 1981 bB; 1982 a; 1983 B
LEDRU, Jean-Rene
Appearances: 1974 B
LOUBET, Serge
Appearances: 1978 W

MACALLI, Christian
Tours: 1981
Appearances: 1981 W,E,NZ2,A2,PNG,B2; 1982 A2;
  1983 B2; 1985 B2
MAGAGNIN, Jean-Pierre
Appearances: 1970 W,E
MAIQUE, Michel
World Cup: 1975
Appearances: 1974 B; 1975 W,**A,w;** 1978 A2;
  1979 WE
MALACAMP, Andre
Tours: 1981
Appearances: 1978 A2, 1979 W,E,PNG: 1980 W,NZ2;
  1981 png
MANTESE, Yannick
Appearances: 1985 NZ; 1987 B
MANTOULAN, Claude
Appearances: 1968 B; 1969 B,W; 1970 W
MARRACQ, Henri
Appearances: 1968 B; 1969 b,W,E
MARSOLAN, Serge
World Cup: 1970, 1972
Appearances: 1968 B; 1969 B,W,E;
  1970 W,E,**NZ,B,A;** 1971 B2; NZ3;
  1972 B,**NZ,B,A;** 1973 A2; 1974 B

MARTY, Jean-Claude
Appearances: 1973 A2; 1974 B2
MAURY, Alain
Appearances: 1986 B,A
MAYORGAS, Jean-Claude
World Cup: 1975, 1977
Appearances: 1975 **NZ,W**
MAZARD, Herve
World Cup: 1970
Appearances: 1969 B,W; 1970 W,**NZ,B;** 1971 B
MAZARE, Michel
World Cup: 1972
Appearances: 1972 **A;** 1973 A; 1975 E; 1980 W,E
MENDES, Luc
Appearances: 1985 b
MEURIN, Jean Louis
Appearances: 1984 B; 1985 B
MOLINER, Jacques
Appearances: 1987 B,PNG; 1988 Bb
MOLINIER, Michel
World Cup: 1970, 1972
Appearances: 1969 W,E; 1970 W,E,**NZ,B,A;**
  1971 B2,NZ3; 1972 B2,**NZ,B,A;** 1973 A2;
  1974 B2; 1975 W,**W,E**
MONTGAILLARD, Pierre
Appearances: 1985 B,NZ2; 1987 PNG; 1988 B2
MOUSSARD, Michel
World Cup: 1977
Appearances: 1974 B; 1975 **a,W,nz;** 1977 **nz**
MOYA, Jose
World Cup: 1977
Appearances: 1977 E,**B,A,NZ;** 1978 A2;
  1979 W,E,PNG; 1981 W,E

NAUDO, Michel
Tours: 1981
Appearances: 1978 A2; 1979 E; 1980 W;
  1981 W,E,NZ
NAUROY, Patrick
Appearances: 1979 PNG2

PALANQUE, Marc
Appearances: 1984 B; 1985 NZ2; 1986 B2; 1987 B2
PALISSES, Roger
Appearances: 1984 B; 1985 B2, NZ2; 1986 A2; 1987 B
PALLARES, Serge
Appearances: 1985 B2,NZ2; 1986 b
PELLERIN, Daniel
World Cup: 1970
Appearances: 1970 **b,A**
PERE, Marcel
Appearances: 1971 B
PEREZ, Andre
Tours: 1981
Appearances: 1981 NZ,a,PNG,B; 1982 A; 1984 B2;
  1985 B,nz2; 1987 B2

259

PEREZ, S
Appearances: 1985 nz
PIERRE, Francis
Appearances: 1972 B; 1974 B2
PILLON, Marcel
Tours: 1981
Appearances: 1975 **NZ,A;** 1978 W;
  1980 W,NZ2; 1981 W,E,NZ,A,PNG,B
PONS, Cyril
Appearances: 1987 B,PNG; 1988 B2
POUGEAU, Jean-Philippe
Appearances: 1987 PNG; 1988 B2
PRUNAC, Didier
Appearances: 1983 b
QUINTILLA, Jean-Louis
Appearances: 1971 NZ
RABOT, Jean-Luc
Appearances: 1986 b2,A; 1987 B2,PNG
RATIER, Hugues
Tours: 1981
Appearances: 1980 NZ2; 1981 W,E,NZ2,A2,PNG,B;
  1984 B; 1985 B2,NZ2; 1986 A2; 1987 B2,PNG;
  1988 B2
REBUJENT, Raymond
Appearances: 1968 B
RIBERE, Francis
Appearances: 1971 NZ
RIVES, Patrick
Appearances: 1973 Aa; 1974 B
ROCCI, Patrick
Appearances: 1987 b
RODRIGUEZ, Guy
World Cup: 1972, 1977
Appearances: 1972 **B;** 1977 **b,a;** 1978 W
RODRIGUEZ, Sebastian
Tours: 1981
Appearances: 1980 W,E; 1981 W,E,NZ2,A2,PNG,B2;
  1986 A
ROOSEBROUCK, Joel
Tours: 1981
World Cup: 1977
Appearances: 1977 w,**B,A,NZ;** 1978 E,a; 1979 PNG;
  1980 W,E,NZ2; 1981 W,E,NZ,A,PNG,B2;
  1982 A2; 1983 B2
ROUANET, Francis
Appearances: 1974 b
RUIZ, Andre
World Cup: 1970, 1972, 1975, 1977
Appearances: 1970 **NZ,B;** 1971 NZ; 1972 B2,**NZ,B,A;**
  1973 A2; 1974 B; 1975 **NZ2,A2,E;** 1977 **B,NZ**
SABATIE, Christian
World Cup: 1970
Appearances: 1969 W,e; 1970 W,E,**NZ,B,A;**
  1971 B2,NZ; 1972 B2
SABOUREAU, Pierre
World Cup: 1977
Appearances: 1968 B; 1971 NZ; 1977 E

SAURET, Jean-Pierre
World Cup: 1972, 1977
Appearances: 1971 B,NZ; 1972 B2,**B;** 1973 A2;
  1975 **NZ,A,W;** 1977 W,E,**B,A,NZ;** 1978 E
SCICCHITANO, Christian
Appearances: 1981 B2; 1983 B; 1984 B2; 1986 A;
  1987 B
SERRANO, Victor
World Cup: 1972
Appearances: 1971 bB, NZ2nz; 1972 B2,**NZ,B,A;**
  1973 a; 1975 E,W,**W,E**
SIRE, Jean-Pierre
Appearances: 1978 E; 1979 E; 1980 NZ2
SOLAL, Patrick
Appearances: 1981 B; 1982 A2; 1983 B; 1984 B2
SOLIER, Jean-Louis
Appearances: 1971 NZ; 1975 E,W
STORER, Yves
Appearances: 1983 B2; 1986 A; 1987 b

TERRATS, Rene
World Cup: 1975, 1977
Appearances: 1971 NZ; 1975 e, W,**W2,E2,NZ2,A2;**
  1977 **A,NZ**
THENEGAL, Charles
Appearances: 1973 A; 1975 **e,NZ,A**
THERON, Max
Appearances: 1971 NZ

TISSEYRE, Marc
Appearances: 1988 B2
TITEUX, Serge
Appearances: 1985 bB,NZ2; 1986 B2,A2; 1987 b
TOUCHAGUES, Alain
Appearances: 1979 E
TOUJAS, Raymond
World Cup: 1972
Appearances: 1968 b; 1972 B,**NZ,B,A**
TRANIER, Francis
World Cup: 1975
Appearances: 1975 **W,E,A,NZ;** 1978 E,A2; 1979 W;
  1980 E
TREMOUILLE, Jean-Pierre
Appearances: 1975 E,NZ,A,W; 1980 NZ; 1981 W
TRINQUE, Patrick
Appearances: 1984 B; 1987 B

VERDES, Daniel
Appearances: 1986 A2; 1987 B2,png; 1988 B2
VERDIERES, Dominique
Appearances: 1980 NZ; 1981 B; 1985 B
VIGOUROUX, Guy
Appearances: 1975 E,W,e
VILA, Jean-Jacques
Tours: 1981
Appearances: 1980 NZ2; 1981 A

FRANCE TOURS OF AUSTRALIA, NEW ZEALAND and PAPUA NEW GUINEA

1951

	P	W	D	L	F	A
Australia	21	15	3	3	582	357

Won Test series 2-1

New Zealand	7	6	0	1	124	62

Lost Test

1955

Australia	25	15	0	10	615	462

Won Test Series 2-1

New Zealand	8	4	0	4	150	129

Drew Test series 1-1

1960

Australia	22	12	2	8	422	390

Drew Test series 1-1-1

New Zealand	9	6	0	3	180	83

Lost Test series 2-0

1964

Australia	25	9	0	16	402	516

Lost Test series 3-0

New Zealand	10	6	0	4	157	117

Lost Test series 3-0

WALIGUNDA, Eric
Appearances: 1978 A2; 1979 W,E,PNG2; 1981 E,B
WOSNIAK, Patrick
Appearances: 1984 B2; 1986 A

ZALDUENDO, Charles
Tours: 1981
World Cup: 1972, 1975
Appearances: 1971 NZ; 1972 **nz,b,A;** 1974 B; 1975 e,w,**NZ2,aA;** 1978 A2w; 1979 W,E,pPNG; 1980 NZnz; 1981 PNG,B; 1982 A

1981

Australia	6	1	0	5	40	141

Lost Test series 2-0

New Zealand	7	5	0	2	89	93

Lost Test series 2-0

Papua New Guinea	2	1	1	0	35	27

Drew Test

● France's World Cup squads also played extra matches Down Under as follows:-
1968 In Australia: Beat Western Suburbs (Sydney) 13-12.
1975 In Australia: Beat Lithgow/Oberon 24-17; lost to Monaro 26-0.
In New Zealand: Lost to Auckland 9-3.
1977 In Australia: Lost to Brisbane 14-12, Toowoomba 14-10, Newcastle 19-12.
In New Zealand: Beat Wellington 8-0.
In Papua New Guinea: Lost unofficial Test 37-6.
● Shortly before Rugby League was founded in France in 1934 they sent a squad on a short tour of England to gain experience.
A French squad also made a three-match trip to England in 1982 as part of their build-up for Test matches against Australia.
Neither of these trips are regarded officially as full tours.

FRANCE TOUR SQUADS TO AUSTRALIA AND NEW ZEALAND
The 1981 tour also included two matches in Papua New Guinea. **Captains in Bold**

1951
Puig-Aubert

M. Andre
Puig-Aubert
A. Audobert
P. Bartoletti
M. Bellan
A. Beraud
E. Brousse
R. Caillou
G. Calixte
V. Cantoni
G. Comes
R. Contrastin
J. Crespo
G. Delaye
J. Dop
R. Duffort
C. Galaup
G. Genoud
O. Lespes
M. Lopez
M. Martin
L. Mazon
J. Merquey
F. Montrucolis
R. Perez
E. Ponsinet
F. Rinaldi
C. Teisseire

Manager: A. Blain
Coaches: J. Duhan
　　　　 R. Samatan
1964
B. Fabre

G. Ailleres
P. Azalbert
M. Bardes
F. Bertrand
A. Bourreil
M. Boule
H. Chamorin
A. Carrere
H. Castel
E. Duseigneur
S. Estiau
R. Eramouspe
J. Etcheberry
B. Fabre
L. Faletti
R. Garnung
J. Graciet
J. Lapoterie
H. Larrue
J-P. Lecompte
C. Mantoulan
F. Mas

1955
J. Merquey

A. Audobert
G. Benausse
G. Berthomieu
F. Cantoni
A. Carrere
R. Contrastin
G. Delaye
A. Delpoux
J. Dop
A. Ducasse
C. Duple
J. Fabre
R. Guilhem
J. Jammes
A. Jiminez
V. Larroude
F. Levy
S. Menichelli
J. Merquey
F. Montrucolis
R. Moulis
J. Pambrun
R. Rey
A. Save
A. Savonne
C. Teisseire
J. Vanel
M. Voron

Manager: A. Blain
Coaches: J. Duhau
　　　　 R. Duffort

J. Panno
P. Plo
C. Sabatie
G. Savonne
L. Verge
J. Villeneuve

Managers: J. Barres
　　　　　 A. Blain
Coaches: R. Duffort
　　　　 F. Bergeze

1981
J. Roosebrouck

G. Alard
M. Ambert
D. Bernard
J.L. Bezard
M. Caravaca
D. Castanon
M. Chantal
H. Daniel
G. Delaunay

1960
A. Jiminez

J. Barthe
G. Benausse
R. Benausse
M. Bescos
A. Boldini
A. Casas
J. Darricau
J. Dubon
R. Eramouspe
B. Fabre
G. Fages
A. Foussat
R. Gruppi
J. Guiraud
A. Jiminez
A. Lacaze
P. Lacaze
R. Majoral
C. Mantoulan
A. Marty
Y. Mezard
R. Moulinas
A. Perducat
L. Poletti
A. Quaglio
F. Rossi
A. Vadon
J. Verges

Managers: A. Blain
　　　　　 G. Vassal
Coaches: J. Duhau
　　　　 R. Duffort
P. Fourquet
J. Gine
H. Guiraud
L. Giradet
P. Gonzales
I. Greseque
D. Hermet
B. Imbert
J. Imbert
G. Laforgue
C. Macalli
A. Malacamp
M. Naudo
A. Perez
M. Pillon
H. Ratier
S. Rodriguez
J. Roosebrouck
J. Vila
C. Zalduendo

Manager:
Coaches: L. Bonnery
　　　　 R. Garrigue

262

FRANCE WORLD CUP SQUADS

Captains in Bold

1954 in France	1957 in Australia	1960 in England
Puig-Aubert	**J. Merquey**	**J. Barthe**
Puig-Aubert	A. Appelian	J. Barthe
J. Audoubert	G. Benausse	A. Boldini
G. Benausse	G. Berthomieu	A. Casas
V. Cantoni	H. Delhoste	J. Dubon
A. Carrere	F. Ferrero	R. Erramouspe
R. Contrastin	J. Foussat	G. Fages
J. Crespo	G. Husson	Y. Gourbal
G. Delaye	R. Jean	R. Gruppi
R. Guilhem	A. Jiminez	J. Guiraud
A. Jiminez	F. Levy	A. Lacaze
J. Krawzyk	R. Medus	C. Mantoulan
J. Merquey	J. Merquey	A. Marty
J. Pambrun	A. Parent	J. Merquey
F. Rinaldi	A. Rives	Y. Mezard
A. Save	J. Rouqueyrol	L. Poletti
C. Teisseire	A. Save	A. Quaglio
G. Verdier	G. Verdie	R. Rey
M. Voron	M. Voron	A. Vadon
Manager: A. Blain	Manager: A. Blain	Manager: A. Blain
Coaches: J. Duhau	Coach: J. Duhau	Coaches: R. Duffort
R. Duffort		D. Duhau

1968 in Australia and New Zealand	1970 in England	1972 in France
G. Ailleres	**J-P. Clar**	**F. de Nadai**
G. Ailleres	R. Biffi	M. Anglade
A. Alesina	E. Bonal	E. Bonal
Y. Begou	F. Bonet	J. Bonal
J. Capdouze	J. Cabero	J. Franc
J-P. Clar	J. Capdouze	M. Frattini
J. Cros	J-P. Clar	J. Garzino
A. Ferren	R. Coquand	S. Gleyzes
M. Frattini	G. Cremoux	B. Guilhem
R. Garrigue	J. Cros	J-M. Imbert
J. Gruppi	R. Garrigue	S. Marsolan
J. Lecompte	J. Gruppi	M. Mazare
J. Ledru	G. Guiraud	M. Molinier
H. Marracq	S. Marsolan	F. de Nadai
H. Mazard	H. Mazard	G. Rodriguez
M. Molinier	M. Molinier	A. Ruiz
F. De Nadai	F. de Nadai	J. Sauret
D. Pellerin	D. Pellerin	V. Serrano
C. Sabatie	A. Ruiz	R. Toujas
V. Serrano	C. Sabatie	C. Zalduendo
Managers: J. Guiraud	Manager: R. Forges	Manager:
F. Soubie	Coach:	Coach:
Coach: R. Lacoste		

**1975 in Australia
and New Zealand**

J. Calle
M. Anglade
E. Bonal
J. Calle
M. Cassin
B. Curt
A. Dumas
S. Gleyzes
A. Gonzales
D. Hermet
J-M. Imbert
F. Kaminski
M. Maique
J-C. Mayorgas
F. de Nadai
A. Ruiz
R. Terrats
F. Tranier
C. Zalduendo
Manager: R. Forges
Coach: Puig-Aubert

**1977 in Australia
and New Zealand**

J. Calle
G. Alard
C. Baile
H. Bonet
J. Bourret
J. Brial
J. Calle
M. Caravaca
M. Cassin
M. Chantal
P. Chauvet
J. Cologni
H. Daniel
G. Garcia
J. Guigue
J. Imbert
J-M. Imbert
C. Laskaweic
J. Mayorgas
M. Moussard
J. Moya
G. Rodriguez
J. Roosebrouck
A. Ruiz
P. Saboureau
J. Sauret
R. Terrats
Manager: P. De Jean
Coach: Y. Begou

● The following players also appeared in the 1975
World Cup in Europe but did not tour Down Under:
Y. Alvernhe, J. Bosc, G. Buchi, P. Chauvet, P.
Clergeau, M. De Matos, F. Duthill, G. Garcia, J.
Gechi, B. Guilhem, M. Laffargue, J. Lacoste, M.
Molinier, M. Moussard, M. Pillan, J. Sauret, V.
Serrano, C. Thenegal, J. Tremoulille, G. Vigouroux.
Non-playing substitutes: J. Castel, G. Laskawieck

RECORDS IN TEST, WORLD CUP AND EUROPEAN CHAMPIONSHIP

For France
Highest score: 42-13 v. England, European
Championship at Marseilles November 25, 1951
(Also widest margin win)
Most tries in a match: No player has scored more than
3
Most goals in a match: 8 by P. Lacaze v. Australia,
First Test at Paris October 31, 1959
Most points in a match: 16 by P. Lacaze (As above)
Most appearances: 45 by Puig-Aubert (1946-1956)
Biggest attendance: 37,471 v. Britain, World Cup at
Toulouse November 7, 1954

Against France
Highest score: 56-6 v. Australia, Second Test at
Brisbane July 2, 1960
Widest margin: 52-0 v. Australia, Second Test at
Carcassonne December 13, 1986
Most tries in a match: 4 by A. Murphy (Britain), First
Test at Leeds March 14, 1959. 4 by K. Fielding
(England), World Cup at Bordeaux October 11,
1975. 4 by D. Shearer (Australia), Second Test at
Carcassonne December 13, 1986
Most goals in a match: 10 by B. Ganley (Britain),
Second Test at Wigan November 23, 1957. 10 by
K. Barnes (Australia), Second Test at Brisbane
July 2, 1960
Most points in a match: 21 (9g, 1t) by B.L. Jones
(Britain), First Test at Leeds January 26, 1957. 21
(9g, 1t) by N. Fox (Britain), Second Test at
Wigan April 3, 1963. 21 (9g, 1t) by N. Fox
(Britain), Second Test at Leigh March 18, 1964

Castleford's Test prop Kevin Ward in action for 1987 Sydney Premiership winners Manly against Canberra Raiders.

DOWN UNDER

THE SYDNEY PREMIERSHIP GRAND FINAL

The Sydney Premiership is Australia's major club competition, concluding with the Grand Final.

A complicated play-off between the top five clubs in the league decides the finalists.

The league leaders, known as the Minor Premiers, are exempt from the first stage which is the preliminary semi-finals. In the minor preliminary semi-final the fourth club meets the fifth, with the major preliminary semi-final between second and third.

The minor semi-final then follows between the minor preliminary winners and the major preliminary losers. The league leaders enter for the major semi-final against the major preliminary winners.

There is then a preliminary final between the minor semi-final winners and the beaten major semi-finalists with the survivors going through to the Grand Final against the major semi-final winners.

The 1987 Grand Final was the last to be played at the Sydney Cricket Ground with the new Sydney Football Stadium replacing the traditional venue.

The Winfield Cup, as the Sydney League is known, was expanded after 1987 to include three clubs from much farther afield — Brisbane, Gold Coast and Newcastle.

BRITISH PLAYERS IN GRAND FINAL

British players who have appeared in the Grand Final are:

Dick Huddart (St. George) 1966 winners, 1 try
Dave Bolton (Balmain) 1966 losers; 1969 winners, 2 drop goals
Mervyn Hicks (Canterbury) 1967 losers
Mal Reilly (Manly) 1972 winners, 1973 winners
Tommy Bishop (Cronulla) 1973 losers

Cliff Watson (Cronulla) 1973 losers
Brian Lockwood (Canterbury) 1974 losers
Gary Stephens (Manly) 1976 winners
Steve Norton (Manly) 1976 winners
Phil Lowe (Manly) 1976 winners, 1 try
Kevin Ward (Manly) 1987 winners

Apart from Hicks all the above have also appeared in the Rugby League Challenge Cup final at Wembley. Len Killeen, the South African winger who began his Rugby League career with St. Helens, got a Grand Final winners medal with Balmain in 1969 when he kicked two goals.

There were a record three British players in the Manly side that won the 1976 Grand Final — Stephens, Norton and Lowe.

There were also three in the 1973 Grand Final, Reilly getting another winners' medal with Manly, while Bishop and Watson played for beaten Cronulla.

Australians who have achieved the Wembley-Grand Final appearance double are: Chris Anderson, Harry Bath, Graham Eadie, John Ferguson, Brett Kenny, John Muggleton and Peter Sterling.

Former St. Helens Test prop Cliff Watson, recipient of a Premiership losers' medal with Cronulla in 1973.

Manly duty...for scrum half Gary Stephens.

Manly duty...for second row man Phil Lowe.

Cronulla duty...for half back Tommy Bishop.

Canterbury duty...for packman Brian Lockwood.

1987 WINFIELD CUP

	P	W	D	L	B*	F	A	Pts
Manly-Warringah	24	18	1	5	2	553	358	41
Eastern Suburbs	24	15	1	8	2	386	353	35
Canberra	24	15	0	9	2	441	321	34
Balmain	24	14	1	9	2	469	349	33
South Sydney	24	13	1	10	2	310	342	31
Canterbury-Bankstown	24	13	0	11	2	353	316	30
Parramatta	24	12	0	12	2	417	411	28
Cronulla-Sutherland	24	11	1	12	2	390	433	27
St. George	24	10	2	12	2	394	409	26
North Sydney	24	11	0	13	2	368	401	26
Illawarra	24	8	0	16	2	374	449	20
Penrith	24	6	1	17	2	274	399	17
Western Suburbs	24	5	2	17	2	339	527	16

* Byes — Each club has two weekends without a match and are awarded two points in lieu.

LEADING SCORERS
Not including play-offs

Tries
Terry Lamb (Canterbury) 16

Goals
Ross Conlon (Balmain) 82

Points
Ross Conlon (Balmain) 184

GRAND FINAL TEAMS...A 20-year review
1967
Souths 12 K. Longbottom; M. Cleary (G. Norgard), R. Moses, E. Simms (3g), B. James; J. Lisle, I. Jones; J. Sattler, E. Walters, J. O'Neill (1t), R. McCarthy (1t), A. Scott, R. Coote
Canterbury 10 L. Johns; B. Reynolds, R. Hagan, J. Greaves, C. Gartner; R. Doyle, R. Kidd; M. Hicks, C. Brown, K. Ryan, K. Goldspink, G. Taylforth (4g), R. Raper (1g)
1968
Souths 13 E. Simms (5g); M. Cleary (1t), A. Branighan, R. Honan, B. James; D. Pittard, R. Grant; Jim Morgan, E. Walters, J.O'Neill, R. Moses, J. Sattler, R. Coote
Manly 9 R. Batty (2g); M. McLean, A. Tennant, F. Stanton, L. Hanigan; R. Fulton (1g), D. Ward; W. Hamilton, F. Jones, N. Pounder, D. Knox, John Morgan (1t), W. Bradstreet (R. Cameron)

1969
Balmain 11 R. Smithies; G. Ruebner (S. Williams 1t), A. Fitzgibbon, T. Parker, L. Killeen (2g); K. Outten, D. Bolton (2g); G. Leo, P. Boulton, B. McTaggart, J. Spencer, J. Walsh, P. Provan
Souths 2 E. Simms (1g); M. Cleary, R. Honan, K. Burke, B. James; D. Pittard, R. Grant; J. Sattler, E. Walters, J. O'Neill, R.McCarthy, R. Moses (P. Sait), R. Coote
1970
Souths 23 E. Simms (7g); M. Cleary, A. Branighan, P. Sait (R. Honan), R. Branighan (1t); D. Pittard, R. Grant (2t); J. Sattler, E. Walters, J. O'Neill, R. McCarthy, G. Stevens, R. Coote
Manly 12 R. Batty (4g); D. Mortiz, R. Fulton (2g), A. Tennant, J. McDonald; I. Martin, E. Whiley; W. Hamilton, F. Jones, J. Bucknell (A. Thomson), J. Morgan, L. Drake, R. Cameron

1971
Souths 16 E. Simms (3g, 1dg); K. Edwards, P. Sait, R. Honan, R. Branighan (1t); D. Pittard, R. Grant; J. Sattler, G. Piggins, J. O'Neill, R. McCarthy (1t), G. Stevens, R. Coote (1t)
St. George 10 G. Langlands (2g); K. Batty, R. Clapham, Ken Maddison, G. Carr; A. Branson, W. Smith; H. Eden, C. Rasmussen, G. Bowen (R. Cox), P. Fitzgerald (M. Dryen), B. Beath (1t), E. Walton (1t)
1972
Manly 19 G. Eadie; K. Irvine, R. Branighan (1t, 6g), R. Fulton (1dg), M. Brown; I. Martin, D. Ward; W. Hamilton, F. Jones (1t), J. O'Neill, A. Thomson, T. Randall, M. Reilly
Easts 14 A. McKean (4g); J. Porter, H. Cameron, M. Harris, W. Mullins (1t); J. Ballesty (1t), K. Junee; J. Armstrong, P. Moscatt, A. Beetson, G. Bandiera (L. Freier), J. Quayle, R. Coote
1973
Manly 10 G. Eadie (2g); K. Irvine, R. Branighan, R. Fulton (2t), M. Brown; I. Martin, J. Mayes; W. Hamilton, F. Jones, J. O'Neill, P. Peters, T. Randall, M. Reilly (J. Bucknell)
Cronulla 7 W. Fisher (R. Bourke 1t); R. Corcoran, S. Rogers (2g), E. Archer, R. Wear; C. Wellman, T. Bishop; C. Watson, R. Turner, G. Bowen, K. Maddison, J. Maguire, G. Pierce
1974
Easts 19 R. Fairfax; J. Porter, J. Brass (2g), M. Harris (1t), W. Mullins (1t); J. Peard (3g), J. Mayes; I. Mackay, E. Walters, K. Jones, A. Beetson (1t), B. Reilly, R. Coote
Canterbury 4 G. Dowling; C. Anderson, S. Cutler (2g), P. Winchester, T. Murphy; M. Hughes, D. Moseley; B. Lockwood, G. Peponis, W. Noonan, G. Connell, J. McDonnell, J. Peek
1975
Easts 38 I. Schubert (1t); B. Pickett (1t), J. Brass (1t), J. Rheinberger, W. Mullins; J. Peard (1t, 7g), J. Mayes (2t); I. Mackay (1t) E. Walters, G. Hedger, A. Beetson (1t) (D. O'Reilly), R. Coote (B. Reilly), K. Stevens
St. George 0 G. Langlands (R. Finch); P. Mills, R. Ferguson, E. Goodwin, J. Chapman; J. Bailey, W. Smith; B. Beath, S. Edge, H. Tatana, P. Fitzgerald, R. Stone (B. Starkey), L. Drake

1976
Manly 13 G. Eadie (5g); T. Mooney, R. Gartner, R. Fulton, R. Jackson; A. Thompson, G. Stephens; J. Harvey, M. Krilich, T. Randall, S. Norton, P. Lowe (1t) (M. Willoughby), I. Martin (G. Thoroughgood)
Parramatta 10 M. Levy; J. Porter (1t), E. Sulkowicz, J. Moran (G. Atkins), N. Glover; J. Peard (2g), J. Kolc; G. Olling, R. Hilditch, D. Fitzgerald, G. Gerard (1t) (J. Baker), R. Higgs, R. Price
1977
Parramatta 9 M. Levy; J. Porter, E. Sulkowicz (1t), M. Cronin (3g), G. Atkins; J. Peard (P. Mann), J. Kolc; G. Olling, R. Hilditch, J. Baker (D. Fitzgerald), G. Gerard, R. Higgs, R. Price
St. George 9 E. Goodwin (1t, 2g) (A. Quirk); S. Butler, G. Quinn, R. Finch, J. Chapman (1g); R. McGregor, M. Shulman (J. Bailey); B. Starkey, S. Edge, C. Young, R. Stone, J. Jansen, R. Reddy
Replay
St. George 22 E. Goodwin (6g, 1dg); S. Butler, G. Quinn, R. Finch, J. Chapman; R. McGregor, J. Bailey (1t); B. Starkey, S. Edge, C. Young, R. Stone (1t), J. Jansen (1t), R. Reddy (B. Beath)
Parramatta 0 M. Levy; J. Porter, M. Cronin, E. Sulkowicz, G. Atkins; J. Peard, J. Kolc; G. Olling, R. Hilditch, J. Baker (D. Fitzgerald), R. Higgs, G. Gerard, R. Price
1978
Cronulla 11 M. Mullane; R. Bourke, S. Rogers (4g), C. Gardner, S. Edmonds (1t); D. Chamberlin, S. Hansard; G. Stares, J. McMartin (R. Beckett), P. Khan, E. Archer, S. Kneen, B. Andrews
Manly 11 G. Eadie (4g); T. Mooney (1t), S. Knight, R. Gartner, S. Booth; A. Thompson, S. Martin; I. Thomson, M. Krilich, J. Harvey, B. Walker, T. Randall, I. Martin.
Replay
Manly 16 G. Eadie (1t, 3g, 1dg); T. Mooney, S. Knight, R. Gartner (2t), S. Booth (R. Branighan); A. Thompson, S. Martin; I. Thomson, M. Krilich, J. Harvey, B. Walker, T. Randall, I. Martin (W. Springall)
Cronulla 0 R. Bourke; C. Gardner, S. Rogers, D. Chamberlin, S. Edmonds; M. Rafferty, S. Hansard; P. Khan, R. Beckett, P. Ryan, S. Kneen, E. Archer, J. Glossop

1979
St. George 17 B. Johnson (1t); M. Brennan (1t), G. Quinn, R. Finch, M Sorridimi (S. Butler); T. Trudgett, S. Morris; B. Starkey, S. Edge, C. Young, G. Grant (4g), G. Wynn, R. Reddy (1t)
Canterbury 13 S. Cutler (1t); C. Anderson, C. Mortimer, P. Mortimer (1t), S. Gearin (1t, 2g) Garry Hughes, S. Mortimer; G. Cook (M. Hughes), G. Peponis, P. Smith, Graeme Hughes, P. Cassilles, S. Folkes
1980
Canterbury 18 G. Brentnall; C. Anderson (1t), C. Mortimer, P. Mortimer, S. Gearin (1t, 6g); Garry Hughes, S. Mortimer; J. Coveney, G. Peponis, G. Robinson, Graeme Hughes, S. Folkes, M. Hughes
Easts 4 M. Gurr; D. Michael, K. Boustead, N. Cleal, S. McFarlane; K. Wright (2g), K. Hastings; J. Harvey, J. Lang, R. Ayliffe, J. Tobin, D. O'Reilly, G. Warnecke
1981
Parramatta 20 S. McKenzie; G. Atkins (1t), M. Cronin (4g), S. Ella (1t), E. Grothe; B. Kenny (2t), P. Sterling; R. O'Reilly, S. Edge, R. Hilditch, K. Stevens (P. Taylor), J. Muggleton, R. Price (S. Sharp)
Newtown 11 P. Sigsworth; J. Ferguson, M. Ryan, B. Hetherington (1t), R. Blacklock (S. McKellar); P. Morris (1g) (K. Wilson), T. Raudonikis (1t); C. Ellis (G. Bugden), B. Jensen (J. Walters), S. Blyth, P. Gould, M. Pitman, G. O'Grady (1t)
1982
Parramatta 21 P. Taylor; N. Hunt (1t), M. Cronin (3g), S. Ella (1t), E. Grothe (1t); B. Kenny (2t) (S. Halliwell), P. Sterling; E. Bugden (G. Martine), S. Edge, C. Phelan, S. Sharp (P. Wynn), J. Muggleton (M. Laurie), R. Price
Manly 8 G. Eadie (1g); J. Ribot, C. Close, M. Blake, P. Carey; A. Thompson, P. Blake (1t); G. Gerard, R. Brown (M. Krilich), T. Randall (I. Thomson), P. Vautin, L. Boyd (1t) (B. Walker), P. McCabe
1983
Parramatta 18 P. Taylor; D. Liddiard, M. Cronin (3g), S. Ella, E. Grothe (1t); B. Kenny (2t) P. Sterling (G. Martine); S. Jurd (C. Phelan), S. Edge (D. Duffy), P. Mares (M. Laurie), P. Wynn, S. Sharp, R. Price

Manly 6 G. Eadie (1g); J. Ribot, C. Close, P. Sigsworth (1t) (M. Blake), K. Boustead; A. Thompson, P. Blake (R. Chisolm); G. Gerard, R. Brown, P. McCabe, P. Vautin (G. Ryan), N. Cleal, I. Schubert
1984
Canterbury 6 M. Potter; S. O'Brien, A. Farrar, C. Mortimer (1g), P. Mortimer; T. Lamb (G. Mullane), S. Mortimer; P. Tunks (G. Robinson), M. Bugden (1t), P. Kelly, B. Battese (D. Brohman), S. Folkes, P. Langmack
Parramatta 4 P. Taylor (R. Quinn); N. Hunt, M. Cronin (1t), S. Ella (D. Liddiard), E. Grothe; B. Kenny, P. Sterling; S. Jurd (S. Sharp) S. Edge, P. Mares (G. Mansfield), C. Phelan, J. Muggleton, R. Price.
1985
Canterbury 7 M. Potter; M. Callinan, C. Mortimer, P. Mortimer (1t), A. Farrar (1g, 1dg) (G. Mullane); M. Hagan, S. Mortimer; P. Kelly, B. Johnstone (M. Bugden), P. Tunks, (D. Gillespie), B. Battese, S. Folkes, P. Langmack
St. George 6 G. Burgess; S. Morris (1t), M. O'Connor (1g), M. Beattie (C. Johns), D. Kinchela; S. Linnane, P. Haddock (A. Neil); P. Jarvis, P. Ritchie (C. Guider), C. Young, B. Noke, G. Wynn (S. Funnell), G. O'Grady
1986
Parramatta 4 P. Taylor; M. Delroy (T. Chalmers), M. Cronin (2g), S. Ella, E. Grothe; B. Kenny, P. Sterling; G. Bugden, M. Moseley, T. Leabetter, M. Laurie, J. Muggleton (P. Wynn), R. Price
Canterbury 2 P. Sigsworth; A. Farrar, M. Hagan, C. Mortimer, S. O'Brien; T. Lamb (1g), S. Mortimer; P. Tunks (G. Robinson), M. Bugden, P. Kelly, P. Dunn, S. Folkes (D. Boyd), P. Langmack.
1987
Manly 18 D. Shearer; D. Ronson, D. Williams, M. O'Connor (1t, 5g), S. Davis; C. Lyons (1t), D. Hasler; P. Daley, M. Cochrane, K. Ward, R. Gibbs (P. Shaw), N. Cleal (M. Pocock) P. Vautin
Canberra 8 G. Belcher (1g); C. Kinna, M. Meninga (1g) (K. Walters), P. Jackson, M. Corkery; C. O'Sullivan (1t), I. Henjak; B. Todd (T. Regan), S. Walters, S. Backo, A. Gilbert, G. Coyne, D. Lance

STATE OF ORIGIN

The State of Origin matches between New South Wales and Queensland began in 1980 and are now established as a major part of the Australian Rugby League scene. Their introduction revived interest in the inter-state matches which had been dominated by New South Wales, who had won the last 15 matches by mainly wide margins.

Under the old system players appeared for the state in which they were playing club rugby at the time and this gave a big advantage to New South Wales because many of Queensland's best players were with Sydney clubs.

But in State of Origin matches players appear for the state in which they were born and this has resulted in the matches becoming more fiercely and evenly fought before increased attendances.

Queensland skipper Wally Lewis.

NEW SOUTH WALES v. QUEENSLAND RESULTS
State of Origin only.

Date	Winner	Score	Venue	Attendance
8 July 1980	Queensland	20 - 10	Brisbane	31,000
28 July 1981	Queensland	22 - 15	Brisbane	25,613
1 June 1982	New South Wales	20 - 16	Brisbane	27,326
8 June 1982	Queensland	11 - 7	Brisbane	19,435
22 June 1982	Queensland	10 - 5	Sydney	20,242
7 June 1983	Queensland	24 - 12	Brisbane	29,412
21 June 1983	New South Wales	10 - 6	Sydney	21,620
28 June 1983	Queensland	43 - 22	Brisbane	26,084
29 May 1984	Queensland	29 - 12	Brisbane	33,662
19 June 1984	Queensland	14 - 2	Sydney	29,088
17 July 1984	New South Wales	22 - 12	Brisbane	16,599
28 May 1985	New South Wales	18 - 2	Brisbane	33,011
11 June 1985	New South Wales	21 - 14	Sydney	39,068
23 July 1985	Queensland	20 - 6	Brisbane	18,825
27 May 1986	New South Wales	22 - 16	Brisbane	33,000
10 June 1986	New South Wales	24 - 20	Sydney	40,707
1 July 1986	New South Wales	18 - 16	Brisbane	21,097
2 June 1987	New South Wales	20 - 16	Brisbane	33,411
16 June 1987	Queensland	12 - 6	Sydney	42,048
15 July 1987	Queensland	10 - 8	Brisbane	33,000
6 Aug. 1987	New South Wales	30 - 18	California	12,349

SUMMARY
New South Wales won 10; Queensland won 11.
Since it became a three-match series in 1982 Queensland have won four series to New South Wales' two.

271

NEW SOUTH WALES v. QUEENSLAND RECORDS
State of Origin only

NEW SOUTH WALES

Highest score:	30-18 at California, 6 August 1987
Widest margin:	18-2 at Brisbane, 28 May 1985
Most appearances:	16+1 sub. by Brett Kenny (Parramatta)
Most tries in a match:	3 by Chris Anderson (Canterbury), 28 June 1983
Most goals in a match:	No player has kicked more than five.
Most points in a match:	18 (2t, 5g) Michael O'Connor (Manly), 28 May 1985
Biggest home attendance:	42,048 16 June 1987

QUEENSLAND

Highest score:	43-22 at Brisbane, 28 June 1983 (Also widest margin)
Most appearances:	21 by Wally Lewis (Fortitude Valley and Wynum Manly)
Most tries:	3 by Kerry Boustead (Manly), 29 May 1984
Most goals:	7 by Mal Meninga (Souths, B) 8 July 1980
Most points:	14 (7g) Mal Meninga (Souths, B) 8 July 1980
Biggest home attendance:	33,662 29 May 1984

Coaches:

New South Wales	Ted Glossop (1980, 1981, 1983); Frank Stanton (1982, 1984); Terry Fearnley (1985); Ron Willey (1986, 1987)
Queensland:	John McDonald (1980); Arthur Beetson (1981, 1982, 1983, 1984); Des Morris (1985); Wayne Bennett (1986, 1987)

English referees
English referees who have taken charge of State of Origin matches are: Billy Thompson on 8 July 1980 and Robin Whitfield on 28 June 1983.

NEW SOUTH WALES TEAMS
NSW teams in State of Origin matches against Queensland up to and including 1987. Only playing substitutes are listed. *Captain. B-Brisbane, S-Sydney

1980 Lost 10-20	**1981 Lost 15-22**	**1982 Won 20-16**
Brisbane: 8 July	**Brisbane: 28th July**	**Brisbane: 1 June**
Eadie (Manly)	Sigsworth (Newtown)	Brentnall (Canterbury)
Anderson (Canterbury)	Fahey (Easts, S)	Anderson (Canterbury)
Cronin (Parramatta) 2g	Cronin (Parramatta) 1t, 3g	Cronin (Parramatta) 4g
Rogers (Cronulla)	*Rogers (Cronulla)	Rogers (Cronulla)
Brentnall (Canterbury) 1t	Grothe (Parramatta) 2t	Niszcot (Souths, S) 2t
Thompson (Manly)	Lamb (Wests, S)	Thompson (Manly)
*Raudonikis (Newtown) 1t	Sterling (Parramatta)	S. Mortimer (Canterbury) 1t
Hambly (Souths, S)	Bowden (Newtown)	Coveney (Canterbury)
Edge (Parramatta)	Jensen (Newtown)	*Krilich (Manly)
Young (St. George)	Hilditch (Parramatta)	Young (St. George)
Cooper (Wests, S)	Tunks (Souths, S)	Rampling (Souths, S)
G. Wynn (St. George)	Boyd (Manly)	Muggleton (Parramatta)
Leis (Wests, S)	Price (Parramatta)	Price (Parramatta)
Sub: Stone (St. George)		Subs: Izzard (Penrith) 1t
		Ayliffe (Easts, S)

1982 Lost 7-11
Brisbane: 8 June
Brentnall (Canterbury)
Niszcot (Souths, S)
Rogers (Cronulla)
Izzard (Penrith) 1t
Melrose (Souths, S) 2g
Thompson (Manly)
S. Mortimer (Canterbury)
Coveney (Canterbury)
*Krilich (Manly)
Young (St. George)
Muggleton (Parramatta)
Rampling (Souths, S)
Price (Parramatta)
Subs: Kenny (Parramatta)
 Ayliffe (Easts, S)

1982 Lost 5-10
Sydney: 22 June
Sigsworth (Newtown)
Dukes (Moree) 1t
Izzard (Penrith)
Cronin (Parramatta) 1g
Fahey (Easts, S)
Kenny (Parramatta)
S. Mortimer (Canterbury)
McKinnon (Norths, S)
*Krilich (Manly)
Ayliffe (Easts, S)
Merlo (Wests, S)
Boyd (Manly)
Price (Parramatta)
Subs: Thompson (Manly)
 Young (St. George)

1983 Lost 12-24
Brisbane: 7 June
Brentnall (Canterbury)
Anderson (Canterbury)
Sigsworth (Manly) 2g
Kenny (Parramatta)
Grothe (Parramatta) 1t
Thompson (Manly)
Sterling (Parramatta)
Gerard (Manly)
*Krilich (Manly)
Bugden (Parramatta)
Boyd (Manly)
Pearce (Balmain)
Price (Parramatta)
Subs: Ella (Parramatta) 1t
 R. Brown (Manly)

1983 Won 10-6
Sydney: 21 June
Gurr (Easts, S)
Hunt (Parramatta) 1t
Cronin (Parramatta) 1g
Ella (Parramatta) 1t
Grothe (Parramatta)
Kenny (Parramatta)
Sterling (Parramatta)
Gerard (Manly)
R. Brown (Manly)
L. Johnston (Norths, S)
Miller (Cronulla)
Field (Cootamundra)
*Price (Parramatta)
Sub: Jurd (Parramatta)

1983 Lost 22-43
Brisbane: 28 June
Gurr (Easts, S)
Hunt (Parramatta)
Cronin (Parramatta) 3g
Ella (Parramatta)
Anderson (Canterbury) 3t
Kenny (Parramatta)
S. Mortimer (Canterbury) 1t
Bugden (Parramatta)
*Krilich (Parramatta)
L. Johnston (Norths, S)
Jurd (Parramatta)
Field (Cootamundra)
Miller (Cronulla)
Subs: Hastings (Easts, S)
 R. Brown (Manly)

1984 Lost 12-29
Brisbane: 29 May
Jack (Balmain)
Grothe (Parramatta)
Ella (Parramatta)
Kenny (Parramatta)
Conlon (Canterbury) 4g
Thompson (Manly)
Sterling (Parramatta)
Roach (Balmain)
Wright (N. Newcastle)
Young (St. George)
Cleal (Manly) 1t
Pearce (Balmain)
*Price (Parramatta)
Subs: Hetherington (Illawarra)
 Jarvis (St. George)

1984 Lost 2-14
Sydney: 19 June
Jack (Balmain)
Conlon (Canterbury) 1g
Kenny (Parramatta)
Farrar (Canterbury)
Grothe (Parramatta)
Lamb (Canterbury)
S. Mortimer (Canterbury)
Tunks (Canterbury)
Simmons (Penrith)
Roach (Balmain)
Cleal (Manly)
Pearce (Balmain)
*Price (Parramatta)
Subs: Ella (Parramatta)
 Jarvis (St. George)

1984 Won 22-12
Brisbane: 17 July
Jack (Balmain)
Morris (St. George)
C. Mortimer (Canterbury)
B. Johnston (St. George) 2t
Conlon (Canterbury) 5g
Kenny (Parramatta)
*S. Mortimer (Canterbury)
Roach (Balmain)
Simmons (Penrith)
Jarvis (St. George)
Walsh (St. George)
Cleal (Manly) 1t
P. Wynn (Parramatta)
Sub: Potter (Canterbury)

1985 Won 18-2
Brisbane: 28 May
Jack (Balmain)
Grothe (Parramatta)
O'Connor (St. George) 2t, 5g
C. Mortimer (Canterbury)
Ferguson (Easts, S)
Kenny (Parramatta)
*S. Mortimer (Canterbury)
Jarvis (St. George)
Elias (Balmain)
Roach (Balmain)
Cleal (Manly)
P. Wynn (Parramatta)
Pearce (Balmain)
Sub: Tunks (Canterbury)

1985 Won 21-14
Sydney: 11 June
Jack (Balmain)
Grothe (Parramatta)
O'Connor (St. George) 4g, 1d
C. Mortimer (Canterbury) 1t
Ferguson (Easts, S)
Kenny (Parramatta) 1t
*S. Mortimer (Canterbury)
Jarvis (St. George)
Elias (Balmain) 1t
Roach (Balmain)
Cleal (Manly)
P. Wynn (Parramatta)
Pearce (Balmain)
Sub: Ella (Parramatta)

1985 Lost 6-20
Brisbane: 23 July
Jack (Balmain)
Ferguson (Easts, S)
C. Mortimer (Canterbury)
O'Connor (St. George) 1g
Grothe (Parramatta)
Kenny (Parramatta)
Hasler (Manly)
Roach (Balmain)
Elias (Balmain)
Jarvis (St. George)
P. Wynn (Parramatta)
Brooks (Balmain)
*Pearce (Balmain)
Subs: Ella (Parramatta) 1t
　　　Rampling (Souths, S)

1986 Won 22-16
Brisbane: 27 May
Jack (Balmain) 1t
Morris (St. George)
C. Mortimer (Canterbury) 1t
O'Connor (St. George) 3g
Farrar (Canterbury) 1t
Kenny (Parramatta)
Sterling (Parramatta)
Roach (Balmain)
Simmons (Penrith) 1t
Tunks (Canterbury)
Folkes (Canterbury)
Cleal (Manly)
*Pearce (Balmain)
Subs: Lamb (Canterbury)
　　　Gillespie (Canterbury)

1986 Won 24-20
Sydney: 10 June
Jack (Balmain)
Hetherington (Illawarra)
O'Connor (St. George) 1t, 2g
C. Mortimer (Canterbury)
Farrar (Canterbury) 1t
Kenny (Parramatta) 1t
Sterling (Parramatta)
Roach (Balmain)
Simmons (Penrith)
Tunks (Canterbury)
Folkes (Canterbury)
Cleal (Manly) 1t
*Pearce (Balmain) 1t
Sub: Gillespie (Canterbury)

1986 Won 18-16
Brisbane: 1 July
Jack (Balmain)
B. Johnston (St. George)
O'Connor (St. George) 1t, 3g
C. Mortimer (Canterbury)
Grothe (Parramatta)
Kenny (Parramatta)
Sterling (Parramatta)
Roach (Balmain)
Simmons (Penrith)
Tunks (Canterbury) 1t
Folkes (Canterbury)
Cleal (Manly)
*Pearce (Balmain) 1t
Subs: Lamb (Canterbury)
　　　Gillespie (Canterbury)

1987 Won 20-16
Brisbane: 2 June
Jack (Balmain)
O'Connor (Manly) 2t, 2g
McGaw (Cronulla) 1t
B. Johnston (St. George)
Ettingshausen (Cronulla)
Kenny (Parramatta)
Sterling (Parramatta)
Davidson (Souths, S) 1t
Simmons (Penrith)
Jarvis (Canterbury)
Folkes (Canterbury)
Cleal (Manly)
*Pearce (Balmain)
Sub: Boyle (Souths, S)

1987 Lost 6-12
Sydney: 16 June
Jack (Balmain)
O'Connor (Manly) 1g
McGaw (Cronulla)
B. Johnston (St. George)
Farrar (Canterbury) 1t
Kenny (Parramatta)
Sterling (Parramatta)
Boyle (Souths, S)
Simmons (Penrith)
Jarvis (Canterbury)
Folkes (Canterbury)
Davidson (Souths, S)
*Pearce (Balmain)
Subs: Hasler (Manly)
　　　Langmack (Canterbury)

1987 Lost 8-10
Brisbane: 15 July
Jack (Balmain)
B. Johnston (St. George)
Kenny (Parramatta)
O'Connor (Manly) 2g
Ettingshausen (Cronulla)
Lyons (Manly)
Sterling (Parramatta)
Tunks (Canterbury)
Simmons (Penrith)
Daley (Manly)
Boyle (Souths, S) 1t
Davidson (Souths, S)
*Pearce (Balmain)
Subs: McGaw (Cronulla)
　　　Folkes (Canterbury)

1987 Won 30-18
California (U.S.A.): 6 August
Docking (Cronulla) 1t
Johnston (St. George)
McGaw (Cronulla) 1t
O'Connor (Manly) 1t, 5g
Ettingshausen (Cronulla) 1t
Lyons (Manly) 1t
*Sterling (Parramatta)
Tunks (Canterbury)
Simmons (Penrith)
Daley (Manly)
Davidson (Souths, S)
Cleal (Manly)
Langmack (Canterbury)
Subs: Hasler (Manly)
　　　Boyle (Souths, S)

NEW SOUTH WALES REGISTER
The following is a register of players who have appeared for New South Wales in the State of Origin series plus the match against Queensland in the United States of America, up to and including 1987. + indicates number of matches played as a substitute. B-Brisbane, S-Sydney.

ANDERSON, Chris (4) Canterbury
AYLIFFE, Royce (1+2) Easts, S

BOWDEN, Steve (1) Newtown
BOYD, Les (3) Manly
BOYLE, David (2+2) Souths, S
BRENTNALL, Greg (4) Canterbury
BROOKS, David (1) Balmain
BROWN, Ray (1+2) Manly
BUGDEN, Geoff (2) Parramatta

CLEAL, Noel (10) Manly
CONLON, Ross (3) Canterbury
COOPER, Bob (1) Wests, S
COVENEY, John (2) Canterbury
CRONIN, Mick (6) Parramatta

DALEY, Phil (2) Manly
DAVIDSON, Les (4) Souths, S
DOCKING, Jonathan (1) Cronulla
DUKES, Phillip (1) Moree

EADIE, Graham (1) Manly
EDGE, Steve (1) Parramattas
ELIAS, Ben (3) Balmain
ELLA, Steve (3+4) Parramatta
ETTINGSHAUSEN, Andrew (3) Cronulla

FAHEY, Terry (2) Easts, S
FARRAR, Andrew (4) Canterbury
FERGUSON, John (3) Easts, S
FIELD, Paul (2) Cootamundra
FOLKES, Steve (5+1) Canterbury

GERARD, Geoff (2) Manly
GILLESPIE, David (+3) Canterbury
GROTHE, Eric (9) Parramatta
GURR, Marty (2) Easts, S

HAMBLY, Gary (1) Souths, S
HASLER, Des (1+2) Manly
HASTINGS, Kevin (+1) Easts, S
HETHERINGTON, Brian (1+1) Illawarra
HILDITCH, Ron (1) Parramatta
HUNT, Neil (2) Parramatta

IZZARD, Brad (2+1) Penrith

JACK, Garry (12) Balmain
JARVIS, Pat (6+2) St. George 4+2, Canterbury 2
JENSEN, Barry (1) Newtown
JOHNSTON, Brian (6) St. George
JOHNSTON, Lindsay (2) Norths, S
JURD, Stan (1+1) Parramatta

KENNY, Brett (16+1) Parramatta
KRILICH, Max (5) Manly

LAMB, Terry (2+2) Canterbury 1+2, Wests, S 1
LANGMACK, Paul (1+1) Canterbury
LEIS, Jim (1) Wests, S
LYONS, Cliff (2) Manly

McGAW, Mark (3+1) Cronulla
McKINNON, Don, (1) Norths, S
MERLO, Paul (1) Wests, S
MELROSE, Tony (1) Souths, S
MILLER, Gavin (2) Cronulla
MORRIS, Steve (2) St. George
MORTIMER, Chris (7) Canterbury
MORTIMER, Steve (8) Canterbury
MUGGLETON, John (2) Parramatta

NISZCOTT, Ziggy (2) Souths, S

O'CONNOR, Michael (10) St. George 6, Manly 4

PEARCE, Wayne (12) Balmain
POTTER, Michael (+1) Canterbury
PRICE, Ray (8) Parramatta

RAMPLING, Tony (2+1) Souths, S
RAUDONIKIS, Tom (1) Newtown
ROACH, Steve (9) Balmain
ROGERS, Steve (4) Cronulla

SIGSWORTH, Phil (3) Newtown 2, Manly 1
SIMMONS, Royce (9) Penrith
STERLING, Peter (11) Parramatta
STONE, Robert (+1) St. George

THOMPSON, Alan (5+1) Manly
TUNKS, Peter (7+1), Souths 1, Canterbury 6+1

WALSH, Chris (1) St. George
WRIGHT, Rex (1) N. Newcastle
WYNN, Graeme (1) St. George
WYNN, Peter (4) Parramatta

YOUNG, Craig (4+1) St. George

QUEENSLAND TEAMS

Queensland teams in State of Origin matches against New South Wales up to and including 1987. Only playing substitutes are listed. *Captain. B-Brisbane, S-Sydney

1980 Won 20-10
Brisbane: 8 July
Scott (Easts, B)
Boustead (Easts, S) 1t
Meninga (Souths, B) 7g
Close (Redcliffe) 1t
Backer (Easts, B)
A. Smith (North, S)
Oliphant (Balmain)
Morris (Balmain)
Lang (Easts, S)
*Beetson (Parramatta)
Hancock (Easts, B)
Reddy (St. George)
Lewis (Fortitude Valley)

1981 Won 22-15
Brisbane: 28 July
Scott (Wynnum Manly)
Backer (Easts, B) 1t
Meninga (Souths, B) 1t, 5g
Close (Redcliffe) 1t
Brennan (South, S)
*Lewis (Fortitude Valley) 1t
Henrick (Norths, B)
Khan (Cronulla)
Conescu (Norths, B)
Morris (Balmain)
Hancock (Toowoomba)
McCabe (Easts, S)
Phelan (Souths, B)

1982 Lost 16-20
Brisbane: 1 June
Scott (Wynnum Manly)
Ribot (Manly) 1t
Brennan (South, S) 1t
Meninga (Souths, B) 5g
Boustead (Easts, S)
*Lewis (Fortitude Valley)
Murray (Fortitude Valley)
Khan (Easts, B)
J. Dowling (St. George)
Hancock (Souths, B)
Walker (Manly)
McCabe (Manly)
Vautin (Manly)

1982 Won 11-7
Brisbane: 8 June
Scott (Wynnum Manly) 1g
Ribot (Manly) 1t
Miles (Wynnum Manly) 1t
Quinn (Ipswich)
Backer (Easts, B)
*Lewis (Fortitude Valley)
Murray (Fortitude Valley)
Morris (Wynnum Manly)
J. Dowling (St. George)
Khan (Easts, B)
McCabe (Manly)
Hancock (Souths, B)
Carr (Wests, B)
Sub: Vautin (Manly) 1t

1982 Won 10-5
Sydney: 22 June
Brennan (Souths, S)
Boustead (Easts, S)
Miles (Wynnum Manly)
Meninga (Souths, B) 2g
Ribot (Manly)
*Lewis (Fortitude Valley) 1t
Murray (Fortitude Valley)
Khan (Easts, B)
J. Dowling (St. George)
Morris (Wynnum Manly)
McCabe (Manly)
Hancock (Souths, B) 1t
Carr (Wests, B)

1983 Won 24-12
Brisbane: 7 June
Scott (Wynnum Manly)
Ribot (Manly)
Meninga (Souths, B) 6g
Miles (Wynnum Manly)
Stacey (Easts, B)
*Lewis (Fortitude Valley) 2t
Murray (Redcliffe) 1t
Tessman (Souths, B)
Conescu (Norths, B)
Brohman (Penrith)
Niebling (Fortitude Valley)
Vautin (Manly)
D. Brown (Manly)

1983 Lost 6-10
Sydney: 21 June
Scott (Wynnum Manly)
Butler (Wynnum Manly)
Meninga (Souths, B) 1t, 1g
Miles (Wynnum Manly)
Close (Manly)
*Lewis (Fortitude Valley)
Murray (Redcliffe)
Tessman (Souths, B)
Conescu (Norths, B)
D. Brown (Manly)
Niebling (Fortitude Valley)
Fullerton-Smith (Redcliffe)
Vautin (Manly)

1983 Won 43-22
Brisbane: 28 June
Scott (Wynnum Manly) 1g
Stacey (Easts, B) 1t
Meninga (Souths, B) 6g
Miles (Wynnum Manly) 1t
Brennan (Redcliffe) 2t
*Lewis (Fortitude Valley) 1dg
Murray (Redcliffe)
Tessman (Souths, B)
Conescu (Norths, B) 1t
D. Brown (Manly) 1t
Niebling (Fortitude Valley) 1t
Fullerton-Smith (Redcliffe)
Vautin (Manly)

1984 Won 29-12
Brisbane: 29 May
Scott (Wynnum Manly)
Boustead (Manly) 3t
Meninga (Souths, B) 2g
Miles (Wynnum Manly) 1t
Close (Manly)
*Lewis (Wynnum Manly) 1t, 1dg
Murray (Redcliffe)
G. Dowling (Wynnum Manly)
Conescu (Gladstone)
D. Brown (Manly)
Niebling (Redcliffe)
Fullerton-Smith (Redcliffe)
Vautin (Manly) 1t

1984 Won 14-2
Sydney: 19 June
Scott (Wynnum Manly)
Bousted (Manly)
Close (Manly)
Miles (Wynnum Manly) 1t
Meninga (Souths, B) 3g
*Lewis (Wynnum Manly)
Murray (Redcliffe)
G. Dowling (Manly) 1t
Conescu (Gladstone)
D. Brown (Manly)
Niebling (Redcliffe)
Fullerton-Smith (Redcliffe)
Vautin (Manly)
Sub: Lindner (Souths, B)

1984 Lost 12-22
Brisbane: 17 July
Scott (Wynnum Manly)
Ribot (Manly)
Meninga (Souths, B) 2g
B. French (Wynnum Manly)
Boustead (Manly) 1t
*Lewis (Wynnum Manly)
Henrick (Fortitude Valley)
G. Dowling (Wynnum Manly)
Conescu (Gladstone)
D. Brown (Manly)
Phelan (Parramatta)
Fullerton-Smith (Redcliffe)
Lindner (Souths, B) 1t
Subs: Kellaway (Souths, B)
Currie (Wests, B)

1985 Lost 2-18
Brisbane: 28 May
Scott (Wynnum Manly)
Ribot (Redcliffe)
Meninga (Souths, B) 1g
Close (Manly)
Shearer (Manly)
*Lewis (Wynnum Manly)
Murray (Redcliffe)
G. Dowling (Wynnum Manly)
Conescu (Redcliffe)
D. Brown (Easts, S)
Vautin (Manly)
McCabe (Manly)
Lindner (Wynnum Manly)

1985 Lost 14-21
Sydney: 11 June
Scott (Wynnum Manly)
Ribot (Redcliffe)
Meninga (Souths, B) 3g
Close (Manly)
Shearer (Manly)
*Lewis (Wynnum Manly)
Murray (Redcliffe)
G. Dowling (Wynnum Manly)
Conescu (Redcliffe)
D. Brown (Easts, S)
Vautin (Manly)
Fullerton-Smith (Redcliffe)
Lindner (Wynnum Manly) 1t
Subs: Currie (Redcliffe)
I. French (Wynnum Manly) 1t

1985 Won 20-6
Brisbane: 23 July
Scott (Wynnum Manly)
Shearer (Manly) 2t
Meninga (Souths, B) 2g
Close (Manly)
Ribot (Redcliffe) 1t
*Lewis (Wynnum Manly)
Murray (Redcliffe)
G. Dowling (Wynnum Manly)
Conescu (Redcliffe)
D. Brown (Easts, S)
I. French (Wynnum Manly) 1t
Fullerton-Smith (Redcliffe)
Vautin (Manly)
Subs: Currie (Redcliffe)
Heugh (Easts, S)

1986 Lost 16-22
Brisbane: 27 May
Scott (Wynnum Manly)
Shearer (Manly)
Meninga (Canberra) 4g
Miles (Wynnum Manly) 1t
Close (Manly)
*Lewis (Wynnum Manly)
Murray (Redcliffe)
G. Dowling (Wynnum Manly) 1t
Conescu (Redcliffe)
D. Brown (Easts, S)
Niebling (Redcliffe)
Jones (Norths, S)
Lindner (Wynnum Manly)
Subs: Jackson (Souths, B)
I. French (Wynnum Manly)

1986 Lost 20-24
Sydney: 10 June
Belcher (Canberra)
Shearer (Manly) 1t
Meninga (Canberra) 2g
Miles (Wynnum Manly)
Kiss (Norths, S) 1t
*Lewis (Wynnum Manly)
Murray (Redcliffe)
Heugh (Easts, B)
Conescu (Redcliffe)
Brohman (Penrith)
Lindner (Wynnum Manly) 1t
Jones (Norths, S)
I. French (Wynnum Manly) 1t
Sub: Tessman (Easts, S)

1986 Lost 16-18
Brisbane: 1 July
Belcher (Canberra) 1t
Shearer (Manly) 1t
Meninga (Canberra)
Miles (Wynnum Manly)
Kiss (Norths, S) 1t
*Lewis (Wynnum Manly)
Murray (Redcliffe)
Tessman (Easts, S)
Conescu (Redcliffe) 1t
Heugh (Easts, B)
Niebling (Redcliffe)
Jones (Norths, S)
Lindner (Wynnum Manly)
Sub: I. French (Wynnum Manly)

1987 Lost 16-20
Brisbane: 2 June
Belcher (Canberra) 1g
Currie (Canterbury) 1t
Jackson (Canberra) 1g
Miles (Wynnum Manly)
Shearer (Manly) 1t
*Lewis (Wynnum Manly)
Langer (Ipswich)
G. Dowling (Norths, B) 1t
Conescu (Redcliffe)
Bella (Norths, S)
Gillmeister (Easts, S)
Vautin (Manly)
I. French (Norths, S)
Sub: G. Smith (Brothers)

1987 Won 12-6
Sydney: 16 June
Belcher (Canberra)
Scott (Wynnum Manly) 1t
Jackson (Canberra)
Miles (Wynnum Manly)
Shearer (Manly) 1t
*Lewis (Wynnum Manly)
Langer (Ipswich)
G. Dowling (Norths, B) 1t
Conescu (Redcliffe)
Bella (Norths, S)
Gillmeister (Easts, S)
Vautin (Manly)
Lindner (Parramatta)
Sub: I. French (Norths, S)

1987 Won 10-8
Brisbane: 15 July
Belcher (Canberra)
Scott (Wynnum Manly)
Jackson (Canberra)
Miles (Wynnum Manly)
Shearer (Manly) 1t, 1g
*Lewis (Wynnum Manly)
Langer (Ipswich)
G. Dowling (Norths, B)
Conescu (Redcliffe)
Niebling (Redcliffe)
Gillmeister (Easts, S)
Vautin (Manly)
Lindner (Parramatta) 1t
Subs: Currie (Canterbury)
I. French (Norths, S)

1987 Lost 18-30
California (U.S.A.): 6 August
Belcher (Canberra)
Currie (Canterbury) 1t
Jackson (Canberra)
Miles (Wynnum Manly) 1t
Shearer (Manly) 3g
*Lewis (Wynnum Manly)
Langer (Ipswich)
G. Dowling (Norths, B)
Conescu (Redcliffe)
Niebling (Redcliffe)
Gillmeister (Easts, S)
Vautin (Manly)
Lindner (Parramatta)
Subs: Scott (Wynnum Manly)
I. French (Norths, S)

QUEENSLAND REGISTER

The following is a register of players who have appeared for Queensland in the State of Origin series plus the match against New South Wales in the United States of America, up to and including 1987. + indicates number of matches played as a substitute. B-Brisbane, S-Sydney.

BACKER, Brad (3) Easts, B
BEETSON, Arthur (1) Parramatta
BELCHER, Gary (6) Canberra
BELLA, Martin (2) North, S
BOUSTEAD, Kerry (6) Easts, S 3; Manly 3
BRENNAN, Mitch (4) Souths, S 3; Redcliffe 1
BROHMAN, Darryl (2) Penrith
BROWN, Dave (10) Manly 6; Easts, S 4
BUTLER, Terry (1) Wynnum Manly

CARR, Norm (2) Wests, B
CLOSE, Chris (9) Manly 7; Redcliffe 2
CONESCU, Greg (17) Norths, B 4; Redcliffe 10; Gladstone 3
CURRIE, Tony (2+3) Wests, B +1; Redcliffe +1; Canterbury 2+1

DOWLING, Greg (11) Wynnum Manly 7; Norths, B 4
DOWLING, John (3) St. George

FRENCH, Brett (1) Wynnum Manly
FRENCH, Ian (3+6) Wynnum Manly 2+3; Norths, S 1+3
FULLERTON-SMITH, Wally (7) Redcliffe

GILLMEISTER, Trevor (4) Easts, S

HANCOCK, Rohan (5) Souths, B 3; Easts, B 1; Toowoomba 1
HENRICK, Ross (2) Norths, B 1; Fortitude Valley 1
HEUGH, Cavill (2+1) Easts, B

JACKSON, Peter (4+1) Canberra 4; Souths, B 1+1
JONES, Gavin (3) Norths, S

KELLAWAY, Bob (+1) Souths, B
KHAN, Paul (4) Easts, B 3; Cronulla 1
KISS, Les (2) Norths, S

LANG, John (1) Easts, S
LANGER, Allan (4) Ipswich
LEWIS, Wally (21) Wynnum Manly 13; Fortitude Valley 8
LINDNER, Bob (9) Souths, B 1; Wynnum Manly 5; Parramatta 3

McCABE, Paul (5) Easts, S 1; Manly 4
MENINGA, Mal (16) Souths, B 13; Canberra 3
MILES, Gene (14) Wynnum Manly
MORRIS, Rod (4) Balmain 2; Wynnum Manly 2
MURRAY, Mark (14) Fortitude Valley 3, Redcliffe 11

NIEBLING, Bryan (9) Fortitude Valley 3; Redcliffe 6

OLIPHANT, Greg (1) Balmain

PHELAN, Chris (2) Souths, B 1; Parramatta 1

QUINN, Graham (1) St. George

REDDY, Rod (1) St. George
RIBOT, John (8) Manly 5; Redcliffe 3

SCOTT, Colin (16+1) Wynnum Manly 15+1; Easts, B 1
SHEARER, Dale (10) Manly
SMITH, Alan (1) Norths, S
SMITH, Gary (+1) Brothers
STACEY, Steve (2) Easts, B

TESSMAN, Brad (4+1) Souths, B 3; Easts, S 1+1

VAUTIN, Paul (13+1) Manly

WALKER, Bruce (1) Manly

NEW ZEALAND TOUR 1987

New Zealand made a four-match tour of Australia and Papua New Guinea in 1987, winning all games including a Test against each country. They also beat a strong Queensland side to make it the best possible start for new coach Tony Gordon, having taken over from Graham Lowe.

The squad included three British-based players in Dean Bell (Wigan), who took over the captaincy when Ron O'Regan dropped out injured four days before departure, Mark Elia (St. Helens) and Joe Ropati (Warrington).

Players who joined British clubs after the tour were: Shane Cooper (St. Helens), Shane Horo (Leigh), Kevin Iro and Adrian Shelford (Wigan), Gary Mercer (Bradford N.) and Ross Taylor (Hull K.R.).

Date	Result	Score	Opposition	Venue	Attendance
July 5	W	44-12	Northern Rivers T: M. Horo (2), Bell (2), Taylor, Iro, Freeman, Elia, Panapa G: Mercer (3), Brown	Lismore	1,500
July 7	W	22-16	Queensland T: M. Horo (2), Elia (2) G: Iro (3)	Brisbane	5,031
July 12	W	36-22	PAPUA NEW GUINEA **Papua New Guinea:** Peter; Kerekere, Kovae (1t,3g), Numapo (Capt, 2t), Kapia; Haili, Kila; Tep, Heni (1t), Lomutopa, Waketsi, Taumaku, Kouro. Subs: Saea, Kombra **New Zealand:** Mercer; Elia (2t), Iro (3t,4g), Bell (Capt, 2t), S. Horo; Freeman, Friend; Taylor, Wallace, Todd, Shelford, M. Horo, Cooper. Subs: Stewart, Lonergan	Port Moresby	15,000
July 21	W	13-6	AUSTRALIA **Australia:** Jack; O'Connor (1g), Miles, Kenny, Shearer; Lewis (Capt), Sterling (1t); Dowling, Simmons, Tunks, Pearce, Niebling, Lindner. Subs: Johnston, Davidson **New Zealand:** Williams; Elia, Iro (2g), Bell, Mercer (1t); Cooper (1dg), Friend; Taylor (1t), Wallace, Shelford, M. Horo, Stewart, McGahan (Capt). Subs: Freeman, Lonergan	Brisbane	16,500

TOUR SUMMARY

P	W	L	T	G	Dr	Pts	T	G	Dr	Pts
4	4	0	22	13	1	115	10	8	0	56

TOUR REGISTER

Player	Club	App.	Sub.	T	G	Pts
BELL, Dean (Capt)	Wigan (England)	4	—	4	—	16
BROWN, Peter	Te Atatu (Auckland)	—	1	—	1	2
COOPER, Shane	Mangere East (Auckland)	4	—	—	— (1)	1
ELIA, Mark	St. Helens (England)	4	—	5	—	20
FREEMAN, Gary	Northcote (Auckland)	3	1	1	—	4
FRIEND, Clayton	N. Sydney (NSW)	2	—	—	—	—
HARVEY, Barry	Randwick (Wellington)	1	—	—	—	—
HORO, Mark	Te Atatu (Auckland)	4	—	4	—	16
HORO, Shane	Te Atatu (Auckland)	2	—	—	—	—
IRO, Kevin	Mt Albert (Auckland)	3	1	4	9	34
LAJPOLD, George	Randwick (Wellington)	1	—	—	—	—
LONERGAN, Dean	Glenora (Auckland)	2	2	—	—	—
McGAHAN, Hugh	Eastern Suburbs (NSW)	1	—	—	—	—
MERCER, Gary	Pikiao (Bay of Plenty)	4	—	1	3	10
PANAPA, Sam	Te Atatu (Auckland)	1	—	1	—	4
ROPATI, Joe	Warrington (England)	1	—	—	—	—
SHELFORD, Adrian	Upper Hutt (Wellington)	3	—	—	—	—
STEWART, Sam	Randwick (Wellington)	3	1	—	—	—
TAYLOR, Ross	Hornby (Canterbury)	4	—	2	—	8
TODD, Brent	Canberra (NSW)	1	—	—	—	—
WALLACE, Wayne	Marist (Canterbury)	3	1	—	—	—
WILLIAMS, Darrell	Manly (NSW)	1	—	—	—	—

(1) Drop goal
Coach: Tony Gordon
Manager: John Bray

The squad included four Sydney-based players in Friend, McGahan, Todd and Williams, who joined the squad after the opening match. McGahan took over the captaincy for his one match, the Test against Australia. Four players returned home after the first two matches — Lajpold and Brown, who were injured, plus Panapa and Ropati.

Great Britain second row man Roy Powell on 1988 duty in Avignon.

GREAT BRITAIN

GREAT BRITAIN

1987-88 TEST REVIEW

Great Britain piled up a century of points in their three-Test build up to the 1988 Lions Tour Down Under.

Coach Malcolm Reilly extended his winning run to five successive Whitbread Trophy Bitter Tests with a clinical 42-0 hammering of Papua New Guinea, playing Test football in Britain for the first time, and the double over the much-improved French, with a record score in France.

Yet the triple success over the bottom two countries in the World Cup table was not deemed to be an accurate form guide for the pending 10-week summer tour featuring three Tests with Australia and one each against Papua New Guinea and New Zealand.

Reilly called on 25 players for the three encounters, giving Test débuts to eight — Karl Fairbank (Bradford N.), Paul Groves (St. Helens), Steve Hampson (Wigan), Paul Loughlin (St. Helens), Paul Medley (Leeds), Martin Offiah (Widnes), Hugh Waddell (Oldham) and David Plange (Castleford).

Britain opened their 1987-88 Test programme with a seven-try rout of the touring Kumuls in the World Cup-rated encounter at Wigan in October, Reilly taking most pleasure from nilling the opposition. *An account of the Papua New Guinea Test is featured in the earlier 1987 KUMULS section.*

Only six of the side to meet Papua were retained for the meeting with France in Avignon three months later, although Wigan, having fielded a Test record of eight players against the Kumuls, were unable to supply Joe Lydon and Andy Goodway, through suspension, and the injured Andy Gregory. Current form sides, John Player Special Trophy finalists St. Helens and Leeds, provided six of the new look line-up.

One of that sextet, Leeds centre Garry Schofield scored a last minute 90-yard interception try to give Britain a record victory on French soil, the 28 points beating the 25-14 record set 31 years earlier. Despite the record score, it was not a totally convincing performance by the British, the exciting rugby with the backs scoring all five tries being negated by poor finishing and a host of defensive errors.

Skipper Ellery Hanley's performance summed up the entire side. While he was the most dangerous attacker, twice in the first half he made the wrong decision. Having broken through in great style, the Wigan utility star held on to the ball to be tackled when a pass would have freed winger Des Drummond. Then Hanley looked a certain tryscorer until he threw out a wild, unnecessary pass that went nowhere.

The stand off finally got it right at the most vital time with Britain hanging on to an 18-14 lead in the 75th minute, supporting substitute Paul Dixon's break to finish off a 50-yard drive between the posts, substitute David Creasser adding the goal to give Britain a 10-point breathing space.

Both Britain's wingers scored a try without being over-burdened with possession. Warrington's Drummond opened the scoring after only seven minutes with a classic touchdown, centre partner Schofield unleashing him on a 75-yard sprint to outpace the French cover and allow him to canter round to the posts.

On the left flank, debutant Martin Offiah owed his first Test try to the skill of scrum half Shaun Edwards who kicked ahead in the middle of the field, regathered and lobbed a pass for the winger to have a clear 30-yard run in.

Equally important in one of the most entertaining Anglo-French meetings was the wing pair's speed in defence, Offiah twice and Drummond once stopping almost certain tries.

After debutant Loughlin had added the goal to Drummond's try, Schofield interchanged passes with full back Hampson to record a 26th minute touchdown and give Britain a 10-4 half-time lead, the French reply being two Gilles Dumas penalties. The home side opened the second half with a shock try. Drummond misfielded France's kick off and within two tackles of winning possession, the Tricolours scored their opening try as second row man Daniel Verdes went through unheeded. Dumas hit the post with his goal attempt, while Loughlin scored a penalty goal before adding the points to Offiah's try on the hour to give Britain an 18-8 lead.

Again the French rallied and a 71st minute try from skipper Hugues Ratier, goalled by Dumas, closed the margin to four points until Hanley and Schofield took Britain to their record score in the last quarter.

In probably the most disciplined Test in France, there was never a hint of trouble and only 15 penalties awarded, while Kevin Beardmore won the scrums 15-10, including three against the head, as a member of a pack which overall lacked authority. Leeds second row man Roy Powell topped the tackle count with 31 on his first full appearance while debutant prop Waddell crowned a hard-working performance by receiving the Whitbread Trophy Bitter Man of the Match award.

Two weeks later at Leeds, Britain marginally improved the scoreline to 30-12, again winning by five tries to two. Yet the British were less adventurous than at Avignon, especially after setting up France for a third consecutive massacre on English soil by racing to a 10-0 lead after only four minutes.

Ironically, with a British victory assured so early on, the wildest reception came from the French when hooker Mathieu Khedimi dashed in for a last minute try, the goal from Frederic Bourrel giving them their highest

The Great Britain squad on duty for the Whitbread Trophy Bitter Test against Papua New Guinea at Wigan in October 1987, from left to right:
Back row: Geoff Plummer (Physio), Zook Ema, Andy Goodway, Paul Medley, Karl Fairbank, John Woods, Phil Ford.
Middle row: Phil Larder (Asst. Coach), Keith Holden, Des Drummond, Brian Case, David Stephenson, Paul Groves, Colin Whitfield, Forbes McKenzie (Doctor).
Front row: Shaun Edwards, Andy Gregory, Malcolm Reilly (Coach), Ellery Hanley (Captain), Les Bettinson (Manager), Joe Lydon, Steve Hampson.

points total in Britain since the last away victory in this country 21 years ago. Such modest French achievement put Britain's performance in perspective.

Britain's centres dominated the scoring with skipper Hanley touching down twice and putting Schofield over for another, the Leeds record recruit also adding five goals.

Wigan full back Hampson received the Whitbread Trophy Bitter Man of the Match award for a performance full of flair, while clubmate Gregory was a dominant figure in the first half, opening the try account after only two minutes.

Britain's backs highlighted the double victory by scoring all 10 tries, overshadowing the forwards with only Waddell maintaining an above average profile throughout to stake a strong, late claim for a tour spot. Beardmore headed the tackle count at Leeds with 30 to add to his 14-12 scrum dominance.

Centre Philippe Fourquet took the French Man of the Match award.

1988 TOUR SQUAD

The naming of Great Britain's squad to tour Papua New Guinea, Australia and New Zealand was a staggered affair.

On 5 April coach Malcolm Reilly announced 23 selected players, with three places left vacant to be filled within three weeks from a stand-by squad of 10 players. Ellery Hanley was appointed captain.

In addition Joe Lydon was named to join the squad in mid-June after completing degree examinations.

The 23 selected players were: Kevin Beardmore (Castleford), Brian Case (Wigan), Paul Dixon (Halifax), Shaun Edwards (Wigan), Karl Fairbank (Bradford N.), Mike Ford (Oldham), Phil Ford (Bradford N.), Henderson Gill (Wigan), Andy Goodway (Wigan), Andy Gregory (Wigan), Mike Gregory (War-

rington), Paul Groves (St. Helens), Steve Hampson (Wigan), Ellery Hanley (Wigan), David Hulme (Widnes), Paul Loughlin (St. Helens), Paul Medley (Leeds), Martin Offiah (Widnes), Andy Platt (St. Helens), Roy Powell (Leeds), Garry Schofield (Leeds), David Stephenson (Leeds), Kevin Ward (Castleford), plus Joe Lydon (Wigan).

The stand-by squad was: Lee Crooks (Leeds), Des Drummond (Warrington), Deryck Fox (Featherstone R.) Roy Haggerty (St. Helens), Les Holliday (Halifax), Colin Maskill (Leeds), David Plange (Castleford), Hugh Waddell (Oldham), Ian Wilkinson (Halifax), Peter Williams (Salford).

The shock choice in the stand-by squad was Salford's former England RU stand off Peter Williams after only three matches of rugby league.

Soon after the squads were named Reilly's tour plans were hit by a series of setbacks.

Wigan full back Steve Hampson broke an arm, but it was hoped he could join the squad three or four weeks after the start of the tour. Days later club mate Andy Goodway withdrew to concentrate on his restaurant business and was replaced by Roy Haggerty.

At the start of May the three vacancies were filled by Lee Crooks and Des Drummond, who had both been left out pending fitness checks, plus Hugh Waddell. Ian Wilkinson was also brought in as cover for Hampson.

There were more problems before the party left on 16 May. Drummond and Lydon were withdrawn from the squad because they were involved in legal proceedings alleging assaults on spectators.

Carl Gibson, the Leeds utility back who was not in the stand-by squad, was called up to replace Drummond but it was decided not to replace Lydon as he had not been due to join the squad until mid-June.

An ankle injury delayed Andy Platt's departure by a week.

● Full tour details will be featured in the 1989-90 edition.

Test debutant Martin Offiah outstrips the French defence in Avignon.

Oldham prop Hugh Waddell, Whitbread Trophy Bitter Man of the Match in Avignon.

285

FIRST WHITBREAD TROPHY BITTER TEST

24 January   Avignon

GREAT BRITAIN 28   FRANCE 14

Steve Hampson (Wigan)	1.	Jean-Philippe Pougeau (St. Esteve)
Des Drummond (Warrington)	2.	Hugues Ratier (Lezignan) Capt.
Garry Schofield (Leeds)	3.	Guy Delaunay (St. Esteve)
Paul Loughlin (St. Helens)	4.	David Fraisse (Le Pontet)
Martin Offiah (Widnes)	5.	Cyrille Pons (St. Gaudens)
Ellery Hanley (Wigan) Capt.	6.	Dominique Espugna (Lezignan)
Shaun Edwards (Wigan)	7.	Gilles Dumas (St. Gaudens)
Kevin Ward (Castleford)	8.	Marc Tisseyre (Pamiers)
Kevin Beardmore (Castleford)	9.	Mathieu Khedimi (St. Esteve)
Hugh Waddell (Oldham)	10.	Pierre Ailleres (Toulouse)
Roy Powell (Leeds)	11.	Pierre Montgaillard (XIII Catalan)
Paul Medley (Leeds)	12.	Daniel Verdes (Villeneuve)
Andy Platt (St. Helens)	13.	Jacques Moliner (Lezignan)
David Creasser (Leeds)	14.	Philippe Gestas (St. Gaudens)
Paul Dixon (Halifax)	15.	Denis Bienes (St. Gaudens)

T: Schofield (2), Drummond, Offiah, Hanley

G: Loughlin (3), Creasser

Substitutions:
Dixon for Medley (65 min.)
Creasser for Loughlin (73 min.)
Manager: Les Bettinson
Coach: Malcolm Reilly

T: Verdes, Ratier

G: Dumas (3)

Substitutions:
Bienes for Fraisse (52 min.)
Gestas for Delaunay (68 min.)
Half-time: 10-4
Referee: Neville Kesha (Auckland)
Attendance: 6,000

Scorechart

Minute	Score	GB	France
7:	Drummond (T)		
	Loughlin (G)	6	0
16:	Dumas (P)	6	2
26:	Schofield (T)	10	2
37:	Dumas (P)	10	4
42:	Verdes (T)	10	8
47:	Loughlin (P)	12	8
60:	Offiah (T)		
	Loughlin (G)	18	8
71:	Ratier (T)		
	Dumas (G)	18	14
75:	Hanley (T)		
	Creasser (G)	24	14
79:	Schofield (T)	28	14
	Scrums	15	10
	Penalties	7	8

Tryscorer Des Drummond.

SECOND WHITBREAD TROPHY BITTER TEST

6 February   Leeds

GREAT BRITAIN 30

Steve Hampson (Wigan)	1.	Jean-Philippe Pougeau (St. Esteve)
David Plange (Castleford)	2.	Hugues Ratier (Lezignan) Capt.
Garry Schofield (Leeds)	3.	Philippe Fourquet (St. Gaudens)
Ellery Hanley (Wigan) Capt.	4.	Guy Delaunay (St. Esteve)
Phil Ford (Bradford N.)	5.	Cyrille Pons (St. Gaudens)
Shaun Edwards (Wigan)	6.	Dominique Espugna (Lezignan)
Andy Gregory (Wigan)	7.	Frederic Bourrel (Limoux)
Kevin Ward (Castleford)	8.	Marc Tisseyre (Pamiers)
Kevin Beardmore (Castleford)	9.	Mathieu Khedimi (St. Esteve)
Hugh Waddell (Oldham)	10.	Pierre Ailleres (Toulouse)
Roy Powell (Leeds)	11.	Pierre Montgaillard (XIII Catalan)
Paul Dixon (Halifax)	12.	Daniel Verdes(Villeneuve)
Andy Platt (St. Helens)	13.	Philippe Gestas (St. Gaudens)
David Stephenson (Leeds)	14.	Jacques Moliner (Lezignan)
Paul Medley (Leeds)	15.	Denis Bienes (St. Gaudens)

FRANCE 12

T: Hanley (2), Gregory, Schofield,
Plange
G: Schofield (5)
Substitutions:
Medley for Powell (60 min.)
Stephenson for Edwards (71 min.)
Manager: Les Bettinson
Coach: Malcolm Reilly

T: Pons, Khedimi
G: Bourrel (2)
Substitution:
Moliner for Ailleres (53 min.)
Half-time: 18-6
Referee: Neville Kesha (Auckland)
Attendance: 7,007

Scorechart

Minute	Score	GB	France
2:	Gregory (T)	4	0
4:	Hanley (T)		
	Schofield (G)	10	0
16:	Schofield (P)	12	0
26:	Pons (T)		
	Bourrel (G)	12	6
30:	Schofield (T)		
	Schofield (G)	18	6
45:	Schofield (P)	20	6
62:	Hanley (T)		
	Schofield (G)	26	6
72:	Plange (T)	30	6
79:	Khedimi (T)		
	Bourrel (G)	30	12
	Scrums	14	12
	Penalties	6	8

Tryscorer Andy Gregory.

287

TESTS

• Although early Tests were played under the titles of Northern Union or England, it is acceptable to regard them as Great Britain.
W-Win, D-Drawn, L-Lost refer to Great Britain.

GREAT BRITAIN v. AUSTRALIA

12 Dec. 1908	D	22-22	QPR, London	2,000
23 Jan. 1909	W	15-5	Newcastle	22,000
15 Feb. 1909	W	6-5	Birmingham	9,000
18 Jun. 1910	W	27-20	Sydney	42,000
2 Jul. 1910	W	22-17	Brisbane	18,000
8 Nov. 1911	L	10-19	Newcastle	6,500
16 Dec. 1911	D	11-11	Edinburgh	6,000
1 Jan. 1912	L	8-33	Birmingham	4,000
27 Jun. 1914	W	23-5	Sydney	40,000
29 Jun. 1914	L	7-12	Sydney	55,000
4 Jul. 1914	W	14-6	Sydney	34,420
26 Jun. 1920	L	4-8	Brisbane	28,000
3 Jul. 1920	L	8-21	Sydney	40,000
10 Jul. 1920	W	23-13	Sydney	32,000
1 Oct. 1921	W	6-5	Leeds	32,000
5 Nov. 1921	L	2-16	Hull	21,504
14 Jan. 1922	W	6-0	Salford	21,000
23 Jun. 1924	W	22-3	Sydney	50,000
28 Jun. 1924	W	5-3	Sydney	33,842
12 Jul. 1924	L	11-21	Brisbane	36,000
23 Jun. 1928	W	15-12	Brisbane	39,200
14 Jul. 1928	W	8-0	Sydney	44,548
21 Jul. 1928	L	14-21	Sydney	37,000
5 Oct. 1929	L	8-31	Hull K.R.	20,000
9 Nov. 1929	W	9-3	Leeds	31,402
4 Jan. 1930	D	0-0	Swinton	34,709
15 Jan. 1930	W	3-0	Rochdale	16,743
6 Jun. 1932	W	8-6	Sydney	70,204
18 Jun. 1932	L	6-15	Brisbane	26,500
16 Jul. 1932	W	18-13	Sydney	50,053
7 Oct. 1933	W	4-0	Belle Vue, Manchester	34,000
11 Nov. 1933	W	7-5	Leeds	29,618
16 Dec. 1933	W	19-16	Swinton	10,990
29 Jun. 1936	L	8-24	Sydney	63,920
4 Jul. 1936	W	12-7	Brisbane	29,486
18 Jul. 1936	W	12-7	Sydney	53,546
16 Oct. 1937	W	5-4	Leeds	31,949
13 Nov. 1937	W	13-3	Swinton	31,724
18 Dec. 1937	L	3-13	Huddersfield	9,093
17 Jun. 1946	D	8-8	Sydney	64,527
6 Jul. 1946	W	14-5	Brisbane	40,500
20 Jul. 1946	W	20-7	Sydney	35,294
9 Oct. 1948	W	23-21	Leeds	36,529
6 Nov. 1948	W	16-7	Swinton	36,354
29 Jan. 1949	W	23-9	Bradford	42,000
12 Jun. 1950	W	6-4	Sydney	47,215
1 Jul. 1950	L	3-15	Brisbane	35,000
22 Jul. 1950	L	2-5	Sydney	47,178
4 Oct. 1952	W	19-6	Leeds	34,505
8 Nov. 1952	W	21-5	Swinton	32,421
13 Dec. 1952	L	7-27	Bradford	30,509
12 Jun. 1954	L	12-37	Sydney	65,884
3 Jul. 1954	W	38-21	Brisbane	46,355
17 Jul. 1954	L	16-20	Sydney	67,577
17 Nov. 1956	W	21-10	Wigan	22,473
1 Dec. 1956	L	9-22	Bradford	23,634
15 Dec. 1956	W	19-0	Swinton	17,542
14 Jun. 1958	L	8-25	Sydney	68,777
5 Jul. 1958	W	25-18	Brisbane	32,965
19 Jul. 1958	W	40-17	Sydney	68,720
17 Oct. 1959	L	14-22	Swinton	35,224
21 Nov. 1959	W	11-10	Leeds	30,184
12 Dec. 1959	W	18-12	Wigan	26,089
9 Jun. 1962	W	31-12	Sydney	70,174
30 Jun. 1962	W	17-10	Brisbane	34,766
14 Jul. 1962	L	17-18	Sydney	42,104
16 Oct. 1963	L	2-28	Wembley	13,946
9 Nov. 1963	L	12-50	Swinton	30,833
30 Nov. 1963	W	16-5	Leeds	20,497
25 Jun. 1966	W	17-13	Sydney	57,962
16 Jul. 1966	L	4-6	Brisbane	45,057
23 Jul. 1966	L	14-19	Sydney	63,503
21 Oct. 1967	W	16-11	Leeds	22,293
3 Nov. 1967	L	11-17	White City, London	17,445
9 Dec. 1967	L	3-11	Swinton	13,615
6 Jun. 1970	L	15-37	Brisbane	42,807
20 Jun. 1970	W	28-7	Sydney	60,962
4 Jul. 1970	W	21-17	Sydney	61,258
3 Nov. 1973	W	21-12	Wembley	9,874
24 Nov. 1973	L	6-14	Leeds	16,674
1 Dec. 1973	L	5-15	Warrington	10,019
15 Jun. 1974	L	6-12	Brisbane	30,280
6 Jul. 1974	W	16-11	Sydney	48,006
20 Jul. 1974	L	18-22	Sydney	55,505
21 Oct. 1978	L	9-15	Wigan	17,644
5 Nov. 1978	W	18-14	Bradford	26,447
18 Nov. 1978	L	6-23	Leeds	29,627
16 Jun. 1979	L	0-35	Brisbane	23,051
30 Jun. 1979	L	16-24	Sydney	26,837
14 Jul. 1979	L	2-28	Sydney	16,844
30 Oct. 1982	L	4-40	Hull C. AFC	26,771
20 Nov. 1982	L	6-27	Wigan	23,216
28 Nov. 1982	L	8-32	Leeds	17,318
9 Jun. 1984	L	8-25	Sydney	30,190
26 Jun. 1984	L	6-18	Brisbane	26,534
7 Jul. 1984	L	7-20	Sydney	18,756
25 Oct. 1986	L	16-38	Man U. AFC	50,583
8 Nov. 1986	L	4-34	Elland Rd, Leeds	30,808
*22 Nov. 1986	L	15-24	Wigan	20,169

* Also World Cup match.

	Played	Won	Drawn	Lost	Tries	Goals	Dr	Pts for
Great Britain	99	49	4	46	242	249	5	1238
Australia	99	46	4	49	282	312	5	1502

GREAT BRITAIN-AUSTRALIA TEST MATCH RECORDS

Britain

Highest score:	40-17 Third Test at Sydney July 19, 1958 (Also widest margin win)
Most tries in a match:	4 by J. Leytham (Wigan) Second Test at Brisbane July 2, 1910
Most goals in a match:	10 by B. L. Jones (Leeds) Second Test at Brisbane July 3, 1954
Most points in a match:	20 by B. L. Jones (as above)
	20 (7g,2t) by R. Millward (Hull KR) Second Test at Sydney June 20, 1970
Biggest attendance:	50,583 First Test at Old Trafford, Manchester, Oct 25, 1986

Australia

Highest score:	50-12 Second Test at Swinton, Nov 9, 1963 (Also widest margin win)
Most tries in a match:	3 by J. Devereux, First Test at QPR, London, Dec 12, 1908
	3 by R. Gasnier, First Test at Swinton, Oct 17, 1959
	3 by R. Gasnier, First Test at Wembley, Oct 16, 1963
	3 by K. Irvine, Second Test at Swinton, Nov 9, 1963
	3 by K. Irvine, Third Test at Sydney, July 23, 1966
	3 by G. Miles, First Test at Old Trafford, Manchester, Oct 25, 1986
	3 by M. O'Connor, First Test at Old Trafford, Manchester, Oct 25, 1986
Most goals in a match:	10 by M. Cronin, First Test at Brisbane, June 16, 1979
Most points in a match:	22 (5g,3t) by M. O'Connor First Test at Old Trafford, Manchester, Oct 25, 1986
Biggest attendance:	70,204 First Test at Sydney, June 6, 1932

● In a World Cup match at Perpignan, France, on October 29, 1972, R. Fulton scored three tries.

Full back Steve Hampson in his second Test, at Avignon.

GREAT BRITAIN v. NEW ZEALAND

25 Jan. 1908	W	14-6	Leeds	8,182	17 Dec. 1955	L	13-28	Leeds	10,438
8 Feb. 1908	L	6-18	Chelsea	14,000	26 Jul. 1958	L	10-15	Auckland	25,000
15 Feb. 1908	L	5-8	Cheltenham	4,000	9 Aug. 1958	W	32-15	Auckland	25,000
30 Jul. 1910	W	52-20	Auckland	16,000	30 Sept. 1961	L	11-29	Leeds	16,540
1 Aug. 1914	W	16-13	Auckland	15,000	21 Oct. 1961	W	23-10	Bradford	19,980
31 Jul. 1920	W	31-7	Auckland	34,000	4 Nov. 1961	W	35-19	Swinton	22,536
7 Aug. 1920	W	19-3	Christchurch	10,000	28 Jul. 1962	L	0-19	Auckland	14,976
14 Aug. 1920	W	11-10	Wellington	4,000	11 Aug. 1962	L	8-27	Auckland	16,411
2 Aug. 1924	L	8-16	Auckland	22,000	25 Sept. 1965	W	7-2	Swinton	8,541
6 Aug. 1924	L	11-13	Wellington	6,000	23 Oct. 1965	W	15-9	Bradford	15,740
9 Aug. 1924	W	31-18	Dunedin	14,000	6 Nov. 1965	D	9-9	Wigan	7,919
2 Oct. 1926	W	28-20	Wigan	14,500	6 Aug. 1966	W	25-8	Auckland	14,494
13 Nov. 1926	W	21-11	Hull	7,000	20 Aug. 1966	W	22-14	Auckland	10,657
15 Jan. 1927	W	32-17	Leeds	6,000	11 Jul. 1970	W	19-15	Auckland	15,948
4 Aug. 1928	L	13-17	Auckland	28,000	19 Jul. 1970	W	23-9	Christchurch	8,600
18 Aug. 1928	W	13-5	Dunedin	12,000	25 Jul. 1970	W	33-16	Auckland	13,137
25 Aug. 1928	W	6-5	Christchurch	21,000	25 Sept. 1971	L	13-18	Salford	3,764
30 Jul. 1932	W	24-9	Auckland	25,000	16 Oct. 1971	L	14-17	Castleford	4,108
13 Aug. 1932	W	25-14	Christchurch	5,000	6 Nov. 1971	W	12-3	Leeds	5,479
20 Aug. 1932	W	20-18	Auckland	6,500	27 Jul. 1974	L	8-13	Auckland	10,466
8 Aug. 1936	W	10-8	Auckland	25,000	4 Aug. 1974	W	17-8	Christchurch	6,316
15 Aug. 1936	W	23-11	Auckland	17,000	10 Aug. 1974	W	20-0	Auckland	11,574
10 Aug. 1946	L	8-13	Auckland	10,000	21 Jul. 1979	W	16-8	Auckland	9,000
4 Oct. 1947	W	11-10	Leeds	28,445	5 Aug. 1979	W	22-7	Christchurch	8,500
8 Nov. 1947	L	7-10	Swinton	29,031	11 Aug. 1979	L	11-18	Auckland	7,000
20 Dec. 1947	W	25-9	Bradford	42,680	18 Oct. 1980	D	14-14	Wigan	7,031
29 Jul. 1950	L	10-16	Christchurch	4,000	2 Nov. 1980	L	8-12	Bradford	10,946
12 Aug. 1950	L	13-20	Auckland	20,000	15 Nov. 1980	W	10-2	Leeds	8,210
6 Oct. 1951	W	21-15	Bradford	37,475	14 Jul. 1984	L	0-12	Auckland	10,238
10 Nov. 1951	W	20-19	Swinton	29,938	22 Jul. 1984	L	12-28	Christchurch	3,824
15 Dec. 1951	W	16-12	Leeds	18,649	28 Jul. 1984	L	16-32	Auckland	7,967
24 Jul. 1954	W	27-7	Auckland	22,097	19 Oct. 1985	L	22-24	Leeds	12,591
31 Jul. 1954	L	14-20	Greymouth	4,240	2 Nov. 1985	W	25-8	Wigan	15,506
14 Aug. 1954	W	12-6	Auckland	6,186	*9 Nov. 1985	D	6-6	Elland Rd,	22,209
8 Oct. 1955	W	25-6	Swinton	21,937				Leeds	
12 Nov. 1955	W	27-12	Bradford	24,443	* Also World Cup match				

	Played	Won	Lost	Drawn	Tries	Goals	Dr	Pts for
Great Britain	70	43	24	3	254	205	3	1186
New Zealand	70	24	43	3	163	204	0	916

GREAT BRITAIN-NEW ZEALAND TEST MATCH RECORDS

Britain

Highest score: 52-20 First Test at Auckland, July 30, 1910 (Also widest margin win)

Most tries in a match: 4 by W. Boston (Wigan) First Test at Auckland, July 24, 1954
4 by G. Schofield (Hull) Second Test at Wigan, Nov 2, 1985

Most goals in a match: 7 by N. Fox (Wakefield T.) Third Test at Swinton, Nov 4, 1961
7 by E. Fraser (Warrington) Second Test at Auckland, Aug 9, 1958

Most points in a match: 16 (4t) by G. Schofield (Hull) Second Test at Wigan, Nov 2, 1985
Biggest attendance: 42,680 Third Test at Bradford, Dec 20, 1947
● In a World Cup match at Pau, France, on November 4, 1972, Britain won 53-19 with J. Holmes (Leeds) scoring 26 points from 10 goals and two tries.
In a World Cup match at Sydney on June 8, 1968, Bev Risman scored 7 goals.

New Zealand
Highest score: 32-16 Third Test at Auckland, July 28, 1984
Widest margin win: 19-0 First Test at Auckland, July 28, 1962
                      27-8 Second Test at Auckland, Aug 11, 1962
No player has scored three tries or more in a Test.
Most goals and points: 7g-14pts by D. White Second Test at Greymouth, July 31, 1954
                       J. Fagan, First Test at Headingley, Sep 30, 1961
                       E. Wiggs, Second Test at Auckland, Aug 20, 1966
Biggest attendance: 34,000 First Test at Auckland, July 31, 1920
● In a World Cup match at Sydney, Australia, on June 25, 1957, W. Sorenson also scored 7 goals, 14 points.

GREAT BRITAIN v. FRANCE
● Results since France were given Test match status.

26 Jan. 1957	W	45-12	Leeds	20,221	2 Mar. 1968	W 19-8	Bradford	14,196
3 Mar. 1957	D	19-19	Toulouse	16,000	30 Nov. 1968	W 34-10	St. Helens	6,080
10 Apr. 1957	W	29-14	St. Helens	23,250	2 Feb. 1969	L 9-13	Toulouse	10,000
3 Nov. 1957	W	25-14	Toulouse	15,000	7 Feb. 1971	L 8-16	Toulouse	14,960
23 Nov. 1957	W	44-15	Wigan	19,152	17 Mar. 1971	W 24-2	St. Helens	7,783
2 Mar. 1958	W	23-9	Grenoble	20,000	6 Feb. 1972	W 10-9	Toulouse	11,508
14 Mar. 1959	W	50-15	Leeds	22,000	12 Mar. 1972	W 45-10	Bradford	7,313
5 Apr. 1959	L	15-24	Grenoble	8,500	20 Jan. 1974	W 24-5	Grenoble	5,500
6 Mar. 1960	L	18-20	Toulouse	15,308	17 Feb. 1974	W 29-0	Wigan	10,105
26 Mar. 1960	D	17-17	St. Helens	14,000	6 Dec. 1981	W 37-0	Hull	13,173
11 Dec. 1960	W	21-10	Bordeaux	8,000	20 Dec. 1981	L 2-19	Marseilles	6,500
28 Jan. 1961	W	27-8	St Helens	18,000	20 Feb. 1983	W 20-5	Carcassonne	3,826
17 Feb. 1962	L	15-20	Wigan	17,277	6 Mar. 1983	W 17-5	Hull	6,055
11 Mar. 1962	L	13-23	Perpignan	14,000	29 Jan. 1984	W 12-0	Avignon	4,000
2 Dec. 1962	L	12-17	Perpignan	5,000	17 Feb. 1984	W 10-0	Leeds	7,646
3 Apr. 1963	W	42-4	Wigan	19,487	1 Mar. 1985	W 50-4	Leeds	6,491
8 Mar. 1964	W	11-5	Perpignan	4,326	17 Mar. 1985	L 16-24	Perpignan	5,000
18 Mar. 1964	W	39-0	Leigh	4,750	*16 Feb. 1986	D 10-10	Avignon	4,000
6 Dec. 1964	L	8-18	Perpignan	15,000	1 Mar. 1986	W 24-10	Wigan	8,112
23 Jan. 1965	W	17-7	Swinton	9,959	*24 Jan. 1987	W 52-4	Leeds	6,567
16 Jan. 1966	L	13-18	Perpignan	6,000	8 Feb. 1987	W 20-10	Carcassonne	2,000
5 Mar. 1966	L	4-8	Wigan	14,004	24 Jan. 1988	W 28-14	Avignon	6,000
22 Jan. 1967	W	16-13	Carcassonne	10,650	6 Feb. 1988	W 30-12	Leeds	7,007
4 Mar. 1967	L	13-23	Wigan	7,448				
11 Feb. 1968	W	22-13	Paris	8,000	* Also World Cup match.			

	Played	Won	Drawn	Lost	Tries	Goals	Dr	Pts for
Great Britain	48	32	3	13	212	206	0	1088
France	48	13	3	32	90	125	3	536

GREAT BRITAIN-FRANCE TEST MATCH RECORDS

Britain
Highest score: 52-4 at Leeds, January 24, 1987
                              (Also widest margin win)
Most tries in a match: 4 by A. Murphy (St. Helens) at Leeds, March 14, 1959
Most goals in a match: 10 by B. Ganley (Oldham) at Wigan, November 23, 1957
Most points in a match: 21 (9g, 1t) by B.L. Jones (Leeds) at Leeds, January 26, 1957
                              21 (9g,1t) by N. Fox (Wakefield T.) at Wigan, April 3, 1963
                              21 (9g,1t) by N. Fox (Wakefield T.) at Leigh, March 18, 1964
Biggest attendance: 23,250 at St. Helens, April 10, 1957

France
Highest score: 24-15 at Grenoble, April 5, 1959
                              24-16 at Perpignan, March 17, 1985
Widest margin win: 19-2 at Marseilles, December 20, 1981
Most tries in a match: 3 by D. Couston at Perpignan, March 17, 1985
Most goals in a match: 7 by P. Lacaze at Wigan, March 4, 1967
Most points in a match: 14 by P. Lacaze (as above).
                              14 (4g,2t) by G. Benausse at Wigan, February 17, 1962
Biggest attendance: 20,000 at Grenoble, March 2, 1958
●In a World Cup match at Toulouse on November 7, 1954, there were 37,471

Additional Great Britain v. France

Pre-Test status
22 May 1952	L	12-22 Paris	16,466
24 May 1953	L	17-28 Lyons	
27 Apr. 1954	W	17-8 Bradford	14,153
11 Dec. 1955	L	5-17 Paris	18,000
11 Apr. 1956	W	18-10 Bradford	10,453

Other match
31 July 1982	L	7-8 Venice	1,500

GREAT BRITAIN v PAPUA NEW GUINEA
5 Aug. 1984	W	38-20 Mt. Hagen	7,510
24 Oct. 1987	W	42-0 Wigan	9,121

Paul Medley, Man of the Match in Great Britain's 42-0 victory over Papua New Guinea in October 1987.

GREAT BRITAIN REPRESENTATION
CLUB-BY-CLUB

Wigan beat their own record by fielding eight players in the Great Britain side which met Papua New Guinea at Wigan on 24 October 1987. The octet was backs Steve Hampson, David Stephenson, Joe Lydon, Shaun Edwards and Andy Gregory, plus forwards Brian Case, Andy Goodway and Ellery Hanley. The previous best of seven were backs Martin Ryan, Gordon Ratcliffe, Ernie Ashcroft, Jack Hilton and Tommy Bradshaw; plus forwards Ken Gee and Joe Egan in the 6-4 victory over Australia at Sydney on 12 June, 1950. Wigan also hold the record for the total of players selected with a remarkable 72.

Mick Sullivan gained Test honours with four clubs—Huddersfield (16), Wigan (19), St. Helens (10) and York (1). Billy Boston gained the most Test honours with a single club, making all 31 of his appearances for

Britain while with Wigan.

Only six of last season's clubs have not had a player selected for Great Britain in Test or World Cup matches — Springfield Borough, Bramley, Doncaster, Carlisle, Mansfield Marksman and Sheffield Eagles. Of the extinct clubs only Broughton Rangers (later Belle Vue Rangers), Merthyr Tydfil, St. Helens Recs and the old Runcorn had players selected for Britain.

The following is a club-by-club register of Great Britain players. The figure in brackets after a player's name is the number of Great Britain appearances he made while serving the club under whose entry he is listed, and the number after the + sign indicates playing substitute. This is followed by the time span between his first and last British cap while at that club.

BARROW (19 players)
W. Burgess (16) 1924-29
W. Burgess (13) 1962-68
D. Cairns (2) 1984
C. Camilleri (2) 1980
C. Carr (7) 1924-26
F. Castle (4) 1952-54
R. Francis (1) 1947
H. Gifford (2) 1908
D. Goodwin (5) 1957-58
J. Grundy (12) 1955-57
P. Hogan (4+1) 1977-78
W. Horne (8) 1946-52
P. Jackson (27) 1954-58
J. Jones (1) 1946
B. Knowelden (1) 1946
E. Szymala (1+1) 1981
E. Toohey (3) 1952
L. A. Troup (2) 1936
J. Woods (1) 1933

BATLEY (4 players)
N. Field (1) 1963
F. Gallagher (8) 1924-26
C. Gibson (+1) 1985
J. Oliver (4) 1928

**BRADFORD NORTHERN
(28 players)**
D. Barends (2) 1979
E. Batten (4) 1946-47
I. Brooke (5) 1966
L. Casey (5) 1979
W. T. H. Davies (3) 1946-47
K. Fairbank (+1) 1987
A. Fisher (8) 1970-78
P. Ford (2) 1987-88
T. Foster (3) 1946-48
J. Grayshon (11) 1979-82
E. Hanley (10+1) 1984-85
R. Jasiewicz (1) 1984
J. Kitching (1) 1946
A. Mann (2) 1908
K. Mumby (11) 1982-84
B. Noble (11) 1982-84
T. Price (1) 1970
J. Rae (1) 1965
W. Ramsey (+1) 1974
A. Rathbone (4+1) 1982-85
A. Redfearn (1) 1979
D. Redfearn (6+1) 1972-74
T. Smales (3) 1965
H. Smith (2) 1926
J. Thompson (1) 1978
K. Traill (8) 1950-54
E. Ward (20) 1946-52
F. Whitcombe (2) 1946

**BROUGHTON/BELLE VUE
RANGERS (8 players)**
W. Bentham (2) 1924
L. Clampitt (3) 1907-14
E. Gwyther (6) 1947-51
A. Hogg (1) 1907
S. McCormick (2) 1948
D. Phillips (1) 1950
J. Price (2) 1921
J. Ruddick (3) 1907-10

CASTLEFORD (23 players)
A. Atkinson (11) 1929-36
K. Beardmore (4+1) 1984-88
W. Bryant (4+1) 1964-67
A. Croston (1) 1937
B. Cunniffe (1) 1937
W. J. Davies (1) 1933
D. Edwards (3+2) 1968-71
K. England (1+1) 1987
A. Hardisty (12) 1964-70
D. Hartley (9) 1968-70
K. Hepworth (11) 1967-70
J. Joyner (14+2) 1978-84
B. Lockwood (7) 1972-74
A. Marchant (3) 1986
R. Millward (1) 1966
S. Norton (2+1) 1974
D. Plange (1) 1988
M. Reilly (9) 1970

P. Small (1) 1962
G. Stephens (5) 1979
D. Walton (1) 1965
J. Ward (3) 1963-64
K. Ward (7) 1984-88

DEWSBURY (6 players)
A. Bates (2+2) 1974
F. Gallagher (4) 1920-21
J. Ledgard (2) 1947
R. Pollard (1) 1950
M. Stephenson (5+1) 1971-72
H. Street (4) 1950

**FEATHERSTONE ROVERS
(13 players)**
T. Askin (6) 1928
K. Bridges (3) 1974
T. Clawson (2) 1962
M. Dixon (2) 1962-64
S. Evans (5+3) 1979-80
Deryck Fox (9) 1985-86
Don Fox (1) 1963
D. Hobbs (7+1) 1984
G. Jordan (2) 1964-67
A. Morgan (4) 1968
S. Nash (16) 1971-74
P. Smith (1+5) 1977-84
J. Thompson (19+1) 1970-77

FULHAM (1 player)
J. Dalgreen (1) 1982

HALIFAX (29 players)
A. Ackerley (2) 1952-58
A. Bassett (2) 1946
J. Beames (2) 1921
N. Bentham (2) 1929
H. Beverley (2) 1937
O. Burgham (1) 1911
A. Daniels (3) 1952-55
W. T. Davies (1) 1911
C. Dixon (1) 1968
P. Dixon (1+2) 1987-88
P. Eccles (1) 1907
T. Fogerty (+1) 1966
A. Halmshaw (1) 1971
N. James (1) 1986
R. Lloyd (1) 1920
A. Milnes (2) 1920
S. Prosser (1) 1914
D. Rees (1) 1926
C. Renilson (7+1) 1965-68
J. Riley (1) 1910
K. Roberts (10) 1963-66
A. Robinson (3) 1907-08
D. Schofield (1) 1955
J. Shaw (5) 1960-62
J. C. Stacey (1) 1920
J. Thorley (4) 1954
J. Wilkinson (6) 1954-55
F. Williams (2) 1914
D. Willicombe (1) 1974

HUDDERSFIELD (24 players)
J. Bowden (3) 1954
K. Bowman (3) 1962-63
B. Briggs (1) 1954
S. Brogden (9) 1929-33
J. Chilcott (3) 1914
D. Clark (11) 1911-20
D. Close (1) 1967
R. Cracknell (2) 1951
J. Davies (2) 1911
F. Dyson (1) 1959
B. Gronow (7) 1911-20
F. Longstaff (2) 1914
K. Loxton (1) 1971
S. Moorhouse (2) 1914
R. Nicholson (3) 1946-48
J. Rogers (7) 1914-21
K. Senior (2) 1965-67
T. Smales (5) 1962-64
M. Sullivan (16) 1954-57
G. Thomas (8) 1920-21
D. Valentine (15) 1948-54
R. Valentine (1) 1967
H. Wagstaff (12) 1911-21
H. Young (1) 1929

HULL (30 players)
W. Batten (1) 1921
H. Bowman (8) 1924-29
F. Boylen (1) 1908
R. Coverdale (4) 1954
M. Crane (1) 1982
L. Crooks (11+2) 1982-87
A. Dannatt (2) 1985
G. Divorty (2) 1985
J. Drake (1) 1960
W. Drake (1) 1962
S. Evans (2) 1982
V. Farrar (1) 1978
R. Gemmell (2) 1968-69
T. E. Gwynne (3) 1928-29
T. Harris (25) 1954-60
M. Harrison (7) 1967-73
W. Holder (1) 1907
A. Keegan (9) 1966-69
E. Morgan (2) 1921
S. Norton (9) 1978-82
W. Proctor (+1) 1984
P. Rose (1) 1982
G. Schofield (15) 1984-87
T. Skerrett (6) 1980-82
W. Stone (8) 1920-21
C. Sullivan (17) 1967-73
H. Taylor (3) 1907
R. Taylor (2) 1921-26
D. Topliss (1) 1982
J. Whiteley (15) 1957-62

**HULL KINGSTON ROVERS
(25 players)**
C. Burton (8+1) 1982-87
A. Burwell (7+1) 1967-69
L. Casey (7+2) 1977-83
G. Clark (3) 1984-85
A. Dockar (1) 1947
G. Fairbairn (3) 1981-82
J. Feetham (1) 1929
P. Flanagan (14) 1962-70
F. Foster (1) 1967
D. Hall (2) 1984
P. Harkin (+1) 1985
S. Hartley (3) 1980-81
P. Hogan (2+2) 1979
R. Holdstock (2) 1980
W. Holliday (8+1) 1964-67
D. Laws (1) 1986
B. Lockwood (1+1) 1978-79
P. Lowe (12) 1970-78
R. Millward (27+1) 1967-78
H. Poole (1) 1964
P. Rose (1+3) 1974-78
M. Smith (10+1) 1979-84
B. Tyson (3) 1963-67
D. Watkinson (12+1) 1979-86
C. Young (5) 1967-68

HUNSLET (23 players)
W. Batten (9) 1907-11
H. Beverley (4) 1936-37
A. Burnell (3) 1951-54
H. Crowther (1) 1929
J. Evans (4) 1951-52
K. Eyre (1) 1965
B. Gabbitas (1) 1959
G. Gunney (11) 1954-65
D. Hartley (2) 1964
J. Higson (2) 1908
D. Jenkins (1) 1929
A. Jenkinson (2) 1911
W. Jukes (6) 1908-10
B. Prior (1) 1966
W. Ramsey (7) 1965-66
B. Shaw (5) 1956-60
G. Shelton (7) 1964-66
F. Smith (9) 1910-14
S. Smith (4) 1954
C. Thompson (2) 1951
L. White (7) 1932-33
R. Williams (3) 1954
H. Wilson (3) 1907

KEIGHLEY (1 player)
T. Hollindrake (1) 1955

LEEDS (63 players)
L. Adams (1) 1932
J. Atkinson (26) 1968-80
J. Bacon (11) 1920-26
R. Batten (3) 1969-73
J. Birch (1) 1907
S. Brogden (7) 1936-37
J. Brough (5) 1928-36
G. Brown (6) 1954-55
M. Clark (5) 1968
T. Clawson (3) 1972
D. Creasser (2 + 2) 1985-88
W. A. Davies (2) 1914
K. Dick (2) 1980
R. Dickinson (2) 1985
L. Dyl (11) 1974-82
A. Fisher (3) 1970-71
R. Gemmell (1) 1964
J. Grayshon (2) 1985
R. Haigh (3 + 1) 1970-71
D. Hallas (2) 1961
F. Harrison (3) 1911
D. Heron (1 + 1) 1982
J. Holmes (14 + 6) 1971-82
S. Hynes (12 + 1) 1970-73

*Leeds centre Les Dyl,
capped 11 times.*

J. W. Jarman (2) 1914
D. Jeanes (3) 1972
D. Jenkins (1) 1947
B. L. Jones (15) 1954-57
K. Jubb (2) 1937
J. Lowe (1) 1932
P. Medley (2 + 1) 1987-88
I. Owens (4) 1946
S. Pitchford (4) 1977
H. Poole (2) 1966
R. Powell (2 + 1) 1985-88
D. Prosser (1) 1937
Keith Rayne (4) 1984
Kevin Rayne (1) 1986
B. Risman (5) 1968
D. Robinson (5) 1956-60
D. Rose (4) 1954
G. Schofield (2) 1988
B. Seabourne (1) 1970
B. Shaw (1) 1961
M. Shoebottom (10 + 2) 1968-71
B. Simms (1) 1962
A. Smith (10) 1970-73
S. Smith (10) 1929-33
D. Stephenson (+ 1) 1988
J. Stevenson (15) 1955-58
S. Stockwell (3) 1920-21
A. Terry (1) 1962
A. Thomas (4) 1926-29
P. Thomas (1) 1907
J. Thompson (12) 1924-32
A. Turnbull (1) 1951
D. Ward (12) 1977-82
W. Ward (1) 1910
F. Webster (3) 1910
R. Williams (9) 1948-51
H. Woods (1) 1937
G. Wriglesworth (5) 1965-66
F. Young (1) 1908

LEIGH (19 players)
K. Ashcroft (5) 1968-70
J. Cartwright (7) 1920-21
D. Chisnall (2) 1970
J. Darwell (5) 1924
S. Donlan (+ 2) 1984
D. Drummond (22) 1980-86
P. Foster (3) 1955
C. Johnson (1) 1985
F. Kitchen (2) 1954
J. Ledgard (9) 1948-54
G. Lewis (1) 1965
M. Martyn (2) 1958-59
W. Mooney (2) 1924
S. Owen (1) 1958
C. Pawsey (7) 1952-54
W. Robinson (2) 1963
Joe Walsh (1) 1971
W. Winstanley (2) 1910
J. Woods (7 + 3) 1979-83

MERTHYR TYDFIL (1 player)
D. Jones (2) 1907

OLDHAM (40 players)
A. Avery (4) 1910-11
C. Bott (1) 1966
A. Brough (2) 1924
T. Clawson (9) 1973-74
A. Davies (20) 1955-60
E. Davies (3) 1920
T. Flanagan (4) 1983-84
D. Foy (3) 1984-85
B. Ganley (3) 1957-58
A. Goodway (11) 1983-85
W. Hall (4) 1914
H. Hilton (7) 1920-21
D. Hobbs (2) 1987
D. Holland (4) 1914
R. Irving (8 + 3) 1967-72
K. Jackson (2) 1957
E. Knapman (1) 1924
S. Little (10) 1956-58
T. Llewellyn (2) 1907
J. Lomas (2) 1911
W. Longworth (3) 1908
L. McIntyre (1) 1963
T. O'Grady (5) 1954
J. Oster (1) 1929
D. Parker (2) 1964
D. Phillips (3) 1946
F. Pitchford (2) 1958-62
T. Rees (1) 1929
S. Rix (9) 1924-26
R. Sloman (5) 1928
A. Smith (6) 1907-08
I. Southward (7) 1959-62
L. Thomas (1) 1947
D. Turner (11) 1956-58
G. Tyson (4) 1907-08
H. Waddell (2) 1988
T. White (1) 1907
C. Winsdale (1) 1959
A. Wood (4) 1911-14
M. Worrall (3) 1984

**ROCHDALE HORNETS
(8 players)**
J. Baxter (1) 1907
J. Bennett (6) 1924
J. Bowers (1) 1920
T. Fogerty (1) 1974
E. Jones (4) 1920
M. Price (2) 1967
J. Robinson (2) 1914
T. Woods (1) 1911

RUNCORN (2 players)
J. Jolley (3) 1907
R. Padbury (1) 1908

**RUNCORN HIGHFIELD/
HUYTON/LIVERPOOL/WIGAN
HIGHFIELD (4 players)**
R. Ashby (1) 1964
W. Belshaw (6) 1936-37
N. Bentham (6) 1928
H. Woods (5) 1936

ST. HELENS (46 players)
C. Arkwright (+2) 1985
L. Aston (3) 1947
W. Benyon (5+1) 1971-72
T. Bishop (15) 1966-69
F. Carlton (1) 1958
E. Chisnall (4) 1974
E. Cunningham (1) 1978
R. Dagnall (4) 1961-65
D. Eckersley (2+2) 1973-74
A. Ellaby (13) 1928-33
L. Fairclough (6) 1926-29
J. Fieldhouse (1) 1986
A. Fildes (4) 1932
A. Frodsham (3) 1928-29
P. Gorley (2+1) 1980-81
D. Greenall (6) 1951-54
P. Groves (1) 1987
R. Haggerty (2) 1987
M. Hicks (1) 1965
N. Holding (4) 1984
R. Huddart (12) 1959-63
L. Jones (1) 1971
A. Karalius (4+1) 1971-72
V. Karalius (10) 1958-61
K. Kelly (2) 1972
B. Ledger (2) 1985-86
P. Loughlin (1) 1988
J. Mantle (13) 1966-73
S. McCormick (1) 1948
T. McKinney (1) 1957
R. Mathias (1) 1979
G. Moses (9) 1955-57
A. Murphy (26) 1958-66
F. Myler (9) 1970
G. Nicholls (22) 1973-79
H. Pinner (5+1) 1980-86
A. Platt (2+3) 1985-88
A. Prescott (28) 1951-58
A. Rhodes (4) 1957-61
J. Stott (1) 1947
M. Sullivan (10) 1961-62
J. Tembey (2) 1963-64
A. Terry (10) 1958-61
John Walsh (4+1) 1972
J. Warlow (3+1) 1964-68
C. Watson (29+1) 1963-71

ST. HELENS RECS (5 players)
F. Bowen (3) 1928
A. Fildes (11) 1926-29
J. Greenall (1) 1921
J. Owen (1) 1921
J. Wallace (1) 1926

SALFORD (27 players)
W. Burgess (1) 1969
P. Charlton (17+1) 1970-74
M. Coulman (2+1) 1971
G. Curran (6) 1946-48
E. Curzon (1) 1910
T. Danby (3) 1950
C. Dixon (11+2) 1969-74
A. Edwards (7) 1936-37
J. Feetham (7) 1932-33
K. Fielding (3) 1974-77
K. Gill (5+2) 1974-77
J. Gore (1) 1926
C. Hesketh (21+2) 1970-74
B. Hudson (8) 1932-37
E. Jenkins (9) 1933-37
J. Lomas (5) 1908-10
T. McKinney (7) 1951-54
A. Middleton (1) 1929
S. Nash (8) 1977-82
M. Richards (2) 1974
A. Risman (17) 1932-46
J. Spencer (1) 1907
J. Ward (1) 1970
S. Warwick (2) 1907
D. Watkins (2+4) 1971-74
W. Watkins (7) 1933-37
W. Williams (2) 1929-32

SWINTON (15 players)
T. Armitt (8) 1933-37
A. Buckley (7) 1963-66
F. Butters (2) 1929
W. Davies (1) 1968
B. Evans (10) 1926-33
F. Evans (4) 1924
J. Evans (3) 1926
K. Gowers (14) 1962-66
H. Halsall (1) 1929
M. Hodgson (16) 1929-37
R. Morgan (2) 1963
W. Rees (11) 1926-29
D. Robinson (12) 1965-67
J. Stopford (12) 1961-66
J. Wright (1) 1932

**WAKEFIELD TRINITY
(22 players)**
I. Brooke (8) 1967-68
N. Fox (29) 1959-69
R. Haigh (2) 1968-70
W. Horton (14) 1928-33
D. Jeanes (5) 1971-72
B. Jones (3) 1964-66
H. Kershaw (2) 1910
F. Mortimer (2) 1956
H. Murphy (1) 1950
H. Newbould (1) 1910
J. Parkin (17) 1920-29
C. Pollard (1) 1924
E. Pollard (2) 1932

H. Poynton (3) 1962
D. Robinson (5) 1954-55
G. Round (8) 1959-62
T. Skerrett (4) 1979
S. Smith (1) 1929
D. Topliss (3) 1973-79
D. Turner (13) 1959-62
D. Vines (3) 1959
J. Wilkinson (7) 1959-62

WARRINGTON (43 players)
J. Arkwright (6) 1936-37
K. Ashcroft (+1) 1974
W. Aspinall (1) 1966
W. Belshaw (2) 1937
N. Bentham (2) 1929
J. Bevan (6) 1974-78
T. Blinkhorn (1) 1929
E. Brooks (3) 1908
J. Challinor (3) 1958-60
N. Courtney (+1) 1982
W. Cunliffe (11) 1920-26
G. Dickenson (1) 1908
W. Dingsdale (3) 1929-33
D. Drummond (2) 1987-88
R. Duane (3) 1983-84
R. Eccles (1) 1982
J. Featherstone (6) 1948-52
M. Forster (2) 1987
E. Fraser (16) 1958-61
L. Gilfedder (5) 1962-63
R. Greenough (1) 1960
A. Gregory (1) 1986
M. Gregory (1) 1987
G. Helme (12) 1948-54
K. Holden (1) 1963
A. Johnson (6) 1946-47
K. Kelly (2) 1980-82
T. McKinney (3) 1955
J. Miller (6) 1933-36
A. Murphy (1) 1971
A. Naughton (2) 1954
T. O'Grady (1) 1961
H. Palin (2) 1947
K. Parr (1) 1968
A. Pimblett (3) 1948
R. Price (9) 1954-57
R. Ryan (5) 1950-52
R. Ryder (1) 1952
F. Shugars (1) 1910
G. Skelhorne (7) 1920-21
G. Thomas (1) 1907
D. Whitehead (3) 1971
J. Woods (+1) 1987

WHITEHAVEN (5 players)
V. Gribbin (1) 1985
W. Holliday (1) 1964
R. Huddart (4) 1958
P. Kitchin (1) 1965
A. Walker (1) 1980

WIDNES (34 players)
M. Adams (11+2) 1979-84
J. Basnett (2) 1984-86
K. Bentley (1) 1980
M. Burke (14+1) 1980-86
F. Collier (1) 1964
R. Dutton (6) 1970
K. Elwell (3) 1977-80
J. Fieldhouse (6) 1985-86
R. French (4) 1968
L. Gorley (4+1) 1980-82
A. Gregory (8+1) 1981-84
I. Hare (1) 1967
F. Higgins (6) 1950-51
H. Higgins (2) 1937
E. Hughes (8) 1978-82
A. Johnson (4) 1914-20
G. Kemel (2) 1965
V. Karalius (2) 1963
D. Laughton (4) 1973-79
J. Lydon (9+1) 1983-85
T. McCue (6) 1936-46
J. Measures (2) 1963
J. Mills (6) 1974-79
A. Myler (14) 1983-86
F. Myler (14+1) 1960-67
G. Nicholls (7) 1971-72
D. O'Neill (2+1) 1971-72
M. O'Neill (3) 1982-83
M. Offiah (1) 1988
H. Pinner (1) 1986
G. Shaw (1) 1980
N. Silcock (12) 1932-37
J. Warlow (3) 1971
S. Wright (7) 1977-78

WIGAN (72 players)
R. Ashby (1) 1965
E. Ashcroft (11) 1947-54
E. Ashton (26) 1957-63
W. Ashurst (3) 1971-72
F. Barton (1) 1951
J. Barton (2) 1960-61
J. Bennett (1) 1926
D. Bevan (1) 1952
W. Blan (3) 1951
D. Bolton (23) 1957-63
W. Boston (31) 1954-63
T. Bradshaw (6) 1947-50
F. Carlton (1) 1962
B. Case (5) 1984-87
W. Cherrington (1) 1960
C. Clarke (7) 1965-73
A. Coldrick (4) 1914
F. Collier (1) 1963
J. Cunliffe (4) 1950-54
S. Edwards (7+2) 1985-88
J. Egan (14) 1946-50
R. Evans (4) 1961-62
G. Fairbairn (14) 1977-80
T. Fogerty (1) 1967
P. Ford (1) 1985
W. Francis (4) 1967-77
D. Gardiner (1) 1965
K. Gee (17) 1946-51
H. Gill (10) 1981-87
A. Goodway (8) 1985-87
J. Gray (5+3) 1974
A. Gregory (3) 1987-88
S. Hampson (3) 1987-88
E. Hanley (10) 1985-88
C. Hill (1) 1966
D. Hill (1) 1971
J. Hilton (4) 1950
T. Howley (6) 1924
W. Hudson (1) 1948
D. Hurcombe (8) 1920-24
B. Jenkins (12) 1907-14
K. Jones (2) 1970
R. Kinnear (1) 1929
N. Kiss (1) 1985
D. Laughton (11) 1970-71
J. Lawrenson (3) 1948
J. Leytham (5) 1907-10
J. Lydon (7) 1986-87
B. McTigue (25) 1958-63
J. Miller (1) 1911
J. Morley (2) 1936-37
I. Potter (7+1) 1985-86
J. Price (4) 1924
R. Ramsdale (8) 1910-14
G. Ratcliffe (3) 1947-50
J. Ring (2) 1924-26
D. Robinson (1) 1970
M. Ryan (4) 1947-50

W. Sayer (7) 1961-63
J. Sharrock (4) 1910-11
N. Silcock (3) 1954
R. Silcock (1) 1908
D. Stephenson (5) 1982-87
J. Sullivan (25) 1924-33
M. Sullivan (19) 1957-60
G. Thomas (1) 1914
J. Thomas (8) 1907-11
S. Wane (2) 1985-86
E. Ward (3) 1946-47
L. White (2) 1947
D. Willicombe (2) 1974
W. Winstanley (3) 1911

WORKINGTON TOWN (9 players)
E. Bowman (4) 1977
P. Charlton (1) 1965
B. Edgar (11) 1958-66
N. Herbert (6) 1961-62
W. Martin (1) 1962
V. McKeating (2) 1951
A. Pepperell (2) 1950-51
I. Southward (4) 1958
G. Wilson (3) 1951

YORK (7 players)
E. Dawson (1) 1956
H. Field (3) 1936
G. Smith (3) 1963-64
J. Stevenson (4) 1959-60
M. Sullivan (1) 1963
B. Watts (5) 1954-55
L. White (4) 1946

Widnes back row forward Mick Adams, 13 caps in a five year Test career.

Wigan utility back Bill Francis, capped four times over a decade.

GREAT BRITAIN TEAMS
... A 20-year review

The following is a compendium of Great Britain Test and World Cup teams since the end of the 1967-68 season.

Initials are included where more than one celebrated player shared a surname in the same era. Only playing substitutes are included on the teamsheet.

(WC): World Cup   t: try   g: goal   dg: drop goal   ★ captain

1968 Australia (WC)
Sydney: 25 May
Lost 10-25
*Risman, B (Leeds) 2g
Brooke (Wakefield) 1t
Burwell (Hull KR)
Shoebottom (Leeds)
Sullivan, C (Hull) 1t
Millward (Hull KR)
Bishop (St. Helens)
Clark, M (Leeds)
Ashcroft, K (Leigh)
Watson (St. Helens)
French (Widnes)
Haigh (Wakefield)
Renilson (Halifax)

1968 France (WC)
Auckland: 2 June
Lost 2-7
*Risman, B (Leeds) 1g
Sullivan, C (Hull)
Brooke (Wakefield)
Burwell (Hull KR)
Atkinson, J (Leeds)
Millward (Hull KR)
Bishop (St. Helens)
Clark, M (Leeds)
Flanagan (Hull KR)
Watson (St. Helens)
Morgan, A (Featherstone)
Haigh (Wakefield)
Renilson (Halifax)
Sub: Warlow (St. Helens)

1968 New Zealand (WC)
Sydney: 8 June
Won 38-14
*Risman, B (Leeds) 7g
Sullivan, C (Hull) 3t
Brooke (Wakefield) 1t
Burwell (Hull KR) 2t
Atkinson, J (Leeds)
Millward (Hull KR)
Bishop (St. Helens)
Clark, M (Leeds)
Flanagan (Hull KR)
Warlow (St. Helens)
French (Widnes)
Morgan, A (Featherstone) 1t
Renilson (Halifax)
Sub: Shoebottom (Leeds) 1t
Watson (St. Helens)

1968 France
St. Helens: 30 Nov
Won 34-10
Keegan (Hull)
Burgess, W (Barrow) 3t
Fox, N (Wakefield) 5g
Gemmell (Hull) 2t
Burwell (Hull KR) 1t
Davies, W (Swinton)
*Bishop (St. Helens)
Hartley, D (Castleford)
Ashcroft, K (Leigh) 1t
Warlow (St. Helens)
Dixon, C (Halifax) 1t
Parr (Warrington)
Renilson (Halifax)

1969 France
Toulouse: 2 Feb
Lost 9-13
Keegan (Hull)
Burgess, W (Salford)
Fox, N (Wakefield) 3g
Gemmell (Hull)
Burwell (Hull KR)
Shoebottom (Leeds)
*Bishop (St. Helens)
Hartley, D (Castleford)
Ashcroft, K (Leigh)
Watson (St. Helens)
Dixon, C (Salford) 1t
Mantle (St. Helens)
Batten, R (Leeds)

1970 Australia
Brisbane: 6 June
Lost 15-37
Price, T (Bradford) 3g
Sullivan, C (Hull)
*Myler (St. Helens)
Shoebottom (Leeds)
Atkinson, J (Leeds)
Hardisty (Castleford)
Hepworth (Castleford)
Chisnall, D (Leigh)
Flanagan (Hull KR) 1t
Watson (St. Helens) 1t
Laughton (Wigan) 1t
Robinson, D (Wigan)
Reilly (Castleford)
Sub: Irving (Oldham)

1970 Australia
Sydney: 20 June
Won 28-7
Edwards, D (Castleford)
Smith, A (Leeds)
Hynes (Leeds) 1g
*Myler (St. Helens)
Atkinson, J (Leeds) 1t
Millward (Hull KR) 7g,2t
Hepworth (Castleford)
Hartley, D (Castleford)
Fisher (Bradford) 1t
Watson (St. Helens)
Laughton (Wigan)
Thompson, J (Featherstone)
Reilly (Castleford)
Sub: Shoebottom (Leeds)

1970 Australia
Sydney: 4 July
Won 21-17
Shoebottom (Leeds)
Smith, A (Leeds)
Hynes (Leeds) 1t
*Myler (St. Helens)
Atkinson, J (Leeds) 2t
Millward (Hull KR) 3g,1t
Hepworth (Castleford)
Hartley, D (Castleford) 1t
Fisher (Bradford)
Watson (St. Helens)
Laughton (Wigan)
Thompson, J (Featherstone)
Reilly (Castleford)

1970 New Zealand
Auckland: 11 July
Won 19-15
Shoebottom (Leeds)
Smith, A (Leeds)
Hynes (Leeds) 2g,1t
*Myler (St. Helens)
Atkinson, J (Leeds) 1t
Millward (Hull KR) 1t
Seabourne (Leeds)
Hartley, D (Castleford)
Fisher (Bradford)
Watson (St. Helens)
Laughton (Wigan) 2t
Thompson, J (Featherstone)
Reilly (Castleford)

1970 New Zealand
Christchurch: 19 July
Won 23-9
Dutton (Widnes) 4g
Smith, A (Leeds)
Hynes (Leeds)
*Myler (St. Helens) 1t
Atkinson, J (Leeds)
Millward (Hull KR) 2t
Hepworth (Castleford)
Hartley, D (Castleford)
Fisher (Bradford)
Watson (St. Helens)
Laughton (Wigan) 1t
Thompson, J (Featherstone)
Reilly (Castleford) 1t

1970 New Zealand
Auckland: 25 July
Won 33-16
Dutton (Widnes) 5g
Smith, A (Leeds) 1t
Hesketh (Salford) 1t
*Myler (St. Helens)
Atkinson, J (Leeds)
Millward (Hull KR) 1g
Hepworth (Castleford) 1t
Watson (St. Helens) 1t
Fisher (Bradford)
Ward, J (Salford)
Irving (Oldham)
Lowe, P (Hull KR) 2t
Reilly (Castleford)
Sub: Hynes (Leeds) 1t

1970 Australia (WC)
Leeds: 24 Oct
Won 11-4
Dutton (Widnes) 3g
Smith, A (Leeds)
Hynes (Leeds) 1t,1g
*Myler (St. Helens)
Atkinson, J (Leeds)
Shoebottom (Leeds)
Hepworth (Castleford)
Hartley, D (Castleford)
Fisher (Bradford)
Watson (St. Helens)
Laughton (Wigan)
Thompson, J (Featherstone)
Reilly (Castleford)

1970 France (WC)
Castleford: 28 Oct
Won 6-0
Dutton (Widnes) 3g
Jones, K (Wigan)
Hynes (Leeds)
*Myler (St. Helens)
Atkinson, J (Leeds)
Shoebottom (Leeds)
Hepworth (Castleford)
Hartley, D (Castleford)
Ashcroft, K (Leigh)
Watson (St. Helens)
Laughton (Wigan)
Thompson, J (Featherstone)
Reilly (Castleford)

1970 New Zealand (WC)
Swinton: 31 Oct
Won 27-17
Dutton (Widnes) 6g
Jones, K (Wigan)
Hynes (Leeds) 1t
Hesketh (Salford) 1t
Atkinson, J (Leeds) 1t
Shoebottom (Leeds)
Hepworth (Castleford)
Chisnall, D (Leigh)
Ashcroft, K (Leigh)
Watson (St. Helens) 1t
Haigh (Leeds)
Thompson, J (Featherstone)
*Laughton (Wigan) 1t
Sub: Charlton (Salford)

1970 Australia (WC)
Leeds: 7 Nov
Lost 7-12
Dutton (Widnes) 1g
Smith, A (Leeds)
Hynes (Leeds) 1g
*Myler (St. Helens)
Atkinson, J (Leeds) 1t
Shoebottom (Leeds)
Hepworth (Castleford)
Hartley, D (Castleford)
Fisher (Leeds)
Watson (St. Helens)
Laughton (Wigan)
Thompson, J (Featherstone)
Reilly (Castleford)
Sub: Hesketh (Salford)
Haigh (Leeds)

1970 tourist Roger Millward.

299

1971 France
Toulouse: 7 Feb
Lost 8-16
Whitehead (Warrington) 1g
Smith, A (Leeds) 1t
*Hynes (Leeds)
Benyon (St. Helens)
Atkinson, J (Leeds)
Hill, D (Wigan)
Shoebottom (Leeds)
Jeanes (Wakefield) 1t
Fisher (Leeds)
Warlow (Widnes)
Mantle (St. Helens)
Haigh (Leeds)
Laughton (Wigan)
Sub: Hesketh (Salford)
    Thompson, J (Featherstone)

1971 France
St. Helens: 17 March
Won 24-2
Whitehead (Warrington) 1t,3g
Smith, A (Leeds) 1t
Hesketh (Salford)
Benyon (St. Helens) 1t
Atkinson, J (Leeds)
Millward (Hull KR) 2t
Nash (Featherstone)
Warlow (Widnes)
Fisher (Leeds)
Watson (St. Helens)
Mantle (St. Helens)
Thompson, J (Featherstone) 1t
*Laughton (Wigan)
Sub: Watkins, D (Salford)
    Coulman (Salford)

1971 New Zealand
Salford: 25 Sep
Lost 13-18
Whitehead (Warrington) 2g
Jones, L (St. Helens)
Benyon (St. Helens) 1t
Hesketh (Salford) 1t
Sullivan, C (Hull)
*Millward (Hull KR)
Nash (Featherstone)
Warlow (Widnes)
Karalius, A (St. Helens)
Jeanes (Wakefield)
Ashurst (Wigan) 1t
Coulman (Salford)
Mantle (St. Helens)
Sub: Edwards, D (Castleford)

1971 New Zealand
Castleford: 16 Oct
Lost 14-17
Edwards, D (Castleford)
Sullivan, C (Hull) 1t
Watkins, D (Salford) 1g
Hesketh (Salford)
Walsh, Joe (Leigh) 1t
*Millward (Hull KR) 1t
Murphy, A (Warrington)
Harrison, M (Hull)
Karalius, A (St. Helens)
Coulman (Salford) 1t
Dixon, C (Salford)
Mantle (St. Helens)
Haigh (Leeds)
Sub: Benyon (St. Helens)
    Stephenson, M (Dewsbury)

1971 New Zealand
Leeds: 6 Nov
Won 12-3
Edwards, D (Castleford)
Sullivan, C (Hull)
Hesketh (Salford)
Holmes (Leeds) 2g,2dg
Atkinson, J (Leeds) 2t
*Millward (Hull KR)
Loxton (Huddersfield)
Harrison, M (Hull)
Karalius, A (St. Helens)
Jeanes (Wakefield)
Irving (Oldham)
Nicholls (Widnes)
Halmshaw (Halifax)
Sub: O'Neill, D (Widnes)

1972 France
Toulouse: 6 Feb
Won 10-9
Charlton (Salford)
*Sullivan, C (Hull) 1t
Holmes (Leeds) 2g
Benyon (St. Helens) 1t
Atkinson, J (Leeds)
Kelly (St. Helens)
Nash (Featherstone)
Harrison, M (Hull)
Karalius, A (St. Helens)
Jeanes (Wakefield)
Ashurst (Wigan)
Lowe, P (Hull KR)
Nicholls (Widnes)

1972 France
Bradford: 12 March
Won 45-10
Charlton (Salford) 1t
*Sullivan, C (Hull) 1t
Holmes (Leeds) 1t,6g
Benyon (St. Helens) 1t
Atkinson, J (Leeds) 1t
Kelly (St. Helens)
Nash (Featherstone)
Harrison, M (Hull)
Stephenson, M (Dewsbury) 1t
Jeanes (Wakefield) 1t
Ashurst (Wigan) 2t
Lowe, P (Hull KR) 1t
Nicholls (Widnes)
Sub: Walsh, John (St. Helens) 1t
    Irving (Oldham)

1972 Australia (WC)
Perpignan: 29 Oct
Won 27-21
Charlton (Salford)
*Sullivan, C (Hull) 1t
Hesketh (Salford)
Walsh, John (St. Helens)
Atkinson, J (Leeds) 1t
O'Neill, D (Widnes) 1t
Nash (Featherstone)
Clawson (Leeds) 6g
Stephenson, M (Dewsbury) 1t
Jeanes (Leeds)
Lockwood (Castleford)
Lowe, P (Hull KR) 1t
Nicholls (Widnes)
Sub: Holmes (Leeds)

1972 France (WC)
Grenoble: 1 Nov
Won 13-4
Charlton (Salford)
*Sullivan, C (Hull) 1t
Hesketh (Salford)
Walsh, John (St. Helens)
Atkinson, J (Leeds)
O'Neill, D (Widnes)
Nash (Featherstone)
Clawson (Leeds) 2g
Stephenson, M (Dewsbury)
Lockwood, B (Castleford)
Dixon, C (Salford)
Lowe, P (Hull KR) 2t
Nicholls (Widnes)

1972 New Zealand (WC)
Pau: 4 Nov
Won 53-19
Charlton (Salford) 1t
*Sullivan, C (Hull) 1t
Hesketh (Salford) 1t
Walsh, John (St. Helens)
Atkinson, J (Leeds) 2t
Holmes (Leeds) 10g,2t
Nash (Featherstone) 1t
Jeanes (Leeds) 1t
Stephenson, M (Dewsbury) 1t
Lockwood (Castleford)
Irving (Oldham)
Lowe, P (Hull KR)
Nicholls (Widnes) 1t
Sub: Redfearn, D (Bradford)
  Karalius, A (St. Helens)

1972 Australia (WC)
Lyon: 11 Nov
Drew 10-10
Charlton (Salford)
*Sullivan, C (Hull) 1t
Hesketh (Salford)
Walsh, John (St. Helens)
Atkinson, J (Leeds)
Holmes (Leeds)
Nash (Featherstone)
Clawson (Leeds) 2g
Stephenson, M (Dewsbury) 1t
Jeanes (Leeds)
Lockwood, B (Castleford)
Lowe, P (Hull KR)
Nicholls (Widnes)
Sub: Irving (Oldham)

1973 Australia
Wembley: 3 Nov
Won 21-12
Charlton (Salford)
*Sullivan (Hull)
Hynes (Leeds)
Hesketh (Salford)
Atkinson, J (Leeds)
Topliss (Wakefield)
Nash (Featherstone) 1dg
Clawson (Oldham) 4g
Clarke (Wigan) 1t
Lockwood (Castleford) 1t
Nicholls (St. Helens)
Lowe, P (Hull KR) 2t
Batten (Leeds)

1973 Australia
Leeds: 24 Nov
Lost 6-14
Charlton (Salford)
*Sullivan (Hull)
Hynes (Leeds)
Hesketh (Salford)
Atkinson, J (Leeds)
Topliss (Wakefield)
Nash (Featherstone)
Clawson (Oldham) 3g
Clarke (Wigan)
Lockwood (Castleford)
Mantle (St. Helens)
Lowe, P (Hull KR)
Batten, R (Leeds)
Sub: Eckersley (St. Helens)
  Dixon, C (Salford)

1973 Australia
Warrington: 1 Dec
Lost 5-15
Charlton (Salford)
Smith, A (Leeds)
Hynes (Leeds)
Hesketh (Salford)
*Sullivan, C (Hull)
Eckersley (St. Helens)
Millward (Hull KR) 1t,1g
Clawson (Oldham)
Clarke (Wigan)
Harrison, M (Hull)
Nicholls (St. Helens)
Lowe, P (Hull KR)
Laughton (Widnes)
Sub: Watkins, D (Salford)
  Dixon, C (Salford)

1974 France
Grenoble: 20 Jan
Won 24-5
Charlton (Salford)
Fielding (Salford) 3t
Willicombe (Halifax) 1t
Hesketh (Salford)
Redfearn, D (Bradford)
Gill, K (Salford) 1t
Bates, A (Dewsbury)
Clawson (Oldham) 3g
Bridges (Featherstone)
Lockwood (Castleford)
Dixon, C (Salford)
Nicholls (St. Helens)
*Laughton (Widnes) 1t
Sub: Watkins, D (Salford)
  Gray (Wigan)

1974 France
Wigan: 17 Feb
Won 29-0
Charlton (Salford) 2t
Fielding (Salford)
Willicombe (Wigan) 1t
Hesketh (Salford)
Redfearn, D (Bradford) 2t
Gill, K (Salford)
Bates, A (Dewsbury)
Clawson (Oldham) 2g
Bridges (Featherstone)
Fogerty (Rochdale)
Dixon, C (Salford)
Nicholls (St. Helens)
*Laughton (Widnes) 1t
Sub: Watkins, D (Salford) 1g
  Gray (Wigan) 1t,1g

1974 Australia
Brisbane: 15 June
Lost 6-12
Charlton (Salford)
Redfearn, D (Bradford)
Watkins, D (Salford) 1g
*Hesketh (Salford)
Bevan, J (Warrington)
Millward (Hull KR)
Nash (Featherstone)
Clawson (Oldham) 2g
Bridges (Featherstone)
Mills (Widnes)
Dixon, C (Salford)
Thompson, J (Featherstone)
Nicholls (St. Helens)
Sub: Eckersley (St. Helens)
  Gray (Wigan)

Prop forward Brian Lockwood.

301

1974 Australia
Sydney: 6 July
Won 16-11
Charlton (Salford)
Dyl (Leeds)
Eckersley (St. Helens)
*Hesketh (Salford)
Millward (Hull KR)
Gill, K (Salford) 1t
Nash (Featherstone)
Mills (Widnes)
Gray (Wigan) 3g,1dg
Thompson, J (Featherstone)
Dixon, C (Salford) 1t
Chisnall, E (St. Helens) 1t
Nicholls (St. Helens)
Sub: Norton (Castleford)

1974 Australia
Sydney: 20 July
Lost 18-22
Charlton (Salford)
Richards (Salford) 1t
Dyl (Leeds) 1t
*Hesketh (Salford)
Bevan, J (Warrington)
Gill, K (Salford)
Nash (Featherstone)
Clawson (Oldham)
Gray (Wigan) 6g
Thompson, J (Featherstone)
Dixon, C (Salford)
Chisnall, E (St. Helens)
Nicholls (St. Helens)
Sub: Millward (Hull KR)
      Rose, P (Hull KR)

1974 New Zealand
Auckland: 27 July
Lost 8-13
Charlton (Salford)
Redfearn, D (Bradford)
Dyl (Leeds)
*Hesketh (Salford)
Bevan, J (Warrington) 1t
Gill, K (Salford)
Nash (Featherstone) 1t
Clawson (Oldham) 1g
Gray (Wigan)
Thompson, J (Featherstone)
Dixon, C (Salford)
Norton (Castleford)
Nicholls (St. Helens)
Sub: Ashcroft (Warrington)

1974 New Zealand
Christchurch: 4 Aug
Won 17-8
Charlton (Salford)
Redfearn, D (Bradford) 1t
Dyl (Leeds) 1t
Dixon, C (Salford)
Richards (Salford)
*Hesketh (Salford) 1t
Nash (Featherstone)
Mills (Widnes)
Gray (Wigan) 4g
Thompson, J (Featherstone)
Chisnall, E (St. Helens)
Norton (Castleford)
Nicholls (St. Helens)
Sub: Bates, A (Dewsbury)

1974 New Zealand
Auckland: 10 Aug
Won 20-0
Charlton (Salford)
Redfearn, D (Bradford)
Willicombe (Wigan)
Dyl (Leeds) 1t
Bevan, J (Warrington) 2t
*Hesketh (Salford) 1t
Nash (Featherstone)
Clawson (Oldham)
Gray (Wigan) 4g
Thompson, J (Featherstone)
Chisnall, E (St. Helens)
Dixon, C (Salford)
Nicholls (St. Helens)
Sub: Bates, A (Dewsbury)
      Ramsey (Bradford)

1977 France (WC)
Auckland: 5 June
Won 23-4
Fairbairn (Wigan) 7g
Fielding (Salford)
Holmes (Leeds)
Dyl (Leeds) 1t
Wright, S (Widnes) 1t
*Millward (Hull KR) 1t
Nash (Salford)
Thompson, J (Featherstone)
Ward, D (Leeds)
Pitchford, S (Leeds)
Bowman, E (Workington)
Nicholls (St. Helens)
Hogan (Barrow)
Sub: Gill, K (Salford)
      Casey (Hull KR)

1977 New Zealand (WC)
Christchurch: 12 June
Won 30-12
Fairbairn (Wigan) 6g
Wright, S (Widnes) 2t
Holmes (Leeds)
Dyl (Leeds)
Francis, W (Wigan)
*Millward (Hull KR) 1t
Nash (Salford)
Thompson, J (Featherstone)
Ward, D (Leeds)
Pitchford, S (Leeds)
Bowman, E (Workington) 1t
Nicholls (St. Helens) 1t
Hogan (Barrow) 1t
Sub: Casey (Hull KR)

1977 Australia (WC)
Brisbane: 18 June
Lost 5-19
Fairbairn (Wigan) 1g
Wright, S (Widnes)
Francis, W (Wigan)
Dyl (Leeds)
Fielding (Salford)
*Millward (Hull KR) 1t
Nash (Salford)
Thompson, J (Featherstone)
Ward, D (Leeds)
Pitchford, S (Leeds)
Bowman, E (Workington)
Nicholls (St. Helens)
Hogan (Barrow)
Sub: Holmes (Leeds)
      Smith, P (Featherstone)

1977 Australia (WC)
Sydney: 25 June
Lost 12-13
Fairbairn (Wigan) 3g
Wright, S (Widnes)
Holmes (Leeds)
Dyl (Leeds)
Francis, W (Wigan)
*Millward (Hull KR)
Nash (Salford)
Thompson, J (Featherstone)
Elwell (Widnes)
Pitchford, S (Leeds) 1t
Bowman, E (Workington)
Casey (Hull KR)
Hogan (Barrow)
Sub: Gill, K (Salford) 1t
      Smith, P (Featherstone)

1978 Australia
Wigan: 21 Oct
Lost 9-15
Fairbairn (Wigan) 3g
Wright, S (Widnes)
Hughes (Widnes)
Cunningham (St. Helens)
Bevan, J (Warrington) 1t
*Millward (Hull KR)
Nash (Salford)
Thompson, J (Bradford)
Ward, D (Leeds)
Rose, P (Hull KR)
Nicholls (St. Helens)
Casey (Hull KR)
Norton (Hull)
Sub: Holmes (Leeds)
    Hogan (Barrow)

1979 Australia
Brisbane: 16 June
Lost 0-35
Woods, J (Leigh)
Barends (Bradford)
Joyner (Castleford)
Hughes (Widnes)
Mathias (St. Helens)
Holmes (Leeds)
Stephens (Castleford)
Mills (Widnes)
Ward, D (Leeds)
Skerrett (Wakefield)
Nicholls (St. Helens)
*Laughton (Widnes)
Norton (Hull)
Sub: Evans, S (Featherstone)
    Hogan (Hull KR)

1979 New Zealand
Auckland: 21 July
Won 16-8
Fairbairn (Wigan) 1t,2g
Evans, S (Featherstone) 1t
Joyner (Castleford)
Smith, M (Hull KR) 1t
Hughes (Widnes) 1t
Holmes (Leeds)
Stephens (Castleford)
Casey (Bradford)
Ward, D (Leeds)
*Nicholls (St. Helens)
Hogan (Hull KR)
Grayshon (Bradford)
Adams, M (Widnes)
Sub: Lockwood (Hull KR)

1978 Australia
Bradford: 5 Nov
Won 18-14
Fairbairn (Wigan) 6g
Wright, S (Widnes) 2t
Joyner (Castleford)
Dyl (Leeds)
Atkinson, J (Leeds)
*Millward (Hull KR)
Nash (Salford)
Mills (Widnes)
Fisher (Bradford)
Lockwood (Hull KR)
Nicholls (St. Helens)
Lowe, P (Hull KR)
Norton (Hull)
Sub: Holmes (Leeds)
    Rose, P (Hull KR)

1979 Australia
Sydney: 30 June
Lost 16-24
Fairbairn (Wigan)
Barends (Bradford)
Joyner (Castleford) 1t
Woods, J (Leigh) 5g
Hughes (Widnes) 1t
Holmes (Leeds)
Stephens (Castleford)
*Nicholls (St. Helens)
Ward, D (Leeds)
Skerrett (Wakefield)
Casey (Bradford)
Grayshon (Bradford)
Adams, M (Widnes)
Sub: Evans, S (Featherstone)
    Watkinson (Hull KR)

1979 New Zealand
Christchurch: 5 Aug
Won 22-7
Fairbairn (Wigan) 5g
Evans, S (Featherstone) 1t
Joyner (Castleford)
Smith, M (Hull KR)
Hughes (Widnes) 1t
Holmes (Leeds)
Stephens (Castleford)
*Nicholls (St. Helens)
Ward, D (Leeds)
Skerrett (Wakefield)
Casey (Bradford) 1t
Grayshon (Bradford) 1t
Adams, M (Widnes)

1978 Australia
Leeds: 18 Nov
Lost 6-23
Fairbairn (Wigan)
Wright, S (Widnes)
Joyner (Castleford)
Bevan, J (Warrington) 1t
Atkinson, J (Leeds)
*Millward (Hull KR) 1t
Nash (Salford)
Mills (Widnes)
Fisher (Bradford)
Farrar (Hull)
Nicholls (St. Helens)
Lowe, P (Hull KR)
Norton (Hull)
Sub: Holmes (Leeds)
    Rose, P (Hull KR)

1979 Australia
Sydney: 14 July
Lost 2-28
Fairbairn (Wigan) 1g
Evans, S (Featherstone)
Joyner (Castleford)
Woods, J (Leigh)
Hughes (Widnes)
Topliss (Wakefield)
Redfearn, A (Bradford)
*Nicholls (St. Helens)
Ward, D (Leeds)
Casey (Bradford)
Hogan (Hull KR)
Grayshon (Bradford)
Norton (Hull)
Sub: Holmes (Leeds)
    Adams, M (Widnes)

1979 tourist John Joyner.

303

1979 New Zealand
Auckland: 11 Aug
Lost 11-18
Fairbairn (Wigan) 1g
Evans, S (Featherstone)
Joyner (Castleford)
Smith, M (Hull KR) 1t
Hughes (Widnes) 1t
Holmes (Leeds)
Stephens (Castleford) 1t
Skerrett (Wakefield)
Ward, D (Leeds)
*Nicholls (St. Helens)
Casey (Bradford)
Grayshon (Bradford)
Adams, M (Widnes)
Sub: Woods, J (Leigh)
    Hogan (Hull KR)

1980 New Zealand
Wigan: 18 Oct
Drew 14-14
*Fairbairn (Wigan) 4g
Camilleri (Barrow) 1t
Joyner (Castleford)
Smith, M (Hull KR) 1t
Bentley (Widnes)
Hartley, S (Hull KR)
Dick (Leeds)
Holdstock (Hull KR)
Watkinson (Hull KR)
Skerrett (Hull)
Gorley, L (Widnes)
Grayshon (Bradford)
Casey (Hull KR)
Sub: Pinner (St. Helens)

1980 New Zealand
Bradford: 2 Nov
Lost 8-12
*Fairbairn (Wigan) 4g
Drummond (Leigh)
Joyner (Castleford)
Smith, M (Hull KR)
Camilleri (Barrow)
Kelly (Warrington)
Dick (Leeds)
Holdstock (Hull KR)
Elwell (Widnes)
Shaw, G (Widnes)
Casey (Hull KR)
Grayshon (Bradford)
Pinner (St. Helens)
Sub: Evans, S (Featherstone)
    Gorley, L (Widnes)

1980 New Zealand
Leeds: 15 Nov
Won 10-2
Burke (Widnes) 2g
Drummond (Leigh) 2t
Joyner (Castleford)
Evans, S (Featherstone)
Atkinson, J (Leeds)
Woods, J (Leigh)
Walker (Whitehaven)
Skerrett (Hull)
Elwell (Widnes)
*Casey (Hull KR)
Gorley, P (St. Helens)
Adams, M (Widnes)
Norton (Hull)

1981 France
Hull: 6 Dec
Won 37-0
Fairbairn (Hull KR) 1g
Drummond (Leigh) 2t
Smith, M (Hull KR)
Woods, J (Leigh) 1t, 7g
Gill (Wigan) 3t
Hartley (Hull KR) 1t
Gregory, A (Widnes)
Grayshon (Bradford)
*Ward, D (Leeds)
Skerrett (Hull)
Gorley, L (Widnes)
Gorley, P (St. Helens)
Norton (Hull)
Sub: Burke (Widnes)
    Szymala (Barrow)

1981 France
Marseilles: 20 Dec
Lost 2-19
Burke (Widnes)
Drummond (Leigh)
Smith, M (Hull KR)
Woods, J (Leigh) 1g
Gill (Wigan)
Hartley (Hull KR)
Gregory, A (Widnes)
*Grayshon (Bradford)
Watkinson (Hull KR)
Skerrett (Hull)
Gorley, L (Widnes)
Szymala (Barrow)
Norton (Hull)
Sub: Gorley, P (St. Helens)

1982 Australia
Hull City FC: 30 Oct
Lost 4-40
Fairbairn (Hull KR)
Drummond (Leigh)
Hughes (Widnes)
Dyl (Leeds)
Evans, S (Hull)
Woods, J (Leigh)
*Nash (Salford)
Grayshon (Bradford)
Ward, D (Leeds)
Skerrett (Hull)
Gorley, L (Widnes)
Crooks, L (Hull) 2g
Norton (Hull)
Sub: D. Heron (Leeds)

1982 Australia
Wigan: 20 Nov
Lost 6-27
Mumby (Bradford) 3g
Drummond (Leigh)
Smith, M (Hull KR)
Stephenson, D (Wigan)
Gill (Wigan)
Holmes (Leeds)
Kelly, K (Warrington)
*Grayshon (Bradford)
Dalgreen (Fulham)
Skerrett (Hull)
Eccles (Warrington)
Burton (Hull KR)
Heron, D (Leeds)
Sub: Woods, J (Leigh)
    Rathbone (Bradford)

1982 Australia
Leeds: 28 Nov
Lost 8-32
Fairbairn (Hull KR)
Drummond (Leigh)
Stephenson, D. (Wigan)
Smith, M (Hull KR)
Evans (Hull) 1t
*Topliss (Hull)
Gregory, A (Widnes)
O'Neill, M (Widnes)
Noble (Bradford)
Rose (Hull)
Smith, P (Featherstone)
Crooks, L (Hull) 2g, 1dg
Crane (Hull)
Sub: Courtney (Warrington)

1983 France
Carcassonne: 20 Feb
Won 20-5
Burke (Widnes) 1g
Drummond (Leigh)
Joyner (Castleford) 1t
Duane, R (Warrington)
Lydon (Widnes) 1t, 3g
Myler, A (Widnes)
Gregory, A (Widnes)
O'Neill, M (Widnes)
Noble (Bradford) 1t
Goodway (Oldham) 1t
*Casey (Hull KR)
Rathbone (Bradford)
Flanagan (Oldham)
Sub: Woods, J (Leigh)
    Smith, P (Featherstone)

1983 France
Hull: 6 March
Won 17-5
Mumby (Bradford) 4g
Drummond (Leigh)
Joyner (Castleford)
Duane, R (Warrington) 1t
Lydon (Widnes)
Myler, A (Widnes)
Gregory, A (Widnes) 1t
O'Neill, M (Widnes)
Noble (Bradford)
Goodway (Oldham)
*Casey (Hull KR)
Rathbone (Bradford)
Flanagan (Oldham)
Sub: Smith, P (Featherstone) 1t

1984 France
Avignon: 29 Jan
Won 12-0
*Mumby (Bradford)
Drummond (Leigh)
Duane, R (Warrington)
Foy, D (Oldham) 1t
Clark (Hull KR)
Lydon (Widnes)
Cairns (Barrow)
Rayne, Keith (Leeds)
Watkinson (Hull KR)
Goodway (Oldham) 1t
Worrall, M (Oldham)
Hobbs, D (Featherstone)
Hall (Hull KR)
Sub: Hanley (Bradford)
    Crooks, L (Hull) 2g

1984 France
Leeds: 17 Feb
Won 10-0
Mumby (Bradford)
Clark (Hull KR)
Joyner (Castleford)
Schofield (Hull)
Basnett (Widnes)
Hanley (Bradford)
Cairns (Barrow)
Rayne, Keith (Leeds)
*Noble (Bradford)
Ward, K (Castleford)
Jasiewicz (Bradford)
Hobbs, D (Featherstone) 5g
Hall (Hull KR)
Sub: Smith, M (Hull KR)
    Smith, P (Featherstone)

1984 Australia
Sydney: 9 June
Lost 8-25
Burke (Widnes) 2g
Drummond (Leigh)
Schofield (Hull) 1t
Mumby (Bradford)
Hanley (Bradford)
Foy, D (Oldham)
Holding (St. Helens)
Crooks, L (Hull)
*Noble (Bradford)
Goodway (Oldham)
Burton (Hull KR)
Worrall, M (Oldham)
Adams (Widnes)
Sub: Lydon (Widnes)
    Hobbs, D (Featherstone)

1984 Australia
Brisbane: 26 June
Lost 6-18
Burke (Widnes) 1g
Drummond (Leigh)
Schofield (Hull) 1t
Mumby (Bradford)
Hanley (Bradford)
Myler, A (Widnes)
Holding (St. Helens)
Rayne, Keith (Leeds)
*Noble (Bradford)
Crooks, L (Hull)
Burton (Hull KR)
Goodway (Oldham)
Worrall (Oldham)
Sub: Gregory, A (Widnes)
    Adams (Widnes)

1984 Australia
Sydney: 7 July
Lost 7-20
Burke (Widnes) 1g
Drummond (Leigh)
Schofield (Hull)
Mumby (Bradford)
Hanley (Bradford) 1t
Myler, A (Widnes)
Holding (St. Helens) 1dg
Hobbs, D (Featherstone)
*Noble (Bradford)
Case (Wigan)
Burton (Hull KR)
Goodway (Oldham)
Adams (Widnes)

1984 New Zealand
Auckland: 14 July
Lost 0-12
Burke (Widnes)
Drummond (Leigh)
Schofield (Hull)
Mumby (Bradford)
Hanley (Bradford)
Smith, M (Hull KR)
Holding (St. Helens)
Hobbs, D (Featherstone)
*Noble (Bradford)
Case (Wigan)
Burton (Hull KR)
Goodway (Oldham)
Adams (Widnes)

1984 tourist Chris Burton.

1984 New Zealand
Christchurch: 22 July
Lost 12-28
Burke (Widnes) 2g
Drummond (Leigh)
Hanley (Bradford) 1t
Mumby (Bradford)
Lydon (Widnes)
Myler, A (Widnes) 1t
Gregory, A (Widnes)
Hobbs, D (Featherstone)
*Noble (Bradford)
Case (Wigan)
Burton (Hull KR)
Goodway (Oldham)
Adams (Widnes)
Sub: Joyner (Castleford)
    Beardmore, K (Castleford)

1984 New Zealand
Auckland: 28 July
Lost 16-32
Burke (Widnes) 4g
Drummond (Leigh)
Hanley (Bradford) 1t
Mumby (Bradford) 1t
Lydon (Widnes)
Myler, A (Widnes)
Gregory, A (Widnes)
Hobbs, D (Featherstone)
*Noble (Bradford)
Case (Wigan)
Adams (Widnes)
Goodway (Oldham)
Flanagan (Oldham)
Sub: Donlan (Leigh)
    Joyner (Castleford)

1984 Papua New Guinea
Mount Hagen: 5 Aug
Won 38-20
Burke (Widnes) 1t, 5g
Drummond (Leigh) 2t
Hanley (Bradford) 1t
Mumby (Bradford) 1t
Lydon (Widnes)
Myler, A (Widnes)
Gregory, A (Widnes)
Rayne, Keith (Leeds) 1t
*Noble (Bradford)
Goodway (Oldham)
Flanagan (Oldham)
Hobbs, D (Featherstone) 1t
Adams (Widnes)
Sub: Donlan (Leigh)
    Proctor (Hull)

1985 France
Leeds: 1 March
Won 50-4
Edwards (Wigan)
Ledger (St. Helens)
Creasser (Leeds) 8g
Gribbin (Whitehaven) 1t
Gill (Wigan) 1t
Hanley (Bradford) 2t
Fox (Featherstone) 2t, 1g
Dickinson (Leeds)
Watkinson (Hull KR) 1t
Dannatt (Hull)
*Goodway (Oldham)
Rathbone (Bradford)
Divorty (Hull) 1t
Sub: Gibson (Batley)
    Platt (St. Helens)

1985 France
Perpignan: 17 March
Lost 16-24
Johnson, C (Leigh)
Clark (Hull KR)
Creasser (Leeds) 1g
Foy, D (Oldham) 1t
Ford, P (Wigan) 2t
*Hanley (Bradford)
Fox (Featherstone)
Dickinson (Leeds)
Kiss (Wigan)
Wane (Wigan)
Dannatt (Hull)
Rathbone (Bradford)
Divorty (Hull) 1g
Sub: Harkin (Hull KR)
    Powell (Leeds)

1985 New Zealand
Leeds: 19 Oct
Lost 22-24
Burke (Widnes) 3g
Drummond (Leigh)
Schofield (Hull)
Hanley (Wigan) 1t
Lydon (Widnes) 1t,2g
Myler, A (Widnes)
Fox (Featherstone)
Crooks, L (Hull)
Watkinson (Hull KR)
Fieldhouse (Widnes)
Goodway (Wigan) 1t
Potter (Wigan)
*Pinner (St. Helens)
Sub: Arkwright (St. Helens)

1985 New Zealand
Wigan: 2 Nov
Won 25-8
Burke (Widnes)
Drummond (Leigh)
Schofield (Hull) 4t
Hanley (Wigan)
Lydon (Widnes) 4g
Myler, A (Widnes)
Fox (Featherstone)
Grayshon (Leeds)
Watkinson (Hull KR)
Fieldhouse (Widnes)
Goodway (Wigan)
Potter (Wigan)
*Pinner (St. Helens) 1dg
Sub: Edwards (Wigan)
    Burton (Hull KR)

1985 New Zealand (Also WC)
Elland Rd, Leeds: 9 Nov
Drew 6-6
Burke (Widnes)
Drummond (Leigh)
Schofield (Hull)
Edwards (Wigan)
Lydon (Widnes)
Hanley (Wigan)
Fox (Featherstone)
Grayshon (Leeds)
Watkinson (Hull KR)
Fieldhouse (Widnes)
Goodway (Wigan)
Potter (Wigan)
*Pinner (St. Helens)
Sub: Arkwright (St. Helens)
    Crooks, L (Hull) 3g

1986 France (Also WC)
Avignon: 16 Feb
Drew 10-10
Burke (Widnes)
Drummond (Leigh)
Schofield (Hull)
Hanley (Wigan) 1t
Gill (Wigan)
Myler, A (Widnes)
Fox (Featherstone)
Crooks, L (Hull) 3g
Watkinson (Hull KR)
Wane (Wigan)
Potter (Wigan)
Fieldhouse (Widnes)
*Pinner (St. Helens)
Sub: Platt (St. Helens)

1986 France
Wigan: 1 Mar
Won 24-10
Lydon (Wigan)
Drummond (Leigh) 1t
Schofield (Hull) 1t,2g
Marchant (Castleford) 1t
Laws (Hull KR)
Myler, A (Widnes)
Fox (Featherstone)
Crooks, L (Hull) 2g
*Watkinson (Hull KR)
Fieldhouse (Widnes)
Rayne, Kevin (Leeds)
James (Halifax) 1t
Potter (Wigan)
Sub: Platt (St. Helens)

1986 Australia
Manch. U. FC: 25 Oct
Lost 16-38
Lydon (Wigan) 1t
Marchant (Castleford)
Schofield (Hull) 2t
Hanley (Wigan)
Gill (Wigan) 1g
Myler, A (Widnes)
Fox (Featherstone)
Ward (Castleford)
*Watkinson (Hull KR)
Fieldhouse (Widnes)
Crooks, L (Hull) 1g
Potter (Wigan)
Goodway (Wigan)

1986 Australia
Elland Rd, Leeds: 8 Nov
Lost 4-34
Lydon (Wigan)
Ledger (St. Helens)
Schofield (Hull) 1t
Marchant (Castleford)
Gill (Wigan)
Myler, A (Widnes)
Fox (Featherstone)
Ward (Castleford)
*Watkinson (Hull KR)
Fieldhouse (St. Helens)
Crooks, L (Hull)
Potter (Wigan)
Goodway (Wigan)
Sub: Edwards (Wigan)
     Platt (St. Helens)

1986 Australia (Also WC)
Wigan: 22 Nov
Lost 15-24
Lydon (Wigan) 2g
Gill (Wigan) 1g
Schofield (Hull) 2t, 1dg
Stephenson (Wigan)
Basnett (Widnes)
Myler, A (Widnes)
Gregory, A (Warrington)
Ward (Castleford)
*Watkinson (Hull KR)
Crooks, L (Hull)
Burton (Hull KR)
Goodway (Wigan)
Pinner (Widnes)
Sub: Potter (Wigan)

1987 France (Also WC)
Leeds: 24 Jan
Won 52-4
Lydon (Wigan) 1t, 8g
Forster (Warrington) 1t
Schofield (Hull)
Stephenson (Wigan)
Gill (Wigan)
*Hanley (Wigan) 2t
Edwards (Wigan) 2t
Hobbs (Oldham)
Beardmore, K (Castleford)
Crooks, L (Hull)
Goodway (Wigan) 1t
Haggerty (St. Helens)
Gregory, M (Warrington) 2t
Sub: Creasser (Leeds)
     England (Castleford)

1987 France
Carcassonne: 8 Feb
Won 20-10
Lydon (Wigan) 4g
Forster (Warrington)
Schofield (Hull)
*Hanley (Wigan) 1t
Gill (Wigan) 1t
Edwards (Wigan)
Gregory, A (Wigan)
Hobbs (Oldham)
Beardmore, K (Castleford) 1t
England (Castleford)
Burton (Hull KR)
Haggerty (St. Helens)
Gregory, M (Warrington)
Sub: Dixon (Halifax)

1987 Papua New Guinea (Also WC)
Wigan: 24 Oct
Won 42-0
Hampson (Wigan)
Drummond (Warrington)
Stephenson (Wigan) 7g
Lydon (Wigan) 1t
Ford (Bradford) 1t
Edwards (Wigan) 2t
Gregory, A (Wigan) 1t
Ward (Castleford)
Groves (St. Helens)
Case (Wigan)
Medley (Leeds) 1t
Goodway (Wigan)
*Hanley (Wigan) 1t
Sub: Woods (Warrington)
     Fairbank (Bradford)

1988 France
Avignon: 24 Jan
Won 28-14
Hampson (Wigan)
Drummond (Warrington) 1t
Schofield (Leeds) 2t
Loughlin (St. Helens) 3g
Offiah (Widnes) 1t
*Hanley (Wigan) 1t
Edwards (Wigan)
Ward (Castleford)
Beardmore, K (Castleford)
Waddell (Oldham)
Powell (Leeds)
Medley (Leeds)
Platt (St. Helens)
Sub: Creasser (Leeds) 1g
     Dixon (Halifax)

1988 France
Leeds: 6 Feb
Won 30-12
Hampson (Wigan)
Plange (Castleford) 1t
Schofield (Leeds) 1t, 5g
*Hanley (Wigan) 2t
Ford (Bradford)
Edwards (Wigan)
Gregory, A (Wigan) 1t
Ward (Castleford)
Beardmore, K (Castleford)
Waddell (Oldham)
Powell (Leeds)
Dixon (Halifax)
Platt (St. Helens)
Sub: Stephenson (Leeds)
     Medley (Leeds)

GREAT BRITAIN RECORDS

Most appearances

46	Mick Sullivan*
31	Billy Boston
29 + 1	Cliff Watson
29	George Nicholls
29	Neil Fox
28 + 1	Roger Millward
28	Alan Prescott
27	Phil Jackson
27	Alex Murphy
26	Eric Ashton
26	John Atkinson
25	Brian McTigue
25	Jim Sullivan
25	Tommy Harris

*Mick Sullivan's record number of appearances include a record run of 36 successive matches. In addition he played in two matches against France before they were given Test status.

Most tries
41, Mick Sullivan, also scoring two against France before they were given Test status.

Most goals and points
93 goals, (14 tries), 228 points, Neil Fox.

Longest Test careers

14 years	—	Gus Risman
1932 to 1946 (17 appearances)		
13 years 9 months	—	Billy Batten
1908 to 1921 (10 appearances)		
13 years 6 months	—	Alex Murphy
1958 to 1971 (27 appearances)		
12 years 9 months	—	Roger Millward
1966 to 1978 (28 + 1 appearances)		
12 years 6 months	—	John Atkinson
1968 to 1980 (26 appearances)		
12 years 6 months	—	Terry Clawson
1962 to 1974 (14 appearances)		

Youngest Test player
Shaun Edwards was 18 years 135 days old when he made his Great Britain Test debut against France at Leeds on 1 March, 1985. Born on 17 October, 1966, he beat the previous record held by Roger Millward (born 16 September, 1947) who was not quite 18 years 6 months old when he made his debut for Britain against France at Wigan on 5 March, 1966. Five months earlier Millward was a non-playing substitute for the second Test against New Zealand.

Oldest Test player
Jeff Grayshon (born 4 March, 1949), was 36 years 8 months when he played in his last Test for Britain, against New Zealand at Elland Road, Leeds, on 9 November, 1985.

Record team changes

The record number of team changes made by the Great Britain selectors is 10. This has happened on three occasions — all against Australia — and in the first two cases resulted in unexpected victories.

In 1929, Britian crashed 31-8 to Australia in the first Test at Hull KR and retained only three players for the second Test at Leeds where they won 9-3.

After their biggest ever defeat of 50-12 in the 1963 second Test at Swinton, Britain dropped nine players and were forced to make another change when Vince Karalius was injured and replaced by Don Fox. Britain stopped Australia making a clean sweep of the series by winning 16-5 at Leeds in the last Test.

Following the 40-4 first Test defeat at Hull City's soccer ground in 1982, the selectors again made 10 changes, not including subsitutes. The changes made little difference this time as Britain went down 27-6 in the second Test at Wigan.

Britain have never fielded the same team for three or more successive Tests.

GREAT BRITAIN REGISTER

The following is a record of the 564 players who have appeared for Great Britain in 244 Test and World Cup matches.
It does not include matches against France before 1957, the year they were given official Test match status.
Figures in brackets are the total of appearances, with the plus sign indicating substitute appearances, e.g. (7 + 3).

For matches against touring teams, the year given is for the first half of the season.
World Cup matches are in bold letters except when also classified as Test matches. Substitute appearances are in lower case letters.
A - Australia, F - France, NZ - New Zealand, P - Papua New Guinea.

ACKERLEY, A (2) Halifax: 1952 A; 1958 NZ
ADAMS, L (1) Leeds: 1932 A
ADAMS, M (11 + 2) Widnes: 1979 Aa, NZ3; 1980 NZ; 1984 A2a, NZ3, P
ARKWRIGHT, C (+2) St. Helens: 1985 nz2
ARKWRIGHT, J (6) Warrington: 1936 A2, NZ; 1937 A3
ARMITT, T (8) Swinton: 1933 A; 1936 A2, NZ2; 1937 A3
ASHBY, R (2) Liverpool: 1964 F; Wigan: 1965 F
ASHCROFT, E (11) Wigan: 1947 NZ2; 1950 A3, NZ; 1954 A3, NZ2
ASHCROFT, K (5 + 1) Leigh: **1968 A**; 1968 F; 1969 F; **1970 F,NZ**; Warrington: 1974 nz
ASHTON, E (26) Wigan: **1957 A,NZ**; 1958 A2,NZ2; 1959 F, A3; 1960 F2; **1960 NZ,A**; 1961 NZ3; 1962 F3,A3; 1963 F,A2
ASHURST, W (3) Wigan: 1971 NZ; 1972 F2
ASKIN, T (6) Featherstone R: 1928 A3,NZ3
ASPINALL, W (1) Warrington: 1966 NZ
ASTON, L (3) St. Helens: 1947 NZ3
ATKINSON, A (11) Castleford: 1929 A3; 1932 A3,NZ3; 1933 A; 1936 A
ATKINSON, J (26) Leeds: **1968 F,NZ**; 1970 A3,NZ3; **1970 A2,F,NZ**; 1971 F2,NZ; 1972 F2; **1972 A2,F,NZ**; 1973 A2; 1978 A2; 1980 NZ
AVERY, A (4) Oldham: 1910 A,NZ; 1911 A2

BACON, J (11) Leeds: 1920 A3,NZ3; 1921 A3; 1924 A; 1926 NZ
BARENDS, D (2) Bradford N: 1979 A2
BARTON, F (1) Wigan: 1951 NZ
BARTON, J. (2) Wigan: 1960 F; 1961 NZ
BASNETT, J. (2) Widnes: 1984 F; 1986 A
BASSETT, A (2) Halifax: 1946 A2
BATES, A (2 + 2) Dewsbury: 1974 F2,nz2
BATTEN, E (4) Bradford N: 1946 A2,NZ; 1947 NZ
BATTEN, R. (3) Leeds: 1969 F; 1973 A2
BATTEN, W (10) Hunslet: 1907 NZ; 1908 A3; 1910 A2,NZ; 1911 A2; Hull: 1921 A

BAXTER, J (1) Rochdale H: 1907 NZ
BEAMES, J (2) Halifax: 1921 A2
BEARDMORE, K (4 + 1) Castleford: 1984 nz; 1987 F2; 1988 F2
BELSHAW, W (8) Liverpool S: 1936 A3,NZ2; 1937 A; Warrington: A2
BENNETT, J (7) Rochdale H: 1924 A3,NZ3; Wigan: 1926 NZ
BENTHAM, N (10) Wigan H: 1928 A3,NZ3; Halifax: 1929 A2; Warrington: 1929(cont) A2
BENTHAM, W (2) Broughton R: 1924 NZ2
BENTLEY, K (1) Widnes: 1980 NZ
BENYON, W (5 + 1) St. Helens: 1971 F2,NZ,nz; 1972 F2
BEVAN, D (1) Wigan: 1952 A
BEVAN, J (6) Warrington: 1974 A2,NZ2; 1978 A2
BEVERLEY, H (6) Hunslet: 1936 A3; 1937 A; Halifax: A2
BIRCH, J (1) Leeds: 1907 NZ
BISHOP, T (15) St. Helens: 1966 A3,NZ2; 1967 A3; 1968 F3; **1968 A,F,NZ**; 1969 F
BLAN, W (3) Wigan: 1951 NZ3
BLINKHORN, T (1) Warrington: 1929 A
BOLTON, D (23) Wigan: 1957 F3; 1958 F,A2; 1959 F,A3; 1960 F2; 1961 NZ3; 1962 F2,A,NZ2; 1963 F,A2
BOSTON, W (31) Wigan: 1954 A2,NZ3; 1955 NZ; 1956 A3; 1957 F5; **1957 F,A**; 1958 F; 1959 A; 1960 F; **1960 A**; 1961 F,NZ3; 1962 F2,A3,NZ; 1963 F
BOTT, C (1) Oldham: 1966 F
BOWDEN, J (3) Huddersfield: 1954 A2,NZ
BOWEN, F (3) St. Helens Rec: 1928 NZ3
BOWERS, J (1) Rochdale H: 1920 NZ
BOWMAN, E (4) Workington T: **1977 F, NZ, A2**
BOWMAN, H (8) Hull: 1924 NZ2; 1926 NZ2; 1928 A2,NZ; 1929 A
BOWMAN, K (3) Huddersfield: 1962 F; 1963 F,A
BOYLEN, F (1) Hull: 1908 A
BRADSHAW, T (6) Wigan: 1947 NZ2; 1950 A3,NZ

BRIDGES, K (3) Featherstone R: 1974 F2,A
BRIGGS, B (1) Huddersfield: 1954 NZ
BROGDEN, S (16) Huddersfield: 1929 A; 1932 A3,
NZ3; 1933 A2; Leeds: 1936 A3,NZ2; 1937 A2
BROOKE, I (13) Bradford N: 1966 A3,NZ2;
Wakefield: 1967 A3; 1968 F2; **1968 A,F,NZ**
BROOKS, E (3) Warrington: 1908 A3
BROUGH, A (2) Oldham: 1924 A,NZ
BROUGH, J (5) Leeds: 1928 A2,NZ2; 1936A
BROWN, G (6) Leeds: **1954 F2,NZ,A**; 1955 NZ2
BRYANT, W (4+1) Castleford: 1964 F2; 1966 Aa;
1967 F
BUCKLEY, A (7) Swinton: 1963 A; 1964 F; 1965
NZ; 1966 F,A2,NZ
BURGESS, W (16) Barrow: 1924 A3,NZ3; 1926 NZ3;
1928 A3,NZ2; 1929 A2
BURGESS, W (14) Barrow: 1962 F; 1963 A; 1965 NZ2;
1966 F,A3,NZ2; 1967 F,A; 1968 F; Salford: 1969 F
BURGHAM, O (1) Halifax: 1911 A
BURKE, M (14+1) Widnes: 1980 NZ; 1981 fF; 1983 F;
1984 A3, NZ3, P; 1985 NZ3; 1986 F
BURNELL, A (3) Hunslet: 1951 NZ2; 1954 NZ
BURTON, C (8+1) Hull KR: 1982 A; 1984 A3, NZ2;
1985 nz; 1986 A; 1987 F
BURWELL, A (7+1) Hull KR: 1967 a; 1968 F3; **1968
A,F,NZ**; 1969 F
BUTTERS, F (2) Swinton: 1929 A2

CAIRNS, D (2) Barrow: 1984 F2
CAMILLERI, C (2) Barrow: 1980 NZ2
CARLTON, F (2) St. Helens: 1958 NZ; Wigan:
1962 NZ
CARR, C (7) Barrow: 1924 A2,NZ2; 1926 NZ3
CARTWRIGHT, J (7) Leigh: 1920 A,NZ3; 1921 A3
CASE, B (5) Wigan: 1984 A, NZ3; 1987 P
CASEY, L (12+2) Hull KR: **1977 f,nz,A**; 1978 A;
Bradford N: 1979 A2,NZ3; Hull KR: 1980 NZ3;
1983 F2
CASTLE, F (4) Barrow: 1952 A3; 1954 A
CHALLINOR, J (3) Warrington: 1958 A,NZ; **1960 F**
CHARLTON, P (18+1) Workington T: 1965 NZ;
Salford: **1970 nz**; 1972 F2; **1972 A2,F,NZ**; 1973 A3;
1974 F2,A3,NZ3
CHERRINGTON, N (1) Wigan: 1960 F
CHILCOTT, J (3) Huddersfield: 1914 A3
CHISNALL, D (2) Leigh: 1970 A; **1970 NZ**
CHISNALL, E (4) St. Helens: 1974 A2,NZ2
CLAMPITT, L (3) Broughton R: 1907 NZ; 1911 A;
1914 NZ
CLARK, D (11) Huddersfield: 1911 A2; 1914 A3; 1920
A3,NZ3
CLARK, G (3) Hull KR: 1984 F2; 1985 F
CLARK, M (5) Leeds: 1968 F2; **1968 A,F,NZ**
CLARKE, C (7) Wigan: 1965 NZ; 1966 F,NZ; 1967 F;
1973 A3
CLAWSON, T (14) Featherstone R: 1962 F2; Leeds:
1972 A2,F; Oldham: 1973 A3; 1974 F2,A2,NZ2

CLOSE, D (1) Huddersfield: 1967 F
COLDRICK, A (4) Wigan: 1914 A3,NZ
COLLIER, F (2) Wigan: 1963 A; Widnes: 1964 F
COULMAN, M (2+1) Salford: 1971 f,NZ2
COURTNEY, N (+1) Warrington: 1982 a
COVERDALE, R (4) Hull: **1954 F2,NZ,A**
CRACKNELL, R (2) Huddersfield: 1951 NZ2
CRANE, M (1) Hull: 1982 A
CREASSER, D (2+2) Leeds: 1985 F2; 1987 f; 1988 f
CROOKS, L (11+2) Hull: 1982 A2; 1984 f, A2; 1985
NZ nz; 1986 F2, A3; 1987 F
CROSTON, A (1) Castleford: 1937 A
CROWTHER, H (1) Hunslet: 1929 A
CUNNIFFE, B (1) Castleford: 1937 A
CUNNINGHAM, E (1) St. Helens: 1978 A
CUNLIFFE, J (4) Wigan: 1950 A,NZ; 1951 NZ; 1954 A
CUNLIFFE, W (11) Warrington: 1920 A,NZ2; 1921
A3; 1924 A3,NZ; 1926 NZ
CURRAN, G (6) Salford: 1946 A,NZ; 1947 NZ;
1948 A3
CURZON, E (1) Salford: 1910 A

DAGNALL, R (4) St.Helens: 1961 NZ2; 1964 F;
1965 F
DALGREEN, J (1) Fulham: 1982 A
DANBY, T (3) Salford: 1950 A2,NZ
DANIELS, A (3) Halifax: 1952 A2; 1955 NZ
DANNATT, A (2) Hull: 1985 F2
DARWELL, J (5) Leigh: 1924 A3,NZ2
DAVIES, A (20) Oldham: 1955 NZ; 1956 A3; **1957
F,A**; 1957 F2; 1958 F,A2,NZ2; 1959 F2,A; **1960
NZ,F,A**; 1960 F
DAVIES, E (3) Oldham: 1920 NZ3
DAVIES, J (2) Huddersfield: 1911 A2
DAVIES, W.A (2) Leeds: 1914 A,NZ
DAVIES, W.J (1) Castleford: 1933 A
DAVIES, W.T (1) Halifax: 1911 A
DAVIES, W.T.H (3) Bradford N: 1946 NZ;
1947 NZ2
DAVIES, W (1) Swinton: 1968 F
DAWSON, E (1) York: 1956 A
DICK, K (2) Leeds: 1980 NZ2
DICKENSON, G (1) Warrington: 1908 A
DICKINSON, R (2) Leeds: 1985 F2
DINGSDALE, W (3) Warrington: 1929 A2; 1933 A
DIVORTY, G (2) Hull: 1985 F2
DIXON, C (12+2) Halifax: 1968 F; Salford: 1969 F;
1971 NZ; **1972 F**; 1973 a2; 1974 F2,A3,NZ3
DIXON, M (2) Featherstone R: 1962 F; 1964 F
DIXON, P (1+2) Halifax: 1987 f; 1988 fF
DOCKAR, A (1) Hull KR: 1947 NZ
DONLAN, S (+2) Leigh: 1984 nz, p
DRAKE, J (1) Hull: 1960 F
DRAKE, W (1) Hull: 1962 F
DRUMMOND, D (24) Leigh: 1980 NZ2; 1981 F2;
1982 A3; 1983 F2; 1984 F, A3, NZ3, P; 1985
NZ3; 1986 F2; Warrington: 1987 P;1988 F

DUANE, R (3) Warrington: 1983 F2; 1984 F
DUTTON, R (6) Widnes: 1970 NZ2; **1970 A2,F,NZ**
DYSON, F (1) Huddersfield: 1959 A
DYL, L (11) Leeds: 1974 A2,NZ3; **1977 F,NZ,A2**;
1978 A; 1982 A

ECCLES, P (1) Halifax: 1907 NZ
ECCLES, R (1) Warrington: 1982 A
ECKERSLEY, D (2+2) St.Helens: 1973 Aa; 1974 Aa
EDGAR, B (11) Workington T: 1958 A,NZ; 1961
NZ; 1962 A3,NZ; 1965 NZ; 1966 A3
EDWARDS, A (7) Salford: 1936 A3,NZ2; 1937 A2
EDWARDS, D (3+2) Castleford: 1968 f; 1970 A;
1971 NZ2nz
EDWARDS, S (7+2) Wigan: 1985 F,nzNZ; 1986a;
1987 F2, P; 1988 F2
EGAN, J (14) Wigan: 1946 A3; 1947 NZ3; 1948 A3;
1950 A3,NZ2
ELLABY, A (13) St.Helens: 1928 A3,NZ2; 1929 A2;
1932 A3,NZ2; 1933 A
ELWELL, K (3) Widnes: **1977 A**; 1980 NZ2
ENGLAND, K (1+1) Castleford: 1987 fF
EVANS, B (10) Swinton: 1926 NZ; 1928 NZ; 1929
A; 1932 A2,NZ3; 1933 A2
EVANS, F (4) Swinton: 1924 A2,NZ2
EVANS, J (4) Hunslet: 1951 NZ; 1952 A3
EVANS, J (3) Swinton: 1926 NZ3
EVANS, R (4) Wigan: 1961 NZ2; 1962 F,NZ
EVANS, S (7+3) Featherstone R: 1979 Aa2,NZ3,
1980 NZnz; Hull: 1982 A2
EYRE, K (1) Hunslet: 1965 NZ

FAIRBAIRN, G (17) Wigan: **1977 F,NZ,A2**; 1978 A3;
1979 A2,NZ3; 1980 NZ2; Hull KR: 1981 F;
1982 A2
FAIRBANK, K (+1) Bradford N: 1987 p
FAIRCLOUGH, L (6) St.Helens: 1926 NZ; 1928
A2,NZ2; 1929 A
FARRAR, V (1) Hull: 1978 A
FEATHERSTONE, J (6) Warrington: 1948 A; 1950
NZ2; 1952 A3
FEETHAM, J (8) Hull KR: 1929 A; Salford: 1932
A2,NZ2; 1933 A3
FIELD, H (3) York: 1936 A,NZ2
FIELD, N (1) Batley: 1963 A
FIELDHOUSE, J (7) Widnes: 1985 NZ3; 1986 F2, A;
St. Helens: 1986 A
FIELDING, K (3) Salford: 1974 F2; **1977 F**
FILDES, A (15) St.Helens Recs: 1926 NZ2; 1928
A3,NZ3; 1929 A3; St.Helens: 1932 A,NZ3
FISHER, A (11) Bradford N: 1970 A2,NZ3; **1970 A**;
Leeds: **A**; 1971 F2; Bradford N: 1978 A2
FLANAGAN, P (14) Hull KR: 1962 F; 1963 F; 1966
A3,NZ; 1967 A3; 1968 F2; **1968 F,NZ**; 1970 A
FLANAGAN, T (4) Oldham: 1983 F2; 1984 NZ, P
FOGERTY, T (2+1) Halifax: 1966 nz; Wigan: 1967 F;
Rochdale H: 1974 F

FORD, P (3) Wigan: 1985 F; Bradford N: 1987 P;
1988 F
FORSTER, M (2) Warrington: 1987 F2
FOSTER, F (1) Hull KR: 1967 A
FOSTER, P (3) Leigh: 1955 NZ3
FOSTER, T (3) Bradford N: 1946 NZ; 1948 A2
FOX, Deryck (9) Featherstone R: 1985 F2, NZ3; 1986
F2, A2
FOX, Don (1) Featherstone R: 1963 A
FOX, N (29) Wakefield T: 1959 F,A2; 1960 F3; 1961
NZ2; 1962 F3,A3,NZ2; 1963 A2,F; 1964 F; 1965
F; 1966 F; 1967 F2,A; 1968 F3; 1969 F
FOY, D (3) Oldham: 1984 F, A; 1985 F
FRANCIS, R (1) Barrow: 1947 NZ
FRANCIS, W (4) Wigan: 1967 A; **1977 NZ,A2**
FRASER, E (16) Warrington: 1958 A3,NZ2; 1959 F2,A;
1960 F3; **1960 F,NZ**; 1961 F,NZ2
FRENCH, R (4) Widnes: 1968 F2; **1968 A,NZ**
FRODSHAM, A (3) St.Helens: 1928 NZ2; 1929 A

GABBITAS, B (1) Hunslet: 1959 F
GALLAGHER, F (12) Dewsbury: 1920 A3; 1921 A;
Batley: 1924 A3,NZ3; 1926 NZ2
GANLEY, B (3) Oldham: 1957 F2; 1958 F
GARDINER, D (1) Wigan: 1965 NZ
GEE, ·K (17) Wigan: 1946 A3,NZ; 1947 NZ3; 1948
A3; 1950 A3,NZ2; 1951 NZ2
GEMMELL, R (3) Leeds: 1964 F; Hull: 1968 F;
1969 F
GIBSON, C (+1) Batley: 1985 f
GIFFORD, H (2) Barrow: 1908 A2
GILFEDDER, L (5) Warrington: 1962 A,NZ2,F;
1963 F
GILL, H (10) Wigan: 1981 F2; 1982 A; 1985 F;
1986 F, A3; 1987 F2
GILL, K (5+2) Salford: 1974 F2,A2,NZ; **1977 f,a**
GOODWAY, A (19) Oldham: 1983 F2; 1984 F, A3,
NZ3, P; 1985 F; Wigan: 1985 NZ3; 1986 A3;
1987 F, P
GOODWIN, D (5) Barrow: 1957 F2; 1958 F,NZ2
GORE, J (1) Salford: 1926 NZ
GORLEY, L (4+1) Widnes: 1980 NZnz; 1981 F2;
1982 A
GORLEY, P (2+1) St.Helens: 1980 NZ; 1981 Ff
GOWERS, K (14) Swinton: 1962 F; 1963 F,A3; 1964
F2; 1965 NZ2; 1966 F2,A,NZ2
GRAY, J (5+3) Wigan: 1974 f2,A2a,NZ3
GRAYSHON, J (13) Bradford N: 1979 A2,NZ3; 1980
NZ2; 1981 F2; 1982 A2; Leeds: 1985 NZ2
GREENALL, D (6) St.Helens: 1951 NZ3; 1952 A2;
1954 NZ
GREENALL, J (1) St.Helens Rec: 1921 A
GREENOUGH, R (1) Warrington: **1960 NZ**
GREGORY, A (12+1) Widnes: 1981 F2; 1982 A;
1983 F2; 1984 a, NZ2, P; Warrington: 1986 A;
Wigan: 1987 F, P; 1988 F
GREGORY, M (2) Warrington: 1987 F2

311

GRIBBIN, V (1) Whitehaven: 1985 F
GRONOW, B (7) Huddersfield: 1911 A2, 1920 A2, NZ3
GROVES, P (1) St. Helens: 1987 P
GRUNDY, J (12) Barrow: 1955 NZ3; 1956 A3; 1957 F3; **1957 F,A,NZ**
GUNNEY, G (11) Hunslet: 1954 NZ3; 1956 A; 1957 F3; **1957 F,NZ**; 1964 F; 1965 F
GWYNNE, T. E (3) Hull: 1928 A,NZ; 1929 A
GWYTHER, E (6) Belle Vue R: 1947 NZ2; 1950 A3; 1951 NZ

HAGGERTY, R (2) St Helens: 1987 F2
HAIGH, R (5+1) Wakefield T: **1968 A,F**; Leeds: **1970 NZ,a**; 1971 F,NZ
HALL, D (2) Hull KR: 1984 F2
HALL, W (4) Oldham: 1914 A3,NZ
HALLAS, D (2) Leeds: 1961 F,NZ
HALMSHAW, A (1) Halifax: 1971 NZ
HALSALL, H (1) Swinton: 1929 A
HAMPSON, S (3) Wigan: 1987 P; 1988 F2
HANLEY, E (20+1) Bradford N: 1984 fF, A3, NZ3, P; 1985 F2; Wigan: 1985 NZ3; 1986 F, A; 1987 F2, P; 1988 F2
HARDISTY, A (12) Castleford: 1964 F3; 1965 F,NZ; 1966 A3,NZ; 1967 F2; 1970 A
HARE, I (1) Widnes: 1967 F
HARKIN, P (+1) Hull KR: 1985 f
HARRIS, T (25) Hull: 1954 NZ2; 1956 A3; 1957 F5; **1957 F,A**; 1958 A3,NZ,F; 1959 F2,A3; 1960 F2; **1960 NZ**
HARRISON, F (3) Leeds: 1911 A3
HARRISON, M (7) Hull: 1967 F2; 1971 NZ2; 1972 F2; 1973 A
HARTLEY, D (11) Hunslet: 1964 F2; Castleford: 1968 F; 1969 F; 1970 A2,NZ2; **1970 A2,F**
HARTLEY, S (3) Hull KR: 1980 NZ; 1981 F2
HELME, G (12) Warrington: 1948 A3; 1954 A3,NZ2; **1954 F2,A,NZ**
HEPWORTH, K (11) Castleford: 1967 F2; 1970 A3,NZ2; **1970 A2,F,NZ**
HERBERT, N (6) Workington T: 1961 NZ; 1962 F,A3,NZ
HERON, D (1+1) Leeds: 1982 aA
HESKETH, C (21+2) Salford: 1970 NZ; **1970 NZ,a**; 1971 Ff,NZ3; **1972 A2,F,NZ**; 1973 A3; 1974 F2,A3,NZ3
HICKS, M (1) St.Helens: 1965 NZ
HIGGINS, F (6) Widnes: 1950 A3,NZ2; 1951 NZ
HIGGINS, H (2) Widnes: 1937 A2
HIGSON, J (2) Hunslet: 1908 A2
HILL, C (1) Wigan: 1966 F
HILL, D (1) Wigan: 1971 F
HILTON, H (7) Oldham: 1920 A3,NZ3; 1921 A
HILTON, J (4) Wigan: 1950 A2,NZ2
HOBBS, D (9+1) Featherstone R: 1984 F2, Aa, NZ3, P; Oldham: 1987 F2

HODGSON, M (16) Swinton: 1929 A2; 1932 A3,NZ3; 1933 A3; 1936 A3,NZ; 1937 A
HOGAN, P (6+3) Barrow: **1977 F,NZ,A2**; 1978 a; Hull KR: 1979 Aa,NZ,nz
HOGG, A (1) Broughton R: 1907 NZ
HOLDEN, K (1) Warrington: 1963 A
HOLDER, W (1) Hull: 1907 NZ
HOLDING, N (4) St. Helens: 1984 A3, NZ
HOLDSTOCK, R (2) Hull KR: 1980 NZ2
HOLLAND, D (4) Oldham: 1914 A3,NZ
HOLLIDAY, W (9+1) Whitehaven: 1964 F; Hull KR: 1965 F,NZ3; 1966 Ff; 1967 A3
HOLLINDRAKE, T (1) Keighley: 1955 NZ
HOLMES, J (14+6) Leeds: 1971 NZ; 1972 F2; **1972 Aa,NZ**; **1977 F,NZ,Aa**; 1978 a3; 1979 A2a,NZ3; 1982 A
HORNE, W (8) Barrow: 1946 A3; 1947 NZ; 1948 A; 1952 A3
HORTON, W (14) Wakefield T: 1928 A3,NZ3; 1929 A; 1932 A3,NZ; 1933 A3
HOWLEY, T (6) Wigan: 1924 A3,NZ3
HUDDART, R (16) Whitehaven: 1958 A2,NZ2; St.Helens: 1959 A; 1961 NZ3; 1962 F2,A3,NZ2; 1963 A
HUDSON, B (8) Salford: 1932 NZ; 1933 A2; 1936 A,NZ2; 1937 A2
HUDSON, W (1) Wigan: 1948 A
HUGHES, E (8) Widnes: 1978 A; 1979 A3,NZ3; 1982 A
HURCOMBE, D (8) Wigan: 1920 A2,NZ; 1921 A; 1924 A2,NZ2
HYNES, S (12+1) Leeds: 1970 A2,NZ2nz; **1970 A2,F,NZ**; 1971 F; 1973 A3

IRVING, R (8+3) Oldham: 1967 F2,A3; 1970 a,NZ; 1971 NZ; 1972 f; **1972 NZ,a**

JACKSON, K (2) Oldham: 1957 F2
JACKSON, P (27) Barrow: 1954 A3,NZ3; **1954 F2,A,NZ**; 1955 NZ3; 1956 A3; **1957 F,NZ**; 1957 F5; 1958 F,A2,NZ
JAMES, N (1) Halifax: 1986 F
JARMAN, J.W. (2) Leeds: 1914 A2
JASIEWICZ, R (1) Bradford N: 1984 F
JEANES, D (8) Wakefield T: 1971 F,NZ2; 1972 F2; Leeds: **1972 A2,NZ**
JENKINS, B (12) Wigan: 1907 NZ3; 1908 A3; 1910 A,NZ; 1911 A2, 1914 A,NZ
JENKINS, D (1) Hunslet: 1929 A
JENKINS, D (1) Leeds: 1947 NZ
JENKINS, E (9) Salford: 1933 A; 1936 A3,NZ2; 1937 A3
JENKINSON, A (2) Hunslet: 1911 A2
JOHNSON, A (4) Widnes: 1914 A,NZ; 1920 A2
JOHNSON, A (6) Warrington: 1946 A2,NZ; 1947 NZ3
JOHNSON, C (1) Leigh: 1985 F

JOLLEY, J (3) Runcorn: 1907 NZ3
JONES, B (3) Wakefield T: 1964 F; 1965 F; 1966 F
JONES, B.L (15) Leeds: 1954 A3,NZ3; 1955 NZ3;
   1957 F3; **1957 F,A,NZ**
JONES, D (2) Merthyr: 1907 NZ2
JONES, E (4) Rochdale H: 1920 A,NZ3
JONES, J (1) Barrow: 1946 NZ
JONES, K (2) Wigan: **1970 F,NZ**
JONES, L (1) St.Helens: 1971 NZ
JORDAN, G (2) Featherstone R: 1964 F; 1967 A
JOYNER, J (14+2) Castleford: 1978 A2; 1979
   A3,NZ3; 1980 NZ3; 1983 F2; 1984 F, nz2
JUBB, K (2) Leeds: 1937 A2
JUKES, W (6) Hunslet: 1908 A3; 1910 A2,NZ

KARALIUS, A (4+1) St.Helens: 1971 NZ3; 1972 F;
   1972 nz
KARALIUS, V (12) St.Helens: 1958 A2,NZ2; 1959
   F; **1960 NZ,F,A**; 1960 F; 1961 F; Widnes:
   1963 A2
KEEGAN, A (9) Hull: 1966 A2; 1967 F2,A3; 1968 F;
   1969 F
KELLY, K (4) St.Helens: 1972 F2; Warrington: 1980
   NZ; 1982 A
KEMEL, G (2) Widnes: 1965 NZ2
KERSHAW, H (2) Wakefield T: 1910 A,NZ
KINNEAR, R (1) Wigan: 1929 A
KISS, N (1) Wigan: 1985 F
KITCHEN, F (2) Leigh: **1954 A,NZ**
KITCHIN, P (1) Whitehaven: 1965 NZ
KITCHING, J (1) Bradford N: 1946 A
KNAPMAN, E (1) Oldham: 1924 NZ
KNOWELDEN, B (1) Barrow: 1946 NZ

LAUGHTON, D (15) Wigan: 1970 A3,NZ2; **1970**
   A2,F,NZ; 1971 F2; Widnes: 1973 A; 1974 F2;
   1979 A
LAWRENSON, J (3) Wigan: 1948 A3
LAWS, D (1) Hull K.R: 1986 F
LEDGARD, J (11) Dewsbury: 1947 NZ2; Leigh:
   1948 A; 1950 A2,NZ; 1951 NZ; **1954 F2,A,NZ**
LEDGER, B (2) St. Helens: 1985 F; 1986 A
LEWIS, G (1) Leigh: 1965 NZ
LEYTHAM, J (5) Wigan: 1907 NZ2; 1910 A2,NZ
LITTLE, S (10) Oldham: 1956 A; 1957 F5; **1957**
   F,A,NZ; 1958 F
LLEWELLYN, T (2) Oldham: 1907 NZ2
LLOYD, R (1) Halifax: 1920 A
LOCKWOOD, B (8+1) Castleford: **1972 A2,F,NZ**;
   1973 A2; 1974 F; Hull KR: 1978 A; 1979 nz
LOMAS, J (7) Salford: 1908 A2; 1910 A2,NZ;
   Oldham: 1911 A2
LONGSTAFF, F (2) Huddersfield: 1914 A,NZ
LONGWORTH, W (3) Oldham: 1908 A3
LOUGHLIN, P (1) St.Helens: 1988 F
LOWE, J (1) Leeds: 1932 NZ
LOWE, P (12) Hull KR: 1970 NZ; 1972 F2; **1972**
   A2,F,NZ; 1973 A3, 1978 A2

LOXTON, K (1) Huddersfield: 1971 NZ
LYDON, J (16+1) Widnes: 1983 F2; 1984 F, a,
   NZ2, P; 1985 NZ3; Wigan: 1986 F, A3; 1987
   F2, P

MANN, A (2) Bradford N: 1908 A2
MANTLE, J (13) St.Helens: 1966 F2,A3; 1967 A2;
   1969 F; 1971 F2,NZ2; 1973 A
MARCHANT, A (3) Castleford: 1986 F, A2
MARTIN, W (1) Workington T: 1962 F
MARTYN, M (2) Leigh: 1958 A; 1959 A
McCORMICK, S (3) Belle Vue R: 1948 A2;
   St.Helens: A
McCUE, T (6) Widnes: 1936 A; 1937 A; 1946 A3,NZ
McINTYRE, L (1) Oldham: 1963 A
McKEATING, V (2) Workington T: 1951 NZ2
McKINNEY, T (11) Salford: 1951 NZ; 1952 A2;
   1954 A3,NZ; Warrington: 1955 NZ3; St.Helens:
   1957 NZ
McTIGUE, B (25) Wigan: 1958 A2,NZ2; 1959 F2,A3;
   1960 F2; **1960 NZ,F,A**; 1961 F,NZ3; 1962
   F,A3,NZ2; 1963 F
MATHIAS, R (1) St.Helens: 1979 A
MEASURES, J (2) Widnes: 1963 A2
MEDLEY, P (2+1) Leeds: 1987 P: 1988 Ff
MIDDLETON, A (1) Salford: 1929 A
MILLER, J (1) Wigan: 1911 A
MILLER, J (6) Warrington: 1933 A3; 1936 A,NZ2
MILLS, J (6) Widnes: 1974 A2,NZ; 1978 A2; 1979 A
MILLWARD, R (28+1) Castleford: 1966 F; Hull
   KR: 1967 A3; 1968 F2; **1968 A,F,NZ**; 1970
   A2,NZ3; 1971 F,NZ3; 1973 A; 1974 A2a; **1977**
   F,NZ,A2; 1978 A3
MILNES, A (2) Halifax: 1920 A2
MOONEY, W (2) Leigh: 1924 NZ2
MOORHOUSE, S (2) Huddersfield: 1914 A,NZ
MORGAN, A (4) Featherstone R: 1968 F2;
   1968 F,NZ
MORGAN, E (2) Hull: 1921 A2
MORGAN, R (2) Swinton: 1963 F,A
MORLEY, J (2) Wigan: 1936 A; 1937 A
MORTIMER, F (2) Wakefield T: 1956 A2
MOSES, G (9) St.Helens: 1955 NZ2; 1956 A; 1957
   F3; **1957 F,A,NZ**
MUMBY, K (11) Bradford N: 1982 A; 1983 F; 1984
   F2, A3, NZ3, P
MURPHY, A (27) St.Helens: 1958 A3,NZ; 1959
   F2,A; **1960 NZ,F,A**; 1960 F; 1961 F,NZ3; 1962
   F,A3; 1963 A2; 1964 F; 1965 F,NZ; 1966 F2;
   Warrington: 1971 NZ
MURPHY, H (1) Wakefield T: 1950 A
MYLER, A (14) Widnes: 1983 F2; 1984 A2, NZ2, P;
   1985 NZ2; 1986 F2, A3
MYLER, F (23+1) Widnes: **1960 NZ,F,A**; 1960 F;
   1961 F; 1962 F; 1963 A; 1964 F; 1965 F,NZ;
   1966 A,NZnz; 1967 F2; St.Helens: 1970
   A3,NZ3; **1970 A2,F**

NASH, S (24) Featherstone R: 1971 F,NZ; 1972 F2;
1972 A2,F,NZ; 1973 A2; 1974 A3,NZ3; Salford:
1977 F,NZ,A2; 1978 A3; 1982 A
NAUGHTON, A (2) Warrington: **1954 F2**
NEWBOULD, H (1) Wakefield T: 1910 A
NICHOLLS, G (29) Widnes: 1971 NZ; 1972 F2;
1972 A2,F,NZ; St.Helens: 1973 A2; 1974
F2,A3,NZ3; **1977 F,NZ,A**; 1978 A3; 1979
A3,NZ3
NICHOLSON, R (3) Huddersfield: 1946 NZ;
1948 A2
NOBLE, B (11) Bradford N: 1982 A; 1983 F2; 1984
F, A3, NZ3, P
NORTON, S (11+1) Castleford: 1974 a,NZ2; Hull:
1978 A3; 1979 A2; 1980 NZ; 1981 F2; 1982 A

O'GRADY, T (6) Oldham: 1954 A2,NZ3;
Warrington: 1961 NZ
OFFIAH, M (1) Widnes: 1988 F
OLIVER, J (4) Batley: 1928 A3,NZ
O'NEILL, D (2+1) Widnes: 1971 nz; **1972 A,F**
O'NEILL, M (3) Widnes: 1982 A; 1983 F2
OSTER, J (1) Oldham: 1929 A
OWEN, J (1) St.Helens Recs: 1921 A
OWEN, S (1) Leigh: 1958 F
OWENS, I (4) Leeds: 1946 A3,NZ

PADBURY, R (1) Runcorn: 1908 A
PALIN, H (2) Warrington: 1947 NZ2
PARKER, D (2) Oldham: 1964 F2
PARKIN, J (17) Wakefield T: 1920 A2,NZ3; 1921
A2;1924 A3,NZ; 1926 NZ2; 1928 A,NZ; 1929 A2
PARR, K (1) Warrington: 1968 F
PAWSEY, C (7) Leigh: 1952 A3; 1954 A2,NZ2
PEPPERELL, A (2) Workington T: 1950 NZ; 1951
NZ
PHILLIPS, D (4) Oldham: 1946 A3, Belle Vue R:
1950 A
PIMBLETT, A (3) Warrington: 1948 A3
PINNER, H (6+1) St.Helens: 1980 nzNZ; 1985
NZ3; 1986 F; Widnes: 1986 A
PITCHFORD, F (2) Oldham: 1958 NZ; 1962 F
PITCHFORD, S (4) Leeds: **1977 F,NZ,A2**
PLANGE, D (1) Castleford: 1988 F
PLATT, A (2+3) St. Helens: 1985 f; 1986 fa;
1988 F2
POLLARD, C (1) Wakefield T: 1924 NZ
POLLARD, E (2) Wakefield T: 1932 A2
POLLARD, R (1) Dewsbury: 1950 NZ
POOLE, H (3) Hull KR: 1964 F; Leeds: 1966 NZ2
POTTER, I (7+1) Wigan: 1985 NZ3; 1986 F2, A2a
POWELL, R (2+1) Leeds: 1985 f; 1988 F2
POYNTON, H (3) Wakefield T: 1962 A2,NZ
PRESCOTT, A (28) St.Helens: 1951 NZ2; 1952 A3;
1954 A3,NZ3; 1955 NZ3; 1956 A3; 1957 F5;
1957 F,A,NZ; 1958 F,A2
PRICE, J (6) Broughton R: 1921 A2; Wigan: 1924
A2,NZ2

PRICE, M (2) Rochdale H: 1967 A2
PRICE, R (9) Warrington: 1954 A,NZ2; 1955 NZ;
1956 A3; 1957 F2
PRICE, T (1) Bradford N: 1970 A
PRIOR, B (1) Hunslet: 1966 F
PROCTOR, W (+1) Hull: 1984 p
PROSSER, D (1) Leeds: 1937 A
PROSSER, S (1) Halifax: 1914 A

RAE, J (1) Bradford N: 1965 NZ
RAMSDALE, R (8) Wigan: 1910 A2; 1911 A2; 1914
A3,NZ
RAMSEY, W (7+1) Hunslet: 1965 NZ2; 1966
F,A2,NZ2; Bradford N; 1974 nz
RATCLIFFE, G (3) Wigan: 1947 NZ; 1950 A2
RATHBONE, A (4+1) Bradford N: 1982 a; 1983 F2;
1985 F2
RAYNE, KEITH (4) Leeds: 1984 F2, A, P
RAYNE, KEVIN (1) Leeds: 1986 F
REDFEARN, A (1) Bradford N: 1979 A
REDFEARN, D (6+1) Bradford N: **1972 nz**; 1974
F2,A,NZ3
REES, D (1) Halifax: 1926 NZ
REES, T (1) Oldham: 1929 A
REES, W (11) Swinton: 1926 NZ2; 1928 A3,NZ3;
1929 A3
REILLY, M (9) Castleford: 1970 A3,NZ3; **1970 A2,F**
RENILSON, C (7+1) Halifax: 1965 NZ; 1967 a;
1968 F3; **1968 A,F,NZ**
RHODES, A (4) St.Helens: **1957 NZ**; **1960 F,A**;
1961 NZ
RICHARDS, M (2) Salford: 1974 A,NZ
RILEY, J (1) Halifax: 1910 A
RING, J (2) Wigan: 1924 A; 1926 NZ
RISMAN, A (17) Salford: 1932 A,NZ3; 1933 A3;
1936 A2,NZ2; 1937 A3; 1946 A3
RISMAN, B (5) Leeds: 1968 F2; **1968 A,F,NZ**
RIX, S (9) Oldham: 1924 A3,NZ3; 1926 NZ3
ROBERTS, K (10) Halifax: 1963 A; 1964 F2; 1965
F,NZ3; 1966 F,NZ2
ROBINSON, A (3) Halifax: 1907 NZ; 1908 A2
ROBINSON, Dave (13) Swinton: 1965 NZ; 1966
F2,A3,NZ2; 1967 F2,A2; Wigan: 1970 A
ROBINSON, Don (10) Wakefield T: **1954 F2,NZ,A**;
1955 NZ; Leeds: 1956 A2; 1959 A2; 1960 F
ROBINSON, J (2) Rochdale H: 1914 A2
ROBINSON, W (2) Leigh: 1963 F,A
ROGERS, J (7) Huddersfield: 1914 A; 1920 A3;
1921 A3
ROSE, D (4) Leeds: **1954 F2,A,NZ**
ROSE, P (2+3) Hull KR: 1974 a; 1978 Aa2; Hull:
1982 A
ROUND, G (8) Wakefield T: 1959 A; 1962
F2,A3,NZ2
RUDDICK, J (3) Broughton R: 1907 NZ2; 1910 A
RYAN, M (4) Wigan: 1947 NZ; 1948 A2; 1950 A
RYAN, R (5) Warrington: 1950 A,NZ2; 1951 NZ;
1952 A

RYDER, R (1) Warrington: 1952 A

SAYER, W (7) Wigan: 1961 NZ; 1962 F,A3,NZ; 1963 A

SCHOFIELD, D (1) Halifax: 1955 NZ

SCHOFIELD, G (17) Hull: 1984 F, A3, NZ; 1985 NZ3; 1986 F2, A3; 1987 F2; Leeds: 1988 F2

SEABOURNE, B (1) Leeds: 1970 NZ

SENIOR, K (2) Huddersfield: 1965 NZ; 1967 F

SHARROCK, J (4) Wigan: 1910 A2,NZ; 1911 A

SHAW, B (6) Hunslet: 1956 A2; **1960 F,A**; 1960 F; Leeds: 1961 F

SHAW, G (1) Widnes: 1980 NZ

SHAW, J (5) Halifax: **1960 F,A**; 1960 F; 1961 F; 1962 NZ

SHELTON, G (7) Hunslet: 1964 F2; 1965 NZ3; 1966 F2

SHOEBOTTOM, M (10+2) Leeds: **1968 A,nz**; 1969 F; 1970 A2a,NZ; **1970 A2,F,NZ**; 1971 F

SHUGARS, F (1) Warrington: 1910 NZ

SILCOCK, N (12) Widnes: 1932 A2,NZ2; 1933 A3; 1936 A3; 1937 A2

SILCOCK, N (3) Wigan: 1954 A3

SILCOCK, R (1) Wigan: 1908 A

SIMMS, B (1) Leeds: 1962 F

SKELHORNE, G (7) Warrington: 1920 A,NZ3; 1921 A3

SKERRETT, T (10) Wakefield T: 1979 A2,NZ2; Hull: 1980 NZ2; 1981 F2; 1982 A2

SLOMAN, R (5) Oldham: 1928 A3,NZ2

SMALES, T (8) Huddersfield: 1962 F; 1963 F,A; 1964 F2; Bradford N: 1965 NZ3

SMALL, P (1) Castleford: 1962 NZ

SMITH, A (6) Oldham: 1907 NZ3; 1908 A3

SMITH, A (10) Leeds: 1970 A2,NZ3; **1970 A2**; 1971 F2; 1973 A

SMITH, F (9) Hunslet: 1910 A,NZ; 1911 A3; 1914 A3,NZ

SMITH, G (3) York: 1963 A; 1964 F2

SMITH, H (2) Bradford N: 1926 NZ2

SMITH, M (10+1) Hull KR: 1979 NZ3; 1980 NZ2; 1981 F2; 1982 A2; 1984 f,NZ

SMITH, P (1+5) Featherstone R: **1977 a2;**1982 A; 1983 f2; 1984 f

SMITH, S (11) Wakefield T: 1929 A; Leeds: A2; 1932 A3,NZ3; 1933 A2

SMITH, S (4) Hunslet: **1954 A,NZ,F2**

SOUTHWARD, I (11) Workington T: 1958 A3,NZ; Oldham: 1959 F2,A2; 1960 F2; 1962 NZ

SPENCER, J (1) Salford: 1907 NZ

STACEY, J.C (1) Halifax: 1920 NZ

STEPHENS, G (5) Castleford: 1979 A2,NZ3

STEPHENSON, D (5+1) Wigan: 1982 A2; 1986 A; 1987 F, P; Leeds: 1988 f

STEPHENSON, M (5+1) Dewsbury: 1971 nz; 1972 F; **1972 A2,F,NZ**

STEVENSON, J (19) Leeds: 1955 NZ3; 1956 A3; 1957 F5; **1957 F,A,NZ**; 1958 F; York: 1959 A2; 1960 F2

STOCKWELL, S (3) Leeds: 1920 A; 1921 A2

STONE, W (8) Hull: 1920 A3,NZ3; 1921 A2

STOPFORD, J (12) Swinton: 1961 F; 1963 F,A2; 1964 F2; 1965 F,NZ2; 1966 F2,A

STOTT, J (1) St.Helens: 1947 NZ

STREET, H (4) Dewsbury: 1950 A3,NZ

SULLIVAN, C (17) Hull: 1967 F; **1968 A,F,NZ**; 1970 A; 1971 NZ3; 1972 F2; **1972 A2,F,NZ**; 1973 A3

SULLIVAN, J (25) Wigan: 1924 A3,NZ; 1926 NZ3; 1928 A3,NZ3; 1929 A3; 1932 A3,NZ3; 1933 A3

SULLIVAN, M (46) Huddersfield: **1954 F2,NZ,A**; 1955 NZ3; 1956 A3; 1957 F3; **1957 F,A,NZ**; Wigan: 1957 F2; 1958 F,A3,NZ2; 1959 F2,A3; 1960 F3; **1960 F,NZ,A**; St.Helens: 1961 F,NZ2; 1962 F3,A3,NZ; York: 1963 A

SZYMALA, E (1+1) Barrow: 1981 fF

TAYLOR, H (3) Hull: 1907 NZ3

TAYLOR, R (2) Hull: 1921 A; 1926 NZ

TEMBEY, J (2) St.Helens: 1963 A; 1964 F

TERRY, A (11) St.Helens: 1958 A2; 1959 F2,A3; 1960 F; 1961 F,NZ; Leeds: 1962 F

THOMAS, A (4) Leeds: 1926 NZ2; 1929 A2

THOMAS, G (1) Warrington: 1907 NZ

THOMAS, G (9) Wigan: 1914 A; Huddersfield: 1920 A3,NZ2; 1921 A3

THOMAS, J (8) Wigan: 1907 NZ; 1908 A3; 1910 A2,NZ; 1911 A

THOMAS, L (1) Oldham: 1947 NZ

THOMAS, P (1) Leeds: 1907 NZ

THOMPSON, C (2) Hunslet: 1951 NZ2

THOMPSON, J (12) Leeds: 1924 A,NZ2; 1928 A,NZ; 1929 A; 1932 A3,NZ3

THOMPSON, J (20+1) Featherstone R: 1970 A2,NZ2; **1970 A2,F,NZ**; 1971 Ff; 1974 A3,NZ3; **1977 F,NZ,A2**; Bradford N: 1978 A

THORLEY, J (4) Halifax: **1954 F2,NZ,A**

TOOHEY, E (3) Barrow: 1952 A3

TOPLISS, D (4) Wakefield T: 1973 A2; 1979 A; Hull: 1982 A

TRAILL, K (8) Bradford N: 1950 NZ2; 1951 NZ; 1952 A3; 1954 A,NZ

TROUP, L A (2) Barrow: 1936 NZ2

TURNBULL, A (1) Leeds: 1951 NZ

TURNER, D (24) Oldham: 1956 A2; 1957 F5; **1957 F,A,NZ**; 1958 F; Wakefield: 1959 A; 1960 F3; **1960 NZ,A**; 1961 F,NZ; 1962 A2,NZ2,F

TYSON, B (3) Hull KR: 1963 A; 1965 F; 1967 F

TYSON, G (4) Oldham: 1907 NZ; 1908 A3

VALENTINE, D (15) Huddersfield: 1948 A3; 1951 NZ; 1952 A2; 1954 A3,NZ2; **1954 F2,NZ,A**

VALENTINE, R (1) Huddersfield: 1967 A

VINES, D (3) Wakefield T: 1959 F2,A

WADDELL, H (2) Oldham: 1988 F2

WAGSTAFF, H (12) Huddersfield: 1911 A2; 1914 A3,NZ; 1920 A2,NZ2; 1921 A2
WALKER, A (1) Whitehaven: 1980 NZ
WALLACE, J (1) St.Helens Recs: 1926 NZ
WALSH, Joe (1) Leigh: 1971 NZ
WALSH, John (4 + 1) St.Helens: 1972 f; **1972 A2,F,NZ**
WALTON, D (1) Castleford: 1965 F
WANE, S (2) Wigan: 1985 F; 1986 F
WARD, D (12) Leeds: **1977 F,NZ,A**; 1978 A; 1979 A3,NZ3;1981 F; 1982 A
WARD, Edward (3) Wigan: 1946 A2; 1947 NZ
WARD, Ernest (20) Bradford N: 1946 A3,NZ; 1947 NZ2; 1948 A3; 1950 A3,NZ2; 1951 NZ3; 1952 A3
WARD, J (4) Castleford: 1963 A; 1964 F2; Salford: 1970 NZ
WARD, K (7) Castleford: 1984 F; 1986 A3; 1987 P; 1988 F2
WARD, W (1) Leeds: 1910 A
WARLOW, J (6 + 1) St.Helens: 1964 F; **1968 f,NZ**; 1968 F; Widnes: 1971 F2,NZ
WARWICK, S (2) Salford: 1907 NZ2
WATKINS, D (2 + 4) Salford: 1971 f,NZ; 1973 a; 1974 f2,A
WATKINS, W (7) Salford: 1933 A; 1936 A2,NZ2; 1937 A2
WATKINSON, D (12 + 1) Hull KR: 1979 a; 1980 NZ; 1981 F; 1984 F; 1985 F, NZ3; 1986 F2, A3
WATSON, C (29 + 1) St.Helens: 1963 A2; 1966 F2,A3,NZ2; 1967 F,A3; 1968 F2; **1968 A,F,nz**; 1969 F; 1970 A3,NZ3; **1970 A2,F,NZ**; 1971 F
WATTS, B (5) York: **1954 F2,NZ,A**; 1955 NZ
WEBSTER, F (3) Leeds: 1910 A2,NZ
WHITCOMBE, F (2) Bradford N: 1946 A2
WHITE, L (7) Hunslet: 1932 A3,NZ2; 1933 A2
WHITE, L (6) York: 1946 A3,NZ; Wigan: 1947 NZ2
WHITE, T (1) Oldham: 1907 NZ
WHITEHEAD, D (3) Warrington: 1971 F2,NZ
WHITELEY, J (15) Hull: **1957 A**; 1958 A3,NZ; 1959 F2,A2; 1960 F; **1960 NZ,F**; 1961 NZ2; 1962 F
WILKINSON, J (13) Halifax: 1954 A,NZ2; 1955 NZ3; Wakefield T: 1959 A; 1960 F2; **1960 NZ,F,A**; 1962 NZ
WILLIAMS, F (2) Halifax: 1914 A2
WILLIAMS, R (12) Leeds: 1948 A2; 1950 A2,NZ2; 1951 NZ3; Hunslet: 1954 A2,NZ
WILLIAMS, W (2) Salford: 1929 A; 1932 A
WILLICOMBE, D (3) Halifax: 1974 F; Wigan: F,NZ
WILSON, G (3) Workington T: 1951 NZ3
WILSON, H (3) Hunslet: 1907 NZ3
WINSLADE, C (1) Oldham: 1959 F
WINSTANLEY, W (5) Leigh: 1910 A,NZ; Wigan: 1911 A3
WOOD, A (4) Oldham: 1911 A2; 1914 A,NZ
WOODS, H (6) Liverpool S: 1936 A3,NZ2; Leeds: 1937 A
WOODS, J (1) Barrow: 1933 A

WOODS, J (7 + 4) Leigh: 1979 A3,nz; 1980 NZ; 1981 F2; 1982 Aa; 1983 f; Warrington: 1987 p
WOODS, T (2) Rochdale H: 1911 A2
WORRALL, M (3) Oldham: 1984 F, A2
WRIGHT, J (1) Swinton: 1932 NZ
WRIGHT, S (7) Widnes: **1977 F,NZ,A2**; 1978 A3
WRIGLESWORTH, G (5) Leeds: 1965 NZ; 1966 A2,NZ2

YOUNG, C (5) Hull KR: 1967 A3; 1968 F2
YOUNG, F (1) Leeds: 1908 A
YOUNG, H (1) Huddersfield: 1929 A

St. Helens and Widnes prop John Warlow, capped seven times between 1964 and 1971.

GREAT BRITAIN TOUR SUMMARIES

1910	P	W	D	L	T	For G	Pts	T	Against G	Pts
In Australia	14	9	1	4	76	56	340	51	47	247
In New Zealand	4	4	0	0	43	29	187	11	7	47
TOTAL	18	13	1	4	119	85	527	62	54	294
1914	P	W	D	L	T	G	Pts	T	G	Pts
In Australia	12	9	0	3	77	55	341	24	31	134
In New Zealand	6	6	0	0	46	28	194	12	13	62
TOTAL	18	15	0	3	123	83	535	36	44	196
1920	P	W	D	L	T	G	Pts	T	G	Pts
In Australia	15	12	0	3	83	64	377	48	42	228
In New Zealand	10	9	0	1	89	47	361	24	16	104
TOTAL	25	21	0	4	172	111	738	72	58	332
1924	P	W	D	L	T	G	Pts	T	G	Pts
In Australia	18	14	0	4	104	77	466	56	45	258
In New Zealand	9	7	0	2	64	40	272	25	21	117
TOTAL	27	21	0	6	168	117	738	81	66	375
1928	P	W	D	L	T	G	Pts	T	G	Pts
In Australia	16	11	1	4	67	60	321	43	45	219
In New Zealand	8	7	0	1	55	36	237	16	12	72
TOTAL	24	18	1	5	122	96	558	59	57	291
1932	P	W	D	L	T	G	Pts	T	G	Pts
In Australia	18	15	1	2	105	84	483	32	38	172
In New Zealand	8	8	0	0	65	52	299	17	18	87
TOTAL	26	23	1	2	170	136	782	49	56	259
1936	P	W	D	L	T	G	Pts	T	G	Pts
In Australia	17	14	0	3	79	82	401	38	45	204
In New Zealand	8	8	0	0	52	27	210	8	16	56
TOTAL	25	22	0	3	131	109	611	46	61	260
1946	P	W	D	L	T	G	Pts	T	G	Pts
In Australia	20	16	1	3	146	100	638	36	45	198
In New Zealand	7	5	0	2	35	20	145	12	21	78
TOTAL	27	21	1	5	181	120	783	48	66	276
1950	P	W	D	L	T	G	Pts	T	G	Pts
In Australia	19	15	0	4	133	102	603	22	56	178
In New Zealand	6	4	0	2	37	25	161	16	20	88
TOTAL	25	19	0	6	170	127	764	38	76	266

1954		P	W	D	L	T	G	Pts	T	G	Pts
In Australia		*22	13	1	7	133	114	627	78	96	426
In New Zealand		10	8	0	2	60	56	292	14	32	106
TOTAL		*32	21	1	9	193	170	919	92	128	532

*One match abandoned. Scores included in points total.

1958		P	W	D	L	T	G	Pts	T	G	Pts
In Australia		21	19	1	1	184	129	810	64	93	378
In New Zealand		9	8	0	1	88	61	386	18	27	108
TOTAL		30	27	1	2	272	190	1,196	82	120	486

1962		P	W	D	L	T	G	Pts	T	G	Pts
In Australia		21	18	0	3	151	113	679	61	60	303
In New Zealand		9	6	0	3	73	50	319	35	28	161
TOTAL		30	24	0	6	224	163	998	96	88	464

1966		P	W	D	L	T	G	Pts	T	G	Pts
In Australia		22	13	0	9	112	85	506	47	83	307
In New Zealand		8	8	0	0	57	47	265	10	24	78
TOTAL		30	21	0	9	169	132	771	57	107	385

1970		P	W	D	L	T	G	Pts	T	G	Pts
In Australia		17	15	1	1	104	92	496	27	66	213
In New Zealand		7	7	0	0	61	37	257	9	24	75
TOTAL		24	22	1	1	165	129	753	36	90	288

1974	P	W	D	L	T	G	DG	Pts	T	G	DG	Pts
In Australia	20	15	0	5	104	93	2	500	38	59	3	235
In New Zealand	8	6	0	2	37	32	0	175	8	27	0	78
TOTAL	28	21	0	7	141	125	2	675	46	86	3	313

1979		P	W	D	L	T	G	DG	Pts	T	G	Pts
In Australia		18	13	1	4	66	73	3	347	39	68	253
In New Zealand		9	8	0	1	48	34	0	212	15	12	69
TOTAL		27	21	1	5	114	107	3	559	54	80	332

1984	P	W	D	L	T	G	DG	Pts	T	G	DG	Pts
In Australia	15	11	0	4	70	59	1	399	40	46	2	254
In New Zealand	8	4	0	4	32	25	1	179	21	21	0	126
In Papua New Guinea	1	1	0	0	7	5	0	38	4	2	0	20
TOTAL	24	16	0	8	109	89	2	616	65	69	2	400

GREAT BRITAIN TOUR SQUADS
Captains in bold

1910 Tour

J. Lomas (Salford)
A. Avery (Oldham)
J. Bartholomew (Huddersfield)
W. Batten (Hunslet)
F. Boylen (Hull)
E. Curzon (Salford)
J. Davies (Huddersfield)
F. Farrar (Hunslet)
T. Helm (Oldham)
B. Jenkins (Wigan)
T. Jenkins (Ebbw Vale)
W. Jukes (Hunslet)
H. Kershaw (Wakefield T.)
J. Leytham (Wigan)
T. Newbould (Wakefield T.)
R. Ramsdale (Wigan)
J. Riley (Halifax)
G. Ruddick (Broughton R.)
J. Sharrock (Wigan)
F. Shugars (Warrington)
F. Smith (Hunslet)
J. Thomas (Wigan)
W. Ward (Leeds)
F. Webster (Leeds)
W. Winstanley (Leigh)
F. Young (Leeds)

Managers: J. Clifford
(Huddersfield) and J.
Houghton (St. Helens)

1914 Tour

H. Wagstaff (Huddersfield)
J. Chilcott (Huddersfield)
J. Clampitt (Broughton R.)
D. Clark (Huddersfield)
A. Coldrick (Wigan)
W. Davies (Leeds)
A. Francis (Hull)
J. Guerin (Hunslet)
W. Hall (Oldham)
D. Holland (Oldham)
J. Jarman (Leeds)
B. Jenkins (Wigan)
A. Johnson (Widnes)
F. Longstaff (Huddersfield)

S. Moorhouse (Huddersfield)
J. O'Garra (Widnes)
W. Prosser (Halifax)
R. Ramsdale (Wigan)
J. Robinson (Rochdale H.)
J. Rogers (Huddersfield)
W. Roman (Rochdale H.)
J. Smales (Hunslet)
F. Smith (Hunslet)
G. Thomas (Wigan)
F. Williams (Halifax)
A. Wood (Oldham)

Managers: J. Clifford
(Huddersfield) and J.
Houghton (St. Helens)

1920 Tour

H. Wagstaff (Huddersfield)
J. Bacon (Leeds)
J. Bowers (Rochdale H.)
J. Cartwright (Leigh)
D. Clark (Huddersfield)
W. Cunliffe (Warrington)
E. Davies (Oldham)
J. Doyle (Barrow)
F. Gallagher (Dewsbury)
B. Gronow (Huddersfield)
H. Hilton (Oldham)
D. Hurcombe (Wigan)
A. Johnson (Widnes)
E. Jones (Rochdale H.)
R. Lloyd (Halifax)
A. Milnes (Halifax)
J. Parkin (Wakefield T.)
G. Rees (Leeds)
W. Reid (Widnes)
J. Rogers (Huddersfield)
G. Skelhorne (Warrington)
J. Stacey (Halifax)
S. Stockwell (Leeds)
W. Stone (Hull)
G. Thomas (Huddersfield)
A. Wood (Oldham)

Managers: S. Foster (Halifax)
and J. Wilson (Hull K.R.)

1924 Tour

J. Parkin (Wakefield T.)
J. Bacon (Leeds)
J. Bennett (Rochdale H.)
W. Bentham (Broughton R.)
H. Bowman (Hull)
A. Brough (Oldham)
W. Burgess (Barrow)
C. Carr (Barrow)
W. Cunliffe (Warrington)
J. Darwell (Leigh)
F. Evans (Swinton)
F. Gallagher (Batley)
B. Gronow (Huddersfield)
T. Howley (Wigan)
D. Hurcombe (Wigan)
E. Knapman (Oldham)
W. Mooney (Leigh)
C. Pollard (Wakefield T.)
J. Price (Wigan)
D. Rees (Halifax)
J. Ring (Wigan)
S. Rix (Oldham)
R. Sloman (Oldham)
J. Sullivan (Wigan)
J. Thompson (Leeds)
S. Whitty (Hull)

Managers: J.H. Dannatt
(Hull) and E. Osborne
(Warrington)

1928 Tour

J. Parkin (Wakefield T.)
T. Askin (Featherstone R.)
N. Bentham (Wigan Highfield)
F. Bowen (St. Helens Recs)
H. Bowman (Hull)
J. Brough (Leeds)
W. Burgess (Barrow)
O. Dolan (St. Helens Recs)
A. Ellaby (St. Helens)
B. Evans (Swinton)
J. Evans (Swinton)
L. Fairclough (St. Helens)
A. Fildes (St. Helens Recs)
A. Frodsham (St. Helens)

319

W. Gowers (Rochdale H.)
T. Gwynne (Hull)
B. Halfpenny (St. Helens)
W. Horton (Wakefield T.)
J. Oliver (Batley)
W. Rees (Swinton)
M. Rosser (Leeds)
R. Sloman (Oldham)
J. Sullivan (Wigan)
J. Thompson (Leeds)
W. Williams (Salford)
H. Young (Bradford N.)

Managers: G. Hutchins
(Oldham) and E. Osborne
(Warrington)

1932 Tour

J. Sullivan (Wigan)
A. Atkinson (Castleford)
L. Adams (Leeds)
S. Brogden (Huddersfield)
F. Butters (Swinton)
I. Davies (Halifax)
W. Dingsdale (Warrington)
A. Ellaby (St. Helens)
B. Evans (Swinton)
J. Feetham (Salford)
N. Fender (York)
A. Fildes (St. Helens)
M. Hodgson (Swinton)
W. Horton (Wakefield T.)
B. Hudson (Salford)
J. Lowe (Leeds)
E. Pollard (Wakefield T.)
A. Risman (Salford)
G. Robinson (Wakefield T.)
N. Silcock (Widnes)
S. Smith (Leeds)
J. Thompson (Leeds)
L. White (Hunslet)
W. Williams (Salford)
J. Woods (Barrow)
J. Wright (Swinton)

Managers: R. Anderton
(Warrington) and G. Hutchins
(Oldham)

1936 Tour

J. Brough (Leeds)
J. Arkwright (Warrington)
T. Armitt (Swinton)
A. Atkinson (Castleford)
W. Belshaw (Liverpool S.)
H. Beverley (Hunslet)
S. Brogden (Leeds)
E. Davies (Wigan)
A. Edwards (Salford)
H. Ellerington (Hull)
G. Exley (Wakefield T.)
H. Field (York)
F. Harris (Leeds)
M. Hodgson (Swinton)
B. Hudson (Salford)
E. Jenkins (Salford)
H. Jones (Keighley)
T. McCue (Widnes)
J. Miller (Warrington)
J. Morley (Wigan)
A. Risman (Salford)
N. Silcock (Widnes)
S. Smith (Leeds)
L. Troup (Barrow)
W. Watkins (Salford)
H. Woods (Liverpool S.)

Managers: R. Anderton
(Warrington) and
W. Popplewell (Bramley)

1946 Tour

A. Risman (Salford)
A. Bassett (Halifax)
E. Batten (Bradford N.)
G. Curran (Salford)
W. Davies (Bradford N.)
J. Egan (Wigan)
T. Foster (Bradford N.)
K. Gee (Wigan)
W. Horne (Barrow)
F. Hughes (Workington T.)
D. Jenkins (Leeds)
A. Johnson (Warrington)
J. Jones (Barrow)
J. Kitching (Bradford N.)

B. Knowelden (Barrow)
J. Lewthwaite (Barrow)
T. McCue (Widnes)
H. Murphy (Wakefield T.)
R. Nicholson (Huddersfield)
I. Owens (Leeds)
D. Phillips (Oldham)
M. Ryan (Wigan)
Edward Ward (Wigan)
Ernest Ward (Bradford N.)
F. Whitcombe (Bradford N.)
L. White (York)

Managers: W. Popplewell
(Bramley) and W. Gabbatt
(Barrow)

1950 Tour

E. Ward (Bradford N.)
E. Ashcroft (Wigan)
T. Bradshaw (Wigan)
J. Cunliffe (Wigan)
A. Daniels (Halifax)
T. Danby (Salford)
J. Egan (Wigan)
J. Featherstone (Warrington)
K. Gee (Wigan)
E. Gwyther (Belle Vue R.)
F. Higgins (Widnes)
J. Hilton (Wigan)
W. Horne (Barrow)
J. Ledgard (Leigh)
H. Murphy (Wakefield T.)
D. Naughton (Widnes)
F. Osmond (Swinton)
A. Pepperell (Workington T.)
D. Phillips (Belle Vue R.)
R. Pollard (Dewsbury)
G. Ratcliffe (Wigan)
M. Ryan (Wigan)
R. Ryan (Warrington)
H. Street (Dewsbury)
K. Traill (Bradford N.)
R. Williams (Leeds)

Managers: G Oldroyd
(Dewsbury) and T. Spedding
(Belle Vue R.)

1954 Tour

R. Williams (Hunslet)
E. Ashcroft (Wigan)
W. Boston (Wigan)
J. Bowden (Huddersfield)
B. Briggs (Huddersfield)
A. Burnell (Hunslet)
E. Cahill (Rochdale H.)
F. Castle (Barrow)
J. Cunliffe (Wigan)
D. Greenall (St. Helens)
G. Gunney (Hunslet)
T. Harris (Hull)
G. Helme (Warrington)
J. Henderson (Workington T.)
P. Jackson (Barrow)
B. L. Jones (Leeds)
T. McKinney (Salford)
T. O'Grady (Oldham)
C. Pawsey (Leigh)
A. Prescott (St. Helens)
R. Price (Warrington)
N. Silcock (Wigan)
K. Traill (Bradford N.)
A. Turnbull (Leeds)
D. Valentine (Huddersfield)
J. Wilkinson (Halifax)

Managers: T. Hesketh
(Wigan) and H. Rawson
(Hunslet)

1958 Tour

A. Prescott (St. Helens)
A. Ackerley (Halifax)
H. Archer (Workington T.)
E. Ashton (Wigan)
D. Bolton (Wigan)
F. Carlton (St. Helens)
J. Challinor (Warrington)
A. Davies (Oldham)
B. Edgar (Workington T.)
E. Fraser (Warrington)
D. Goodwin (Barrow)
T. Harris (Hull)
R. Huddart (Whitehaven)
K. Jackson (Oldham)
P. Jackson (Barrow)
V. Karalius (St. Helens)

M. Martyn (Leigh)
B. McTigue (Wigan)
G. Moses (St. Helens)
A. Murphy (St. Helens)
F. Pitchford (Oldham)
I. Southward (Workington T.)
M. Sullivan (Wigan)
A. Terry (St. Helens)
J. Whiteley (Hull)
W. Wookey (Workington T.)

Managers: B. Manson
(Swinton) and T. Mitchell
(Workington T.)
Coach: J. Brough
(Workington T.)

1962 Tour

E. Ashton (Wigan)
D. Bolton (Wigan)
W. Boston (Wigan)
F. Carlton (Wigan)
G. Cooper (Featherstone R.)
B. Edgar (Workington T.)
R. Evans (Wigan)
E. Fraser (Warrington)
N. Fox (Wakefield T.)
D. Fox (Featherstone R.)
L. Gilfedder (Warrington)
N. Herbert (Workington T.)
R. Huddart (St. Helens)
B. McTigue (Wigan)
A. Murphy (St. Helens)
K. Noble (Huddersfield)
H. Poynton (Wakefield T.)
G. Round (Wakefield T.)
W. Sayer (Wigan)
J. Shaw (Halifax)
P. Small (Castleford)
M. Sullivan (St. Helens)
I. Southward (Workington T.)
J. Taylor (Hull K.R.)
D. Turner (Wakefield T.)
J. Wilkinson (Wakefield T.)

Managers: S. Hadfield
(Wakefield T.) and A. Walker
(Rochdale H.)
Coach: C. Hutton (Hull K.R.)

1966 Tour

H. Poole (Leeds)
W. Aspinall (Warrington)
T. Bishop (St. Helens)
I. Brooke (Bradford N.)
W. Bryant (Castleford)
A. Buckley (Swinton)
W. Burgess (Barrow)
C. Clarke (Wigan)
G. Crewdson (Keighley)
C. Dooler (Featherstone R.)
B. Edgar (Workington T.)
P. Flanagan (Hull K.R.)
T. Fogerty (Halifax)
K. Gowers (Swinton)
A. Hardisty (Castleford)
B. Jones (Wakefield T.)
A. Keegan (Hull)
J. Mantle (St. Helens)
F. Myler (Widnes)
W. Ramsey (Hunslet)
K. Roberts (Halifax)
D. Robinson (Swinton)
G. Shelton (Hunslet)
J. Stopford (Swinton)
C. Watson (St. Helens)
G. Wriglesworth (Leeds)

Managers: W. Spaven (Hull
K.R.) and J. Errock (Oldham)

1970 Tour

F. Myler (St. Helens)
J. Atkinson (Leeds)
D. Chisnall (Leigh)
R. Dutton (Widnes)
D. Edwards (Castleford)
A. Fisher (Bradford N.)
P. Flanagan (Hull K.R.)
A. Hardisty (Castleford)
D. Hartley (Castleford)
K. Hepworth (Castleford)
C. Hesketh (Salford)
S. Hynes (Leeds)
R. Irving (Oldham)
D. Laughton (Wigan)
P. Lowe (Hull K.R.)
R. Millward (Hull K.R.)
T. Price (Bradford N.)

M. Reilly (Castleford)
D. Robinson (Wigan)
B. Seabourne (Leeds)
M. Shoebottom (Leeds)
A. Smith (Leeds)
C. Sullivan (Hull)
J. Thompson (Featherstone R.)
J. Ward (Salford)
C. Watson (St. Helens)

Manager: J. Harding (Leigh)
Coach: J. Whiteley (Hull)

1974 Tour

C. Hesketh (Salford)
K. Ashcroft (Warrington)
J. Atkinson (Leeds)
A. Bates (Dewsbury)
J. Bates (Dewsbury)
J. Bevan (Warrington)
J. Bridges (Featherstone R.)
J. Butler (Rochdale H.)
P. Charlton (Salford)
E. Chisnall (St. Helens)
T. Clawson (Oldham)
C. Dixon (Salford)
L. Dyl (Leeds)
D. Eckersley (St. Helens)
K. Gill (Salford)
J. Gray (Wigan)
J. Mills (Widnes)
R. Millward (Hull K.R.)
S. Nash (Featherstone R.)
G. Nicholls (St. Helens)
S. Norton (Castleford)
D. Redfearn (Bradford N.)
P. Rose (Hull K.R.)
J. Thompson (Featherstone R.)
D. Watkins (Salford)
D. Willicombe (Wigan)

Replacements during tour
W. Ramsey (Bradford N.) for
J. Bates; M. Richards
(Salford) for Atkinson

Manager: R. Parker
(Blackpool B.)
Coach: J. Challinor
(St. Helens)

1979 Tour

D. Laughton (Widnes)
M. Adams (Widnes)
D. Barends (Bradford N.)
L. Casey (Bradford N.)
S. Evans (Featherstone R.)
P. Glynn (St. Helens)
J. Grayshon (Bradford N.)
P. Hogan (Hull K.R.)
J. Holmes (Leeds)
E. Hughes (Widnes)
M. James (St. Helens)
J. Joyner (Castleford)
G. Liptrot (St. Helens)
B. Lockwood (Hull K.R.)
T. Martyn (Warrington)
R. Mathias (St. Helens)
J. Mills (Widnes)
R. Millward (Hull K.R.)
K. Mumby (Bradford N.)
S. Nash (Salford)
G. Nicholls (St. Helens)
S. Norton (Hull)
A. Redfearn (Bradford N.)
T. Skerrett (Wakefield T.)
M. Smith (Hull K.R.)
G. Stephens (Castleford)
C. Stone (Hull)
D. Ward (Leeds)
D. Watkinson (Hull K.R.)
J. Woods (Leigh)

Replacements during tour
J. Burke (Wakefield T.) for
Mills; G. Fairbairn (Wigan)
for Martyn; D. Topliss
(Wakefield T.) for Millward

Managers: H. Womersley
(Bradford N.) and
R. Gemmell (Hull)
Coach E. Ashton (St. Helens)

1984 Tour

B. Noble (Bradford N.)
M. Adams (Widnes)
R. Ashton (Oldham)
K. Beardmore (Castleford)
M. Burke (Widnes)

C. Burton (Hull K.R.)
B. Case (Wigan)
G. Clark (Hull K.R.)
L. Crooks (Hull)
S. Donlan (Leigh)
D. Drummond (Leigh)
R. Duane (Warrington)
T. Flanagan (Oldham)
D. Foy (Oldham)
A. Goodway (Oldham)
A. Gregory (Widnes)
E. Hanley (Bradford N.)
D. Hobbs (Featherstone R.)
N. Holding (St. Helens)
J. Joyner (Castleford)
J. Lydon (Widnes)
K. Mumby (Bradford N.)
A. Myler (Widnes)
M. O'Neill (Widnes)
H. Pinner (St. Helens)
W. Proctor (Hull)
Keith Rayne (Leeds)
G. Schofield (Hull)
M. Smith (Hull K.R.)
M. Worrall (Oldham)

Replacement during tour
J. Basnett (Widnes) for Duane

Managers: R. Gemmell (Hull)
and R. Davis (RLHQ)
Coach: Frank Myler (Oldham)

GREAT BRITAIN IN THE WORLD CUP

A — Australia, Fr — France, GB — Great Britain, NZ — New Zealand

1954 in France   *Winners:* Great Britain

30 Oct.	Fr	22	NZ	13	Paris	13,240
31 Oct.	GB	28	A	13	Lyons	10,250
7 Nov.	GB	13	Fr	13	Toulouse	37,471
7 Nov.	A	34	NZ	15	Marseilles	20,000
11 Nov.	GB	26	NZ	6	Bordeaux	14,000
11 Nov.	A	5	Fr	15	Nantes	13,000

Play off

| 13 Nov. | GB | 16 | Fr | 12 | Paris | 30,368 |

Final Table

	P.	W.	D.	L.	F.	A.	Pts.
Great Britain	3	2	1	0	67	32	5
France	3	2	1	0	50	31	5
Australia	3	1	0	2	52	58	2
New Zealand	3	0	0	3	34	82	0

1957 in Australia   *Winners:* Australia

15 June	GB	23	Fr	5	Sydney	50,007
15 June	A	25	NZ	5	Brisbane	29,636
17 June	GB	6	A	31	Sydney	57,955
17 June	NZ	10	Fr	14	Brisbane	28,000
22 June	A	26	Fr	9	Sydney	35,158
25 June	GB	21	NZ	29	Sydney	14,263

Final Table

	P.	W.	D.	L.	F.	A.	Pts.
Australia	3	3	0	0	82	20	6
Great Britain	3	1	0	2	50	65	2
New Zealand	3	1	0	2	44	60	2
France	3	1	0	2	28	59	2

1960 in England   *Winners:* Great Britain

24 Sept.	GB	23	NZ	8	Bradford	20,577
24 Sept.	A	13	Fr	12	Wigan	20,278
1 Oct.	A	21	NZ	15	Leeds	10,773
1 Oct.	GB	33	Fr	7	Swinton	22,923
8 Oct.	A	3	GB	10	Bradford	32,773
8 Oct.	NZ	9	Fr	0	Wigan	2,876

Final Table

	P.	W.	D.	L.	F.	A.	Pts.
Great Britain	3	3	0	0	66	18	6
Australia	3	2	0	1	37	37	4
New Zealand	3	1	0	2	32	44	2
France	3	0	0	3	19	55	0

1968 in Australia   *Winners:* Australia
and New Zealand

25 May	A	25	GB	10	Sydney	62,256
25 May	Fr	15	NZ	10	Auckland	18,000
1 June	A	31	NZ	12	Brisbane	23,608
2 June	Fr	7	GB	2	Auckland	15,760
8 June	A	37	Fr	4	Brisbane	32,600
8 June	GB	38	NZ	14	Sydney	14,105

Final Table

	P.	W.	D.	L.	F.	A.	Pts.
Australia	3	3	0	0	93	26	6
France	3	2	0	1	26	49	4
Great Britain	3	1	0	2	50	46	2
New Zealand	3	0	0	3	36	84	0

Play off final

| 10 June | A | 20 | Fr | 2 | Sydney | 54,290 |

1970 in England   *Winners:* Australia

21 Oct.	A	47	NZ	11	Wigan	9,586
24 Oct.	GB	11	A	4	Leeds	15,084
25 Oct.	NZ	16	Fr	15	Hull	3,824
28 Oct.	GB	6	Fr	0	Castleford	8,958
31 Oct.	GB	27	NZ	17	Swinton	5,609
1 Nov.	Fr	17	A	15	Bradford	6,215

Final Table

	P.	W.	D.	L.	F.	A.	Pts.
Great Britain	3	3	0	0	44	21	6
Australia	3	1	0	2	66	39	2
France	3	1	0	2	32	37	2
New Zealand	3	1	0	2	44	89	2

Play off final

| 7 Nov. | A | 12 | GB | 7 | Leeds | 18,776 |

1972 in France   *Winners:* Great Britain

28 Oct.	Fr	20	NZ	9	Marseilles	20,748
29 Oct.	GB	27	A	21	Perpignan	6,324
1 Nov.	A	9	NZ	5	Paris	8,000
1 Nov.	GB	13	Fr	4	Grenoble	5,321
4 Nov.	GB	53	NZ	19	Pau	7,500
5 Nov.	A	31	Fr	9	Toulouse	10,332

Final Table

	P.	W.	D.	L.	F.	A.	Pts.
Great Britain	3	3	0	0	93	44	6
Australia	3	2	0	1	61	41	4
France	3	1	0	2	33	53	2
New Zealand	3	0	0	3	33	82	0

Play off final

| 11 Nov. | GB | 10 | A | 10 | Lyon | 4,231 |

No further score after extra-time so Great Britain took the championship because they had scored the greatest number of points in the qualifying League table.

1977 in Australia and New Zealand   *Winners:* Australia

29 May	A	27	NZ	12	Auckland	18,000
5 June	GB	23	Fr	4	Auckland	10,000
11 June	A	21	Fr	9	Sydney	13,231
12 June	GB	30	NZ	12	C'church	7,000
18 June	A	19	GB	5	Brisbane	27,000
19 June	NZ	28	Fr	20	Auckland	8,000

Final Table

	P.	W.	D.	L.	F.	A.	Pts.
Australia	3	3	0	0	67	26	6
Great Britain	3	2	0	1	58	35	4
New Zealand	3	1	0	2	52	77	2
France	3	0	0	3	33	72	0

Play off final

| 25 June | A | 13 | GB | 12 | Sydney | 24,457 |

● Details of the current World Cup series which began in 1985 will be given in the next edition.

GREAT BRITAIN WORLD CUP SQUADS

Captains in bold

1954 IN FRANCE

D. Valentine (Huddersfield)
W. Banks (Huddersfield)
H. Bradshaw (Huddersfield)
G. Brown (Leeds)
R. Coverdale (Hull)
G. Helme (Warrington)
P. Jackson (Barrow)
F. Kitchen (Leigh)
J. Ledgard (Leigh)

A. Naughton (Warrington)
D. Robinson (Wakefield T)
D. Rose (Leeds)
R. Rylance (Huddersfield)
S. Smith (Hunslet)
M. Sullivan (Huddersfield)
J. Thorley (Halifax)
B. Watts (York)
J. Whiteley (Hull)

Manager: G. Shaw (Castleford)

1957 IN AUSTRALIA

A. Prescott (St. Helens)
E. Ashton (Wigan)
W. Boston (Wigan)
A. Davies (Oldham)
J. Grundy (Barrow)
G. Gunney (Hunslet)
T. Harris (Hull)
P. Jackson (Barrow)
L. Jones (Leeds)

S. Little (Oldham)
T. McKinney (St. Helens)
G. Moses (St. Helens)
R. Price (Warrington)
A. Rhodes (St. Helens)
J. Stevenson (Leeds)
M. Sullivan (Huddersfield)
D. Turner (Oldham)
J. Whiteley (Hull)

Managers: W. Fallowfield (RL Secretary) and H. Rawson (Hunslet)

1960 IN ENGLAND

E. Ashton (Wigan)
W. Boston (Wigan)
J. Challinor (Warrington)
A. Davies (Oldham)
E. Fraser (Warrington)
R. Greenough (Warrington)
T. Harris (Hull)
V. Karalius (St. Helens)
B. McTigue (Wigan)

A. Murphy (St. Helens)
F. Myler (Widnes)
A. Rhodes (St. Helens)
B. Shaw (Hunslet)
J. Shaw (Halifax)
M. Sullivan (Wigan)
D. Turner (Wakefield T)
J. Whiteley (Hull)
J. Wilkinson (Wakefield T)

Manager: W. Fallowfield (RL Secretary)

1968 IN AUSTRALIA AND NEW ZEALAND

B. Risman (Leeds)
J. Atkinson (Leeds)
K. Ashcroft (Leigh)
T. Bishop (St. Helens)
I. Brooke (Wakefield T)
A. Burwell (Hull KR)
M. Clark (Leeds)
D. Edwards (Castleford)
P. Flanagan (Hull KR)

R. French (Widnes)
R. Haigh (Wakefield T)
R. Millward (Hull KR)
A. Morgan (Featherstone R)
C. Renilson (Halifax)
M. Shoebottom (Leeds)
C. Sullivan (Hull)
J. Warlow (St. Helens)
C. Watson (St. Helens)
C. Young (Hull KR)

Manager: W. Fallowfield (RL Secretary)

Coach: C. Hutton (Hull KR)

1970 IN ENGLAND

F. Myler (St. Helens)
K. Ashcroft (Leigh)
J. Atkinson (Leeds)
P. Charlton (Salford)
D. Chisnall (Leigh)
R. Dutton (Widnes)
A. Fisher (Bradford N & Leeds)
R. Haigh (Leeds)
D. Hartley (Castleford)
C. Hesketh (Salford)

K. Hepworth (Castleford)
S. Hynes (Leeds)
K. Jones (Wigan)
D. Laughton (Wigan)
M. Reilly (Castleford)
M. Shoebottom (Leeds)
A. Smith (Leeds)
J. Thompson (Featherstone R)
C. Watson (St. Helens)

Manager: J. Harding (Leigh)

Coach: J. Whiteley (Hull KR)

1972 IN FRANCE

C. Sullivan (Hull)
J. Atkinson (Leeds)
P. Charlton (Salford)
T. Clawson (Leeds)
C. Dixon (Salford)
C. Hesketh (Salford)
J. Holmes (Leeds)
R. Irving (Oldham)
D. Jeanes (Leeds)
A. Karalius (St. Helens)

Manager: W. Spaven (Hull KR)

B. Lockwood (Castleford)
P. Lowe (Hull KR)
S. Nash (Featherstone R)
G. Nicholls (Widnes)
D. O'Neill (Widnes)
D. Redfearn (Bradford N)
M. Stephenson (Dewsbury)
D. Topliss (Wakefield T)
John Walsh (St. Helens)

Coach: J. Challinor (St. Helens)

1977 IN AUSTRALIA AND NEW ZEALAND

R. Millward (Hull KR)
E. Bowman (Workington T)
L. Casey (Hull KR)
L. Dyl (Leeds)
K. Elwell (Widnes)
G. Fairbairn (Wigan)
K. Fielding (Salford)
W. Francis (Wigan)
K. Gill (Salford)
A. Hodkinson (Rochdale H)

Manager: R. Parker (Blackpool B)

P. Hogan (Barrow)
J. Holmes (Leeds)
S. Lloyd (Castleford)
S. Nash (Salford)
G. Nicholls (St. Helens)
S. Pitchford (Leeds)
P. Smith (Featherstone R)
J. Thompson (Featherstone R)
D. Ward (Leeds)
S. Wright (Widnes)

Coach: D. Watkins (Salford)

Wigan's Ian Gildart splashes his way through the St. Helens mudbath.

UNDER-21s

Great Britain's young Lions crashed to a first-ever double defeat by their French counterparts in the 23-year history of Under-24 and Under-21 internationals.

A last minute touchline penalty goal inflicted a 14-13 defeat at Aussillon — Malcolm Reilly's first reversal in seven internationals since his January 1987 appointment — while France scored the only try in a quagmire for an 8-4 victory at St. Helens two weeks later.

Britain again had an under-24 age limit while France included some older players. Under new coach Jacques Jorda, France deserved success in both encounters, a complete contrast to 12 months earlier when Britain rattled up 94 points in a double record breaker.

In the opening international at Aussillon it looked as though Hull K.R. drop kick ace Wayne Parker had snatched victory when he coolly hit his 13th of the season five minutes from the end. With a minute to go, Castleford full back Gary Lord obstructed winger Jean-Philippe Pougeau and substitute Freddy Bourrel struck a superb 40-yard penalty goal from the touchline to record only the third French success at this level since Under-24 football was first introduced in 1965.

Britain looked the sharper side in the opening quarter, skipper Martin Dermott providing a slick pass to send second row man Dean Sampson crashing over for a seventh minute try. Hull K.R. marksman Mike Fletcher added the goal and then kicked a 19th minute penalty goal.

The French, with six Test men in their ranks, hit back in style after 27 minutes with classy centre David Fraisse scoring a superb try and adding the goal. Six minutes after the break, second row man Daniel Divet crashed through a two-man tackle, Eric Vergniol tacking on the goal.

After hookers Dermott and Thierry Valero were sent to the sin bin by referee John McDonald, Castleford prop Kenny Hill hauled Britain back into the game by setting up a try for Leeds winger Richard Pratt to level the scores and set up an exciting finale.

A fortnight later, Reilly brought back Featherstone Rovers full back Chris Bibb and Wigan utility man Richard Russell, both ruled out of the first encounter by injury, but lost flu victim Darren Wright which forced a reshuffle in the back division.

The Under-21 match was preceded by the Colts international as part of an Anglo-French doubleheader, leaving the Knowsley Road pitch mudbound. With the rain driving down relentlessly, the fixture would normally have been postponed.

Both sides earned full credit for commitment and effort but the atrocious conditions ruled out any positive football. The Whitbread Trophy Bitter Man of the Match was shared between both teams as individual performances were difficult to sustain in the strength-sapping conditions.

With Britain again lacking flair, France always looked the better side and took the lead with the only touchdown of the game after 24 minutes. Stand off Dominique Espugna dived over by the posts, centre Fraisse adding the goal, British centre Fletcher reducing the arrears with a penalty goal on the stroke of half-time.

Fraisse put France further ahead with a penalty goal on the hour as the St. Helens pitch deteriorated into a bog, Fletcher completing the scoring eight minutes later with his second penalty goal.

Ironically, the first-ever double defeat coincided with the announcement of plans for the reshaping of junior football in Britain with the likelihood of a new under-19 set-up bringing about the end of Under-21 and Colts internationals.

6 March		Aussillon

GREAT BRITAIN 13 and **FRANCE 14**

Gary Lord (Castleford)	1.	Jean Frison (Toulouse)
Richard Pratt (Leeds)	2.	Laurent Toniol (Toulouse)
Mike Fletcher (Hull K.R.)	3.	Eric Vergniol (Villeneuve)
Darren Wright (Widnes)	4.	David Fraisse (Le Pontet)
Errol Johnson (Leeds)	5.	Jean-Philippe Pougeau (St. Esteve)
Shaun Irwin (Castleford)	6.	Dominique Espugna (Lezignan), Capt.
Wayne Parker (Hull K.R.)	7.	Ronel Zenon (Chatillon)
Ian Lucas (Wigan)	8.	Amar Mimouni (Pia)
Martin Dermott (Wigan), Capt.	9	Thierry Valero (Lezignan)
Kenny Hill (Castleford)	10.	Georges Grandjean (Lezignan)
Ian Gildart (Wigan)	11.	Daniel Divet (Limoux)
Dean Sampson (Castleford)	12.	Thierry Blachere (Le Pontet)
Gary Sanderson (Warrington)	13.	Jacques Moliner (Lezignan)
Frank Cassidy (Swinton)	14.	Freddy Bourrel (Limoux)
Neil Harmon (Warrington)	15.	Jean-Luc Bardes (St. Esteve)

T: Sampson, Pratt
G: Fletcher (2), Parker (dg)
Substitutions:
Harmon for Sampson (55 min.)
Cassidy for Wright (70 min.)
Manager: Les Bettinson
Coach: Malcolm Reilly
Attendance: 400

T: Fraisse, Divet
G: Fraisse, Pougeau, Bourrel
Substitutions:
Bardes for Moliner (10 min.)
Bourrel for Fraisse (44 min.)
Half-time: 8-6
Referee: John McDonald (Wigan)

19 March		St. Helens

GREAT BRITAIN 4 and **FRANCE 8**

Chris Bibb (Featherstone R.)	1.	Jean Frison (Toulouse)
Richard Pratt (Leeds)	2.	Phillipe Chiron (Carpentras)
Mike Fletcher (Hull K.R.)	3.	Jean-Philippe Pougeau (St. Esteve)
Frank Cassidy (Swinton)	4.	David Fraisse (Le Pontet)
Errol Johnson (Leeds)	5.	Alain Carriere (Lezignan)
Steve Robinson (Halifax)	6.	Dominique Espugna (Lezignan), Capt.
Wayne Parker (Hull K.R.)	7.	Ronel Zenon (Chatillon)
Ian Lucas (Wigan)	8.	Amar Mimouni (Pia)
Martin Dermott (Wigan), Capt.	9.	Thierry Valero (Lezignan)
Kenny Hill (Castleford)	10.	Georges Grandjean (Lezignan)
Ian Gildart (Wigan)	11.	Thierry Blachere (Le Pontet)
Neil Harmon (Warrington)	12.	Daniel Divet (Limoux)
Gary Sanderson (Warrington)	13.	Jacques Pech (Limous)
Richard Russell (Wigan)	14.	Franz Martial (Paris)
Gary Price (Wakefield T.)	15.	Jean-Luc Bardes (St. Esteve)

G: Fletcher (2)
Substitutions:
Russell for Robinson (52 min.)
Price for Hill (70 min.)
Manager: Les Bettinson
Coach: Malcolm Reilly
Attendance: 852

T: Espugna
G: Fraisse (2)
Substitution:
Martial for Carriere (52 min.)
Half-time: 2-6
Referee: Robert Belle (France)

GREAT BRITAIN
UNDER-21s RESULTS

25 Nov. 1984	W 24-8	v. F	Castleford
16 Dec. 1984	W 8-2	v. F	Albi
9 Oct. 1985	L 12-16	v. NZ	Bradford
19 Jan. 1986	L 6-19	v. F	St. Esteve
2 Feb. 1986	W 6-2	v. F	Whitehaven
8 Mar. 1987	W 40-7	v. F	St. Jean de Luz
21 Mar. 1987	W 54-6	v. F	St. Helens
6 Mar. 1988	L 13-14	v. F	Ausillon
19 Mar. 1988	L 4-8	v. F	St. Helens

Key: A - Australia, F - France,
NZ - New Zealand

GREAT BRITAIN
UNDER-21s REGISTER

The following is a register of appearances for Great Britain Under-21s since this classification of match was introduced in 1984.

Figures in brackets are the total appearances, with the plus sign indicating substitute appearances, e.g. (3 + 1).

Away matches are in bold letters. Substitute appearances are in lower case letters.

ALLEN, S. (1) St. Helens: 1984 F

BECKWITH, M. (1 + 1) Whitehaven: 1986 f, F
BIBB, C. (3) Featherstone R.: 1987 F, F; 1988 F
BISHOP, P. (1 + 1) Warrington: 1987 F, f

CARBERT, B. (3) Warrington: 1985 NZ; 1986 F, F
CASSIDY, F. (1 + 1) Swinton: 1988 f, F
CLARK, G. (2) Hull K.R.: 1984 F, F
CONWAY, M. (1) Leeds: 1984 F
CREASSER, D. (5) Leeds: 1984 F, F; 1985 NZ; 1986 F, F
CROOKS, L. (2) Hull: 1984 F, F
CURRIER, A. (2) Widnes: 1984 F, F

DALTON, J. (3) Whitehaven: 1985 NZ; 1986 F, F
DANNATT, A. (6) Hull: 1984 F, F; 1985 NZ; 1986 F; 1987 F, F
DERMOTT, M. (4) Wigan: 1987 F, F; 1988 F, F
DISLEY, G. (+ 1) Salford: 1987 f
DIVORTY, G. (6) Hull: 1984 F; 1985 NZ; 1986 F, F; 1987 F, F

Warrington packman Neil Harman fends off French centre David Fraisse in the St. Helens mud.

EASTWOOD, P. (2) Hull: 1987 **F**, **F**
EDWARDS, S. (4) Wigan: 1984 F; 1985 NZ;
1987 **F**, **F**

FLETCHER, M. (2) Hull K.R.: 1988 **F**, **F**
FORD, M. (3+1) Wigan: 1985 NZ; 1986 **F**;
Leigh: 1987 f, **F**
FORSTER, M. (3) Warrington: 1985 NZ; 1986 **F**, **F**
FOX, D. (1) Featherstone R.: 1984 **F**

GILDART, I. (2) Wigan: 1988 **F**, **F**
GREGORY, M. (1) Warrington: 1984 **F**
GRIBBIN, V. (1+1) Whitehaven: 1984 f, **F**
GROVES, P. (3) Salford: 1984 F, **F**; 1985 NZ

HARCOMBE, K. (1) Rochdale H.: 1986 F
HARMON, N. (1+1) Warrington: 1988 f, **F**
HILL, B. (+1) Leeds: 1986 f
HILL, K. (2) Castleford: 1988 **F**, **F**
HUGHES, G. (1) Leigh: 1986 F
HULME, D. (2+1) Widnes: 1985 nz; 1986 **F**, **F**

IRWIN, S. (1) Castleford: 1988 **F**

JOHNSON, E. (2) Leeds: 1988 **F**, **F**

LORD, G. (1) Castleford: 1988 **F**
LOUGHLIN, P. (2) St. Helens: 1987 **F**, **F**
LUCAS, I. (2) Wigan: 1988 **F**, **F**
LYMAN, P. (3) Featherstone R.: 1985 NZ; 1986 **F**, **F**
LYON, D. (2) Widnes: 1985 NZ; 1986 **F**

McCORMACK, K. (2) St. Helens: 1987 **F**, **F**
MEDLEY, P. (2) Leeds: 1987 **F**, **F**
MOUNTAIN. D. (+1) Castleford: 1987 f

PARKER, W. (2) Hull K.R.: 1988 **F**, **F**
POWELL, R. (5) Leeds: 1984 F, **F**; 1985 NZ;
1986 **F**, **F**
PRATT, R. (2) Leeds: 1988 **F**, **F**
PRICE, G. (+1) Wakefield T.: 1988 f
PROCTOR, W. (+1) Hull: 1984 f
PUCKERING, N. (4) Hull: 1986 F, **F**; 1987 **F**, **F**

RIPPON, A. (1) Swinton: 1984 **F**
ROBINSON, S. (1) Halifax: 1988 **F**
ROUND, P. (1+1) St. Helens: 1984 F, f
RUSSELL, R. (1+1) Wigan: 1987 F; 1988 f

SAMPSON, D. (1) Castleford: 1988 **F**
SANDERSON, G. (4) Warrington: 1987 **F**, **F**;
1988 **F**, **F**
SCHOFIELD, G. (2) Hull: 1984 **F**, **F**

WANE, S. (3) Wigan: 1984 **F**; 1985 NZ; 1986 **F**
WESTHEAD, J. (1+2) Leigh: 1985 nz; 1986 f, **F**
WRIGHT, D. (2) Widnes: 1987 **F**; 1988 **F**

GREAT BRITAIN UNDER-24s RESULTS

3 Apr.	1965	W 17-9	v. F	Toulouse
20 Oct.	1965	W 12-5	v. F	Oldham
26 Nov.	1966	L 4-7	v. F	Bayonne
17 Apr.	1969	W 42-2	v. F	Castleford
14 Nov.	1976	W 19-2	v. F	Hull K.R.
5 Dec.	1976	W 11-9	v. F	Albi
12 Nov.	1977	W 27-9	v. F	Hull
18 Dec.	1977	W 8-4	v. F	Tonneins
4 Oct.	1978	L 8-30	v. A	Hull K.R.
14 Jan.	1979	W 15-3	v. F	Limoux
24 Nov.	1979	W 14-2	v. F	Leigh
13 Jan.	1980	W 11-7	v. F	Carcassonne
5 Nov.	1980	L 14-18	v. NZ	Fulham
10 Jan.	1981	W 9-2	v. F	Villeneuve
16 Jan.	1982	W 19-16	v. F	Leeds
21 Feb.	1982	W 24-12	v. F	Tonneins
16 Jan.	1983	W 19-5	v. F	Carpentras
11 Nov.	1983	W 28-23	v. F	Villeneuve
4 Dec.	1983	W 48-1	v. F	Oldham

GREAT BRITAIN UNDER-24s REGISTER
Since reintroduction in 1976

The following is a register of appearances for Great Britain Under-24s since this classification of match was reintroduced in 1976, until it was replaced by the new Under-21 level in 1984.

Figures in brackets are the total appearances, with the plus sign indicating substitute appearances, e.g. (7+3).

Away matches are in bold letters. Substitute appearances are in lower case letters.

ARKWRIGHT, C. (1) St. Helens: 1982 F
ASHTON, R. (3) Oldham: 1983 **F**, **F**, **F**

BANKS, B. (1) York: 1979 F
BELL, K. (2) Featherstone R.: 1977 F, **F**
BENTLEY, K. (+1) Widnes: 1980 nz
BURKE, M. (5) Widnes: 1979 F; 1980 **F**, NZ;
1982 F; 1983 **F**
BURTON, B. (2) Castleford: 1976 F, **F**

CAIRNS, D. (2) Barrow: 1979 F; 1982 **F**
CASE, B. (3 + 1) Warrington: 1979 **F**; 1980 NZ: 1981 **F**; 1982 f
CLARK, G. (3) Hull K.R.: 1983 **F, F, F**
CRAMPTON, J. (4) Hull: 1976 F, **F**; 1977 F, **F**
CROOKS, L. (1) Hull: 1983 F

DICKINSON, R. (5) Leeds: 1976 F, **F**; 1977 F, **F**; 1978 A
DRUMMOND, D. (5) Leigh: 1979 F; 1980 **F**; 1981 F; 1982 F, **F**
DUANE, R. (2) Warrington: 1983 **F, F**
DUNN, B. (2) Wigan: 1983 **F, F**

ECCLES, R. (2) Warrington: 1978 A; 1979 F
ENGLAND, K. (+ 1) Castleford: 1983 f
EVANS, S. (3) Featherstone R.: 1980 NZ; 1981 **F**; Hull: 1982 **F**

FENNELL, D. (1) Featherstone R.: 1978 A
FENTON, S. (6) Castleford: 1977 F, **F**; 1979 F; 1980 **F**, NZ; 1981 **F**
FIELDHOUSE, J. (1 + 1) Warrington: 1983 **F**, f
FLANAGAN, T. (5) Oldham: 1980 NZ; 1981 **F**; 1983 **F, F, F**
FORD, Phil (1) Warrington: 1982 **F**
FOX, V. (1) Whitehaven: 1980 NZ
FOY, D. (2) Oldham: 1983 **F, F**

GIBBINS, M. (2) Featherstone R.: 1977 F, **F**
GILBERT, J. (2 + 1) Featherstone R.: 1977 F; 1977 f; 1981 **F**
GILL, H. (1) Wigan: 1982 F
GOODWAY, A. (2) Oldham: 1983 **F, F**
GREGORY, A. (1) Widnes: 1982 F

HALL, D. (+ 1) Hull K.R.: 1976 f
HANLEY, E. (2) Bradford N.: 1982 F; 1983 F
HARKIN, P. (1) Hull K.R.: 1981 **F**
HARTLEY, I. (1) Workington T.: 1979 F
HOBBS, D. (2) Featherstone R.: 1982 F, **F**
HOGAN, P. (2) Barrow: 1978 A; Hull K.R.: 1979 **F**
HOLDING, N. (4) St. Helens: 1979 F; 1980 **F**, NZ; 1983 **F**
HOLDSTOCK, R. (3) Hull K.R.: 1978 A; 1979 **F**; 1980 **F**
HORNBY, J. (2) Wigan: 1978 A; 1979 **F**
HYDE, G. (1 + 1) Castleford: 1980 NZ; 1982 f

JAMES, K. (1) Bramley: 1980 **F**
JOHNSON, B. (2) Castleford: 1982 F, **F**
JOYNER, J. (4 + 1) Castleford: 1976 f; 1977 F, **F**; 1978 A; 1979 F

LEDGER, B. (2) St. Helens: 1983 **F, F**
LIPTROT, G. (4) St. Helens: 1977 F, **F**; 1978 A; 1979 **F**
LYDON, J. (3) Widnes: 1983 **F, F, F**

MASKILL, C. (1) Wakefield T.: 1983 **F**
MOLL, D. (1) Keighley: 1983 **F**
MUMBY, K. (6) Bradford N.: 1976 F, **F**; 1977 F, **F**; 1978 A; 1981 **F**
MUSCROFT, P. (3) New Hunslet: 1976 F, **F**; 1978 A
MYLER, A. (3) Widnes: 1982 **F**; 1983 **F, F**
MYLER, J. (1 + 1) Widnes: 1982 f; **F**

NOBLE, B. (4) Bradford N.: 1982 F, **F**; 1983 **F, F**
NULTY, J. (2) Wigan: 1976 F, **F**

O'NEILL, M. (3 + 2) Widnes: 1980 nz; 1982 F, f; 1983 **F, F**
O'NEILL, P. (3) Salford: 1980 **F**, NZ; 1981 **F**
O'NEILL, S. (2) Wigan: 1979 **F**; 1981 **F**

PINNER, H. (4 + 4) St. Helens: 1976 F, **F**; 1977 f, f; 1978 a; 1979 f, **F**; 1980 **F**
POTTER, I. (4) Warrington: 1979 **F**; 1981 **F**; Leigh: 1982 F, **F**
PROCTOR, W. (1) Hull: 1983 **F**

RATHBONE, A. (+ 1) Leigh: 1979 f
RAYNE, Keith (2) Wakefield T.: 1979 **F**; 1980 **F**
RICHARDSON, T. (1) Castleford: 1979 **F**
ROE, P. (4) Bradford N.: 1976 F, **F**; 1977 F, **F**
RUDD, I. (1 + 1) Workington T.: 1979 f; 1980 **F**

SCHOFIELD, G. (+ 2) Hull: 1983 f, f
SHEPHERD, M. (2) Huddersfield: 1977 F, **F**
SKERRETT, T. (1) Wakefield T.: 1977 **F**
SMITH, D. (2) Leeds: 1976 F, **F**
SMITH, Malcolm (1) Wigan: 1979 F
SMITH, Mike (7) Hull K.R.: 1976 F, **F**; 1977 **F**; 1978 A; 1979 **F, F**; 1980 **F**
SMITH, P. (1) Featherstone R.: 1978 A
SMITH, R. (+ 1) Salford: 1983 f
STEPHENSON, D. (5) Salford: 1979 F; 1980 **F**, NZ; 1982 F; Wigan: 1982 **F**
SWANN, M. (1) Leigh: 1979 F
SYZMALA, E. (2) Barrow: 1976 F, **F**

THACKRAY, R. (1) Warrington: 1980 NZ
TIMSON, A. (2) Castleford: 1982 F, **F**
TURNBULL, S. (2) Salford: 1976 F, **F**

VAN BELLEN, G. (2) Bradford N.: 1980 NZ; 1982 **F**

WARD, D. (+ 2) Leeds: 1976 f, f
WARD, K. (3) Castleford: 1980 **F**, NZ; 1981 **F**
WHITFIELD, C. (1) Salford: 1981 **F**
WILKINSON, A. (1) Leigh: 1977 **F**
WOOD, J. (2) Widnes: 1977 F, **F**
WOODS, J. (5) Leigh: 1977 F, **F**; 1978 A; 1979 **F, F**
WORRALL, M. (3) Oldham: 1983 **F, F, F**

ENGLAND AND WALES

Wales scrum half Peter Banner.

England packman Tommy Martyn.

England prop John Millington.

Six-cap Welshman Mike Nicholas.

England centre Derek Noonan.

One cap Englishman Barry Philbin.

Clive Sullivan, capped 14 times for Wales.

England centre John Walsh.

Frank Wilson, holder of 13 Welsh caps.

ENGLAND & WALES

The following is a register of England and Wales appearances since the reintroduction of European and World Championship matches in 1975, but does not include England's challenge match against Australia played after the 1975 World Championship.

Figures in brackets are the total appearances since 1975, with the plus sign indicating substitute appearances, e.g. (7+3).

A few players also played in the 1969-70 European Championship and this is shown as an additional total outside bracket, e.g. (11)2.

World Championship matches are in bold letters. Substitute appearances are in lower case letters.

A - Australia, E - England, F - France, NZ - New Zealand, W - Wales.

ENGLAND REGISTER
Since reintroduction in 1975

ADAMS, M. (3+2) Widnes: 1975 **NZ**, a; 1978 F; 1979 W; 1981 w
ARKWRIGHT, C. (+1) St. Helens: 1984 w
ATKINSON, J. (7) 4 Leeds: 1975 W, **F, W, NZ, W**; 1978 F, W

BANKS, B. (+1) York: 1979 f
BEARDMORE, K. (1) Castleford: 1984 W
BEVERLEY, H. (1) Workington T: 1979 W
BRIDGES, K. (7) Featherstone R: 1975 **NZ, A, W, F, NZ, A**; 1977 W
BURKE, M. (1) Widnes: 1984 W

CAIRNS, D. (1) Barrow: 1984 W
CASE, B. (1) Warrington: 1981 F
CASEY, L. (5) Hull K.R.: 1978 F, W; 1980 W; 1981 F, W
CHARLTON, P. (1) Salford: 1975 **F**
CHISNALL, D. (3+1) Warrington: 1975 w, **F, W, NZ**
CHISNALL, E. (3+1) St. Helens: 1975 F, **W, NZ**, a
CLARK, G. (1) Hull K.R.: 1984 W
COOKSON, P. (2) Leeds: 1975 **NZ, A**
COULMAN, M. (5) Salford: 1975 F, W, **W, A**; 1977 F
CUNNINGHAM, J. (2) Barrow: 1975 F, W

DONLAN, S. (1) Leigh: 1984 W
DRUMMOND, D. (5) Leigh: 1980 W, F; 1981 F, W; 1984 W
DUNN, G. (6) Hull K.R.: 1975 W, **A, F, NZ, A**; 1977 F
DYL, L. (12+1) Leeds: 1975 F, W, **F, W, NZ, A**, nz, A; 1977 W, F; 1978 F, W; 1981 W
ECKERSLEY, D. (+5) St. Helens: 1975 f, w, f; Widnes: 1977 w; 1978 w
ELWELL, K. (2) Widnes: 1978 F, W
EVANS, S. (3) Featherstone R: 1979 F; 1980 W, F

FAIRBAIRN, G. (15) Wigan: 1975 **W, NZ, A, W, F, NZ, A**; 1977 W, F; 1978 F; 1980 W, F; 1981 F, W; Hull K.R.: 1981 W

FARRAR, V. (1) Featherstone R: 1977 F
FENTON, S. (2) Castleford: 1981 F, W
FIELDING, K. (7) Salford: 1975 F, **F, W, NZ, A**, W, F
FORSYTH, C. (3) Bradford N: 1975 **W, F, NZ**

GILL, H. (1) Wigan: 1981 W
GILL, K. (9+2) Salford: 1975 W, **F, w, NZ, a**, W, F, **NZ, A**; 1977 W, F
GLYNN, P. (2) St. Helens: 1979 W, F
GOODWAY, A. (1) Oldham: 1984 W
GORLEY, L. (1+1) Workington T: 1977 W. Widnes: 1981 w
GORLEY, P. (2+1) St. Helens: 1980 W, f; 1981 W
GRAY, J. (3) Wigan: 1975 F, W, **F**
GRAYSHON, J. (9+1) Dewsbury: 1975 **W, F, NZ, A**; 1977 W. Bradford N: 1979 W, F; 1980 w, F; 1981 W

HANLEY, E. (1) Bradford N.: 1984 W
HARRISON, M. (2) Leeds: 1978 F, W
HOBBS, D. (1) Featherstone R.: 1984 W
HOGAN, B. (5) Wigan: 1975 **W, F, NZ, A**; 1977 W
HOGAN, P. (1) Hull K.R.: 1979 F
HOLDING, N. (1) St. Helens: 1980 W
HOLDSTOCK, R. (3) Hull K.R.: 1980 W, F; 1981 W
HOLMES, J. (5+2) Leeds: 1975 **W, F, NZ, A**; 1977 W, f; 1978 f
HUDDART, M. (1) Whitehaven: 1984 W
HUGHES, E. (8+1) Widnes: 1975 **W, F, NZ**, a; 1977 F; 1978 F, W; 1979 W, F
IRVING, R. (3) Wigan: 1975 **W, F, A**

JACKSON, P. (2) Bradford N.: 1975 W, **F**
JONES, L. (1) St. Helens: 1977 W
JOYNER, J. (4) Castleford: 1980 W, F; 1981 W, W
KELLY, A. (1) Hull K.R.: 1984 W
KELLY, K. (3) Warrington: 1979 W; 1981 F, W
LAUGHTON, D. (1) Widnes: 1977 W
LEDGER, B. (+1) St. Helens: 1984 w

334

LIPTROT, G. (2) St. Helens: 1979 W, F
LOCKWOOD, B. (2)+1 Hull K.R.: 1979 W, F
LOWE, P. (3)2 Hull K.R.: 1977 F; 1978 F; 1981 W

MARTYN, T. (4+1) Warrington: 1975 W, F, w;
   1979 W, F
MILLINGTON, J. (2) Hull K.R.: 1975 F; 1981 W
MILLWARD, R. (13)3+1 Hull K.R.: 1975 F, W,
   F, W, A, W, F, NZ, A; 1977 W, F; 1978 F, W
MORGAN, M. (3+3) Wakefield T: 1975 f, W, f, W,
   nz, A
MUMBY, K. (2) Bradford N: 1979 W, F
MURPHY, M. (1) Oldham: 1975 F

NASH, S. (7) Featherstone R: 1975 W, NZ, A.
   Salford: 1978 F, W; 1981 W, W
NICHOLLS, G. (7+4) St. Helens: 1975 F, F, W, NZ,
   A, w, nz, f; 1977 f; 1978 F, W
NOONAN, D. (3) Warrington: 1975 W, F, W
NORTON, S. (11) Castleford: 1975 W, NZ, A, W, F,
   NZ, A; 1977 F. Hull: 1978 W; 1981 W, W

O'NEILL, S. (1) Wigan: 1981 F

PATTINSON, W. (1+1) Workington T: 1981 f, W
PHILBIN, B. (1) Warrington: 1975 F
PIMBLETT, G. (1) St. Helens: 1978 W
PINNER, H. (3) St. Helens: 1980 W, F; 1981 F
POTTER, I. (2) Warrington: 1981 F, W

RAYNE, Keith (2) Wakefield T: 1980 W, F

REDFEARN, A. (2) Bradford N: 1979 F; 1980 F
REDFEARN, D. (2) Bradford N: 1975 F, A
REILLY, M. (+1)2 Castleford: 1977 w
RICHARDSON, T. (1) Castleford: 1981 W
ROSE, P. (2) Hull K.R.: 1977 F; 1978 W

SCHOFIELD, G. (1) Hull: 1984 W
SHEARD, L. (1) Wakefield T: 1975 W
SMITH, D. (1) Leeds: 1977 F
SMITH, K. (1) Wakefield T: 1979 W
SMITH, M. (5) Hull K.R.: 1980 W, F; 1981 F, W, W
SMITH, P. (1) Featherstone R: 1980 F
STEPHENS, G. (1) Castleford: 1979 W
SZYMALA, E. (+1) Barrow: 1979 f

THOMPSON, J. (2+1)1 Featherstone R: 1975 A;
   1977 W. Bradford N: 1978 w
TINDALL, K. (1) Hull: 1979 F
TOPLISS, D. (1) Wakefield T: 1975 F

WADDELL, H. (1) Blackpool B.: 1984 W
WALKER, A. (1) Whitehaven: 1981 W
WALSH, J. (3) St. Helens: 1975 F, NZ, A
WARD, D. (6) Leeds: 1977 F; 1980 W, F;
   1981 F, W, W
WATKINSON, D. (+1) Hull K.R.: 1977 w
WOODS, J. (3+4) Leigh: 1979 w, F; 1980 w, F;
   1981 f, w, W
WRIGHT, S. (7) Wigan: 1975 NZ. Widnes: 1977 W;
   1978 F, W; 1979 W, F; 1980 W

WALES REGISTER
Since reintroduction in 1975

BANNER, P. (9) Salford: 1975 F, E, F, E, NZ.
   Featherstone R: 1975 (cont.) E, A, NZ, F
BAYLISS, S. (1) St. Helens: 1981 E
BEVAN, J. (17) Warrington: 1975 F, E, E, A, NZ, F;
   1977 E, F; 1978 A; 1979 F, E; 1980 F, E;
   1981 F, E, E; 1982 A
BOX, H. (5) Featherstone R: 1979 F, E; 1980 F, E.
   Wakefield T: 1981 F
BUTLER, B. (2+2) Swinton: 1975 F, nz. Warrington:
   1975 (cont.) f; 1977 F

CAMBRIANI, A. (3) Fulham: 1981 F, E, E
CAMILLERI, C. (3) Barrow: 1980 F. Widnes:
   1982 A. Bridgend: 1984 E
COSLETT, K. (8)2 St. Helens: 1975 F, E, F, E, A,
   NZ, E, A
CUNNINGHAM, E (8) St. Helens: 1975 E, A, E, A;
   1977 E; 1978 F, E, A
CUNNINGHAM, T. (2) Warrington: 1979 F, E
CURLING, D. (+1) Warrington: 1977 f

DAVID, T. (2) Cardiff C: 1981 E; 1982 A
DAVIES, F. (1) New Hunslet: 1978 E
DAVIES, M. (1) Bridgend: 1984 E
DIAMOND, S. (2+1) Wakefield T: 1980 F, e; 1981 F
DIXON, C. (10)3 Salford: 1975 F, E, F, E, NZ, A;
   1977 E, F; 1978 F. Hull K.R.: 1981 E

EVANS, R. (5) Swinton: 1975 E, F, F; 1978 F;
   Salford: 1978 E

FENWICK, S. (2) Cardiff C: 1981 E; 1982 A
FISHER, A. (10)4 Leeds: 1975 F, E, A, NZ.
   Castleford: 1975 (cont.) E, A, NZ; 1977 E, F.
   Bradford N: 1978 A
FLOWERS, N. (4) Wigan: 1980 F, E; 1981 E.
   Bridgend: 1984 E
FORD, Phil (1) Warrington: 1984 E
FRANCIS, W. (19) Wigan: 1975 F, E, F, E, A, NZ,
   E, A, NZ, F; 1977 E, F. St. Helens: 1978 F, E,
   A; 1979 F, E. Oldham: 1980 F, E

335

GALLACHER, S. (3+1) Keighley: 1975 f, E, **NZ, F**
GREGORY, B. (3) Wigan: 1975 **E, NZ, F**
GRIFFITHS, C. (+2) St. Helens: 1980 f; 1981 f

HALLETT, L. (2) Cardiff C: 1982 A. Bridgend:
1984 E
HERDMAN, M. (2+1) Fulham: 1981 e, E; 1982 A
HOPKINS, L. (1) Workington T: 1982 A

JAMES, M. (11) St. Helens: 1975 **E**; 1978 F, E, A;
1979 F, E; 1980 F, E; 1981 F, E, E
JOHNS, G. (+2) Salford: 1979 f. Blackpool B: 1984 e
JONES, C. (1+3) Leigh: 1975 **nz, F**; 1978 f, e
JULIFF, B. (8) Wakefield T: 1979 F, E; 1980 F, E;
1981 F, E: Wigan: 1982 A; 1984 E

McJENNETT, M. (2+1) Barrow: 1980 F; 1982 a;
1984 E
MANTLE, J. (11+1)3 St. Helens: 1975 F, E, **F, e,
A, NZ, E, A, NZ, F**; 1977 E; 1978 E
MATHIAS, R. (20) St. Helens: 1975 F, E, **F, E, A,
NZ, A, NZ, F**; 1977 E, F; 1978 F, E, A;
1979 F, E; 1980 F, E; 1981 F, E
MILLS, J. (13)4 Widnes: 1975 F, E, **E, A, NZ, A,
NZ**; 1977 E, F; 1978 F, E, A; 1979 E
MURPHY, M. (4+1) Bradford N: 1975 **F, NZ, F**;
1977 f. St. Jacques, France: 1979 F

NICHOLAS, M. (4+2) Warrington: 1975 F, e;
1977 E, F; 1978 F; 1979 e

O'BRIEN, C. (1) Bridgend: 1984 E
OWEN, G. (2) Oldham: 1981 E, F
OWEN, R. (+2) St. Helens: 1981 f, e

PARRY, D. (6) Blackpool B: 1980 F, E; 1981 F, E, E:
1982 A
PREECE, C. (1) Bradford N: 1984 E
PRENDIVILLE, P. (4+2) Hull: 1979 e; 1980 E;
1981 F, e; 1982 A; 1984 E
PRITCHARD, G. (1+2) Barrow: 1978 f, e;
Cardiff C.: 1981 E

RICHARDS, M. (2)1 Salford: 1975 **F**; 1977 E
RINGER, P. (2) Cardiff C: 1981 E; 1982 A
RISMAN, J. (2+1) Workington T: 1978 F; 1979 f, E
ROWE, P. (4+3)2 Blackpool B: 1975 a, e, a.
Huddersfield: 1977 E, F; 1979 F, E
RULE, S. (1) Salford: 1981 E

SELDON, C. (1+1) St. Helens: 1980 f, E
SHAW, G. (7) Widnes: 1978 F, A; 1980 F, E; 1981 E.
Wigan: 1982 A; 1984 E
SKERRETT, T. (7) Wakefield T: 1978 A; 1979 F, E;
1980 F. Hull: 1981 F, E; 1984 E
SULLIVAN, C. (10)4 Hull K.R.: 1975 **E, A, NZ, E**;
1977 F; 1978 F, E, A; 1979 F, E

TREASURE, D. (5) Oldham: 1975 **E, A, NZ, E**;
1977 F
TURNER, G. (3+3) Hull K.R.: 1975 e, **A, e, A, f.**
Hull: 1978 E

WALLACE, R. (+1) York: 1975 f
WALTERS, G. (2+1) Hull: 1980 E. 1981 E.
Bridgend 1984 e
WANBON, R. (3)3+1 Warrington: 1975 **E, A, NZ**
WATKINS, D. (14) Salford: 1975 F, E, **F, E, A, NZ,
E, A, NZ, F**; 1977 E; 1978 E, A; 1979 F
WILKINS, R. (1+1) Workington T: 1977 e, F
WILLIAMS, B. (1) Cardiff C: 1982 A
WILLICOMBE, D. (11)+2 Wigan: 1975 F, E, **F, E,
A, NZ, NZ, F**; 1978 F, E, A
WILSON, D. (4) Swinton: 1981 F, E, E; 1984 E
WILSON, F. (7+2)4 St. Helens: 1975 F, E, **F, e, a,
E, A, NZ, F**
WOODS, P. (10) Widnes: 1977 E, F; 1978 F, E, A.
Rochdale H: 1979 F, E. Hull: 1980 E; 1981 F, E

The medal awarded to each member of the Hall of Fame.

HALL OF FAME

Rugby League's first-ever Hall of Fame — designed to pay tribute to the game's select band of legendary personalities — was scheduled to be opened in October 1988.

Sponsored by Whitbread Trophy, the shrine to the 13-a-side code's heritage was also to feature memorabilia of the full League scenario, including great players, memorable matches, record achievements and trophies.

Housed at the Bentley Arms restaurant at Oulton, near Leeds, the £250,000 project was conceived by Rugby League PRO David Howes as a major feature of a two-year sponsorship deal with Whitbread launched in 1987.

A five-man panel of selectors was given the awesome task of choosing the Hall of Fame entrants. Rugby League Chairman Bob Ashby, Secretary-General David Oxley, PRO David Howes, journalist Raymond Fletcher and historian Robert Gate decided to restrict the Hall of Fame entry to the highest echelon of players, based on playing records and a rating as a legend in the annals of the game.

Specially designed commemorative medals were struck by the Queen's jewellers for presentation to the living entrants among the nine selected Hall of Fame entrants.

Two major ground rules were that Hall of Fame entry was open to any player who had graced the British scene for the majority of his career and that a player had been retired for at least 10 years.

Many hours were spent considering the candidates following discussions with former players, officials and even veteran supporters who could give some insight into the reputations of the game's greatest personalities.

There was no plan to have a set number of players who would enter the Hall of Fame, but from a long list of possibilities just nine players stood out as fulfilling the highest qualifications. They were, in alphabetical order: Billy Batten, Brian Bevan, Billy Boston, Alex Murphy, Jonty Parkin, Gus Risman, Albert Rosenfeld, Jim Sullivan and Harold Wagstaff.

BILLY BATTEN
1905-1927

The centre was a member of two great teams — the Hunslet *All Four Cups* team of 1907-08 and Hull's Northern Union Challenge Cup winning team of 1914.

His transfer from Hunslet to Hull in 1913 caused a sensation with the £600 fee doubling the previous record. Batten's pay of £14 per game was more than five times the average.

His benefit match cheque for £1,079 was another record at that time. But Batten gave value for money in a career spanning 22 years following his signing as a 17-year-old for Hunslet in 1905.

Although Batten made his first impact as a winger it was as a powerful centre that he is remembered. A superbly fit, heavily built athlete, his knees-up running action and famous 'Batten Leap' over opponents made him one of the most feared players the game has known.

Batten made only one tour of Australasia — in 1910 — but turned down a 1914 trip and his refusal to play in a trial match ruled him out of the 1920 tour. Nevertheless, Batten's 10 Test appearances covered almost 14 years.

After 11 memorable years at Hull, he moved to briefer spells at Wakefield Trinity and Castleford. He played in two Yorkshire Cup finals for Wakefield...the last 19 years after his first with Hunslet.

BRIAN BEVAN
1945-1964

The Australian was the most extraordinary player of them all. His bald head, spindly legs and frail-looking body belied an amazing talent for scoring tries.

The winger's record total of 796 touchdowns is over 200 more than the second best. Nine times he scored more than 50 tries in a season, including six in succession, with a top total of 72. He finished at the top of the tryscoring list on five occasions in an era of great tryscoring wingers.

The Antipodean wonder scored a hat-trick of tries or more in a match exactly 100 times, twice scoring a Warrington record of seven.

Other Warrington records still held by him are 66 tries in a season in 1952-53, 740 in a career and 620 appearances.

Bevan arrived at Warrington unannounced in 1945 while on leave from the Australian Navy. He played one match in 1945-46 before returning and scoring 48 tries in his first full season.

Having left Sydney before he was 22, Bevan had made little impact on the Australian scene but was soon to become a legend in England. He stayed at Warrington for 16 full seasons before moving to Blackpool Borough for two years, scoring 17 tries.

Bevan made a total of 26 appearances for a strong Other Nationalities side and other representative teams which brought him another 39 tries.

BILLY BOSTON
1953-1970

The Welshman burst on to the Rugby League scene with an impact never achieved by any other former Rugby Union player. After only five matches for Wigan, the 19-year-old soldier was chosen for Great Britain's 1954 tour of Australasia and went on to score a then record 36 tries in 18 appearances.

It was the start of a glorious wing career that was to bring him 571 tries — the most ever by a British player and beaten only by Australian Brian Bevan.

The total included a Wigan career record of 478, while he twice equalled the club best of seven tries in a match.

Three times he scored 50 tries or more in a season with a top total of 60 in 1956-57 being one of two occasions that he finished at the head of the try-scoring chart.

Boston was a surprise omission from the 1958 tour of Australasia but toured again four years later. In all, he made 31 Test appearances for Britain and scored 24 tries.

Starting as an athletically built 12½st winger of graceful pace, Boston grew into a 15st player of destructive power.

After 15 great seasons at Wigan he came out of retirement to play just 11 matches for Blackpool Borough, playing his last match as a second row forward in 1970.

ALEX MURPHY
1956-1975

Murphy was a star from the moment he signed for St. Helens on his 16th birthday in 1955. Three years later he became the then youngest-ever Great Britain tourist to Australasia and was immediately hailed as one of the greatest scrum halves of all time.

Murphy toured again in 1962 and was selected for the 1966 trip — at centre — but withdrew. Even so, he went on to make 27 appearances for Britain with his last in 1971.

From a cheeky, ebullient half back who teased opposition and referees alike, Murphy matured into a captain and player-coach of exceptional quality though still occasionally upsetting authority.

Wembley was his speciality. He captained St. Helens to victory in 1966, then as player-coach led Leigh and Warrington to wins in 1971 and 1974. He won the Lance Todd Trophy with Leigh and was also in St. Helens' 1961 team, thus sharing the record of being on the winning side in four Wembley finals.

Murphy played in three different positions at Wembley — stand off, centre and twice at scrum half and was a scorer in each final with a total of five drop goals and a try.

Although Murphy was a master at creating tries he was also a devastating finisher who scored 275 including a record-equalling four for Britain in a Test.

JONTY PARKIN
1913-1932

The Wakefield Trinity half back reigned supreme with Great Britain in the 1920s. Playing at either stand off or scrum half, he appeared in 17 Test matches between 1920 and 1930, being on the losing side only three times.

He was the first of a still small band of players to complete three tours of Australasia — in 1920, 1924 and 1928 — joining Harold Wagstaff as the only captain to lead two tour squads. Parkin was unique in twice bringing back the Ashes.

In all, he captained Great Britain in 11 Test matches, the last being in 1930 when he was 35. He also played 12 times for England and gained 17 caps with Yorkshire.

Although noted more for his try-making ability and tactical skills than as a scorer, Parkin still holds the county record of five tries in a match for Yorkshire. He also scored a hat-trick for Great Britain against New Zealand and finished with a career total of 157 touchdowns.

Parkin was 18 when he signed for Wakefield in 1913 and stayed with them for 17 years before leaving for two seasons with Hull Kingston Rovers. His move to Rovers caused a change in the bye-laws after he paid his own £100 transfer fee.

GUS RISMAN
1929-1954

The Welshman maintained a high level of consistency longer than any other player. Twenty-five years after making his Rugby League debut with Salford, he made 45 appearances in his last full season of 1953-54, scoring 294 points for Workington Town with 138 goals and six tries. He was 43.

Risman's Test career of 17 matches covered a record span of 14 years from 1932. He toured Australasia in 1932, 1936 and 1946 when he was captain. But for the war he would almost certainly have completed a unique four tours.

His Wembley career also covered a record span of 14 years, leading Salford to victory in 1938 and Workington Town in 1952 when at 41 he became the oldest to play at the stadium.

In addition, he appeared for Salford in the 1939 final and proved his versatility by playing at Wembley in three different positions — stand off, centre and full back. He achieved a similar feat with Great Britain.

Goal kicking was another feature of Risman's brilliant all-round game, finishing with a career total of 1,678. He twice kicked a club record 13 goals in a match for Salford.

At the end of an 873-match career, Risman had also scored 232 tries for a points total of 4,052, finishing with a brief spell at Batley.

ALBERT ROSENFELD
1909-1924

Rosenfeld is a name printed indelibly in the record books. It is said records are made to be broken, but the Huddersfield winger's 80 tries in 1913-14 remain the most scored in a season with no sign of it ever being beaten.

Although that record alone gives Rosenfeld a strong claim to fame, the Australian was much more than a one-season wonder. Two years earlier he had scored 78 tries, which remains the second best season's haul.

Rosenfeld was a tryscoring phenomenon, finishing at the top of the game's try chart in five successive seasons. Until his arrival no player had scored 50 tries in a season, but Rosenfeld passed the half century in four successive campaigns with totals of 78, 56, 80 and 56.

Only the First World War prevented him adding to the sequence but he still finished with a total of 374 tries in eight full seasons with Huddersfield.

They had signed 'Rozzy' after he toured Britain with the first Kangaroos in 1908-09. He played in one Test on tour to go with three against New Zealand when he was at half-back.

Rosenfeld was a member of Huddersfield's *Team of All The Talents* that won a succession of trophies including *All Four Cups* in 1914-15.

He was transferred to Wakefield Trinity in 1921 and then moved on to Bradford Northern where he finished his career in December 1924, having amassed 392 tries.

JIM SULLIVAN
1921-1946

The Welshman dominated Rugby League for more than 20 years in which he was acknowledged as the greatest ever full back and goalkicker.

He was a Welsh Rugby Union wonder boy when Wigan signed him from Cardiff, making his professional debut in 1921 while still only 17.

It was the beginning of a remarkable one club career which stretched to 1946 and resulted in a succession of goalkicking records. Some have since been broken but others could last for ever, including a career total of 2,867 goals. From his first season until the outbreak of the Second World War, Sullivan kicked a century of goals in 18 successive seasons.

His records of 22 goals and 44 points for Wigan in a Cup game against Flimby and Fothergill amateurs have stood for more than 60 years.

A total of 928 club and representative appearances make him the most durable player of all time. It includes a record 60 international appearances, 25 of them Tests. His international totals of 160 goals and 329 points are also records.

But Sullivan was much more than a record breaker. He was a great leader who captained Britain in 15 Tests and led the 1932 tourists. He also toured in 1924 and 1928, but turned down a 1936 trip that would have given him a unique record four tours.

HAROLD WAGSTAFF
1906-1925

The Prince of Centres made his debut for Huddersfield at Bramley on 10 November 1906 while only 15½ years old — the youngest recorded age for a first team player.

Disbelief of his age caused Huddersfield to publish a facsimile of the boy's birth certificate showing he was born at Underbank, Holmfirth, on 19 May 1891.

Wagstaff was still only 17 years when he played for England against Australia in January 1909. Although it was not a Test match Wagstaff went on to make 12 Test appearances and two tours of Australasia, both as captain, in 1914 and 1920.

He led the Lions in the famous *Rorke's Drift* Test of 1914 when the tourists beat Australia 14-6 despite injuries reducing the team to 10 men in the closing stages.

Huddersfield handed Wagstaff the captaincy when he was only 20 to begin one of the greatest eras in club rugby. Known as *The Team of All The Talents,* Huddersfield dominated the game for a decade, winning all the trophies time and again.

They achieved the rare *All Four Cups* feat in 1914-15 and only the First World War prevented them adding to their haul.

Wagstaff remained with Huddersfield throughout his career which ended in March 1925.

Lancashire stand off John Woods (left) and Yorkshireman Chris Burton in the 1987 War of the Roses battle.

WAR OF THE ROSES

WAR OF THE ROSES

1987 WAR OF THE ROSES

Yorkshire completed a hat-trick of Rodstock War of the Roses victories but only after weathering Lancashire's most determined challenge in the three-year history of the new style encounter.

The home county bounced back from a controversial White Rose touchdown on the hour to close the gap to six points and set the scene for a frantic last five minutes of intense pressure on the visitors' line.

Yorkshire held out, despite the absence of second row man Chris Burton in the sin bin, and fully deserved to maintain their unbeaten record in the County of Origin series.

With Lancashire coach Alex Murphy and Yorkshire's Peter Fox retained for a third confrontation and the billing as an official Test trial, the inter-county meeting at Wigan attracted 9,748 spectators, the best crowd for a county fixture for 21 years.

Yorkshire loose forward Andy Goodway received the Rodstock Man of the Match award, selected by Great Britain coach Malcolm Reilly, but the evening was also a huge success for captain Ellery Hanley. The

Wigan teammates linked up over 75 yards for Hanley to open the scoring after 15 minutes. Having taken Goodway's pass just inside the Lancashire half, the White Rose stand off raced 45 yards to touch down, shrugging off two Lancashire challenges and selling Wigan clubmate Steve Hampson a clinical dummy to record his 1,000th career point. Bradford Northern prop David Hobbs added the goal.

Lancashire replied 10 minutes later when skipper Andy Gregory, leading the side for the third successive time, hoisted a kick which bounced awkwardly for the visiting defence but kindly for debutant full back Hampson to touch down, too wide out for Colin Whitfield to add the goal, giving Yorkshire a 6-4 interval lead.

The first half had seen Lancashire, with seven debutants on duty, making a significant impression in the forwards despite conceding weight to the powerful Yorkshire six. The tempo of a hard fought game slowed down after the break when the visitors' extra strength began to take toll.

A hat-trick of Rodstock War of the Roses victories for jubilant Yorkshire with captain Ellery Hanley and Coach Peter Fox holding the trophy.

344

In Hampson, Lancashire had an enterprising attacker, keen to impress the watching Great Britain management, but even the former Vulcan RU full back was powerless to prevent Yorkshire's next score.

Arguably the turning point of the contest, the 58th minute touchdown came as Lancashire were threatening Yorkshire's dominance of the tournament. Against the run of play, Yorkshire mounted an attack on the home line and scrum half Deryck Fox put in a short kick which bounced off the legs of Lancashire stand off John Woods, visiting centre Tony Marchant pouncing for the crucial try.

Lancashire players protested, none more vehemently than captain Gregory, who was sent to the sin bin by referee John Holdsworth. As the number seven trotted off, Fox added the goal to give the visitors a 12-4 lead.

During Gregory's absence, Yorkshire struck again, moving the ball in classic style with Wakefield Trinity centre Andy Mason bursting onto Goodway's pass to feed wing partner Henderson Gill for a 67th minute touchdown.

Hull K.R. second row man Burton was sent to the sin bin in the 71st minute for a foul tackle on Lancashire prop Tony Humphries, leaving his colleagues to survive the most intense 10 minutes of the three Rodstock encounters.

Lancashire, at last showing the expected county passion, stormed the visitors' defence and Oldham second row man Paul Round set up a breathtaking finish by following Gregory's kick to dive over for a 74th minute try, to which Halifax centre Whitfield added the goal to leave the home side trailing by only six points.

Despite being a man short, Yorkshire battled desperately during the final five minutes and held out to gain an impressive victory and enable coach Fox to maintain his winning record in county football.

RODSTOCK WAR OF THE ROSES

16 September   **Wigan**

LANCASHIRE 10		YORKSHIRE 16
Steve Hampson (Wigan)	1.	Ian Wilkinson (Halifax)
Kevin McCormack (St. Helens)	2.	Carl Gibson (Leeds)
Paul Cullen (Warrington)	3.	Tony Marchant (Castleford)
Colin Whitfield (Halifax)	4.	Andy Mason (Wakefield T.)
Darren Wright (Widnes)	5.	Henderson Gill (Wigan)
John Woods (Warrington)	6.	Ellery Hanley (Wigan) Capt.
Andy Gregory (Wigan) Capt.	7.	Deryck Fox (Featherstone R.)
Brian Case (Wigan)	8.	Kevin Ward (Castleford)
Martin Dermott (Wigan)	9.	Kevin Beardmore (Castleford)
Tony Humphries (Warrington)	10.	David Hobbs (Bradford N.)
Paul Round (Oldham)	11.	Lee Crooks (Leeds)
Ian Potter (Wigan)	12.	Chris Burton (Hull K.R.)
Mike Gregory (Warrington)	13.	Andy Goodway (Wigan)
Neil McCulloch (Leigh)	14.	John Joyner (Castleford)
Billy McGinty (Warrington)	15.	Paul Dixon (Halifax)

T: Hampson, Round
G: Whitfield
Substitutions:
McCulloch for McCormack (Half-time)
McGinty for Case (68 min.)
Coach: Alex Murphy
Referee: John Holdsworth (Kippax)

T: Hanley, Marchant, Gill
G: Hobbs, Fox
Substitution:
Dixon for Crooks (46 min.)
Coach: Peter Fox
Half-time: 4-6
Attendance: 9,748

LANCASHIRE v. YORKSHIRE RESULTS
All county championship matches except where stated.

Date	Result		Score	Venue	Attendance
7 Dec. 1895	Yorkshire	won	8 - 0	Oldham	9,059
29 Feb. 1896	Lancashire	won	8 - 3	Huddersfield	5,300
21 Nov. 1896	Lancashire	won	7 - 3	Oldham	15,000
20 Nov. 1897	Yorkshire	won	7 - 6	Bradford P.A.	11,000
5 Nov. 1898	Yorkshire	won	20 - 9	Salford	8,000
4 Nov. 1899	Lancashire	won	16 - 13	Halifax	9,000
3 Nov. 1900	Lancashire	won	24 - 5	Rochdale	18,000
15 Feb. 1902	Yorkshire	won	13 - 8	Hull	15,000
15 Nov. 1902	Lancashire	won	13 - 0	Salford	14,000
14 Nov. 1903	Lancashire	won	8 - 0	Leeds	11,000
12 Nov. 1904	Yorkshire	won	14 - 5	Oldham	8,500
4 Nov. 1905	Lancashire	won	8 - 0	Hull	8,000
3 Nov. 1906	Lancashire	won	19 - 0	Salford	5,000
2 Nov. 1907	Yorkshire	won	15 - 11	Halifax	7,000
31 Oct. 1908	Lancashire	won	13 - 0	Salford	5,000
4 Nov. 1909	Yorkshire	won	27 - 14	Hull	6,000
7 Nov. 1910	Lancashire	won	17 - 3	Wigan	2,000
25 Jan. 1912	Lancashire	won	13 - 12	Halifax	3,199
16 Dec. 1912	Yorkshire	won	20 - 8	Oldham	4,000
10 Dec. 1913	Yorkshire	won	19 - 11	Huddersfield	3,500
24 Sept. 1919	Lancashire	won	15 - 5	Broughton	5,000
21 Oct. 1920	Yorkshire	won	18 - 3	Hull	7,000
4 Oct. 1921	Yorkshire	won	5 - 2	Rochdale	4,000
7 Dec. 1922	Match drawn	—	11 - 11	Hull K.R.	8,000
8 Dec. 1923	Lancashire	won	6 - 5	Oldham	8,000
29 Nov. 1924	Lancashire	won	28 - 9	Halifax	6,000
12 Dec. 1925	Lancashire	won	26 - 10	St. Helens	13,000
30 Oct. 1926	Lancashire	won	18 - 13	Wakefield	9,000
29 Oct. 1927	Lancashire	won	35 - 19	Warrington	12,000
3 Nov. 1928	Lancashire	won	33 - 10	Halifax	6,520
22 Mar. 1930	Lancashire	won	18 - 3	Rochdale	4,000
18 Oct. 1930	Yorkshire	won	25 - 15	Wakefield	9,000
17 Oct. 1931	Lancashire	won	11 - 8	Warrington	10,049
*29 Oct. 1932	Yorkshire	won	30 - 3	Wakefield	4,000
25 Sept. 1933	Yorkshire	won	15 - 12	Oldham	2,000
*9 Jan. 1935	Match drawn	—	5 - 5	Leeds	1,500
12 Oct. 1935	Lancashire	won	16 - 5	Widnes	6,700
21 Oct. 1936	Lancashire	won	28 - 6	Castleford	7,648
12 Feb. 1938	Lancashire	won	10 - 9	Rochdale	3,653
*26 Oct. 1938	Match drawn	—	10 - 10	Leeds	3,000
10 Nov. 1945	Lancashire	won	17 - 16	Swinton	11,059
9 Nov. 1946	Yorkshire	won	13 - 10	Hunslet	5,000
12 Nov. 1947	Lancashire	won	22 - 10	Wigan	6,270
3 May 1949	Lancashire	won	12 - 3	Halifax	7,000

Date	Result		Score	Venue	Attendance
5 Oct. 1949	Lancashire	won	22 - 13	Warrington	15,000
18 Oct. 1950	Yorkshire	won	23 - 15	Huddersfield	6,547
10 Oct. 1951	Yorkshire	won	15 - 5	Leigh	11,573
28 Apr. 1953	Yorkshire	won	16 - 8	Hull	8,400
14 Oct. 1953	Lancashire	won	18 - 10	Leigh	12,870
6 Oct. 1954	Yorkshire	won	20 - 10	Bradford	8,500
26 Sept. 1955	Lancashire	won	26 - 10	Oldham	8,000
26 Sept. 1956	Lancashire	won	35 - 21	Hull	8,500
23 Sept. 1957	Yorkshire	won	25 - 11	Widnes	6,200
24 Sept. 1958	Yorkshire	won	35 - 19	Hull K.R.	5,000
29 Oct. 1958	Yorkshire	won	16 - 15	Leigh	8,500
11 Nov. 1959	Yorkshire	won	38 - 28	Leigh	6,417
31 Aug. 1960	Lancashire	won	21 - 20	Wakefield	15,045
9 Oct. 1961	Lancashire	won	14 - 12	Leigh	4,970
26 Sept. 1962	Yorkshire	won	22 - 8	Wakefield	7,956
11 Sept. 1963	Lancashire	won	45 - 20	St. Helens	11,200
23 Sept. 1964	Yorkshire	won	33 - 10	Hull	7,100
10 Nov. 1965	Yorkshire	won	16 - 13	Swinton	5,847
21 Sept. 1966	Lancashire	won	22 - 17	Leeds	10,528
24 Jan. 1968	Lancashire	won	23 - 17	Widnes	8,322
25 Sept. 1968	Yorkshire	won	10 - 5	Hull K.R.	6,656
3 Sept. 1969	Lancashire	won	14 - 12	Salford	4,652
13 Jan. 1971	Yorkshire	won	32 - 12	Castleford	2,000
24 Feb. 1971	Yorkshire	won	34 - 8	Castleford	4,400
29 Sept. 1971	Yorkshire	won	42 - 22	Leigh	4,987
11 Oct. 1972	Yorkshire	won	32 - 18	Castleford	2,474
19 Sept. 1973	Lancashire	won	17 - 15	Widnes	3,357
25 Sept. 1974	Yorkshire	won	20 - 14	Keighley	1,219
16 Oct. 1974	Lancashire	won	29 - 11	Widnes	3,114
20 Dec. 1975	Yorkshire	won	17 - 7	Wigan	700
1 Mar. 1977	Yorkshire	won	18 - 13	Castleford	2,730
††19 Oct. 1977	Lancashire	won	33 - 8	Widnes	5,056
27 Sept. 1978	Lancashire	won	23 - 7	Widnes	4,283
12 Sept. 1979	Yorkshire	won	19 - 16	Castleford	2,738
24 Sept. 1980	Lancashire	won	17 - 9	Widnes	1,593
9 Sept. 1981	Yorkshire	won	21 - 15	Castleford	1,222
26 May 1982	Yorkshire	won	22 - 21	Leigh	1,738
WR11 Sept. 1985	Yorkshire	won	26 - 10	Wigan	6,743
WR17 Sept. 1986	Yorkshire	won	26 - 14	Leeds	5,983
WR16 Sept. 1987	Yorkshire	won	16 - 10	Wigan	9,748

* Match abandoned but result stands   †† Queen's Jubilee match   WR War of the Roses
● There were also a few Lancashire-Yorkshire matches played during the war years but not of a competitive nature.

SUMMARY
Lancashire won 41   Yorkshire won 40   Drawn 3

White Rose centre Tony Marchant evades Lancashire loose forward Mike Gregory.

Yorkshire's Lee Crooks off loads despite the efforts of Brian Case and Paul Round (right).

LANCASHIRE v. YORKSHIRE RECORDS

LANCASHIRE

Highest score:	45-20 at St. Helens, 11 Sept. 1963
Widest margin win:	As above and 33-8 at Widnes, 19 Oct. 1977
Most tries in a match:	No player has scored more than 3
Most goals in a match:	9 by L. Gilfedder (Wigan) at St. Helens, 11 Sept. 1963
Most points in a match:	18 by L. Gilfedder (Wigan) as above
Biggest home attendance:	18,000 at Rochdale, 3 Nov. 1900

OTHER RECORDS (not involving Yorkshire)

Highest score:	60-12 v. Cumberland at Wigan, 10 Sept. 1958
Most tries in a match:	4 by T. O'Grady (Oldham) v. Cumberland at Wigan, 6 Sept. 1956
	4 by W. Burgess (Barrow) v. Cumberland at Widnes, 12 Sept. 1962
Most goals in a match:	12 by E. Fraser (Warrington) v. Cumberland at Wigan, 10 Sept. 1958
Most points in a match:	24 by E. Fraser (Warrington) as above
Biggest home attendance:	24,000 v. Australia at Warrington, 26 Sept. 1929

YORKSHIRE

Highest score:	42-22 at Leigh, 29 Sept. 1971
Widest margin win:	30-3 at Wakefield, 29 Oct. 1932
Most tries in a match:	No player has scored more than 3
Most goals in a match:	10 by V. Yorke (York) at Hull K.R., 24 Sept. 1958
Most points in a match:	20 by V. Yorke (York) as above
Biggest home attendance:	15,045 at Wakefield, 31 Aug. 1960

OTHER RECORDS (not involving Lancashire)

Highest score:	51-12 v. Cumberland at Hunslet, 17 Oct. 1923
Highest against:	55-11 v. Australia at Huddersfield, 26 Nov. 1952
Most tries in a match:	5 by J. Parkin (Wakefield T.) v. Cumberland at Halifax, 14 Nov. 1921
Most goals in a match:	10 also by N. Fox (Wakefield T.) v. Australia at York, 28 Sept. 1959
Most points in a match:	23 by N. Fox (Wakefield T.) as above
Biggest home attendance:	19,376 v. Australia at Wakefield, 4 Oct. 1967

LANCASHIRE TEAMS

. . . A 20-year review. Initials are included where more than one celebrated player shared a surname in the same era. Only playing substitutes are listed.

Tommy Bishop.

Ray French.

1968 Yorkshire
Hull K.R.: 25 Sept.
Lost 5-10
Dutton (Widnes) 1g
D. Whitehead (Oldham)
Benyon (St. Helens)
Glover (Warrington)
Jones (St. Helens)
D. O'Neill (Widnes)
Williams (Swinton)
Halliwell (Salford)
Taylor (Oldham)
Fletcher (Oldham)
French (Widnes)
S. Whitehead (Salford)
Lyon (Wigan)
Subs: Hesketh (Salford) 1t
J. Stephens (Wigan)

1968 Cumberland
St. Helens: 6 Nov.
Won 24-19
Dutton (Widnes) 3g
Burgess (Barrow) 2t
Hesketh (Salford)
Gemmell (Hull) 2t
Tickle (Leigh)
Brophy (Barrow)
Bishop (St. Helens)
J. Stephens (Wigan)
Sayer (St. Helens)
Brown (Rochdale)
E. Chisnall (St. Helens) 2t
Welding (Leigh)
Robinson (Swinton)
Sub: D. O'Neill (Widnes)

1969 Yorkshire
Salford: 3 Sept.
Won 14-12
Dutton (Widnes) 4g
Jones (St. Helens)
Hesketh (Salford)
Benyon (St. Helens)
Murray (Barrow) 1t
W. Davies (Swinton)
Gordon (Warrington)
J. Stephens (Wigan)
Taylor (Oldham)
Fletcher (Wigan)
Nicholls (Widnes)
Welding (Leigh)
Laughton (Wigan) 1t
Subs: Tees (Rochdale)
       B. Hogan (Wigan)

1969 Cumberland
Workington: 24 Sept.
Won 30-10
Dutton (Widnes) 6g
Burgess (Salford)
Hesketh (Salford)
F. Myler (St. Helens)
Murray (Barrow)
A. Murphy (Leigh) 3t
Gordon (Warrington) 1t
J. Stephens (Wigan)
Ashcroft (Leigh)
Sanderson (Barrow)
Robinson (Swinton) 1t
Welding (Leigh)
Laughton (Wigan) 1t
Sub: D. Hill (Wigan)

1970 Cumberland
Barrow: 11 Nov.
Won 28-5
John Walsh (St. Helens) 5g
S. Wright (Wigan) 1t
Benyon (St. Helens)
Hesketh (Salford) 1t
Joe Walsh (Leigh)
F. Myler (St. Helens) 2t
Boylan (Widnes)
D. Chisnall (Leigh)
Ashcroft (Leigh) 1t
Brown (Rochdale)
E. Prescott (St. Helens) 1t
E. Chisnall (St. Helens)
Laughton (Wigan)
Subs: Martin Murphy (Oldham)
       Nicholls (Widnes)

1971 Yorkshire
Castleford: 13 Jan.
Lost 12-32
Dutton (Widnes) 3g
S. Wright (Wigan)
Benyon (St. Helens)
D. O'Neill (Widnes)
Joe Walsh (Leigh)
W. Davies (Swinton) 1t
A. Murphy (Leigh)
Mick Murphy (Barrow)
Clarke (Wigan)
Brown (Rochdale)
E. Chisnall (St. Helens)
E. Prescott (St. Helens)
Laughton (Wigan) 1t
Subs: Boylan (Widnes)
       Nicholls (Widnes)

1971 Yorkshire (Play-off)
Castleford: 24 Feb.
Lost 8-34
Tyrer (Wigan) 1g
Joe Walsh (Leigh)
Buckley (Swinton)
Hesketh (Salford)
Jones (St. Helens) 1t
D. O'Neill (Widnes)
Boylan (Widnes)
J. Stephens (St. Helens)
Ashcroft (Leigh)
B. Hogan (Wigan)
Nicholls (Widnes) 1t
Cramant (Swinton)
Robinson (Wigan)
Subs: Eckersley (Leigh)
       Clarke (Wigan)

1971 Cumberland
Workington: 15 Sept.
Lost 7-17
Dutton (Widnes) 2g
Keiron O'Loughlin (Wigan)
Benyon (St. Helens) 1t
Eckersley (Leigh)
Fuller (Wigan)
D. O'Neill (Widnes)
Boylan (Leigh)
D. Chisnall (Warrington)
A. Karalius (St. Helens)
Brown (Rochdale)
Cunningham (Wigan)
Wills (Huyton)
Nicholls (Widnes)
Subs: Whittle (St. Helens)
       Welding (Rochdale)

1971 Yorkshire
Leigh: 29 Sept.
Lost 22-42
Dutton (Widnes) 5g
Jones (St. Helens)
Benyon (St. Helens)
Hesketh (Salford)
Joe Walsh (Leigh)
D. O'Neill (Widnes)
Kenny (Swinton) 1t
J. Stephens (St. Helens) 1t
A. Karalius (St. Helens)
Mick Murphy (Barrow)
Lester (Leigh)
Ashurst (Wigan)
Clark (Oldham) 1t
Subs: Eckersley (Leigh)
       Welding (Rochdale) 1t

1972 Cumberland
Warrington: 27 Sept.
Won: 26-16
Martin Murphy (Oldham)
Hodgkinson (Oldham)
Benyon (St. Helens)
John Walsh (St. Helens) 1t, 4g
E. Hughes (Widnes)
K. Kelly (St. Helens) 1t
Banner (Salford)
Halsall (Swinton)
A. Karalius (St. Helens) 2t
J. Stephens (St. Helens)
E. Prescott (Salford)
B. Gregory (Warrington) 1t
Nicholls (Widnes) 1t
Subs: Hesketh (Salford)
       Birchall (Rochdale)

1972 Yorkshire
Castleford: 11 Oct.

Lost 18-32

Dutton (Widnes) 2g
Hodgkinson (Oldham) 1t
Benyon (St. Helens)
John Walsh (St. Helens) 1g
E. Hughes (Widnes) 1t
D. O'Neill (Widnes) 1t
Banner (Salford)
Halsall (Swinton)
A. Karalius (St. Helens)
J. Stephens (St. Helens) 1t
E. Chisnall (St. Helens)
B. Gregory (Warrington)
Ashurst (Wigan)

1973 Cumbria
Barrow: 5 Sept.

Won 18-6

D. Whitehead (Warrington) 3g
Brelsford (Rochdale)
Benyon (St. Helens) 1t
Hesketh (Salford)
E. Hughes (Widnes) 1t
Eckersley (St. Helens)
Gordon (Warrington)
Fiddler (Leigh) 1t
Evans (Swinton)
Brady (Warrington)
Nicholls (St. Helens)
Welding (Rochdale)
Laughton (Widnes)
Sub: Noonan (Warrington) 1t

1973 Yorkshire
Widnes: 19 Sept.

Won 17-15

D. Whitehead (Warrington) 3g
Brelsford (Rochdale)
Benyon (St. Helens) 1t
Hesketh (Salford)
E. Hughes (Widnes)
Eckersley (St. Helens)
Gordon (Warrington)
Fiddler (Leigh) 1g
Evans (Swinton)
Brady (Warrington)
Nicholls (St. Helens) 1t
Welding (Rochdale)
E. Prescott (Salford) 1t
Subs: Noonan (Warrington)
Briggs (Warrington)

1974 Other Nationalities
Salford: 11 Sept.

Won 14-13

D. Whitehead (Warrington) 1g
S. Wright (Wigan)
John Walsh (St. Helens)
Noonan (Warrington)
Jones (St. Helens)
Whittle (Warrington) 1t
Gordon (Warrington)
D. Chisnall (Warrington)
Evans (Swinton)
Fiddler (Leigh) 3g
Nicholls (St. Helens)
E. Prescott (Salford)
B. Philbin (Warrington)
Sub: B. Gregory (Oldham) 1t

1974 Cumbria
Warrington: 18 Sept.

Won 29-4

D. Whitehead (Warrington) 4g, 1t
S. Wright (Wigan) 1t
Noonan (Warrington) 2t
Hesketh (Salford)
E. Hughes (Widnes) 1t
Whittle (Warrington)
Nulty (Wigan)
D. Chisnall (Warrington) 1t
Evans (Swinton)
Fiddler (Leigh)
Robinson (Wigan)
B. Gregory (Oldham)
T. Martyn (Leigh) 1t

1974 Yorkshire
Keighley: 25 Sept.

Lost 14-20

D. Whitehead (Warrington) 4g
S. Wright (Wigan)
John Walsh (St. Helens)
Hesketh (Salford) 1t
E. Hughes (Widnes)
Whittle (Warrington)
Gordon (Warrington)
D. Chisnall (Warrington)
Evans (Swinton)
Fiddler (Leigh)
T. Martyn (Leigh) 1t
B. Gregory (Oldham)
B. Philbin (Warrington)
Sub: Robinson (Wigan)

1974 Yorkshire (Play-off)
Widnes: 16 Oct.

Won 29-11

Dutton (Widnes) 7g
S. Wright (Wigan) 1t
Hesketh (Salford) 1t
Noonan (Warrington) 2t
E. Hughes (Widnes)
Gill (Salford) 1t
Gordon (Warrington)
D. Chisnall (Warrington)
Ashcroft (Warrington)
Brady (Warrington)
Nicholls (St. Helens)
E. Prescott (Salford)
B. Philbin (Warrington)
Subs: Aspey (Widnes)
T. Martyn (Leigh)

1975 Other Nationalities
St. Helens: 25 Nov.

Won 36-7

Dutton (Widnes) 6g
J. Davies (Leigh)
Pimblett (St. Helens)
Butler (Salford)
George (Widnes)
Gill (Salford) 1t
Bowden (Widnes) 1t
B. Hogan (Wigan)
Elwell (Widnes) 1t
Nelson (Widnes)
Nicholls (St. Helens) 1t
T. Martyn (Warrington) 2t
Adams (Widnes) 1t
Subs: Eckersley (St. Helens)
Hodkinson (Rochdale) 1t

1975 Cumbria
Workington: 6 Dec.

Won 22-17

Dutton (Widnes) 5g
Davies (Leigh) 1t
Butler (Salford) 1t
George (Widnes)
Jones (St. Helens)
Gill (Salford)
Bowden (Widnes) 2t
B. Hogan (Wigan)
Elwell (Widnes)
Hodkinson (Rochdale)
Nicholls (St. Helens)
T. Martyn (Warrington)
Adams (Widnes)
Subs: Eckersley (St. Helens)
Turnbull (Salford)

1975 Yorkshire
Wigan: 20 Dec.
Lost 7-17
Dutton (Widnes) 2g
Jones (St. Helens)
Butler (Salford)
George (Widnes)
E. Hughes (Widnes)
Gill (Salford)
Bowden (Widnes)
B. Hogan (Wigan)
Evans (Swinton)
Hodkinson (Rochdale)
Turnbull (Salford) 1t
T. Martyn (Warrington)
Adams (Widnes)
Subs: Benyon (St. Helens)
   Nelson (Widnes)

1977 Cumbria
Leigh: 2 Feb.
Won 18-14
M. Hogan (Leigh)
Fielding (Salford) 1t
Stacey (Leigh)
Butler (Salford)
S. Wright (Widnes) 1t
Gill (Salford)
Bowden (Widnes)
Coulman (Salford) 1t
Elwell (Widnes)
Wilkinson (Leigh)
T. Martyn (Warrington)
Adams (Widnes)
Boyd (Leigh)
Sub: Hesford (Warrington) 1t, 3g

1977 Yorkshire
Widnes: 1 March
Lost 13-18
Fairbairn (Wigan) 3g
Fielding (Salford)
Hughes (Widnes) 1t
Hesford (Warrington)
S. Wright (Widnes)
Gill (Salford)
Bowden (Widnes)
Hodkinson (Rochdale)
Elwell (Widnes) 1dg
J. Wood (Widnes)
T. Martyn (Warrington) 1t
Adams (Widnes)
Boyd (Leigh)
Subs: Aspey (Widnes)
   Pinner (St. Helens)

1977 Yorkshire (Jubilee)
Widnes: 19 Oct.
Won 33-8
Pimblett (St. Helens) 5g
Jones (St. Helens)
Aspey (Widnes) 1t
Woods (Leigh) 2t, 2g
S. Wright (Widnes) 1t
Gill (Salford)
Bowden (Widnes)
Wilkinson (Leigh) 1t
Elwell (Widnes) 1t
Gourley (Rochdale)
Adams (Widnes) 1dg
Nicholls (St. Helens)
E. Prescott (Salford)
Sub: Macko (Leigh)

1978 Yorkshire
Widnes: 27 Sept.
Won 23-7
Fairbairn (Wigan) 4g
Fielding (Salford) 2t
Aspey (Widnes)
Cunningham (St. Helens) 1t
Bevan (Warrington) 1t
K. Kelly (Warrington) 1t
Bowden (Widnes)
D. Chisnall (St. Helens)
Elwell (Widnes)
Hodkinson (Rochdale)
Adams (Widnes)
Nicholls (St. Helens)
E. Prescott (Salford)
Subs: Glynn (St. Helens)
   Pinner (St. Helens)

1978 Cumbria
Whitehaven: 11 Oct.
Lost 15-16
Glynn (St. Helens) 3g
S. Wright (Widnes) 2t
Aspey (Widnes)
E. Hughes (Widnes)
Jones (St. Helens)
K. Kelly (Warrington)
Bowden (Widnes)
D. Chisnall (St. Helens)
Liptrot (St. Helens)
Hodkinson (Rochdale)
Adams (Widnes)
Nicholls (St. Helens)
E. Prescott (Salford)
Subs: Keiron O'Loughlin (Wigan) 1t
   Pinner (St. Helens)

1979 Cumbria
St. Helens: 5 Sept.
Won 23-15
Eckersley (Widnes) 2g
Arkwright (St. Helens) 1t
Woods (Leigh) 1t, 3g
E. Hughes (Widnes) 2t
Hornby (Wigan)
K. Kelly (Warrington)
Bowden (Widnes)
B. Hogan (Widnes)
Elwell (Widnes)
S. O'Neill (Wigan)
W. Melling (Wigan)
Nicholls (St. Helens)
Pinner (St. Helens) 1dg
Subs: Glynn (St. Helens)
   E. Prescott (Salford)

1979 Yorkshire
Castleford: 12 Sept.
Lost 16-19
Eckersley (Widnes) 1t
Arkwright (St. Helens)
Keiron O'Loughlin (Wigan)
E. Hughes (Widnes)
Glynn (St. Helens)
Burke (Widnes) 3g
Bowden (Widnes)
S. O'Neill (Wigan)
Elwell (Widnes)
Gourley (Salford)
Adams (Widnes)
W. Melling (Wigan)
Pinner (St. Helens) 2t, 1dg
Subs: Hull (Widnes)
   E. Prescott (Salford)

1980 Cumbria
Barrow: 3 Sept.
Lost 16-19
Burke (Widnes) 2g
Bilsbury (Leigh) 1t
Stephenson (Salford)
Glynn (St. Helens)
Bentley (Widnes)
Woods (Leigh) 2t
Holding (St. Helens)
M. O'Neill (Widnes)
Elwell (Widnes)
Eccles (Warrington) 1t
Dearden (Widnes)
Gittins (Leigh)
Adams (Widnes)
Sub: Flanagan (Oldham)

1980 Yorkshire
Widnes: 24 Sept.
Won 17-9
C. Whitfield (Salford) 4g
Bentley (Widnes)
Bilsbury (Leigh) 1t
M. Foy (Wigan)
Hornby (Wigan) 1t
Woods (Leigh)
Holding (St. Helens) 1t
M. O'Neill (Widnes)
Liptrot (St. Helens)
Eccles (Warrington)
S. O'Neill (Wigan)
Dearden (Widnes)
Adams (Widnes)
Subs: A. Fairhurst (Leigh)
    Gittins (Leigh)

1981 Yorkshire
Castleford: 9 Sept.
Lost 15-21
C. Whitfield (Salford) 3g
Drummond (Leigh) 2t
Stephenson (Salford)
M. Foy (Wigan)
Bentley (Widnes) 1t
K. Kelly (Warrington)
A. Gregory (Widnes)
M. O'Neill (Widnes)
Kiss (Wigan)
Case (Warrington)
Potter (Warrington)
Adams (Widnes)
Pinner (St. Helens)
Sub: Donlan (Leigh)

1981 Cumbria
Wigan: 16 Sept.
Lost 15-27
C. Whitfield (Salford) 3g
Drummond (Leigh) 1t
George (Widnes)
Glynn (St. Helens) 1t
Bentley (Widnes)
K. Kelly (Warrington) 1t
Peters (St. Helens)
Hodkinson (Wigan)
Kiss (Wigan)
M. O'Neill (Widnes)
Potter (Warrington)
Case (Warrington)
Pinner (St. Helens)
Subs: Kirwan (Oldham)
    Yates (Salford)

1982 Yorkshire
Leigh: 26 May
Lost 21-22
Burke (Widnes) 1t, 6g
Drummond (Leigh)
Stephenson (Wigan) 1t
Woods (Leigh)
Basnett (Widnes)
A. Myler (Widnes) 1t
A. Gregory (Widnes)
M. O'Neill (Widnes)
Kiss (Wigan)
Wilkinson (Leigh)
Potter (Leigh)
F. Whitfield (Widnes)
Flanagan (Oldham)
Sub: Fieldhouse (Warrington)

1982 Cumbria
Workington: 30 May
Won 46-8
Burke (Widnes) 8g
Meadows (St. Helens) 3t
Stephenson (Wigan) 2t
Donlan (Leigh) 3t
Basnett (Widnes)
Keiron O'Loughlin (Widnes)
A. Gregory (Widnes)
M. O'Neill (Widnes) 1t
Kiss (Wigan)
Wilkinson (Leigh)
Potter (Leigh)
Tabern (Leigh) 1t
Flanagan (Oldham)
Subs: C. Whitfield (Wigan)
    Fieldhouse (Warrington)

1985 Yorkshire
Wigan: 11 Sept.
Lost 10-26
Burke (Widnes) 1g
Ledger (St. Helens)
Stephenson (Wigan)
Keiron O'Loughlin (Salford)
Lydon (Widnes)
A. Myler (Widnes)
A. Gregory (Warrington) 1t
M. O'Neill (Widnes)
Webb (Warrington)
Forber (St. Helens)
Eccles (Warrington) 1t
Fieldhouse (Widnes)
Pendlebury (Salford)
Subs: Edwards (Wigan)
    Wane (Wigan)

1986 Yorkshire
Leeds: 17 Sept.
Lost 14-26
Lydon (Wigan)
Forster (Warrington)
R. Duane (Warrington)
Stephenson (Wigan) 1t, 3g
Basnett (Widnes) 1t
Edwards (Wigan)
A. Gregory (Warrington)
Pyke (Leigh)
Liptrot (St. Helens)
Fieldhouse (Widnes)
Arkwright (St. Helens)
Platt (St. Helens)
M. Gregory (Warrington)
Subs: Henderson (Leigh)
    Haggerty (St. Helens)

1987 Yorkshire
Wigan: 16 Sept.
Lost 10-16
Hampson (Wigan) 1t
McCormack (St. Helens)
Cullen (Warrington)
Whitfield (Halifax) 1g
D. Wright (Widnes)
Woods (Warrington)
A. Gregory (Wigan)
Case (Wigan)
Dermott (Wigan)
Humphries (Warrington)
Round (Oldham) 1t
Potter (Wigan)
M. Gregory (Warrington)
Subs: McCulloch (Leigh)
    McGinty (Warrington)

1987 Papua New Guinea
St. Helens: 14 Oct.
Drew: 22-22
Hampson (Wigan)
Drummond (Warrington)
Lydon (Wigan) 1t, 1g
Henderson (Leigh) 1t
Offiah (Widnes)
Edwards (Wigan) 2t
A. Gregory (Wigan)
Pyke (Leigh)
Groves (St. Helens)
Round (Oldham)
M. Gregory (Warrington)
Roberts (Warrington) 1t
Arkwright (St. Helens)
Subs: D. Hulme (Widnes)
    Cottrell (Leigh)

353

LANCASHIRE REGISTER

The following is a register of current players who have appeared for Lancashire. Each played at least one first team game last season.

ARKWRIGHT, C. (4) St. Helens
BASNETT, J. (3) Widnes
BENTLEY, K. (4) Widnes
BURKE, M. (5) Widnes
CASE, B. (3) Warrington 2, Wigan
COTTRELL, A. (+1) Leigh
CULLEN, P. (1) Warrington
DERMOTT, M. (1) Wigan
DONLAN, S. (1+1) Leigh
DRUMMOND, D. (4) Leigh 3, Warrington
DUANE, R. (1) Warrington
ECCLES, R. (3) Warrington
EDWARDS, S. (2+1) Wigan
FAIRBAIRN, G. (2) Wigan
FAIRHURST, A. (+1) Leigh
FIELDHOUSE, J. (2+2) Warrington +2, Widnes 2
FLANAGAN, T. (2+1) Oldham
FORBER, P. (1) St. Helens
FORSTER, M. (1) Warrington
GITTINS, T. (1+1) Leigh
GLYNN, P. (4+2) St. Helens
GREGORY, A. (7) Widnes 3, Warrington 2, Wigan 2
GREGORY, M. (3) Warrington
GROVES, P. (1) St. Helens
HAGGERTY, R. (+1) St. Helens
HAMPSON, S. (2) Wigan
HENDERSON, J. (1+1) Leigh
HOLDING, N. (2) St. Helens
HUGHES, E. (12) Widnes
HULME, D. (+1) Widnes
HUMPHRIES, A. (1) Warrington

KIRWAN, P. (+1) Oldham
KISS, N. (4) Wigan
LEDGER, B. (1) St. Helens
LIPTROT, G. (3) St. Helens
LYDON, J. (3) Widnes, Wigan 2
McCORMACK, K. (1) St. Helens
McCULLOCH, N (+1) Leigh
McGINTY, W (+1) Warrington
MEADOWS, K. (1) St. Helens
MYLER, A. (2) Widnes
OFFIAH, M (1) Widnes
O'LOUGHLIN, Keiron (4+1) Wigan 2+1, Widnes, Salford
O'NEILL, M. (7) Widnes
O'NEILL, S. (3) Wigan
PENDLEBURY, J. (1) Salford
PETERS, S. (1) St. Helens
PINNER, H. (4+3) St. Helens
PLATT, A. (1) St. Helens
POTTER, I. (5) Warrington 2, Leigh 2, Wigan
PRESCOTT, E. (9+2) Salford 7+2, St. Helens 2
PYKE, D. (2) Leigh
ROBERTS, M. (1) Warrington
ROUND, P. (2) Oldham
STEPHENSON, D. (6) Salford 2, Wigan 4
TABERN, R. (1) Leigh
WANE, S. (+1) Wigan
WEBB, C. (1) Warrington
WHITFIELD, C. (4+1) Salford 3, Wigan +1, Halifax
WOODS, J. (6) Leigh 5, Warrington
WRIGHT, D. (1) Widnes

YORKSHIRE TEAMS

. . . **A 20-year review.** Initials are included where more than one celebrated player shared a surname in the same era. Only playing substitutes are listed.

Bill Francis.

Mick Harrison.

1968 Cumberland
Whitehaven: 11 Sept.
Won 23-10
Keegan (Hull)
Hurl (Hunslet)
A. Burwell (Hull KR) 1t
Wriglesworth (Bradford) 2t
Atkinson (Leeds) 1t
Millward (Hull KR) 4g,1t
Seabourne (Leeds)
Clark (Leeds)
C. Dickinson (Castleford)
Scroby (Halifax)
Ramsey (Leeds)
A. Morgan (Featherstone)
Reilly (Castleford)

1968 Lancashire
Hull KR: 25 Sept.

Won 10-5

Keegan (Hull) 1t
Francis (Wigan)
Hynes (Leeds)
Wriglesworth (Bradford)
Atkinson (Leeds)
Millward (Hull KR) 2g
Seabourne (Leeds) 1t
Denis Hartley (Castleford)
C. Dickinson (Castleford)
J. Ward (Castleford)
P. Lowe (Hull KR)
A. Morgan (Featherstone)
Reilly (Castleford)

1969 Lancashire
Salford: 3 Sept.

Lost 12-14

Keegan (Hull)
A. Smith (Leeds)
Hynes (Leeds)
A. Burwell (Hull KR)
Francis (Wigan)
Millward (Hull KR) 2g
K.Hepworth (Castleford) 1t
Denis Hartley (Castleford)
C. Dickinson (Castleford)
Macklin (Hull) 1g
P. Lowe (Hull KR) 1t
Lockwood (Castleford)
Batten (Leeds)
Subs: Edwards (Castleford)
      A. Morgan (Featherstone)

1969 Cumberland
Hull KR: 1 Oct.

Won 42-3

Keegan (Hull) 1t
Lowndes (Castleford) 1t
Moore (Hull KR) 3t
A. Burwell (Hull KR)
T. Thompson (Hunslet) 1t
Millward (Hull KR) 6g, 2t
Davidson (Hull) 1t
Harrison (Hull)
M. Stephenson (Dewsbury)
J. Ward (Castleford)
Haigh (Wakefield) 1t
J. Thompson (Featherstone)
Doyle (Batley)

1970 Cumberland
Whitehaven: 14 Sept.

Lost 15-21

Edwards (Castleford)
Slater (Wakefield)
Shoebottom (Leeds)
Watson (Leeds)
Lamb (Bradford) 1t
Wolford (Bramley)
Davidson (Hull)
Denis Hartley (Castleford)
M. Stephenson (Dewsbury) 1t
Clawson (Hull KR) 3g
Lockwood (Castleford)
J. Thompson (Featherstone) 1t
Batten (Leeds)
Sub: Firth (Hull)

1971 Lancashire
Castleford: 13 Jan.

Won 32-12

Jefferson (Keighley) 6g
A. Smith (Leeds) 2t
Hynes (Leeds) 1t
N. Stephenson (Dewsbury) 2t
Atkinson (Leeds)
Topliss (Wakefield)
Shoebottom (Leeds) 1g
Clawson (Hull KR)
C. Dickinson (Castleford)
Jeanes (Wakefield)
Haigh (Leeds)
J. Thompson (Featherstone)
Batten (Leeds) 1t

1971 Lancashire (Play-off)
Castleford: 24 Feb.

Won 34-8

Jefferson (Keighley) 1t,1g
Slater (Wakefield) 2t
Stenton (Castleford)
N. Stephenson (Dewsbury) 3g, 2t
Young (York)
Hardisty (Castleford) 1g
K. Hepworth (Castleford)
Clawson (Hull KR)
C. Dickinson (Castleford)
Jeanes (Wakefield) 1t
Lockwood (Castleford)
Irving (Oldham) 1t
Halmshaw (Halifax)
Subs: Topliss (Wakefield) 1t
      M. Stephenson (Dewsbury)

1971 Lancashire
Leigh: 29 Sept.

Won 42-22

Edwards (Castleford)
Slater (Wakefield)
Watson (Bradford) 1t
N. Stephenson (Dewsbury) 5g,1t
Lamb (Bradford) 1t
Millward (Hull KR) 4g,1t
Nash (Featherstone) 1t
Harrison (Hull)
M. Stephenson (Dewsbury)
Jeanes (Wakefield)
Boxall (Hull)
Irving (Oldham)
Halmshaw (Halifax) 1t
Subs: Topliss (Wakefield) 1t
      Farrar (Featherstone) 1t

1971 Cumberland
Wakefield: 20 Oct.

Won 17-12

Edwards (Castleford)
Slater (Wakefield)
Watson (Bradford) 2t
N. Stephenson (Dewsbury) 2t
Lamb (Bradford)
Millward (Hull KR) 1g
A. Bates (Dewsbury)
Harrison (Hull)
M. Stephenson (Dewsbury)
Farrar (Featherstone)
Boxall (Hull) 1t
Irving (Oldham)
Halmshaw (Halifax)

1972 Cumberland
Whitehaven: 13 Sept.

Lost: 14-23

Rushton (Dewsbury)
A. Smith (Leeds)
Dyl (Leeds)
N. Stephenson (Dewsbury) 4g
D. Redfearn (Bradford)
Millward (Hull KR)
Nash (Featherstone) 2t
Clawson (Leeds)
M. Stephenson (Dewsbury)
Jeanes (Wakefield)
Cookson (Leeds)
J. Bates (Dewsbury)
Halmshaw (Halifax)
Subs: Wraith (Wakefield)
      Irving (Oldham)

1972 Lancashire
Castleford: 11 Oct.
Won 32-18
Jefferson (Keighley) 7g
Lamb (Bradford) 2t
Worsley (Castleford) 1t
Pickup (Huddersfield) 1t
D. Redfearn (Bradford) 1t
Blacker (Bradford)
A. Bates (Dewsbury)
Naylor (Batley)
M. Stephenson (Dewsbury)
T. Lowe (Dewsbury)
Irving (Oldham) 1t
Lockwood (Castleford)
Norton (Castleford)
Subs: Wraith (Wakefield)
      C. Dickinson (Castleford)

1973 Lancashire
Widnes: 19 Sept.
Lost 15-17
Jefferson (Keighley) 3g
A. Smith (Leeds) 1t
Hynes (Leeds)
Holmes (Leeds)
Atkinson (Leeds) 1t
Topliss (Wakefield)
Nash (Featherstone)
Harrison (Hull)
M. Morgan (Wakefield)
Davies (Huddersfield) 1t
Grayshon (Dewsbury)
J. Thompson (Featherstone)
Stone (Featherstone)
Sub: J. Bates (Dewsbury)

1974 Lancashire
Keighley: 25 Sept.
Won 20-14
Marshall (Leeds) 4g
D. Redfearn (Bradford)
Hughes (Bramley)
Roe (Keighley)
Atkinson (Leeds) 1t
Millward (Hull KR) 1t
A. Bates (Dewsbury) 1t
Dixon (York)
Raistrick (Keighley)
Irving (Wigan) 1t
Grayshon (Dewsbury)
Idle (Bramley)
Norton (Castleford)
Subs: Clark (N. Hunslet)
      J. Bates (Dewsbury)

1973 Cumberland (Play-off)
Leeds: 17 Jan.
Won 20-7
Jefferson (Keighley) 4g
Lamb (Bradford)
Worsley (Castleford)
Dyl (Leeds)
D. Redfearn (Bradford) 1t
Topliss (Wakefield) 1t
Hudson (Hull KR)
Dixon (York) 1t
M. Stephenson (Dewsbury)
Lyons (Wakefield) 1t
Irving (Oldham)
Lockwood (Castleford)
Batten (Leeds)
Subs: N. Stephenson (Dewsbury)
      B. Kear (Featherstone)

1974 Cumbria
Workington: 11 Sept.
Lost 7-10
Jefferson (Keighley) 2g
Lamb (Bradford)
Dave Hartley (Featherstone) 1t
M. Smith (Featherstone)
D. Redfearn (Bradford)
Topliss (Wakefield)
Nash (Featherstone)
Harrison (Leeds)
Spurr (Castleford)
Farrar (Featherstone)
Grayshon (Dewsbury)
J. Bates (Dewsbury)
Norton (Castleford)
Subs: Burton (Halifax)
      Ramsey (Bradford)

1974 Lancashire (Play-off)
Widnes: 16 Oct.
Lost 11-29
Sheard (Wakefield)
Lamb (Bradford)
Roe (Keighley) 1t
Burton (Halifax) 1g
Atkinson (Leeds) 1t
Topliss (Wakefield)
A. Bates (Dewsbury)
Dixon (York)
Raistrick (Keighley)
Millington (Hull KR)
Grayshon (Dewsbury)
Irving (Wigan)
Norton (Castleford) 1t

1973 Cumbria
Bramley: 12 Sept.
Won 37-12
Jefferson (Keighley) 7g, 1t
A. Smith (Leeds) 3t
Newlove (Featherstone)
Dyl (Leeds)
Atkinson (Leeds)
Topliss (Wakefield) 1t
Nash (Featherstone) 1g
Ballantyne (Wakefield)
M. Morgan (Wakefield) 1t
Davies (Huddersfield)
Irving (Wigan)
J. Thompson (Featherstone) 1t
Stone (Featherstone)
Sub: Idle (Bramley)

1974 Other Nationalities
Hull KR: 18 Sept.
Won 22-15
Marshall (Leeds) 5g
D. Redfearn (Bradford)
Hughes (Bramley)
M. Smith (Featherstone) 1t
Atkinson (Leeds) 1t
Burton (Halifax) 1t
A. Bates (Dewsbury)
Harrison (Leeds)
Farrar (Featherstone)
Ramsey (Bradford) 1t
Grayshon (Dewsbury)
J. Thompson (Featherstone)
Norton (Castleford)
Subs: Langley (Leeds)
      J. Bates (Dewsbury)

1975 Cumbria
Dewsbury: 19 Nov.
Won 10-7
Wraith (Castleford)
D. Smith (Wakefield) 1t
Holmes (Leeds) 1t, 2g
Dyl (Leeds)
Dunn (Hull KR)
Newlove (Featherstone)
Millward (Hull KR)
Beverley (Dewsbury)
Bridges (Featherstone)
J. Thompson (Featherstone)
Grayshon (Dewsbury)
Irving (Wigan)
Norton (Castleford)
Subs: N. Stephenson (Dewsbury)
      M. Morgan (Wakefield)

1975 Other Nationalities
Bradford: 6 Dec.
Drew 16-16
Wraith (Castleford)
D. Smith (Wakefield) 1t
Holmes (Leeds) 2g
N. Stephenson (Dewsbury)
Dunn (Hull KR)
Newlove (Featherstone)
Nash (Salford)
Beverley (Dewsbury)
Bridges (Featherstone) 1t
J. Thompson (Featherstone) 2t
Grayshon (Dewsbury)
Irving (Wigan)
Norton (Castleford)
Subs: Topliss (Wakefield)
    M. Morgan (Wakefield)

1977 Lancashire
Castleford: 1 Mar.
Won 18-13
Mumby (Bradford) 1g
Muscroft (N. Hunslet) 1t
Crook (Wakefield)
Francis (Wigan)
Atkinson (Leeds)
Topliss (Wakefield)
Stephens (Castleford)
J. Thompson (Featherstone)
D. Ward (Leeds) 1t
Farrar (Featherstone)
Rose (Hull KR) 1t
P. Lowe (Hull KR)
Norton (Castleford)
Subs: N. Stephenson (Dewsbury) 1t
    Lloyd (Castleford) 2g

1978 Cumbria
Hull: 20 Sept.
Won 37-9
Mumby (Bradford) 4g
T. Morgan (York)
Joyner (Castleford) 1t
N. Stephenson (Dewsbury) 1t, 1g
Atkinson (Leeds)
Francis (St. Helens) 2t
Nash (Salford)
Harrison (Leeds)
Dalgreen (Warrington) 1t
Pitchford (Leeds) 1t
Casey (Hull KR) 1t
P. Lowe (Hull KR) 1t
Crane (Leeds) 1t
Subs: Topliss (Wakefield)
    Farrar (Hull)

1975 Lancashire
Wigan: 20 Dec.
Won 17-7
Langley (Dewsbury)
D. Smith (Wakefield)
Holmes (Leeds) 4g
Dyl (Leeds)
Atkinson (Leeds) 1t
Topliss (Wakefield)
Stephens (Castleford)
Millington (Hull KR)
Bridges (Featherstone)
Farrar (Featherstone)
Grayshon (Dewsbury)
M. Morgan (Wakefield) 2t
Norton (Castleford)
Subs: Hancock (Hull)
    J. Thompson (Featherstone)

1977 Cumbria (Jubilee)
York: 5 Oct.
Won 28-10
Banks (York)
D. Smith (Leeds) 2t
Marston (York) 1t
Quinn (Featherstone) 5g
Atkinson (Leeds) 2t
Hancock (Hull)
Shepherd (Huddersfield)
Beverley (Dewsbury)
Bridges (Featherstone)
Farrar (Featherstone)
M. Morgan (York)
Boxall (Hull) 1t
Bell (Featherstone)
Subs: Hague (Leeds)
    Branch (Huddersfield)

1978 Lancashire
Widnes: 27 Sept.
Lost 7-23
Mumby (Bradford)
Muscroft (N. Hunslet)
Joyner (Castleford)
M. Smith (Hull KR) 1t
D. Redfearn (Bradford)
Francis (St. Helens)
Stephens (Castleford)
Ballantyne (Castleford)
Wileman (York)
Pitchford (Leeds)
Lloyd (Hull) 2g
P. Smith (Featherstone)
Branch (Huddersfield)
Subs: Topliss (Wakefield)
    Farrar (Hull)

1977 Cumbria
Whitehaven: 15 Feb.
Drew 12-12
Wraith (Castleford)
Muscroft (N. Hunslet)
Joyner (Castleford) 1t
Roe (Bradford)
Atkinson (Leeds)
Topliss (Wakefield) 1t
Stephens (Castleford)
J. Thompson (Featherstone)
D. Ward (Leeds)
A. Dickinson (Castleford)
Grayshon (Dewsbury)
Lloyd (Castleford) 3g
M. Morgan (Wakefield)

1977 Lancashire (Jubilee)
Widnes: 19 Oct.
Lost 8-33
Mumby (Bradford)
D. Smith (Leeds)
Hague (Leeds)
Quinn (Featherstone) 1g
Atkinson (Leeds) 1t
Francis (Wigan)
Nash (Salford)
J. Thompson (Bradford)
Bridges (Featherstone)
Farrar (Featherstone)
M. Morgan (York) 1t
Branch (Huddersfield)
Bell (Featherstone)
Subs: Hancock (Hull)
    Griffiths (N. Hunslet)

1979 Cumbria
Workington: 29 Aug.
Lost 13-17
Box (Featherstone)
Fletcher (Wakefield) 1t
M. Parrish (Hunslet) 3g
Banks (York) 1t
Fenton (Castleford)
Evans (Featherstone)
Dean (Hunslet) 1dg
Tindall (Hull)
Wileman (Hull)
Gibbins (Featherstone)
Grayshon (Bradford)
Hankins (Dewsbury)
Bell (Featherstone)
Sub: G. Smith (York)

357

1979 Lancashire
Castleford: 12 Sept.
Won 19-16
Box (Featherstone) 3g
Fletcher (Wakefield)
Joyner (Castleford)
Evans (Featherstone)
Fenton (Castleford)
Burton (Castleford) 1t
Stephens (Castleford)
Beverley (Workington)
Raistrick (Halifax) 1t, 1dg
Gibbins (Featherstone)
Branch (Huddersfield) 1t
Hankins (Dewsbury)
Adams (Leeds) 1t
Subs: P. Johnson (Castleford)
      R. Dickinson (Leeds)

1980 Cumbria
Hull KR: 17 Sept.
Lost 16-17
Wraith (Castleford)
Fletcher (Wakefield) 1t
Joyner (Castleford)
Quinn (Featherstone) 4g
Fenton (Castleford)
Hague (Leeds)
Dick (Leeds) 1t, 2dg
Holdstock (Hull KR)
Spurr (Castleford)
Skerrett (Hull)
Grayshon (Bradford)
Kevin Rayne (Wakefield)
Norton (Hull)
Sub: D. Heron (Leeds)

1980 Lancashire
Widnes: 24 Sept.
Lost 9-17
Wraith (Castleford)
Fletcher (Wakefield) 1t
Joyner (Castleford)
Quinn (Featherstone) 3g
Fenton (Castleford)
Topliss (Wakefield)
Stephens (Castleford)
Holdstock (Hull KR)
Watkinson (Hull KR)
Skerrett (Hull)
Grayshon (Bradford)
Kevin Rayne (Wakefield)
Norton (Hull)
Subs: Wilby (Hull)
      D. Heron (Leeds)

1981 Lancashire
Castleford: 9 Sept.
Won 21-15
Mumby (Bradford) 1t
Richardson (Castleford)
Joyner (Castleford) 2t
Dyl (Leeds) 1t
Fenton (Castleford)
Holmes (Leeds)
Nash (Salford)
Grayshon (Bradford)
D. Ward (Leeds) 1t
Millington (Hull KR)
Finch (Castleford) 3g
P. Smith (Featherstone)
Norton (Hull)

1981 Cumbria
Whitehaven: 23 Sept.
Lost 10-20
Box (Wakefield)
Richardson (Castleford)
Hague (Leeds)
Quinn (Featherstone) 1g
A. Parker (Bradford) 1t
Holmes (Leeds)
Nash (Salford)
R. Dickinson (Leeds)
D. Ward (Leeds)
Standidge (Halifax)
Finch (Castleford) 1t, 1g
Idle (Bradford)
Bell (Featherstone)
Subs: Evans (Featherstone)
      White (York)

1982 Cumbria
Castleford: 23 May
Won 22-7
Mumby (Bradford)
Richardson (Castleford) 3t
Joyner (Castleford) 2t
Day (Hull)
Gant (Bradford)
Holmes (Leeds)
Dick (Leeds) 1t, 2g
Tindall (Hull)
D. Ward (Leeds)
R. Dickinson (Leeds)
G. Van Bellen (Bradford)
Casey (Hull KR)
Norton (Hull)
Subs: Dyl (Leeds)
      D. Hobbs (Featherstone)

1982 Lancashire
Leigh: 26 May
Won 22-21
Mumby (Bradford)
Pryce (York) 3t
Joyner (Castleford)
Day (Hull)
Gant (Bradford)
Holmes (Leeds)
Dick (Leeds) 1t, 3g, 1dg
Tindall (Hull)
D. Ward (Leeds)
R. Dickinson (Leeds)
G. Van Bellen (Bradford)
P. Smith (Featherstone)
K. Ward (Castleford) 1t
Subs: Dyl (Leeds)
      Keith Rayne (Leeds)

1985 Lancashire
Wigan: 11 Sept.
Won 26-10
Kay (Hunslet)
Gibson (Batley)
Hyde (Castleford) 1t
Mason (Bramley) 2t
Laws (Hull KR)
Joyner (Castleford)
Fox (Featherstone) 3g
Hill (Leeds)
Watkinson (Hull KR)
M. Morgan (Oldham)
D. Hobbs (Oldham) 1t
Burton (Hull KR)
D. Heron (Leeds) 1t
Subs: Lyman (Featherstone)
      Dannatt (Hull)

1985 New Zealand
Bradford: 23 Oct.
Won 18-8
Mumby (Bradford)
Gibson (Batley) 1t
Creasser (Leeds)
Schofield (Hull) 1dg
Mason (Bramley)
Hanley (Wigan) 1t, 1dg
Fox (Featherstone) 2g
Grayshon (Bradford)
Noble (Bradford)
Skerrett (Hull)
Crooks (Hull)
Goodway (Wigan) 1t
D. Heron (Leeds)
Subs: Steadman (York)
      Lyman (Featherstone)

1986 Lancashire	1987 Lancashire	1987 Papua New Guinea
Leeds: 17 Sept.	Wigan: 16 Sept.	Leeds: 27 Oct.
Won 26-14	Won 16-10	Won 28-4
Wilkinson (Leeds)	Wilkinson (Halifax)	Mumby (Bradford)
Gibson (Leeds)	Gibson (Leeds)	Eastwood (Hull)
Marchant (Castleford) 1t	Marchant (Castleford) 1t	Marchant (Castleford) 1t
Hanley (Wigan) 1t	Mason (Wakefield)	Gibson (Leeds) 3t
Gill (Wigan) 1t	Gill (Wigan) 1t	Mason (Wakefield)
Joyner (Castleford)	Hanley (Wigan) 1t	Joyner (Castleford)
Fox (Featherstone)	Fox (Featherstone) 1g	Fox (Featherstone)
Kelly (Hull KR)	Ward (Castleford)	Hobbs (Bradford) 2g
Noble (Bradford)	K. Beardmore (Castleford)	McCallion (Halifax)
Hobbs (Oldham) 5g	Hobbs (Bradford) 1g	Powell (Leeds)
P. Smith (Featherstone)	Crooks (Leeds)	Burton (Hull K.R.)
Price (York)	Burton (Hull K.R.)	K. Fairbank (Bradford) 1t
Lyman (Featherstone) 1t	Goodway (Wigan)	Dixon (Halifax)
Subs: Mason (Bramley)	Sub: Dixon (Halifax)	Subs: Creasser (Leeds) 1t
Medley (Leeds)		D. Heron (Leeds)

YORKSHIRE REGISTER

The following is a register of current players who have appeared for Yorkshire. Each played at least one first team game last season.

BEARDMORE, K. (1) Castleford
BELL, K. (4) Featherstone R.
BURTON, C. (3) Hull K.R.

CREASSER, D. (1+1) Leeds
CROOKS, L. (2) Hull, Leeds

DANNATT, A (+1) Hull
DICK, K. (3) Leeds
DICKINSON, R. (3+1) Leeds
DIXON, P. (1+1) Halifax

EASTWOOD, P. (1) Hull

FAIRBANK, K. (1) Bradford N.
FLETCHER, A. (4) Wakefield T.
FOX, D. (5) Featherstone R.

GIBSON, C. (5) Batley 2, Leeds 3
GILL, H. (2) Wigan
GOODWAY, A. (2) Wigan
GRAYSHON, J. (14) Dewsbury 9, Bradford N. 5

HAGUE, N. (3+1) Leeds
HANLEY, E. (3) Wigan
HERON, D. (2+3) Leeds
HILL, B. (1) Leeds
HOBBS, D. (4+1) Featherstone R. +1, Oldham 2, Bradford N. 2
HOLMES, J. (8) Leeds
HYDE, G. (1) Castleford

IDLE, G. (1+1) Bramley +1, Bradford N.

JOHNSON, Phil. (+1) Castleford
JOYNER, J. (12) Castleford

KAY, A. (1) Hunslet
KELLY, A. (1) Hull K.R.

LAWS, D. (1) Hull K.R.
LYMAN, P. (1+2) Featherstone R.

McCALLION, S. (1) Halifax
MARCHANT, A, (3) Castleford
MASON, A. (4+1) Bramley (2+1), Wakefield T. 2
MEDLEY, P. (+1) Leeds
MUMBY, K. (9) Bradford N.

NASH, S. (10) Featherstone R. 5, Salford 5
NOBLE, B. (2) Bradford N.

PARRISH, M. (1) Hunslet
POWELL, R. (1) Leeds
PRICE, G. (1) York
PRYCE, G. (1) York

QUINN, S. (5) Featherstone R.

RAYNE, Keith (+1) Leeds
RAYNE, Kevin (2) Wakefield T.
REDFEARN, D. (7) Bradford N.
ROE, P. (3) Keighley 2, Bradford N.

SCHOFIELD, G. (1) Hull
SKERRETT, T. (3) Hull
SMITH, G. (+1) York
SMITH, M. (1) Hull K.R.
SMITH, P. (4) Featherstone R.
SPURR, R. (2) Castleford
STEADMAN, G. (+1) York
STEPHENS, G. (6) Castleford
STEPHENSON, N. (7+3) Dewsbury

TOPLISS, D. (10+5) Wakefield T.

VAN BELLEN, G. (2) Bradford N.

WARD, K. (2) Castleford
WATKINSON, D. (2) Hull K.R.
WHITE, B. (+1) York
WILKINSON, I. (2) Leeds, Halifax

COUNTY CHAMPIONSHIP TITLES
(including joint titles)

Lancashire 34
Yorkshire 24
Cumbria 16
Cheshire 1

Year	Winner	Year	Winner
1895-96	Lancashire	1937-38	Lancashire
1896-97	Lancashire	1938-39	Lancashire
1897-98	Yorkshire	1945-46	Lancashire
1898-99	Yorkshire	1946-47	Yorkshire
1899-1900	Lancashire	1947-48	Lancashire
1900-01	Lancashire	1948-49	Cumberland
1901-02	Cheshire	1949-50	Undecided
1902-03	Lancashire	1950-51	Undecided
1903-04	Lancashire	1951-52	Yorkshire
1904-05	Yorkshire	1952-53	Lancashire
1905-06	Lancashire / Cumberland	1953-54	Yorkshire
1906-07	Lancashire	1954-55	Yorkshire
1907-08	Cumberland	1955-56	Lancashire
1908-09	Lancashire	1956-57	Lancashire
1909-10	Cumberland / Yorkshire	1957-58	Yorkshire
1910-11	Lancashire	1958-59	Yorkshire
1911-12	Cumberland	1959-60	Cumberland
1912-13	Yorkshire	1960-61	Lancashire
1913-14	Undecided	1961-62	Cumberland
1919-20	Undecided	1962-63	Yorkshire
1920-21	Yorkshire	1963-64	Cumberland
1921-22	Yorkshire	1964-65	Yorkshire
1922-23	Lancashire / Yorkshire	1965-66	Cumberland
1923-24	Lancashire	1966-67	Cumberland
1924-25	Lancashire	1967-68	Lancashire
1925-26	Lancashire	1968-69	Yorkshire
1926-27	Lancashire	1969-70	Lancashire
1927-28	Cumberland	1970-71	Yorkshire
1928-29	Lancashire	1971-72	Yorkshire
1929-30	Lancashire	1972-73	Yorkshire
1930-31	Yorkshire	1973-74	Lancashire
1931-32	Lancashire	1974-75	Lancashire
1932-33	Cumberland	1975-76	Yorkshire
1933-34	Cumberland	1976-77	Yorkshire
1934-35	Cumberland	1977-78	Not Held
1935-36	Lancashire	1978-79	Lancashire
1936-37	Lancashire	1979-80	Lancashire
		1980-81	Cumbria
		1981-82	Cumbria
		1982-83	Yorkshire

Garry Schofield — record £155,000 transfer from Hull to Leeds.

TRANSFERS

TRANSFERS

TRANSFER REVIEW
1 June 1987 to 31 May 1988

Leeds twice shattered the cash record transfer fee with the signing of Hull Test players Lee Crooks and Garry Schofield for £150,000 and £155,000 respectively.

Crooks signed on 2 June for £150,000 with the international prop or second row forward interrupting a summer spell with Australian club Balmain to complete the deal. He had not sought a transfer and expressed reluctance at leaving his home town club, but Hull were in financial trouble and needed the money.

The fee beat the previous cash record of £130,000 when Test scrum-half Andy Gregory moved from Warrington to Wigan on 11 January 1987. It also equalled the £150,000 rated cash plus two players deal which took Test player Ellery Hanley from Bradford Northern to Wigan in September 1985. Crooks' fee more than doubled the previous cash record for a forward of £65,000 set when Wigan signed Test star Andy Goodway from Oldham on 29 July 1985.

Five months after signing Crooks, Leeds broke the transfer record again when they signed his friend and former Hull colleague Schofield for £155,000 on 23 October 1987. Following a contract dispute the Test centre had been placed on the transfer list at a then world record listing of £200,000 and had not played for Hull since returning from a summer spell with Balmain, Australia.

First reports of the Crooks and Schofield transfers put the fees much higher with some confusion over the inclusion of 15 per cent Value Added Tax. It was later explained that the original figures of £172,000 for Crooks and £178,250 for Schofield had included VAT which the paying club retrieves from the Customs and Excise.

In between the two signings Leeds also paid a record fee for a winger when they gave Widnes £50,000 for Test player John Basnett on 20 August which was broken later in the season by St. Helens. The previous highest fee for a winger had been £40,000 when Des Drummond moved from Leigh to Warrington in February 1987 and Phil Ford left Warrington for Wigan in February 1985.

Leeds were also involved with Wakefield Trinity in the most remarkable players plus cash deal of all time. It included six players, two joining Leeds and four going to Wakefield plus a cash balance which made the deal an estimated £120,000.

Full back Gary Spencer and half-back John Lyons joined Leeds with Wakefield obtaining centre Andy Mason, winger Phil Fox, half back Mark Conway and forward Keith Rayne. Spencer had been on the transfer list at £90,000 and Rayne at £35,000.

David Stephenson (£75,000) from Wigan and Alan Rathbone (£32,000) from Warrington were other major Leeds signings. In addition they recruited top-ranked Australian players Marty Gurr, Peter Jackson, Steve Morris, and Peter Tunks plus New Zealand RU All Black Mark Brooke-Cowden. Great Britain BARLA forward John Fairbank was also signed from Elland in a club record deal for an amateur.

The massive spending spree took Leeds' total outlay for 12 months well past half-a-million pounds. They accounted for four of the period's nine £50,000 plus cash transfers.

The others were £65,000: Paul Round from St. Helens to Oldham and Les Holliday from Swinton to Halifax; £55,000: Mick Worral from Oldham to Salford and Les Quirk from Barrow to St. Helens; £50,000: Derek Pyke from Leigh to Widnes who also included Harry Pinner in part exchange. Pinner was valued at about £45,000.

The £65,000 fee for Round was a record for a Division Two club, Oldham having just been relegated.

Quirk's £55,000 transfer was a record for a winger, beating the £50,000 Basnett figure a little earlier.

St. Helens equalled the record fee for a hooker when they signed Paul Groves from Salford for £40,000. The record was set when Colin Maskill moved from Wakefield to Leeds in 1985.

Wigan listed Ellery Hanley at a world record £225,000 after coach Graham Lowe accused the Great Britiain Test captain of 'unco-operative behaviour'. But the fee frightened off interested clubs and after peace moves from both sides Hanley was taken off the list after three weeks.

There was a total of 168 transfers between clubs plus 20 players going on loan including those who returned to their original club. A few years ago the annual total of loan transactions was well over 100 dropping to 63 in 1986-87.

NEW TRANSFER SYSTEM

The transfer system underwent the biggest change in the game's history with the introduction of a new players' contract ruling during the 1987 close season. It meant players were no longer tied to a club indefinitely but could arrange their own contracts.

At the end of the contract period the player is free to negotiate a new one with the club or seek one with another club. A transfer fee would still have to be paid but if the clubs concerned fail to agree on the amount then it would be decided by an independent tribunal of three members.

The first ruling by the new tribunal was on 27 August and involved Ged Byrne's transfer from Salford to Wigan. The centre had been transferred 10 days earlier and already played for Wigan in the Okells Charity Shield match.

Salford sought £75,000 for Byrne, Wigan offered only £20,000 and the tribunal fixed the fee at £40,000.

RUGBY UNION SIGNINGS

The recruitment of top-rated rugby union players was the busiest for many years and included four internationals. They were Stuart Evans (Wales) to St. Helens, Peter Williams (England) to Salford, Alan Tait (Scotland) to Widnes, and Mark Brooke-Cowden (New Zealand) to Leeds.

All signed for substantial amounts but it was more difficult than ever to know what the exact fees were. Their contracts covered several years with most of the money being paid in instalments. Since April 1987 the Rugby League and the Inland Revenue had reached an agreement that the first £6,000 of any signing-on fee should be tax free and this resulted in a reluctance for players to receive an initial lump sum.

In the circumstances the record signing-on fee for a rugby union player is generally still recognised as the £80,000 Terry Holmes received from Bradford Northern in 1985.

Evans' contract with St. Helens was believed to be well in excess of £50,000 which would make the prop easily the costliest RU forward convert. The Neath RU captain won nine caps for Wales.

Williams, the Orrell and England stand-off, was a controversial selection for Great Britain's tour standby squad after playing only three matches for Salford, all in the centre.

Tait, the Kelso and Scotland centre, picked up a Stones Bitter Premiership winners medal without having played a full game of rugby league. His three appearances were all as substitute.

Brooke-Cowden was a surprise capture by Leeds after the New Zealand All Black forward had approached them following his appearance in the 1987 RU World Cup.

Of the other prominent RU players to switch codes the most successful was Martin Offiah, the Rosslyn Park winger who broke the Widnes try record in his first season, topped the game's touchdown chart and was selected for Great Britain's tour of Australasia.

Mark Preston, the Fylde and England B winger, also made an immediate impact scoring five tries in only his fifth match for Wigan.

Charlie McAlister, a New Zealand Maoris player appearing with Bradford and Bingley RU club, made a quicker than intended switch to rugby league when a newspaper report named him as the trialist apppearing for Oldham. The wing or centre signed for Oldham soon after.

David Bishop, the Pontypool and Wales scrum half, was involved in an extraordinary on-off signing episode with St. Helens. They arranged a Press conference on 24 September to announce his signing for a reported £100,000 but with Bishop there ready to sign the deal was called off when a medical report declared that a broken neck he suffered six years earlier made him still unfit for rugby. Bishop then returned to rugby union with the Wales RU stating that they had no evidence of him having broken any of their rules on professionalism.

But a total of 18 rugby union players did switch to professional rugby league, an increase of five on the previous year.

AMATEUR SIGNINGS

A total of 227 amateur RL players turned professional compared with 159 the previous year. Two were reported to have received contracts worth £40,000, believed to be a record for an amateur signing.

Sixteen-year-old Graham Southernwood signed as an amateur for Castleford with the Redhill junior scrum half or hooker to take up the professional contract on his 17th birthday.

Jason Ramshaw, aged 18, signed for Halifax after the Lock Lane (Castleford) hooker had gained junior international honours.

A year earlier Halifax had set the record with the £40,000 signing of Simon Longstaff.

OVERSEAS SIGNINGS

The Rugby League tightened up the rules regarding the signing of overseas players. Under the old quota system each club was allowed to sign three overseas players. But some recruited additional players from abroad who qualified for British passports and did not need work permits.

The system was obviously being abused and in February it was decided that in 1988-89 clubs would be allowed only one such signing and from the following season there would be a strict quota of three overseas players per club.

The 1987-88 season was the first under the supposed three-player quota but it did not curb the import of overseas signings. A total of 128 overseas players appeared in first team rugby during the season — only four down on the previous season's record total.

The total of Australian players was down from 95 to 79 but there were 47 New Zealanders compared with 35 the previous year.

A record 16 New Zealand Test players appeared during the season with Wigan's signing of teenage centre Kevin Iro making the biggest impact.

The major Australian signing was Salford's coup in obtaining Test full back Garry Jack. Other Test players having their first experience of English club rugby were Steve Morris and Peter Tunks (Leeds), Dale Shearer (Widnes) and Rod Reddy (Barrow).

The following is a list of all overseas players who made at least one first team appearance during the season.

OVERSEAS REGISTER 1987-88
*Test players as at 1 June 1988
AUSTRALIA (79)

Aitken, David	(Fulham)
Allen, Jamie	(Bramley)
Anast, Theo	(Hunslet)
Anderson, Tony	(Halifax)
Austin, Greg	(Salford)
Beattie, Michael	(Castleford)
Benson, Trevor	(Hunslet)
*Boyd, Les	(Warrington)
Brooks, David	(Hull)
Butcher, Jeffrey	(Barrow)
Butler, Warren	(Barrow)
Byron, Gerry	(Rochdale H.)
Clark, Robert	(Mansfield M.)
Cogger, Jamie	(Runcorn H.)
Cogger, John	(Runcorn H.)
Denson, Alan	(Bramley, Featherstone R.)
*Eadie, Graham	(Halifax)
Ewer, Steve	(Runcorn H.)
Fifita, John	(Castleford)
French, Gary	(Springfield B.)
Gale, Scott	(Hull)
Gearin, Paul	(Sheffield E.)
Gibson, Kerry	(Runcorn H.)
Gibson, Steven	(Salford)
Gillespie, David	(Hunslet)
Graham, Mal	(Oldham)
Grogan, Bob	(Halifax)
Gurr, Marty	(Leeds)
Halliwell, Steve	(Wakefield T.)
Hamilton, Scott	(Huddersfield B.)
Hanson, Dean	(Halifax)
Hohn, Mark	(Hunslet)
Hytch, Peter	(Sheffield E.)
*Jack, Garry	(Salford)
Jackson, Mark	(Warrington)
Jackson, Peter	(Leeds)
Jackson, Robert	(Warrington)
Johnson, Brian	(Warrington)
Kelly, Shane	(Fulham)
Lamb, Derek	(Mansfield M.)
Lawrie, Geordie	(Fulham)
Lennon, Gregg	(Wakefield T.)
*Lindner, Bob	(Castleford)
Louis, Stephen	(Doncaster)
Lulham, Rickie	(Hunslet)
McCaffery, Paul	(Hull)
McCarthy, Brian	(Oldham, Salford)

McInerney, Mark	(Keighley)
McKenzie, Phil	(Widnes)
Manning, Kevin	(Fulham)
Marsden, Peter	(Runcorn H.)
Masa, Santiago	(Fulham)
Meredith, Martin	(Halifax)
*Morris, Steve	(Leeds)
Mortimer, Peter	(Hull K.R.)
Mulherin, Paul	(York)
Neller, Keith	(Halifax)
O'Riley, Paul	(Fulham)
Penola, Colin	(Hunslet)
Pocock, Mark	(Barrow)
*Reddy, Rod	(Barrow)
Regan, Terry	(Hull)
Robinson, Michael	(York, Bramley)
Ryan, Glenn	(Hull K.R.)
Sartor, John	(Doncaster)
Sawyer, Aaron	(Rochdale H.)
Schubert, Gary	(Carlisle)
*Shearer, Dale	(Widnes)
Skinner, Matthew	(Bramley)
Stevens, Darren	(Leeds)
Stutchbury, John	(Bramley, Doncaster)
Tarry, William	(Whitehaven)
Taylor, Craig	(Fulham)
*Tunks, Peter	(Leeds)
Vievers, Phil	(St. Helens)
Vohland, Wayne	(Huddersfield B.)
Walsh, Peter	(Oldham)
Warnecke, Gary	(Oldham)
Webb, Terry	(Hunslet)

Les Boyd of Warrington.

365

NEW ZEALAND (47)

Barrow, Scott	(Rochdale H.)
*Bell, Dean	(Wigan)
*Bell, Ian	(Whitehaven)
Bell, Todd	(Whitehaven)
Brooke-Cowden, Mark	(Leeds)
Cambell, Danny	(Runcorn H.)
Clarke, Jeff	(Leigh)
Connell, Pomare	(Rochdale H.)
*Cooper, Shane	(St. Helens)
*Elia, Mark	(St. Helens)
Frame, Mark	(Leigh)
Gillan, Dave	(Fulham)
Glenn, Ricky	(Whitehaven)
Grima, Joe	(Swinton, Widnes)
*Horo, Shane	(Leigh)
*Iro, Kevin	(Wigan)
Iro, Tony	(Wigan)
Jenkins, Terry	(Doncaster)
*Leuluai, James	(Hull)
Lloyd, Chris	(Widnes)
McAlister, Charles	(Oldham)
McFarland, David	(Swinton, Springfield B.)
McKenzie, Ian	(Springfield B.)
Mehand, Mike	(Mansfield M.)
*Mercer, Gary	(Bradford N.)
Miller, Craig	(Fulham)
Muller, Robert	(Swinton)
*O'Hara, Dane	(Hull)
O'Shea, Terry	(Salford)
*Ropati, Joe	(Warrington)
Schaumkell, Kevin	(Bramley)
*Shelford, Adrian	(Wigan)
Shelford, Kelly	(Whitehaven)
*Smith, Gordon	(Hull K.R.)
Smith, Joe	(Springfield B.)
*Sorensen, Kurt	(Widnes)
Stewart, Russell	(Bradford N.)
Subritzky, Peter	(Carlisle)
*Tamati, Kevin	(Warrington)
Tarawhiti, Clarke	(Whitehaven)
*Taylor, Ross	(Hull K.R.)
Tuimavave, Paddy	(Leigh, Swinton)
Tupaea, Ashley	(Mansfield M.)
Tupaea, Shane	(Mansfield M.)
Vaafusu, Olsen	(Rochdale H.)
Watson, David	(Whitehaven)
*West, Graeme	(Wigan)

SOUTH AFRICA (1)

Du Toit, Nicholas	(Barrow)

MOROCCO (1)

M'Barki, Hussein	(Hull)

Kevin Iro, Wigan's New Zealand Test centre, shows his power against Salford.

RECORD TRANSFERS

The first £1,000 transfer came in 1921 when Harold Buck joined Leeds from Hunslet, although there were reports at the time that another player was involved in the deal to make up the four-figure transfer. Other claims for the first £1,000 transfer are attached to Stan Brogden's move from Bradford Northern to Huddersfield in 1929.

The following list gives an indication of how transfer fees have grown this century in straight cash deals only:

Season	Player	Position	From	To	Fee
1901-02	Jim Lomas	Centre	Bramley	Salford	£100
1910-11	Jim Lomas	Centre	Salford	Oldham	£300
1912-13	Billy Batten	Centre	Hunslet	Hull	£600
1921-22	Harold Buck	Wing	Hunslet	Leeds	£1,000
1929-30	Stanley Smith	Wing	Wakefield T.	Leeds	£1,075
1933-34	Stanley Brogden	Wing/centre	Huddersfield	Leeds	£1,200
1937-38	Billy Belshaw	Full back	Liverpool S.	Warrington	£1,450
1946-47	Bill Davies	Full back/centre	Huddersfield	Dewsbury	£1,650
1947-48	Bill Hudson	Forward	Batley	Wigan	£2,000
1947-48	Jim Ledgard	Full back	Dewsbury	Leigh	£2,650
1948-49	Ike Owens	Forward	Leeds	Castleford	£2,750
1948-49	Ike Owens	Forward	Castleford	Huddersfield	£2,750
1948-49	Stan McCormick	Wing	Belle Vue R.	St. Helens	£4,000
1949-50	Albert Naughton	Centre	Widnes	Warrington	£4,600
1950-51	Bruce Ryan	Wing	Hull	Leeds	£4,750
1950-51	Joe Egan	Hooker	Wigan	Leigh	£5,000
1950-51	Harry Street	Forward	Dewsbury	Wigan	£5,000
1957-58	Mick Sullivan	Wing	Huddersfield	Wigan	£9,500
1958-59	Ike Southward	Wing	Workington T.	Oldham	£10,650
1960-61	Mick Sullivan	Wing	Wigan	St. Helens	£11,000
1960-61	Ike Southward	Wing	Oldham	Workington T.	£11,002 10s
1968-69	Colin Dixon	Forward	Halifax	Salford	£12,000
1969-70	Paul Charlton	Full back	Workington T.	Salford	£12,500
1972-73	Eric Prescott	Forward	St. Helens	Salford	£13,500
1975-76	Steve Nash	Scrum half	Featherstone R.	Salford	£15,000
1977-78	Bill Ashurst	Forward	Wigan	Wakefield T.	£18,000
1978-79	Clive Pickerill	Scrum half	Castleford	Hull	£20,000
1978-79	Phil Hogan	Forward	Barrow	Hull K.R.	£35,000
1979-80	Len Casey	Forward	Bradford N.	Hull K.R.	£38,000
1980-81	Trevor Skerrett	Forward	Wakefield T.	Hull	£40,000
1980-81	George Fairbairn	Full back	Wigan	Hull K.R.	£72,500
1985-86	Ellery Hanley	Centre/stand off	Bradford N.	Wigan	£85,000
1985-86	Joe Lydon	Centre	Widnes	Wigan	£100,000
1986-87	Andy Gregory	Scrum half	Warrington	Wigan	£130,000
1987-88	Lee Crooks	Forward	Hull	Leeds	£150,000
1987-88	Garry Schofield	Centre	Hull	Leeds	£155,000

MOST MOVES

Geoff Clarkson extended his record number of transfers to 12 when he left Leigh for Featherstone Rovers on 27 October 1983. He played for 10 different English clubs and had a brief spell in Australia.

Clarkson, born on 12 August 1943 was 40 years old when he finished playing regular first team rugby in 1983-84. He turned professional with Wakefield Trinity in 1966 after gaining Yorkshire County forward honours with Wakefield Rugby Union Club.

Clarkson's club career in England is as follows:

1966 — Wakefield T.
1968 — Bradford N.
1970 — Leigh
1971 — Warrington
1972 — Leeds
1975 — York
1976 — Bramley
1978 — Wakefield T. and Hull K.R.
1980 — Bradford N. and Oldham
1981 — Leigh
1983 — Featherstone R.

1987-88 SIGNINGS

The following is a register of signings by clubs from 1 June 1987 to 31 May 1988. The right-hand column lists the club from which the player was recruited (ARL Amateur Rugby League, RU — Rugby Union).

In some instances a player who wishes to retain his amateur status is not registered although he may be named in the club's list of appearances.

Although this is a register of signings, it is possible to trace a club's transfers by scrutinising the right hand column.

Indicates where clubs have agreed to a player being signed 'on loan', a temporary transfer, the Rugby Football League prohibiting a subsequent transfer within 28 days. Where a player on loan has not been retained his return to his original club is also marked.

BARROW

Signed	Player	Club From
7.8.87	Stott, Philip	Wigan
16.9.87	Butcher, Jeffrey	Manly, Aus
30.9.87	Pocock, Mark	Manly, Aus
30.9.87	Reddy, Rod	Centrals, Aus
15.10.87	*Blacker, Brian	Salford
16.10.87	Trainer, Patrick	Walney Central, ARL
29.10.87	Burns, Howard	Workington T.
15.12.87	Hall, John	Barrow Island ARL
30.12.87	Butler, Warren	Wauchope, Aus
6.1.88	Shaw, Neil	Barrow Island ARL
16.2.88	Brown, Ralph	Holker Pioneers
16.2.88	Marwood, Dean	Barrow Island ARL
3.3.88	Mossop, Andrew	Warrington
15.4.88	Kendall, Simon	Barrow Island ARL

BATLEY

Signed	Player	Club From
18.9.87	Mitchell, Keith	Hunslet
5.10.87	Bowness, Mark	Dewsbury Crown ARL
9.11.87	Fortis, Mark	Dewsbury Moor ARL
4.12.87	Parrish, Steve	Bradford N.
10.12.87	*Parrish, Michael	Oldham
20.12.87	Geary, Paul	Featherstone R.
8.1.88	Cook, Mark	Mansfield M.
6.2.88	Jones, David	Featherstone R.
26.4.88	McCleary, Jack	Doncaster

BRADFORD NORTHERN

Signed	Player	Club From
19.7.87	Seabourne, Peter	Hunslet Parkside ARL
2.9.87	Mercer, Gary	Pikiao, NZ
2.9.87	Stewart, Russell	Ngongotaha, NZ
15.9.87	Rhodes, Paul	Garforth ARL
15.9.87	Duggen, Chris	West Bowling ARL
15.9.87	Richards, Craig	Queensbury ARL
1.10.87	Skerrett, Kelvin	Hunslet
21.10.87	*Moulden, Darren	York
21.10.87	*Parrish, Steve	York
9.1.88	Barraclough, Glenn	Bramley
9.1.88	Clarkson, Allan	Bramley

John Fifita — Castleford's Australian signing.

BRAMLEY

Signed	Player	Club From
20.8.87	Hunter, Damian	Stanningley ARL
20.8.87	Savage, David	Thornbury ARL
20.8.87	Greenwood, Russell	Bramley Colts
20.8.87	Hazelwood, Gary	Stanningley ARL
20.8.87	Webster, Gino	Broadway ARL
20.8.87	Langley, Paul	Castleford RU
20.8.87	Booth, Simon	Royal Navy RU
20.8.87	Barik, Tony	—
20.8.87	Potapi, Victor	Thornbury ARL
25.8.87	Johnson, Phil	Huddersfield B.
8.9.87	Hendry, Paul	Wakefield T.
10.9.87	Spedding, Paul	Mansfield M.
12.9.87	Lewis, Peter	Hanging Heaton ARL
25.9.87	Crawford, Adrian	Bradford N.
25.9.87	Gill, Anthony	Bradford N.
30.9.87	Owen, Philip	Leeds
11.10.87	Allen, Jamie	St. Dominics, Aus
12.11.87	Farrar, Andrew	Bramley ARL
17.11.87	Skinner, Matthew	Terrigal Womberal, Aus
17.11.87	Denson, Allan	Terrigal Womberal, Aus
10.12.87	Gascoigne, Andy	Leeds
13.12.87	Olpherts, Eric	Queens ARL
4.1.88	Hussey, Graham	Torre Road ARL
9.1.88	Woolford, William	Leeds
9.1.88	Cross, David	Eastern Suburbs, Aus
9.1.88	Cleary, James	Brisbane Easts, Aus
9.1.88	Bond, Steven	Bradford N.
10.1.88	Race, Wayne	Bradford N.
29.1.88	Kenworthy, Martin	West Park RU
4.2.88	Brentley, Gary	Bradford N.
7.2.88	Wood, Darren	Milford ARL
9.2.88	Hardisty, Ian	Castleford
5.3.88	Senior, Daryl	Shaw Cross ARL
5.3.88	Turner, Michael	Shaw Cross ARL
5.3.88	*Aston, Mark	Sheffield E.

CARLISLE

Signed	Player	Club From
1.9.87	Scott, Ian	Ellenborough ARL
5.9.87	Mills, Steve	Fulham
23.9.87	Stafford, Peter	Workington T.
8.10.87	Courty, David	Workington T.
8.10.87	Coles, Colin	Glesson Rangers ARL
4.12.87	Murdock, Paul	Ellenborough ARL
24.2.88	Vickers, Barry	Netherhall RU

CASTLEFORD

Signed	Player	Club From
8.6.87	Fifita, John	St. George, Aus
12.6.87	Beattie, Michael	St. George, Aus
13.8.87	Lindner, Bob	Parramatta, Aus
10.11.87	Blankley, Dean	Normanton ARL
14.11.87	Mirfin, Phillip	Castleford Colts
10.12.87	Juliff, Brian	Halifax
21.1.88	Smith, Anthony	Wheldale ARL
24.3.88	Horo, Shane,	Leigh

DEWSBURY

Signed	Player	Club From
30.6.87	Hinchcliffe, Stephen	Gate Inn ARL
30.6.87	Bowie, Iain	Castleford Colts
30.6.87	Coen, Darren	Castleford
30.6.87	Overend, Richard	Gate Inn ARL
30.6.87	Cornell, Paul	Dewsbury Colts
30.6.87	Oxley, Richard	Gate Inn ARL
20.7.87	Hoyle, Robert	Gate Inn ARL
15.8.87	Shaw, Alan	Wakefield T.
2.9.87	Cocks, Gary	Wakefield T.
15.9.87	Hughes, Michael	York
24.9.87	Wilkinson, Andrew	Wakefield T.
24.9.87	Hartley, Iain	Castleford
12.10.87	Joyce, Philip	Halifax Colts
5.11.87	Clayforth, Shaun	Halifax
8.1.88	Reed, Steven	Batley
8.1.88	Grix, Wayne	Mansfield M.
9.1.88	Cochrane, Anthony	Mansfield M.
14.4.88	Gregoire, Don	Huddersfield

DONCASTER

Signed	Player	Club From
1.7.87	Beardmore, Paul	Doncaster Colts
18.8.87	Flynn, Mark	—
20.8.87	Evans, John	Bentley Yarborough ARL
20.8.87	Wilkinson, Anthony	—
20.8.87	Cook, Darrell	—
20.8.87	Cutts, Lee	Brodsworth ARL
21.8.87	Beddon, Alan	Askern Miners ARL
21.8.87	Jones, Gary	Fryston Crown ARL
21.8.87	O'Grady, Chris	Askern Miners ARL
21.8.87	Ford, Brian	Askern Miners ARL
21.8.87	Smith, Simon	York Colts
21.8.87	Maxwell, Terence	—
21.8.87	Muir, Leslie	Brodsworth ARL
21.8.87	Milner, Paul	—
21.8.87	Morgan, Wayne	Hunslet Parkside ARL
27.8.87	Stutchbury, John	W. Belconnen, Aus
28.8.87	Payne, Phil	Castleford
1.9.87	Dickinson, Malcolm	Lock Lane ARL
17.9.87	Louis, Stephen	S. Newcastle, Aus
9.10.87	Jenkins, Terry	Marist ARL
3.11.87	Rowlandson, Ian	Rockware ARL
10.11.87	Duxbury, Darren	Ackworth ARL
11.11.87	Greenfield, Paul	Ackworth ARL
12.11.87	Robinson, Kevin	Anvil Inn, ARL
13.11.87	Newman, David	Houghton Greyhounds ARL
24.11.87	Grace, Michael	Brodsworth ARL
3.12.87	Sartor, John	Wallaman, Aus
6.1.88	Hooper, Trevor	York
6.1.88	Tansley, Ian	York
9.2.88	Clawson, Martin	Bradford N.

FEATHERSTONE ROVERS

Signed	Player	Club From
16.7.87	Sharp, Timothy	Travellers Sts ARL
15.10.87	Busby, David	Hull K.R.
8.11.87	Bastian, John	Milford ARL
8.11.87	Hughes, Paul	Travellers Sts ARL
10.11.87	Gilbert, John	Widnes
11.12.87	Bannister, Andrew	Walton ARL
8.1.88	Sykes, David	Travellers Sts ARL
26.4.88	Fox, Martin	Gate Inn ARL

FULHAM

Signed	Player	Club From
20.8.87	Alexander, Adrian	Oldham
20.8.87	Chatterton, Ian	Underbank ARL
20.8.87	Gundry, Simon	Fulham Travellers ARL
20.8.87	Fearnly, Derek	Ealing ARL
20.8.87	Hutchinson, Mike	Peckham ARL
20.8.87	Guyett, Stephen	—
20.8.87	Grimoldby, Nicholas	Peckham ARL
30.8.87	Masa, Santiago	Cronulla, Aus
18.9.87	O'Riley, Paul	Guilford Leagues, Aus
27.9.87	Manning, Kevin	Guilford Leagues, Aus
27.9.87	Johansson, Lawrence	—
27.9.87	Francis, Hugh	Liverpool Univ. ARL
1.11.87	Kelly, Shane	Seagulls Diehards, Aus
8.11.87	Aitken, David	Ipswich Jets, Aus
15.11.87	Cheetham, Paul	Keighley
4.1.88	Mayo, John	Swinton
13.3.88	Wightman, Ian	—
20.3.88	*Elgar, Nicky	Hull
20.3.88	Justin, Herbert	Surrey Heath ARL
1.4.88	Mighty, Andrew	South London ARL
3.4.88	Wing, Jason	W. London Inst. ARL
10.4.88	Leslie, Roy	South London ARL

HALIFAX

Signed	Player	Club From
21.7.87	Taylor, Mick	Oldham
21.7.87	Hanson, Dean	Illawara, Aus
21.7.87	Meredith, Martin	Manly-Warringah, Aus
27.8.87	Wilkinson, Ian	Leeds
24.9.87	Grogan, Bob	Brothers, Aus
23.10.87	Longstaff, Simon	Normanton ARL
1.1.88	Twist, David	Salford
10.1.88	Holliday, Les	Swinton

HUDDERSFIELD BARRACUDAS

No signings

HULL

Signed	Player	Club From
3.7.87	Milnes, Ian	Hull Colts
3.7.87	Price, Richard	Sharlston ARL
14.7.87	Mason, Lee	Hull Colts
28.8.87	Fletcher, Paul	Salford
25.9.87	Leuluai, James	Leigh
25.9.87	Blanchard, Philip	BP ARL
25.9.87	Nolan, Robert	Hull Colts
2.10.87	Gale, Scott	Balmain, Aus
2.10.87	Brooks, David	Balmain, Aus
2.10.87	M'Barki, Hussein	Oldham
2.10.87	Ellis, Ian	Heworth ARL
16.10.87	Regan, Terry	Canberra, Aus
6.11.87	McCaffery, Paul	North Sydney, Aus
23.11.87	Blowers, Stephen	Hull Boys Club ARL
1.1.88	Carroll, John	Batley

HULL KINGSTON ROVERS

Signed	Player	Club From
30.7.87	Mortimer, Peter	Canterbury Banks, Aus
18.8.87	Cator, Michael	Hull K.R. Colts
18.8.87	Swinney, Terence	Hull K.R. Colts
21.8.87	Lawler, Kenneth	West Hull ARL
21.8.87	Pennock, Paul	Myson ARL
21.8.87	Thompson, Andrew	Hull K.R. Colts
28.8.87	Fletcher, Paul	Eureka ARL
2.9.87	Taylor, Ross	Hornby, NZ
18.9.87	Matthews, Lee	Ace ARL
18.9.87	Robinson, Kevin	Wakefield T.
15.10.87	Ryan, Glenn	Manly, Aus
27.11.87	Sullivan, Anthony	Hull K.R. Colts
1.1.88	*Harrison, David	St. Helens

HUNSLET

Signed	Player	Club From
15.6.87	Hohn, Mark	Seagulls Diehards, Aus
15.6.87	Benson, Trevor	Redcliffe, Aus
11.8.87	Gillespie, David	Canterbury Banks, Aus
20.8.87	Thompson, Lee	Belle Isle ARL
4.10.87	Hart, Robin	Shaw Cross ARL
13.11.87	Mitchell, Keith	—
30.12.87	Lulham, Rickie	Caringbah, Aus
1.1.88	Anast, Theo	Canterbury Banks, Aus
24.3.88	Farrar, Andrew	Bramley

KEIGHLEY

Signed	Player	Club From
25.8.87	Moorby, Gary	Leeds
25.8.87	Skerrett, Trevor	Leeds
27.8.87	Hirst, Carl	Siddal ARL
29.8.87	Fairbank, John	Elland ARL
29.8.87	White, Brendan	Bradford N.
27.9.87	Newton, Steven	—
31.10.87	Manning, Terence	Elland ARL
12.11.87	O'Grady, Gerry	Boothtown ARL
11.12.87	Fairbank, Mark	Oldham
12.12.87	Rose, Gary	Yew Tree ARL
9.1.88	Fairbank, David	Elland ARL

LEEDS

Signed	Player	Club From
2.6.87	Crooks, Lee	Hull
4.6.87	Rathbone, Alan	Warrington
20.7.87	Lyons, John	Wakefield T.
20.7.87	Spencer, Gary	Wakefield T.
21.7.87	Brooke-Cowden, Mark	Ponsonby RU, NZ
27.7.87	Gurr, Marty	Manly, Aus
10.8.87	Jackson, Peter	Sydney Souths, Aus
20.8.87	Basnett, John	Widnes
30.8.87	Tunks, Peter	Canterbury Banks, Aus
10.9.87	Stevens, Darren	Mansfield M.
17.9.87	Rowse, Martin	Hunslet Boys ARL
29.9.87	Morris, Steve	Sydney Easts, Aus
23.10.87	Schofield, Garry	Hull
3.11.87	Chisnall, Thomas	Milford ARL
9.11.87	Fairbank, John	Elland ARL
13.11.87	Fawcett, Vincent	Middleton ARL
1.1.88	Stephenson, David	Wigan
2.3.88	*Stephens, Gary	Halifax
12.3.88	Chick, Stuart	Littleborough RU
3.5.88	Jones, Gary	Lock Lane ARL

LEIGH

Signed	Player	Club From
6.7.87	Worgan, Graham	Widnes
1.10.87	Frame, Mark	Canterbury, NZ
9.10.87	Clarke, Jeff	Northcote, NZ
25.10.87	Willis, Chris	Mansfield M.
15.11.87	Burrill, Craig	Orrell RU
16.11.87	Horo, Shane	Northcote, NZ
18.12.87	Richardson, Geoff	Rose Bridge ARL
18.12.87	Waterworth, Keith	Rose Bridge ARL
31.12.87	Cooper, Mark	Blackbrook ARL
10.1.88	Holliday, Mike	Swinton
10.1.88	Lang, Shaw	Leigh Miners ARL
10.1.88	Pinner, Harry	Widnes
11.1.88	Earner, Adrian	St. Helens Colts
3.2.88	Ruane, David	Widnes
3.2.88	Tuimavave, Paddy	Swinton
10.2.88	Dowlings, Anthony	Leigh Miners ARL
11.2.88	Melling, Alex	Swinton
8.3.88	Kelly, Shaun	Leigh Miners ARL
20.3.88	Donohue, Jason	—
20.3.88	Ogden, Michael	Golborne ARL
20.3.88	Dean, Shaun	Leigh Miners ARL
26.3.88	Peters, Steve	Oldham
26.3.88	Webb, Carl	Warrington

MANSFIELD MARKSMAN

Signed	Player	Club From
30.6.87	Edge, Philip	Rochdale H.
3.7.87	Tupaea, Ashley	Redcliffe, NZ
7.7.87	Ince, Ian	Wigan St. Patricks ARL
30.7.87	Lamb, Derek	The Oaks, Aus
23.8.87	Moore, Ian	Hatfield ARL
23.8.87	Whitehead, Craig	Rochdale H.
25.8.87	Deakin, Chris	Rochdale H.
31.8.87	Swift, Michael	St. Anne's ARL
3.9.87	Sanderson, Mark	Milford ARL
19.10.87	Mehand, Michael	Mt. Wellington, NZ
24.10.87	Hawkyard, Kevin	Deighton ARL
26.11.87	Cook, Mark	Hare and Hounds ARL
8.1.88	Willis, Chris	Leigh
1.2.88	Stones, Chris	Bradford N.
18.2.88	Johnson, William	Swinton
20.3.88	Sheldon, Michael	Jubilee ARL
27.3.88	Davies, Paul	Jubilee ARL

OLDHAM

Signed	Player	Club From
15.7.87	Nadiole, Tom	Leigh
5.8.87	Meadows, Kevin	Warrington
5.8.87	Peters, Steve	Warrington
17.8.87	Graham, Mal	Bradford N.
18.8.87	Irving, Richard	Moldgreen ARL
21.8.87	Round, Paul	St. Helens
2.9.87	Bates, Ian	Gate Inn ARL
4.9.87	Copeland, Tony	Broughton Park RU
7.9.87	*Lowndes, Paul	Warrington
22.9.87	Walsh, Peter	Newcastle, Aus
26.9.87	McCarthy, Brian	Canterbury Banks, Aus
20.11.87	Robinson, Stephen	Saddleworth R. ARL
11.12.87	Coston, Trevor	Wigan St. Patricks ARL
9.1.88	Ford, Mike	Leigh
17.2.88	McAlister, Charles	Bradford & Bingley RU
28.3.88	*Nadiole, Tom	Salford

ROCHDALE HORNETS

Signed	Player	Club From
2.7.87	Ruane, Andrew	Widnes
5.8.87	Clucus, Geoff	Fitton Hill ARL
7.8.87	Whittle, Jason	Wigan St. Patricks ARL
10.8.87	Mellor, Terence	Lowerhouse ARL
10.8.87	Aspey, Stephen	Wigan St. Patricks ARL
19.8.87	Morris, John	Waterhead ARL
21.8.87	Dalton, Alan	Saddleworth ARL
25.8.87	Yates, Andrew	Waterhead ARL
25.8.87	Ruane, Dennis	Simms Cross ARL
25.8.87	Parkinson, Thomas	Heywood ARL
27.8.87	Kelly, Mark	Littleborough ARL
15.9.87	Hoare, Shaun	Fulham
18.9.87	Sawyer, Aaron	Manly-Warringah, Aus
24.9.87	Barrow, Scott	Addington, NZ
29.10.87	Vaafusu, Olsen	Mosman
20.11.87	*Dobson, Mark	Wigan
12.1.88	Cowie, Neil	Todmorden ARL
23.3.88	Nanyn, Michael	Springfield B.

371

RUNCORN HIGHFIELD

Signed	Player	Club From
20.6.87	Ashall, Paul	Rose Bridge ARL
22.7.87	Middlehurst, Chris	Simms Cross ARL
22.7.87	Dean, Geoff	Wigan St. Judes ARL
21.8.87	Cogger, Jamie	Berala Bears, Aus
25.8.87	Rose, Terry	Westbank ARL
3.9.87	Ewer, Steve	Berala Bears, Aus
24.9.87	Shaw, Glyn	Warrington
31.10.87	Marsden, Peter	Northern Suburbs, Aus
8.1.88	Pojunas, Christopher	Parkside Colliery ARL
31.1.88	Glover, Michael	Springfield B.
15.2.88	*Day, Sean	St. Helens
2.3.88	Gibson, Kerry	Western Suburbs, Aus

ST. HELENS

Signed	Player	Club From
2.7.87	Neill, John	Kells ARL
2.7.87	Price, Philip	St. Helens Colts
2.7.87	Large, David	UGB ARL
22.8.87	Cooper, Shane	Mt. Albert, NZ
26.8.87	Dudley, Steven	Thatto Heath ARL
1.9.87	Tanner, David	Fylde RU
10.9.87	Evans, Stuart	Neath RU
1.10.87	Quirk, Les	Barrow
14.10.87	Groves, Paul	Salford
3.11.87	Haggerty, Paul	Thatto Heath ARL
14.12.87	Souto, Peter	—
22.12.87	Harrison, John	Parkside ARL

SALFORD

Signed	Player	Club From
20.7.87	Cairncross, Chris	Dewsbury
22.7.87	Jones, Ken	Swinton
12.8.87	Ratcliffe, David	Leigh Miners ARL
14.8.87	Shaw, David	Wigan St. Patricks ARL
17.8.87	Potts, Ian	Irlam Hornets ARL
10.9.87	*Blacker, Brian	Barrow
10.9.87	Gibson, Steve	Brisbane Souths, Aus
28.9.87	Cairns, David	Barrow
29.9.87	Jack, Garry	Balmain, Aus
1.10.87	O'Shea, Terry	Te Atatu, NZ
4.10.87	Austin, Greg	Manly-Warringah, Aus
15.10.87	Walsh, Joseph	Wigan St. Patricks ARL
15.10.87	Warrall, Michael	Oldham
3.11.87	Warhurst, Glenn	Oldham St. Annes ARL
10.12.87	Fox, Kevin	Langworthy ARL
23.12.87	O'Loughlin, Jason	Wigan St. Patricks ARL
25.2.88	*Nadiole, Tom	Oldham
1.3.88	Brook, Jason	Oldham St. Annes ARL
6.3.88	McCarthy, Brian	Oldham
21.3.88	Gormley, Ian	Widnes
22.3.88	Williams, Peter	Orrell RU
28.3.88	Worrall, Tony	Warrington

SHEFFIELD EAGLES

Signed	Player	Club From
18.7.87	Cook, Michael	Hunslet Junction ARL
20.7.87	Wilson, Andy	Queens Park ARL
29.7.87	Oldridge, Paul	Hillsborough H. ARL
28.8.87	Nelson, David	Queens Park ARL
28.8.87	Ward, Martin	Carlisle
17.10.87	Gearin, Paul	North Sydney, Aus
24.10.87	Broadbent, Paul	Lock Lane ARL
14.11.87	McDermott, Christopher	Kasimoor ARL
14.11.87	Young, Andy	Kasimoor ARL
14.11.87	McDermott, Paul	Whitehaven
18.11.87	Cook, Michael	—
18.11.87	Hytch, Peter	Bribie Island, Aus
18.11.87	Lamb, Michael	Bribie Island ARL
22.1.88	Fleming, Mark	Bradford N.
5.4.88	*Aston, Mark	Bramley

Stuart Evans — St. Helens' Welsh capture.

SPRINGFIELD BOROUGH

Signed	Player	Club From
7.7.87	Karalius, Graham	Simms Cross ARL
16.7.87	Bimson, Jeff	Wigan St. Patricks ARL
10.8.87	Eccles, Bob	Warrington
10.8.87	Hodson, Tony	Warrington
11.8.87	Garner, Steve	Fulham
11.8.87	Thompson, Courtney	Mansfield M.
16.8.87	Smith, Michael	Wigan St. Patricks ARL
16.8.87	Swindells, Adrian	Crosfields ARL
16.8.87	Ellis, John	Wigan St. Patricks ARL
16.8.87	Gee, Barry	Ashton Blurbrill ARL
27.8.87	Eccles, Clifford	Leigh Miners ARL
27.8.87	Pucill, Andrew	Crosfields ARL
28.8.87	Seabrook, Derrick	St. Helens
28.8.87	Walsh, David	Huddersfield B.
28.8.87	McLarmey, Ian	Crosfields ARL
28.8.87	Gordon, John	Crosfields ARL
28.8.87	Barber, Thomas	Crosfields ARL
28.8.87	Vernon, Neil	Thames Board ARL
28.8.87	Tomes, Lawrence	Wigan St. Judes ARL
29.8.87	Jamieson, Ged	Salford
30.8.87	Duane, Ian	Rochdale H.
5.9.87	Gittins, St.an	Swinton
5.9.87	Wells, Richard	Union, Aus
12.9.87	Peers, Michael	Swinton
17.9.87	French, Gary	Brisbane Souths, Aus
18.9.87	Iddon, Timothy	Crosfields ARL
18.9.87	Emson, John	Crosfields ARL
18.9.87	Winnard, Ian	St. Cuthberts ARL
2.10.87	Robinson, Michael	Mareeba, Aus
22.10.87	Brown, David	Rochdale H.
24.10.87	Smith, Joe	Blackpool St. Annes ARL
31.10.87	McKenzie, Ian	Brisbane Norths, Aus
31.10.87	Harborow, Jason	Wigan Colts
14.11.87	Berry, David	Crown Springs ARL
14.11.87	Frain, Simon	Boars Head ARL
19.12.87	Griffiths, St.eve	Salford
19.12.87	Boxton, Paul	Rose Bridge ARL
23.12.88	Donlan, Steve	Bradford N.
9.1.88	Tarawhiti, Clarke	Whitehaven
9.1.88	McFarland, David	Swinton
9.1.88	Parkes, David	St. Helens
10.1.88	Litherland, Dennis	St. Helens
10.1.88	Wilson, Donald	Swinton
10.1.88	Green, Jimmy	Carlisle
6.2.88	Regan, David	Leigh
6.2.88	Dwyer, Mark	Rochdale H.
13.2.88	Guest, Neil	Latchford Albion ARL
4.3.88	Mahoney, David	Swinton
19.3.88	Viller, Mark	Swinton
23.3.88	Wood, David	Rochdale H.

SWINTON

Signed	Player	Club From
29.8.87	Thompson, Ian	Whitehaven
9.10.87	McFarland, David	Ponsonby, NZ
2.11.87	Ronson, Scott	Thatto Heath ARL
5.11.87	Tuimavave, Paddy	Mt. Albert, NZ
21.11.87	Skeech, Ian	Newton-le-Willows RU
28.12.87	Gelling, Bryan	Leigh
5.1.88	Abram, Darren	Warrington
7.1.88	Brown, Andrew	Thatto Heath ARL
9.1.88	Frodsham, Tommy	Springfield B.
16.1.88	Frazer, Neil	Workington T.
24.1.88	Bilby, Bernard	Thatto Heath ARL
18.2.88	Forber, Gary	Thatto Heath ARL
13.3.88	Melling, Alex	Leigh
19.3.88	Howarth, Roy	Springfield B.

WAKEFIELD TRINITY

Signed	Player	Club From
22.7.87	Fox, Phil	Leeds
22.7.87	Conway, Mark	Leeds
22.7.87	Mason, Andy	Leeds
22.7.87	Rayne, Keith	Leeds
23.7.87	Topliss, David	Oldham
31.7.87	Tolson, Mark	Wakefield T. Colts
31.7.87	Stevenson, Sean	Wakefield T. Colts
31.7.87	Russell, Julian	Wakefield T. Colts
31.7.87	Rollin, Paul	Wakefield T. Colts
31.7.87	Moore, John	Wakefield T. Colts
31.7.87	Haigh, Paul	Wakefield T. Colts
14.9.87	Lennon, Gregg	Brisbane Norths, Aus
28.10.87	Dack, Andrew	—
7.12.87	*Fletcher, Andrew	Mansfield M.
8.1.88	Kelly, Andy	Hull K.R.

Mark Conway — Leeds to Wakefield Trinity.

373

WARRINGTON

Signed	Player	Club From
14.8.87	Lyon, David	Widnes
14.8.87	Geary, Nigel	Wigan St. Judes ARL
23.8.87	Bacon, Michael	Thatto Heath ARL
1.10.87	Jackson, Mark	S. Suburbs, Aus
4.11.87	Williamson, Paul	Woolston ARL
1.12.87	Sumner, Phillip	Wigan St. Patricks ARL
7.2.88	Rudd, Christopher	Kells ARL
7.2.88	Chambers, Gary	Kells ARL

WHITEHAVEN

Signed	Player	Club From
20.6.87	Tarry, William	Thangool, Aus
1.7.87	Mounsey, Gary	Glasson
20.7.87	McDermott, Paul	Wakefield T.
27.8.87	Wilson, Rae	Whitehaven
27.8.87	Bell, Ian	Manukau, NZ
27.8.87	Shelford, Kelly	Glenora, NZ
10.9.87	Tarawhiti, Clarke	McMahons Pt, NZ
24.9.87	Glenn, Ricky	W. Suburbs RU, Aus
29.9.87	Thomson, Ian	Swinton
31.10.87	Watson, David	Manukau, NZ
3.11.87	Ryan, Mark	Mirehouse ARL
24.11.87	Bell, Todd	Manukau, NZ
4.12.87	Brennan, Robert	Ellenborough, ARL
8.1.88	*Rose, Tony	York
9.2.88	Arnor, Martin	Wathbrow ARL
19.2.88	Howland, Kevin	Wathbrow ARL
19.2.88	Burney, Philip	Egremont ARL
19.2.88	Brannon, Robert	Ellenborough ARL
18.3.88	Branthwaite, Steven	Gosforth RU

WIDNES

Signed	Player	Club From
27.7.87	Offiah, Martin	Rosslyn Park RU
1.10.87	Jackson, Steve	Canberra, Aus
2.10.87	Jackson, Mark	Brisbane Souths, Aus
29.10.87	Shearer, Dale	Manly-Warringah, Aus
16.11.87	Lloyd, Christopher	Teatatu, NZ
24.12.87	Marsh, David	Blackbrook ARL
10.1.88	Grima, Joe	Swinton
10.1.88	Pyke, Derek	Leigh
9.3.88	Kebbie, Brimah	Broughton Park RU
23.4.88	Tait, Alan	Kelso RU

WIGAN

Signed	Player	Club From
4.7.87	Marshall, David	Wigan St. Patricks ARL
6.8.87	O'Donnell, Augustus	Wigan St. Patricks ARL
17.8.87	Byrne, Ged	Salford
21.8.87	Shelford, Adrian	Upper Hut Tigers, NZ
21.9.87	Iro, Kevin	Mt. Wellington, NZ
22.10.87	Clarke, Philip	Wigan St. Patricks ARL
2.12.87	Ingram, David	—
5.1.88	Iro, Tony	Mt. Albert, NZ
15.1.88	Frost, Stephen	Wigan St. Judes ARL
4.2.88	Goulding, Robert	Widnes St. Maries
8.3.88	Preston, Mark	Fylde RU

WORKINGTON TOWN

Signed	Player	Club From
3.7.87	Riley, Peter	Gt Clifton ARL
3.7.87	Penrice, Paul	Gt Clifton ARL
3.7.87	Shearman, Robert	Gt Grasslot ARL
12.7.87	Roach, Tony	—
21.7.87	Little, Andrew	Gt Clifton ARL
23.7.87	Thurnow, George	Gt Clifton ARL
31.7.87	Stafford, Peter	Carlisle
27.8.87	Stoddart, Peter	Whitehaven
28.8.87	Gorge, Paul	Ellenborough ARL
23.9.87	Smith, David	Carlisle
1.10.87	Clewes, Andrew	Leigh Colts
8.10.87	Phillips, Graham	Carlisle
6.1.88	Priestley, Stephen	Corckickle ARL
11.2.88	Pickering, Brendan	Gt Clifton ARL
10.3.88	Atherton, Wayne	Leigh
11.3.88	Lomax, William	Swinton

YORK

Signed	Player	Club From
7.7.87	Dobson, Stephen	Wakefield T.
7.7.87	Morrell, Wayne	Doncaster
21.7.87	Sullivan, Graham	Punch Bowl ARL
21.8.87	Lilley, Mark	Leeds Colts
23.8.87	Hague, Neil	Halifax
27.8.87	Hammerton, Chris	Heworth ARL
27.8.87	Horton, Stuart	Castleford
27.8.87	Fletcher, Ian	Castleford
10.9.87	Mulherin, Paul	Parramatta, Aus
22.9.87	*Parrish, Steve	Bradford N.
22.9.87	*Moulden, Darren	Bradford N.
23.10.87	Davis, Alexander	Hunslet
31.10.87	Pever, Ian	Heworth ARL
12.11.87	Robinson, Michael	Maruba, Aus
16.11.87	Rose, Tony	Whitehaven
29.11.87	Douglas, Michael	Heworth ARL
12.12.87	Wheatley, Stephen	Southlands ARL
12.12.87	Moore, Ian	Hatfield ARL
7.1.88	Timson, Andy	Doncaster
20.1.88	Shillito, Alan	Castleford

Steve Hampson — Player of the Year.

AWARDS

THE 1988 MAN OF STEEL AWARDS

Launched in the 1976-77 season, the Rugby Football League's official awards are presented to the Man of Steel, the personality judged to have made the most impact on the season; the First and Second Division Players of the Year, decided by a ballot of the players; the Young Player of the Year, under 21 at the start of the season; the Coach of the Year and Referee of the Year all chosen by a panel of judges.

Having been sponsored by Trumanns Steel for the first seven years, the awards were taken over by Greenall Whitley in 1983-84. Last season they presented a record £7,000 in prizes at the Variety Centre, Salford.

Greenalls Man of Steel

In his debut season, Widnes winger Martin Offiah carried off the coveted title worth £1,750 and a £300 silver champagne goblet. The former Rosslyn Park RU speedster topped the try chart with 44 touchdowns, created a new club record with 42 tries for Widnes and equalled the First Division record by scoring in 11 successive league matches. The college student made his representative debut for Great Britain, Lancashire and the Chairman's XIII before being selected for the 1988 tour Down Under.

Greenalls First Division Player of the Year

Wigan full back Steve Hampson topped the poll of fellow Stones Bitter Championship players, votes being cast in January and April. Hampson made his debut for Lancashire and then Great Britain, taking his tally to three caps against France, being rated Man of the Match at Leeds. He played in every match for Wigan until breaking an arm which ruled him out of a Wembley appearance for the third time.

Greenalls Second Division Player of the Year

His fellow players' choice in the twin ballot was Featherstone Rovers' veteran packman Peter Smith who missed only one of the Colliers' 36 matches, scoring 21 tries to equal the record tally by a Featherstone forward and including his 100th touchdown for the club. He finished seventh in the top ten try chart.

Greenalls Young Player of the Year

Wigan stand off Shaun Edwards created Man of Steel history by receiving his hat-trick of category awards. Appointed skipper of Wigan early in the new year, Edwards became the youngest-ever captain at Wembley, lifting the Silk Cut Challenge Cup. A regular selection for both Great Britain and Lancashire, he completed his collection of honours with a trip Down Under with the 1988 Lions. He finished seventh in the try chart with 21 touchdowns.

Greenalls Referee of the Year

Wakefield man-in-the-middle Fred Lindop celebrated his compulsory retirement by receiving the award for a record fourth time having been nominated for the 11th time in the 12-year history of the award scheme.

Greenalls Coach of the Year

For the first time an award was held over at the presentation ceremony. The judges were in deadlock between nominees Doug Laughton (Widnes) and Alex Murphy (St. Helens), the destiny of the award being determined by the following Sunday's Premiership final, the victor being Laughton following a 38-14 defeat of the Saints at Old Trafford.

● Each of the five category winners received a cheque for £650 and an inscribed silver wine goblet worth £200.

THE MAN OF STEEL AWARDS ROLL OF HONOUR SINCE 1978

	Man of Steel	1st Division Player	2nd Division Player	Young Player	Coach	Referee
1978	George Nicholls (St. Helens)	George Nicholls (St. Helens)	John Woods (Leigh)	John Woods (Leigh)	Frank Myler (Widnes)	Billy Thompson (Huddersfield)
1979	Doug Laughton (Widnes)	Mick Adams (Widnes)	Steve Norton (Hull)	Steve Evans (Featherstone R.)	Doug Laughton (Widnes)	Mick Naughton (Widnes)
1980	George Fairbairn (Wigan)	Mick Adams (Widnes)	Steve Quinn (Featherstone R.)	Roy Holdstock (Hull K.R.)	Peter Fox (Bradford N.)	Fred Lindop (Wakefield)
1981	Ken Kelly (Warrington)	Ken Kelly (Warrington)	John Crossley (York)	Des Drummond (Leigh)	Billy Benyon (Warrington)	John Holdsworth (Kippax)
1982	Mick Morgan (Carlisle)	Steve Norton (Hull)	Mick Morgan (Carlisle)	Des Drummond (Leigh)	Arthur Bunting (Hull)	Fred Lindop (Wakefield)
1983	Allan Agar (Featherstone R.)	Keith Mumby (Bradford N.)	Steve Nash (Salford)	Brian Noble (Bradford N.)	Arthur Bunting (Hull)	Robin Whitfield (Widnes)
1984	Joe Lydon (Widnes)	Joe Lydon (Widnes)	David Cairns (Barrow)	Joe Lydon (Widnes)	Tommy Dawes (Barrow)	Billy Thompson (Huddersfield)
1985	Ellery Hanley (Bradford N.)	Ellery Hanley (Bradford N.)	Graham Steadman (York)	Lee Crooks (Hull)	Roger Millward MBE (Hull K.R.)	Ron Campbell (Widnes)
1986	Gavin Miller (Hull K.R.)	Gavin Miller (Hull K.R.)	Derek Pyke (Leigh)	Shaun Edwards (Wigan)	Chris Anderson (Halifax)	Fred Lindop (Wakefield)
1987	Ellery Hanley (Wigan)	Andy Gregory (Wigan)	John Cogger (Runcorn H.)	Shaun Edwards (Wigan)	Graham Lowe (Wigan)	John Holdsworth (Kippax)
1988	Martin Offiah (Widnes)	Steve Hampson (Wigan)	Peter Smith (Featherstone R.)	Shaun Edwards (Wigan)	Doug Laughton (Widnes)	Fred Lindop (Wakefield)

NOMINEES:

1978 *1st Division Player:* Roger Millward (Hull K.R.), Harry Pinner (St. Helens). *2nd Division Player:* Phil Hogan (Barrow), Mick Morgan (York). *Young Player:* Neil Hague (Leeds), Keith Mumby (Bradford N.). *Coach:* Eric Ashton MBE (St. Helens), John Mantle (Leigh). *Referee:* Ron Campbell (Widnes), Fred Lindop (Wakefield).

1979 *1st Division Player:* Brian Lockwood (Hull K.R.), Tommy Martyn (Warrington). *2nd Division Player:* Barry Banks (York), John Wolford (Dewsbury). *Young Player:* Mick Burke (Widnes), John Woods (Leigh). *Coach:* Billy Benyon (Warrington), Arthur Bunting (Hull). *Referee:* Fred Lindop (Wakefield), Billy Thompson (Huddersfield).

1980 *1st Division Player:* Len Casey (Hull K.R.), George Fairbairn (Wigan). *2nd Division Player:* Mick Blacker (Halifax), John Wolford (Dewsbury). *Young Player:* Steve Hubbard (Hull K.R.), Harry Pinner (St. Helens). *Coach:* Maurice Bamford (Halifax), Arthur Bunting (Hull). *Referee:* Ron Campbell (Widnes), Billy Thompson (Huddersfield).

1981 *1st Division Player:* Mick Adams (Widnes), Tommy Martyn (Warrington). *2nd Division Player:* Arnie Walker (Whitehaven), Danny Wilson (Swinton). *Young Player:* Paul Harkin (Hull K.R.), Keith Mumby (Bradford N.). *Coach:* Reg Bowden (Fulham), Peter Fox (Bradford N.). *Referee:* Ron Campbell (Widnes), Fred Lindop (Wakefield).

1982 *1st Division Player:* Jeff Grayshon (Bradford N.), Andy Gregory (Widnes). *2nd Division Player:* Denis Boyd (Carlisle), Alan Fairhurst (Swinton). *Young Player:* Lee Crooks (Hull), Andy Gregory (Widnes). *Coach:* Doug Laughton (Widnes), Alex Murphy/Colin Clarke (Leigh). *Referee:* Gerry Kershaw (York), Billy Thompson (Huddersfield).

1983 *1st Division Player:* Bob Eccles (Warrington), David Topliss (Hull). *2nd Division Player:* Tommy David (Cardiff C.), Mike Lampkowski (Wakefield T.). *Young Player:* Ronnie Duane (Warrington), Andy Goodway (Oldham). *Coach:* Alex Murphy (Wigan), Frank Myler (Oldham). *Referee:* John Holdsworth (Leeds), Fred Lindop (Wakefield).

1984 *1st Division Player:* Garry Schofield (Hull), John Woods (Leigh). *2nd Division Player:* Lynn Hopkins (Workington T.), John Wolford (Hunslet). *Young Player:* Gary Divorty (Hull), Garry Schofield (Hull). *Coach:* Arthur Bunting (Hull), Roger Millward MBE (Hull K.R.). *Referee:* Derek Fox (Wakefield), Fred Lindop (Wakefield).

1985 *1st Division Player:* Harry Pinner (St. Helens), Gary Prohm (Hull K.R.). *2nd Division Player:* Terry Langton (Mansfield M.), Peter Wood (Runcorn H.). *Young Player:* Deryck Fox (Featherstone R.), Andy Platt (St. Helens). *Coach:* Arthur Bunting (Hull), Colin Clarke/Alan McInnes (Wigan). *Referee:* Fred Lindop (Wakefield), Stan Wall (Leigh).

1986 *1st Division Player:* Steve Ella (Wigan), John Fieldhouse (Widnes). *2nd Division Player:* John Henderson (Leigh), Graham King (Hunslet). *Young Player:* Paul Lyman (Featherstone R.), Roy Powell (Leeds). *Coach:* Roger Millward MBE (Hull K.R.), John Sheridan (Doncaster). *Referee:* John Holdsworth (Kippax), Robin Whitfield (Widnes).

1987 *1st Division Player:* Lee Crooks (Hull), Ellery Hanley (Wigan). *2nd Division Player:* Andy Bateman (Hunslet), Les Holliday (Swinton). *Young Player:* Paul Loughlin (St. Helens), Kevin McCormack (St. Helens). *Coach:* Chris Anderson (Halifax), Alex Murphy (St. Helens). *Referee:* Kevin Allatt (Southport), Fred Lindop (Wakefield).

1988 *1st Division Player:* Martin Offiah (Widnes), Kurt Sorensen (Widnes). *2nd Division Player:* Deryck Fox (Featherstone R.), Hugh Waddell (Oldham). *Young Player:* Paul Medley (Leeds), Steve Robinson (Halifax). *Coach:* Doug Laughton (Widnes), Barry Seabourne (Bradford N.). *Referee:* John Holdsworth (Kippax), Ray Tennant (Castleford).

DAILY MIRROR-STONES BITTER AWARDS

Introduced in the 1979-80 season, the scheme acknowledges the adjudged Team of the Month in both Division One and Two.

A panel of judges representing the Daily Mirror, Stones Bitter and the Rugby League selected the two monthly winners, the First Division winners receiving £400, the Second Division £300, plus a framed citation.

Promoted by the Daily Mirror, the awards were sponsored for the first four seasons by Shopacheck before Lada Cars took over in the 1983-84 season and introduced the first-ever £1,000 Team of the Year title. Stones Bitter took over the sponsorship in 1987-88.

The Daily Mirror-Stones Bitter Awards Roll of Honour

	1979-80 First Division	1980-81 First Division	1981-82 First Division	1982-83 First Division
Aug./Sept.	Salford	Hull K.R.	Leigh	Leeds
Oct.	Leigh	Castleford	Widnes	Hull
Nov.	Leeds	Featherstone R.	Hull K.R.	Castleford
Dec.	Hull	Warrington	Hull*	Wigan
Jan.	Bradford N.	Halifax		Wigan
Feb.	Widnes	Wakefield T.	Leigh	Castleford
Mar.	Hull	Widnes	Bradford N.	Hull
Apr./May	Leigh	Bradford N.	Hull	Widnes

	Second Division	Second Division	Second Division	Second Division
Aug./Sept.	Halifax	Huddersfield	Oldham	Fulham
Oct.	Batley	Fulham	Swinton	Huyton
Nov.	Featherstone R.	Wigan	Carlisle	Wakefield T.
Dec.	Oldham	Blackpool B.	Carlisle*	Salford
Jan.	Whitehaven	Keighley		Whitehaven
Feb.	Halifax	York	Huyton	Hunslet
Mar.	Barrow	Whitehaven	Oldham	Fulham
Apr./May	Swinton	Batley	Oldham	Cardiff C.

*A double-money award to cover both months, badly hit by adverse weather.
†Not awarded due to bad weather.

Team of the Year
1983-84: Widnes
1984-85: Hull K.R.
1985-86: Halifax
1986-87: Wigan
1987-88: Widnes

GREENALL WHITLEY TOP SCORERS AWARDS

Launched in the 1976-77 season, the scheme was designed to reward the top try and goal scorers. Sponsored by brewers Greenall Whitley, the 1987-88 awards were worth £25 a try and £5 a goal.

In his first season, ex-Rosslyn Park RU winger Martin Offiah topped the try chart with 44 touchdowns, featuring 42 for Widnes, one for Great Britain and one for the Chairman's XIII. His Greenall Whitley prize amounted to £1,100.

Veteran stand off John Woods celebrated his move from Bradford N. to Warrington by leading the goal chart with 152, receiving a cheque for £760.

Sammy Lloyd: Twice top goalscorer.

Greenall Whitley Top Scorers Awards Roll of Honour

Top Tries		Top Goals	
1976-77 Stuart Wright (Widnes): 31	**1982-83** Bob Eccles (Warrington): 37	**1976-77** Sammy Lloyd (Castle'd): 163	**1983-84** Bob Beardmore (Castleford): 142 Steve Hesford (Warrington): 142
1977-78 Stuart Wright (Widnes): 33	**1983-84** Garry Schofield (Hull): 38	**1977-78** Geoff Pimblett (St. Helens): 178	**1984-85** Sean Day (St. Helens): 157
1978-79 Steve Hartley (Hull K.R.): 35	**1984-85** Ellery Hanley (Bradford N.): 55	**1978-79** Sammy Lloyd (Hull): 172	**1985-86** Chris Johnson (Leigh): 173
1979-80 Keith Fielding (Salford): 30 Steve Hubbard (Hull K.R.): 30	**1985-86** Steve Halliwell (Leigh): 49	**1979-80** Steve Quinn (F'stone R.): 163	**1986-87** Paul Loughlin (St. Helens): 190
1980-81 John Crossley (York): 35	**1986-87** Ellery Hanley (Wigan): 63	**1980-81** Steve Hesford (Warrington): 147	**1987-88** John Woods (Warrington): 152
1981-82 John Jones (Work'ton T.): 31	**1987-88** Martin Offiah (Widnes): 44	**1981-82** Lynn Hopkins (Work'ton T.): 190	
		1982-83 Steve Diamond (Fulham): 136	

	1983-84 First Division	1984-85 First Division	1985-86 First Division	1986-87 First Division	1987-88 First Division
Aug./ Sept.	Bradford N.	Hull K.R.	Hull K.R.	St. Helens	Wigan
Oct.	Hull K.R.	St. Helens	Wigan	Wigan	Bradford N.
Nov.	Widnes	Featherstone R.	Oldham	Warrington	Leeds
Dec.	Leeds	Halifax	Wigan	Warrington	St. Helens
Jan.	Hull	Hull K.R.	Widnes	Wigan	St. Helens
Feb.	Castleford	Wigan	†	Halifax	Wigan
Mar.	Wigan	Wigan	St. Helens	Leigh	Hull
Apr./ May	St. Helens	St. Helens	Warrington	Halifax	Widnes

	Second Division	Second Division	Second Division	Second Division	Second Division
Aug./ Sept.	Barrow	Mansfield M.	Wakefield T.	Sheffield E.	Workington T.
Oct.	Halifax	Carlisle	Rochdale H.	Doncaster	Springfield B.
Nov.	Swinton	Dewsbury	Leigh	Hunslet	Oldham
Dec.	Batley	Batley	Blackpool B.	Rochdale H.	Bramley
Jan.	Barrow	Batley	Doncaster	Swinton	Featherstone R.
Feb.	Hunslet	Bramley	†	Whitehaven	Wakefield T.
Mar.	Huddersfield	Dewsbury	Batley	Doncaster	York
Apr./ May	Blackpool B.	Swinton	Leigh	Hunslet	Oldham

Team of the Month for January: St. Helens with Paul Loughlin inspiring them to the John Player Special Trophy.

381

STONES BITTER – DAILY STAR STARMEN AWARDS

Introduced in 1982-83, the scheme was sponsored by Stones Bitter and promoted by the *Daily Star*. For 1987-88 the top three players for each side in every Stones Bitter Championship and Second Division game were awarded a rating out of 10. The top pollster in the Championship received £1,000 and a trophy, with £500 and a trophy being presented to the top Second Division player.

Championship

1982-83	Harry Pinner (St. Helens)	
1983-84	John Woods (Leigh)	
1984-85	Ellery Hanley (Bradford N.)	
1985-86	Deryck Fox (Featherstone R.)	
1986-87	Deryck Fox (Featherstone R.)	
1987-88	Kurt Sorensen (Widnes)	

Second Division

1982-83	Graham Beale (Keighley)
1983-84	John Wolford (Hunslet)
1984-85	Graham Steadman (York)
1985-86	Dean Carroll (Carlisle)
1986-87	Billy Platt (Mansfield M.)
1987-88	Chris Vasey (Dewsbury)

1987-88 FINAL TABLES

Stones Bitter Championship

Kurt Sorensen (Widnes)	29
Paul Harkin (Bradford N.)	27
Andy Goodway (Wigan)	22
Mike Smith (Hull K.R.)	22
John Woods (Warrington)	18
Martin Offiah (Widnes)	18
Ellery Hanley (Wigan)	18
Harry Pinner (Leigh)	16
Paul Groves (St. Helens)	16
Wayne Parker (Hull K.R.)	16

Second Division

Chris Vasey (Dewsbury)	32
Deryck Fox (Featherstone R.)	32
Mark Conway (Wakefield T)	24
Bob Eccles (Springfield B.)	18
Steve Carroll (Bramley)	17
Derek Lamb (Mansfield)	16
Andy Ruane (Rochdale H.)	16
Ian Fletcher (York)	16

WALLACE ARNOLD – SUNDAY MIRROR ENTERTAINER AWARDS

Introduced in 1986-87, the scheme was sponsored by Wallace Arnold and promoted by the *Sunday Mirror*.

Each month an adjudged player was chosen as Entertainer of the Month to receive a Wallace Arnold holiday voucher for £250. The Entertainer of the Year was awarded a £1,000 holiday voucher, the 1988 winner being Widnes winger Martin Offiah, the league's top try scorer, Great Britain debutant and tourist.

Mirror Entertainer of the Month

Sept.	Andy Goodway (Wigan)
Oct.	Martin Offiah (Widnes)
Nov.	Paul Round (Oldham)
Dec.	Garry Schofield (Leeds)
Jan.	Hugh Waddell (Oldham)
Feb.	Steve Hampson (Wigan)
Mar.	Gary Divorty (Hull)
Apr./ May	—

Entertainer of the Year

1987:	Martin Offiah (Widnes)

TRAVELEADS TOP FAN AWARD

The fourth Traveleads Top Fan award as Rugby League's official Supporter of the Year — a 17-day trip to Australia to watch the second and third Tests — was presented to schoolteacher Sue Walford, a Hull K.R. fanatic who also supported a number of Second Division clubs.

REFEREES

REFEREES' HONOURS 1987-88

Silk Cut Challenge Cup final:
Fred Lindop

John Player Special Trophy final:
Fred Lindop

Stones Bitter Premiership final:
John Holdsworth

Second Division Premiership:
Robin Whitfield

Grunhalle Lager Lancashire Cup final:
Fred Lindop

John Smiths Yorkshire Cup final:
Kevin Allatt (+replay)

Under-21. France v Britain:
John McDonald

RL Chairman's XIII v Auckland:
John Holdsworth

Cumbria v Papua New Guinea:
Ray Tennant

Yorkshire v Papua New Guinea:
Fred Lindop

Lancashire v Papua New Guinea:
John Kendrew

World Club Challenge
John Holdsworth

Rodstock War of the Roses:
John Holdsworth

Okells Charity Shield:
John Holdsworth

SENIOR REFEREES 1987-88

KEVIN ALLATT (Southport)
Date of birth: 29.12.42
Grade Two: 1970-71
Grade One: 1972-73
Premiership Trophy 1986-87
Lancashire Cup 1983-84
Yorkshire Cup 1987-88 (+replay)
Lancashire v Yorkshire 1975-76

GEOFF BERRY (Batley)
Date of birth: 26.4.54
Grade Two: 1981-82
Grade One: 1983-84

ALEX BOWMAN (Whitehaven)
Date of birth: 20.9.56
Grade One: 1986-87

ALAN BURKE (Oldham)
Date of birth: 21.1.57
Grade One: 1987-88

DAVE CARTER (Widnes)
Date of birth: 29.11.55
Grade One: 1984-85

STEVE CROSS (Hull)
Date of birth: 23.3.50
Grade One: 1986-87

KEVIN DOCKRAY (Leeds)
Date of birth: 5.3.52
Grade One: 1987-88

DENNIS DRINKWATER (Warrington)
Date of birth: 17.11.48
Grade One: 1987-88

BRIAN GALTRESS (Bradford)
Date of birth: 9.8.60
Grade One: 1988-89

STEPHEN HAIGH (Ossett)
Date of birth: 5.4.45
Grade Two: 1980-81
Grade One: 1983-84

JOHN HOLDSWORTH (Kippax)
Date of birth: 25.1.47
Grade Two: 1979-80
Grade One: 1980-81
Challenge Cup 1986-87
John Player Trophy 1985-86, 1986-87
Premiership Trophy 1980-81
Lancashire Cup 1982-83, 1985-86
World Club Challenge 1987-88
Wales v England 1980-81
RL Chairman's XIII v Papua New Guinea 1987-88
Cumbria v Yorkshire 1981-82
France v Great Britain Under-24s 1982-83
War of the Roses 1987-88
Charity Shield 1987-88

GARY HOLGATE (Barrow)
Date of birth: 26.4.48
Grade One: 1987-88

PAUL HOUGHTON (Warrington)
Date of birth: 1.10.51
Grade One: 1985-86

JOHN KENDREW (Castleford)
Date of birth: 22.4.50
Grade Two: 1982-83
Grade One: 1983-84
Lanchashire v Papua New Guinea 1987-88

GERRY KERSHAW (Easingwold)
Date of birth: 24.10.43
Grade Two: 1969-70
Grade One: 1970-71
Challenge Cup 1980-81
Lancashire Cup 1980-81
Floodlit Trophy 1973-74
John Player Trophy 1973-74
Wales v England 1981-82
Wales v Australia 1982-83
France v Great Britain Under-24s 1981-82
Lancashire v Yorkshire 1971-72
Lancashire v Cumbria 1972-73
Cumbria v Other Nationalities 1974-75
Cumbria v Lancashire 1978-79, 1980-81

KEIRON MORRIS (Widnes)
Date of birth: 29.9.48
Grade One: 1988-89

BRIAN SIMPSON (Manchester)
Date of birth: 23.6.44
Grade One: 1985-86

JIM SMITH (Halifax)
Date of birth: 2.3.44
Grade Two: 1977-78
Grade One: 1983-84
Lancashire Cup 1986-87

KEN SPENCER (Warrington)
Date of birth: 29.8.47
Grade Two: 1974-75
Grade One: 1983-84

COLIN STEELE (Dalton-in-Furness)
Date of birth: 11.9.60
Grade One: 1987-88

RAY TENNANT (Castleford)
Date of birth: 7.4.49
Grade One: 1985-86
Cumbria v Papua New Guinea 1987-88

FRANK TICKLE (St. Helens)
(Date of birth: 26.10.45
Grade One: 1984-85

CHARLIE TIDBALL (Wakefield)
Date of birth: 25.12.48
Grade One: 1987-88

PAUL VOLANTE (Batley)
Date of birth: 30.6.52
Grade One: 1983-84

JOHN WHITELAM (Hull)
Date of birth: 11.5.53
Grade One: 1988-89

ROBIN WHITFIELD (Widnes)
Date of birth: 26.11.43
Grade Two: 1979-80
Grade One: 1980-81
Challenge Cup 1982-83, 1985-86
Yorkshire Cup 1981-82
Second Division Premiership 1987-88
France v Australia (2) 1982-83
New Zealand v Australia 1983
Australia v New Zealand (3) 1986
Yorkshire v Lancashire 1981-82

THE ALLIANCE

SLALOM LAGER ALLIANCE
FINAL TABLES 1987-88

FIRST DIVISION

	P.	W.	D.	L.	Dr.	FOR Gls.	FOR Trs.	FOR Pts.	Dr.	AGAINST Gls.	AGAINST Trs.	AGAINST Pts.	Pts.
Leeds	24	20	0	4	3	84	118	643	2	45	51	296	40
Widnes	24	16	0	8	2	82	96	550	7	68	57	371	32
Halifax	24	14	0	10	1	75	89	507	3	64	75	431	28
Castleford	24	13	0	11	3	68	77	447	3	59	73	413	26
Warrington W.	24	13	0	11	9	74	86	501	1	76	86	497	26
Salford	24	13	0	11	6	65	77	444	6	73	87	500	26
St. Helens	24	12	1	11	5	79	94	539	2	69	79	456	25
Wigan	24	12	0	12	2	53	84	444	2	62	81	450	24
Hull	24	11	1	12	2	78	93	530	3	62	85	467	23
Hunslet	24	8	3	13	3	73	75	449	4	77	99	554	19
Hull K.R.	24	9	0	15	5	71	68	419	8	67	90	502	18
Swinton C.	24	8	1	15	3	52	70	387	6	78	95	542	17
Leigh	24	4	0	20	5	45	51	299	2	99	120	680	8

● Bottom two clubs relegated

SECOND DIVISION

	P.	W.	D.	L.	Dr.	FOR Gls.	FOR Trs.	FOR Pts.	Dr.	AGAINST Gls.	AGAINST Trs.	AGAINST Pts.	Pts.
Whitehaven	26	18	2	6	2	83	111	612	4	56	60	356	38
Carlisle	26	18	2	6	14	83	91	544	9	49	56	331	38
Blackpool S.	26	18	1	7	6	77	100	560	9	57	64	379	37
Bradford N.	26	16	2	8	6	66	93	506	2	57	70	396	34
Oldham	26	15	3	8	0	85	113	622	3	76	83	487	33
Wakefield T.	26	15	1	10	6	70	98	538	10	50	66	374	31
Featherstone R.	26	15	1	10	0	74	91	512	4	67	71	422	31
Batley	26	14	1	11	6	55	74	412	2	66	78	446	29
Barrow	26	13	2	11	7	87	115	641	3	69	77	449	28
Dewsbury	26	11	0	15	1	63	61	371	5	66	82	465	22
Huddersfield P.	26	9	3	14	6	53	73	408	5	79	119	639	21
Rochdale H.	26	10	0	16	5	72	83	481	7	61	84	465	20
Workington T.	26	8	0	18	8	63	72	422	10	67	81	468	16
Doncaster	26	6	1	19	3	54	61	355	4	97	121	682	13
Bramley	26	6	1	19	7	54	60	355	4	91	128	698	13
York	26	5	2	19	7	47	53	313	3	78	109	595	12

● Top three clubs promoted

1987-88 RESULTS

FIRST DIVISION

Home: (rows) — Away: (columns)

Home \ Away	Castleford	Halifax	Hull	Hull K.R.	Hunslet	Leeds	Leigh	St. Helens	Salford	Swinton C.	Warrington W.	Widnes	Wigan
Castleford	—	30-10	26-10	19-8	16-12	8-20	34-14	23-16	38-30	36-12	32-13	6-16	20-10
Halifax	10-4	—	28-10	26-7	19-18	22-18	48-6	14-20	40-0	28-12	30-18	26-10	36-18
Hull	26-14	17-10	—	24-8	32-22	14-19	42-10	22-28	30-36	34-0	58-6	16-24	24-20
Hull K.R.	12-16	18-10	8-39	—	37-10	20-23	32-5	38-14	46-14	4-7	14-15	6-18	25-4
Hunslet	16-20	14-18	12-12	24-14	—	8-34	32-12	26-26	30-16	20-20	20-12	21-28	6-44
Leeds	24-8	18-16	58-0	54-10	20-30	—	30-9	26-12	19-12	42-4	36-6	28-12	40-10
Leigh	30-20	22-34	6-26	10-24	16-20	16-28	—	10-27	11-6	12-6	22-16	15-28	10-14
St. Helens	30-14	17-18	21-16	22-12	27-30	17-24	34-4	—	24-25	28-12	20-30	34-10	40-4
Salford	30-16	20-10	18-10	2-12	46-8	10-12	31-14	16-10	—	23-16	22-16	2-16	18-17
Swinton C.	12-11	22-12	16-36	16-43	40-26	0-16	30-4	32-8	27-28	—	14-11	25-30	30-14
Warrington W.	24-0	60-26	37-12	24-0	26-22	30-10	20-16	24-26	27-28	16-6	—	16-12	2-48
Widnes	10-20	32-6	26-18	84-0	10-4	22-18	58-13	16-10	34-13	18-16		—	18-6
Wigan													—

SECOND DIVISION

Home: (rows) — Away: (columns)

Home \ Away	Barrow	Batley	Blackpool S.	Bradford N.	Bramley	Carlisle	Dewsbury	Doncaster	Featherstone R.	Huddersfield P.	Oldham	Rochdale H.	Wakefield T.	Whitehaven	Workington T.	York
Barrow	—	24-8	14-26	14-4	91-6	16-16	29-16	30-4	4-24	72-4	38-16	26-5	17-14	21-12	23-20	66-0
Batley	24-14	—	20-15	6-18	16-6	14-12	11-8	20-10	24-14	16-16	30-20	42-14	15-8	24-32	—	11-4
Blackpool S.	26-16	16-6	—	—	30-6	20-7	14-16	12-12	34-12	42-0	12-12	26-14	28-20	30-6	19-10	44-8
Bradford N.	24-16	6-20	14-18	—	24-20	7-4	10-12	24-18	24-24	12-13	30-10	21-10	29-10	42-12	12-8	16-16
Bramley	13-35	14-38	22-14	12-22	—	2-25	46-6	25-17	25-0	12-24	—	36-8	1-8	8-6	16-6	—
Carlisle	33-14	30-12	29-16	14-11	56-16	—	—	26-12	14-22	18-10	10-16	20-6	21-19	—	14-12	16-12
Dewsbury	14-8	4-11	9-16	—	46-7	14-12	—	—	10-44	22-10	8-20	10-8	6-16	16-48	12-13	28-20
Doncaster	—	6-22	—	6-38	6-38	18-22	28-20	—	—	8-10	10-8	24-16	—	10-22	28-26	14-8
Featherstone R.	28-12	—	28-15	20-14	36-12	32-22	28-12	12-20	—	—	6-28	24-18	20-12	14-14	42-6	38-18
Huddersfield P.	22-22	20-6	16-18	21-24	25-10	8-10	28-20	16-20	17-16	—	12-42	30-24	14-31	26-21	52-14	32-12
Oldham	22-20	30-16	6-8	38-6	44-0	13-22	16-6	62-22	17-16	42-6	—	27-10	18-18	18-20	16-6	30-4
Rochdale H.	—	34-4	21-14	12-16	48-4	22-18	22-2	26-8	6-16	40-12	27-10	—	—	2-13	18-7	28-3
Wakefield T.	12-14	20-14	33-18	26-25	12-7	10-10	44-8	32-8	26-12	32-7	39-14		—	7-10	16-12	50-6
Whitehaven	30-6	70-6	—	14-16	12-18	10-16	28-8	44-9	11-10	56-10	16-4		22-16	—	—	21-10
Workington T.	18-19	—	10-17	34-24			0-4	21-24	18-4	14-28	48-12		18-23	5-16	—	
York	17-16	10-6	18-28	18-26							24-24		4-13		12-6	—

Mark Bailey of St. Helens is well tackled in the Slalom Lager Alliance Challenge Cup final against Barrow.

The victorious St. Helens team with the Alliance Challenge Cup.

SLALOM LAGER ALLIANCE CHALLENGE CUP 1988

First Round

Blackpool S.	14	Doncaster	0
Bradford N.	26	Wakefield T.	11
Carlisle	17	Leigh	14
Castleford	44	Dewsbury	2
Hull	44	Workington T.	2
Hull K.R.	16	Halifax	14
Hunslet	22	Wigan	16
Leeds	66	Batley	0
Oldham	12	Huddersfield P.	6
Rochdale H.	22	Swinton C.	4
Warrington W.	20	Whitehaven	8
Widnes	18	Salford	6
York	10	Bramley	18

Byes: Barrow, Featherstone R., St. Helens.

Second Round

Carlisle	25	Hunslet	18
Castleford	12	Barrow	15
Featherstone R.	10	Leeds	30
Hull	30	Bramley	16
Hull K.R.	19	Bradford N.	8
St. Helens	26	Rochdale H.	10
Warrington W.	32	Blackpool S.	16
Widnes	22	Oldham	24

Third Round

Barrow	20	Oldham	6
Carlisle	12	Hull	6
Hull K.R.	10	St. Helens	12
Leeds	30	Warrington	4

Semi-Finals

Carlisle	6	Barrow	21
St. Helens	14	Leeds	11

Final

St. Helens	16	Barrow	14

LANCASHIRE COUNTY CHALLENGE SHIELD 1987-88

First Round

Carlisle	28	Wigan	20
Crosfields	17	Widnes	12
Leigh	15	Rochdale H.	15
Oldham	22	Thatto Heath	20
Salford	26	Whitehaven	12
Swinton	28	Blackpool S.	22
Warrington	36	Barrow	10
Workington T.	22	St. Helens	46

Replay

Rochdale H.	15	Leigh	10

Second Round

Crosfields	23	Carlisle	7
Salford	25	St. Helens	12
Swinton	16	Rochdale H.	13
Warrington	18	Oldham	5

Semi-Finals

Crosfields	7	Warrington	23
Swinton	14	Salford	2

Final

Warrington	21	Swinton	19

YORKSHIRE SENIOR COMPETITION CHALLENGE CUP 1987-88

First Round

Bramley	14	Dewsbury	6
Castleford	34	Bradford N.	16
East Leeds	4	Leeds	62
Featherstone R.	8	Wakefield T.	32
Halifax	22	Hunslet	12
Huddersfield P.	18	Doncaster	12
Hull	62	Batley	10
Hull K.R.	40	York	4

Second Round

Castleford	10	Hull K.R.	22
Halifax	50	Bramley	6
Huddersfield P.	4	Wakefield T.	11
Hull	6	Leeds	24

Semi-Finals

Halifax	16	Wakefield T.	2
Hull K.R.	13	Leeds	12

Final

Halifax	2	Hull K.R.	5

COLTS

COLTS LEAGUE

FINAL TABLES 1987-88

FIRST DIVISION

	P.	W.	D.	L.	Dr.	FOR Gls.	Trs.	Pts.	Dr.	AGAINST Gls.	Trs.	Pts.	Pts.
Hull	18	17	0	1	0	63	95	506	3	24	19	127	34
Hull K.R.	17	13	0	4	2	54	84	446	1	24	38	201	26
Castleford	18	12	0	6	2	52	82	434	2	51	61	348	24
Bradford N.	18	10	1	7	8	61	68	402	4	47	48	290	21
Wigan	18	10	0	8	4	52	77	416	4	43	59	326	20
Wakefield T.	17	7	0	10	2	25	39	208	2	48	65	358	14
St. Helens	18	6	1	11	1	38	46	261	5	48	60	341	13
Halifax	18	5	0	13	7	33	43	245	5	34	62	321	10
Leeds	18	5	0	13	2	32	40	226	2	60	90	482	10
Hunslet	18	3	0	15	1	29	34	195	1	60	106	545	6

SECOND DIVISION

	P.	W.	D.	L.	Dr.	FOR Gls.	Trs.	Pts.	Dr.	AGAINST Gls.	Trs.	Pts.	Pts.
Doncaster	18	17	1	0	0	90	141	744	2	21	32	172	35
Dewsbury	17	13	1	3	0	65	98	522	3	24	39	207	27
Sheffield	18	8	0	10	1	34	61	313	3	54	69	387	16
York	18	6	0	12	3	35	57	301	1	55	90	471	12
Huddersfield	12	3	0	9	4	17	28	150	1	47	79	411	6
Fulham	19	3	0	16	4	29	36	206	2	69	112	588	6

COLTS CHAMPIONSHIP ROLL OF HONOUR

1975-76	Wigan
1976-77	Bradford N.
1977-78	Bradford N.
1978-79	Hull K.R.
1979-80	Oldham
1980-81	Hull
1981-82	Hull
1982-83	Hull
1983-84	Castleford

	Division One	Division Two
1984-85	Wakefield T.	St. Helens
1985-86	Wigan	Leigh
1986-87	Hull	Hunslet
1987-88	Hull	Doncaster

COLTS LEAGUE

1987-88 RESULTS

FIRST DIVISION

Home: \ Away:	Bradford N.	Castleford	Halifax	Hull	Hull K.R.	Hunslet	Leeds	St. Helens	Wakefield T.	Wigan
Bradford N.	—	19-21	26-9	14-16	16-22	30-7	26-2	14-14	36-8	16-26
Castleford	20-40	—	20-16	6-26	26-8	52-4	28-8	50-12	8-6	50-24
Halifax	4-15	18-20	—	0-20	2-22	30-6	30-4	34-10	24-4	11-20
Hull	32-16	36-2	30-8	—	50-6	26-6	30-10	22-2	44-10	24-0
Hull K.R.	40-4	44-14	32-1	3-14	—	66-12	26-0	10-8	48-0	42-16
Hunslet	18-25	16-36	6-32*	6-34	0-32	—	18-8	16-6	4-20	22-30
Leeds	18-27	8-26	24-14	10-56	12-22	34-18	—	18-12	26-10	10-2
St. Helens	0-22	14-21	26-6	3-10	16-12	10-16	66-12	—	24-10	0-52
Wakefield T.	8-38	15-14	5-4	4-28	—	24-0	26-12	14-20	—	20-12
Wigan	25-18	34-20	31-2	21-8	10-11	50-20	45-10	2-18	16-24	—

*Abandoned after 70 minutes

SECOND DIVISION

Home: \ Away:	Dewsbury	Doncaster	Fulham	Huddersfield	Sheffield	York
Dewsbury	—	14-14 / 20-24	74-12 / 30-16	60-13	20-6 / 38-7	32-4
Doncaster	32-20 / 22-20	—	40-2 / 58-4	42-8	74-20 / 34-4	50-13 / 62-10
Fulham	10-12 / 4-30	16-48 / 10-20	—	23-6 / 6-14	15-28 / 11-18	14-9 / 19-18
Huddersfield	10-56	1-62	37-8	—	11-24	38-20 / 2-48
Sheffield	6-8 / 14-28	10-28 / 6-46	32-6 / 32-4	28-8	—	28-8* / 28-4
York	9-26 / 4-34	0-50 / 4-38	46-10 / 36-16	34-2	32-12 / 12-10	—

*Abandoned after 50 minutes

COLTS CHALLENGE CUP 1988

First Round

Bradford N.	8	Wakefield T.	9
Dewsbury	8	Hull	30
Fulham	10	Doncaster	20
Halifax	42	Sheffield E.	0
Hunslet	10	Castleford	28
Leeds	18	Hull K.R.	30
St. Helens	36	York	2

Bye: Wigan awarded tie with Huddersfield who could not raise a team.

Second Round

Halifax	4	Wakefield T.	16
Hull K.R.	23	Castleford	6
St. Helens	4	Hull	20
Wigan	22	Doncaster	14

Semi-Finals

Hull	26	Wigan	0
Hull K.R.	2	Wakefield T.	2

Replay

Wakefield T.	12	Hull K.R.	14

Final at Hull K.R.

Hull K.R.	26	Hull	9

COLTS CHALLENGE CUP
ROLL OF HONOUR

1976
Wigan	24	Hull K.R.	12

at Wigan

1977
Hull K.R.	15	St. Helens	13

at Leeds

1978
Castleford	19	Wakefield T.	10

at Leeds

1979
Hull	17	Widnes	17

at Bradford
Replay
Hull	22	Widnes	14

at Wakefield

1980
Leeds	25	Widnes	14

at Wigan

1981
Hull	32	Castleford	17

at Leeds

1982
Hull	19	Hull K.R.	16

at Leeds

1983
Hunslet	11	Hull K.R.	3

at Hull K.R.

1984
Castleford	24	Hull	11

at Hull K.R.

1985
Wakefield T.	23	Bradford N.	10

at Leeds

1986
St. Helens	16	Wigan	16

at St. Helens
Replay
Wigan	18	St. Helens	9

at Wigan

1987
St. Helens	48	Barrow	6

at Wigan

1988
Hull K.R.	26	Hull	9

at Hull K.R.

The Jim Challinor Memorial Trophy for the Man-of-the-Match in the Final:

1977   Steve Crooks (Hull K.R.)
1978   Paul Bastow (Castleford)
1979   Gary Peacham (Hull)
1980   Ian Mackintosh (Leeds)
1981   Lee Crooks (Hull)
1982   Tracey Lazenby (Hull K.R.)
1983   Andrew Tosney (Hunslet)
1984   Dean Mountain (Castleford)
1985   Billy Conway (Wakefield T.)
1986   Richard Russell (Wigan)
1987   Mark Lee (St. Helens)
1988   Rob Nolan (Hull)

COLTS PREMIERSHIP 1988

First Round

Hull	38	Bradford N.	14
Hull K.R.	26	Castleford	20

Final at Hull

Hull	18	Hull K.R.	14

COLTS PREMIERSHIP ROLL OF HONOUR

1976
Hull K.R.	26	Wakefield T.	12

at Swinton

1977
Bradford N.	29	Hull K.R.	15

at Swinton

1978
Wakefield T.	23	Hull K.R.	20

at Swinton

1979
Hull	17	Hull K.R.	9

at Huddersfield

1980
Oldham	21	Leeds	13

at Swinton

1981
Hull K.R.	27	Hull	21

at Leeds

1982
Hull	19	Hull K.R.	11

at Leeds

1983
Hull	34	Leigh	5

at Leeds

1984
Leeds	24	Hull	8

at Leeds

1985
Hull K.R.	18	Wakefield T.	8

at Elland Road, Leeds

1986
Wigan	21	Hull K.R.	6

at Elland Road, Leeds

1987
Wigan	19	Hull	12

at Wigan

1988
Hull	18	Hull K.R.	14

at Hull

The Dave Valentine Memorial Trophy for the Man-of-the-Match in the Final:

1977 Paul Harkin (Bradford N.)
1978 David Wandless (Wakefield T.)
1979 Kevin Hickman (Hull K.R.)
1980 Andrew Mackintosh (Leeds)
1981 Malcolm Beall (Hull K.R.)
1982 Shaun Patrick (Hull)
1983 Andrew Kamis (Hull)
1984 Paul Medley (Leeds)
1985 Paul Speckman (Hull K.R.)
1986 Jeff Bimpson (Wigan)
1987 Lee Jackson (Hull)
1988 Rob Nolan (Hull)

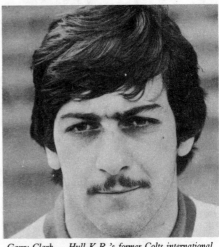

Garry Clark — Hull K.R.'s former Colts international who gained senior Test honours.

Wayne Proctor of Hull, another Colts international who won senior honours.

OLTS INTERNATIONALS

3 January, 1988   Salon

GREAT BRITAIN 17		FRANCE 10
imon Longstaff (Halifax)	1.	Alain Etienne (Roanne)
nthony Sullivan (Hull K.R.)	2.	Jean-Marie Bourrell (S.C. Limoux)
ichard Price (Hull)	3.	Christophe Nadalin (R.C. Albi)
rant Anderson (Castleford)	4.	Eric Vergniol (U.S. Villeneuve)
nthony Farrell (Huddersfield B.)	5.	Laurent Toniol (Toulouse XIII)
haun Irwin (Castleford)	6.	Didier Foulquier (Limoux)
aul Delaney (Leeds)	7.	Frederic Mas (Entraigues)
onathan Neil (St. Helens)	8.	Yannick Quillien (Carpentras)
ee Jackson (Hull)	9.	Charles Giudicelli (Albi)
enny Hill (Castleford), Capt.	10.	Patrick Costes (Carcassonne)
n Gildart (Wigan)	11.	Bruno Alibert (Albi), Capt.
enis Betts (Wigan)	12.	Didier Cabestany (St. Esteve)
ary Price (Wakefield T.)	13.	David Amat (Carcassonne)
eil Roebuck (Bradford N.)	14.	Bruno Luchese (Aussillion)
ram Butt (Leeds)	15.	Regis Ascencio (Carcassonne)
avid Amann (Leeds)	16.	Sylvain Christmanowich (Chatillion)

T: Price, Betts, Hill
G: Longstaff, Roebuck, Hill (dg)
ubstitutions:
utt for Longstaff (half-time)
oebuck for Delaney (61 min.)
mann for Betts (75 min.)
Manager: Harry Jepson
Coach: Geoff Lyon

T: Mas, Toniol
G: Verniol
Substitution:
Christmanowich for Mas (68 min.)
Luchese for Alibert (75 min.)
Ascencio for Cabestany (77 min.)
Half-time: 11-0
Referee: Ray Tennant (Castleford)

9 March, 1988   St. Helens

GREAT BRITAIN 18		FRANCE 6
imon Longstaff (Halifax)	1.	Jean-Christophe Simon (Limoux)
hil Price (St. Helens)	2.	Nicholas Reyre (Avignon)
ichard Price (Hull)	3.	Eric Vergniol (Villeneuve)
rant Anderson (Castleford)	4.	Didier Foulquier (Limoux)
nthony Farrell (Huddersfield B.)	5.	Lucien Foual (Le Pontet)
haun Irwin (Castleford), Capt.	6.	Sylvain Christmanowitch (Chatillion)
aul Delaney (Leeds)	7.	Frederic Mas (Entraigues)
onathan Neil (St. Helens)	8.	Yannick Quillien (Carpentras)
ee Jackson (Hull)	9.	Regis Ascencio (Carcassonne)
avid Amann (Leeds)	10.	Stephane Boyer (Villeneuve)
ob Nolan (Hull)	11.	Didier Cabestany (St. Esteve)
ennis Betts (Wigan)	12.	Patrick Jammes (Limoux)
eil Roebuck (Bradford N.)	13.	David Amat (Carcassonne)
ince Fawcett (Leeds)	14.	Patrick Coste (Carcassonne)
ram Butt (Leeds)	15.	Bruno Luchese (Aussillion)
like Forshaw (Wigan)	16.	Oliver Hourcault (Villeneuve)

T: Farrell, Delaney, Irwin, Anderson
G: Longstaff
ubstitutions:
utt for Longstaff (52 min.)
orshaw for Amann (62 min.)
awcett for Farrell (77 min.)
Manager: Harry Jepson
Coach: Geoff Lyon

T: Vergniol
G. Christmanowitch
Substitutions:
Coste for Quillien (22 min.)
Luchese for Foulquier (54 min.)
Half-time: 18-0
Referee: Alain Sablayrolles (France)

COLTS COUNTY CHAMPIONSHIP

25 November, 1987　　　　　　　Halifax

YORKSHIRE 44		LANCASHIRE 8
Brendan Carlyle (York)	1.	Phil Ball (Wigan)
Anthony Sullivan (Hull K.R.)	2.	Lee Webb (Wigan)
Richard Price (Hull)	3.	Neil Gavin (St. Helens)
Simon Longstaff (Halifax)	4.	Paul Haggerty (St. Helens)
Giles Boothroyd (Castleford)	5.	Austin O'Donnell (Wigan)
Neil Roebuck (Bradford N.)	6.	Wayne Reid (Wigan)
Stephen Blowers (Hull)	7.	Sean Devine (St. Helens)
David Amann (Leeds)	8.	Jon Neil (St. Helens), Capt.
Kenneth Hill (Castleford), Capt.	9.	Shaun Bannister (St. Helens)
David McAreavy (Hull K.R.)	10.	Steven Dunbar (Wigan)
Martin Smithson (Leeds)	11.	Ian Gildart (Wigan)
Sonny Nickle (Hunslet)	12.	Dave Gaskell (St. Helens)
Gary Price (Wakefield T.)	13.	Mike Forshaw (Wigan)
Anthony Farrell (Huddersfield B.)	14.	Tony Greenall (St. Helens)
Lee Jackson (Hull)	15.	Dave Bate (St. Helens)

T: Longstaff (2), Farrell (2), Roebuck,
　Boothroyd, Price G., Price R.
G: Longstaff (6)
Substitutions:
Farrell for Carlyle (half-time)
Jackson for Smithson (62 min.)
Coach: David Redfearn (Bradford N.)
Half-time: 10-0

T: O'Neill
G: Devine (2)

Substitutions:
Greenall for Webb (half-time)
Bate for Gaskell (68 min.)
Coach: Eric Chisnall (St. Helens)
Referee: K. Spencer (Warrington)

POT POURRI

DIARY OF LANDMARKS

1895 August 29... the beginning. The Northern Rugby Football Union formed at St. George's Hotel, Huddersfield, following the breakaway from the English RU by 21 clubs who wanted to pay players for taking time off work to play.
September 7... season opens with 22 clubs.
Joseph Platt appointed Rugby League Secretary.

1897 April 24... Batley won the first Northern Union — later Rugby League — Challenge Cup final.
Line-out abolished and replaced by punt from touch.
All goals to be worth two points.

1898 Professionalism allowed but players must be in full-time employment.

1899 Scrum if player cannot release the ball after a tackle.

1901 Punt from touch replaced by 10-yard scrum when ball is carried into touch.

1902 Two divisions introduced.
Punt from touch abolished completely.
Touch-finding rule introduced with the ball having to bounce before entering touch.

1905 Two divisions scrapped.
Lancashire and Yorkshire County Cup competitions inaugurated.

1906 Thirteen-a-side introduced, from traditional 15.
Play-the-ball introduced.

1907 First tour — New Zealand to England. The tour party were RU 'rebels'.
First Top Four play-off for championship.

1908 Australia and New Zealand launch Rugby League.
First Australian tour of England.

1910 First British tour of Australia and New Zealand.

1915 Competitive rugby suspended for duration of First World War.

1919 Competitive rugby resumed in January.

1920 John Wilson appointed Rugby League Secretary.

1922 Title of Northern Rugby Football Union changed to Rugby Football League.
Goal from a mark abolished.

1927 First radio broadcast of Challenge Cup Final — Oldham v. Swinton at Wigan.

1929 Wembley staged its first RL Challenge Cup final — Wigan v. Dewsbury.

1932 London exhibition match under floodlights at White City — Leeds v. Wigan.

1933 France staged its first Rugby League match — an exhibition between England and Australia in Paris.
London Highfield, formerly Wigan Highfield, became capital's first Rugby League team, also first to play regularly under floodlights.

1934 A French squad made a short tour of England before Rugby League was officially launched in France.

1935 European Championship introduced, contested by England, France and Wales.

1939 Second World War. Emergency war-time competitions introduced.

1945 War-time emergencies over.
Bill Fallowfield appointed Rugby League Secretary.

1946 First all-ticket match — Hull v. Hull K.R.

1948 King George VI became first reigning monarch to attend Rugby League match — Wigan v. Bradford Northern Cup final at Wembley.
First televised match — at Wembley — but shown only in London area.
Wembley's first all-ticket final.
International Board formed.

1949 Welsh League formed.

1950 Italian squad made brief tour of England.

1951   First televised match in the North — Britain v. New Zealand at Swinton. First floodlights installation by Northern club, Bradford Northern.

1952   First nationally televised Challenge Cup final — Workington Town v. Featherstone Rovers.

1954   First World Cup competition, staged in France.

1955   London staged series of televised floodlit matches for the Independent Television Association Trophy. Welsh League disbanded.

1956   Sunday rugby for amateurs permitted by the Rugby Football League.

1962   Two divisions reintroduced, with Eastern and Western Divisions also formed.

1964   Substitutes allowed for injuries, but only up to half-time. Two division and regional leagues scrapped. One league system with Top-16 play-off for championship.

1965   BBC-2 Floodlit Trophy competition began with regular Tuesday night series. Substitutes allowed for any reason up to and including half-time. English Schools Rugby League formed.

1966   Four-tackle rule introduced for Floodlit Trophy competition in October, then for all games from December.

1967   First Sunday fixtures played, two matches on December 17th.

1969   Substitutes allowed at any time. University Rugby League Association formed.

1971   John Player Trophy competition launched.

1972   Six-tackle rule introduced. Timekeepers with hooter system to signal end of match introduced. Colts League formed.

1973   Two divisions re-introduced. March 4... British Amateur Rugby League Association formed.

1974   Drop goal value halved to one point. Had been reduced earlier in internation matches. David Oxley appointed Rugby League Secretary. David Howes appointed first full-time Public Relations Officer to the Rugby Football League. National Coaching Scheme launched.

1975   Premiership Trophy competition launched.

1976   Differential penalty introduced for technical scrum offences.

1977   County Championship not held for first time since 1895, excluding war years. Anglo-Australian transfer ban agreed.

1978   Papua New Guinea admitted as full members of International Board.

1981   Rugby League Professional Players Association formed.

1982   County Championship scrapped.

1983   January 1... Sin bin introduced. Try value increased to four points. Handover after sixth tackle introduced among several other new or amended law following meeting of International Board. Anglo-Australia transfer ban lifted.

1984   Alliance League introduced in reserve grade reorganisation.

1985   First Charity Shield match played in Isle of Man. War of the Roses launched on Lancashire v. Yorkshire county of origin basis. Relegation-promotion reduced to three down, three up.

1986   Relegation-promotion altered for one year only to four down, two up to provide a 14 strong First Division for the 1987-8 season.

1987   Division Two Premiership Trophy competition launched. New players' contracts system introduced

1988   Colts scrapped for new youth scheme.

DISCIPLINARY RECORDS

This sub-section is a compilation of sendings off and disciplinary verdicts for first team players.

The following information is based on the workings of the League's Disciplinary Committee which meets twice-monthly during a season.

Andy Goodway — four match ban.

DISMISSALS .... A review

The following is a review of the number of first team players sent off in each season since 1981-82.

— indicates where a club was not in existence.

	1987-88	1986-87	1985-86	1984-85	1983-84	1982-83	1981-82
Barrow	4	4	3	6	2	2	2
Batley	1	7	3	3	3	4	3
Bradford N.	2	2	4	0	3	3	11
Bramley	4	3	3	2	3	2	0
Bridgend	—	—	—	4	6	2	7
Carlisle	9	3	2	3	8	4	3
Castleford	3	1	3	1	5	4	7
Dewsbury	5	3	4	4	2	5	10
Doncaster	3	2	4	1	10	2	4
Featherstone R.	2	0	0	3	1	1	9
Fulham	0	6	5	4	6	8	3
Halifax	1	2	1	5	3	4	3
Huddersfield B.	0	4	4	4	4	2	3
Hull	2	5	5	2	3	4	3
Hull K.R.	1	4	8	2	5	4	13
Hunslet	2	1	2	4	3	1	4
Keighley	5	7	8	7	0	3	3
Leeds	2	1	2	4	0	3	5
Leigh	6	2	1	1	3	2	6
Mansfield M.	2	6	3	3	—	—	—
Oldham	4	3	6	5	5	3	8
Rochdale H.	5	1	3	4	9	1	7
Runcorn H.	3	3	12	5	5	3	3
St. Helens	1	3	0	4	3	3	2
Salford	2	5	6	5	5	6	3
Sheffield E.	0	3	6	4	—	—	—
Southend I.	—	—	—	3	3	—	—
Springfield B.	2	4	5	4	3	3	2
Swinton	3	3	2	2	0	4	1
Wakefield T.	5	5	6	7	5	2	6
Warrington	3	6	6	1	6	5	10
Whitehaven	3	2	3	3	6	2	4
Widnes	2	4	5	6	7	4	3
Wigan	5	3	3	2	2	3	5
Workington T.	5	5	9	5	4	3	3
York	4	3	2	1	4	2	3
Totals	**101**	**116**	**139**	**124**	**137**	**104**	**159**

DISCIPLINARY ANALYSIS 1987-88

The following is a club-by-club disciplinary record for last season, showing the players sent off in first team matches and the findings of the League's Disciplinary Committee.

The committee's verdict is featured in the brackets after the player's name, each number indicating the match ban imposed. SOS stands for sending off sufficient and NG for not guilty. A suspension reduced or increased on appeal is shown as follows, 6 to 4.

The sin bin suspensions were imposed under the totting-up system where two points were issued for a 10-minute temporary dismissal. A one-match ban was imposed when the running total reached six points.

SB indicates in brackets the number of one-match bans imposed under the sin bin totting-up system. It does not include a record of players' sin bin dismissals which have not reached the six-point total.

* indicates where video evidence was submitted. The 1984-85 season was the first time video action other than official BBC or ITV tapes could be offered in evidence. In 1987-88 the committee considered video evidence in 31 individual cases, four more than during 1986-87. Two cases were considered by the committee after viewing a video, the player not having been dismissed.

Club	Total sent off	Dismissed Player	Sin Bins
Barrow	4	G. Kendall (SOS), P. Pocock (2), T. Kay (3), W. Butler (2)	M. Pocock (1SB)
Batley	1	P. Geary (3)	
Bradford N.	2	D. Hobbs (*3 to 2, *4)	B. Hill (1SB)
Bramley	4	C. Bowman (2), P. Spedding (6 to 4), P. Fletcher (2), W. Race (2)	P. Lister (1SB)
Carlisle	9	K. Pape (*1), S. Langton (4), C. Armstrong (1), K. Green (6), A. McMullen (*NG), P. Subritzky (8), G. Schubert (SOS), S. Kirkby (6), M. Thomason (2)	
Castleford	3	K. England (*3), B. Juliff (1), G. Anderson (2)	
Dewsbury	5	J. Moore (4), G. Cocks (2), P. Shuttleworth (4), S. Morris (4), S. Hinchcliffe (4)	P. Shuttleworth (1SB)
Doncaster	3	J. Green (4 to 3), M. Gibbon (2), K. Jones (NG)	
Featherstone R.	2	K. Harrison (2), K. Bell (2)	M. Campbell (1SB)
Fulham	0		K. Manning (1SB), D. Aitken (1SB)
Halifax	1	G. Beevers (*NG)	
Huddersfield B.	0		A. Farrell (1SB)
Hull	2	A. Dannatt (4), T. Wilby (1)	

Club	Total sent off	Dismissed Player	Sin Bins
Hull K.R.	1	C. Burton (*3 to 2)	
Hunslet	2	S. Nickle (*2), S. Lay (*NG)	R. Sampson (1SB), P. Tate (1SB), A. Sykes (1SB)
Keighley	5	G. Moorby (2), C. Atkinson (2,3), T. Skerrett (*2), G. Rose (2)	M. Fairbank (1SB) R. Winterbottom (1SB)
Leeds	2	K. Rayne (4), L. Crooks (*2)	
Leigh	6	A. Cottrell (3,*SOS, *2), B. Dunn (*1) C. Johnson (NG), M. Dean (3)	D. Evans (1SB)
Mansfield M.	2	J. Warburton (*SOS), N. Rudd (*SOS)	
Oldham	4	S. Peters (6,8), M. Bardsley (4), D. Foy (*3)	
Rochdale H.	5	A. Ruane (2,4), D. Williams (4), A. Fairhurst (3), P. Cartwright (2)	
Runcorn H.	3	P. Durnin (2), A. Jackson (4), G. Shaw (SOS)	T. Rose (1SB)
St. Helens	1	A. Platt (*4)	C. Arkwright (1SB)
Salford	2	P. Glynn (2), D. Bullough (4)	
Springfield B.	2	D. Wilson (4), J. Emson (3)	
Swinton	3	G. Ainsworth (2), J. Grima (*SOS), J. Percival (*2)	F. Cassidy (1SB) D. Wilson (1SB)
Wakefield T.	5	I. Hopkinson (3), I. Jowitt (4), K. Harcombe (2), K. Rayne (*2), P. Mallinder (*4)	B. Conway (1SB) K. Harcombe (1SB)
Warrington	3	M. Gregory (3), P. Cullen (*2), A. Humphries (*2)	D. Drummond (1SB)
Whitehaven	3	B. Fisher (2), I. Bell (2), R. Glen (2)	
Widnes	2	T. Stockley (4), K. Sorensen (3)	P. Hulme (1SB), D. Pyke (1SB)
Wigan	5	J. Lydon (*SOS), A. Goodway (*SOS,*4) A. Shelford (*SOS,*NG)	A. Gregory (1SB)
Workington T.	5	N. Frazer (6), R. Tabern (2), P. Stoddart (4), C. Falcon (*2), G. Burgess (*2)	
York	4	S. Horton (4,4), S. Ellis (4), A. Timson (6)	

● In addition, the Disciplinary Committee carried out two 'trials by video,' calling up players who had not been dismissed after viewing video tapes. Joe Lydon of Wigan and Don Duffy of Carlisle were both given a four match ban.

SPONSORSHIP
This updated sub-section is a record of the sponsorship programme under the control of the Rugby Football League.

1978-88 COMPETITIONS:

Silk Cut Challenge Cup	£160,000
John Player Special Trophy	£150,000
Stones Bitter Championship and Premiership	£130,000
Whitbread Trophy Bitter Tests	£ 80,000
British Coal Nines	£ 25,000
Okells Charity Shield	£ 6,000
Rodstock War of the Roses	£ 4,000
	£555,000

Awards:

Greenalls Man of Steel Awards	£ 9,000
Daily Mirror/Stones Bitter Teams of the Month and Year	£ 7,000
Traveleads Top Fan	£ 4,000
Sunday Mirror/Wallace Arnold Entertainer Awards	£ 4,000
Greenall Whitley Top Scorers Award	£ 2,500
Daily Star/Stones Bitter Star Men	£ 1,500
	£ 28,000

Miscellaneous:	£ 45,000
GRAND TOTAL	£628,000

COMPETITION SPONSORSHIP
The following is a review of sponsorship of the game's major competitions.

SILK CUT CHALLENGE CUP

	Prel.	1st	2nd	3rd	S.F.	R.U.	Winners	Development Fund	Total
	£	£	£	£	£	£	£	£	£
1979	—	750	1,160	2,000	3,555	6,555	12,555	4,500	60,000
1980	—	750	1,160	2,000	3,555	6,555	12,555	19,500	75,000
1981	—	750	1,160	2,000	3,555	6,555	12,555	29,500	85,000
1982	1,000	1,000	1,400	2,400	4,325	8,000	14,555	30,000	100,000
1983	1,000	1,000	1,400	2,400	4,325	8,000	14,555	40,000	110,000
1984	1,000	1,000	1,400	2,400	4,325	8,000	14,555	48,000	120,000
1985	1,100	1,100	1,500	2,500	4,500	9,000	16,000	47,600	130,000
1986	1,100	1,100	1,500	2,500	4,500	9,000	16,000	57,600	140,000
1987	1,200	1,200	1,650	2,750	4,500	9,000	16,000	58,200	150,000
1988	1,200	1,200	1,800	3,000	5,000	10,000	18,000	62,000	160,000

● Sponsored by State Express 1979-84.

JOHN PLAYER SPECIAL TROPHY

	Prel.	1st	2nd	3rd	S.F.	R.U.	Winners	Development Fund	Total
	£	£	£	£	£	£	£	£	£
1971-72	—	—	—	—	1,000	2,500	5,000	—	9,500
1972-73	—	150	300	450	1,000	2,500	5,000	—	16,100
1973-74	—	150	300	450	1,000	2,500	5,000	—	16,100
1974-75	—	150	300	450	1,000	2,500	5,000	—	16,100
1975-76	—	300	450	600	1,500	3,000	6,000	—	22,800
1976-77	—	400	550	700	1,500	3,000	6,000	—	25,600
1977-78	—	450	600	750	1,750	3,500	8,000	—	30,000
1978-79	—	550	700	900	1,750	3,500	8,000	—	33,000
1979-80	—	600	800	1,000	2,000	4,000	8,500	—	36,500
1980-81	—	600	800	1,000	2,000	4,000	8,500	3,500	40,000
1981-82	700	700	900	1,175	2,500	4,500	9,000	7,000	50,000
1982-83	700	700	900	1,175	2,500	5,000	10,000	10,500	55,000
1983-84	700	700	900	1,175	2,500	5,000	10,000	15,500	60,000
1984-85	750	750	1,000	1,500	2,500	5,000	10,000	20,000	75,000
1985-86	750	750	1,000	1,500	2,750	5,500	11,000	26,000	80,000
1986-87	800	800	1,100	1,700	3,000	6,000	12,000	26,200	85,000
1987-88	1,100	1,100	1,600	2,825	4,750	9,000	16,000	65,000	150,000

STONES BITTER

	Championship winners	R.U.	2nd Division winners	R.U.	Premiership winners	R.U.	2nd Division Premiership winners	R.U.	Development Fund	Total
	£	£	£	£	£	£	£	£	£	£
1980-81	6,000	—	3,000	—	4,000	—	—	—	42,000	55,000
1981-82	10,000	—	6,000	—	6,000	—	—	—	48,000	70,000
1982-83	12,000	—	7,000	—	7,000	—	—	—	54,000	80,000
1983-84	12,000	—	7,000	—	7,000	—	—	—	59,000	85,000
1984-85	13,000	—	9,000	—	8,000	—	—	—	60,000	90,000
1985-86	13,000	—	9,000	—	8,000	—	—	—	65,000	95,000
1986-87	20,000	8,000	10,000	4,000	9,000	3,500	4,000	1,500	60,000	120,000
1987-88	20,000	8,000	10,000	4,000	9,000	3,500	4,000	1,500	70,000	130,000

● Sponsored by Slalom Lager from 1980-86

GRUNHALLE LAGER LANCASHIRE CUP

	Winners	Total
	£	£
1976	1,000	4,000
1977	1,500	5,000
1978	1,800	5,500
1979	1,900	6,000
1980	2,530	10,000
1981	2,700	11,000
1982	3,000	11,500
1983	3,200	12,500
1984	3,400	13,250
1985	3,400	13,250
1986	4,300	17,000
1987	4,600	18,000

● Sponsored by Burtonwood Brewery 1976-85

YORKSHIRE CUP

	Sponsor	Winners	Total
		£	£
1972	Esso	800	4,000
1973	Esso	1,500	6,000
1974	Esso	1,400	6,000
1975	Esso	1,200	6,000
1976	Esso	1,200	6,000
1977	Esso	1,600	8,000
1978	Esso	2,000	9,000
1979	Esso	2,000	9,500
1980	Websters Brewery	2,750	13,000
1981	Websters Brewery	3,000	14,000
1982	Websters Brewery	2,500	15,000
1983	Philips Video	2,500	15,000
1984	Philips Video	2,500	15,000
1985	John Smiths	2,500	5,000
1986	John Smiths	2,500	12,500
1987	John Smiths	3,000	12,500

INTERNATIONAL

Great Britain v Australia Tests 1978
Forward Chemicals: £17,500

Great Britain v Australia Tests 1982
Dominion Insurance: £40,000

Great Britain v France Tests 1983
Dominion Insurance: £5,000

Great Britain v France Tests 1984
Dominion Insurance: £5,000

Great Britain Tour 1984
Modern Maintenance Products: £100,000

Great Britain 1985-86
Whitbread Trophy Bitter: £85,000

Great Britain 1986-87
Whitbread Trophy Bitter: £85,000

Great Britain 1987-88
Whitbread Trophy Bitter: £80,000

NINE-A-SIDES

For the first time, the League staged a nine-a-side competition, the one-night event being featured on BBC TV's Sportsnight. Backed by a £25,000 sponsorship from British Coal, the 2½ hour tournament was staged at Central Park, Wigan and the eight teams invited to take part were tourists Papua New Guinea and Auckland, plus the top six British club sides in the 1986-87 league table. All matches were played seven minutes each way, except the final which was extended to nine minutes each half. First round losers received £2,000 each, semi-finalists £3,000 each, the runners-up £4,000 and the winners £6,000, the remaining £1,000 being allocated to travel expenses. The inaugural 1987 results were:

First Round

Auckland	8	Halifax	0
Castleford	8	Hull K.R.	6
St. Helens	14	Warrington	10
Wigan	12	Papua New Guinea	4

Semi-Finals

Castleford	20	Auckland	6
Wigan	16	St. Helens	0

Final

Wigan	10	Castleford	0

Attendance: 6,529
Man of the Tournament: Richard Russell (Wigan)

Crowd boom! Rockets herald the entry of the Wigan and Manly teams for the Fosters World Club Challenge match which drew 36,895 spectators.

Crowd pleasers: Graham Eadie of Halifax moves in on Wigan's Henderson Gill.

ATTENDANCES

CLUB ATTENDANCE REVIEW

The following is a review of clubs' home attendances for league matches from 1979-88.

The main figure is the individual club's average gate for league games during that season. The figure in brackets indicates an upward or downward trend compared with the previous season.

Also indicated is the division the club competed in that season, i.e. 1 — First Division, 2 — Second Division.

Club	79-80	80-81	81-82	82-83	83-84	84-85	85-86	86-87	87-88
Barrow	2 3143 (+155)	1 4065 (+922)	1 4162 (+97)	1 3852 (−310)	2 3218 (−450)	1 2728 (−490)	2 1926 (−802)	1 2664 (+738)	2 1624 (−1040)
Batley	2 1330 (+415)	2 1329 (−1)	2 1052 (−277)	2 916 (−136)	2 864 (−52)	2 1015 (+151)	2 930 (−85)	2 744 (−186)	2 859 (+115)
Bradford N.	1 6236 (+585)	1 6105 (−131)	1 5816 (−289)	1 4920 (−896)	1 5316 (+386)	1 4251 (−1065)	1 3975 (−276)	1 4312 (+377)	1 4723 (+411)
Bramley	2 1204 (−4)	2 1050 (−154)	2 928 (−122)	2 809 (−119)	2 759 (−50)	2 858 (+99)	2 831 (−27)	2 737 (−94)	2 858 (+121)
Bridgend	—	—	2 2008 —	2 854 (−1154)	2 581 (−273)	2 510 (−70)	—	—	—
Carlisle	—	—	2 2950 (−1026)	1 1924 (−1172)	2 752 (+244)	2 986 (−368)	2 618 (+171)	2 789 (+171)	2 763 (−26)
Castleford	1 3714 (+42)	1 4612 (+898)	1 3791 (−821)	1 3548 (−243)	1 4288 (+740)	1 3217 (−1071)	1 3701 (+430)	1 4758 (+1057)	1 4520 (−238)
Dewsbury	2 1552 (+78)	2 1377 (−175)	2 1048 (−329)	2 779 (−269)	2 706 (−73)	2 995 (+189)	1 1819 (+824)	2 669 (−1150)	2 658 (−41)
Doncaster	2 428 (−191)	2 628 (+200)	2 556 (−72)	2 441 (−115)	2 255 (−186)	2 266 (+11)	2 689 (+423)	2 1543 (+854)	2 1450 (−93)
Featherstone R.	2 2301 (−360)	1 3007 (+706)	1 2806 (−201)	1 2647 (−159)	1 3032 (+385)	1 2541 (−491)	1 2320 (−221)	1 2606 (+286)	2 1879 (−727)
Fulham	—	2 6096 —	1 4321 (−1775)	2 2688 (−1633)	1 2238 (−450)	2 949 (−1289)	2 817 (−132)	2 684 (−133)	2 615 (−69)
Halifax	2 2969 (+655)	1 4090 (+1121)	2 2818 (−1272)	1 2270 (−548)	2 1254 (−1016)	1 3497 (+2243)	1 4944 (+1447)	1 4891 (−53)	1 6521 (+1630)
Huddersfield B.	2 1654 (−879)	2 1769 (+115)	2 1185 (−584)	2 776 (−409)	2 699 (−77)	2 905 (+206)	2 678 (−227)	2 524 (−154)	2 601 (+77)
Hull	1 10021 (+3168)	1 11711 (+1690)	1 13190 (+1479)	1 11525 (−1665)	1 10679 (−846)	1 8525 (−2154)	1 6245 (−1280)	1 5538 (−707)	1 5111 (−427)
Hull K. R.	1 6953 (+1008)	1 8904 (+1951)	1 8723 (−181)	1 7379 (−1344)	1 6966 (−413)	1 6715 (−215)	1 4855 (−1860)	1 4651 (−204)	1 4186 (−465)
Hunslet	1 1718 (+249)	2 921 (−797)	2 744 (−177)	2 1195 (+451)	2 1338 (+143)	1 2246 (+908)	2 722 (−1524)	1 1050 (+338)	1 2678 (+1050)
Keighley	2 1593 (−1)	2 1612 (+19)	2 1576 (−36)	2 1085 (−491)	2 734 (−351)	2 822 (+88)	2 685 (−137)	2 445 (−240)	2 958 (+503)

Club	79-80	80-81	81-82	82-83	83-84	84-85	85-86	86-87	87-88
Leeds	1 6681 (+1520)	1 5934 (−747)	1 5599 (−335)	1 5893 (+294)	1 6542 (+649)	1 7330 (+788)	1 6928 (−402)	1 6393 (−535)	1 9911 (+3518)
Leigh	1 4418 (+1099)	1 4498 (+80)	1 5939 (+1441)	1 4617 (−1322)	1 4434 (−183)	1 3822 (−612)	2 2710 (−1112)	1 4232 (+1522)	1 4516 (+284)
Mansfield M.	—	—	—	—	—	2 1020 —	2 487 (−553)	2 368 (−119)	2 368 —
Oldham	2 2367 (+1160)	1 3220 (+853)	1 2395 (−825)	1 3721 (+1326)	1 4138 (+417)	1 4562 (+424)	1 4333 (−229)	1 3915 (−418)	2 3790 (−125)
Rochdale H.	2 1210 (−479)	2 1149 (−61)	2 888 (−261)	2 619 (−269)	2 538 (−81)	2 542 (+4)	2 1267 (+725)	2 877 (−390)	2 1106 (+229)
Runcorn H.	2 238 (−161)	2 270 (+32)	2 385 (+115)	2 224 (−161)	2 172 (−52)	2 509 (+337)	2 363 (−146)	2 331 (−35)	2 515 (+184)
St. Helens	1 5577 (−81)	1 4934 (−643)	1 4862 (−72)	1 4543 (−319)	1 4656 (+113)	1 7336 (+2680)	1 6022 (−1314)	1 7341 (+1391)	1 8417 (+1076)
Salford	1 4846 (+746)	1 3458 (−1388)	2 2404 (−1054)	2 1928 (−476)	1 2399 (+471)	2 1795 (−604)	1 2520 (+725)	1 2826 (+306)	1 3747 (+921)
Sheffield E.	—	—	—	—	—	2 885 —	2 698 (−187)	2 708 (+10)	2 847 (+139)
Southend Invicta	—	—	—	—	2 731 —	2 216 (−515)	—	—	—
Springfield B.	1 1576 (+339)	2 684 (−892)	2 768 (+84)	2 679 (−89)	2 625 (−54)	2 555 (−70)	2 534 (−21)	2 475 (−59)	2 922 (+447)
Swinton	2 1509 (+178)	2 1935 (+426)	2 1567 (−368)	2 1314 (−253)	2 1077 (−237)	2 1590 (+513)	1 2706 (+1116)	2 1622 (−1084)	1 2987 (+1365)
Wakefield T.	1 4559 (+491)	1 4814 (+255)	1 3716 (−1098)	2 2344 (−1372)	1 3483 (+1139)	2 1568 (−1915)	2 1714 (+146)	1 2637 (+923)	2 2416 (−221)
Warrington	1 5122 (−72)	1 4917 (−205)	1 3838 (−1079)	1 3824 (−14)	1 4059 (+235)	1 3801 (−258)	1 3618 (−183)	1 4172 (+554)	1 4974 (+820)
Whitehaven	2 1761 (+397)	2 2733 (+972)	1 2710 (−23)	2 1742 (−968)	1 1639 (−103)	2 1540 (−99)	2 1878 (+333)	2 1800 (−78)	2 1772 (−28)
Widnes	1 6143 (−608)	1 5306 (−837)	1 5485 (+179)	1 4703 (−782)	1 4687 (−16)	1 4266 (−421)	1 4019 (−247)	1 3840 (−179)	1 6262 (+2422)
Wigan	1 4665 (+160)	2 4693 (+28)	1 5497 (+804)	1 7426 (+1929)	1 7479 (+53)	1 10056 (+2577)	1 12515 (+2459)	1 12732 (+217)	1 13021 (+289)
Workington T.	1 1834 (−321)	1 2188 (+354)	2 1969 (−219)	1 1470 (−499)	2 934 (−536)	1 920 (−14)	2 702 (−218)	2 653 (−49)	2 737 (+84)
York	1 3934 (+669)	2 3827 (−107)	1 3677 (−150)	2 1685 (−1992)	2 1215 (−470)	2 1528 (+313)	1 2828 (+1300)	2 1520 (−1380)	2 1406 (−114)

COMPETITION ATTENDANCE REVIEW

		79-80	80-81	81-82	82-83	83-84	84-85	85-86	86-87	87-88
FIRST	Total	1,169,956	1,226,428	1,264,520	1,113,915	1,140,548	1,137,195	1,100,329	1,162,666	1,060,296
DIVISION	Av.	4,875	5,110	5,268	4,641	4,752	4,738	4,585	4,844	5,826
SECOND	Total	302,345	420,994	403,652	321,226	279,673	266,730	310,311	217,552	381,825
DIVISION	Av.	1,661	2,005	1,484	1,181	914	953	1,014	863	1,364
LEAGUE TOTALS (1st & 2nd)	Total	1,472,301	1,647,422	1,668,172	1,435,141	1,420,221	1,403,925	1,410,640	1,380,218	1,442,121
	Av.	3,489	3,661	3,258	2,803	2,601	2,700	2,584	2,805	3,121
R.L. CUP	Av.	10,370	9,993	11,388	8,355	8,399	8,497	8,280	6,965	8,764
JOHN PLAYER	Av.	4,314	5,362	5,590	4,219	3,893	4,881	4,232	4,122	3,570
PREMIER	Av.	7,343	11,689	9,454	10,099	8,136	10,115	9,273	15,154	13,462
10,000+ (No. of)		20	36	36	37	26	27	36	43	46

20,000-plus crowds . . . . A 10-year review

All matches except the Rugby League Challenge Cup final at Wembley

26,447	Britain v. Australia	Second Test	Bradford	5 Nov. 1978
29,627	Britain v. Australia	Third Test	Leeds	18 Nov. 1978
20,775	Bradford N. v. Hull	RL Cup round 3	Bradford	9 Mar. 1980
29,448	Hull v. Hull K.R.	Premiership final	Leeds	16 May 1981
25,245	Hull v. Hull K.R.	John Player final	Leeds	23 Jan. 1982
21,207	Hull v. Castleford	RL Cup semi-final	Leeds	27 Mar. 1982
41,171	Hull v. Widnes	RL Cup final replay	Elland Rd, Leeds	19 May 1982
26,771	Britain v. Australia	First Test	Hull C. FC	30 Oct. 1982
23,216	Britain v. Australia	Second Test	Wigan	20 Nov. 1982
26,031	Hull v. Castleford	RL Cup semi-final	Elland Rd, Leeds	2 Apr. 1983
20,569	Hull v. Hull K.R.	Division One	Hull	8 Apr. 1983
20,077	St. Helens v. Wigan	RL Cup round 3	St. Helens	11 Mar. 1984
25,237	Hull v. Hull K.R.	Yorks Cup final	Hull C. FC	27 Oct. 1984
26,074	St. Helens v. Wigan	Lancs Cup final	Wigan	28 Oct. 1984
25,326	Hull v. Hull K.R.	John Player final	Hull C. FC	26 Jan. 1985
20,982	Hull v. Castleford	RL Cup semi-final	Leeds	6 Apr. 1985
20,968	Hull v. Castleford	RL Cup semi-final replay	Leeds	10 Apr. 1985
22,209	Britain v. New Zealand	Third Test	Elland Rd, Leeds	9 Nov. 1985
21,813	Wigan v. St. Helens	Division One	Wigan	26 Dec. 1985
23,866	Hull K.R. v. Leeds	RL Cup semi-final	Elland Rd, Leeds	29 Mar. 1986
32,485	Hull K.R. v. Leeds	RL Cup semi-final replay	Elland Rd, Leeds	3 Apr. 1986
28,252	Wigan v. St. Helens	Lancs Cup semi-final	Wigan	1 Oct. 1986
30,622	Wigan v. Australia	Tour	Wigan	12 Oct. 1986
20,180	Oldham v. Wigan	Lancs Cup final	St. Helens	19 Oct. 1986
50,583	Britain v. Australia	First Test	Manchester U. FC	25 Oct. 1986
30,808	Britain v. Australia	Second Test	Elland Rd, Leeds	8 Nov. 1986

(continued)

20,169	Britain v. Australia	Third Test	Wigan	22 Nov. 1986
21,214	St. Helens v. Wigan	Division One	St. Helens	26 Dec. 1986
21,144	Warrington v. Wigan	John Player final	Bolton W. FC	10 Jan. 1987
20,355	Wigan v. St. Helens	Division One	Wigan	17 Apr. 1987
22,457	Wigan v. Halifax	Premiership semi-final	Wigan	10 May 1987
38,756	Warrington v. Wigan	Premiership final	Manchester U. FC	17 May 1987
36,895	Wigan v. Manly	World Club Challenge	Wigan	7 Oct. 1987
20,234	Wigan v. Warrington	Lancs Cup final	St. Helens	11 Oct. 1987
23,809	Wigan v. St. Helens	Division One	Wigan	27 Dec. 1987
25,110	Wigan v. Leeds	RL Cup round 2	Wigan	14 Feb. 1988
20,783	Salford v. Wigan	RL Cup semi-final	Bolton W. FC	12 Mar. 1988
20,534	Halifax v. Hull	RL Cup semi-final	Leeds	26 Mar. 1988
25,117	Hull v. Halifax	RL Cup semi-final replay	Elland Rd, Leeds	30 Mar. 1988
21,812	St. Helens v. Wigan	Division One	St. Helens	1 Apr. 1988
35,252	St. Helens v. Widnes	Premiership final	Manchester U. FC	15 May 1988

1987-88 ANALYSIS

FIRST DIVISION

Total attendance 1,060,296
Average 5,826

Gates rose by 20 per cent compared with the 1986-87 average attendance of 4,844. Wigan topped the gates chart for the fourth successive season, further increasing their average turnout to 13,021. Twelve of their 13 home league matches attracted gates of 10,000 plus. A total of 10 of the 14 First Division clubs increased their average attendances with Leeds and Widnes recording upsurges of more than 50 per cent.

SECOND DIVISION

Total attendance.............. 381,825
Average·......................... 1,364
A massive rise of 40 per cent was recorded for the average gate in the 20-strong Second Division compared with the 1986-87 figure of 863. The promoted trio of clubs headed the gates chart with champions Oldham the best supported with an average home return of 3,790, only 125 per game down on their previous season in the First Division. Half of the clubs recorded increases in attendances, led by Keighley with a 100 per cent upsurge and Springfield Borough who almost doubled their gates with the move to Wigan.

LEAGUE CHAMPIONSHIP

Aggregate..................... 1,442,121
Average 3,121
The average attendance for the 34 clubs competing in the two-division league set-up was up 11 per cent compared with the 1986-87 figure of 2,805.

SILK CUT CHALLENGE CUP

Attendances on the Wembley trail went up by 26 per cent, the 1988 tournament attracting a total of 341,812 fans, an average of 8,764 for the 37 ties plus two replays. The previous season's average figure was 6,965. The traditional top attendance was for the final at Wembley which attracted a capacity 94,273.

JOHN PLAYER SPECIAL TROPHY

The 36 ties in the 1987-88 competition attracted a total of 128,526 fans, an average of 3,570. Compared with the previous campaign's tally of 4,122, this was a 13 per cent downward trend.

STONES BITTER PREMIERSHIP

The end of season top-eight tournament attracted a total of 94,235 for the seven ties. The second staging of the final at Manchester United's Old Trafford ground attracted 35,252 fans. The average gate for the competition was 13,462. The 1987 figures were a total of 106,076, averaging 15,154.

SECOND DIVISION PREMIERSHIP

The second staging of the tournament featured six ties staged on the grounds of the qualifying clubs with the final being the first stage of the new-style Stones Bitter Premiership double-header at Manchester United's Old Trafford ground. The half dozen ties attracted an average gate of 2,845, an increase of 40 per cent. A crowd of 22,500 was recorded for the start of the Second Division showpiece final at Old Trafford, the gate ultimately reaching 35,252.

GRUNHALLE LAGER LANCASHIRE CUP

After three years of substantial increases, the 1987 Lancashire Cup campaign suffered a 25 per cent decrease with the 1986 average gate of 7,250 falling to 5,410. The 15 ties tallied 81,151 fans, with the final between Warrington and Wigan at St. Helens pulling in 20,234 of those.

JOHN SMITHS YORKSHIRE CUP

The 1987 competition recorded an 18 per cent increase in gates for the 17 ties plus a replay of the final. The aggregate turnout of 77,889 produced an average of 4,327 compared with the figure of 3,784 12 months earlier.

FIVE-FIGURE CROWDS

There were 47 five-figure gates, a record during the two-division era since re-introduction in 1973. As per tradition the top gate was for the Wembley final of the Silk Cut Challenge Cup which attracted 94,273, only the sixth capacity attendance. Gates of 20,000-plus featured at ten of the 47 games with Wigan featuring in seven of them. Nineteen of the five-figure gates were for Wigan home matches, 12 of them for the Riversiders' 13 Stones Bitter Championship matches at Central Park. The Leeds revival was reflected in the staging of 10 five-figure crowds for matches at Headingley. The 10,000-plus gates were divided into the following categories:

League	29
Challenge Cup	7
Premiership Trophy	4
John Player Special Trophy	3
Lancashire Cup	2
Yorkshire Cup	1
World Club Challenge	1

Wigan's Joe Lydon applauds the fans at Wembley.

FIRST DIVISION

	1987-88 Average	Annual Difference
Wigan	13021	(+ 289)
Leeds	9911	(+3518)
St. Helens	8417	(+1076)
Halifax	6521	(+1630)
Widnes	6262	(+2422)
Hull	5111	(− 427)
Warrington	4974	(+ 820)
Bradford Northern	4723	(+ 411)
Castleford	4520	(− 238)
Leigh	4516	(+ 284)
Hull Kingston Rovers	4186	(− 465)
Salford	3747	(+ 921)
Swinton	2987	(+1365)
Hunslet	2678	(+1050)

SECOND DIVISION

	1987-88 Average	Annual Difference
Oldham	3790	(− 125)
Wakefield Trinity	2416	(− 221)
Featherstone Rovers	1879	(− 727)
Whitehaven	1772	(− 28)
Barrow	1624	(−1040)
Doncaster	1450	(− 93)
York	1406	(− 114)
Rochdale Hornets	1106	(+ 229)
Keighley	958	(+ 503)
Springfield Borough	922	(+ 447)
Batley	859	(+ 115)
Bramley	858	(+ 121)
Sheffield Eagles	847	(+ 139)
Carlisle	763	(− 26)
Workington Town	737	(+ 84)
Dewsbury	658	(− 41)
Fulham	615	(− 69)
Huddersfield Barracudas	601	(+ 77)
Runcorn Highfield	515	(+ 184)
Mansfield Marksman	368	(−)

FIXTURES

PRINCIPAL DATES 1988-89

1988
21 August	Okells Charity Shield: Widnes v. Wigan (Isle of Man)
28 August	League season commences
18 September	County Cup Competitions (1)
21 September	Rodstock War of the Roses, Yorkshire v. Lancashire County of Origin (Headingley, Leeds)
28 September	County Cup Competitions (2)
5 October	County Cup Competitions (SF)
16 October	John Smiths Yorkshire Cup (F)
23 October	Grunhalle Lager Lancashire Cup (F)
26 October	British Coal Nines
29 October	Whitbread Trophy Hall of Fame Celebration: Great Britain v. Rest of the World (Headingley, Leeds)
13 November	John Player Special Trophy (1)
27 November	John Player Special Trophy (2)
4 December	John Player Special Trophy (3)
10 December	John Player Special Trophy (SF)
17 December	John Player Special Trophy (SF)

1989
7 January	John Player Special Trophy (F)
20 January	Great Britain Under-20s v. France
21 January	Whitbread Trophy Test: Great Britain v. France
29 January	Silk Cut Challenge Cup (1)
4 February	France v. Great Britain Under-20s
5 February	Whitbread Trophy Test: France v. Great Britain
12 February	Silk Cut Challenge Cup (2)
26 February	Silk Cut Challenge Cup (3)
11 March	Silk Cut Challenge Cup (SF)
25 March	Silk Cut Challenge Cup (SF)
23 April	Stones Bitter Premiership (1)
29 April	Silk Cut Challenge Cup (F) (Wembley)
7 May	Stones Bitter Premiership (SF)
14 May	Stones Bitter Premiership (F)

STONES BITTER CHAMPIONSHIP 1988-89

SUNDAY, 28th AUGUST, 1988

Featherstone R.	v.	Leeds
Halifax	v.	Widnes
Hull	v.	Castleford
St. Helens	v.	Bradford N.
Salford	v.	Hull K.R.
Wakefield T.	v.	Warrington
Wigan	v.	Oldham

SUNDAY 4th SEPTEMBER, 1988

Bradford N.	v.	Salford
Castleford	v.	Halifax
Hull K.R.	v.	Featherstone R.
Oldham	v.	Leeds
Wakefield T.	v.	Wigan
Warrington	v.	St. Helens
Widnes	v.	Hull

SUNDAY, 11th SEPTEMBER, 1988

Featherstone R.	v.	Oldham
Halifax	v.	Bradford N.
Hull	v.	Wakefield T.
Leeds	v.	Widnes
St. Helens	v.	Castleford
Salford	v.	Warrington
Wigan	v.	Hull K.R.

SUNDAY, 25th SEPTEMBER, 1988

Bradford N.	v.	Wigan
Castleford	v.	Oldham
Hull K.R.	v.	Halifax
Leeds	v.	St. Helens
Wakefield T.	v.	Salford
Warrington	v.	Hull
Widnes	v.	Featherstone R.

SUNDAY, 2nd OCTOBER, 1988

Featherstone R.	v.	Bradford N.
Halifax	v.	Warrington
Hull	v.	Leeds
Oldham	v.	Hull K.R.
St. Helens	v.	Wakefield
Salford	v.	Widnes
Wigan	v.	Castleford

SUNDAY, 9th OCTOBER, 1988

Bradford N.	v.	Hull
Castleford	v.	Salford
Hull K.R.	v.	St. Helens
Leeds	v.	Wigan
Wakefield T.	v.	Oldham
Warrington	v.	Featherstone R.
Widnes	v.	Halifax

SUNDAY, 16th OCTOBER, 1988

Featherstone R.	v.	Halifax
Hull K.R.	v.	Bradford N.
St. Helens	v.	Hull
Salford	v.	Leeds
Widnes	v.	Castleford
Wigan	v.	Wakefield
Warrington	v.	FRANCE

SUNDAY, 23rd OCTOBER, 1988

Castleford	v.	Warrington
Hull	v.	Wigan
Leeds	v.	Hull K.R.
Oldham	v.	St. Helens
Salford	v.	Featherstone R.
Wakefield T.	v.	Widnes
Halifax	v.	FRANCE

SUNDAY 6th NOVEMBER, 1988

Bradford N.	v.	Leeds
Featherstone R.	v.	Castleford
Halifax	v.	Hull
Hull K.R.	v.	Wakefield T.

St. Helens	v.	Salford
Warrington	v.	Oldham
Wigan	v.	Widnes

SUNDAY, 20th NOVEMBER, 1988

Castleford	v.	St. Helens
Hull	v.	Featherstone R.
Leeds	v.	Warrington
Oldham	v.	Halifax
Salford	v.	Wigan
Wakefield T.	v.	Bradford N.
Widnes	v.	Hull K.R.

SUNDAY, 4th DECEMBER, 1988

Bradford N.	v.	Oldham
Featherstone R.	v.	Salford
Hull K.R.	v.	Leeds
St. Helens	v.	Halifax
Warrington	v.	Castleford
Widnes	v.	Wakefield T.
Wigan	v.	Hull

SUNDAY, 11th DECEMBER, 1988

Castleford	v.	Widnes
Halifax	v.	Wigan
Hull	v.	St. Helens
Leeds	v.	Featherstone R.
Oldham	v.	Warrington
Salford	v.	Bradford N.
Wakefield	v.	Hull K.R.

SUNDAY, 18th DECEMBER, 1988

Bradford N.	v.	Castleford
Widnes	v.	Leeds

BOXING DAY, MONDAY, 26th DECEMBER, 1988

Castleford	v.	Hull K.R.
Featherstone R.	v.	Wakefield T.
Leeds	v.	Halifax
Oldham	v.	Salford
St. Helens	v.	Wigan
Warrington	v.	Widnes

1989

NEW YEAR'S DAY, 1st JANUARY, 1989

Castleford	v.	Bradford N.
Leeds	v.	Oldham
Wakefield T.	v.	Featherstone R.
Widnes	v.	St. Helens
Wigan	v.	Warrington

MONDAY, 2nd JANUARY, 1989

Hull K.R.	v.	Hull

SUNDAY, 8th JANUARY, 1989

Featherstone R.	v.	Wigan
Halifax	v.	Castleford
Hull	v.	Bradford N.
Oldham	v.	Widnes
St. Helens	v.	Leeds
Salford	v.	Wakefield T.
Warrington	v.	Hull K.R.

SUNDAY, 15th JANUARY, 1989

Bradford N.	v.	Warrington
Featherstone R.	v.	St. Helens
Hull K.R.	v.	Oldham
Wakefield T.	v.	Hull
Widnes	v.	Salford
Wigan	v.	Halifax

SUNDAY, 22nd JANUARY, 1989

Castleford	v.	Wakefield T.
Halifax	v.	Featherstone R.
Hull	v.	Widnes

Leeds	v.	Salford
Oldham	v.	Bradford N.
St. Helens	v.	Hull K.R.
Warrington	v.	Wigan

SUNDAY, 5th FEBRUARY, 1989

Bradford N.	v.	Halifax
Hull K.R.	v.	Warrington
Salford	v.	Hull
Wakefield T.	v.	Leeds
Widnes	v.	Oldham

FRIDAY, 17th FEBRUARY, 1989

Salford	v.	Castleford

SUNDAY, 19th FEBRUARY, 1989

Bradford N.	v.	St. Helens
Featherstone R.	v.	Widnes
Halifax	v.	Hull K.R.
Oldham	v.	Hull
Wigan	v.	Leeds
Warrington	v.	Wakefield T.

SUNDAY, 26th FEBRUARY, 1989

Hull	v.	Halifax
St. Helens	v.	Oldham
Wakefield T.	v.	Castleford
Wigan	v.	Featherstone R.

WEDNESDAY, 1st MARCH, 1989

Le Pontet	v.	Widnes

WORLD CLUB CHAMPIONSHIP

SUNDAY, 5th MARCH, 1989

Castleford	v.	Hull
Halifax	v.	Salford
Hull K.R.	v.	Wigan
Leeds	v.	Wakefield T.
Oldham	v.	Featherstone R.
Warrington	v.	Bradford N.

SUNDAY, 12th MARCH, 1989

Featherstone R.	v.	Hull K.R.
Halifax	v.	Oldham
Hull	v.	Warrington
Salford	v.	St. Helens
Wigan	v.	Bradford N.

WEDNESDAY, 15th MARCH, 1989

Widnes	v.	Le Pontet

WORLD CLUB CHAMPIONSHIP

SUNDAY, 19th MARCH, 1989

Bradford N.	v.	Widnes
Hull K.R.	v.	Salford
Leeds	v.	Castleford
Oldham	v.	Wakefield T.
St. Helens	v.	Featherstone R.
Warrington	v.	Halifax

GOOD FRIDAY, 24th MARCH, 1989

Castleford	v.	Featherstone R.
Hull	v.	Hull K.R.
Leeds	v.	Bradford N.
Salford	v.	Oldham
Wakefield T.	v.	Halifax
Widnes	v.	Warrington
Wigan	v.	St. Helens

MONDAY, 27th MARCH, 1989

Featherstone R.	v.	Hull
Halifax	v.	Leeds
Hull K.R.	v.	Castleford
Oldham	v.	Wigan
St. Helens	v.	Widnes
Warrington	v.	Salford

TUESDAY, 28th MARCH, 1989

Bradford N.	v.	Wakefield T.

SUNDAY, 2nd APRIL, 1989

Castleford	v.	Wigan
Hull	v.	Oldham
Salford	v.	Halifax
Wakefield T.	v.	St. Helens
Warrington	v.	Leeds
Widnes	v.	Bradford N.

SUNDAY 9th APRIL, 1989

Bradford N.	v.	Featherstone R.
Halifax	v.	Wakefield T.
Hull K.R.	v.	Widnes
Leeds	v.	Hull
Oldham	v.	Castleford
St. Helens	v.	Warrington
Wigan	v.	Salford

SUNDAY, 16th APRIL, 1989

Bradford N.	v.	Hull K.R.
Castleford	v.	Leeds
Featherstone R.	v.	Warrington
Halifax	v.	St. Helens
Hull	v.	Salford
Widnes	v.	Wigan

413

2ND DIVISION FIXTURES
Preliminary draft subject to Club amendments

SUNDAY, 28th AUGUST, 1988

Dewsbury	v.	Runcorn H.
Doncaster	v.	Fulham
Hunslet	v.	Chorley B.
Keighley	v.	Whitehaven
Mansfield M.	v.	Huddersfield B.
Rochdale H.	v.	Barrow
Sheffield E.	v.	Bramley
Swinton	v.	Carlisle
Workington T.	v.	Leigh
York	v.	Batley

WEDNESDAY, 31st AUGUST, 1988

Mansfield M.	v.	Dewsbury

SUNDAY, 4th SEPTEMBER, 1988

Barrow	v.	Mansfield M.
Bramley	v.	Doncaster
Carlisle	v.	Batley
Chorley B.	v.	Workington T.
Fulham	v.	Sheffield E.
Huddersfield B.	v.	Rochdale H.
Hunslet	v.	Swinton
Leigh	v.	Runcorn H.
Whitehaven	v.	Dewsbury
York	v.	Keighley

WEDNESDAY, 7th SEPTEMBER, 1988

Bramley	v.	Huddersfield B.
Keighley	v.	Chorley B.

SUNDAY, 11th SEPTEMBER, 1988

Dewsbury	v.	Hunslet
Doncaster	v.	York
Huddersfield B.	v.	Fulham
Keighley	v.	Leigh
Mansfield M.	v.	Bramley
Rochdale H.	v.	Whitehaven
Runcorn H.	v.	Batley
Sheffield E.	v.	Barrow
Swinton	v.	Chorley B.
Workington T.	v.	Carlisle

WEDNESDAY, 14th SEPTEMBER, 1988

Hunslet	v.	Batley
Swinton	v.	Runcorn H.

WEDNESDAY, 21st SEPTEMBER, 1988

Sheffield E.	v.	Mansfield M.

SUNDAY, 25th SEPTEMBER, 1988

Barrow	v.	Whitehaven
Batley	v.	Hunslet
Fulham	v.	Bramley
Leigh	v.	Sheffield E.
Rochdale H.	v.	Keighley
Runcorn H.	v.	Doncaster
Swinton	v.	Mansfield M.
Workington T.	v.	Chorley B.
York	v.	Dewsbury

SUNDAY, 2nd OCTOBER, 1988

Batley	v.	Huddersfield B.
Bramley	v.	Swinton
Carlisle	v.	Leigh
Chorley B.	v.	Barrow
Doncaster	v.	Dewsbury
Keighley	v.	Workington T.
Mansfield M.	v.	Hunslet
Sheffield E.	v.	York
Whitehaven	v.	Rochdale H.

SUNDAY, 9th OCTOBER, 1988

Barrow	v.	Keighley
Carlisle	v.	Doncaster

Chorley B.	v.	Sheffield E.
Dewsbury	v.	Rochdale H.
Fulham	v.	Batley
Leigh	v.	Hunslet
Runcorn H.	v.	Whitehaven
Swinton	v.	York
Workington T.	v.	Huddersfield B.

SUNDAY, 16th OCTOBER, 1988

Batley	v.	Mansfield M.
Bramley	v.	Fulham
Doncaster	v.	Workington T.
Huddersfield B.	v.	Dewsbury
Hunslet	v.	Barrow
Keighley	v.	Carlisle
Rochdale H.	v.	Chorley B.
Sheffield E.	v.	Leigh
Whitehaven	v.	Runcorn H.
York	v.	Swinton

SUNDAY, 23rd OCTOBER, 1988

Barrow	v.	Rochdale H.
Carlisle	v.	Runcorn H.
Chorley B.	v.	Bramley
Dewsbury	v.	York
Fulham	v.	Huddersfield B.
Leigh	v.	Whitehaven
Mansfield M.	v.	Doncaster
Sheffield E.	v.	Batley
Swinton	v.	Keighley

SUNDAY, 30th OCTOBER, 1988

Batley	v.	Rochdale H.
Bramley	v.	Dewsbury
Carlisle	v.	Barrow
Huddersfield B.	v.	Workington T.
Keighley	v.	Hunslet
Mansfield M.	v.	Swinton
Runcorn H.	v.	Fulham
Whitehaven	v.	Chorley B.
York	v.	Leigh

SUNDAY, 6th NOVEMBER, 1988

Barrow	v.	Swinton
Batley	v.	Carlisle
Chorley B.	v.	Runcorn H.
Fulham	v.	York
Hunslet	v.	Dewsbury
Leigh	v.	Mansfield M.
Rochdale H.	v.	Huddersfield B.
Sheffield E.	v.	Keighley
Workington T.	v.	Doncaster

SUNDAY, 20th NOVEMBER, 1988

Chorley B.	v.	Carlisle
Dewsbury	v.	Workington T.
Doncaster	v.	Hunslet
Huddersfield B.	v.	Sheffield E.
Leigh	v.	Bramley
Mansfield M.	v.	Fulham
Runcorn H.	v.	Rochdale H.
Whitehaven	v.	Batley
York	v.	Barrow

SUNDAY, 4th DECEMBER, 1988

Barrow	v.	Leigh
Batley	v.	Runcorn H.
Bramley	v.	Mansfield M.
Carlisle	v.	Dewsbury
Chorley B.	v.	Whitehaven
Hunslet	v.	Huddersfield B.
Keighley	v.	Swinton
Workington T.	v.	Fulham
York	v.	Doncaster

414

SUNDAY, 11th DECEMBER, 1988

Dewsbury	v.	Mansfield M.
Doncaster	v.	Bramley
Fulham	v.	Hunslet
Huddersfield B.	v.	Runcorn H.
Keighley	v.	Sheffield E.
Leigh	v.	Carlisle
Rochdale H.	v.	Batley
Swinton	v.	Workington T.
Whitehaven	v.	Barrow
York	v.	Chorley B.

SUNDAY, 18th DECEMBER, 1988

Batley	v.	Fulham
Bramley	v.	York
Carlisle	v.	Swinton
Hunslet	v.	Keighley
Mansfield M.	v.	Leigh
Runcorn H.	v.	Huddersfield B.
Sheffield E.	v.	Dewsbury
Workington T.	v.	Rochdale H.

BOXING DAY, MONDAY, 26th DECEMBER, 1988

Barrow	v.	Runcorn H.
Bramley	v.	Hunslet
Chorley B.	v.	Leigh
Dewsbury	v.	Batley
Doncaster	v.	Sheffield E.
Huddersfield B.	v.	Carlisle
Rochdale H.	v.	Swinton
Whitehaven	v.	Workington T.
York	v.	Mansfield M.

NEW YEAR'S DAY, SUNDAY, 1st JANUARY, 1989

Batley	v.	Dewsbury
Carlisle	v.	Whitehaven
Doncaster	v.	Huddersfield B.
Fulham	v.	Rochdale H.
Hunslet	v.	York
Keighley	v.	Bramley
Mansfield M.	v.	Sheffield E.
Runcorn H.	v.	Chorley B.
Swinton	v.	Leigh
Workington T.	v.	Barrow

SUNDAY, 8th JANUARY, 1989

Barrow	v.	Hunslet
Bramley	v.	Batley
Carlisle	v.	Fulham
Chorley B.	v.	Keighley
Dewsbury	v.	Doncaster
Huddersfield B.	v.	Mansfield M.
Leigh	v.	Workington T.
Rochdale H.	v.	Runcorn H.
Whitehaven	v.	Swinton

SUNDAY, 15th JANUARY, 1989

Batley	v.	Sheffield E.
Bramley	v.	Barrow
Doncaster	v.	Carlisle
Fulham	v.	Whitehaven
Keighley	v.	Rochdale H.
Mansfield M.	v.	Chorley B.
Runcorn H.	v.	Leigh
Swinton	v.	Hunslet
Workington T.	v.	Dewsbury
York	v.	Huddersfield B.

SUNDAY, 22nd JANUARY, 1989

Barrow	v.	Chorley B.
Carlisle	v.	Rochdale H.
Dewsbury	v.	Fulham
Huddersfield B.	v.	Bramley
Leigh	v.	Keighley
Mansfield M.	v.	York
Runcorn H.	v.	Workington T.
Sheffield E.	v.	Swinton
Whitehaven	v.	Doncaster

SUNDAY, 5th FEBRUARY, 1989

Bramley	v.	Sheffield E.
Carlisle	v.	Keighley
Chorley B.	v.	Hunslet
Dewsbury	v.	Whitehaven
Doncaster	v.	Runcorn H.
Fulham	v.	Mansfield M.
Huddersfield B.	v.	York
Rochdale H.	v.	Leigh
Swinton	v.	Barrow
Workington T.	v.	Batley

SUNDAY, 19th FEBRUARY, 1989

Barrow	v.	Carlisle
Batley	v.	Doncaster
Chorley B.	v.	Mansfield M.
Hunslet	v.	Leigh
Keighley	v.	York
Rochdale H.	v.	Workington T.
Runcorn H.	v.	Swinton
Sheffield E.	v.	Huddersfield B.
Whitehaven	v.	Fulham

SUNDAY, 26th FEBRUARY, 1989

Carlisle	v.	Chorley B.
Dewsbury	v.	Bramley
Doncaster	v.	Rochdale H.
Fulham	v.	Runcorn H.
Huddersfield B.	v.	Whitehaven
Leigh	v.	Barrow
Mansfield M.	v.	Batley
Swinton	v.	Sheffield E.
Workington T.	v.	Keighley

SUNDAY, 5th MARCH, 1989

Barrow	v.	York
Batley	v.	Bramley
Chorley B.	v.	Swinton
Fulham	v.	Workington T.
Hunslet	v.	Mansfield M.
Rochdale H.	v.	Dewsbury
Runcorn H.	v.	Carlisle
Sheffield E.	v.	Doncaster
Whitehaven	v.	Keighley

SUNDAY, 12th MARCH, 1989

Bramley	v.	Chorley B.
Dewsbury	v.	Carlisle
Doncaster	v.	Whitehaven
Huddersfield B.	v.	Batley
Leigh	v.	Rochdale H.
Mansfield M.	v.	Barrow
Sheffield E.	v.	Hunslet
Workington T.	v.	Runcorn H.
York	v.	Fulham

SUNDAY, 19th MARCH, 1989

Barrow	v.	Sheffield E.
Batley	v.	Workington T.
Carlisle	v.	Huddersfield B.
Chorley B.	v.	York
Hunslet	v.	Doncaster
Keighley	v.	Mansfield M.
Rochdale H.	v.	Fulham
Runcorn H.	v.	Dewsbury
Swinton	v.	Bramley
Whitehaven	v.	Leigh

GOOD FRIDAY, 24th MARCH, 1989

Fulham	v.	Doncaster
Hunslet	v.	Bramley
Leigh	v.	Chorley B.
Runcorn H.	v.	Keighley
Swinton	v.	Rochdale H.
Workington T.	v.	Whitehaven
York	v.	Sheffield E.

EASTER MONDAY, 27th MARCH, 1989

Barrow	v.	Workington T.
Bramley	v.	Keighley
Chorley B.	v.	Rochdale H.
Dewsbury	v.	Huddersfield B.
Doncaster	v.	Batley
Leigh	v.	Swinton
Sheffield E.	v.	Fulham
Whitehaven	v.	Carlisle
York	v.	Hunslet

SUNDAY, 2nd APRIL, 1989

Batley	v.	York
Bramley	v.	Leigh
Fulham	v.	Carlisle
Huddersfield B.	v.	Hunslet
Keighley	v.	Barrow
Rochdale H.	v.	Doncaster
Sheffield E.	v.	Chorley B.
Swinton	v.	Whitehaven

SUNDAY, 9th APRIL, 1989

Barrow	v.	Bramley
Carlisle	v.	Workington T.
Dewsbury	v.	Sheffield E.
Doncaster	v.	Mansfield M.
Hunslet	v.	Fulham
Keighley	v.	Runcorn H.
Leigh	v.	York
Whitehaven	v.	Huddersfield B.

SUNDAY, 16th APRIL, 1989

Batley	v.	Whitehaven
Fulham	v.	Dewsbury
Huddersfield B.	v.	Doncaster
Hunslet	v.	Sheffield E.
Mansfield M.	v.	Keighley
Rochdale H.	v.	Carlisle
Runcorn H.	v.	Barrow
Workington T.	v.	Swinton
York	v.	Bramley